WOMEN
AND THE MAKING
OF AMERICA

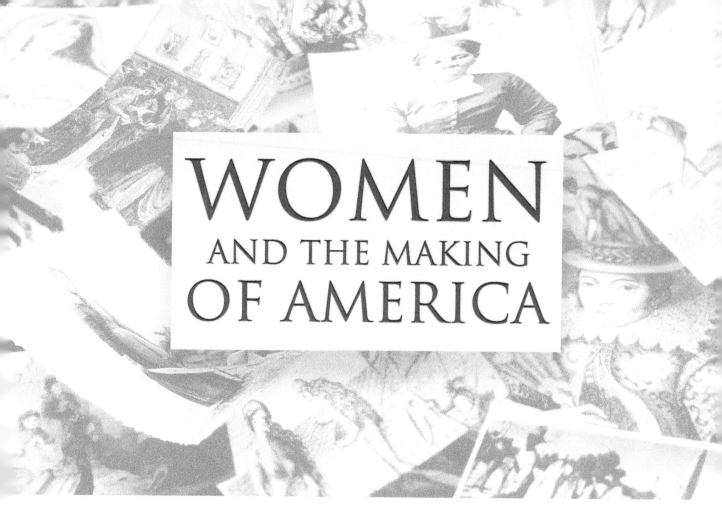

WOMEN
AND THE MAKING
OF AMERICA

VOLUME 1

MARI JO BUHLE
Brown University

TERESA MURPHY
George Washington University

JANE GERHARD
Mount Holyoke College

PEARSON

Prentice
Hall

Library of Congress Cataloging-in-Publication Data

Buhle, Mari Jo
  Women and the making of America / Mari Jo Buhle, Teresa Murphy, Jane Gerhard.
    p. cm.
  Includes bibliographical references and index.
  ISBN-13: 978-0-13-183916-8 (combined, vols. 1 and 2)
  ISBN-13: 978-0-13-812688-9 (vol. 1)
  ISBN-13: 978-0-13-812687-2 (vol. 2)
  1. Women's studies—United States—History. 2. Feminism—United States—History. I.
Murphy, Teresa. II. Gerhard, Jane F. III. Title.
  HQ1181.U5B84 2008
  305.40973—dc22

                                  2008015611

VP/Publisher: Priscilla McGeehon
Publisher: Charlyce Jones Owen
Senior Editorial Assistant: Maureen Diana
Developmental Editor: Carolyn Viola-John
Executive Marketing Manager: Sue Westmoreland
Marketing Assistant: Athena Moore
Managing Editor (Production): Lisa Iarkowski
Project Manager: Marianne Peters-Riordan
Operations Specialist: Maura Zaldivar
Senior Art Director: Maria Lange
Interior Design: Ilze Lemesis
Cover Design: Maria Lange
Cover Illustration/Photo: (From bottom center): Courtesy of the Library of Congress (a, c-d, f, h-k); U.S. Department of Agriculture; The Public Archives of Canada; Corbis/Bettmann.

Cover Art Creation: Cory Skidds
AV Project Manager: Mirella Signoretto
Director, Image Resource Center: Melinda Patelli
Manager, Rights and Permissions: Zina Arabia
Manager, Visual Research: Beth Brenzel
Manager, Cover Visual Research & Permissions: Karen Sanatar
Image Permission Coordinator: Craig A. Jones
Photo Researcher: Julie Tesser
Composition/Full-Service Project Management: Emily Bush/S4Carlisle Publishing Services
Printer/Binder: Courier
Credits and acknowledgments borrowed from other sources and reproduced, with permission, in this textbook appear on appropriate page within text or on page C-1.

Pearson Education LTD., London
Pearson Education Singapore, Pte. Ltd
Pearson Education, Canada, Ltd
Pearson Education–Japan
Pearson Education Australia PTY, Limited

Pearson Education North Asia Ltd
Pearson Educación de Mexico, S.A. de C.V.
Pearson Education Malaysia, Pte. Ltd
Pearson Education, Upper Saddle River, New Jersey

10 9 8 7 6

ISBN-13: 978-0-13-812688-9
ISBN-10: 0-13-812688-7

BRIEF CONTENTS

CONTENTS

CHAPTER 3   EIGHTEENTH-CENTURY REVOLUTIONS, 1700–1800   64

Maps, Tables, and Figures

Overview Tables

Figures

WOMEN'S LIVES

WOMEN'S VOICES

ABOUT THE AUTHORS

Mari Jo Buhle

Mari Jo Buhle is William R. Kenan Jr. University Professor and Professor of American Civilization and History at Brown University, specializing in American women's history. She received her B.A. from the University of Illinois, Urbana–Champaign, and her Ph.D. from the University of Wisconsin, Madison. She is the author of *Women and American Socialism, 1870–1920* (1981) and *Feminism and Its Discontents: A Century of Struggle with Psychoanalysis* (1998). She is also coeditor of *Encyclopedia of the American Left*, second edition (1998). Professor Buhle held a fellowship (1991–1996) from the John D. and Catherine T. MacArthur Foundation.

Teresa Murphy

Teresa Murphy is Associate Professor of American Studies at George Washington University. Born and raised in California, she received her B.A. from the University of California, Berkeley and her Ph.D. from Yale University. She is the author of *Ten Hours Labor: Religion, Reform, and Gender in Early New England* (1992) and is currently completing a study about the origins of women's history in the late eighteenth and early nineteenth centuries. She is the former Associate Editor of *American Quarterly*.

Jane Gerhard

Jane F. Gerhard is a visiting assistant professor of History at Mount Holyoke College, specializing in American women's history and the history of sexuality in America. She received her B.A. from Hampshire College in Amherst, Massachusetts, and her Ph.D. from Brown University. She is the author of *Desiring Revolution: Second Wave Feminism and the Rewriting of American Sexual Thought, 1920 to 1982* (2001).

PREFACE

Women and the Making of America writes—and rewrites—the history of women and gender in the United States from the era of the first cultural contact between indigenous peoples and Europeans in the fifteenth century to the new globalism of the twenty-first century. This narrative is organized around an exploration of the dynamics of power—between women and men, as well as among different women. As a result, the chapters in this book return repeatedly to the meaning of diversity in American history; the meaning of sexuality; and the changing nature of gender, of definitions of masculinity and femininity, in the history of the United States. This is an approach that builds on recent interpretive trends that have moved beyond the "separate spheres" paradigm that governed the scholarship in women's history during its formative years in the 1970s. Rather than focusing on the status of women in the shifting relationship between the ostensibly "private" affairs of the family and the "public" dimensions of society and politics, this book recognizes that women cannot be studied apart from the world of politics and diplomacy. Women and issues of gender have been deeply enmeshed in the creation of both society and the political order in the United States.

Women and the Making of America explores the lives of a broad spectrum of women because it recognizes that diversity is a central factor in the history of women and gender. Each chapter explores, in one way or another, how relationships among women were determined by differences of race, ethnicity, class, age, region, or religion. Hierarchies and inequalities occurred within families, communities, and the nation. These differences affected both personal encounters, such as among friends and family, and major institutions, such as education and the labor market. For example, at the end of the nineteenth century, groups of reform-minded white women in the western United States, filled with the fervor of evangelical Protestantism, extended aid and protection to groups of women who shared few of their values or enjoyed little of their power: Chinese prostitutes in San Francisco and Mormon plural wives in Utah. The story that comes into focus is complex, situating missionary women and their clients within a historical context that highlights competing notions of sexuality and agency. This sort of attention to diversity reveals the power dynamics among various groups of women that were central to the overlapping—mutually constitutive—hierarchies that have shaped all women's lives.

Women and the Making of America not only highlights these power dynamics but pays special attention to the history of social activism that addressed inequalities. Women of all groups participated—albeit to varying degrees and in distinctive ways—in political affairs that extended from family to community to nation. By the end of the eighteenth century, groups of women began to form their own organizations for social betterment. By the end of the nineteenth century, many of these organizations came together to create a variety of social movements that made women's diverse voices heard. Even before the passing of the Nineteenth Amendment to the Constitution, which granted women the right to vote, many women found ways to challenge existing dynamics of power and to represent their own interests as members of communities and as women. These more informal challenges necessarily figure prominently in the chapters ahead, recognizing power in the most personal and intimate relationships between men and women and among women themselves.

Women and the Making of America explores the power of these intimate relationships in the historical realm of sexuality. As seen through various lenses—reproduction, health, pleasure, reigning definitions of normality and deviancy, laws, and reform agendas, sexuality serves as an enduring benchmark for assessing power dynamics. From the early-nineteenth-century "passionless" republican mothers to the sexually expressive "women adrift" during the Progressive Era to the celebrants of the 1960s sexual revolution, women often relied on sexuality for their authority. This book explores the meaning of these forms of sexual expression, as well as exploring the female subcultures organized around sexuality. The development of lesbian subcultures in the twentieth century, for example, provides opportunities for exploring the links between gender, sexuality, and social hierarchies.

Women and the Making of America underscores the significance of the United States as a "nation of immigrants." From the appearance of the first European explorers and settlers in the fifteenth century to the recent upsurge and shifting patterns of immigration in the twenty-first century, women have taken part in a larger world system of global exchange in people, trade, and ideas. A continental perspective additionally emphasizes the great expanse of the nation, including shifting boundaries and territorial acquisitions that add to population diversity. Equally important, the rise of the United States as a global power plays a major role in the nation's history, engaging women in military actions and war and forcing them into an international market for goods and services. Within such context, several chapters raise questions about the sources of influence and control within the family, the market economy, and nation state and necessarily foreground issues of citizenship.

Women and the Making of America ultimately explores both the political economy and the sphere of reproduction to shape a narrative. Changing patterns of women's labor, household as well as market, and the relationship of both to issues of power within the family and society at large are central to the stories of diverse groups of women. The achievements of women, individually and collectively, in fields ranging from the arts and sciences, education, and humanitarian reform to politics broadly defined illustrate various dimensions of power. At the same time, conventional signposts in the history of the United States figure prominently. Students new to the study of American history will find these signposts helpful as context; advanced students will find ways to reconstruct and reshape the familiar historical narrative.

SPECIAL FEATURES

Introduction A separate introductory chapter summarizes various approaches to the study of women and gender in history, provides an overview of historiography focused on the scholarship since the 1970s, and introduces the concept of power and explains it as the principal category of analysis. It also provides examples of diversity, sexuality, and global perspective that shape the overall narrative.

Chapter Opening Each chapter begins with a short first-person account that sets the scene for the major themes considered.

Women's Lives Each chapter has two short biographies, which all together highlight the themes of diversity, sexuality, and global perspective. These biographies demonstrate the way the history presented in the main body of the chapter affected individuals.

Women's Voices Each chapter has two primary source excerpts from letters, personal diaries, public statements, or first-person accounts that offer perspectives of well-known or ordinary women on the events considered in the chapter.

Maps, Graphs, Charts, and Tables Maps in each chapter situate the history of women spatially in the United States. Most chapters offer a graph, chart, or table to suggest longer trends.

Overview Tables These special tables provide students with a summary of complex issues.

Photos and Illustrations Each of the photos and illustrations date from the historical period under discussion and aid the student in visualizing the world in which women have lived and the relationships in which they were engaged.

Time Lines Each chapter includes a time line that integrates major events in U.S. history and the special events of women's history.

Review Questions Review questions at the end of each chapter help students review, reinforce, and retain the material in each chapter and encourage them to relate the material to broader issues in American history.

Recommended Reading The works in the short, annotated Recommended Reading list at the end of each chapter have been selected with the undergraduate college student in mind.

Additional Bibliography The Additional Bibliography contains additional readings for both instructors and students interested in pursuing topics in women's history in more depth.

Glossaries A Glossary of Key Terms provides definitions of key concepts.

SUPPLEMENTARY MATERIAL

Instructor's Manual with Test Item File The *Instructor's Manual* contains everything instructors need for developing and preparing lecture presentations, including chapter outlines and overviews, lecture topics, discussion questions, and information about audiovisual resources. It also includes a Test Item File of over 1,500 multiple-choice, short-answer, and essay questions.
ISBN: 0-13-2278040-5; 978-0-13-2278040-9

Test Generator This computerized test management program, available for Windows and Macintosh environments, allows instructors to design their own exams by selecting items from the Test Item File. The Test Generator software is available by download from the Pearson Instructor Resource Center. http://www.prenhall.com/irc

Primary Sources in Women's History A collection of 300 primary source documents and images organized by the content of the chapters in the text.
ISBN: 0-13-227842-1; 978-0-13-227842-3

Prentice Hall and Penguin Bundle Program Prentice Hall and Penguin are pleased to provide adopters of *Women and the Making of America* with an opportunity to receive significant discounts when orders for the text are bundled together with Penguin titles in women's history.

 **http://www.myhistorykit.com** Prentice Hall's exclusive *MyHistoryKit*™ offers unique tools and support that make it easy for students and instructors to integrate this online study guide with the text.

Instructors can elect to use a gradebook to monitor student assignments. This helpful student resource is organized according to the main subtopics of each chapter.

 **Research Navigator**™ Prentice Hall's Research Navigator™ helps your students make the most of their study and research time. From finding the right articles and journals to citing sources, drafting and writing effective papers, and completing research assignments, Research Navigator™ simplifies and streamlines the entire process.

Complete with extensive help on the research process and three exclusive databases full of relevant and reliable source material including EBSCO's *ContentSelect* Academic Journal Database, the *New York Times* Search by Subject Archive, and Best of the Web Link Library, Research Navigator™ is the one-stop research solution for your students. Take a tour on the Web at http://www.researchnavigator.com.

ACKNOWLEDGMENTS

We wish to thank our collaborators at Pearson/Prentice Hall: Charlyce Jones Owen, Publisher; Charles Cavaliere, Executive Editor; Sue Westmoreland, Executive Marketing Manager; Marianne Peters-Riordan, Production Editor; Carolyn Viola-John, Development Editor, Maureen Diana, Editorial Assistant; Emily Bush, Project Editor.

We wish to also thank the reviewers for providing insightful comments:

Carli Schiffner, *SUNY Canton*
Elizabeth Hayes Turner, *University of North Texas*
Nancy Rosenbloom, *Canisius College*
Kathleen A. Laughlin, *Metropolitan State University*
Michael Goldberg, *University of Washington, Bothell*
Louise Newman, *University of Florida*
Angela Boswell, *Henderson State University*
Margaret A. Spratt, *California University of Pennsylvania*
Joyce L. Broussard, *California State University, Northridge*
Alice Kessler-Harris, *Columbia University*
Jimmie McGee, *South Plains College*
Thomas Dublin, *SUNY Binghamton*
Karen Blair, *Central Washington University*
Margaret Lowe, *Bridgewater State College*
Richard Godbeer, *University of California, Riverside*
Sharon Hartman Strom, *University of Rhode Island*
John McClymer, *Assumption College*
Marguerite Renner, *Glendale Community College*

We authors shared equally in the writing of *Women and the Making of America*. Although we take collective responsibility for the book, we each authored specific chapters. Teresa Murphy wrote chapters 1–8; Mari Jo Buhle wrote chapters 9–15; and Jane Gerhard wrote chapters 16–22.

For assistance in research, our thanks go to John O'Keefe, Laurel Clark, Karen Inouye, Nicole Eaton, and Laura Prieto.

We thank our friends and family for their support: Jean Wood; Susan Smulyan; Paul Buhle; David Stern; and Joel, Max, Nicholas, and Grace Kuipers.

INTRODUCTION

CLASSIFIE

ACTIVIS

WOM
OWN
BUSINES

WHAT'S
NEW

RESOURCES
AND LINKS

E-MAIL

ARTICLES AND
SPEECHES

FEMINIST.
COM

WOMEN'S
HEALTH ISSUES

While students today may think it
obvious that women have a history worth studying, it was not always
the case. Historians of women, beginning at
the turn of the twentieth century, had to win
a place for their field by establishing that conventional histories neglected women's contributions to U.S. society and too often left out
the experiences of ordinary people in the
United States. Along with scholars of African
American and Native American histories,
historians of women participated in larger
trends in academic life that altered the definition of what counted as "history."

*Home page of Feminist.com website. (Reprinted with the per-
mission of the Women's College Coalition.)*

This introduction looks at the origins of the field of women's history, but it does more than historicize the field. It also introduces three central frameworks used by historians to analyze women's diverse experiences: the social construction of gender, public/private spheres, and the category of woman. Last, it introduces the organization and layout of the textbook, highlighting what students can expect to see, read, and learn as they use it.

WRITING U.S. WOMEN'S HISTORY

The field of U.S. women's history has ties to movements for social change, specifically the broad social and political movement—Progressivism—that flourished in the United States between 1890 and 1920 and the protest movements of the 1960s and 1970s. At both moments, teachers and students discovered that the study of history connected them not only to the past but to the future.

Anarchist Emma Goldman, an early advocate for feminism, called for women to be as free as their male counterparts, demanding in a 1897 speech that women required "freedom of action, freedom in love and freedom in motherhood."

Why History?

In 1916, Caroline F. Ware enrolled in Vassar College, where she met a remarkable group of faculty. Her teachers, representatives of the first generation of women to support themselves as "professional" historians, took pride in their rigorous course offerings in historical methodology. They also taught their students, Ware recalled later in life, that the study of history could serve as the "prelude to responsible social action."

Ware's mentor was Lucy Maynard Salmon, who in 1897 published *Domestic Service*, a detailed examination of household workers in the United States. Salmon and her Vassar students had gathered mountains of data on wages, hours, conditions of labor, and relationships with employers—all for the specific purpose of finding remedies for the "social disadvantages" borne by the many women who worked as servants. Although the bulk of the study focused on contemporary conditions, Salmon opened with a lengthy historical review and explained to her readers that insights into the current situation depended on an understanding of the past.

Salmon, who helped to pioneer the new field of women's history, insisted that her own historical research effectively guided her down the path of social reform. Through the administrative offices of the American Historical Association, the major professional society in the field, she worked to promote the study of history in the public school system. She also campaigned steadily for woman's rights, serving on the boards of several suffrage organizations. Much to the dismay of Vassar's president, Salmon encouraged students to demonstrate their own dedication to the cause by holding suffrage meetings on the campus. Meanwhile, Salmon played an active role in civic betterment in the surrounding community of Poughkeepsie, New York.

Carolyn F. Ware, who proudly admitted that she "got her education at Vassar," learned these lessons well. As an undergraduate, she excelled in her coursework and, following Salmon's advice, interned during her junior year at a social service organization in New York. Later, at Harvard University, she chose to write a dissertation on the first modern industry to employ women, cotton textile manufacturing in early New England. Then, after receiving her doctorate, Ware returned to Vassar to instruct yet another generation of women students in the "service ideals" that she had imbibed from her own mentors.

The field of women's history emerged at the turn of the twentieth century as a distinct product of scholar-activists like Salmon and Ware. Wedded to the social idealism of the Progressive Era, these historians determinedly studied various aspects of women's past—work, family, and politics—to provide the requisite knowledge necessary for planning the future, a future when the relationships between men and women would be more equitable than they were during their own times. Despite their innovations and accomplishments, their project had come to a near halt in the late 1920s when first-wave feminism, the movement for woman suffrage that began with the historic meeting at Seneca Falls, New York, in 1848 went into retreat.

In the late 1960s, with the emergence of second-wave feminism, often referred to as the *women's liberation movement*, the field of women's history revived. A new generation of scholars eagerly embraced the mantle of the scholar-activist and set themselves, in their own words, to "constructing usable pasts." This time around, they enlarged the research agenda in new and exciting ways.

In 1969, Roxanne Dunbar unwittingly echoed her predecessors in insisting that, for feminists, "It is not enough that we take collective action. We must know where we come from historically and personally and how we can most effectively break the bonds." Unlike Ware, Dunbar had not found someone like Salmon to inspire her to study history. To the contrary, by the time she had come of age, there were few courses being taught by women professors and none that focused on the history of women. Dunbar instead came to this conclusion through her political activism.

In the 1960s, when Dunbar moved from her home in Oklahoma to the San Francisco Bay Area in California, she found her inspiration in a vibrant movement for social change. This inspiration deepened after she moved to Boston, where she met a group of women who were deeply involved in the women's liberation movement. Together they founded the radical feminist Cell 16 and published *No More Fun and Games: A Journal of Female Liberation*. Ultimately, it was her political activism that led her to deepen her study of history. After receiving a doctorate from UCLA, Dunbar took a position at California State University–Hayward, where she helped to found programs in Native American studies, ethnic studies, and women's studies.

Dunbar and Ware, working in different historical moments, each found a synergy between her study of history and her political hopes. For these two women, history provided new ways to approach pressing contemporary social questions. While individuals studied the history of women in the early years of the century, a critical mass of interested scholars grew in the 1970s, enabling the field of women's history to grow rapidly and achieve a place in the academic world.

Origins of the Field

After nearly a half century of quiescence, the academic study of women across several disciplines took off. In 1969, U.S. colleges and universities offered only seventeen courses on women. A year later, there were more than one hundred women's studies courses; and by 1973 there were more than two hundred. No single feminist organization directed this growth. The courses cropped up spontaneously all over the country, with some campuses implementing new programs in response to sit-ins and strikes conducted jointly by students and faculty. In other places, faculty women privately pressured their departments to sponsor women's studies classes. The first women's studies program was established in 1970 at San Diego State College after a year of intense organizing.

Activist and scholar Catherine Stimpson later recalled that for both faculty and students, the discovery of women's studies was exhilarating and challenging as it often "began with a sense of rupture and estrangement from accepted knowledge" in their academic disciplines. Professional organizations for feminist scholars formed. Journals for feminist scholarship came into existence, including *Signs*, *Frontiers*, and *Feminist Studies*, which worked in tandem with programs and conferences to build the field of women's history. Ann Calderwood, the first editor of *Feminist Studies*, recalled that the journal "grew out of the women's movement at its early, spontaneous and energetic phase, bringing together political commitment and scholarship. Then merely to assert that women should be studied was a radical act."

According to the American Historical Association, the concentration in women's history and gender studies is currently one of the fastest-growing areas of the discipline. Several colleges and universities now offer advanced degrees in women's history, and courses in the area are now offered at most colleges and universities in the United States.

Standard Approaches to Women's History

Perhaps the most long-lived approach to women's history is what scholars in the field term "compensatory." Historians readily acknowledge that women have played only a minor role in history as conventionally defined by men's achievements. For the most part, women have not served as heads of state; generals in armies; or leaders of business, religion, or the arts. However, a few exceptional women have stood out for their distinctive accomplishments.

Many of us have grown up reading biographies about these famous—and occasionally infamous—women. It is now nearly common knowledge that: beginning in 1804, the teenage Sacagawea of the Shoshone tribe helped to guide the Lewis and Clark expedition; in the mid-nineteenth century, activist Dorothea Dix first brought the plight of the mentally ill to public attention and helped create the first generation of U.S. mental asylums; Martha Jane Canary, better known as Calamity Jane, achieved fame as a gunslinger and cross-dresser; and Amelia Earhart drew international attention in 1933 as the first woman to fly unaccompanied across the Atlantic Ocean. However entertaining and rich as appealing anecdotes, biographies of such "women worthies" often tell very little of the lives of the majority of women. To the contrary, such biographies tend to emphasize their subjects' unique or quaint qualities as well as remarkable achievements.

"Contribution" history, a variation on this theme, builds on the premise that women have played important roles in history that have not yet been sufficiently recognized. A popular example of this category, the history of women's participation in social reform, dutifully records their activities in movements ranging from antislavery to the social settlements to civil rights. In such studies, biographies—of Sojourner Truth, Jane Addams, and Ella Baker, for example—once again figure prominently to highlight the activities of the leaders of these important movements.

Like "compensatory" history, a focus on women's contributions sheds little light on the majority of women. We may come to appreciate that a group of women led by Jane Addams and her friend and colleague Ellen Gates Starr in 1889 founded Hull House, the leading social settlement of the Progressive Era. Usually, what we do not learn is the means by which these women managed such an extraordinary feat at a time when the majority of women not only lacked even the right to vote but held no public office outside the realm of local school boards.

In other words, "contribution" history tends to focus narrowly on women's previously unrecognized role in, for example, reform movements but typically fails to examine the ways these women made their way past the many barriers against their participation in the masculine realm of politics. That they devoted much of their lives to improving women's condition usually remains unexamined, figuring only incidentally among their achievements in promoting social betterment in general. In sum, the main "story" of history remains centered on familiar events, such as wars, politics, and presidents' administrations, and men continue to serve as the principal actors. What is unique to the "contribution" approach is the recognition that women have played at least a small role in the standard story of U.S. history.

Perhaps the most enduring topic in the model of contribution history is the woman suffrage movement. Recent U.S. history textbooks provide some coverage of the struggle for the vote, noting its beginning at the Seneca Falls, New York, meeting in 1848 and celebrating its conclusion in the ratification of the Nineteenth Amendment to the Constitution in 1920. The participants themselves in this great campaign inaugurated this tradition by crafting numerous books and essays on the subject dearest to their heart. Moreover, these novice historians did this work not just to gather recollections but to supply future generations with the requisite knowledge to carry on the struggle.

The leading example, still an invaluable resource, is the massive collection of documents compiled over forty years by Elizabeth Cady Stanton, Susan B. Anthony, Matilda Joslyn Gage, and Ida Husted Harper. The unwieldy six-volume *History of Woman Suffrage*, which the editors described as an "arsenal of facts," warrants its prominent status among the "classics" in the field of women's history. Shortly before women won the right to vote, a sympathetic reviewer praised the collection for offering "glowing records of as wonderful women as the world ever saw." Other prominent suffragists also supplied memoirs that

Pilot Amelia Earhart became a celebrity in the 1920s when she became the first woman to cross the Atlantic Ocean in a plane, an act that challenged the ideas that women were too weak for demanding physical and mental tasks.

included vivid descriptions of the campaigns they led. Since 1920, scholars have been building on these early efforts to produce an abundance of excellent books on the topic. Still, especially in U.S. history textbooks, the history of women begins and ends with the campaign for the ballot, thereby relegating to the margins the many other facets of a broader—and unending—movement to expand woman's rights and excluding the history of the majority of women who did not join in the struggle.

Since the late 1960s, when the field of women's history revived alongside second-wave feminism, scholars have created for themselves a much more ambitious agenda. Neither content with the results of "compensatory" or "contribution" histories nor satisfied by the noble accounts of the campaign for suffrage, they have aspired to create a framework suitable for encompassing the lives of women who, for the most part, have been absent in our stories of the past. This ambitious project required a reassessment of the measure of historical significance and what the main story line would ultimately be.

FRAMEWORKS OF WOMEN'S HISTORY

Since the 1960s, historians have created new frameworks for the writing of U.S. women's history. Three frameworks have proved most important to the field. The first is a framework that emphasizes that gender is a product of society and culture, not only biology. The second is that the division of social life into public and private realms simplifies what is in fact a far more complex and dynamic field of social relations. Last is the understanding that women have multiple identities that are rooted in race, class, sexuality, and religion, as well as gender.

The Social Construction of Gender

Historians of women drew from a range of disciplines and none proved more useful than anthropology. Feminist anthropologists gave historians of women an approach to the study of the social construction of gender. Anthropologists demonstrated the wide variety of social roles women played across time and place, including public and private roles. They demonstrated that societies create gender differences differently in different places; that a great variety existed in women's social roles and powers, their public status, and their cultural definitions of femininity; and that the nature, quality, and social significance of women's activities vary more than had previously been assumed. In short, anthropologists offered historians tools for analyzing the links between work, status, and gender.

One crucial insight came from Michelle Zimbalist Rosaldo in her groundbreaking introduction to the anthology *Women, Culture and Society*, published in 1974. Rosaldo set out important distinctions between biological sex and the social construction of gender. She argued that while biology dictates that women lactate and bear children, societies construct—and thus can change—the meanings attached to those biological facts. She and other feminist anthologists argued that woman's ability to

Portrait of Camille Clifford in 1906, the woman who inspired illustrator Charles Gibson's "Gibson Girl," an idealized representation of white femininity that appeared in magazines at the turn of the 20th century.

bear children must be uncoupled from a set of assumptions about woman's nature—assumptions that have gained the appearance of universal truth and have been used to justify women's subordination. Rosaldo wrote, "That women have been seen as wives and more particularly mothers; that their lives have been defined in terms of reproductive functions; that their personalities have been shaped by ties with 'mothers' who in turn are women—all of these are human products that we feel account for women's secondary status."

Rosaldo and other feminist anthropologists found help in the work of Margaret Mead. Mead's study of adolescence and sexuality in *Coming of Age in Samoa* (1928) and *Sex and Temperament in Three Primitive Societies* (1935) demonstrated varieties in the social construction of gender and in women's status. Mead herself was very much a product of the sea change in U.S. gender roles that took place in the 1910s and 1920s, particularly the gains women made in education and in the professions. She graduated from Barnard College in 1923 and was among the first graduates of Columbia University to earn a doctorate in anthropology, which she completed in 1929. Until 1933, Mead studied in New Guinea where she observed three specific cultures: Arapesh, Mundugumor, and the Tchambuli. Each culture displayed distinctive gender roles. In one culture, both the women and men were cooperative; in the second, they were both ruthless and aggressive; and in the Thambuli culture, the women were dominant and the men more submissive. These findings led Mead to propose that masculine and feminine characteristics reflected cultural conditioning (or socialization), not fundamental biological differences. She wrote in *Sex and Temperament* that "If those temperamental attitudes which we have traditionally regarded as feminine—such as passivity, responsiveness, and a willingness to cherish children—can so easily be set up as the masculine pattern in one tribe, and, in another, be outlawed for the majority of women as for the majority of men, we no longer have any basis for regarding aspects of such behavior as sex linked."

While Rosaldo claimed Mead as an important forerunner, she and her peers strove to explain the deeper structures that shaped what they understood as the persistent, cross-cultural devaluation of women. She agreed with Mead that women engaged in a variety of social behaviors. Yet, cross-cultural studies indicated that, despite such variations, women's responsibility for child rearing was so commonplace as to be nearly universal. The conflation of childbearing and child rearing was a situation that tied most women to the "private" sphere of the family while at the same time freed men for "public" activities of society. Rosaldo concluded that "the opposition between domestic and public orientations provides the necessary framework for an examination of male and female roles in any society."

While the structure of private/public spheres explained much, Rosaldo and her peers were keenly aware of the role that ideology played in the production of gender. Saturated in the U.S. world of television, movies, and advertisements on the one hand and that of sermons, marriage experts, doctors, and advice columnists on the other, this generation of feminists appreciated that the representations of gender mattered to men's and women's understanding of themselves as much as did the economic and political dimensions of society. They argued that it was not only the actual division between "public" and "private" but the meanings people express about it that mattered. Rosaldo ultimately concluded that "woman's place in human social life is not in any direct sense a product of the things she does, but of the meaning her activities acquire through concrete social interaction." Building on this insight, feminist anthropologists offered historians of women an important framework for thinking about the public/private distinction as firmly rooted in both material and ideological realms.

Public/Private and Separate Spheres

The public/private distinction and its relationship to gender—the associations between men, masculinity, and the public sphere and those between women, femininity, and the private sphere—gave historians a pliable framework for examining change and continuity in women's history. It enabled historians to examine the ongoing connection of women to domesticity, or the private sphere, which has remained strong, while assessing the significant changes in women's economic, political, and legal opportunities. As the field took off in the 1960s, historians of women wrote accounts of ordinary women in their daily lives framed by their familial roles and responsibilities. They aimed to return both women and the importance of private life to the historical record.

The field of social history, which also took shape in the mid-1960s, proved to be the defining characteristic of recent scholarship on women's history. In choosing topics of everyday life and the experiences of "ordinary" people, social historians contributed new information about the history of the "private" sphere as well as its connection to the public. By using census data and court records, for example, they shed light on the historical dimensions of sex ratios, fertility rates, family size, and various life-cycle patterns, such as age of first marriage, births of first and last children, first menstruation and menopause, and death. They told of the food people ate and the way they procured and prepared it. They provided literacy rates and documented the rise of school systems and coeducation. All of these new explorations shed new light on the "private" sphere of the family and allowed women's historians to redirect the beam to the social relations between the sexes.

Private life, however, comprised more than motherhood and food. Thanks to insights gained from the second wave of feminism, historians of women understood the private realm as one also of conflict and violence as much as pleasure and satisfaction. Historians introduced such topics as birth control and abortion, women's physical and mental health, childbirth and child rearing, sexual pleasure, rape, and domestic violence. That personal and private events, events that took place typically in the home and outside of the purview of public notice, could be part of the historical record drew on and embodied the famous feminist slogan "the personal is political." Personal life and issues of identity had roots in social life and as such could not be classified as merely "personal." To answer questions concerning women's subjective experiences that cannot be found in published sources, historians turned to diaries, letters, memoirs, and other literary sources. Recovering women's voices from the past became a central part of rebuilding a historical record, including the most intimate details, of women's lives. These explorations developed more nuanced accounts of women's difference from men as well as from each other. Historians of women discovered a distinctive culture of women.

Yet, the view of men and women as living in separate and distinctive worlds was also a product of nineteenth-century gender ideology. Historians of the private realm found the notion of "separate spheres" in published essays, diaries, and sermons and adopted it as a way to explain nineteenth-century women's experiences as well as their understandings of themselves as women. Separate spheres neatly mapped gender on to the public/private divide. Men ruled the public world of work and politics, women the private world of home. Yet, so tight was the mapping of gender on to the categories of public and private that the trope, or metaphor, of separate spheres threatened to obscure its function as a discourse of gender. Women never existed purely in the private realm, historians ultimately concluded, and neither were the issues of politics or economy separate from the home.

Women's historians did not study gender as a feature only of the "private" realm. They also studied the role gender played in the public world of work, economics, and politics. Historians demonstrated that the association of women with the realm of family, home, and children affected the entire course of U.S. economic history. From the onset of industrial capitalism in the late eighteenth century through the era of deindustrialization that shaped the last half of the twentieth century, the presumed natural or biological differences between men and women served as the ideological foundation for what has become known as the family wage, the notion that societies thrive only when men earn wages sufficient to meet the needs of their family. A corollary to the family wage is the belief that societies run best when women stay home and tend to the domestic needs of families. Yet, the ideal of the family wage, with its deeply gendered scripts of male breadwinner and female caretaker, rarely captured the complex reality of women's wage work. From the first textile mills of the early nineteenth century to the service occupations that have increasingly sustained the U.S. economy since World War II, women have worked outside the home. Indeed, by the first years of the twenty-first century, women in every age group, from twenty to seventy and more, are much more likely to be working than they were twenty years ago; while men in their prime, that is, between the ages twenty to fifty-four, are less likely to be employed. Still, the nexus of "woman" and "family" remains strong.

New studies of the gendered dimensions of the public sphere underscore that gender is not a concept with relevance only to the private sphere. Rather, it is an analytic tool that casts light on the ways that ideas about masculinity and femininity shape economic, legal, and political systems, not only individuals.

Identity and Diversity

A fundamental building block of U.S. women's history has been the idea that women, in addition to their class, racial, and religious differences, share a common experience of being "women." While central to the enterprise of writing women's history, the category of "woman" has nonetheless been controversial. In the 1970s, feminists argued that women faced a uniquely gendered form of discrimination. This view of women's shared experiences of femininity and of subordination affirmed the idea of the connectedness of women across time and culture. It identified the common and unifying feature of women to be the female body. The female body did not "cause" women's secondary status, but the meanings attached to the female body nearly universally emphasized women's subordination to men. Ironically, the female body—the physical difference between men and women—was understood by many second-wave feminists as the point of origin for both women's oppression and feminist activism. Just as women's biological difference from men served to justify the historical subordination of women to men, that same biological difference, in the hands of feminists, justified political action undertaken to dismantle women's subordination.

Initially, the sense of a shared female identity across culture and history was empowering. However, in asserting the idea that women were oppressed as women and that, therefore, women should band together regardless of other kinds of differences among them, led second-wave feminists into uncomfortable discussions about alternative forms of identity to which women lay claim (such as race, religion, and nation). It raised thorny questions about the essential or fundamental nature of women that held the category together and justified its existence. By the mid-1970s, women of color and Chicana feminists had pioneered an alternative politics of identity that shaped the practice of both feminism and women's history. Feminists of color demanded that activists and scholars alike address the simultaneous and interlocking forms of inequality that shaped women's experiences. Poverty, racism, homophobia, and sexism converged in powerful ways, they insisted, and could not be ranked and ordered.

As a result of minority feminist theory and activism, the field of U.S. women's history questions accounts of women's lives that segregate gender identities from those forged in and through race, class, and sexuality. For example, women in the antebellum South experienced their womanhood in markedly different ways. Enslaved women may have shared the material space of the plantation with their white mistresses, but their experiences of femininity, from childbirth to death, were not at all similar. While free African American and enslaved women tended to children and the needs of their families, they had little control over the material conditions of their lives or that of their children. White women, rich and poor, had more options but often found their privileges undercut by their dependency on men.

Similarly, women's historians have shown that individuals have harnessed notions of womanhood to a wide variety of political aims. When African American Sojourner Truth, a former slave and abolitionist, famously explained in 1851 that "nobody helps me into carriages or over puddles or gives me the best place—ain't I a woman?" she challenged her listeners to come to terms with the different value placed on the femininity of white and black women, of poor and landed whites, of freed and bonded African American women. For Truth, laying claim to respectable womanhood was a savvy political tactic. Elizabeth Cady Stanton, who also blended abolitionism with woman's rights activism, embraced a different tactic. She found that the answer to women's secondary status lay in casting off the limits womanhood placed on woman's rights and choices. In recognition of the nation's 1876 centennial, Stanton proposed that "woman was made first for her own happiness, with the absolute right to herself—to all the opportunities and advantages life affords for her complete development; and we deny the dogma of the centuries, incorporated in the codes of all nations—that woman was made for man—her best interests, in all cases, to be sacrificed to his will." As an educated, white, middle-class woman, Stanton rejected contemporary notions of womanhood as a limitation on her agency and thereby stood in stark contrast to Truth who viewed these notions as a potential resource to be mobilized.

Unity among women, then, is no longer assumed by historians of women. As a field of inquiry, U.S. women's history examines the relationships of power between groups of women at the same time it continues to emphasize the reality that women, as women, face historically specific experiences and oppressions. Far from being a natural difference or biological fact, womanhood is an experience saturated with history and politics.

FUNDAMENTAL ASSUMPTIONS AND PREMISES OF THIS BOOK

In their different ways, both Truth and Stanton would have endorsed a principle that has guided scholars: the importance of recognizing that women were agents of change rather than compliant victims of oppressive circumstances or restrictive ideology. For example, when the first textile factories appeared in the late eighteenth century, women and children constituted the first workforce; and as the system of industrial production expanded in subsequent decades, women continued to staff the mills and assess their situation. In the early 1820s, women weavers in Pawtucket, Rhode Island, protested their low wages and poor conditions, leading to what is considered to be the first strike of factory workers in the United States. Within the family, women also acted forcefully. One historian has gone so far as to trace the rise of "domestic feminism" as evidenced in the declining size of families of the white, urban, middle class in the nineteenth century. Without relying on new contraceptive techniques or mechanisms, women were gaining more control over reproduction, this historian concluded, by assuming the right to determine the timing and frequency of sexual intercourse within marriage. As a consequence, over the course of the nineteenth century, the average number of children per family dropped from seven to four.

In the late 1940s, one of the most distinguished historians in the United States, Mary R. Beard, warned against using "oppression" or "subjection" as a baseline for writing women's history. Such a formulation does disservice to the rich historical record, she insisted. Beard made her case vividly in *Woman as Force in History*, a book illustrating the way "civilization" has depended on women's work and contributions, especially in the realm of private life. It was women, whose primary role has always been the preservation of life, who, in essence, nurtured the development of society from its beginning. Beard emphasized not only women's achievements but went to great lengths to document their enormous contributions to community life that other historians had overlooked in their misguided focus on the nation-state and its male leaders.

Recently, historians of women have continued down this path, once again examining the tremendous role that women have played within their communities. Lacking access to the formal mechanisms of power, women instead formed their own networks of kin and friends to take responsibility for the welfare of the poor and the indigent, the mentally or physically disabled, the unemployed and uprooted, and especially dislocated women and their children. By the early twentieth century, the organizations and institutions they had established were so extensive and well-rooted that they formed the basis of what historians would later term the "welfare state."

The main narrative line of this book builds on these premises, viewing the division between "private" and "public" as important primarily in a rhetorical sense, that is, as a language of gender rather than a description of material reality. Instead, agency or *power* emerges as a central category of analysis. This category facilitates a study of relationships between men and women (rather than a study of women in isolation) as well as relationships among women, either as friends or relatives, and as antagonists. The category *power* also prompts a consideration of the changing nature of those relationships, thereby making gender—masculinity as well as femininity—a central feature of the narrative. Finally, this category recognizes that these relations of *power* are structured as well by other factors. The relationships among women—as determined, for example, by differences of race, ethnicity, class, age, region, and religion—are part of a dynamic history of hierarchy and inequality within families, communities, and nation. This textbook examines how women of varying backgrounds have negotiated their differences both in personal encounters and institutional movements. The category *power* is used to examine the social relationships between men and women, specifically within the realm of sexuality. In line with recent scholarship, sexuality emerges as a major dimension in the history of women and gender. A focus on sexuality, defined through reproduction, women's health, reigning definitions of sexual normality and deviance, and as an enduring benchmark for measuring gender equality, provides an important means through which to analyze changes in women's lives. From the early-nineteenth-century "passionless" republican mothers to sexually expressive African American blues singers of the 1930s, notions of ideal or deviant womanhood often rely on sexuality for their authority. Lesbian subcultures also serve as analytic opportunities to explore the relationship between gender and sexuality.

Photographers and journalists documented the impact of the Depression on communities across the country, like this photo of a breadline in Harlem, New York, in the early 1930s. Such images also record the racial and gendered hierarchies involved in relief efforts.

This book deploys *power*, then, as an expansive category. Individual chapters cover familiar topics, such as the shift of production of goods from home to factory, as events that affected the power dynamics within the family, that is, between husband and wife as well as between parents and children, and as events that reconfigured relationships among women of different social standings, particularly among those who earned wages for their labors, either in the home or in the factory, and those who did not. Individual chapters also highlight topics that have more recently come to the fore of scholarship, such as the role of U.S. women in establishing an imperialist agenda for the United States in the late nineteenth century. Within such contexts, this textbook raises questions about the sources of influence or control within the family, the market economy, the community, and the nation state. Moreover, the analysis of power necessarily emphasizes issues of gender, class, race, and citizenship and illustrates the fluidity between what are conventionally distinguished as the "private" and "public" arenas.

In using power as a category of analysis, this textbook develops a narrative focused on both the sphere of reproduction and the political economy. Of special interest are the changing patterns of women's labor, household as well as market, and the relationship of both to issues of power within the family and society at large. A large component of the text concerns activism and political organization, including such conventional topics as voting rights and unionism. Moreover, the achievements and contributions of women, individually and collectively, serve not so much to lionize these pioneers but to illustrate various dimensions of the operation of power in U.S. society.

However, despite the analytical emphasis on power, the conventional signposts in the history of the United States figure prominently. These signposts provide background for the novice and at the same time serve to orient more advanced students to events encountered in other contexts or courses.

The stories thus unfold in several major sections: the era of exploration and colonization; the American Revolution and the creation of a new nation; the industrialization of the economy and expansion of territories; the Civil War and the abolition of slavery; the expansion of the nation both within the North American continent and overseas; the push toward reform and the increasing participation of women in the labor market; and the consolidation of mass consumer society as shaped by the major events of the twentieth century, including the Great Depression, World War II, the cold war, and the civil rights movements that led up to second-wave feminism. However, at the heart of this organization is a mix of methodologies—an examination of the changing social relationships that constitute the history of women as well as a consideration of social constructions, that is, of gender.

RECOMMENDED READING

Julie Des Jardins. *Women and the Historical Enterprise in America: Gender, Race, and the Politics of Memory, 1880–1945*. Chapel Hill: University of North Carolina Press, 2003. A detailed examination of women in the profession of history, which includes a highly informative chapter on the first women to write and teach on U.S. women's history.

Nancy A. Hewitt. "Beyond the Search for Sisterhood: American Women's History in the 1980s." *Social History* 10 (1985): 299–321. Warns against assuming that what women share in common supersedes the differences based in class and racial inequalities.

Evelyn Brooks Higginbotham. "African-American Women's History and the Metalanguage of Race." *Signs* 17 (Winter 1992): 251–74. A key text on theoretical and methodological issues concerning the place of race in women's history.

Joan Kelly-Gadol. "The Social Relations of the Sexes: Methodological Implications of Women's History." *Signs* 1 (Summer 1976): 809–82. One of the first essays to specify the theoretical dimensions of the project of women's history.

Linda K. Kerber. "Separate Spheres, Female Worlds, Woman's Place: The Rhetoric of Women's History." *Journal of American History* 75 (1988): 9–39. Argues against the notion that men and women actually lived in "separate spheres" and replaces it with an emphasis on rhetoric.

Denise Riley. *"Am I That Name?": Feminism and the Category of "Women" in History*. Minneapolis: University of Minnesota Press, 1988. Offers an analysis of the way rhetorical conventions have helped to fashion our understanding of gender differences, especially as embodied in the term "woman."

Joan Wallach Scott. "Gender: A Useful Category of Historical Analysis." *American Historical Review* 92 (December 1986). Argues that not just women's history but all history can be retold if gender is used as the primary means of analysis.

ADDITIONAL BIBLIOGRAPHY

Mary R. Beard. *Woman as Force in History: A Study in Traditions and Realities*. New York: The Macmillan Company, 1946.

Berenice A. Carroll, ed. *Liberating Women's History: Theoretical and Critical Essays*. Urbana: University of Illinois Press, 1976.

Blanche Wiesen Cook. "The Historical Denial of Lesbianism." *Radical History Review* 20 (Spring/Summer 1979): 60–65.

Martin Duberman, Martha Vicinus, and George Chancey, eds. *Hidden from History: Reclaiming the Gay and Lesbian Past*. New York: NAL Books, 1989.

Lisa Duggan. "The Discipline Problem: Queer Theory Meets Lesbian and Gay History." *Gay and Lesbian Quarterly* 2 (1995): 179–91.

Judith Grant. *Fundamental Feminism: Contesting the Core Concepts of Feminist Theory*. New York: Routledge, 1993.

Mary S. Hartman and Lois Banner, eds. *Clio's Consciousness Raised: New Perspectives in the History of Women*. New York: Harper & Row, 1974.

Nancy Isenberg. "Second Thoughts on Gender and Women's History." *American Studies* 36 (1995): 93–105.

Joan Kelly. "The Doubled Vision of Feminist History." *Feminist Studies* 5 (Spring 1979): 216–27.

Gerda Lerner. *The Majority Finds Its Past: Placing Women in History*. New York: Oxford University Press, 1979.

———. *Why History Matters*. New York: Oxford University Press, 1997.

Tessie Liu. "Teaching the Differences among Women from a Historical Perspective: Rethinking Race and Gender as Social Categories." *Women's Studies International Forum* 14, no. 4 (1991): 265–76.

Patrice McDermott. *Politics and Scholarship: Feminist Academic Journals and the Production of Knowledge*. Urbana: University of Illinois Press, 1994.

Sue Morgan, ed. *The Feminist History Reader*. London; New York: Routledge, 2006.

Louise M. Newman. "Dialogue: Critical Theory and the History of Women: What's at Stake in Deconstructing Women's History." *Journal of Women's History* 2 (Winter 1991): 58–68.

Karen Offen, Ruth Roach Pierson, and Jane Rendall, eds. *Writing Women's History: International Perspectives.* Bloomington: Indiana University, 1991.

Benita Roth. *Separate Roads to Feminism: Black, Chicana, and White Feminist Movements in America's Second Wave.* Cambridge, UK; New York: Cambridge University Press, 2004.

Daniel Scott Smith. "Family Limitation, Sexual Control, and Domestic Feminism in Victorian America." In *Clio's Consciousness Raised: New*

Perspectives on the History of Women, edited by Mary Hartman and Luis W. Banner, New York: Harper & Row, 1974, 119–36.

Carroll Smith-Rosenber. "The Female World of Love and Ritual: Relations between Women in Nineteenth Century America." *Signs* 1 (1975): 1–29.

Manuela Thurner. "Subject to Change: Theories and Paradigms of U.S. Feminist History." *Journal of Women's History* 9 (Summer 1997): 122–46.

Barbara Welter. "The Cult of True Womanhood, 1820–1860." *American Quarterly* 18 (1966): 151–74.

WORLDS APART, TO 1700

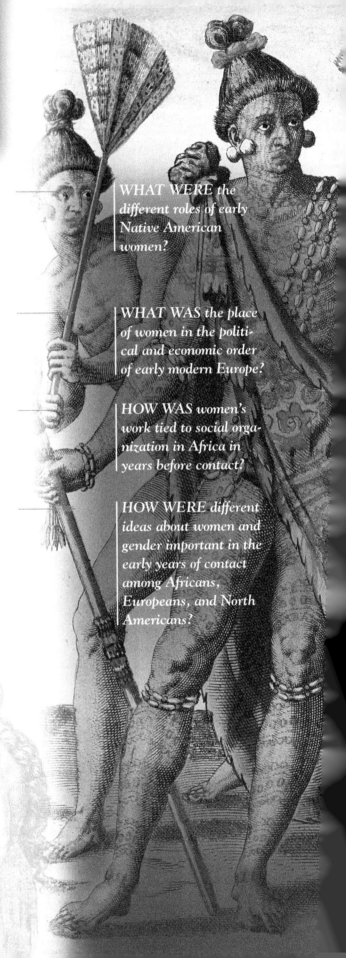

WHAT WERE the different roles of early Native American women?

WHAT WAS the place of women in the political and economic order of early modern Europe?

HOW WAS women's work tied to social organization in Africa in years before contact?

HOW WERE different ideas about women and gender important in the early years of contact among Africans, Europeans, and North Americans?

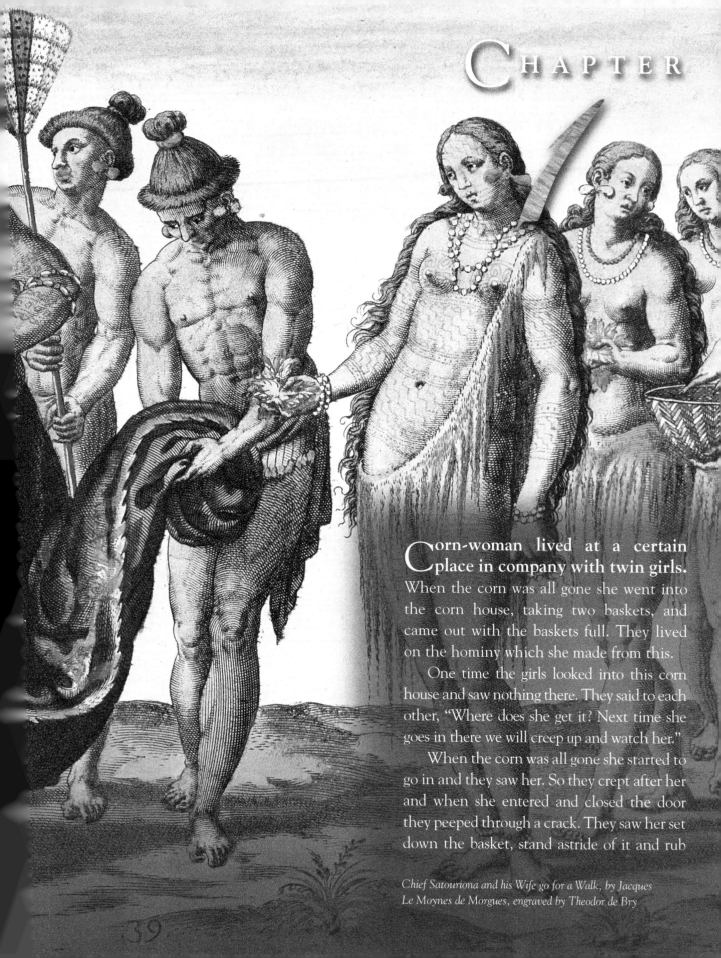

Corn-woman lived at a certain place in company with twin girls. When the corn was all gone she went into the corn house, taking two baskets, and came out with the baskets full. They lived on the hominy which she made from this.

One time the girls looked into this corn house and saw nothing there. They said to each other, "Where does she get it? Next time she goes in there we will creep up and watch her."

When the corn was all gone she started to go in and they saw her. So they crept after her and when she entered and closed the door they peeped through a crack. They saw her set down the basket, stand astride of it and rub

Chief Satouriona and his Wife go for a Walk, by Jacques Le Moynes de Morgues, engraved by Theodor de Bry

and shake herself, and there was a noise, tsagȧk, as if something fell off. In this way she filled one basket with corn. Then she stood over the other, rubbed herself and shook, the noise tsagȧk was heard and that basket was full of beans. After that the girls ran away.

"Let us not eat it," they said. "She defecates and then feeds us with the excrement." So when the hominy was cooked they did not eat it, and from that she knew they had seen her. "Since you think it is filthy, you will have to help yourselves from now on. Kill me and burn my body. When summer comes things will spring up on the place where it was burned and you must cultivate them, and when they are matured they will be your food."

They killed Corn-woman and burned her body and when summer came, corn, beans, and pumpkins sprang up.

Source: The Natchez Myth from John R. Swanton, "The Origin of Corn" Myths and Tales of the Southeastern Indians, Bureau of American Ethnology Bulletin 88 (Washington, DC: U.S. Government Printing Office, 1929), 230.

ariations of the stories of Corn-woman, or Corn Mother, have been told for centuries in different Native American communities throughout North America. The powerful fertility myths that circulated orally joined the woman who produced food with the woman who produced children. Similar traditions prevailed throughout history in Africa and Europe, where women were also of critical importance in feeding their societies and rearing their children. Indeed, these roles were so important that their societies not only saw the productive and reproductive roles of women as linked, they also evolved complex laws to regulate how women produced and reproduced. Community strategies to grow food and trade goods included alliances created by marriage or other kinds of sexual relationships.

These alliances varied tremendously throughout the Americas, Africa, and Europe, creating different household structures. Women might live in small families with only their husbands and children, or they might be part of a more extended lineage in which they were one of several wives, or they might live in a society in which their relationships with their mothers were more important than their relationships with their husbands. In some societies, women controlled the farmlands and took primary responsibility for agricultural production, whereas in other places their husbands or fathers were more likely to control these resources. As a result, women in different parts of the world exercised power in diverse ways, and women in some societies had more power than women in other societies.

In the thousands of years before the end of the fifteenth century, when the continents of the Americas, Africa, and Europe came into explosive contact, these different forms of social organization evolved, to a large extent, independently of one another. However, as Europeans developed deeper trade relations with Africa beginning in the middle of the fifteenth century, discovered the Americas at the end of the fifteenth century, and soon after began the forced transport of African slaves across the

Atlantic, these different forms of social organization became the subject of intense scrutiny. As men and women in Africa, Europe, and the Americas took each others' measure in the years following contact, they noted with unease different patterns of dress and social life, family organization and work, and religion and governance. While occasionally these encounters with different cultures prompted self-reflection, more often they provided fodder for misunderstanding and conflict.

WOMEN IN THE AMERICAS

Between twenty thousand and thirty thousand years ago, men and women began to enter the North American continent by crossing the Bering Strait from Asia. The men hunted game while women tended the base camp, foraging for nuts and berries wherever they landed. These bands of hunter-gatherers moved both south and east, over thousands of years, usually in search of food. By the time Europeans arrived in the New World at the end of the fifteenth century, approximately sixty million people inhabited North and South America, speaking more than one thousand different languages. About six million people lived in North America where hundreds of different cultural traditions continued to evolve. At this point, the Aztecs had conquered many of the peoples living in central Mexico, the Pueblo cultures of the Southwest had been weakened by devastating droughts, and warring tribes in the New York area had not yet begun to negotiate the truce that would lead to the creation of the Iroquois League. Women's roles in each of these societies varied with historical circumstances; but particularly in less hierarchical societies, these women exercised considerable power in their control over food and access to their communities.

Hunting and Gathering

During the thousands of years in which inhabitants of the Americas evolved from bands of hunters and gatherers to societies in which agriculture played an increasingly important role, women often had both status and power because the food they provided was of critical importance. In most of these societies, men were responsible for hunting, but women were the foragers and, eventually, the farmers. Communities were small and decision making was relatively egalitarian, often focusing on questions of when and where to move.

Hunting and gathering societies were organized in small bands that moved from one place to another as resources were depleted. While men hunted game, women usually maintained the base camp, tending to children while they also foraged for roots and berries or turned animal skins into clothing and carcasses into meat. The big game hunted by men began to disappear around 8000 BCE, so that men shifted to hunting smaller animals, and women's foraging activities became even more critical to community survival because the smaller animals did not provide as much meat as the larger ones. As communities increasingly relied on foraging, women were more likely than men to determine when it was time to move on, particularly because they were more likely to exhaust their supply of nuts and berries before men exhausted the supply of game.

This leadership role provided power to women, but power did not always translate into a better life. As an investigation of the Eva site in Tennessee demonstrated, women buried there had significantly shorter life spans than did the men of their community. Many women died before reaching age thirty, whereas men often lived past the age of sixty. This might have been because men no longer hunted large game and thus faced less mortal danger, whereas women continued to face the same dangers of death in childbirth. Indeed, as life became more sedentary, women might have started bearing more children, an activity that would have resulted in more deaths for the mothers.

Because women were the ones who usually gathered plants and seeds, they were probably the ones who scattered seeds purposefully to encourage further growth. Eventually, this experimentation led to the development of agriculture, first in the valleys around Mexico City as early as 5000 BCE and in the area that is now the southwestern United States by about 1500 BCE. In most indigenous societies in North America, women became the farmers. Where groups continued to rely on game for part of their diet, men were the hunters, though sometimes they helped to prepare the fields. Women's crops of corn and beans and cotton supported increasing numbers of people and more complex forms of society composed of permanent settlements and expanding trade networks. As women faced a more demanding schedule of tending crops, harvesting, and organizing food processing, societies may have begun creating ideas about gender to organize work. Children, for example, may have been more likely to be assigned specific jobs by gender, which ingrained such distinctions more clearly than in the past.

Farming provided more food than hunting did so that populations could grow. However, women faced new challenges in their living conditions. Because they moved less often, the lack of sanitation in these camps was a growing problem. Disease could spread quickly, more often striking the women and children, who were permanent inhabitants, than the men, who were off hunting. Women also shouldered an increasingly heavy workload as the primary farmers in many of these societies. In the southeastern part of the United States, for example, women increasingly began to suf-

Native American women were often responsible for planting crops. Jacques Le Moyne de Morgues captured this gendered division of labor among Timucua women during the 1560s, when he traveled with an expedition through what is now Florida. His artwork was later desseminated in engravings made by Theodor de Bry at the end of the sixteenth century.

fer from osteoarthritis because of their farming chores. The work that women undertook with the advent of agriculture not only was demanding but also varied in significant ways from one region to another.

Cultural Differences

By 1000 CE, densely populated, architecturally sophisticated, and complex societies that were rooted in agricultural production had emerged not only in Mexico, with the successive domination of the Olmecs, the Mayans, and the Aztecs, but also in the southwestern United States, with the development of the Pueblo cultures, and farther east, with the Mississippian cultures that flourished along the banks of the Mississippi River. In areas farther north, other groups such as the Iroquois combined a semimobile existence with farming and hunting, while in some places to the west, the California and Northwest Coast Indians shared forests and streams that were so abundant they had little use for agriculture. Each of these societies used ideas about gender to organize work and the distribution of resources. However, because gender is a socially constructed category, the activities of women in one society were not necessarily the same as those of women in another. These gender distinctions were some of the most important ways in which cultural differences were manifested among the many peoples living throughout North America during this time period.

Among the Iroquois peoples of the northeastern United States, women not only farmed the land but also were the ones who inherited it, a system that worked well in a society in which men were often gone. The Iroquois League, initially composed of the Senecas, the Mohawks, the Oneidas, the Onondagas, and the Cayugas, had been formed in the fifteenth century to bring peace to these tribes. However, during the spring, summer, and fall, men continued to fight as well as hunt, leaving women behind to tend to the land. Before departing, the men cleared new fields for planting with a slash-and-burn technique, but women then planted and harvested the crops of corn, beans, and squash. Women worked in their fields communally and then distributed and prepared the food for their families. Indeed, the women controlled not only the distribution of food from their crops but also the distribution of animal meat that men obtained through hunting.

In the fortified villages of Iroquoia, women were a dominant force. Multiple families lived in longhouses, twenty feet wide and as much as two hundred feet long. Matrons, representing the oldest generation of women, presided over these households in which husbands came to live with their daughters and granddaughters in **matrilocal** societies. Each nuclear family occupied a small compartment of the longhouse, sharing fires and food. Iroquois societies were not only matrilocal but also **matrilineal**, because goods, including their homes and the rights to their land, were inherited through the mothers' families. Iroquois women did not inherit specific parcels of land, because such concepts of ownership did not exist among the Iroquois. Rather, they inherited rights to farm certain areas of land through their mothers' families.

The role of women is less clear in the Mississippian societies that developed during this same period in cities and villages stretching from Louisiana and Alabama in the South to Illinois and Iowa in the North. The vast urban center of Cahokia, populated by probably twenty thousand to thirty thousand people at its peak in the twelfth century CE, was the most spectacular of these settlements. This complex culture was extremely hierarchical, composed of political and religious elites who were supported by large groups of artisans and farmers. Cahokia used the agricultural produce of outlying

matrilocal Living with the wife's family.

matrilineal Tracing inheritance and descent through the female line.

MAP 1-1 NORTH AMERICAN CULTURE AREAS, C. 1500

A variety of Native American cultures adapted to distinctive climates throughout the Americas.

farmlands for its subsistence, and Cahokian leaders marshaled the labor of thousands to build huge pyramids for ritual purposes. While both men and women of the peasant class may have been farmers in this society, women were ritually linked to agriculture and fertility in figurines depicting them with farming tools and produce.

Women were also closely tied to agriculture in the Pueblo societies that emerged in the Southwest. By the time Europeans arrived at the beginning of the sixteenth cen-

Michael Hampshire, "Community Life at Cahokia. This rendering of the Cahokia community by a modern day artist suggests the densely populated and urban characteristics of the community when it was at its height.

tury, many of these Pueblo societies were organized both matrilineally and matrilo-cally. Like the Iroquois, women owned the homes that their families lived in and the fields that they farmed; the goods that their families accumulated passed through the female line. However, unlike the Iroquois, husbands and sons of Pueblo women often did the actual farming, in addition to hunting small game to supplement the family diet. Women prepared the food that was produced and crafted beautiful pottery jars and tightly woven baskets that were dense enough to carry water and store excess food. They also built the homes where their families lived. Men cut and hauled the timber that was used to frame their pueblos, but women were responsible for the rest of the construction. While women controlled the household, Pueblo men controlled the *kivas*. Central to every Pueblo town, kivas were build-ings that men shared for socializing, for ritual practices, and for weaving. Although women in southwestern societies also wove, weaving was clearly an important activity for men in Pueblo societies.

patrilineal Tracing in-heritance and descent through the male line.

patrilocal Living with the husband's family.

Not all societies in the Americas were matrilineal. Among the Aztecs who rose to power in central Mexico beginning in the twelfth century CE, women lived in a society that was both **patrilineal** and **patrilocal**. Men were responsible for the farming, while women were responsible for do-mestic activities. Girls married young in Aztec society—sometimes when they were ten or twelve years old—and went to live with their husbands' families. While much of their responsibility centered on the home, one of their activities, weaving, took on broader significance. As the Aztecs ex-panded their conquest to surrounding areas, they taxed both the men and the women in the societies they conquered. While men paid their tributes through work or warfare, women paid their tributes in cloth. Demands for cloth tributes increased over the years so that women had trouble produc-ing enough to meet their obligations. Thus, some households who could af-ford to do so acquired female slaves to help with the weaving or husbands took additional wives.

Aztec girls were trained in domestic skills such as grinding maize and weaving, as is revealed in this page of the Codex Men-doza, which was created in Mexico City in 1541–1542.

Marriage, Family, and Gender Identities

Just as practices of work and inheritance varied among Native Americans, so too did ideas about family. Each society created distinctive forms of family organization that were well suited to the way they used their resources. Among those who communally owned agricultural fields and shared hunting lands, for example, family lineages and clans were more socially significant than the smaller units formed by husbands, wives, and their children. A woman's relationship to her parents or siblings who controlled the land she farmed were usually much more important than her relationship to her husband. To the extent that marriages created alliances between different lineages, parents took an interest in the choices their children made. But because individual family units were absorbed into larger households, and because land was communally owned or managed, marriage negotiations were simple, and little property changed hands. Small gifts were exchanged between husband and wife as a show of reciprocity, but legal obligations beyond that were uncommon.

Marriages were primarily personal relationships that could be dissolved if the relationship deteriorated. Among some Indian groups of the eastern United States, a young husband and wife would limit their sexual encounters during their first year of marriage while they established their relationship. It was during this time that the couple would also be most likely to divorce if their relationship did not work out. Once they began to have children, divorce was less likely, though still accepted. Divorce did not necessarily lead to disruptions in child rearing among the Iroquois, for example, because the children of these marriages became a part of the mother's lineage. Uncles were the important authority figures who were responsible for discipline, while fathers could be more indulgent.

polygamy Marriage to more than one spouse.

Not only was divorce accepted by many Indians; so too was **polygamy**, the practice of having more than one spouse at a time. Where circumstances warranted, a man took more than one wife. Some of the higher-status Indians of the eastern United States, particularly chiefs, had extensive social responsibilities that were too onerous for one wife to shoulder. An extra wife in that case was an important way to extend additional hospitality. Where warfare had reduced the proportion of men in a society, more than one sister sometimes married the same husband who would contribute hunting goods for them to share. This practice of **soral polygamy** was particularly useful in matrilineal societies, because when a man married two sisters he was still a part of the same lineage.

soral polygamy Marriage to two sisters by the same man.

Because marriage had a very different meaning for Native Americans, so too did sexuality. For many Indians, sexual relations were important not only for procreation but also for other forms of sociability. Women sometimes welcomed new men into their community by sleeping with them. Pueblo women viewed sex as a way of not only welcoming strangers but also limiting their power. The same was true of Algonquian women in the Chesapeake region and the Huron women near the Saint Lawrence River. Indeed, unmarried women in Indian societies were usually free to engage in sexual relations with as many men as they wished. In some cases, women expected a demonstration of reciprocity when they engaged in sexual relations with men who were not their husbands. Pueblo women, for example, expected a gift such as a blanket or piece of meat. Such exchanges were not required for sex that occurred within marriage, because by the very nature of the relationship, such obligations had already been worked out.

Even after marriage, women in some tribes continued to have sex with men who were not their husbands. Women of the matrilineal Huron, Ottawa, and Montagnais groups in the Quebec area, for example, were free to engage in sexual relations with men who were not their husbands. One Montagnais husband scoffed at the concern expressed by an early Jesuit missionary who wanted to know how Indian men could be sure their sons really belonged to them. "You French people love only your own children," he pointed out, "but we love all the children of our tribe." The patrilineal Miami and Illinois Indians of the Great Lakes region, by way of contrast, frowned upon such practices. Women in these tribes were sometimes mutilated by their husbands, gang-raped by their husbands' friends, or executed if they had sex with someone besides their husbands. Even among these groups that more carefully policed the sexuality of women, however, divorce was still an option for wives dissatisfied with their husbands.

Some women in the Great Lakes region preferred temporary relationships with male hunting companions to the commitments that marriage demanded and constructed a gender identity that was neither male nor female. These hunting women never married. They preferred traveling with men through the forests to staying with women in the villages to raise children. Their relationship with a particular man usually only lasted as long as a hunt. They provided food and clothing for their companions and expected compensation in return. They enjoyed sex with their partners and if children were produced returned them to their villages to be raised by their families. These children did not have the status that would allow them to marry into the higher ranks of their governing class, but they were otherwise accepted by their relatives, suggesting the extent to which the alternative gender identity of their mothers was accepted.

While hunting women in the Great Lakes region represented one important variation on the basic gender divisions between men and women, an even more widespread variation in gender distinctions occurred in the case of people who were biologically male but who dressed like and took on the roles of women in their society. Today they are referred to as *two-spirit people* or *men-women*, though in precontact times the names for this alternative gender identity varied. Although they were never very numerous in any given community, two-spirit people could be found in most areas of North America except the Northeast where the Iroquois dominated. Two-spirit people were highly valued in their communities and sometimes functioned as spiritual leaders or took on other jobs of ritual importance such as burying the dead. In other cases, they were prized for their ability to apply the strength of a man to the jobs usually undertaken by women, such as grinding corn. The sexual relationships that were allowed for two-spirit people varied with their tribes. Among the Pueblo Indians, for example, they were allowed to have sex only with men, not women. Indeed, they were not allowed to refuse demands for sex from young men. In other groups, they had stable marriages with individual men. While most of their sexual relations were with men, this was not always the case, and sometimes they did have sexual relations with women. Indian cultures observed a strong binary division of gender between men and women, but the presence of hunting women and two-spirit people shows how these cultures also included third and even fourth gender identities for some of their members.

Exercising Power

How women exercised power was largely a result of the kind of society they lived in. In hierarchical and highly stratified societies, such as those found among the Mayans and Aztecs in Mexico or the Mississippian cultures surrounding Cahokia, power was exercised by elite classes of royalty and nobles. Women who were born into those classes sometimes wielded significant power, but they did so because of their elite status rather than their gender. Among the less-stratified, mobile or semimobile societies that stretched across vast areas of North America, however, decision making often occurred on a community level and in a more egalitarian fashion, giving both individual women and groups of women opportunities to exercise power.

sovereign Autonomous ruler or chief of state.

Among the Mayans in Mexico, some women exercised the power of **sovereigns**. Both Princess Kanal Ikal, who ruled from 583 CE to 604 CE, and Princess Zak-Kuk, who ruled shortly after, inherited their positions and ruled independently of any power held by their husbands. They are commemorated in numerous monuments that remain at Palenque in central Mexico. Lady Xoc, who was married to a powerful Mayan king, Shield Jaguar, participated in important rituals and was honored with her own temple in Yaxchilan. Among the Aztecs, who dominated central Mexico several centuries later, women of the royal line made strategic marriages to maintain the power of their family. Women also ruled in some of the Mississippian groups that survived in the southeastern United States into the period of contact with Europeans. The men traveling with explorer Hernando de Soto on his search for treasure in 1540 recorded an encounter with a female leader whom they called the Lady of Cofachiqui. She arrived in a canoe with six noblewomen, pulled by another canoe filled with rowers and noblemen. Jacques Le Moyne, an artist who came to Florida with French explorers in 1564, described another queen being carried on a litter by six men in Florida.

shaman Spiritual leader, often with the power to heal.

Women occasionally took on the role of **shaman** in some Indian societies. Shamans, spiritual leaders who had supernatural powers to communicate with the spirit world and to heal in the natural world, were usually men, but not always. In the Great Lakes region, both men and women were shamans. They were often sought to predict the future or dance in a curing ceremony. In one case from 1636, a particularly powerful female shaman was called in to cure a sick woman when three male shamans had failed. According to the Jesuit priest who watched, she "began to shake the house and to sing and cry so loudly that she caused the devil to come who told them more than they wanted."

In some tribes, such as those of the Iroquois, women participated in many crucial decisions. While the chief of their tribes was always a man, Iroquois matrons chose him—and they removed him if necessary. They also chose men to speak for them at council meetings. They sometimes even demanded captives in warfare or kept men from participating in war. Thus, although men and women engaged in very different roles in society and exercised different kinds of power, Iroquois women were not subordinate to men. Buttressing their political voice, however, was their control over the distribution of food.

In many of the less-hierarchical societies, in which the household was a key social component of the larger social system, women most clearly exercised power when they controlled their bodies or the distribution of resources. When women in matrilineal societies decided whom to have sex with, they controlled access to their lineages and the inheritances that passed through their lineages. If they decided to end a pregnancy, they also controlled who would be a member of their societies. By providing food to their households, they were responsible for the physical survival of their communities. In both symbolic and real terms, these were crucial areas of power that complemented the power exercised by men in hunting, warfare, and diplomatic negotiations and that spilled over into more formal political activities as well. These were also forms of power that differed significantly from the customs that had evolved in European societies.

WOMEN'S LIVES

LADY XOC

On October 28, 709 CE, Lady Xoc of Yaxchilan pierced a hole in her tongue and pulled a rope of thorns through it. As the first (and most powerful) wife of the Mayan king, Shield Jaguar, Lady Xoc was enacting a ritual that both recognized the important alignment of Jupiter with Saturn that year and that commemorated the birth of Shield Jaguar's son, Bird Jaguar, by a younger wife. Lady Xoc apparently did not have any children who would inherit the throne, but she was powerful enough that she was not displaced by the younger wife who bore Bird Jaguar, the heir to the kingdom. Indeed, a temple was built in Lady Xoc's honor, commemorating her blood sacrifice and other key aspects of her leadership.

That Temple, now known as "Structure 23," was strategically placed on the main plaza, signifying Lady Xoc's importance. Over the doorways, three critical scenes were portrayed that attest to her influence. In one, she calls on the founders of the royal line to legitimize her husband's claim to the throne. In another, she helps her husband dress for battle. And in a third, she pulls the rope of thorns through her tongue. Lady Xoc is the focus of each scene, a high honor seldom accorded to women in Mayan art. In part, this

was because Lady Xoc was not only Shield Jaguar's senior wife but also his cousin and she brought to their marriage a powerful alliance with her birth family that helped her husband's rise to power. But it is also clear that Lady Xoc exercised power from the female space created in her temple, a power that lasted throughout her life. ∎

EUROPEAN WOMEN

Europe was in a state of upheaval in the two centuries that preceded its discovery of the Americas in 1492. Various parts of the continent were being transformed socially and economically by growing trade with Asia and Africa. A new class of wealthy merchants began to rival nobles for power. Peasants struggled to survive while landholders, eager to graze their own herds for commercial purposes, claimed pasturelands the peasants had been using. This social and economic dislocation was compounded by the demographic catastrophe of the bubonic plague, introduced into Europe by rats from a ship bringing merchandise from Asia. The **Black Death**, as the plague was called, struck originally in the 1340s, wiping out about twenty-five million people within three years. Periodic outbreaks added to the death toll, and within fifty years, Europe's population declined by 40 percent. Finally, the Hundred Years' War, fought

Black Death Bubonic plague that swept Europe beginning in the 1340s and continuing particularly through the seventeenth century.

Queen Elizabeth Playing a Lute, *by Nicholas Hilliard.* *Queen Elizabeth I was known for her accomplishments in the arts as well as in politics. This portrait by Nicholas Hilliard suggests her artistic accomplishments. (Nicholas Hilliard (1547–1619) Queen Elizabeth I playing the lute/Berkeley Castle, Gloucesterhsire, UK/Bridgeman Art Library)*

largely on French soil from the middle of the fourteenth to the middle of the fifteenth century, not only exacerbated the chaos and misery caused by the plague and the demands of trade but also ended with the emergence of more modern nation states in Europe.

All of these changes had consequences for women. In some cases, powerful female leaders such as Elizabeth I of England and Isabella of Castile gained power as a result of inheritance or marriage. With social and political hierarchies shaken to the point of collapse, gender roles adapted. Women took on new jobs, but their very flexibility in the face of catastrophe itself became a subject of debate and concern, particularly because they lived in societies that were organized around male leadership in both the home and the government.

Flexible Labor Force

Throughout Europe, many peasant women lived on small farms. Their activities were mostly confined to the household while men took charge of the fields. The household, however, was an expansive concept. Women's work included child rearing; tending gardens where they grew peas, turnips, and onions; processing food; and baking bread. During cold winter months, women turned to spinning so that they could make clothes for their family. Where possible, women collected nuts and berries from nearby woods and often tended the pigs and chickens that provided meat and eggs.

Women's work was crucial to the family's subsistence, but women also performed other valuable tasks beyond the household. At harvest time, women helped the men to cut the grains and bind the sheaves. They also herded the cattle into the field after the harvest to eat what was left. Women's flexibility to work beyond the household was crucial as land became so scarce that peasant families could not support themselves with their produce and as money was demanded in the payment of rent. Women made butter and cheese and soap, not just for their own consumption but for sale at local markets. Women—more than men—also worked as day laborers for wealthy families and sold produce or animals that they raised to earn the extra money families needed to survive as the economy around them became increasingly commercialized. In 1450, for example, Katherine Rolf of Cambridge, England, earned money weeding for the local convent, selling chickens, and cleaning wool. Other women picked up work as dairymaids and laundresses for wealthy families.

Many urban women also demonstrated their flexibility in the wake of the disruptions caused by the Black Death when they moved into trades formerly the province of men. In England, many of the guilds that determined how trades would be practiced in a city allowed the wives and daughters of their members to join as well as permitting the widows of their members to carry on their husbands' trades. As a result, in 1419, thirty-nine of the members of the Brewers' Company in England were women. These women joined a small number of other female craftsmen who had established themselves in trades throughout Europe even before the plague had struck. In Paris, for example, five exclusively female guilds were operating at the end of the thirteenth century. Women were particularly active in the silk trades, which required careful handling of the delicate threads and cloth. By the end of the fifteenth century, however, as the population returned to earlier levels, women began to disappear from the guild rosters. A few hung on as grocers, locksmiths, brewers, and weavers; but most did not. Men who wanted their jobs pushed women out, and guilds changed their rules to favor men. As women moved in and out of fields and crafts and took on wage work to supplement family incomes, their flexibility provided an important cushion for both families and the larger economies in which they lived. At the same time, this flexibility meant that women were more difficult to categorize and their engagement in nontraditional jobs was seen as a threat to the social order.

In all circumstances, women earned less than men for their work, usually significantly less. As one contemporary writer during this period put it, women were "half-men" whose jobs were not as important and who worked more slowly than men. Only during the peak years of the plague did women's wages more closely approximate those of men. Even with the market on their side, however, laws were passed that enforced inequality. Dairymaids were supposed to earn a shilling less per year than a plowman according to an English law enacted in 1388. Lower wages not only led to increased poverty for women but to other forms of discrimination as well. In sixteenth-century England, as men and women moved from place to place in search of work, towns worried particularly about the ability of female vagrants to support themselves on the meager wages they were paid and feared they might end up on poor relief.

Patriarchal Societies

Women in Europe were paid less than men as part of a larger ideology that argued women were inferior to men in both mind and body. They had proven their weakness when Eve had tempted Adam in the biblical account of creation. Medical doctors believed a woman's temperament was ruled by her womb, which severely impaired her judgment. As a result, women were considered disorderly and irrational and could not be trusted because they lied. They caused social discord with their gossip. And because they lacked self-control, women could not control their sexual appetites. A woman's lusty sexuality was one of her most prominent weaknesses. Some writers argued that women were sexually insatiable (and thus more like animals than men were) because they could have multiple orgasms.

These beliefs were particularly clear in the witch hunts that spread like wildfire in northern Europe beginning in the fifteenth century and exploding in the sixteenth and seventeenth centuries. Many believed the ignorance and lustiness of women made them particularly vulnerable to Satan's temptations. Between fifty thousand and one hundred thousand people were executed for witchcraft, most of them women.

This view of the female character provided strong justification for not only treating women as inferior but also making sure they were under the control of men. By the sixteenth century, a lively pamphlet debate had emerged in England in which one side warned of the dangers of women's inherently shrewish natures and uncontrollable sexual urges. The other side argued that women's weaknesses were more the result of poor socialization and that if women were properly trained they could be modest and pious. Indeed, many women already measured up to this standard, their defenders claimed. Of course, there were strong class overtones to this distinction as well. In Spain,

W̲OMEN'S V̲OICES

LIVING AS A MAN

Elena de Céspedes was an Afro-Spanish woman who lived as both a man and a woman at different times in sixteenth-century Spain. When finally she faced the judges of the Inquisition in 1587, Elena claimed that although she had begun her life as a woman, she was a hermaphrodite. This physical condition, she argued, allowed her to marry both a man and a woman and to leave behind female labor for male jobs that were more lucrative. Historians have found her case interesting because of what it reveals about sexuality during the sixteenth century, but it is also important for what it tells us about the way in which different opportunities for work were limited by gender.

I was born in the city of Alhama, in the house of Benito de Medina, my mother's master. I was born a slave . . . but my master freed me. . . . I lived with my mother until I was fifteen or sixteen years old, at which time I married Cristobal Lombardo. . . . But because I got along badly with him, he left, leaving me pregnant. . . . I learned the trade of making hose and became a hosier. From there, I began to work as a weaver. . . . But after six months, I couldn't find anything to weave, so I began to work as a tailor and a hosier. . . . I went to Jerez de la Frontera, where I practiced the same trades of hosier and tailor. But there I got into a fight with a pimp called Heredia. I stabbed him and they arrested me. When I got out of jail, because of the threat this Heredia and his other pimp friends made against me, I decided to disguise myself in men's garb, so I left off wearing women's garb, which until then I'd always worn. . . .

I went to the Court [Madrid] for about two years and set up shop as a tailor. At Court I became friends with a surgeon from Valencia who took me into his home for a while and began to teach me to cure. . . . Because I learned so quickly and in so little time to cure as well as he did and

since the trade proved advantageous to me, I left off the tailor's trade and took up that of surgeon. . . . I became fond of Maria del Cano, daughter of Francisco del Cano, and Maria became fond of me, so I asked for her hand in marriage. . . .

[W]e went to Yepes, where we were married . . . in the parish of San Benito. . . . [W]e stayed in Yepes for more than a year, living together as man and wife until around Christmas, when, since there was no surgeon in Ocana, I went to live there. Then the *alcalde mayor*, named Ortega, sent a letter to the governor that . . . he'd known me and that it had been said by some that I was a woman and by others that I was male and female. Because of this letter the governor . . . Abraumel, arrested me. From there I was brought as a prisoner to this Holy Office. . . .

I've had carnal relations with many other women. . . . At Court, I took as my friend Isabel Ortiz and had relations with her as a man. Isabel never knew I had a woman's nature. My wife Maria del Cano never knew I had a woman's nature. Even though it's true that many times Maria desired to put her hand on my shameful parts, I never let her do it, even though she wanted to very much. . . .

Source: *Richard L. Kagan and Abigail Dyer, eds.,* Inquisitorial Inquiries: Brief Lives of Secret Jews and Other Heretics *(Baltimore, MD: Johns Hopkins University Press) 2004, 40–49.*

Questions

1. Elena claims that she began to dress as a man to escape attack in Jerez de la Frontera, but this does not explain why she continued to dress as a man. What professional opportunities opened up for Elena as a man?

2. What does Elena's testimony tell us about sex in sixteenth-century Spain?

wealthier women upheld their families reputations with their virtue. Their sexuality had to be carefully policed lest whole families' suffered dishonor, so they therefore appeared more modest than poorer women. Among the lower classes, family honor did not have the same value, so the virtue of these women did not have to be protected or policed in the same way. It was these women who were seen as promiscuous.

Throughout Europe, regardless of their class position, women—wives and daughters—were legally under the control of their husbands and fathers. This **patriarchal order** extended from household to government, as men were expected to rule their families and their communities. In countries that followed Roman law, such as Spain, the Netherlands, and France, women still maintained important rights of inheritance and property holding. In Spanish law, for example, girls and boys inherited property from both their mothers and their fathers, just as they inherited both their parents' names. Spanish women kept the right to the property they brought into marriage; and if they died childless, their siblings and parents laid claim to the property, not their husbands. Husbands in Spain still usually managed their wives' property, and wives had to get their husbands' permission before buying or selling it, but married women made contracts and used the courts when necessary to protect themselves.

Farmyard with Woman Milking a Cow, Da Costa Book of Hours, *Bruges, 1515. The work a woman did in her dairy was a valuable resource for farm families in Europe.*

In England, a different set of legal rights evolved for women under what eventually became known as common law. Married women in England merged their legal identities with that of their husbands. In this system of **coverture**, a married woman surrendered her property to her husband along with her name. As a **feme covert**, she could not make contracts, testify against her husband in court, or engage in any other legal transactions. Only those women who never married or who became widows assumed the status of **feme sole** and were able to engage independently in legal transactions. Unless a husband made specific arrangements specifying otherwise, his widow usually received the interest in one-third of his estate when he died rather than simply regaining the property she brought with her into the marriage.

Whether structured around Roman law or common law, these patriarchal households not only were necessary to compensate for the perceived weaknesses of women, but also were part of a larger political order. Families were viewed as the building blocks of the state; they were the first line of defense in maintaining a larger patriarchal order. A man ruled over his wife and children just as a king ruled over his kingdom. As Thomas Hobbes pointed out in *Leviathan,* his famous book on political philosophy published in 1651, a family was "a little monarchy." Thus, in England, if a servant killed his master or if a wife killed her husband, the crime was one of petty treason, not homicide. Female subordination was a part of political as well as family ideology.

Because marriage was crucial to both the political and social order, marriages in Europe were increasingly regulated by the sixteenth century. Many people at this time resisted actually formalizing their marriages legally. A large segment of the poor in Europe married informally, sometimes by jumping over a broom. Such informal marriages had the advantage of being broken without expensive divorce fees, should the divorce even be allowed. In Spain, a couple could establish a relationship simply by having a contract notarized, and they could end the relationship with a second notarized contract.

patriarchal order Society in which the father is the head of the family and the rest of the society is based on this hierarchy.

coverture Legal status of a woman upon marriage under common law, in which her legal identity is merged with that of her husband.

feme covert Status of married woman under common law in which her legal identity is merged with that of her husband.

feme sole Status of a single woman under common law in which her legal identity is independent of a man.

WOMEN'S VOICES

LOVE AND MONEY

Margery Brews, a young woman living in fifteenth-century England, faced a crisis when her father refused to come up with the money her fiancé, John Paston, had been expecting. Her father limited her dowry to one hundred pounds. Fortunately, the two families were able to reach an agreement and the couple married, but Margery did not know if this would be the outcome when she penned this letter to her sweetheart.

1477

To my Right Well beloved Cousin John Paston, Esquire, be this Letter delivered, &c.

Right worshipful and well beloved Valentine, in my most humble wise, I recommend me unto you, &c. And heartily I thank you for the Letter, which that ye send me by John Breckerton, whereby I understand and know, that ye be purposed to come to Topcroft in a short time, and without any errand or matter, but only to have a conclusion of the matter betwixt my father and you; I would be most glad of any Creature alive, so that the matter might grow to effect. And thereas ye say, and ye come and find the matter no more towards you than ye did aforetime, ye would no more put my father and my Lady my Mother to no cost nor business for that cause a good while after, which causeth my heart to be full heavy; and if that ye come, and the matter take to none effect, then should I be much more sorry, and full of heaviness.

And as for myself I have done and understand in the matter [all] that I can or may, as God knoweth; and I let you plainly understand, that my father will no more money part withal in that behalf, but an 100 l. and 50 marks, which is right far from the accomplishment of your desire.

Wherefore, if that ye could be content with that Good, and my poor Person, I would be the merriest maiden on ground; and if ye think not yourself so satisfied, or that ye might have much more Good, as I have understood by you afore; good, true, and loving Valentine, that ye take no such labour upon you, as to come more for that matter, But let [what] is, pass, and never more to be spoken of, as I may be your true Lover and Beadwoman during my life.

No more unto you at this time, but Almight Jesu preserve you both body and soul, &c.

By your Valentine, Margery Brews

Source: *Catherine Moriarty, ed.,* The Voice of the Middle Ages in Personal Letters 1100–1500 *(New York: Peter Bedrick Books, 1989), 208.*

Questions

1. Although the marriage negotiations are between Margery's father and fiancé, how does she participate in the negotiations?

2. How are love and money balanced in the relationship between Margery and John?

Concubinage, or barragania, as the practice was known, was well established in medieval Spain. Indeed, in medieval Spain, couples even performed the marriage ceremonies themselves with only two witnesses present. The marriage was usually preceded by an engagement, which was considered to be so legally binding that many couples felt it was acceptable to have sex after an engagement agreement had been signed. The Catholic Church attacked these practices at the Council of Trent in the 1560s by declaring marriage a sacrament and demanding that marriages take place inside a church, in the presence of a priest. Protestant clergy also demanded a more formal ceremony and required their followers to "post banns" before they married, announcing their intentions for all. In both ways, the churches were making sure that couples recognized the public importance of their personal relationships.

Whether formal or informal, European marriages were **monogamous**. Most people in northwestern Europe lived in fairly small households of six to eight people composed of parents and children during the fourteenth and fifteenth centuries. Larger, more extended households that included grandparents and other relatives were more common in southern Europe. In either case, peasant families were careful to control the number of children they had. In northwestern Europe, where many couples waited until their late twenties to marry because they were setting up independent households, the number of children they had was automatically reduced by their late start. But couples also controlled family size through abstinence, coitus interuptus, abortion, or infanticide. The Catholic Church condemned abortion, forbidding it in the twelfth century after the first month or two of conception and banning it altogether in the sixteenth century. But the practice still continued. In poorer areas, some families that simply could not afford to feed more children also practiced infanticide. Girls were more likely to be killed than boys, as was clear in the gender ratios that emerged in which more men than women were present. Methods were subtle: girls were weaned earlier than boys in some areas, thus exposing them to the risk of disease, or parents might "accidentally" roll over on a baby while sleeping, thus smothering it. In a society in which men were expected to rule, boys were more likely to survive infancy than girls were.

Challenges to Patriarchy

The patriarchal order in Europe confronted an important wrinkle in its gendered hierarchy as the wives and daughters of kings took the reins of power. By the sixteenth century, women had assumed the crown in some of the most important new countries in Europe. Isabella of Castile inherited this position, as did both Mary I and her half sister Elizabeth I in England. Women did not inherit the throne in France, but Anne of Austria and Catherine de Medici assumed powerful roles as **regents** while their royal children were young. In each case, as these women held on to their power and ruled decisively, debates erupted about their competence. Were women, even when royally born, really fit to take the reins of power? Some argued that women, even if educated, could not overcome the limitations of their bodies. Others, however, distinguished between the personal body of the queen (which could be female) and her public persona (which could assume the characteristics of a male leader), a distinction commonly made when Elizabeth I ruled England. As she herself declared, "I know I have the body of a weak and feeble woman, but I have the heart and stomach of a king."

Most women of lower status, of course, held no political power, although neither did their husbands. Like the men in their societies, their engagement with the government tended to surface sporadically in the protests and revolts that arose around taxes, unfair prices, or other injustices. Kerstine and Sophia Hoofs, for example, were forced to leave Flanders in 1329 because they had incited a

monogamous Marriage to one spouse.

regent Person who rules when a king or monarch is too young or enfeebled to do so.

Ferdinand II of Aragon and Isabella of Castile. In their marriage, Ferdinand II of Aragon and Isabella of Castile formed a powerful royal alliance during the fifteenth century, driving out the Moors and Jews at the same time that they funded Christopher Columbus in his historic exploration of the New World.

riot. Later in the century, Zoetin Houdewin was fined for her riot activities. Women were most likely to riot about the price of food but not always. When the peasants revolted against a new head tax in England in 1381, women participated along with men. While women used the streets to express their political opinions in these instances, legislative assemblies and legal proceedings were other matters. Common women could not hold office and, except in countries following Roman law, did not have access to the courts for settling disputes.

One realm in which women were able to exert significantly more control over their lives was in the convents. Although convents in the early modern period had lost many of the religious privileges they held during the medieval period, they still continued to offer an important alternative to marriage for women who had the means to enter them. Women in convents were expected to live cloistered lives of prayer, and their families were expected to make a significant financial contribution upon the entry of a daughter or widow to support this sort of life. Still, nuns often conducted small schools (though forbidden to do so) or produced crafts that helped to provide for their livelihoods because most convents were not self-supporting. To run their convents, nuns often had to take on a variety of supervisory tasks connected with their lands and formal operations. Women in religious orders not only took on jobs that were usually reserved for men; they also adopted lifestyles that allowed them to live with other women, free from the day-to-day supervision of men that characterized most households of the time.

Convents, along with monasteries, came under attack during the Protestant Reformation. Beginning with Martin Luther's Ninety-Five Theses in 1517, and following with the wide-ranging theological treatises of men such as John Calvin, new Protestant denominations were created in the sixteenth century that not only undermined the power of the Catholic Church but also affected the terms by which many women exercised power in their lives. Protestants, for example, argued that the celibacy of priests and nuns was an undesirable state of existence more likely to result in sinful than saintly behavior. They thus eliminated convents from their religious practices and urged all women, as well as men, to marry. Given the power of men over women in marriage, some women certainly found their options for exercising power curtailed. On the other hand, most Protestant religions moved away from the Catholic practice of accepting all children born of their followers into the church. Many Protestant denominations, particularly those influenced by the teachings of John Calvin, began to demand a conversion experience of all members, women as well as men. Women thus joined Protestant congregations as individuals rather than as family members, therefore assuming a kind of spiritual equality with men.

The ability of ordinary women to form a relationship to a church independent of their families did represent an important break with tradition. In European societies, most women derived their status and power from their rank (as members of a royal family, for example) or from their positions in their households. Women who lived in countries that adopted Roman law generally had more legal rights than those who did not. But in either case, they operated in societies in which male control of family and governance were closely intertwined norms, thus limiting the power that women might derive from their important activities within the home. In both the work they did and the positions they achieved, women in Europe differed not only from women in the Americas but also from women in Africa.

AFRICAN WOMEN

By the sixteenth century, the vast continent of Africa supported a wide variety of societies that ranged from complex urban traders to agriculturalists to wide-ranging groups of hunter-gatherers. While some people farmed, others herded cattle, sheep, and goats, and still others mined the rich natural resources that included gold. Salt, nuts, ivory, gold, and slaves became important commodities for trade throughout Africa and beyond. Patrilineal households were increasingly the norm by this time as Islam spread from the North into the trading cities along both the eastern and western coasts and into interior cities such as Timbuktu. Women participated actively in these urban economies, producing and trading goods. They also tended the crops on many of the inland farms, shouldering their responsibilities sometimes as wives and daughters or, if they were less fortunate, as pawns or slaves.

Work and Power

In Africa, as in all parts of the world, there was a clear, gendered division of labor in the work women did. Their economic activities varied, depending on their particular culture, but women south of the Sahara Desert tended to engage in jobs of central economic importance. They not only had primary responsibility for rearing their children, but also took an active role in the farming, craft making, and trading that sustained their societies.

Throughout Africa, women were farmers. In many of the settlements of southern Africa, women were responsible for farming while men were responsible for herding the animals. The distinction was so important that men were sometimes buried beneath the animal pens in their villages while women were buried on the outskirts of town where their fields would have been. In West Africa, where agriculture was also the predominant mode of living, labor was divided differently. Women cared for children, collected firewood and nuts, and watched after small livestock while men prepared the fields for planting. Both men and women in West Africa planted the fields, but they tended different crops.

Women were responsible for weaving cloth in West Africa; and throughout Africa, they wove mats and baskets and crafted pottery. While many of these items were designed for home use, women also traded their goods at local markets, along with any surplus produce they had. In most cases, women entered the markets on very different terms from men. Among the Yorubas of West Africa, for example, men controlled the more far-flung trade of luxury items that brought a profit, while women dominated the local markets that focused on the use value of the items they exchanged. As such, men's and women's trade affected their societies in very different ways. Women's trade did not lead to stratification in society the way men's trade did because it simply did not generate the profits that would allow some to become wealthy. Instead, women's trade facilitated the day-to-day living requirements of all community members.

The creation of some crafts gave women, as well as men, high status in their societies. Throughout West Africa, iron workers and woodworkers, leather workers, and bards (poets or singers) were particularly revered for their abilities to work with metal and fire, animal hides, and words. Within families, these artisans passed their skills from one generation to the next, so that women as well as men sometimes entered these trades. While men initiated young boys into the mysteries of their trades, women did the same

WOMEN'S LIVES

IDIA, FIRST IYOBA OF BENIN

Idia was one of the most powerful women in the history of Benin. At the end of the fifteenth century, when her husband died, her son Esigie struggled with his half brother Arhuaran (who had a different mother) for control of the kingdom. It is said Idia assisted her son in the struggle for power, raising an army to support him and drawing on her magical powers. Once Esigie gained the throne, he created the title of Queen Mother, or Iyoba, for Idia and built her a beautiful palace. Esigie's domain grew with the help of Portuguese traders, as well as with the help of his mother. Idia acquired both prestige and wealth as a result. With the title of Queen Mother, she was given powers equal to that of one of the village chiefs.

Images of Idia became an important part of court art. Carved ivory masks of Idia, marked by two slashes above her nose, were worn by the king for ceremonial occasions. According to tradition, Idia's parents did not want her to marry the king. They made two cuts between Idia's eyes and inserted magical medicines there to drive the king

away. The king discovered the plan and had the medicines removed before proceeding to marry Idia. The incisions remained, however, and provided a source of power to Idia. ■

for young girls, creating craft associations that exerted great influence in their societies. Female bards gained status not only because of their ability to sing or perform music but also because they were hairdressers who attended to the personal needs of the elite. These women were particularly powerful because they were privy to gossip that came from the private chambers of the wealthy and because they could cast powerful spells.

At the highest levels, women in West African societies balanced the power held by male leaders. While most kingdoms were ruled by a king, the position of queen mother was also extremely important. She could intercede for those who had offended the king, and in certain circumstances, her influence could lead to the removal of a king. Idia, the mother of Esigie, was a particularly important queen mother in the sixteenth century who was credited with providing her son with the advice, medicine, and magic he needed to assert his power in the kingdom of Benin. In other cases, women assumed direct power. Queen Aminatu of Zazzau was one of the most famous to do so at the end of the sixteenth century. She not only fought with her kingdom's soldiers; she successfully extended the trading empire of her region leading to a powerful economic expansion.

Family Economies

Ibn Battuta was shocked by the women he met in West Africa in 1352. The Islamic scholar and explorer who traveled thirty years throughout the Islamic world writing about his experiences met elite Muslims in the kingdom of Mali whose religious practices were far different from his own. Battuta noted with dismay that although the women were quite devoted to their prayers, they did not veil themselves. Even more disturbing, the women maintained friendships with men who were not members of their immediate families. When Battuta pressed one of his hosts on the friendship his wife maintained with another man, pointing out that this violated Islamic law, his host retorted, "Women's companionship with men in our country is honourable and takes place in a good way: there is no suspicion about it. They are not like the women in your country."

Battuta's encounters suggest the ways in which Africans south of the Sahara Desert adapted the Islamic practices that filtered into their societies with the trade routes that developed after 1100 CE. Islam had a powerful influence on both marriage and the status of women, but it existed in a distinct form among many of the Africans who practiced it. Islamic religious practices had been introduced into sub-Saharan Africa through the marriages of northern traders intent on establishing outposts farther south. Along the east coast of Africa, matrilineal societies were the norm when Muslim traders arrived seeking entrée into society. Marriage to local women allowed traders access to land, trade, and political influence. In towns where political power was transmitted through the mothers' lines, their children reinforced the power of traders until some of these societies shifted to a patrilineal system in an attempt to undercut this access.

In West Africa, where Battuta visited, systems of patrilineal descent also came to predominate over matrilineal lines by about 1200 CE, though women still maintained some important forms of control over their lives. In some of these societies, they were still able to obtain a divorce easily, for example, if they became dissatisfied with their husbands. Indeed, divorced women could maintain a position of high status in their societies, as was clear in the case of the *karuwai*, divorced women who were leaders in the bori possession cult among the Hausa people. In part, divorce was accepted because in many West African societies, ties to one's birth family were more important than ties to a spouse, so that birth and death were more important causes for celebration than were marriages.

Marriage, however, was a crucial way of organizing labor. Land was shared communally in many African societies and use of it was determined by village elders. A man's claim on the labor of both wife and children was extremely important because labor was a relatively scarce commodity. Thus, men derived their wealth through the control of labor rather than through ownership of land. A man paid a "bride price" for a wife because women were recognized as important workers and a woman significantly increased her husband's wealth when they married. Without such a payment—in cattle, cash, or other valuables—a marriage was not legitimate and a man had no claim to his children. Most young men did not have the resources to pay a bride price, so their relatives were often intimately involved in the selection and negotiations that took place around a marriage.

Wealthy men could expand their resources even further by acquiring more than one wife. Polygamy was an accepted practice throughout Africa, though it was limited by the economic practicality of bride price. Most men had a hard enough time coming up with the bride price for one wife, let alone two. In polygamous households, each woman was likely to have her own hut on her husband's compound and to keep her children with her until they were grown. When boys reached manhood, they would then go to live with their fathers. Until then, each mother was responsible for feeding her children through the crops she raised or the food she purchased. In this way, matrilocal living arrangements flourished in the midst of patrilineal kinship systems.

Dependence and Freedom: Slavery in Africa

pawn A person who is held as security for a debt.

While marriage was one way for a family to acquire workers, pawnship and slavery were two other ways to build a family's labor force. **Pawns** were literally people who had been pawned to pay for a debt. Often they were children—and often they were girls—who were held by the creditor until the family could pay its debt and redeem them. Until that time, the pawn's labor belonged to the creditor. Because pawns still had known kin who were often nearby, they were unlikely to be mistreated or to be sold to anyone else. Slaves, by definition, had no kin and had no rights. They were outsiders in the communities where they lived. Perhaps they had been seized in warfare or perhaps simply kidnapped for sale as a slave. They could be resold and their children could be held as slaves also.

In Africa, women were twice as likely as men were to be held as slaves. They were prized for both their productive and their reproductive value, and it showed in their price. Women cost twice as much as men in the African slave market. Given the work that women could do, this is not surprising. They were trained in crafts, farming, and domestic work. They might also be given as gifts to reward valiant warriors. For men looking to increase the labor they needed for farming, purchasing a slave to be a concubine could be cheaper than paying the bride price for a wife. These unions were viewed as inferior to marriages between free people but were particularly common when a man wished to take a second wife and could not afford the marriage costs. Slave women who were not taken as concubines by their masters often found themselves given to other men in the family. Thus, unlike free women, slave women had little control over sexual access to their bodies.

Slave women did find one advantage in the sexual relations their masters demanded of them. If they bore children of their union, both they and their children could be set free. This was also true if they bore children as a result of relationships with other free men in the masters' households. What this represented, in fact, was the slow incorporation of a "kinless" slave into the household of the master. Faced with the loss of control such freedom could entail, some groups changed this custom. In the West African kingdom of Songhay, for example, slave women were not allowed to marry free men, to ensure that their children were kept as slaves. Askia Muhammad, who came to rule the kingdom in 1493, changed the law to allow slave women to marry free men but decreed their children should still remain as slaves. However, in most cases, within a generation or two, children or grandchildren were incorporated into the family lineage.

Women not only were more likely to be held as slaves in Africa but also were more likely to value the labor of slaves. Because women were responsible for so many agricultural and domestic duties, one way to manage that workload was to draw on the labor of slave women. Even in cases in which a slave woman was owned by a man, her labor was often very much at the service of another woman. Wealthy women sometimes purchased their own slaves. By forcing slave women to take over their domestic duties, these women could pursue other activities, including more lucrative trading practices. Slave women who were relocated to Islamic societies in North Africa or the Middle East faced the harshest conditions. Free women in Islamic societies north of the Sahara Desert were sequestered from public life, so the duties of slave women who worked for them were extensive.

Whether they were wives, slaves, or pawns, women were highly valued workers in households that by the fifteenth century were organized patrilineally in most African societies. In places where gender-specific craft societies existed, women translated their skills into broader forms of collective power. As was the case in Europe and in the Americas, women seldom held the role of sovereign in the kingdoms that evolved in some areas. As these Europeans, Africans, and Native Americans came into contact, though, their focus was more often on differences than on similarities.

THE GENDERED DYNAMICS OF CONTACT

The European discovery of the New World in 1492 and the slave trade with Africa that developed soon after brought the peoples of three continents into growing contact. Over the course of the next three centuries, the Native American population was decimated as a result of disease and warfare, while large segments of the population of Africa were forcibly transported to the New World as slaves. Europeans, who looked not only for profit but also for legitimacy in these activities, argued that they

MAP 1-2 ATLANTIC TRADE AMONG THE AMERICAS, GREAT BRITAIN, AND WEST AFRICA DURING THE SEVENTEENTH AND EIGHTEENTH CENTURIES

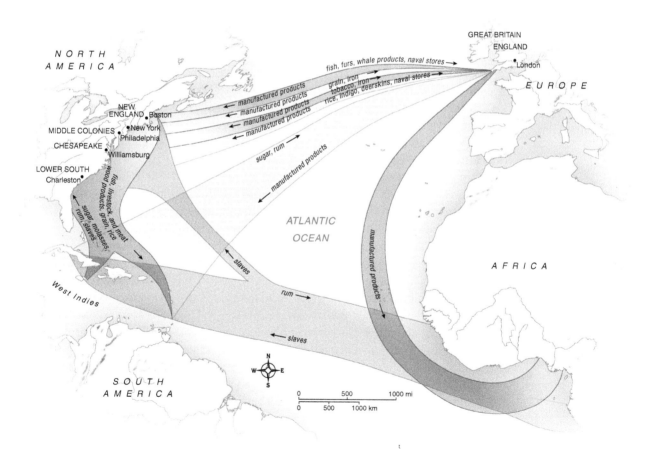

The trans-Atlantic trading network that emerged from the sixteenth century through the eighteenth century involved the trade of slaves, who produced some of the most valuable crops in the New World. England exchanged manufactured products for these raw materials.

were conquering inferior peoples lacking in the essentials of civilization. Central to these arguments was the view that women and gender relationships in Africa and the New World were not simply different but degraded.

Discovering New Worlds

European merchants and monarchs began searching in earnest for new passages to Asia in the middle of the fifteenth century after conflicts with Islamic officials of the Ottoman Empire disrupted the trade routes that they had been cultivating for a couple of centuries. Portugal, drawing on advanced research in navigation, had already developed trade with Africa when Bartholomeu Dias, a Portuguese sea captain, successfully navigated the southern edge of Africa in 1488. Four years later, Christopher Columbus succeeded in persuading the monarchs of a newly consolidating Spain to fund his attempt to find a westward route to Asia. Ferdinand and Isabella were looking for new sources of wealth to support the military they had built up to drive both Muslims and Jews out of Spain. In the wake of Columbus' discovery, Spain sent a succession of explorers and conquerors to establish its empire, including Hernán Cortés, who conquered the mighty Aztecs of central Mexico in 1521.

The Europeans who explored the Americas returned with stories of wonder not only about the riches of the New World but of the men and women who inhabited it. Many of these stories concerned dangerous women in narratives that seem to have symbolized the fears of the explorers rather than portraying the actual societies they encountered. Amerigo Vespucci, traveling through the New World in 1503 and 1504, described female cannibals who attacked and ate a Spanish sailor. At another point, he described women who forced their husbands to enlarge their penises to satisfy their sexual cravings, even though the practice was dangerous to the men. Spanish explorers, including Columbus and Cortés, wrote of islands of Amazonlike women (heard about but never quite discovered) who lived without men (except to mate) and fiercely protected their riches of gold and jewels. California's name was derived from a fictional Spanish story about an island of pagan women who were conquered, Christianized, and married by Spanish soldiers. In cases like these, explorers carried with them European myths of strange lands and used them to embellish their stories of adventure in a new world in which anything seemed possible.

Even more important, Europeans routinely characterized the New World in feminine terms—as a body both fertile and ripe to be conquered. Sir Walter Raleigh famously described Guiana at the end of the sixteenth century as "a countrey that hath yet her maidenhead." In other words, he compared Guiana to a virgin, waiting for the right man to penetrate and possess it. As Raleigh elaborated, "It hath never bene entred by any armie of strength, and never conquered or possessed by any christian Prince." Visually, America was repeatedly depicted in feminine form, greeting male European explorers. Soldiers and explorers were invited to engage in a conquest that was not only economic and political but also sexual and predicated on ideas of gender hierarchy.

Complementing this gendered ideology of European male conqueror and virgin land was the image of the impotent or dissipated Indian male who had failed to properly cultivate the nature surrounding him. As one English writer noted, the "womb" of Indian land was "barren" because it was unknown to the Indians. In making this argument, European conquerors returned repeatedly to their perception that Indian men were lazy because they hunted rather than farmed. In Europe, hunting was a leisure activity for the upper classes and farming was officially the activity of men. By this logic, Indian men who hunted were loafing and thus not entitled to their lands.

Sexuality and Claims of Civilization

Europeans not only viewed these new worlds in gendered terms; they regarded the sexuality and sexual practices of the people living there as degraded. Repeatedly, explorers from one continent judged the practices of another by their own standards and found the others wanting. Systematically, they came to understand differences in female behavior as an indication of a society's savagery and its need to be conquered by "civilized" people.

One early English trader, venturing to the west coast of Africa in the sixteenth century, was both fascinated and repelled by the women he saw who did not cover their breasts. Describing their breasts as "very foule and long, hanging down like the udder of a goate," the trader suggested the way in which he perceived these Africans as more animal than human. European Explorers in the New World made similar observations of the Native American women they encountered.

While lack of clothing was equated with a lack of civilization, African and Indian attitudes toward sex suggested immorality to Europeans. In Africa, the Dutch trader Nicolas van Wassenaer was disgusted by the women he met in the early seventeenth century. "The women take little heed concerning their virtue," he reported, "besides which they are dirty by nature, because they smell bad due to the palm oil which they pour on their hair, which in hot weather drips the length of the body." In the New World, European men repeatedly commented on encounters they had with Indian women in which it was expected they would have sex. Father Gabriel Sagard bemoaned the wickedness of young Huron women who "vie with one another as to which shall have the most lovers," and the husband who "offers his wife, if she be willing, for some small and trifling present." Others expressed shock that some Indian women expected gifts from men when they had sex with them. To Europeans, this did not represent the reciprocity that it did to Indians but, rather, smacked of prostitution.

Europeans were equally appalled by the two-spirit people they met in Indian villages. Their perspective was clear in the European name that emerged for this third gender: *berdache*. The term was derived from the Arabic word *bardag* that had been adapted in Italian, French, and Spanish languages to describe the passive male in same-sex encounters. Spanish conquistadors called these men *bardaje*, a term of condemnation. Spaniards also called them *putos*, male whores, perhaps because these men-women in the Southwest were expected to have sex with any young man who demanded it of them.

The mathematician John White and Thomas Hariot, a cartographer, were more respectful in their depictions of Native Americans near the Roanoke colony where they lived at the end of the sixteenth century, but they still saw them as savages. White produced many pictures of Algonquian women that appeared in Hariot's widely circulated *A Brief and True Report of the New Found Land of Virginia*. Most of these portraits emphasized the domestic qualities of the women and portrayed them with their hands strategically placed to cover their breasts, but the women were still clearly lacking in the culture of Europeans. This point was particularly driven home by the inclusion in his collection of watercolors of early Britons before being civilized by the Romans. These women, also bare breasted and scantily clad, were evidence of how far Europe had come since the Roman conquest; and White and Hariot implied that Europe could now offer the same civilization to the New World.

John White, "A Cheife Herowans Wyfe of Pomeoc and her daughter of the age of 8 or 10 yeares". Europeans such as John White were fascinated by the domestic arrangements of the peoples they encountered in the New World. This portrait, drawn at the Roanoke settlement at the end of the sixteenth century, conveyed a sense of motherly nurture that Europeans would understand.

Gender and the Emergence of the Slave Trade

Heavily armed with guns and a strong sense of cultural superiority, Europeans had expected the natives of the New World to work for them in the mines and plantations they set up. This expectation was challenged during the sixteenth century, however, as conflict, resistance, and disease decimated the Indian population. Thus Europeans quickly turned to an additional source of forced labor that they had discovered early in the fifteenth century: the slaves of Africa. Patronizing the trading ports on the west coast of Africa that had begun to send slaves to Europe, they expanded this traffic in human beings during the sixteenth century to include New World destinations as well. During the next three centuries, slave-trading ports grew large and merchants grew wealthy as they increasingly financed slave raids into the interior of Africa to feed the demand for labor.

In the slave trade that developed, gender mattered. Europeans were looking primarily for agricultural laborers for their colonial plantations and mines and thus preferred men to women when purchasing their human cargo because they assumed men worked better in the fields than women. Africans, on the other hand, highly valued women as both agricultural workers and slaves. To a certain extent, this meant that the labor demands of the two continents complemented each other, with the New World taking a larger proportion of men as slaves and Africa retaining a larger proportion of women as slaves, creating gender imbalances on both continents among the slave populations. This situation had become more complicated, at least by the seventeenth century, however, as African slave traders insisted on selling more women than Europeans wanted, arguing that women could do the agricultural work demanded on New World plantations. In the give and take that took place in the African slave markets, more men than women were still loaded onto the ships headed for the Americas but Europeans were also clearly forced to accept more female slaves than they would have preferred.

As the world's population was rebalanced with both forced migrations from Africa and free migrations from Europe during the sixteenth through the eighteenth centuries, far more Africans than Europeans sailed for the Americas. In North America, as opposed to Latin America, European women outnumbered African immigrants, one element that made North American colonies distinct from those farther south. However, even in North America, Europeans were forced to accept the ability of women to do the same agricultural work as men—and they did. Although many new arrivals died, particularly in the early years of colonization, enough women were transported as slaves to allow for the eventual creation of families and cultures in slavery. In some areas of West Africa, however, where the loss of men to slavery was most acute, polygamy appears to have become more common.

In the great trade cities that developed along the west coast of Africa, a cosmopolitan culture emerged in which mixed-race people known as Luso-Africans assumed an important role as cultural brokers. They emerged in the fifteenth century as Portugese traders intermarried with African women who provided them not only with the domestic skills of a wife but also with access to society and trade in their cultures. In some of the African societies, the children of these marriages became outcasts; but in others, the children (as well as their mothers) were able to parley their novel connections into lucrative commercial undertakings. By the seventeenth century, a group of Luso-African women called *nhares* had emerged as wealthy entrepreneurs who headed extensive households staffed by servants and slaves and far-flung business ventures. Often these women became wives of English and French traders who followed the Portuguese into African trade.

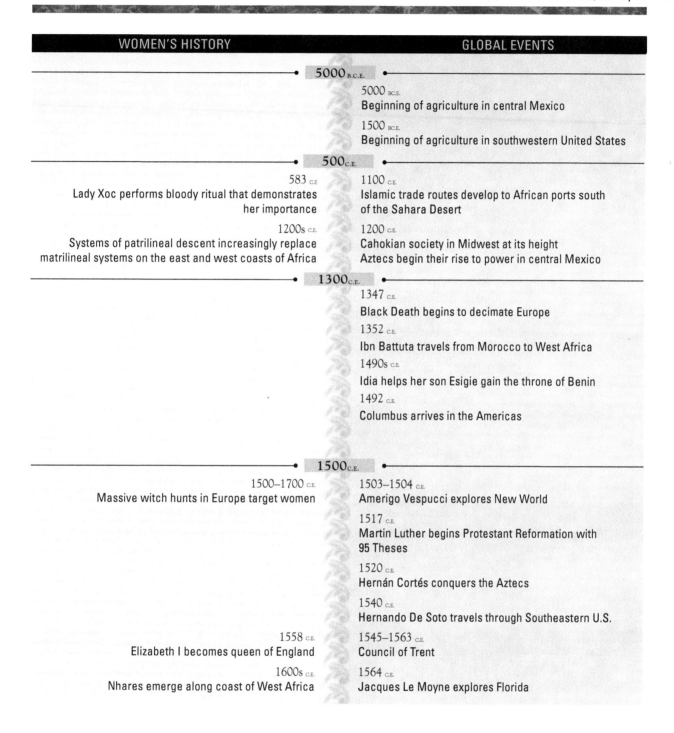

WOMEN'S HISTORY	GLOBAL EVENTS

5000 B.C.E.

5000 B.C.E.
Beginning of agriculture in central Mexico

1500 B.C.E.
Beginning of agriculture in southwestern United States

500 C.E.

583 C.E.
Lady Xoc performs bloody ritual that demonstrates her importance

1100 C.E.
Islamic trade routes develop to African ports south of the Sahara Desert

1200s C.E.
Systems of patrilineal descent increasingly replace matrilineal systems on the east and west coasts of Africa

1200 C.E.
Cahokian society in Midwest at its height
Aztecs begin their rise to power in central Mexico

1300 C.E.

1347 C.E.
Black Death begins to decimate Europe

1352 C.E.
Ibn Battuta travels from Morocco to West Africa

1490s C.E.
Idia helps her son Esigie gain the throne of Benin

1492 C.E.
Columbus arrives in the Americas

1500 C.E.

1500–1700 C.E.
Massive witch hunts in Europe target women

1503–1504 C.E.
Amerigo Vespucci explores New World

1517 C.E.
Martin Luther begins Protestant Reformation with 95 Theses

1520 C.E.
Hernán Cortés conquers the Aztecs

1540 C.E.
Hernando De Soto travels through Southeastern U.S.

1558 C.E.
Elizabeth I becomes queen of England

1545–1563 C.E.
Council of Trent

1600s C.E.
Nhares emerge along coast of West Africa

1564 C.E.
Jacques Le Moyne explores Florida

For most African women who encountered the slave trade, the experience was quite different. Women who were transported to the Americas came from areas near the trading ports from which they were shipped. They could have fetched a higher price if sold farther inland, but transportation costs were high. Instead, they were shipped to the New World in a journey called the Middle Passage, the second leg of a three-part transatlantic trading network. European captains exchanged their goods for slaves in Africa. Fully loaded with human cargo, ships then sailed for the Americas, where slaves were sold for sugar, tobacco, or other products destined for the European market. Packed so tightly into a ship that many on board died, slaves endured a dangerous and terrifying experience. Women faced not only the dangers of disease but also sexual abuse from the ship's crew. For the women who survived, enslavement in the New World would be a more brutal experience than what they had known in Africa.

CONCLUSION

The slave trade, along with the decimation of the Native American populations, constituted the most devastating results of the contact that began to unfold in the sixteenth century. As Europeans, Africans, and Native Americans intermingled, the consequences were social as well as physical. Household arrangements, key to the social organization of societies on all three continents, varied greatly, as did the place of women within these households. In some Native American societies, women exercised tremendous power. In both Africa and the Americas, women were often the farmers. In Europe, their rights to own property varied depending on whether their countries followed common law or Roman law. In Africa, women could be held as slaves but not necessarily for their entire lives. When new households were forged in the Americas following contact, these different conventions collided and evolved as families continued to be crucial building blocks of the new frontier. As a result, women were key players in the age of discovery that was unfolding.

REVIEW QUESTIONS

1. How were the sexual and family lives of Indian women related to the ways in which their societies allocated resources?
2. What did patriarchy mean for women in European society?
3. Why were women more important than men in African slavery?
4. In what ways were women important in misunderstandings about what constituted civilization?

RECOMMENDED READING

Bonnie S. Anderson and Judith P. Zimmerman. *A History of Their Own: Women in Europe from Prehistory to the Present*, vol. 1. New York: Harper & Row, 1988. Lively and wide-ranging survey of women in European history.

Iris Berger and E. Frances White. *Women in Sub-Saharan Africa*. Bloomington: Indiana University Press, 1999. Best available introduction to the lives of women on African continent.

Karen Olsen Bruhns and Karen E. Stothert. *Women in Ancient America*. Norman: University of Okla-

homa Press, 1999. Clear and current overview of women's lives and their place in different hierarchies in precontact America.

David Eltis. *The Rise of African Slavery in the Americas*. Cambridge: Cambridge University Press, 2000. Overarching survey of how slavery evolved in Africa and the Americas that pays particular attention to the role of Africans as well as Europeans in the slave trade, including an important chapter on the role of women and gender.

ADDITIONAL BIBLIOGRAPHY

Native American Women

James Axtell, ed. *The Indian Peoples of Eastern America: A Documentary History of the Sexes.* New York: Oxford University Press, 1981.

Charles Callendar and Lee M. Kochens. "The North American Berdache." *Current Anthropology* 24, no. 4 (1983): 443–70.

Cheryl Claasen and Rosemary A. Joyce. *Women in Prehistory: North America and Mesoamerica.* Philadelphia: University of Pennsylvania Press, 1997.

Thomas D. Dillehay. *The Settlement of the Americas: A New Prehistory.* New York: Basic Books, 2000.

Stuart J. Fiedel. *Prehistory of the Americas.* Cambridge: Cambridge University Press, 1987.

Joan M. Gero and Margaret W. Conkey, eds. *Engendering Archaeology: Women and Prehistory.* Cambridge, MA: Basil Blackwell, 1995.

Takeshi Inomata and Stephen D. Houston, eds. *Royal Courts of the Ancient Maya.* Vol. 1, *Theory, Comparison, and Synthesis.* Boulder, CO: Westview Press, 2001.

Daniel K. Richter. *The Ordeal of the Longhouse: The Peoples of the Iroquois League in the Era of European Colonization.* Chapel Hill: University of North Carolina Press, 1992.

Linda Schele and David Freidel. *A Forest of Kings: The Untold Story of the Ancient Maya.* New York: William Morrow, 1990.

Michael E. Smith *The Aztecs.* Malden, MA: Basil Blackwell, 2003.

Margaret Supplee Smith and Emily Herring Wilson. *North Carolina Women Making History.* Chapel Hill: University of North Carolina Press, 1999.

European Women

Natalie Zemon Davis. *Society and Culture in Early Modern France.* Stanford: Stanford University Press, 1975.

Barbara A. Hanawalt. *The Ties That Bind: Peasant Families in Medieval England.* New York: Oxford University Press, 1986.

Ellen E. Kittell. "Women, Audience, and Public Acts in Medieval Flanders." *Journal of Women's History* 10, No. 3 (1988). 74–96.

Catherine Moriarty, ed. *The Voices of the Middle Ages in Personal Letters 1100–1500.* New York: Peter Bedrick Books, 1989.

Retha M. Warnicke. *Women of the English Renaissance and Reformation.* Westport, CT: Greenwood Press, 1983.

Merry E. Weisner. *Women and Gender in Early Modern Europe,* 2nd ed. Cambridge: Cambridge University Press, 2000.

African Women

Basil Davidson. *A History of West Africa 1000–1800.* London: Longman, 1965.

Toyin Falola, ed. *Africa: African History Before 1885,* vol. 1. Durham, NC: Carolina Academic Press, 2003.

Said Hamdum and Noel King. *Ibn Battuta in Black Africa.* Princeton, NJ: Markus Wiener, 1994.

Darlene Clark Hine and David Barry Gaspar. *More Than Chattell: Black Women and Slavery in the Americas.* Bloomington: Indiana University Press, 1996.

Flora Kaplan. "Images of the Queen Mother in Benin Court Art." *African Arts* 26, no. 3 (July 1993): 54–63, 86–88.

Paul Lovejoy. *Transformations in Slavery: A History of Slavery in Africa,* 2nd ed. Cambridge: Cambridge University Press, 2000.

Claire Robertson and Martin Klein, eds. *Women and Slavery in Africa.* Madison: University of Wisconsin Press, 1983.

Contact

George E. Brooks. *Commerce, Social Status, Gender, and Religious Observance from the Sixteenth to the Eighteenth Century.* Athens: Ohio University Press, 2003.

Robert Fulton and Steven W. Anderson. "The Amerindian 'Man-Woman': Gender, Liminality, and Cultural Continuity." *Current Anthropology* 3, no. 5 (December 1992): 603–10.

Louis Montrose. "The Work of Gender in the Discourse of Discovery." *Representations* 33 (Winter 1991): 1–41.

Jennifer Morgan. *Laboring Women: Reproduction and Gender in New World Slavery.* Philadelphia: University of Pennsylvania Press, 2004.

Biographies, Autobiographies, and Memoirs

Richard L. Kagan and Abigail Dyer, eds. *Inquisitorial Inquiries: Brief Lives of Secret Jews and Other Heretics.* Baltimore, MD: Johns Hopkins University Press, 2004.

CONTACT AND CONQUEST, 1500–1700

HOW DID women shape the settlement of New Spain?

HOW WERE Native American women central to the political and economic structure of New France?

HOW DID patriarchy and slavery emerge together in the Chesapeake region?

HOW DID family structure and the status of women evolve in New England?

Chapter 2

Desired and beloved brother of my heart:

. . . I ask you for the love of God to spare me such pain from your absence, and yourself such necessity, when I have the means to give you relief. Do be sure to come quickly now, and don't make your children endure hunger and necessity. I would have sent money for your trip, but since I have had no reply to my letters, I didn't dare. Go to Ronda and collect the rent from my houses, and if you wish to, mortgage them and take four or five years' income in advance; I leave it to your discretion. And invest all except what you need for

De espanol y mulata, produce morisca, *attributed to Juan Juarez, 1715.*

travel in fine cloths, in Rouen and Dutch linens; be sure you do it yourself, and don't trust it to others. . . .

Do everything in your power to bring along with you two masters of weaving coarse woolens and carding, for they will profit us greatly, and also a candlemaker, who should be an examined journeyman and good at his trade. Buy their provisions and make a contract with them from the day they sail, and I will fulfill whatever you agree to; I will pay their passage and any debts they have when they arrive. And you can do all this much better than I could....

Tell the sister of my soul to consider this letter hers; how is it that her heart doesn't melt like mine for us to see each other? I understand that she is the reason you haven't come, yet she is the one who loses and has lost in not enjoying a land where food is plenteous and she can give me a good old age. I ask her, since it is in her own favor, to come quickly and make my old age happy with her arrival and that of my longed-for nephews.

Source: Maria de Carranza to her brother Hernando de Soto in Seville, 1589, reprinted from James Lockhart and Enrique Otte, eds. and trans., Letters and People of the Spanish Indies, Sixteenth Century (*New York: Cambridge University Press, 1976) 136–138.*

Maria de Carranza was a wealthy and powerful woman in both the New World and the Old. Her husband, Diego Sánchez Guadalupe, ran a textile mill in Puebla, Mexico, while Maria ran the household, but her powers were many. She controlled land in Spain and labor in Mexico, using her economic resources to bring her far-flung family together and to produce a wide range of goods. In the sixteenth and seventeenth centuries, households such as Maria's were crucial components of the societies emerging on the frontiers of the New World. However, the activities of those households and the women who supervised them varied from one region of the Americas to the next. Women's lives were shaped around not only issues of class but also the laws of the different countries who engaged in the conquest and the relationships settlers established with the indigenous peoples of their regions.

Frontiers emerged throughout North America during the sixteenth and seventeenth centuries, as Europeans and Native Americans fought, traded, and intermarried. These frontiers were defined not simply by the violent conflicts that took place, though there were plenty of those. Rather, the frontiers of the New World were created as different cultures came into contact, forcing both newcomers and indigenous peoples to adapt their social practices to new circumstances. While the Spanish claimed much of what is now Mexico, the Southwest of the United States, California, and Florida, French traders pushed down the Mississippi River from what is now Canada, establishing outposts by the beginning of the eighteenth century at New Orleans on the Gulf of Mexico. British settlers established colonies in the Chesapeake region and farther south in the Carolinas, as well as in New England and in various parts of the middle Atlantic region, surrounding the smaller Dutch colony in New York. While European countries made great claims about their control over vast territories, in fact, these frontier societies were characterized by their fragility and frequent challenges to their power, both within and without.

In this fluid social atmosphere, in which state power was often limited, household organization was critical. Households organized production, facilitated intermarriage (or at least sex), and provided a fundamental form of social hierarchy. As a result, women were key players on the frontier. But the different economic goals and migration patterns of each European empire meant that household structures varied in important ways. The Spanish and French, for example, counted on and acknowledged intermarriage with indigenous peoples in a way that the English did not. British immigrants in the southern colonies of North America relied on plantation slavery and the labor of imported Africans in a way that those farther north did not. For women, the implications of those variations were enormous. Each frontier was different.

SPANISH CONQUEST IN THE SOUTHWEST

During the sixteenth century, the Spanish dominated exploration and conquest in the New World. The vice royalty of New Spain was established in 1535, governing a growing number of colonies founded and led by conquistadors such as Francisco Vásquez de Coronado, Pedro Menéndez de Avilés, and Juan de Oñate. With forced labor from conquered Indians and enslaved Africans, the Spanish extracted gold and silver to feed the growing empire. Expeditions north of Mexico yielded far less in the way of riches. Nonetheless, by the end of the sixteenth century, Spain had expanded its northern border to include parts of what are now Florida and New Mexico. In 1565, Pedro Menéndez de Avilés wiped out a small settlement of French Protestants who had established a fort in Florida and erected the new Spanish colony of St. Augustine nearby. Juan de Oñate drew on the enormous wealth his father had amassed in the silver mines of Mexico to establish the colony of New Mexico in 1598. Neither outpost was very large or prosperous, but each introduced the government and customs of New Spain into areas that would later become the United States.

Immigration and Work

Spanish women began arriving in the New World before the end of the fifteenth century. When Columbus made his third voyage in 1498, thirty women traveled with him to the colony of Hispaniola. In the first decades of the sixteenth century, Spanish women constituted about 10 percnt of the Spanish immigrants, though as the century progressed, their proportion grew. As a result, the number of Spanish women sailing to various parts of the growing empire during the sixteenth and seventeenth centuries probably averaged close to three thousand women per year. The first

MAP 2-1 NEW MEXICO IN THE SEVENTEENTH CENTURY

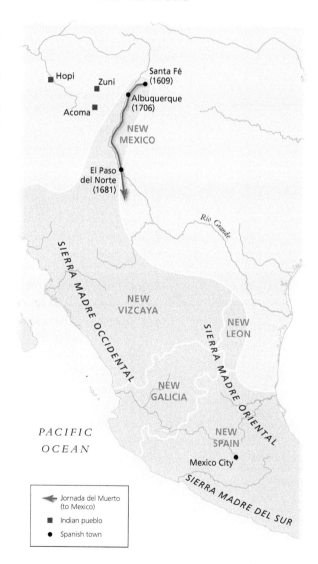

The Spanish empire extended to Santa Fe by 1609. The road leading from Santa Fe, *Jornada del Muerto*, which means Road to Death, suggests how little control Spain actually had over this territory.

female slaves came from Spain as well, though very quickly they began to be imported from Africa as part of the transatlantic slave trade. Close to half a million slaves were transported into New Spain during the sixteenth and seventeenth centuries, and probably 30 to 40 percent were female. Both African and Spanish women lived, worked, and fought with the indigenous women who managed to survive the diseases and attacks of the Spanish conquistadors.

Some of the Spanish women arriving in the New World were the wives, daughters, and nieces of conquistadors or, later, government officials and merchants. Even the Spanish wives of powerful men found themselves working hard because a lack of resources and conquests of the Indian population drew all members of the outposts into service. A couple of generations of settlement were necessary before elite Spanish women began to live in luxurious circumstances. Even then, some of those women managed businesses that they ran with the assistance of male kin who handled public exchanges when necessary.

More often, women who came to New Spain during the sixteenth and seventeenth centuries were artisans who worked as bakers, midwives, and shopkeepers; or they were servants or slaves who worked in households. Slave women were most likely to live in the cities of New Spain, working as house servants or doing more specialized jobs such as cooking, sewing, or washing clothes. Widows who needed the wages of their slaves for survival sent them out to do those jobs or to become street vendors or prostitutes. Because slave women were "without honor," they could appear in public without regard to protecting their sexual virtue whereas elite women could not.

Indian women, like Indian men, fought the Spanish and died from their new diseases. In some rural regions of Mexico throughout the sixteenth century, women wove cloth not only for their families but also as tribute for their new Spanish conquerors (just as they had done in previous years for their Aztec conquerors). In other places, as their men headed into forced labor in the mines or to cattle ranches established by the Spanish, Indian women went with them, sometimes hauling metal or clearing land, as well as engaging in more traditional female activities of housekeeping and child rearing. Others found their way to new Spanish cities by the seventeenth century. They, like slaves, worked as domestics or sold goods in the marketplace, adapting some of their traditional skills to a new market relationship.

The Spanish were not always pleased to have women working on tasks they felt men should do, but often they were forced to accept it. When Juan de Oñate's followers established their fledgling colony of New Mexico, for example, Indian women rather than men built their houses and churches. The Pueblo women resisted Spanish gender conventions that prohibited them from construction work, but they did accept some Spanish changes to their technology. They quickly began to use sheepskin, for example, rather than twigs to hold the plaster together in their buildings. Women's insistence that they continue their responsibilities of building became a part of a new culture that mixed European and Indian traditions in the Southwest during the ensuing centuries.

Captivity and Kinship

mestizo Person of mixed Spanish and Indian heritage.

This **mestizo** society, composed of people part Spanish and part Indian, was born in the exchange of women that took place through captivity, marriage, or less formal agreements somewhere in between. When Hernán Cortés and his soldiers landed in Mexico in 1519, for example, the Tabascan Indians gave them twenty female slaves including a young Mayan woman the Spaniards named Doña Marina, who became both a concubine and an advisor of the conquistador. The status of women such as Doña Marina reflects the complex nature of the relationships formed by women in New Spain in the years of conquest. As slaves, concubines, and go-betweens, they brought different worlds together linguistically, culturally, and physically. The power that they were able to exert, however, was usually focused on their own survival. To be a concubine was probably better than being raped or enslaved, but it was not clear where one condition left off and another began. It was possible to be both slave and mistress, and it is hard to know what kind of choice these women had in forming their relationships.

WOMEN'S LIVES

DOÑA MARINA

Doña Marina was born into a noble family in Pay-nala, near the town of Coatzacoalcos on the Yucatan Peninsula of Mexico around the start of the sixteenth century. Her father died when she was quite young, and her mother married another nobleman (cacique) in the vicinity. However, after her brother was born, her mother and stepfather decided that Marina's brother should inherit the political power both parents held and they decided to get rid of Marina to keep her from challenging her brother's inheritance. They gave her away to a group in another town, who eventually traded her as a slave to the nearby Indians in Tabasco. This was how she came to be included in a group of slave women offered to Cortés.

Cortés baptized the slave women and distributed them as concubines among his men, giving Marina to Alonzo Hernández Puertocarrero. But when Puertocarrero returned to Spain, Cortés took her for his own. Marina was fluent in several local Indian languages as a result of her having lived among different groups, and her knowledge of Indian politics was invaluable: she explained to the Spaniards that many Indians resented their Aztec conquerors and she helped the Spaniards in various diplomatic negotiations with the Indians they met as they marched toward the Aztec capital. She also bore a son, Martin, as a result of her relationship with Cortés. Soon after, Cortés married her to one of his soldiers, Juan Jaramillo de Salvatierra, giving her both freedom and legitimacy in the new empire.

Her role in the conquest has become both mythical and contested in Latin American history. Many reviled her memory because they felt she betrayed her people and gave her the derogatory nickname "La Malinche." In the Chicano movement that developed in the United States in the 1970s, this view of her persisted in much of the original literature surrounding the movement. However, Chicana women soon challenged this view, arguing that Doña Marina had adapted to her circumstances as best she could and that in her diplomacy and in giving birth to her son, she had founded the *mestizo* nation that grew out of the Spanish conquest. ∎

Certainly some Indian women encountered worse brutality. Francisco Vásquez de Coronado, governor of New Spain's northwestern province of New Galicia, pushed toward the Rio Grande in 1540 searching for riches. As he moved north, he and his men sacked Indian villages and raped Indian women, sparking bloody resistance.

At various points during the Spanish conquest of the New World, conquistadors were urged to marry Indian women as a way of gaining access to their lands and power, as well as to Christianize them. These marriages were most likely to occur with high-status women such as Isabel Moctezuma, daughter of the last Aztec emperor, who outlived all three of her Spanish husbands. In a similar vein, Pedro Menéndez de Avilés married the sister of a local Indian chief when he established St. Augustine in Florida. More often, however, Spanish men took Indian women as concubines. The Catholic Church was highly critical of such practices, urging marriage instead. But the practice was so widespread that even priests engaged in informal marriages, leading the Catholic Church to encourage the friars to employ only old women as servants. These informal marriages were one of the reasons that women headed so many households in New Spain: informal marriages were more easily dissolved or ignored than formal ones. By the middle of the sixteenth century in Mexico, for example, women headed one-fourth of all households recorded.

crillo Person of Spanish heritage born in a colony.

casta Person of mixed heritage.

The first-generation mestizo children were accepted as Spaniards whether they were born of legal marriages or not, and many entered into the Spanish project of conquest as soldiers. However, within a couple of generations, mestizos faced growing discrimination in colonial society as they were branded with the stigma of illegitimacy and impure blood. The few mestizo children born to legally married parents were simply accepted as **crillos** (Spaniards born in the New World), but the vast majority of children born through informal unions were less likely to gain such acceptance. Yet from the northern frontiers of New Spain to its southern borders, the mestizo population was rapidly becoming dominant. By 1650, mestizos probably outnumbered Spaniards in the New World. Spain's strategy of conquest thus created a "frontier of inclusion," in which the blood of Europeans and Indians mixed in ways that were officially recognized though increasingly difficult to classify.

The problem of classification was an important one in New Spain. When Spaniards first arrived, they established a caste society in which a Spanish elite ruled both conquered Indians and African slaves. Intermarriage and informal sexual relationships among these different groups challenged that hierarchy. **Castas**, those born of some sort of cultural intermixing, could be wealthy or poor, high status or low status, depending upon the particular circumstances of their parents. A mestizo woman's marriage to a Spaniard would elevate her status while marriage to an African would lower it. Elites and government officials in New Spain devoted some time to categorizing and ranking these different combinations, an obsession that was reflected in a new genre of art emerging in eighteenth-century Mexico, the casta painting. These paintings addressed the issue of ethnic intermixing by carefully portraying the physical features of racially mixed parents and the children they produced.

In the eighteenth century, artists in Mexico created paintings that depicted the physical characteristics of children produced by intermarriage among Europeans, Africans, and Indians. These casta paintings depicted a social hierarchy that was rooted in the physical characteristics produced through intermarriage.

Religion and Conquest

The inclusive frontier of Spain's empire in the Americas was religious as well as familial. Catholic priests traveled with the conquistadors throughout New Spain, building churches, monasteries, and convents and attempting to convert the indigenous population through persuasion—or force, if necessary. For crillo women, the convents of New Spain offered an important alternative to marriage, just as they did in Europe. In some orders, women brought dowries of land, slaves, and jewels, which they retained and managed. Convents sometimes became repositories of vast amounts of capital and offered important credit opportunities for the families of nuns who belonged.

As missionaries moved through the countryside, they often promoted not only the worship of God but also reverence for the Virgin Mary, particularly around devotion to the Virgin of Guadalupe. Of brown skin rather than white, the Virgin of Guadalupe was both Indian and European. She became the new symbol of fertility, motherhood, and religious belief in New Spain, displacing the fertility goddesses and Corn Mothers that had been worshipped by the Indians. First embraced by the crillo population of Mexico during the seventeenth century, over the next couple of centuries the Virgin of Guadalupe eventually was revered by a large segment of the Mexican population as a national symbol. But the cult of the Virgin had special meanings for women. As a protector of female virtue, she became a focus for instilling Christian standards of sexual purity at the same time she inspired women to resist acts of abuse by men.

The Virgin of Guadalupe combined characteristics of the Christian Virgin Mary with indigenous Indian beliefs, becoming the national symbol of Mexico and other countries in Latin America.

In addition to spreading devotional practices, the friars worked hard to change the ways in which Native Americans worked and lived. The Franciscans on the frontier of New Mexico, for example, objected to the fact that Pueblo women, rather than men, built their homes. Nor did the priests accept weaving as a male activity. Believing that they were civilizing the Indians, the Franciscans encouraged the men to do construction work and the women to weave cloth. The Catholic priests also attacked the sex and marriage practices of the Indians they sought to rule. They condemned the positions used by Indians when having intercourse as bestial. They demanded an end to premarital sex and insisted on monogamy. And because the Spanish controlled many of the resources young Indians would need, the Franciscans, rather than Pueblo elders, were able to exert a powerful influence on marriage practices.

Witchcraft, Resistance, and Revolt

Both church and government officials also had to contend with witchcraft accusations, an issue that often concerned women. Those accused of witchcraft were of low status and hence almost never Spanish. Indian, African, and mixed-caste women trafficked in charms and magical potions that they shared with Spanish women as well. In almost all cases, their witchcraft was gendered (practiced by women to control men) and sexual—meant to arouse a man's ardor, punish unfaithful husbands and lovers, or end abusive behavior. While many of these spells were drawn from African or Indian traditions, they were mixed with European ideas of witchcraft as well. Despite complaints from afflicted men, Spanish authorities by and large ignored these witches, viewing sexual witchcraft as having more personal than political significance. It was a sin, but it was not treason to manipulate a man's behavior with magic potions.

Even Antonia de Soto escaped censure, at least from the church. A twenty-year-old mulatto slave living on the northern frontier of New Spain at the end of the seventeenth century, Antonia fled her master, donned men's clothing, chewed peyote, and under its spell made a pact with the devil to "be his" in exchange for her freedom. Antonia traversed the countryside in her new identity as a man, though her carousing and gambling soon degenerated into theft and murder. Eventually regretting her deeds, Antonia confessed to the church authorities and was pardoned by them because of her contrition. It is not known what happened to Antonia when the case was handed over to civil authorities.

Although colonial officials often dismissed witchcraft in the Spanish Empire as unimportant to larger power relations, it sometimes did have political consequences; in those cases, the punishments were far more severe. A woman in Guachichil, Mexico, who was accused of using her witchcraft to incite a revolt against Spain, was executed. More often, however, when witchcraft was associated with a political challenge, the practitioners were men. The authorities in New Mexico, for example, viewed the hexes of Pueblo shamans with great alarm. During the 1670s, the witchcraft of Pueblo shamans was considered responsible for killing seven Franciscan friars and was closely associated with talk of rebellion by Indians who were fed up with Spanish rule. Governor Juan Francisco Treviño of New Mexico hanged several of these men in 1675 and attempted to sell about forty-seven others into slavery after subjecting them to a severe beating. They were saved, however, by Pueblo warriors who forced the governor to relinquish his captives.

The attack on Pueblo shamans sparked a growing resistance movement among many of the Indians in New Mexico. The economic and political oppression of Spanish rule and a growing cynicism over the spiritual powers exercised by the Catholic friars fueled the rebellion. The attack on Pueblo gender relations that had been carried out in the name of Christianity and civilization added to Indian discontent with the Spanish. Pope, one of the shamans who had been beaten by Spanish authorities in the 1670s, rallied Indian men and women to the cause. The Indians attacked in August of 1680, sacking Catholic churches, martyring Franciscan priests, and murdering settlers in the Spanish towns of New Mexico.

As the Pueblo Revolt unfolded beginning in August of 1680, Pope linked the rewards of warfare with a new regime of matrimony by claiming that the Indian "who shall kill a Spaniard will get an Indian woman for a wife, and he who kills four will get four women, and he who kills ten or more will have a like number of women." As the Spanish retreated, Pope urged his followers to please their gods by returning to their old ways of farming and worship and to abandon any wife they had married by Spanish law. Pueblo women as well as men had attended Pope's planning meetings. Indeed, according to the testimony at a later inquiry, it was "particularly the women" who wanted to drive the Spanish out. Despite their dramatic success, however, the Indians only succeeded in expelling the Spanish for a decade; by the 1690s, the Spanish government had launched a successful reconquest of New Mexico.

The Christian tradition demanded a household structure that challenged the gender hierarchy of many indigenous societies. Some Indians continued to resist, but others were drawn in. In many cases, women became part of new mestizo households in which social, religious, and cultural practices merged into a new frontier culture. Those women who became Christian found powerful inspiration in the Virgin of Guadalupe, but it came at the price of traditional forms of behavior that had also empowered women. Indigenous women farther North faced similar issues.

TRADING VENTURES IN THE NORTH

While Spain reaped riches from the gold and silver mines of its New World empire, those treasures proved elusive for other European colonies. Both France and the

Netherlands focused instead on developing a lucrative fur trade farther north. By the middle of the sixteenth century, the French had established a trading post near what is now Quebec. They pushed down the Mississippi River during the seventeenth century and by the beginning of the eighteenth century had established the port of New Orleans on the Gulf of Mexico. The Dutch gained a toehold in North America in 1624 when the Dutch West India Company sent thirty-five Flemish families to New Netherland and began organizing European trade in beaver pelts in the area that is now New York. Their colony came to encompass much of what is now New York State, but in 1664 the Dutch surrendered control to the English.

While both the French and the Dutch focused on the fur trade, their colonizing methods were different, creating two very distinct trading frontiers. A key difference developed in the domestic arrangements of the traders and the roles women played in their economies. Both colonies were dominated by single men, though by the 1650s the Dutch were sending more families. Among Dutch women who did arrive, some became quite active in the mercantile activities of the colony. The French, by way of contrast, sought to facilitate trade through marriages to Indian women. Like the Spanish, the French created a frontier of inclusion.

MAP 2-2   NEW FRANCE IN THE SEVENTEENTH CENTURY

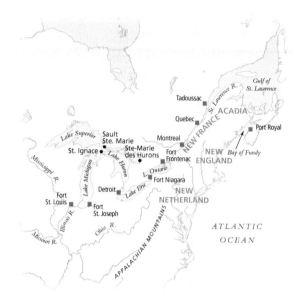

French trading settlements were scattered along a broad swath of northern waterways by the seventeenth century.

The Fur Trade

The French quickly discovered that Indian women were important participants in the development of the fur trade. Before trapping became a widely commercialized trade, men hunted while women processed and distributed the meat and hides that were produced. Women not only prepared the meat for eating but also turned the animal skins into leggings, jackets, and moccasins; they also transformed the bones of the animals into needles, ladles, and other tools for survival.

The French were amazed that the men handed over the animal carcasses from their hunts to the women and accepted their control of distribution. The Jesuit missionary Paul Le Jeune, described the domestic arrangements of the Montagnais Indians of Quebec by saying, "Men leave the arrangement of the household to the women, without interfering with them; they cut, and decide, and give away as they please, without making the husband angry." But for the Montagnais Indians and other tribes, the exchange between hunters and processors was an even one. Decision making was done by those responsible for the tasks, whether it be distribution or moving when food production demanded it.

As the trade developed with the French, both Indian men and women altered some of their patterns of work. Men increased the bounty of their hunt with muskets and steel traps. Women also acquired goods from the French, but the goods were materials that offered the women respite from their labor rather than tools to increase agricultural production. Indian women, for example, found the copper pots they obtained from the French to be lighter and more portable than the wooden ones they had previously used. As Indian men became increasingly involved in the fur trade, their families began to rely more and more on some of the food they acquired from the Europeans—whether it was dried peas or bread—rather than food that women gathered. However, in fur trade communities that relied on agriculture, women continued to be busy tending their crops.

Those Indian women who married French fur traders found new kinds of work opening up for them as cultural brokers between the French and their Indian tribes. Such women not only processed and repaired animal skins for their husbands but also provided crucial access to trade networks through their kin. As translators of languages and customs, these women could assist not only in trading ventures but also in diplomatic negotiations.

Catholicism and Conversion

The French hoped not only to establish a trading empire in the New World but to re-create French society. Two of their most important cultural weapons for doing so were religion and education, both of which would bring with them the values of French culture. The French viewed Indian women as central agents of this civiliz-

ing effort and thus focused a large part of their efforts on converting them. Father Paul Le Jeune argued in the 1630s that the girls must be converted first and that they would convert the boys. The Ursuline Sisters were encouraged to set up their convents and educate Indian girls in Christian and civilized ways. This is how Marie de l'Incarnation, one of the first female missionaries to the New World, found herself cleaning, clothing, and instructing young Indian girls in seventeenth-century Quebec.

Not all Indian women welcomed these efforts at evangelization, however. French priests who interacted with the Huron and Montagnais societies between the Great Lakes and the Saint Lawrence River reported great resistance among the Indian women they tried to convert—indeed, they struggled more with the women than with the men. One Indian woman reportedly threw a knife at her husband as he pressured her to convert. "Dost thou not see that we are all dying since they told us to pray to God?" Women may have been particularly resistant to Christianity when it was tied to increasing their subordination to men. Father Le Jeune encouraged one Indian man to stand up to his wife. "I told him he was the master," reported the priest, "and that in France women do not rule their husbands."

Marie l'Incarnation left her only son behind in Paris when she became a nun and traveled to New France in the seventeenth century to convert the Indians living there. Her letters back to France provided an important glimpse of interactions that took place between the French and the Native Americans they encountered.

The French priests extended their arguments about male leadership to include political organization as well as family relationships. Troubled by the relative egalitarianism in the decision-making processes of the Montagnais society, for example, the priests urged the men to choose some male leaders who would lead the decision-making process. It was the logical next step in the kind of family-building authority structure they were trying to construct. Meeting in council, some of the men who agreed to this plan and who elected three leaders informed the women and children of their communities, "Know that you will obey your husbands and you young people know that you will obey your parents, and our captains. . .".

WOMEN'S VOICES

CONFLICTS WITH THE HURON

Marie de l'Incarnation, a French widow, left her young son in France and became an Ursuline missionary in Quebec during the seventeenth century. She wrote extensively to both her son and to members of her religious order, including the Mother Superior of her convent, about the Huron peoples that she met and tried to convert.

Quebec, September 13, 1640

My reverend and very dear Mother:

. . . The demons have conspired to destroy the Huron mission if they can and arrange that all the calumnies brought against the missionaries seem to be truths. Great assemblies have been held with the purpose of exterminating the Revered Fathers but, far from being afraid, they waited for death with marvelous constancy and even hastened to the places where the conspiracy was most heated.

One of the oldest and most prominent women of this nation harangued an assembly in this way: "It is the Black Robes that make us die by their spells. Harken to me. I am proving it by arguments you will know to be true. They lodged in a certain village where everyone was well. As soon as they were established there, everyone was dead except for three or four persons. They went elsewhere and the same thing happened. They visited the cabins in other villages and only those they did not enter were free of mortality and sickness. Do you not see that when they move their lips—what they call prayers—those are spells that come from their mouths? It is the same way when they read in their books. Besides, in their cabins they have big pieces of wood (those are guns) with which they make a great noise and spread their magic everywhere. If they are not promptly put to death, they will finally ruin the country so that neither small nor great will remain. . . ."

The Reverend Fathers are held actually to be sorcerers inasmuch as, wherever they go, God permits death to accompany them, to purify the faith of those they have converted. They have been reduced to the extremity of hiding their breviaries and of no longer praying aloud. . . .

Source: Marie de l'Incarnation to Mother Ursule de Sainte-Catherine, Mother Superior of the Ursulines of Tours, in Joyce Marshall, ed. and trans., Word From New France: The Selected Letters of Marie de L'Incarnation *(Toronto: Oxford University Press, 1967), 8–83.*

Questions

1. Why did Huron women think that their people were dying?

2. What was Marie de l'Incarnation's explanation for the deaths taking place among the Hurons?

While Indian women sometimes resisted the subordination that came with conversion, at other times they deployed Catholicism to defend their status. Women who feared physical abuse from their husbands found advocates in the French priests. Indian women also experimented with ideals of sexual chastity and religious sisterhoods as new sources of female power. As in New Spain, some Christianized Indian women in New France developed a cult around the figure of the Virgin Mary. The Virgin was, after all, a very powerful mother—an image that would resonate with Indians who

Catherine Tegakwitha (also known as Kateri, Tekawitha) was an Indian orphan who converted to Christianity in the seventeenth century while she was quite young. She gained great respect from both the Indians surrounding her and the French for her piety and acts of penitence.

organized their societies matrilineally. As a result, by the middle of the seventeenth century, 40 percent of the Hurons had converted to Christianity.

Kateri Tekakwitha was one of the most famous of the female Indian converts in New France. Born near what is now Albany in 1656 to an Algonquian mother and a Mohawk father, Kateri was orphaned as a young girl when her family died of smallpox; she herself was permanently disfigured and almost blinded by the epidemic. Tekakwitha rebuffed the approaches of young men whom her relatives suggested as potential mates and eventually fled north to Kahnawake, just south of Montreal, where the Jesuits had established a mission. Converting to Christianity, she engaged in acts of physical penitence that included fasting, self-flagellation, and burning her feet with hot coals. She also attempted to set up a convent with two of her friends, though the Jesuits intervened to prevent it. When she died at the age of twenty-four, both the French and the Indians in her village revered her for her piety. For Tekakwitha, conversion to Christianity may have been a way to avoid a marriage that she did not want and a way to assert power that both French and Indians would admire.

Marriage, Sex, and Survival in the Middle Ground

French priests who tried to convert Indian women were particularly shocked by their attitudes toward sex and marriage. It was a clash in attitudes that led to repeated conflicts. The Montaignais women were quite distressed in the 1630s, for example, when Father Le Jeune began his campaign against polygamy. Years of warfare had depleted the male population so that it had become increasingly common for an Indian man to marry sisters. Monogamy, the Indians felt, would create suffering for the many women who would not be afforded the benefits that came with a husband. Indians also resisted the attempts of the Jesuits to curtail divorce. With a strong sense of practicality, they pointed out to Father Le Jeune that they could not "persevere in the state of matrimony with a bad wife or a bad husband." Nor did they see a reason to stay married to someone they did not love or (in the case of women) to stay married to a man who did not hunt.

Regardless of what the priests thought of Indian customs, the French government counted on intermarriage between French men and Indian women, at least throughout much of the seventeenth century. France, unlike many other European countries, worried that weakness would result from a loss of population to new colonies; thus, the government was reluctant to promote immigration. The trading empire that France envisioned required few Frenchmen, relying instead on cooperative Indians for trading partners. Thus, during the seventeenth century, fewer than thirteen thousand men and only about two thousand women (excluding nuns) emigrated from France to North America. Few French women were involved in the initial century of French colonization in the New World. With so few men and almost no women emigrating from France to the New World, French society would have to be created not only through conversion but also through marriages to Indian women. Because the French thought in both patriarchal and patrilineal terms, they assumed that cultural affinities would be tied to the father and not to the mother; they assumed the women would become French rather than the men becoming Indian. Government officials did not originally see any social distance between the commoners from France who were trying to eke out a living in New France and the Indian women they married. Indians also supported intermarriage as a way to facilitate trading relationships with the French. The **coureurs de bois**, French fur traders, were particularly interested in obtaining Indian wives. There were few French women to choose from, even if they were interested, and Amerindian women offered valuable family ties and knowledge of trapping.

coureurs de bois French trappers.

The coureurs de bois, however, seemed to enter more into Indian life than to carry with them French civilization, providing an important wrinkle in French policy. Most of the traders and their wives, for example, married according to Indian custom rather than French law. Such marriages could be dissolved far more easily than French marriages, leaving French missionaries to complain that morality was declining rather than improving as civilization met savagery. Indeed, as French fur trappers were assimilated into the families of their wives, they became increasingly difficult for French authorities to control, ignoring restrictions the government tried to place on the fur trade. It was only as French authorities began to shut down outposts in remote areas of the colony and order fur traders back into the interior that many coureurs de bois began to marry their wives according to French law, thus giving them stronger claim to remain with their wives' families. Local French military commanders may have winked at this behavior, both as a way to ease relationships with local Indians and as a way to promote their own side deals in the fur trade.

Through these relations between French men and Indian women, a new fur-trading society—the **metis**—began to emerge around the Great Lakes region. Some of the children of this new society were educated by the French and married French immigrants or joined Catholic religious orders. Others continued the fur trade through the colonial period, relying on a pidgin language that mixed French and Indian languages, and creating a culture that had elements of both European and Native American society. Their villages continued to flourish around the Great Lakes until the early nineteenth century, when most were overwhelmed by new settlers from the East.

metis Mixture of French and Indian cultures.

New Netherland Trade

Like France, the Netherlands sent few people to its North American colonies. In the 1620s, the Dutch economy was booming, and few people were interested in leaving the Old World. As a result, about half of those immigrating to New Netherland were from other European countries, and approximately 80 percent of the immigrants were young single men. By the 1650s, the Dutch economy had slowed down and opportunities in the New World began to seem more attractive, particularly to families interested in acquiring land for farming. As a result of this growth in immigration, there were approximately nine thousand settlers in New Netherland by 1664 when the English conquered the colony, and an increasing percentage of them were women.

Some women came to the colony as indentured servants, but more commonly they came as part of a family, assisting on farms and in shops. In other cases, women managed their own businesses. Some brewed or sold beer. Others traded or managed the family estate. By 1664, there were 46 female traders operating in Albany and 134 in New Amsterdam. An additional 13 women ran their own shops in Albany as did 50 women in New Amsterdam.

Both married and unmarried women actively participated in commerce because the Dutch followed Roman law and allowed married women to operate their own businesses

Female traders were more common in New Amsterdam than in the British colonies during the seventeenth century because the Dutch followed Roman Civil Law while the British followed Common Law. As a result, Dutch women had more legal rights than did British women.

and to make their own contracts. They appeared in court when necessary and inherited property equally with their brothers.

Some women exercised considerable economic power in this system. Maria van Cortlandt, for example, not only managed the brewery her father gave her but also took charge of the wide-ranging activities of the Van Rensselaer estate after her husband Jeremias van Rensselaer died in 1674. Margaret Hardenbroeck arrived in New Amsterdam in 1659 as an agent for one of her cousins in the Netherlands, trading European goods such as pins and vinegar in exchange for furs. When she died in 1691, she was one of the wealthiest women in New York.

The Dutch demonstrated that women could enter their trading ventures in ways quite different from those of the French. The French, reluctant to send their own settlers, had relied on Indian women as go-betweens who became key participants on the French trading frontier. Dutch women, once they actually began to settle in New Netherland, undertook trading activities themselves. The British would introduce yet other variations on this theme as English women began to immigrate to both the Chesapeake and New England regions.

PLANTATION SOCIETIES OF THE SOUTHEAST

While the French pushed farther through Canada and down the Mississippi River, the British developed large settlements along the Atlantic coast during the seventeenth century. Among the earliest and most enduring were those established in the Chesapeake region. These settlements were partly set up as a beachhead to challenge the Spanish empire and to plunder Spanish ships sailing back to Europe with gold. But British adventurers also hoped to reap riches in whatever trade they could establish in the New World. The Virginia Company, operating under a royal charter from King James I, established Jamestown in 1607 for the Virginia Colony. In 1634, the Calvert family, Catholic supporters of King Charles I, began settling a large tract of land at the northern end of the Chesapeake region, which they named Maryland. Although Maryland differed from Virginia in its inclusion of a large Catholic minority, in most other respects, the colonies were similar.

The Virginia Company that established the new colony of Virginia had originally viewed its venture as one rooted in the extraction and trade of natural resources—a male venture not unlike the trapping culture of the French farther north and inland. The Chesapeake region proved worthless in terms of minerals, but the British discovered an appealing variety of tobacco and moved with speed to develop commercial agriculture. By 1630, a million and a half pounds of tobacco were exported from the fledgling colony. With the development of this early plantation economy, the British turned to Africans for labor power, shaping a powerful variant of slavery that would become a crucial underpinning of the New World experience.

More than the French and the Spanish, the British tried to set up their own communities independent of the Indians who surrounded them. The British distinguished themselves from other Europeans by arguing that they would not take up with Indian women and bragged about the way in which their men resisted their advances. Because the British had little interest in staking their economic claims on trade with the Indians (as France did), there was little reason to officially promote intermarriage between British men and Indian women. Thus, when British men did marry or become otherwise involved with such women, their relationships were ignored. Their frontier was thus one of exclusion rather than inclusion.

MAP 2-3 EUROPEAN COLONIES OF THE ATLANTIC COAST 1607–1639

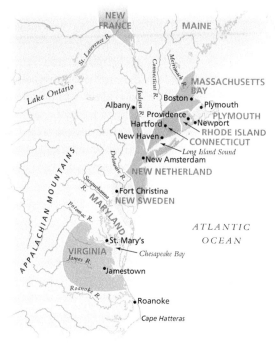

In addition to France and England, Sweden and the Netherlands established colonies along the eastern seaboard of North America early in the seventeenth century.

The Tobacco Economy

Few women immigrated to the Chesapeake region in its early years. Unlike France, England was eager to export its inhabitants to the New World, particularly the poor who had been dispossessed of their farms and pasturelands. Most of those who came to the early colonies of the Chesapeake region were men. In Virginia, there were more than three men for every woman in the early decades of settlement. As a result, the Virginia Company began recruiting English women, who were viewed as crucial components of an agricultural society both for the stability they were thought to bring and the kinds of rural domestic work they could do. Pamphleteers enticed British women by promising them the opportunities to live much as they did in England, arguing that only "nasty" wenches worked in the fields.

In fact, throughout most of the seventeenth century, women continued the tradition of flexible labor patterns that existed in Europe: tobacco was the most important crop in the colony, and when necessary, women worked alongside men tending it. As a result, women did not have the time to sustain the subsistence crops and create the local markets of exchange that were so important in England. There were few spinning wheels to be found in Virginia and Maryland during the first decades of settlement. Instead, the cash generated by women's labor in the tobacco fields was used to purchase supplies imported from elsewhere. In the 1680s, as tobacco became less profitable, many women finally turned to more traditional kinds of female work such as raising vegetables, milking cows, making butter and cheese, washing clothes, and preparing food. Because there were few mills available, women also faced the exhausting labor of beating and grinding grain such as corn. When their financial circumstances permitted, they did hire indentured servants to take over this onerous task. "Beating the mortar," as it was called, was no more popular with servants than with housewives, and some complained that such demands violated the agreements they had made with their masters.

indentured servant
Person bound to work for a master for four to seven years as payment for transportation to the New World.

Indentured servants, female as well as male, constituted three-fourths of the British immigrants to the southern colonies. However, only one-fourth of the indentured servants were female. Young women agreed to work for their masters and mistresses for a stipulated amount of time—usually four to seven years—in return for the payment of their passage to the New World as well as room and board while they were in service. Some of these young women found themselves literally worked to death. Ellinor Hues was beaten repeatedly and eventually died in the tobacco fields of Virginia.

Increasingly during the seventeenth century, slave women from Africa began to replace indentured servants on southern plantations. African women were experienced agricultural workers, and while some helped with housework, masters expected them to hoe tobacco along with the men. Both female and male slaves were only a small part of the workforce in the Chesapeake during the first half of the seventeenth century. Slaves cost more than indentured servants because masters held them in bondage for life rather than for a few years. Because so many immigrants died within a few months of arrival, there was little point in paying for an expensive slave when she could die soon; a cheaper indentured servant would do just as well. By the last quarter of the seventeenth century, as immigrants began to live longer in the Chesapeake region, slaves were a better investment. By the 1660s, there were slightly more slave women in Virginia than there were indentured serving women.

While British as well as African women actually worked in the fields, African women became associated with agricultural labor while British women did not. This distinction became clear in the laws of Virginia as early as 1643, when a tax was placed on all those expected to be working in profitable enterprises. Not only were all men over the age of sixteen supposed to pay this tax, so too were "all Negro women" whether slave or free. African women were considered producers for a market economy while European women were not—regardless of whether the work they did was really different. The taxes that either free black women or that free black families paid for all women associated with them thus created an additional economic burden for black families that white families did not face.

Wealthy Widows and Serving Wenches

Women were important for the new colonies of the Chesapeake region not only as workers but also as wives. Because England wanted to export part of its population, its vision of colonization was one that was rooted in the establishment of British families who would displace indigenous ones. However, because men were much more likely to immigrate to the New World than women were, some unintended economic opportunities opened up for those women who survived the diseases of the new continent. Many of these women married older men of some wealth who not only died before them but also left them in control of their entire estates. The "**tobacco brides**" who were brought to the colony by the Virginia Company in the early 1620s, for example, could only marry men who paid the exorbitant rate of 120 pounds of tobacco for their transportation. Women such as these became widows within a few years and sometimes inherited large estates as well as the right to administer them. There were few uncles or brothers from an extended family network to manage a widow's inheritance as there were in England. Also, because disease killed many children, family size was small and there were relatively few surviving heirs to divide an estate. It was unusual for British women at this time to inherit a large estate and even more unusual to have the right to administer it. Widows in the Chesapeake region assumed far greater responsibilities than their counterparts in England during the seventeenth century.

Free white women exercised power not only through the control of property when widowed but also through the informal networks of gossip, nursing, and trade that they created. Midwives often forced an unmarried woman to name the father of her child at the moment she gave birth and provided testimony to local authorities attempting to determine which man needed to be punished for unlawful behavior. Midwives and other matrons could also be called upon to examine women who complained of spousal abuse. Whether through court testimony or informal networks, women created and maintained community standards of decency.

Indentured servants, however, found their opportunities far more limited. They faced the same risks of dying, particularly in their first year, as did free women, but they faced other risks as well. Female servants were not allowed to marry without their master's permission, something that was difficult to obtain because a husband's authority would conflict with a master's and it was expected that a married woman's work would be interrupted by pregnancies. Thus, men who wanted to marry indentured servants were expected to pay masters for the amount of time the women still owed. For those couples that did not have the money or the inclination to wait, the punishments were drastic. A single woman who became pregnant while she was indentured could have her term of service extended by up to two years. She could also be whipped and fined, and she faced the real possibility of having her child taken away from her by the courts, a common occurrence for women who fell in love with other servants, slaves, or poor men who could not pay for their freedom. Even women who became pregnant because they were sexually abused by their masters got little sympathy from the courts. Most judges continued to assume that women were sexual creatures who encouraged sexual liaisons with the men they knew. In addition, folk wisdom at the time suggested that a woman could only become pregnant if she had an orgasm, which would be an obvious indicator that she had enjoyed the sexual activity.

The failure of the courts to protect servant women from abusive masters in the Chesapeake region was part of a general policy of the government to stay out of household matters, which was also one of the reasons widows were able to take over their husbands' estates. Women found little protection from husbands, fathers, or masters who mistreated them. One young servant, Elizabeth Abbott, was beaten viciously, repeatedly, by John and Alice Proctor before she died in 1624. While neighbors tended her wounds, no one stopped the beatings; nor were the Proctors convicted of any crime. Neither did courts in the Chesapeake region show much interest in wife beating. Because the colonial governments were reluctant to intervene in household relations, many settlers ignored rules that required the official sanction of the government

tobacco brides Young women brought to Virginia in the 1620s who promised to marry men who would pay for their passage.

and the church in the creation of a marriage. Instead, settlers commonly felt mutual consent and sex were all they required. As long as a woman was free, she was unlikely to be prosecuted for an informal marriage.

Slavery, Race, and Intermarriage

Elizabeth Keys sued for her freedom in 1656 and won. Born the daughter of a slave woman and a free English man, Keys pointed out that she not only was a Christian, which had long been a basis for declaring freedom, but also was the daughter of a free man. In arguing for the importance of her father's status in determining her own, Keys followed the logic of English law, which recognized patrilineal descent in determining a child's status. Keys challenged the way in which planters were trying to maintain power over their slaves through future generations by tying a child's status to that of its mother. Keys' local court had granted her freedom, but the General Court of Virginia overturned that decision. The General Assembly eventually sided with Elizabeth Keys, but only after she married Englishman William Greensted, her lawyer and the father of two of her children.

Keys' case reveals the fluidity of slave law in Virginia during the first half of the seventeenth century. While slaves had always had a different status from indentured servants, the exact nature of that difference was not clear. Some slaves purchased their freedom or the freedom of their loved ones and went on to moderately successful lives. Anthony and Mary Johnson both arrived in Virginia on some of the earliest slave ships, and they had managed to buy their way out of slavery and even acquire property on the eastern shore of Virginia by the 1650s. Although they faced growing racial discrimination—such as the tax placed on black women that was not placed on white women, they still managed to live decently. After 1662, though, the laws in Virginia began to make it harder for slaves and the children of slaves to gain their freedom. A law passed in 1662 made it clear that in the case of slave women, their children's condition would be determined not by who their father was but by who their mother was—if the mother was a slave, then her child also belonged to her master. Similar laws were passed in Maryland. In this way, planters laid claim to not only the productive labors of their female slaves but also their reproductive labors.

Virginia's laws on interracial sexual relations also marked African Americans as a degraded race. Unmarried couples who had children could be prosecuted for fornication, but in 1662 the fines were doubled for cases of interracial sex. Because the law only concerned free people, masters who had sexual relationships with their slave women were not prosecuted. Most of those who were punished by the law were free white women who had sex with Afro-Virginian men, be they free or slave.

Three decades later, even legal relationships between blacks and whites were outlawed. Before 1691, Africans and Europeans could intermarry if both parties were free—and they sometimes did. After 1691, however, children of interracial relationships in Virginia automatically became illegitimate and were unable to inherit property.

With so many avenues for legitimate marriage shut off, it is not surprising that many Afro-Virginian women headed their own households and that in many cases they were responsible for protecting their children. While a difficult burden to bear, it may have been a role that free black women could adapt to because many came from parts of Africa where the mother-child bond was strong.

WOMEN'S LIVES

POCAHONTAS

Matoaka, better known by her nickname of Pocahontas, was born in the Chesapeake region at the end of the sixteenth century. She was one of many children of Powhatan, a particularly powerful chief, who had taken numerous wives from different villages as part of his strategy to consolidate power in his region. Pocahontas, like her siblings, was born as a result of her father's strategy to create political alliances, and the life she led reflected her understanding of the political importance of kinship and marriage.

She was only about twelve or thirteen when she "saved" one of the strange new men who had intruded on her territory. John Smith, a British captain, had been first welcomed by Powhatan but then captured and forced to lie flat on stones as Indians from the village prepared to beat him. The young girl flung herself over his body to protect him. As the Indians drew back, she pulled Smith to his feet and her father then adopted him as one of his sons. Pocahontas not only acted as a go-between in cementing an alliance with the British by protecting John Smith; she created another powerful alliance with the British in 1614 when she married John Rolfe, after converting to Christianity the year before and taking the new name of Rebecca. The couple had a son named Thomas in 1615 and traveled to England the following year, where Pocahontas was greeted as royalty. Pocahontas was well aware of her role in joining the two cultures into an alliance, a perception she made particularly clear when she encountered John Smith in England. She was offended that he had taken so long to come to see her in England; when they finally did meet, she chastised him, demanding that he call her child and she call him father, "so I will bee for ever and ever your

Ætatis suæ 21. Aᵒ 1616.

Countrieman." Unfortunately, Pocahontas also became ill and died in England at the age of twenty-two after suffering from what appeared to be pneumonia.

The marriage of Pocahontas and John Rolfe suggests the way in which interracial and intercultural marriage practices were in flux in the very early years of settlement around the Chesapeake region, though such a marriage became problematic for subsequent generations. By the middle of the seventeenth century, Virginia had outlawed interracial marriage; and by 1691, the assembly had passed a law to make it clear that Indians were included in this prohibition. As the Indian population in Virginia declined during the eighteenth century and ceased to be a threat, some local writers began to reconsider these prohibitions. Would the British conquest of the New World

(continued)

have been better executed, they wondered, if there had been more marriages such as the one between Pocahontas and Rolfe? Prominent Virginians, including Thomas Jefferson, searched their genealogies for connections. Other southerners, however, were more ambivalent about the idea of interracial marriage and preferred to emphasize the protection Pocahontas had offered John Smith as well as her conversion to Christianity. This viewpoint is most famously depicted in a painting for the U.S. Capitol Rotunda from 1840. Pocahontas is portrayed with lighter skin than the other Indians in the painting and with her back to the Indians, facing both the minister and the Englishmen of the colony, suggesting the ways in which Americans of European heritage wanted to imagine her.

Throughout the colonial period and the nineteenth century, the legend of Pocahontas evolved as one that explored and denied the possibilities of interracial marriage. That ambivalence has continued into the twenty-first century in the current manifestations of the Pocahontas legend. In the popular Disney version of *Pocahontas*, the Indian princess champions cross-cultural toleration. She sings "Colors of the Wind" as a poetic rendering of this goal and rebukes those Europeans who see her people as savages. Yet the original movie does not acknowledge her marriage to John Rolfe. ▪

Anxious Patriarchs

Planters moved to define the laws of slavery in the Chesapeake region in part because slaves were becoming a more economical alternative to indentured servants but also because they were worried that white servants and ex-servants might join together with slaves and free blacks as a large and unruly underclass to overthrow the gentry. Those fears were realized in 1676 when an interracial alliance materialized in Bacon's Rebellion, led rather improbably by an elite newcomer who felt shut out of power in Virginia by Governor Berkeley and his officials. Nathaniel Bacon rallied back-country settlers from the western frontier, many of them former servants or slaves, in attacks on Indian villages during 1675. Berkeley was fearful that these raids would destabilize the colony's relationships with the Indians, so he moved quickly against Bacon and his followers. As a result, in 1676, the men turned their fury on what they called the "grandees" of Jamestown, burning to the ground much of the capital. This attack on the wealthy and ruling elite brought fears of class conflict to the forefront of the colony.

While Bacon's armed followers were men, many of his supporters were women and they too rallied to his cause. Bacon relied on informal networks of communication to spread news of his cause—networks that women often fostered through their gossip. Mrs. Haviland traveled throughout the countryside promoting Bacon's cause, though Sarah Drummond was perhaps the most spirited of Bacon's female supporters, at one point claiming in a meeting of the rebels, "I fear the power of England no more than a broken straw...." Regardless of Sarah Drummond's brave words, the Rebellion collapsed with the death of Nathaniel Bacon that year. Rebels were rounded up and executed; and though female participants escaped with their lives, they still faced harassment and economic hardship.

Even before Bacon's Rebellion, the colonial government had begun to crack down on the power women exercised through their gossip. In 1662, they passed a law allowing women to be ducked (instead of paying a fine) if convicted of slander, a much more public and particularly humiliating form of punishment. In the years following Bacon's Rebellion, white women found their independence curtailed in other significant ways as a more patriarchal society asserted itself. After 1680, courts were more likely to remind married women of their feme covert status and to demand the presence of a husband if they wished to proceed with their cases. Widows also faced more questions as they tried to control inheritances or lead households on their own.

By curtailing the power of white women, the government in Virginia established a stronger system of patriarchal authority by the end of the seventeenth century. White men gained power from changes in the laws concerning not only women but also black men. In 1692, slaves also lost the right to own property, including livestock they raised to feed their families. For male slaves who came from African areas where men were responsible for herding, this was a powerful attack on their gender roles. The Assembly had begun to restrict slave access to guns in the years before Bacon's Rebellion and in the years following the Rebellion looked suspiciously at free blacks as well. In 1723, free black men were barred from the colony's militias. By allowing all white men to own guns and property and to participate in the militia, the Virginia Assembly effectively manipulated ideas of gender and race to undermine the class alignments that had developed among the poor in Bacon's Rebellion. Poor white men joined with wealthy white men in an assertion of male patriarchy.

Thus, by the end of the seventeenth century, the fluid frontier settlements in the Chesapeake region had yielded to a more settled society of racial and gender hierarchy. The division of labor was clearer as respectable white women were less likely to be found in the fields and extended family networks afforded multiple layers of male leadership. The control of slave women's sexuality ensured a permanent underclass of workers, and the stigmatization of their agricultural work ensured that race would be an important qualifier of gender. Further restrictions on black men, meanwhile, contributed to a belief in the privileged status of white men.

GODLY SOCIETIES OF NEW ENGLAND

The British settlers who landed farther north on the eastern seaboard in the early seventeenth century found a climate and rocky soil that were hostile to the commercial plantation agriculture growing in the South. In addition, while the immigrants to the north expected to set up successful commercial ventures, many were also immigrating for another reason: they were fleeing what they felt to be the unholy religious practices of England and hoping to set up a new world that would honor God in a way they felt was impossible to achieve in the Old World. This was particularly true for the Pilgrims who established Plymouth Colony in 1620 and for the Puritans who established Massachusetts Bay Colony in 1626. These economic and religious differences had an important impact on the presence of women in the New England colonies. Because Pilgrims and Puritans were migrating for religious reasons as much as for economic ones and because they expected to engage broadly in subsistence rather than in commercial farming, they tended to migrate as families rather than as individuals. From the beginning of settlement in New England, English women were present in approximately equal numbers to English men. Moreover, family structures similar to those in England were established quickly, conditions that were not true in the more heavily male Chesapeake region.

Goodwives

The Puritans who immigrated to Massachusetts Bay were committed to maintaining traditional social hierarchies and ways of living, and the families they brought with them ensured this development. Over 40 percent of the immigrants were women and only 17 percent were servants. The few single men who arrived in New England during these early days quickly married, so that early English setters in New England created a strong family structure as a basis for their social and economic order. The women of these families were expected to replicate their work in England, and within a couple of generations they had. As frontier areas became settled, women tended to their dairy work and their spinning. They also slaughtered small animals, brewed beer and cider, cooked, cleaned, mended clothes, and tended children.

When necessary, women assisted their husbands in their shops and taverns or stood in for them if their husbands were unavailable. Anne Devorix of Massachussetts supervised servants and interacted with merchants who had an interest in her husband's fishing business during the 1660s, as well as overseeing the planting of the family farm when her husband was gone. Anne Dering received power of attorney from her husband to collect his debts in 1674. As such, these women fulfilled a clearly defined role, not as independent women but as **deputy husbands**. They were expected as partners in a marriage to step in for their husbands if necessary.

Other women took on traditional female roles, including nursing and midwifery. Midwives were perceived by their patients as having practical experience in healing, as opposed to male healers and doctors who were perceived as having a more intellectual approach, whether or not they had been formally trained in medicine in a university. Midwives, along with other neighbors, assisted women when they gave birth, coaxing out newborns and making sure that after the birth women were properly cleaned to avoid future infection. Midwives also tended both men and women who fell sick and were particularly important in neighborhoods where no doctor was present. While a midwife was unlikely to be paid cash for her work, she received gifts of cloth or other goods.

As women engaged in nursing or assisted their husbands with their farms and their businesses, they not only contributed to the well-being of their families but also created and solidified the ties that held their communities together. They traded extra yarn or preserves at the local store, using the credit to purchase goods needed for their homes and providing useful commodities for their neighbors. Likewise, as they filled in for their husbands, they ensured the smooth functioning of larger economic transactions; and in caring for the sick, they attended to the physical well-being of their communities. These activities were also times to socialize, to exchange news, and to share opinions. As in the southern colonies, if a young woman gave birth without being married, the women who attended her delivery expected her to name the father as the baby was born and they testified about their knowledge in court. Women's work in New England carried with it an important element of social responsibility.

Girls were trained for these roles from a young age, both at home and at school. In many towns, girls attended "dame schools" taught by women rather than men. Their curriculum usually differed from that of boys, focusing on cooking and sewing as well as reading and writing. Wealthier girls could receive a more extensive education at home if their parents could afford a tutor, but even in these cases their training was generally geared toward their future roles as goodwives.

deputy husband
Position assumed by a woman who took on the responsibilities of her husband while he was gone.

WOMEN'S VOICES

A GOODWIFE

Anne Bradstreet (1612–1672) was the daughter of one Massachusetts governor and the wife of another. She was also one of the first English poets in the New World. She wrote this epitaph for her mother Dorothy Dudley, who died in 1643.

Here lyes

A Worthy Matron of unspotted life,

A loving Mother and obedient wife,

A friendly Neighbor, pitiful to poor,

Whom oft she fed, and clothed with her store;

To Servants wisely aweful, but yet kind,

And as they did, so they reward did find:

A true Instructer of her Family,

The which she ordered with dexterity.

The publick meetings ever did frequent,

And in her Closet constant hours she spent;

Religious in all her words and wayes,

Preparing still for death, till end of dayes:

Of all her Children, Children liv'd to see,

Then dying, left a blessed memory.

Source: *Anne Bradstreet, 1643, quoted in Helen Stuart Campbell, Anne Bradstreet and Her Time, Project Gutenberg, etext 6854, http://infomotions.com/etexts/gutenberg/dirs/etext04/nnbst10.htm*

Questions

1. What were the most important duties of a woman in Puritan society?
2. How does this poem describe the work that women did holding society together?

Family Government

Because of both migration patterns and geographical differences, family structure in New England differed in significant ways from that in the Chesapeake region though the settlers of both regions were from England. Not only did more families (and hence more women) immigrate to the New England colonies, but members of those families lived longer lives in the seventeenth century than did their contemporaries in old England or in the Chesapeake region. Whereas a woman in the Chesapeake region could expect to live to the age of thirty-nine during the seventeenth century, a woman in New England could expect to live between sixty and seventy years. Men were similarly healthy and long-lived. New England did not have the health problems that came from the overcrowded cities of England or from the diseased swamps of the southern colonies. These women also married younger than their southern contemporaries, in part because many of them were not indentured. As a result, they began having children at a younger age and bore more children. With children also more likely to survive than those in the South, large families quickly became the norm in New England. Eighty percent of the children born in New England during the seventeenth century survived to adulthood whereas only 40 to 50 percent of the children born in the Chesapeake region did.

Elizabeth Clark Freake was a prominent Puritan woman in Massachusetts Bay colony. As the portrait reveals, her childrearing responsibilities were of central importance in her life.

The implications of these hardy families for the women who lived in them were enormous, as an English patriarchal family structure took root more successfully in early New England than was possible in the Chesapeake region. Women were not so likely to become widows as they were in the South, and they were much more likely to have a large number of surviving children. A father was more likely to stay alive in New England to rule his family—and his sons were likely to be grown and ready to assume control of family property by the time he died, thus eliminating the need for women to take over. Families could indeed function as the basis for government in New England, and they did. Those individuals who entered Massachusetts Bay Colony without a spouse or parent were expected to live in a household nonetheless.

The importance of the family as a basis for political order shaped the sexual relations of the men and women in the colony. Puritans expected men and women alike to enjoy sex. Indeed, like most Europeans during this period, Puritans did not believe conception was possible unless both the woman and man experienced orgasm. However, they expected sex to be procreative and to occur within the bounds of formal, state-sanctioned marriages. Sodomy, which was prosecuted more extensively in New England than in the Chesapeake region, could result in the death penalty. More commonly, New England courts meted out light punishments to the numerous couples who conceived children before being formally married. Many considered their betrothal to one another enough of a commitment to legitimize sexual intercourse, and others shared the popular belief at the time that marriages could be private affairs between two individuals. New England courts rejected both arguments, prosecuting these couples for fornication more consistently than did courts farther south.

For married couples, patriarchal order prevailed. Married women followed British law in assuming the legal status of feme coverts, merging their legal identities with those of their husbands; they could not own property or make contracts. Although a

TABLE 2-1 Life Expectancy at Age 20 for Whites in British North America: North vs. South

Salem, Massachusetts	17th Century	36 years
Plymouth Colony	17th Century	48 years
Andover, Massachusetts	1670-1699	45 years
Charles Country, Maryland	1652-1699 (native born)	26 years
Charles Parish, Virginia	1655-1699	21 years
Perquimans Country, NC	17th Century	30.5 years

(Source: Henry A Germany, "The White Population of the Colonial United States, 1607–1790," in Michael R. Haines and Richard H. Steckel, A Population History of North America, New York: Cambridge University Press, 163–164)

Life expectancy in the northern British colonies was significantly higher than in southern British colonies.

woman assumed an independent legal identity when widowed, her expected inheritance of one-third share in the interest from her husband's estate was calculated not to breed economic independence but, rather, to prevent her from becoming an impoverished dependent supported by her neighbors. Similarly, children paid careful attention to the wishes of their parents, who controlled their inheritances. Although New Englanders believed strongly in the importance of sexual attraction in a marriage and expected their children to engage in a lively courtship, they did not hesitate to advise their children about the economic and social suitability of potential partners.

Female Piety

Religious practices in New England were important means for reinforcing the gender hierarchy in families because religious commitments had driven so many into the northern colonies. Many of those immigrating to New England did not believe that the Anglican church created by Henry VIII in the sixteenth century went far enough in reforming the corrupt practices they saw in Catholicism, and they worried that God would be displeased with them for failing to bring the society around them into line with their religious practices. Starting out fresh in the New World where they could use their religious beliefs to organize society had a lot of appeal. In the New World, they could live as they believed God demanded and set an example to the rest of the world. This urge was strengthened at the end of the 1620s as King Charles I began to persecute the Puritans in England, forcing their exodus. By 1643, twenty thousand Puritans had immigrated across the Atlantic in the **Great Migration**. Other religious groups such as the Pilgrims and the Quakers began leaving for similar reasons, creating a world full of religious fervor.

Great Migration Movement of Puritans from England to New England between the 1620s and 1650s as a result of religious persecution.

Religion sustained women as they faced both the challenges and dangers of the New World. When Mary Rowlandson was captured by Indians in 1676 during King Philip's War, she viewed her experience as a religious trial and took comfort in her spiritual devotion. Held for three months before being ransomed, Rowlandson was relieved to return to her family and famously recounted her adventure in one of the early best sellers of New England, *A True History of the Captivity and Restoration of Mrs. Mary Rowlandson*. Repeatedly, she reminded her readers that God had tested her faith during her captivity but that He had never deserted her.

Unlike Catholicism and Anglicanism, Puritanism and most other Protestant denominations demanded a conversion experience as a central criteria of membership. Parents were expected to bring their children to church for religious training, but membership was not automatically conveyed at birth or by baptism. It was usually during teenage years that young people went through a period of self-doubt and self-examination, trying to determine if they were one of the **elect**—people chosen by God to be saved. Those who reached a positive conclusion came before church members to describe their soul-searching experiences. In the early years of the Puritan experiment, women appeared just as men did and were admitted as full members in the church as a result of their narratives.

elect People chosen by God to be saved.

Such active participation in religion clearly brought women growing respect. Although they were viewed as subordinate to their husbands, they were also seen as important helpers in the religious education of their children. Their spiritual nurturing moved children toward productive self-examination and (one hoped) conversion.

Suspicions continued about the evil nature of women, but some ministers began to speak in favor of women's spirituality. John Cotton, one early minister, suggested that because of Eve's sin, women were acutely aware of their weaknesses and prone to be more careful because of past failures. Women were not considered the spiritual equals of men—that would challenge the patriarchal order of Puritan society—but their souls were equal to men's. More important, women became more likely to have conversion experiences than men, so that women were becoming the majority of the congregants in Puritan churches by the end of the seventeenth century. Not only were they more numerous; they also had their conversion experiences at a younger age than men, often joining congregations independently of their husbands.

While women comprised the majority of members in Puritan churches, they were not allowed to control church property, to appoint ministers, or to be ministers. They did meet, however, in the homes of older women to discuss a minister's sermon or their own spiritual condition. Even these meetings could lead to trouble if a woman questioned the teachings of church elders. This is precisely what happened to Anne Hutchinson, who was expelled from Massachusetts Bay Colony after she was tried by both the General Court in 1637 and by an ecclesiastical court in 1638 for holding meetings in which she suggested that many local ministers were deviating from Puritan theology in their sermons. As Reverend Hugh Peter reprimanded her, "You have stept out of your place, you have rather bine a Husband than a Wife and a preacher than a Hearer; and a Magistrate than a Subject."

Mary Dyer, a follower of Anne Hutchinson, was also banished. Moving to Rhode Island with her husband, she eventually became a Quaker. Quakers were considered religious radicals in the seventeenth century, in part because they allowed women as well as men to speak on religious matters. Their founder, George Fox, argued that God had created men and women equal. Although women had lost that status after Eve's sin, Fox believed women regained their equality once they experienced conversion. As a result, not only did Quaker women speak in their meetings but some felt moved to become missionaries or to travel the countryside as lay preachers. Mary Dyer was repeatedly banished from Boston and New Haven for her preaching, but she was not successfully silenced until 1660 when she was hanged in Boston for her religious zeal.

Witchcraft and Danger

While authorities in the Spanish Empire ignored most witchcraft accusations (just as authorities did in Spain), the New England colonies, following the lead of northern Europe, took witchcraft far more seriously. During the first century of settlement, between 1620 and 1725, at least 344 people were accused of witchcraft, 78 percent (267) of them women. About forty-five of these women were convicted and twenty-eight were executed.

Most of these women were older, and many had challenged patriarchal conventions in wrangling over inheritances that were unusually large. Katherine Harrison, who was convicted of witchcraft and expelled from Connecticut as punishment in 1669, was the sole heir of her husband's estate. Other women who were convicted in the famous witchcraft trials of Salem, Massachusetts, in 1692 had also faced conflicts over family bequests. Rachel Clinton and Sarah Good, for example, had engaged in protracted court battles as they tried to claim their inheritances.

The Salem witch trials, by far the most wide-reaching in their scope—and quickly regretted by many who participated—brought to an end most trials for witchcraft in the colonies. By the time the outbreak had passed, 144 people had been charged with witchcraft (106 of them women), while four women and six men had been executed. The Salem outbreak was unusual, however, in that many of those who did the accusing were female rather than male, and many accusers were quite young or servants in households—the kind of people not usually taken seriously in a courtroom.

The outbreak may have been the result of tensions over female assertiveness, but there were other factors at work here as well. Many of those accused of witchcraft were associated with families who were promoting economic development in their community. It is possible that fellow townsmen viewed them with suspicion for the changes they encouraged. Another factor may have been the previous experiences of the young accusers. Many of the girls who claimed to have been tortured by witches were refugees from the Maine frontier where they had seen friends and family murdered in conflicts with Indians. They may have been traumatized as a result of their experiences. Whatever the reasons, the excesses of the Salem trials spelled the demise of witch hunting in New England.

While the witchcraft trials exemplified the continuing distrust that existed about women, the collapse of these witch hunts indicated the respect for women that had been growing during the seventeenth century. Women in New England were increasingly revered for their piety and valued as both mothers and deputy husbands. These gains in status, however, were clearly circumscribed by their subordinate place within a patriarchal family and political order.

OVERVIEW

Conflicts and Conquest

1664	**The British conquer New Netherland**	The Dutch surrendered soon after being attacked by the British because they were heavily outnumbered, though the attack triggered a larger war between the Dutch and the English that lasted until 1667
1675	**King Philip's War**	Metacomet, an Indian leader known as King Philip by the English, led a coalition of Narragansett and Wampanoag Indians against British rule. In the two years of warfare, which the Indians ultimately lost, approximately 4,000 Indians and 2,000 English died.
1676	**Bacon's Rebellion**	Nathaniel Bacon led disgruntled backcountry settlers first against Indians in the western territories of Virginia and then, when the Virginia government tried to stop them, against the colonial leadership is Jamestown.
1680	**Pueblo Revolt**	Pueblo Indians in New Mexico, led by shaman Pope, rebel against Spanish rule, murdering Franciscan priests and driving the Spanish out of New Mexico for the next decade.

CONCLUSION

By the end of the seventeenth century, colonial societies had developed throughout the New World with the Spanish, French, and British, in particular, facing off against one another and struggling with the Native American groups who had survived disease and warfare. In some cases, women were key cultural brokers, uniting different societies through their marriages and sexual relationships. Their households were

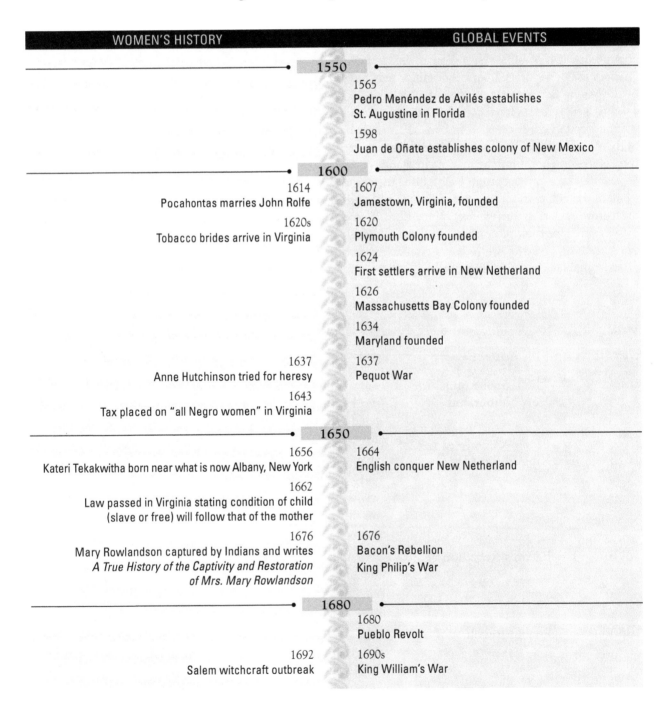

WOMEN'S HISTORY	GLOBAL EVENTS
	1550
	1565 Pedro Menéndez de Avilés establishes St. Augustine in Florida
	1598 Juan de Oñate establishes colony of New Mexico
	1600
1614 Pocahontas marries John Rolfe	1607 Jamestown, Virginia, founded
1620s Tobacco brides arrive in Virginia	1620 Plymouth Colony founded
	1624 First settlers arrive in New Netherland
	1626 Massachusetts Bay Colony founded
	1634 Maryland founded
1637 Anne Hutchinson tried for heresy	1637 Pequot War
1643 Tax placed on "all Negro women" in Virginia	
	1650
1656 Kateri Tekakwitha born near what is now Albany, New York	1664 English conquer New Netherland
1662 Law passed in Virginia stating condition of child (slave or free) will follow that of the mother	
1676 Mary Rowlandson captured by Indians and writes *A True History of the Captivity and Restoration of Mrs. Mary Rowlandson*	1676 Bacon's Rebellion King Philip's War
	1680
	1680 Pueblo Revolt
1692 Salem witchcraft outbreak	1690s King William's War

expansive, as they facilitated production and trade as well as providing models of government. These were forms of social organization that would continue to be vital in the eighteenth century, though as the colonial political order matured, both the household and the place of women within it faced reassessment.

REVIEW QUESTIONS

1. How did Christianity affect the status of women in the New World?

2. Compare and contrast the attitudes toward intermarriage in the empires of Spain, France, and England. How did these attitudes affect the status of women and the development of their colonies?

3. Why were women so important as cultural go-betweens in the New World?

4. Compare and contrast the witchcraft cases in New Spain with those in New England.

RECOMMENDED READINGS

Kathleen Brown. *Good Wives, Nasty Wenches, and Anxious Patriarchs: Gender, Race, and Power in Colonial Virginia*. Chapel Hill: University of North Carolina Press, 1996. A powerful and complex study of the ways in which ideas about gender and race evolved in tandem in the slave society of colonial Virginia.

Ramon Gutierrez. *When Jesus Came, the Corn Mothers Went Away: Marriage, Sexuality, and Power in New Mexico, 1500–1846*. Stanford: Stanford University Press, 1991. A path-breaking interpretation of the ways in which sexuality and gender relations were of central importance in the conquest of New Mexico.

Susan Midgen Socolow. *The Women of Colonial Latin America*. Cambridge: Cambridge University Press, 2000. A well-written summary of the personal, religious, and working lives of the diverse women who lived in New Spain.

Laurel Ulrich. *Good Wives: Image and Reality in the Lives of Women in Northern New England, 1650–1750*. New York: Vintage, 1991. Beautifully written analysis of the material and social lives of women on the New England frontier.

ADDITIONAL BIBLIOGRAPHY

Spanish Conquest in the Southwest

Juliana Barr. "A Diplomacy of Gender: Rituals of First Contact in the 'Land of the Tejas.'" *William and Mary Quarterly*, Third Series LXI, no. 3 (July 2004): 393–434.

Ruth Behar. "Sexual Witchcraft, Colonialism, and Women's Powers: Views from the Mexican Inquisition." In *Sexuality and Marriage in Colonial Latin America*, edited by Asuncion Lavrin. Lincoln: University of Nebraska Press, 1989.

Virginia Bouvier. *Women and the Conquest of California, Codes of Silence: 1542–1840*. Tucson: University of Arizona Press, 2001.

James F. Brooks. *Captives and Cousins: Slavery, Kinship, and Community in the Southwest Borderlands*. Chapel Hill: University of North Carolina Press, 2002.

Susan Deeds. "Subverting the Social Order: Gender, Power, and Magic in Nueva Vizcaya." In *Choice, Persuasion, and Coercion: Social Control on Spain's North American Frontiers*, edited by Jesus F. de La Teja and Ross Frank. Albuquerque: University of New Mexico Press, 2005.

David Eltis. *The Rise of African Slavery in the Americas*. Cambridge: Cambridge University Press, 2000.

Cheryl J. Foote and Sandra K. Schackel. "Indian Women of New Mexico, 1535–1680." In *New*

Mexico Women, edited by Joan M. Jensen and Darlis A. Miller. Albuquerque: University of New Mexico Press, 1986.

Salome Hernandez. "*Nueva Mexicanas* as Refugees and Reconquest Settlers, 1680-1696." In *New Mexico Women*, edited by Joan M. Jensen and Darlis A. Miller. Albuquerque: University of New Mexico Press, 1986.

Ilona Katzew. *Casta Painting: Images of Race in Eighteenth-Century Mexico*. New Haven, CT: Yale University Press, 2004.

Laura Lewis. *Hall of Mirrors: Power, Witchcraft, and Caste in Colonial Mexico*. Durham, NC: Duke University Press, 2003.

Mangus Morner. *Race Mixture in the History of Latin America*. Boston: Little, Brown & Company, 1967.

Marysa Navarro, and Virginia Sanchez Korrol. *Women in Latin America and the Carribbean: Restoring Women to History*. Bloomington: Indiana University Press, 1999.

Stafford Poole. *Our Lady of Guadalupe: The Origins and Sources of a Mexican National Symbol, 1531–1797*. Tucson: University of Arizona Press, 1995.

Bruce G. Trigger and Wilcomb E. Washburn. *The Cambridge History of the Native Peoples of the Americas*. Vol. 1, *North America, Part I*. Cambridge: Cambridge University Press, 1996.

Trading Ventures in the North

Karen Anderson. *Chain Her by One Foot: The Subjugation of Native Women in Seventeenth-Century New France*. New York: Routledge, 1991.

Saliha Belmessous. "Assimilation and Racialism in Seventeenth and Eighteenth-Century French Colonial Policy." *American Historical Review* 110, no. 2 (April 2005).

Charles Callendar. "Miami." In Vol. 15 of *Handbook of North American Indians*, edited by William C. Sturtevant. Washington, DC: Smithsonian Institution, 1978.

Carol Devens. *Countering Colonization: Native American Women and Great Lakes Missions, 1630–1900*. Berkeley: University of California Press, 1992.

Eleanor Leacock. "Montagnais Women and the Jesuit Program for Colonization." In *Women and Colonization*, edited by Mona Etienne and Eleanor Leacock. New York: Praeger, 1980.

Jacqueline Peterson. "Many Roads to Red River: Metis Genesis in the Great Lakes Region, 1680–1815." In *The New Peoples: Being and Becoming Metis in North America*, edited by Jacqueline Peterson and Jennifer S. H. Brown. Lincoln: University of Nebraska Press, 1885.

Susan Sleeper-Smith. *Indian Women and French Men: Rethinking Cultural Encounter in the Western Great Lakes*. Amherst: University of Massachusetts Press, 2001.

Richard White. *The Middle Ground: Indians, Empires, and Republics in the Great Lakes Region, 1650–1815*. Cambridge: Cambridge University Press, 1991.

Plantation Societies of the Southeast

Lois G. Carr, and Lorena Walsh. "The Planter's Wife: The Experience of White Women in Seventeenth-Century Maryland," *William and Mary Quarterly* 34 (1977): 542–571.

Kirsten Fischer. *Suspect Relations: Sex, Race, and Resistance in Colonial North Carolina*. Ithaca, NY: Cornell University Press, 2002.

David W. Galenson. *White Servitude in Colonial America: An Economic Analysis*. Cambridge: Cambridge University Press, 1981.

Jennifer Morgan. *Laboring Women: Reproduction and Gender in New World Slavery*. Philadelphia: University of Pennsylvania Press, 2004.

Mary Beth Norton. *Founding Mothers and Fathers: Gendered Power and the Forming of American Society*. New York: Alfred A. Knopf, 1996.

Terri L. Snyder. *Brabbling Women: Disorderly Speech and the Law in Early Virginia*. Ithaca, NY: Cornell University Press, 2003.

Michael Zuckerman. "Identity in British America: Unease in Eden." In *Colonial Identity in the Atlantic World, 1500–1800*, edited by Nicholas Canny and Anthony Pagden. Princeton, NJ: Princeton University Press, 1989.

New England

Richard Godbeer. *Sexual Revolution in Early America*. Baltimore, MD: Johns Hopkins University Press, 2002.

Jane Kamensky. *Governing the Tongue: The Politics of Speech in Early New England.* New York: Oxford University Press, 1997.

Carol F. Karlsen. *The Devil in the Shape of a Woman: Witchcraft in Colonial New England.* New York: Norton, 1987.

Mary Beth Norton. *Founding Mothers and Fathers: Gendered Power and the Forming of American Society.* New York: Random House, 1992.

Mary Beth Norton. *In the Devil's Snare: The Salem Witchcraft Crisis of 1692.* New York: Alfred A. Knopf, 2002.

Anne Marie Plane. *Colonial Intimacies: Intimacies: Indian Marriage in Early New England.* Ithaca, NY: Cornell University Press, 2000.

Elizabeth Reis. *Damned Women: Sinners and Witches in Puritan New England.* Ithaca, NY: Cornell University Press, 1999.

Rebecca J. Tannenbaum. *The Healer's Calling: Women and Medicine in Early New England.* Ithaca, NY: Cornell University Press, 2002.

Paula A. Treckel. *To Comfort the Heart: Women in Seventeenth-Century America.* New York: Twayne, 1996.

Biographies, Autobiographies, and Memoirs

Natalie Zemon Davis. *Women on the Margins: Three Seventeenth Century Lives.* Cambridge, MA: Harvard University Press, 1995.

Nancy Shoemaker. "Kateri Tekakwitha's Tortuous Path to Sainthood," *Negotiators of Change: Historical Perspectives on Native American Women,* edited by Nancy Shoemaker. New York: Routledge, 1995.

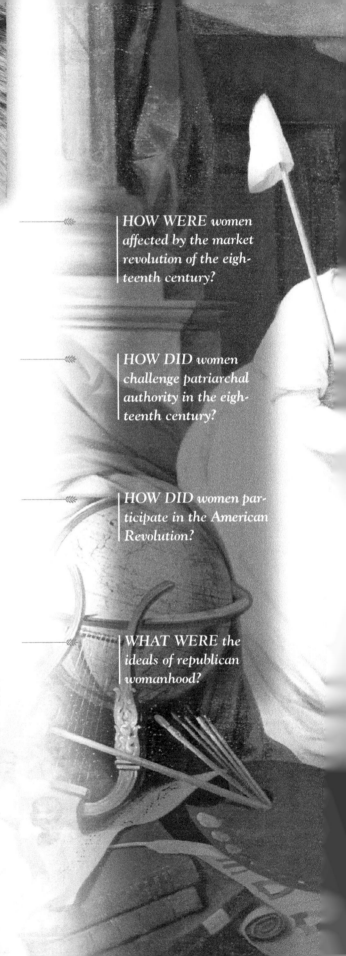

EIGHTEENTH-CENTURY REVOLUTIONS, 1700-1800

HOW WERE women affected by the market revolution of the eighteenth century?

HOW DID women challenge patriarchal authority in the eighteenth century?

HOW DID women participate in the American Revolution?

WHAT WERE the ideals of republican womanhood?

CHAPTER 3

The Humble Petition of Mary Prat Sheweth

. . . Your Petitioner was many years ago appointed Housekeeper for the State House with an allowance of Two Hundred Pounds Currency p[er] year which place she held until the Capture of Charlestown when...she was discharged and turned out of it to make room for another Person who was more attached to the British Government, at that time she had due to her upwards of a year and four months Salary. . . . Since the Evacuation of this Capital she has had to her great satisfaction the good fortune to be reinstated in her former post but thro' the Cruel and inhuman treatment of

"Liberty Displaying the Arts & Sciences," Samuel Jennings, 1792 (The Library Company of Philadelphia)

the British she is so much reduced in her circumstances as to be nearly in want of all the necessaries of life. She therefore begs leave to submit her case to this Honourable House humbly hoping they will take it into their most serious consideration and allow her, her arrears of Salary or such other relief as they in their Wisdom shall think fit.

Source: *Quoted in Cynthia Kierner*, Southern Women in Revolution, 1776–1800, Personal and Political Narratives *(Columbia: University of South Carolina Press, 1998) 63–64.*

Mary Prat Sheweth petitioned the South Carolina Assembly for her back pay in 1783, a couple of years after the American Revolution had come to a close. Like many women in the new republic, she now felt empowered to approach her government in a way she had not in the years before the Revolution. Her political consciousness had no doubt grown with her support for the patriot cause. She had risked her job before war had been officially declared by refusing to reveal the names of rebels who had stolen gunpowder from the Charleston storage depot, and she had continued to funnel supplies to the patriots as the war unfolded. Small wonder she was fired when the British briefly took control of Charleston.

Sheweth felt empowered to petition her state legislature after the Revolution, but her wartime patriotism had gained her little else. For women in the new republic, husbands or fathers were supposed to be their political representatives. Although women participated widely in the Revolution and their political consciousness had grown, the rights they gained were different from those given to men. Rather than gaining full status as citizens, women were entrusted with the responsibility of training their children to be responsible leaders of the new republic. While men assumed an increasingly direct relationship with the state, women's relationships to their government continued to be mediated largely through their households.

Households of the eighteenth century had undergone important transformations, however, in British North America. The religious enthusiasm of the Great Awakening and the intellectual challenges of the Enlightenment undermined fundamental assumptions about patriarchal authority. Even the consumer items increasingly available for purchase had begun to transform social relationships within households. Women and men increasingly viewed themselves as companions in marriage. As a result, women were mistresses of a new kind of household, and the power they wielded within their homes was necessarily transformed.

THE MARKET REVOLUTION

English control of the eastern seaboard expanded dramatically in the last half of the seventeenth century as England conquered New Netherland in 1664, transforming it into New York, and set up the new colonies of Carolina, New Jersey, and Pennsylvania. Additional colonization took place with the creation of Georgia, New Hampshire, and Vermont in the eighteenth century. The British Empire expanded even farther at the conclusion of the Seven Years' War between France and England. Known as the **French and Indian War** in North America, France surrendered its claims east of the Mississippi River to England in the **Treaty of Paris** of 1763. These colonization efforts took a toll, of course. Thousands of settlers in frontier areas lost their lives in Indian attacks during the French and Indian War. Urban dwellers, particularly in Boston, faced other dangers. Approximately thirty-five hundred men were recruited into service for British campaigns in Latin America during the Anglo-Spanish War of the 1740s, and most of those men never returned home.

The expansion of the British Empire in North America went hand in hand with a growing capitalist revolution in which new consumer goods from abroad—exchanged for raw materials from the colonies—transformed the lives of women as well as men. Indeed, while men were almost always the merchants who arranged this transcontinental trade, women were also at the forefront of these activities, selling goods in their shops or hawking their produce on city streets, cultivating rice in the Carolinas or tending tobacco in the Chesapeake region and farther inland, supervising dairy work on their farms, or presiding over their tea tables in the cities. The exchange of goods created in different parts of the world and increasingly sold for money formed the basis of an expanding market economy that began to affect both social relationships and personal identities.

French and Indian War Also known as the Seven Years' War in Europe, it was fought between France and England from 1754 to 1763 in both Europe and North America.

Treaty of Paris Treaty that ended the French and Indian War between France and England.

Cities of Women

Cities such as Boston, New York, Philadelphia, and Charleston were small by European standards but they were growing at a phenomenal rate. Between 1720 and 1790, New York grew from 8,000 to 33,000 residents, Philadelphia from 10,000 to 28,000, and Charleston from 3,500 to 16,000. A booming Atlantic trade of consumer goods and slaves circulated through their ports, dominating these and other cities. Immigrants included Sephardic Jews from Spain and Huguenots from France, as well as Catholics and Protestants from Ireland, Wales, and Germany. Slaves, increasingly

TABLE 3-1   Four Largest Cities in British North America

	1720	1742	1790
Boston	12,000	16,000	18,300
Philadelphia	10,000	13,000	28,500
New York	7,000	11,000	33,100
Charlestown	3,500	6,800	16,300

(From: Carl Bridenbaugh, Cities in the Wilderness: The First Century of Urban Life (1966), p.303 and Goldfield, David, Urban America: From Downtown to No Town (1979))

By the end of the eighteenth century, New York and Philadelphia had overtaken Boston as the largest cities in the new United States.

imported straight from Africa, poured into not only southern ports such as Charleston but also northern cities such as New York.

In many of these cities, the presence of women, particularly single women, distinguished urban areas from rural ones. By 1765, white women outnumbered white men in Boston and other New England port cities by a ratio of five to four. In Philadelphia, the sex ratio was more even, with women probably making up about 48 percent of the population, but the abundance of single women enhanced their significance. About one-third of the adult women in Philadelphia were single at the time of the Revolution. Many had migrated to the cities to find work. Although women were not paid as much as men, single women still found more economic opportunities in cities than on local farms, so many preferred to take their chances there.

This high percentage of single women meant women were much more likely to head households in the cities than they were in the countryside. In Boston, women headed 20 percent of the city's households by the end of the eighteenth century; and in Philadelphia, the percentage never dropped below 12 percent. A similar situation prevailed in Charleston, where women headed 18 percent of the city's households when the first census was taken in 1790. These were much higher percentages than existed in rural areas, where farms continued, by and large, to be run by men.

A New World of Goods

In large cities and small, women participated extensively in local businesses. Anne Shields and Jane Vobe, for example, both ran taverns in Williamsburg, Virginia. Their work was not uncommon. Women ran most of the taverns in Virginia. If the women were married, their husbands might have held the licenses, but advertisements made it clear that women were in charge of the taverns. Officials in northern cities also granted licenses to widows in need so that they would not require public assistance. In South Carolina, married women actually owned as well as operated taverns because South Carolina had the strongest laws in the colonies protecting the rights of married businesswomen. They were allowed to sign legal documents and contract debts independent of their husbands, a privilege the women of Charleston were not reluctant to use in setting up their shops.

In Boston and Philadelphia, women operated close to 50 percent of the city's shops. Mary Channing supervised a large dry goods store in Boston, while Lydia Hyde sold tea and dry goods from her shop in Philadelphia. Other women worked as artisans, making candles or buttons or tailored clothing. While women were seldom legally apprenticed to learn these trades, they often picked up their skills informally from their fathers and husbands; and it was not uncommon for a widow to take over her husband's business when he died.

While cities were the epicenters of the new consumer economy, women in rural areas were hardly isolated from the growing marketplace. In the eighteenth century, women on farms and in villages throughout New England learned to spin and sew at a young age. Often working together, they manufactured fabrics for their clothes and linens for their households, "signing" their pieces with their initials. A woman from a more prosperous family could even acquire a cabinet in which to keep her goods, taking it with her when she married. More than women of the early seventeenth century, the women of the eighteenth century cherished their embroidered bedspreads and tablecloths and napkins, all carefully spun, cut, and sewn, as the movable property they brought with them into their marriages. As men became busier with farm work and trades during the course of the eighteenth century, women also increasingly took over the weaving that many men had previously done, particularly in New England and the South. While much of what they produced was meant for their families, they also traded extra cloth for manufactured items at their local stores. Without actually working for wages, they still participated in the growing consumer revolution. Other women used their skills in casual wage work. In Maryland, for example, several white women from local farms worked for John Gresham, a prosperous plantation owner, spinning and knitting wool from his large flock of sheep to clothe his slaves.

The goods that began to circulate in the colonies during the eighteenth century were not only making domestic life more pleasurable but also creating new forms of social distinction. Wealthy shoppers could now choose from a variety of silks to make their clothing and an even wider variety of carpets to furnish their homes. These luxury items were beyond the reach of more common folk, but this was not true of cheaper items such as the highly prized Irish soap that many now purchased instead of making their own from ashes. And while wealthy matrons acquired elaborate tea services, even poorer consumers could purchase the tea that had become a popular new beverage. Throughout the colonies, households began to acquire plates, cutlery, and chairs, which allowed a family to sit at the same time when they ate dinner—without using their hands or without eating from the same bowl.

These consumer products brought not only comfort to eighteenth-century households but also a struggle over social hierarchy as the wealthy sought to distinguish themselves from more common folk—and common folk just as quickly sought to close the gap. Women became key players in the pursuit of status, and the proper use of these domestic goods became just as important as their acquisition. It was not enough to own a fancy tea service; a woman had to know how to properly serve tea and make polite conversation in the ritual that surrounded a tea party. More common women who found their families sitting around a dinner table together also had to orchestrate this new social event by providing greater attention to both the food they served and the conversation at mealtimes. By experimenting with these trappings of gentility, they could also experiment with new identities and new forms of sociability in their homes.

Issues of Inequality

Despite widespread participation as both producers and consumers in the market revolution unfolding around them, women did not necessarily fare well in this new economy. Changing patterns of inheritance, decreased access to the courts, and low wages were some of the problems women faced in the eighteenth century. As a result, economic participation did not translate into economic independence for most women.

Although cities were growing during the eighteenth century, most colonists were farmers, and each generation struggled to provide enough land for the next. Some parents bought land farther west for their sons (provoking continuing conflicts with Indians). But they also made hard choices about inheritance. As land became more scarce, men became more likely to shortchange the inheritances of their wives and daughters to provide for their male heirs. In Pennyslvania, for example, women were increasingly less likely to inherit the traditional one-third share in their husbands' estates. By the 1790s, a man could demand that the son who inherited the homestead take care of his mother, alleviating the man's need to leave any property to his wife so that she could support herself. Thus, widows began losing what little economic independence they had had in earlier years.

In New York, the loss of economic independence among women was even more pronounced as English law supplanted Dutch law following the conquest of New York in 1664. The British allowed the Dutch to retain their inheritance laws, which allowed a widow one-half of her husband's estate and allowed married women the right to own property. But families gradually intermarried with the British, and Dutch customs faded. There were 134 female merchants in New Amsterdam when the British took over in 1664, but only 43 could be found in its incarnation as New York City a century later. Inheritance patterns also changed. Although Dutch men continued to will greater amounts of property to their wives and daughters than British men did, that custom, too, began to fade during the eighteenth century. Not surprisingly, as new forms of women's work, such as commercial dairy farming, expanded in New York during the eighteenth century, men commonly owned the equipment, though their wives and daughters did the work.

In areas where British law had always dominated, women also faced increasing difficulties accessing the courts. In New Haven, Connecticut, for example, the courts of the seventeenth century had been dedicated to maintaining community harmony and had operated in a fairly casual fashion. Women as well as men participated in the informal proceedings, either testifying as witnesses or bringing forth their own grievances on issues that ranged from slander to economic disputes. This use of the courts became more difficult during the eighteenth century as local merchants began to hire lawyers rather than representing themselves, and most women were unable to afford the legal representation that eighteenth-century courts were coming to expect.

Women also faced increasing economic hardship in the more complex economy of the eighteenth century because they simply were not paid as much as men when they were compensated in cash wages. In the previous century, women might have achieved greater value for their work if they bartered their products—exchanging bread for rum, for example. Such exchanges became less common in the eighteenth century, particularly in urban areas where cash was more likely to be used. Wages for women fluctuated throughout the century, but women usually made only half as much as men.

Poverty thus loomed as a real threat to women, particularly widows, whose numbers were growing as a result of the many wars of the eighteenth century. In Boston (as in other New England seaports), the number of widows had grown to twelve hundred by mid-century, partly because so many men had died in various British military campaigns in Latin America. Most of these widows were quite poor and desperate to find support for themselves and their children. The Society for Encouraging Industry and the Employment of the Poor attempted to put these women to work in a small spinning factory, but the results were disappointing. Many women did not know how to spin, and others needed to work at home where they could care for their children and rely on their neighbors for help. As their struggles made clear, the new market economy offered little improvement in the lives of many poor women.

Slavery in a Market Economy

The market revolution that brought new consumer goods to the shores of the colonies and kept shops up and down the eastern seaboard humming also underlay the explosive growth in the slave trade. Slavery supplied the demand for labor in seaport cities, in the rice and tobacco fields of the South, and on the smaller farms of the North. The different economic needs of each of these areas shaped the lives of slave women and gender roles in regionally distinct ways.

Slaves and workers picking leaves and operating machinery at a tobacco factory in North America. Slaves worked with free whites and indentured servants on plantations in the South. Men and women both worked in the tobacco fields, but they could be assigned different jobs.

As artisans and domestic workers, slaves were also ubiquitous in eighteenth-century American cities, constituting 14 percent of the population of New York City at the time of the Revolution and 20 percent of the workingmen in Philadelphia at mid-century. Because so many slaves in northern cities worked as artisans, slave men outnumbered slave women by a significant proportion. The case was reversed in the southern cities of Savannah and Charleston, however, where slave women were used extensively for domestic work.

In cities such as Charleston, slave women who worked as weavers and seamstresses and cooks also controlled much of the petty merchandizing in their towns. Working from their street carts, they hawked goods grown by female slaves in the countryside or fish caught and meat butchered by their menfolk. White citizens often complained of their noisy and aggressive behavior, branding the street hawkers as immoral women. Equally upsetting to whites was the way in which some urban slaves used their earnings to buy fine consumer goods, so that some slave women were alleged to dress as well as their mistresses. Outraged citizens repeatedly passed legislation forbidding slaves to wear such clothing, but the constant stream of laws suggests not only how threatening whites found this behavior but also how little their legislation did to stop it. Thus, consumer goods provoked status conflicts not only between rich and poor but also between slave and free.

While urban slave women were sometimes able to manipulate the market economy in acquiring goods, they faced more of a challenge in having children. In cities such as New York, where masters had little extra space, slaves were often crammed into a back room and discouraged from marrying. Although a female slave could increase an urban slaveholder's capital by bearing children, most masters did not think the children worth the trouble. By the time of the Revolution, few slave women in either New York or Philadelphia were having children; if they did have children, they often died as infants.

In the more settled areas of the Chesapeake region and farther inland in the newly cleared lands of the Piedmont region, balanced sex ratios helped slaves there to form families. Slaves living on smaller farms were more likely to be separated from their families than those living on large plantations; but in the Chesapeake region, a stable slave community was emerging in which many families were able to stay together. Children on larger plantations of the Chesapeake region were often able to live with their mothers—and possibly their fathers, though about one-third of these families were split up as slaves were moved farther inland to open up new tobacco fields in the Piedmont region.

Farther south, in the Carolinas and Georgia, slaves faced unbalanced sex ratios that affected both how they lived and how they worked. In the rice fields that dominated plantation life in this region, new slaves from Africa took on the grueling task of tending crops. In Africa, women had been responsible for this task, but in these areas of the South, where male slaves outnumbered female slaves by a substantial margin, men were expected to farm as well. Slave men, many just arrived from Africa, thus faced not only the degradation of slavery but the further humiliation of being forced to do "women's work."

Slaves, like free people, were vital to the market economy of the eighteenth century. For women, this new world of goods could bring pleasure and new forms of socializing but it could exacerbate poverty as well. In either case, women's lives were being transformed.

FAMILY RELATIONS AND SOCIAL RESPONSIBILITIES

Although men usually exerted more power through their access to the courts or in deciding who would receive an inheritance, traditional patterns of authority were questioned in other ways. In a wide variety of social and sexual relations, strict patriarchal control of the household, in particular, was challenged. As a result, women not only negotiated a new place in the market economy of the eighteenth century; they also negotiated new social and sexual identities.

Passions and Patriarchal Authority

Eliza Lucas of South Carolina adored Pamela, the heroine of Samuel Richardson's 1740s novel, *Pamela: Or, Virtue Rewarded*, one of the most popular English novels of the eighteenth century. "She is a good girl and as such I love her dearly," she wrote to her friend Mary Barrett. Lucas and many other young women who could read made books one of the most popular British imports circulating throughout the colonies. Fictional works such as *Pamela* and *Clarissa* (also by Richardson) were tales of love and seduction that might end well—but might not. Key to their outcome was the moral backbone of the heroine, cultivated by loving parents who valued her personal feelings and self-reliance over her blind obedience. Pamela had the moral strength to resist the sexual demands of her employer. In Richardson's *Clarissa: Or the History of a Young Lady* (1748), on the other hand, tragedy resulted as an overbearing father prodded the heroine to marry a wealthy man she did not love and in desperation she fled into the hands of an evil seducer. This was the fate of a child who knew only how to slavishly follow the will of her parents.

Sentimental novels such as these were not only exciting to read, they popularized new ideas about human nature and social authority that were central to philosophical treatises written by Enlightenment philosophers such as John Locke. Locke had challenged Puritan beliefs that children were born with sinful natures and, instead, argued that children learned to be good or evil as a result of their upbringing. Parents had to

WOMEN'S VOICES

LETTER TO A FATHER

Eliza Lucas was an educated young woman in South Carolina who managed her family's plantation outside of Charleston, South Carolina, because her father was away in Antigua serving with the British army and her mother was too frail to take on the responsibilities of running the family estate. She avidly read the new books circulating in the colonies, including works by John Locke and novels such as Richardson's Pamela. She eventually married Charles Pinckney, a man who shared her intellectual passions.

Hond. Sir

. . . .

As you propose Mr. L. to me I am sorry I can't have Sentiments favourable enough of him to take time to think on the Subject, as your Indulgence to me will ever add weight to the duty that obliges me to consult what best pleases you, for so much Generosity on your part claims all my Obedience, but as I know tis my happiness you consult [I] must beg the favour of you to pay my thanks to the old Gentleman for his Generosity and favourable sentiments of me and let him know my thoughts on the affair in such civil terms as you know much better than any I can dictate; and beg leave to say to you that the riches of Peru and Chili if he had them put together could not purchase a sufficient Esteem for him to make him my husband.

As to other Gentlemen you mention, Mr. Walsh, you know, Sir, I have so slight a knowledge of him I can form no judgment of him, and a Case

of such consiquence requires the Nicest distinction of humours and Sentiments. But give me leave to assure you, my dear Sir, that a single life is my only Choice and if it were not as I am yet but Eighteen, hope you will [put] aside the thought of my marrying yet these 2 or 3 years at least.

You are so good to say you have too great an Opinion of my prudence to think I would entertain an indiscreet passion for any one, and I hope heaven will always direct me that I may never disappoint you; and which indeed could induce me to make a secret of my Inclination to my best friend, as I am well aware you would not disapprove it to make me a Sacrifice to Wealth, and I am as certain I would indulge no passion that had not your approbation, as I truly am

Dr. Sir, Your most dutiful and affecte. Daughter
E. Lucas

Source: *Elise Pinckney, ed.,* The Letterbook of Eliza Lucas Pinckney 1739–1762 *(Chapel Hill: The University of North Carolina Press, 1972) 5–6.*

Questions

1. In this letter to her father, what does Eliza imply is important in choosing a marriage partner? What should be avoided?

2. How does Eliza respond to her father's authority over her?

3. How do you think Eliza has been influenced by the books she has read?

educate their children not only formally but also through example to act virtuously and independently. In both Locke's philosophy and in the popular literature that celebrated it, mindless subservience to one's father was not only unnecessary but also dangerous. Voluntary allegiance rather than patriarchal control was championed as the new basis for authority in the eighteenth-century family.

This was a message that resonated with many young people in the colonies as they created their own forms of independence. Lucy Barnes of Massachusetts, for example, had no love for her wealthy cousin John, whom her father wished her to marry. She chose Joseph Hosmer instead and made sure her parents would accept her choice by becoming pregnant. Barnes was not unusual in her behavior. By the time of the Revolution, one in three brides was pregnant when she married. Ideas of independence that young women picked up from popular literature were reinforced by the changing economic structure of the countryside. Fewer parents were able to provide inheritances for all of their children in the eighteenth century because fathers no longer had the land or wealth that had given economic clout to their patriarchal control in earlier generations. With little property at stake, daughters felt more freedom to choose a spouse they liked, even if their parents did not approve.

Even more possibilities for sexual independence existed in cities. Particularly in the rapidly growing multiethnic neighborhoods of Philadelphia, a tolerance for casual sexual encounters emerged along with a commitment to personal satisfaction in marital relationships. As the number of illegitimate children born each year increased, city officials made sure that fathers paid child support, but neither parent was punished for fornication. Popular forms of literature, such as almanacs, featured bawdy jokes about both men and women who reveled in their lusty behavior. And although legal divorces were hard to get, many spouses divorced informally by placing an advertisement in the local newspaper claiming to have been deserted. Most commonly, a man would claim his wife had left him and that he would no longer be liable for her debts. But wives seldom contested such claims, suggesting they were comfortable with the announcement. Thus, in 1771, Robert Hill placed a notice in the Philadelphia newspapers that his wife Hannah had declared "that another man hath a better right to her than I have, and that she is desirous of parting from me, and being *extremely* willing to gratify her, I took her at her word. . . ."

In both popular literature and in popular practice, ideals of household organization and household authority were being revised. Individuals looked more for personal satisfaction in their relationships and worried less about responding to their parents' wishes. Fathers often had fewer economic resources to offer their children, which undercut their authority. A new ideal of personal independence and fulfillment was emerging.

Disorderly Women: The Challenge of the Great Awakening

Great Awakening
Series of religious revivals that swept the colonies in the middle of the eighteenth century.

New Lights People converted to evangelical religious beliefs in the Great Awakening.

Old Lights People who supported the status quo in churches and opposed the religious changes promoted by New Lights.

Challenges to household authority also emerged from the fires of the **Great Awakening** that engulfed both men and women in the flames of religious enthusiasm during the eighteenth century. Beginning in the middle colonies as early as the 1720s, cresting in New England during the 1740s and 1750s, and continuing in the South through the 1760s, most parts of the Atlantic seacoast shared in the powerful and emotional religious experiences that not only transformed the lives of individuals but also bound them together with believers across the Atlantic in various parts of Protestant Europe, extending into the Caribbean and even Africa. New religious denominations, such as the Methodists, arose as part of this fervor, while established denominations such as the Congregationalists and Presbyterians were torn apart. **New Lights**, as the revivalists were called, fought bitterly with the **Old Lights**, who sought to preserve the status quo within their churches. The New Lights emphasized the need for a powerful, physically felt conversion experience. Preachers encouraged such transformations with evocative, heart-felt preaching, quite distinct from the dry and learned sermons of many ministers. Hannah Heaton, a young woman from Connecticut, represented the response of many young converts when she recalled, "[I] did vent out my anguish with tears and groans and a few broken speches."

Critics argued that the emotionalism of the preaching and the enthusiasm of the audiences could easily turn a heavenly experience into an earthly one in which lust replaced piety. Certainly the sight of swooning young women in the throes of religious ecstasy involved a lack of decorum that suggested sexual impropriety even where none existed. And a few very radical converts did leave their spouses for new ones after they were baptized. However, the greater challenge to family relations probably lay in the way that converted children declared independence from unconverted parents, or a converted wife from her husband.

The challenge to gender hierarchy became particularly clear as some women were inspired to preach God's word. Women's preaching usually began with witnessing, as they spoke about God from their hearts to members of their congregation. But some women carried their role further, exhorting those who would listen to hear the word of God. Bathsheba Kingsley of Massachusetts, for example, was repeatedly hauled before her church elders and rebuked for her tendency to ride throughout the countryside urging her neighbors to change their wicked ways. Because this new evangelical preaching was emotional and evocative, and because it required little in the way of formal theological training, anyone with a powerful voice and powerful convictions could become a preacher. Established clergymen bemoaned this challenge to the traditional order as not only women but also African Americans and other members of the lower classes took to "ranting" in the countryside—and as large audiences flocked to hear them.

Other women actually created new religions in this period of spiritual ferment, challenging gender ideals in their process of challenging accepted religions. Jemima Wilkinson, who was strongly influenced by Quaker beliefs, claimed to have died of typhus in 1776 and to have been resurrected as the Public Universal Friend who brought word to those on Earth about the imminent arrival of God's second coming. As her new name—Public Universal Friend—suggested, she was neither a man nor a woman; and to further confuse gender issues, she eschewed traditional female clothing, choosing instead long flowing gowns that drew on male forms of dress as well as female. Like many of the preachers traveling the countryside, she preached spontaneously on biblical texts in a powerful voice that moved her audiences. Ann Lee, founder of the Shakers, arrived from England in the latter part of the eighteenth century and was equally charismatic. As an illiterate preacher, Lee had little use for a Bible she could not read and promoted instead a religion focused more on singing and dancing than on formal sermons.

The Great Awakening was not meant to challenge hierarchies of gender. Indeed, men were as likely as women to join the evangelical churches. However, the women who preached and exhorted the word of God stepped far beyond the usual roles accorded to women in eighteenth-century society. In doing so, they undermined common assumptions about female subservience that underlay both household hierarchy and government authority.

Female Companions: The Gendered Enlightenment

Other women fostered new ideas of gender relationships in the social activities they organized in their homes. This was particularly true in more elite households where

Salon Regular reception, usually held in the home of a wealthy woman, where social, intellectual, and political leaders mixed.

complementarity Idea that men and women have different characteristics that complement one another.

Enlightenment Intellectual movement stressing human reason and the ability to achieve progress by applying reason to problems of science and society.

Scottish Enlightenment Intellectual movement centered in Scotland that assumed inequalities and hierarchies were natural and necessary in society.

women hosted social events promoting intellectual conversations and civilized discourse. Men in urban settings carried on political debates in the coffeehouses and taverns that filled the cities. There they made business deals or discussed politics while sharing newspapers, playing cards, and drinking their favorite beverages. But in most cases, these spaces were off-limits to women. As an alternative, elite women hosted afternoon tea parties at which men and women could mingle and share in light conversation. Critics sometimes dismissed such gatherings as little more than frivolous occasions for gossip, but their barbs inspired some women to improve the quality of conversation rather than to abandon their efforts at sociability. Elizabeth Magawley of Philadelphia, for example, bemoaned the idle chatter of teatime and undertook a more ambitious project of promoting **salons** on the European model. Here, men and women shared in more elevated conversation about politics and literature, comparable to what might be found in coffeehouses. Magawley did not suggest that women use these events to decide political issues, but she did argue that women would provide an important level of refinement in the ensuing discussions.

In promoting such interactions, Magawley was drawing on new ideals of **complementarity** between men and women that emphasized differences between the sexes. While one important strain of **Enlightenment** thinking had followed Locke's emphasis on the natural rights of men, another group associated with the **Scottish Enlightenment** asserted that society was inherently unequal but that each individual occupied an important position in the social hierarchy that carried both responsibilities and rights. This group emphasized the need for complementary roles between men and women in promoting social progress. Civilization reached its apex, many of these writers argued, when men and women worked together, each making different but complementary contributions to the social order that were best suited to their natural abilities. *Sketches of the History of Man* by Lord Kames was one of the most widely circulated books to make such an argument, identifying key areas where women and men best used their different natures to advance society. Kames argued, for example, that men were strong so that they should be protectors of society while women were delicate and better suited to being caregivers. Men had the intellectual abilities to rule while women had the intellectual abilities to obey. Men were more creative and thus able to produce great art and literature, whereas female capabilities lay in promoting manners and civilization. Finally, men were more patriotic and dedicated to their government while women were devoted to their families. All of these differences were good, Kames argued, because they allowed men and women to complement each other as they promoted social harmony rather than struggling against each other for power. Of course, men had the abilities that rendered them worthy of ruling while women only possessed the capabilities to obey. Thus, complementarity meant that a new system of subordination could easily replace the older one.

Whether stressing the importance of an individual's choice in marriage partner or the complementarity of the sexes, new ideas about patriarchal authority and women's roles within the family were emerging in the eighteenth century. As young couples courted (and cavorted) and as matrons sought the attention of their husbands, women demanded respect for their opinions and their choices. To a certain extent, ideals of complementarity represented a new way of constituting family hierarchy as patriarchal authority was challenged. But these issues of authority were not only played out in eighteenth-century families. In the Revolutionary struggle for independence that engulfed the colonies during the 1760s and 1770s, the attack on patriarchal authority took on political ramifications as colonists debated the practical applications of Enlightenment ideals such as natural rights, voluntary allegiance, and complementarity in the old government they attacked and the new government they created.

DECLARING INDEPENDENCE

Colonial dissatisfaction with British rule began to crystallize in the French and Indian War that had raged through the frontier from 1756 to 1763. Although the British wrested control from the French of the territory east of the Mississippi River, they still had to worry about many of the Indians still living there. Many of the tribes had sided with the French and killed more than four thousand British settlers during the course of the war, but the British government sought to build peaceful relationships by designating the land west of the Appalachians as Indian territory. Anglo colonists hungry for land were outraged by British policy. Colonists were further angered when the British government began to tax them to pay off the war debt.

Protests turned to armed conflict by 1775, when shots were fired at Lexington and Concord. By the following year, colonial leaders calling themselves **Patriots** were moving resolutely toward establishing a new government. Members of the **Second Continental Congress** meeting in Philadelphia issued the **Declaration of Independence** in July 1776. As fighting continued, the former colonies scrambled to write new state constitutions that reflected not only their transformation from colonial status but also a broadening spectrum of participation by colonists in both the Revolution and their governments.

Thomas Paine, a failed corset maker who had recently immigrated to Philadelphia from London, popularized many Revolutionary ideas about popular political participation when he published *Common Sense* in 1776. The pamphlet went through numerous editions over the next few years as colonists read and debated the issues he raised. Most important, Paine challenged the idea that any king had a divine right to rule a country and argued instead that governments could and should be constituted by a social compact among individuals. This argument promoted the idea that each individual citizen, in making this social compact, should be granted the opportunity to participate in the government he had created. In this way, Paine popularized the important political concept of rights advanced by Enlightenment thinkers such as John Locke that men were born free in a state of nature and endowed equally with natural rights but that in order to live in harmony and gain protection, they created a government to which they surrendered some of their rights. Just as novelists had popularized Locke's ideas of the importance of voluntary allegiance in the family, Paine popularized Locke's ideas of voluntary allegiance in the state. Inhabitants of the colonies who had not dreamed of participating in politics before now began to imagine a new political order in which they might have rights and responsibilities.

MAP 3-1   DEMONSTRATIONS AGAINST THE STAMP ACT IN 1765

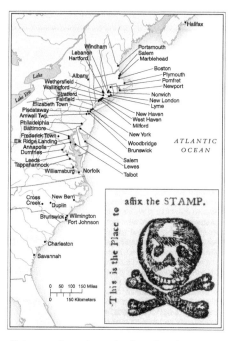

Colonists throughout the British colonies protested the Stamp Act in 1765.

Patriots Colonists who opposed Britain during the American Revolution.

Second Continental Congress Representatives of the thirteen colonies in rebellion against England, meeting as a government body from 1775 to 1781 to direct the Patriot cause.

Declaration of Independence Written by the Second Continental Congress in 1776 rejecting the King of England as the leader of the British colonies and asserting the right of men to form their own government.

OVERVIEW

British Measure Leading to the Revolution

1764	Sugar Act	Taxes sugar imported into colonies at a very high rate and imposes regulations to end smuggling by colonists
1765	Stamp Act	Taxes documents and papers by requiring the purchase of stamps for newspapers, legal documents, playing cards, licenses, and other paper documents. Repealed in 1766
1765	Quartering Act	Requires colonists to house British soldiers in their homes
1767	Townshend Acts	Taxes imported goods such as glass, paper, lead, and tea. Repealed in 1770
1773	Tea Act	Exempts the British East India Company from paying taxes on tea the company imported into the colonies, giving them an unfair advantage over colonial merchants in the sale of tea

Abigail Adams not only managed the family farm while her husband was away fighting the Revolution, she kept close tabs on political events in Massachusetts, providing her husband with important insights about how the Revolution was proceeding in his home state while he was engaged with the Continental Congress in Philadelphia.

Sons of Liberty
Organization of Patriots opposed to British taxes.

Abigail Adams, who possessed the intelligence, curiosity, and stamina to not only complement but challenge her politically ambitious husband John, recognized what these ideas could mean for women. Most famously, she sparred with her husband in the spring of 1776 as he debated with delegates of the Second Continental Congress about what their new government could look like. Pointing out to him that men were "naturally tyrannical," Abigail enjoined her husband, "Remember, all men would be tyrants if they could. If particular care and attention is not paid to the ladies, we are determined to foment a rebellion and will not hold ourselves bound by any laws in which we have no voice or representation." John, clearly flustered at the unraveling of the social order implied in his wife's suggestion, could only reply in strained fashion that he had heard "that our struggle has loosened the bonds of government everywhere; that children and apprentices were disobedient; that schools and colleges were grown turbulent; that Indians slighted their guardians, and Negroes grew insolent to their masters." As he contemplated the ramifications of Abigail's demands, he concluded, "[Y]our letter was the first intimation that another tribe, more numerous and powerful than all the rest, were grown discontented." He should not have been surprised though, for women were active participants in the political struggles engulfing their lives.

Daughters of Liberty

By 1765, men throughout the colonies had begun to protest the oppressive taxes levied to pay for the French and Indian War. The Sugar Act of 1764 had been followed by the Stamp Act and the Quartering Act in 1765, and the Townshend Duties in 1767. Young Patrick Henry pushed resolutions against the duties through the Virginia House of Burgesses while the **Sons of Liberty** in Boston roused angry crowds in Boston and artisans in South Carolina hanged the stamp distributor in effigy. Resistance grew from New Hampshire through the Carolinas as colonists vowed to boycott British goods and to demonstrate their independence by providing for themselves. This strategy quickly drew women into the fray, for women were important consumers and producers of most household items.

Young women began meeting together in spinning bees by 1769 in order to produce "homespun" cloth to replace English textiles. Often calling themselves **Daughters of Liberty**, as many as ninety women met at a time, sometimes in the home of their local Congregational minister—if he supported the cause. They produced not only yarn and cloth but also a patriotic spectacle. Neighbors came by to watch the women and cheer them on. The *Boston Evening Post* celebrated the patriotism of New England women in helping "to bring about the salvation of a whole continent." The activities of southern women in producing homespun cloth were less likely to be noticed because they often lived on farms at great distances from one another and thus they tended to spin alone without public recognition.

Daughters of Liberty Women who organized to support the Patriot cause.

Women soon joined with male patriots in boycotting other consumer goods that had become popular during the eighteenth century. Perhaps most notable was the boycott of tea. The Tea Act of 1773 had given the British East India Company the right to sell tea in the colonies without paying the same taxes as colonial merchants. The colonists viewed this favoritism as unfair to their own economic aspirations and responded by boycotting tea—an activity that women led because they were the chief consumers of tea. In Edenton, North Carolina, in 1774, fifty-one women highlighted the political implications of their activities by writing and signing a statement that they would not consume items that were being boycotted. Their behavior garnered attention on both sides of the Atlantic as one Englishman compared the women to Amazons.

By the time of the Revolution, some women were even more aggressive in their policing of consumption activities. As the war dragged on during the late 1770s, many items were in short supply, and prices skyrocketed. Some merchants hoped to make a profit selling food, in particular, to the warring armies at whatever price they could fetch. Members of their communities, however, expected merchants to sell their goods at a price locals could afford. Patriot governments mandated price controls and set up committees to make sure they were enforced. Women as well as men were in the forefront of this movement. In Poughkeepsie, New York, for example, twenty-two women demanded that a merchant's wife sell her tea to her local community at a fair price in 1777; and the following day, several of them joined with men in the neighborhood to break into the house and open casks of liquor in further protest.

About one-third of the food riots that took place during the Revolution involved women, either partially or exclusively. In Fishkill, New York, women were outraged when Jacobus Lefferts refused to sell his tea at the price established by the Continental Congress in 1776. Seizing his goods and selling it for the price approved by the patriots, the women promised to donate the proceeds to the Revolutionary cause. In the summer of 1777, women in Boston rioted over food prices and at one point captured Thomas Boylston and liberated the coffee he was hoarding. In each case, women connected their role as consumers with the Revolutionary cause they were supporting.

This famous British cartoon lampooned the ladies of Edenton, North Carolina, who showed their political commitment by agreeing to boycott tea in 1774. The cartoon suggests that these women were immoral, manly, boisterous, and bad mothers.

Women also worked tirelessly throughout the colonies as fundraisers for the Patriot cause. The most successful effort occurred as Esther

De Berdt Reed and Sarah Franklin Bache (the daughter of Benjamin Franklin) spearheaded a major fund-raising drive in Philadelphia to provide money to the soldiers in the Continental Army. Organizing women to go door-to-door asking for donations, the campaign was a stunning success, garnering $300,000. Reed had hoped to give each soldier $2.00 in **specie**, but Washington forbade her, arguing that the money would undercut his own attempts to pay his men in paper currency and that they were likely to spend it inappropriately anyway. Finally, he agreed to let the women contribute over two thousand shirts to the troops. Women in other states followed suit with their own fund-raising drives. In addition to shirts, however, many women were kept busy at their spinning wheels and looms providing cloth and blankets for army procurement officers. Though the production of clothes and the purchase of foods were traditional female activities, they took on important political overtones as the Revolution unfolded.

specie Coin rather than paper money.

Women's feelings of independence also surfaced as they expanded their roles as deputy husbands, taking over the farms and shops of their husbands who had headed off to battle. One woman remembered the way her grandmother would saddle her horse and supervise workers on their extensive farm and iron works before breakfast and then turn her attention to the children and household after breakfast. Mary Bartlett of New Hampshire gradually shifted her reports on the farm she had taken over for her husband, referring at first to "your farming business" but later to "our farming business." Less-fortunate women had to scramble to earn whatever money they could to make up for the lack of an income from their spouses.

Loyalist Wives

Loyalists Colonists who sided with Britain during the American Revolution.

Those women who supported the **Loyalist** cause—and they were a significant minority—occupied a more politically ambiguous and economically vulnerable position than did women who supported the Patriot cause. As tensions with England began to unfold, their local social networks collapsed, leaving them isolated from friends and neighbors. Whether they wished it or not, a political identity was thrust upon them.

For Loyalist women, feelings of isolation began with the growing hostilities over British taxes. Social events became occasions for political debate, driving wedges into friendships. Shopkeepers who refused to participate in boycotts found their goods and homes under attack. Christian Barnes of Boston complained bitterly of the attacks on her and her husband by the Sons of Liberty, whom she condemned as a "set of wretches."

After war broke out, many men were forced to take a loyalty oath to the Patriot cause or face imprisonment. Loyalist men either joined the British forces or moved into territory controlled by the British. Their wives often stayed behind, trying to protect their homes and their children as the war unfolded around them. Patriot forces regarded them with suspicion, however, and expelled them when they gained sufficient control of an area. The wives of many Loyalists were driven from Newark, New Jersey, in 1777, as were Loyalist wives of Philadelphia in 1780.

Those who had not already left their homes by the end of the war certainly did so after the British surrender. They left behind their land, most of their valuables, and the people they had known. Some settled in England, while others headed to Canada or even the Caribbean. In their petitions to the British government, many revealed their loneliness and desolation as they requested financial assistance. They highlighted not only their poverty but also their isolation from friends and family they had left behind. "I am without Friends or Money," one petitioner explained, "a friendless, forlorn Woman."

WOMEN'S LIVES

MERCY OTIS WARREN

Mercy Otis Warren came from a prominent Massachusetts family and received an excellent education with her brothers. Her education was put to good use as resistance to Great Britain mounted in the colonies and her brothers and husband were drawn into the fray. Patriot leaders quickly came to appreciate Warren's intelligence—so much so that they counted on her writings to defend and spur the Patriot cause.

Writing anonymously during the 1770s, Warren published a string of plays and poems lampooning the British and urging on the colonists in their resistance. She skewered the British governor, Thomas Hutchinson, in two plays, *The Adulateur* and *The Defeat*. After the Boston Tea Party, John Adams encouraged her to memorialize the event and she did in a poem entitled "The Squabble of the Sea Nymphs." She encouraged women to support the boycott of British goods in a later poem and celebrated the virtue of the colonists in yet another. Her pamphlet *The Group*, published as war broke out in 1775, satirized the Loyalists of Boston. As the Revolution progressed and later, as the infant republic faced its earliest crises, Warren continued to write poems about the importance of the republican vision and her fears that many Patriots were straying from the path of political virtue. This was the theme that would animate her greatest work, *History of the American Revolution*, written over thirty years and finally published in 1805.

While Mercy Otis Warren ventured further than any other woman during the Revolution in engaging in the political debates that animated colonial resistance, she did not translate that activism

(John Singleton Copley (American, 1738-1815), Mrs. James Warren (Mercy Otis)," ca. 1763. Oil on canvas. 49 5/8 x 39 1/2 in. (126 x 100.3 cm). Bequest of Winslow Warren. Courtesy Museum of Fine Arts, Boston (31.212). Reproduced with permission. © 2000 Museum of Fine Arts, Boston. All Rights Reserved.)

into a larger critique of her place in a patriarchal society. She engaged in political debate with both men and women, and she believed that political ideas that came from women were as valid as those espoused by men. But she also believed that men and women were different in nature and that because of their different natures women were suited to the domestic world while men were suited to the world of politics and economy. Her writing was important, but her family duties were paramount. ∎

Fighting the War

Whether they sided with the Patriots or the Loyalists, women could not help but be caught up in the military conflict. Although both the British and colonial armies were composed of men, a straggling crew of the poorest women and children who had no way to support themselves with their husbands off fighting a war were present as camp followers. Washington found them a nuisance, but he also recognized that

By the nineteenth century, the term Molly Pitcher had become embodied in the body of a real person, who symbolized the patriotic activities of women in war. Currier and Ives lithographs, such as this one, circulated widely throughout the United States in the late nineteenth century.

many of his men would desert if they felt their families needed them at home. Making the best of what he considered a bad situation, Washington allowed them to receive partial rations and encouraged them to make themselves useful.

Women were indeed useful in the war effort. They sold food and supplies to the troops as they moved from place to place, as well as cooking, sewing, and washing clothes for their husbands and other soldiers. Indeed, the British soldiers, who traveled with women as well, had noted as early as the French and Indian War that the colonial soldiers were a ragged looking lot because they did not have enough women to clean and mend their clothes. Women also nursed their husbands or worked officially in foul-smelling army hospitals. Though women were paid for their labors, their pay was lower than what men received for comparable jobs. Female nurses and matrons earned less money than male stable hands. Not surprisingly, the laundresses in one camp went on strike to demand fair pay.

Some women even moved with their husbands to the battlefront, carrying buckets of water to quench the thirst of fighting men and to douse the over-heated canons the men were firing. The name "Molly Pitcher" evolved as a term for women who took on this task, and was applied most famously to Mary Ludwig Hays, who took over loading her husband's canon at the Battle of Monmouth in 1778. Deborah Sampson, who had no menfolk to follow, disguised herself and served as a soldier for several years before she was wounded and her true sexual identity became clear to an army surgeon.

Class also played an important role in the way women participated in military life. The poor and ragged camp followers were viewed as troublesome and dangerous by commanding officers who commented on their ugliness, dirtiness, and need for discipline. Officers' wives, however, were another matter. Officers from Washington down welcomed their female family members, particularly during long winters when balls and teas created a lively social season in the homes where officers had taken up temporary residence. Elizabeth Schuyler met her future husband Alexander Hamilton in this context, and she was not the only young lady to snag a dashing officer.

As the battlefields shifted up and down the colonial coast, even women who were not camp followers found themselves pressed into military service. When troops they supported moved into the vicinity, women would vie for opportunities to house the men they supported, particularly if there was a chance they would be paid for their efforts. At other times, women were forced to house soldiers of the opposing army when their land fell into enemy possession. In those cases, women might be less welcoming. Their homes were not only invaded but vandalized. Lydia Mintern Post of Long Island complained bitterly of the damage her Hessian "guests" did to her property as she was forced to lodge them. Elizabeth Wilstee, a Loyalist of New Hampshire, stood by helplessly while Patriot forces stole her furniture, destroyed her bedding, and pried the logs off her house.

A few women faced even greater trials when subjected to violence by opposing troops. Women in Staten Island and New Jersey were raped by invading British and Hessian soldiers in 1776 as were women in New Haven and Fairfield, Connecticut, during 1779. Abigail Palmer of New Jersey was only thirteen when she was raped by British troops in 1777. Farther south, several of the McDonald girls were stripped by Patriot soldiers in North Carolina. Other women lost their lives, including Hannah Caldwell who was murdered by a British soldier in search of loot. Caldwell's murder became a rallying cry for the Patriot forces, as did the death of Jane McCrea. McCrea's family was split, with some supporting the Loyalist cause and others supporting the Patriot cause. She herself was engaged to a Loyalist officer when Indians who were allied with the British captured her. In a dispute over the young woman, the Indians scalped her, galvanizing the Patriot troops her fiancé opposed. Indeed, in frontier areas where conflict with Indians was endemic, women were sometimes taken captive. In the largest of these raids, 170 women and children from Kentucky were captured by Indians and taken to Canada.

Deborah Sampson achieved fame in the early nineteenth century after her biography was published and she traveled around the country describing her experiences during the Revolutionary War, when she dressed as a man and enlisted in the Continental Army. Although her activities were unusual, she was not the only woman to secretly enlist.

Some women retaliated, though. While soldiers thought nothing of imposing on female hospitality and more or less expected women to be nonpolitical bystanders in the war, some women took advantage of this naïveté and bravely crossed enemy lines to share the information they had gathered with the side they supported. Others, in less dramatic fashion, simply provided a place for soldiers to stay as they tried to elude capture from their enemies. Facing severe punishments if they were caught, Patriot and Loyalist women secretly assisted soldiers and spied for the forces they supported.

Seize the Day: Indian and Slave Women of the Revolution

For Native American women and for slave women, the Revolution raised issues of independence that were different from those confronting Euro-American women. Native American women and men had to calculate which side in this colonial struggle was more likely to protect them from land-hungry colonists. Slaves calculated questions of independence in terms of freedom from bondage. They recognized that the demands for freedom being voiced by the colonists could be extended into a critique of slavery as well. However, while some slaves fought for freedom within the rhetoric of revolution, others thought their chances for freedom were better with the British. Most Native Americans agreed with them. Neither Indians nor slaves, however, were particularly interested in the political differences between the Patriots and the Loyalists. Neither were the Euro-Americans much interested in the oppression faced by their allies. The alliances these groups formed were purely strategic.

Most Indian tribes fought with the British, calculating that the British were more likely to honor their boundaries than the colonists were. Despite various efforts by the British to hold back Anglo settlements west of the Appalachians, thousands of farmers, hunters, traders, and land speculators had pushed into those lands during the eighteenth century, sparking a series of bloody conflicts (see chapter 4). Compared to these rapacious colonists, the British government seemed like the lesser of two evils.

Many Indian groups had hoped to avoid participating in the conflict at all, viewing it as a conflict among Europeans. However, as conflict spread from New England to Canada as early as 1777, the Iroquois confederacy realized it would be drawn in. Mary (Molly) Brandt, a powerful Mohawk matron who had been married to Sir William Johnson, the British superintendent of Indian Affairs in the North, worked assiduously to build support for the British among the Iroquois confederacy. She used her membership in the Society of Six Nations Matrons to persuade other women to support the war—and to encourage their men to join the Loyalists. Like most Loyalist women, Brandt was eventually forced to leave her home and all her possessions for a new life in Canada.

Regardless of which side Indians fought on, conflict on the frontier was vicious; and as a result, Indian women and children left behind in the villages suffered some of the worst excesses of military brutality. One chief claimed that Patriot troops had "put to death all the Women and Children" in his village, saving only a few girls "whom they carried away for the use of their soldiers." Some Indian women were mutilated after they were murdered, as their wombs were torn out of their bodies. Those who survived such attacks faced starvation and bitter cold as troops burned their fields and their houses. Mary Jemison, who had been captured by the Seneca Indians when a child and who had chosen to stay with the Senecas even though she was later ransomed by her relatives, described vividly how Patriot forces had destroyed their crops and their homes. They had "not a mouthful of any kind of sustenance left, not even enough to keep a child one day from perishing of hunger." Meslamonehonqua, a Miami Indian woman, echoed that desperation when she demanded support from the British in Detroit, saying "I am Deputized by the Women of our Villages, to pray you to send them Ammunition for to support their families."

Slaves had also been drawn into the war early on when in 1775 Lord Dunmore, governor of Virginia, issued a proclamation that any slaves in his colony willing to take up arms against their masters would be granted their freedom. Three hundred male slaves quickly mustered into the "Ethiopian Regiment." During the course of the war, over eighty thousand slaves fled their masters, many taking their chances with the British. The offer of potential freedom behind British lines had a particularly powerful impact on women. Slave women had been much less likely than slave men to run away during the colonial period because they often had small children who could not travel long distances to freedom in Florida or other colonies on the frontier. However, as the British army drew closer to slave populations in both the North and the South during different periods of the war, that calculation changed and women became much more likely to make a bid for freedom. Of the twenty-three slaves who fled Thomas Jefferson's Virginia plantation, more than half were female. Over 40 percent of more than twenty-eight hundred ex-slaves who left with the British at the end of the war were female.

WOMEN'S VOICES

CONCERNS OF AN INDIAN MATRON

Mary (Molly) Brandt, born a Mohawk Indian, was the sister of Joseph Brandt, Chief of the Six Nations, and wife of Sir William Johnson, the British Superintendent of Indian Affairs in New York. Because of these ties, she was an important go-between for the British and the Iroquois. Although Johnson died just before the outbreak of the American Revolution, Molly maintained that role, rallying the Iroquois to the British cause. That loyalty cost her dearly when she and her people were forced to flee to Canada as the British lost the war.

Carleton Island, 5th October 1779

Sir

We arraived here the 29th last month after Tedaous and dissagreable Voyage; where we remain and by all Appearance may be for the winter I have rote to Colo Butler and my brother Acquainting them of my Situation, desireing there advice, as I was left no Directions Concerning my self or family. Only when a Vessel Arraived, I Could get a passage to Niagara—I have been promised by Colo Johnson at Montreal that I Should hear from the Genl [Haldimand] and have his directions & order to be provided at whatever place my little service should be wanted which

you know I am always ready to do, Should you think proper to speak to the Genl on that head will be much Oblidged to You. the Indians are a Good deele dissatisfied on acct of the Colo.s hasty temper which I hope he will soon drop Otherwise it may be Dissadvantageous I need not tell You whatever is promised or told them it ought to be perform'd—

Those from Canada are much Dissatisfied on Account of his taking more Notice of those that are suspected than them that are known to be Loyal, I tell this only to you that you advise him on that head—Meantime beg leave to be remembered to all Your family from Sir—

Your wellwisher
Mary Brant

Source: *Letter of Molly Brandt to Judge Daniel Claus, in Sharon Harris, ed.,* American Women Writers to 1800 *(New York: Oxford University Press,) 280–281.*

Questions

1. How does Molly Brandt demonstrate her confidence in representing the needs of her Indian people?

2. Does Molly Brandt regard herself as an equal to the British or their inferior?

Once behind British lines, however, slave women faced a new set of trials. Women were not allowed to bear arms, but they took on other duties of camp followers in nursing the sick, cooking, and doing laundry. Many died in these camps as epidemics repeatedly struck. When Lord Dunmore evacuated Virginia, for example, a smallpox epidemic broke out on his ships and he left his African American followers on an island in the Chesapeake Bay, where many died alone and unattended.

Not all slaves supported the British. Others assisted Patriot troops and attempted to extend Revolutionary rhetoric about freedom into their own lives. As the Revolution drew to a close, the Massachusetts slave Mumbet (who would later take the name Elizabeth Freeman) sued for her freedom and won. She argued that her enslavement violated the promise of liberty that was central to the state constitution; and, eventually, slavery was ruled unconstitutional in Massachusetts. Slowly, other states in the North also abolished the practice, though slaves could be found in some parts of the North through the 1820s. In the South, such arguments for African American freedom largely fell on deaf ears. Some southern slave owners did free their slaves, but by the end of the century, slavery in the South was stronger than ever. Although women such as Elizabeth Freeman had tried to extend arguments for liberty to include slavery, their impact was limited.

Female Citizens

In the heady days of 1776, as states debated the nature of their new governments, most men were no more interested in extending political rights to women than extending them to slaves. Delegates to constitutional conventions were much more focused on the extent to which uneducated and propertyless men would have access to political power. Elites worried that a completely democratic society would degenerate into the tyranny of ignorant masses with little respect for property rights. Poor farmers and artisans who were fighting to defend the Patriot cause argued that such mistrust was unfair. In New Jersey, however, this debate unexpectedly affected women when the state constitution was written in 1776. The New Jersey constitution dealt with the conflict between property holders and commoners by extending the right to vote to women but insisting on a property qualification. All adults who possessed at least fifty pounds of property were given the right to vote. Married women would not have qualified under these rules because they legally could not own property, but some single women did. Most likely, these women were being counted upon to uphold the rights of property holders in case poorer men challenged them. As a result, single women with property received an important new right—and they used it.

The inclusion of women as voters in the New Jersey constitution did not arouse much comment, though by the 1790s criticism was growing. This was due in no small part to the growing competition between the **Federalists** and the **Jeffersonian Republicans** for the allegiance of voters. The Federalists were committed to a strong central government and the promotion of commerce, while the Republicans were committed to a weaker central government and the interests of farmers. Each faction viewed the other with alarm. As the two young parties jockeyed to promote their particular causes, they calculated where their support might be found; and among the groups they sized up and courted were the female voters of the state. The Federalists rounded up women in a hotly contested election in 1797. However, they soon began to fear that women might favor the Republicans. In the end, neither the Republicans nor the Federalists felt there was enough to be gained in courting the women and both sides dropped support for the female franchise when the state constitution was rewritten in 1807. Although women had actively used the vote while they had it, they did not protest their disenfranchisement when it occurred.

While the New Jersey experiment with female voting was an anomaly in female political participation during the Revolutionary period, petitioning was not. Petitions were a way subjects could approach their government directly to request anything from personal assistance to a change in the law. Few women used petitions before the Revolution, but during and after the war, an increasing number of women began to petition their governments. Some petitioned the Continental Congress or various state legislatures for economic relief if widowed or economic payment if they had rendered

Federalists Political faction that supported the Constitution and a strong central government.

Jeffersonian Republicans Political faction that opposed the Federalists and favored limited government and an agrarian republic.

WOMEN'S LIVES

PHILLIS WHEATLEY

Phillis Wheatley was also caught up in the intellectual revolution that engulfed the colonies, but her status as an African American and a slave gave her a very different perspective from that of white women. Wheatley had been born in Africa in 1753 and sold into slavery as a child. She was purchased by John and Susannah Wheatley, a pious couple in Boston, who recognized the intellectual aptitude of the girl and taught her to read not only in English but also in Latin and Greek. The young slave was not only smart but pious, caught up in the fires of the Great Awakening. Inspired by her reading and her religion, Phillis Wheatley began to write poetry as a teenager. In 1773, as Revolutionary fervor began to build in Boston, the Wheatleys granted Phillis her freedom, and in 1778, she married John Peters.

As Wheatley sought to gain an audience for her poetry, first as a slave and later as an impoverished freedwoman, her dependence on the patronage of others was always painfully clear. She spoke to and of people whom she acknowledged as her social superiors, whether it be the great evangelical preacher, George Whitefield; her patroness in England, the Countess of Huntington; or George Washington. But she also spoke with a clear sense of herself as an African sold into slavery. And those who read her work, or knew of it, had to confront the double problem of the clear intellectual capabilities of someone who was not only a woman but also an African American. Many scoffed at her work, including Thomas Jefferson, who found her writing "below the dignity of criticism." Indeed, her first volume of poetry was published in England rather than in Massachusetts, because she could not attract enough of a following in Boston to warrant publication there.

Despite these problems, Wheatley wrote patriotic and religious verse throughout the Revolutionary period, championing freedom for the colonies but reminding her readers that there were others in need of freedom as well. Writing to the Earl of Dartmouth, Wheatley joined the personal pain caused by her capture with a larger lament about tyranny. "What pangs excruciating must molest, What sorrows labour in my parent's breast?" she asked. And joining her plight to that of the colonists, she concluded, "Such, such is my case. And can I then but pray/Others may never feel tyrannic sway?" Using her religious beliefs to articulate a shared humanity with whites, she carefully reminded readers in another of her poems, "Remember Christians; Negroes, black as Cain, May be refin'd, and join th' angelic train." ∎

Although the experiment allowing women to vote in New Jersey ended in 1807, it was not forgotten. As this drawing from Harper's Magazine in 1880 makes clear, women's voting practices were not only remembered in a popular magazine, but depicted as a respectable activity.

service to the government. Abigail Ott and Mary Munn of Pennsylvania no longer had their husbands to support them and were starving. Nonhelema, an Indian woman, requested payment for tending the cattle of Americans fighting at Fort Randolph on the Ohio River. Mary Sansum of Charleston petitioned the state of South Carolina for back pay she believed owed her dead husband. Hundreds of these petitions flooded the legislatures of the states during and after the war.

As women became more comfortable petitioning the government, they also began to use this approach collectively in a few instances to address issues of policy. In Charleston, nine slave-owning widows protested legislation in 1783 that prohibited slave women from selling their goods in the streets. Many of these slaves were there at the behest of their mistresses who counted on the income to support themselves. A few years later, sixty-seven seamstresses in South Carolina signed another petition requesting a higher tariff on the imported clothing that was providing stiff competition to their goods and driving them out of business. As their behavior made clear, women did not have the same political rights as men but they did have a political consciousness.

A Virtuous Republic

Articles of Confederation
Document adopted by Second Continental Congress in 1777 to create first government of the United States as a loose confederation of states.

United States Constitution Document adopted by Constitutional Convention in 1787 to replace Articles of Confederation and to provide for a stronger centralized government of the United States.

The new United States government faced constant turmoil in its early years. The **Articles of Confederation**, which had been adopted by the Second Continental Congress in 1777, was abandoned ten years later as too weak to hold the new national government together. The **United States Constitution** replaced it in 1787. Debates about the national government were echoed in each state as separate constitutions were written and rewritten. Repeatedly, Americans asked themselves and each other how far the Revolution would go in granting rights and promoting democracy. Debates such as these framed questions about the rights of women in the new republic.

MAP 3-2 NORTH AMERICA AFTER THE TREATY OF PARIS 1783

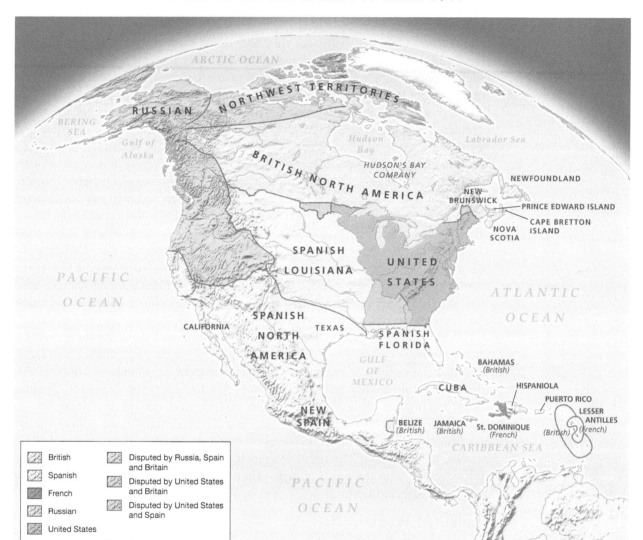

After the conclusion of the American Revolution, the new United States extended largely from the Atlantic Ocean to the Mississippi River, with Spain controlling most of the land to the west and Britain controlling much of the land that would become Canada.

Republican Mothers and Virtuous Wives

In the celebrations that followed the Revolutionary victory, the citizens of the new republic repeatedly toasted the role of patriotic women. Their fortitude, their virtue, and their good sense were widely acknowledged. Women themselves boasted of their political acumen. Margaret Manigault, for example, claimed she could "read the papers, & talk learnedly about them all," when she described herself as "a great Politician." Young women in the North and the South talked freely of the new president, the Constitution, and other more local political affairs.

This political awareness, however, did not lead women into political power. Rather, a consensus rapidly developed that women had proven themselves worthy and capable of rearing virtuous citizens in the new republic. This emphasis on child rearing was a serious concern. In the uncharted waters of a new republican form of government, citizens worried about whether or not the electorate would be suitably trained to govern itself. Although they had grown frustrated with British rule, the Revolutionary generation had grown up with a belief that the monarchy provided crucial stability in a government. Citizens of the United States took seriously the need to create stability in new ways with an educated and selfless public. Elites had viewed property holding as one way of ensuring the capabilities of voters, but a new confidence also began to emerge in the capabilities of women. A well-educated and virtuous woman would be a valuable sounding board for her husband and a trusted educator of their children.

Journals of the time thus suggested that men look for wisdom and patience in a wife rather than beauty and wealth. And women were urged to wed men who would treat them as friends. These would be marriages in which men and women could share advice and contemplate problems that could have political ramifications as well as personal. Child rearing should have a similar purpose. Thus, Mary Cranch was proud of developing her son's capacity to reason. "When any thing was demanded of you the reason was given why it ought to be done," she told him later. This youthful training, her comment implied, had given him the skills to listen thoughtfully to political debate and act judiciously for the common good.

Those who championed the responsibility of women to educate their children and advise their husbands argued that it was not only their duty but also their right. Men had the right to vote, but women had the right to influence. The Lockean ideas of natural equality and social contract that had been popularized by Thomas Paine and written into the Declaration of Independence were not applied to women. The belief that men and women had different rights came from the Scottish Enlightenment tradition that stressed that individuals had different rights depending on their rank. The rights of women, when conceived in this way, were not only different from the rights of men—they were actually derived from a very different political tradition.

Educated Women

The most significant change in the lives of women following the Revolution was their growing access to education so that they could successfully assume their roles within their families. Advanced academies for elite girls proliferated, particularly in the North, where even the daughters of farmers and shopkeepers were more likely to gain a basic knowledge of reading and writing at local schools.

Girls of modest backgrounds usually received their educations in summer sessions at the town school. Of course, not all towns had schools; and even if they did, they would not necessarily allow girls to enroll or they could refuse to pay for the instruction of girls. But in Masssachusetts, for example, girls were more likely to find these opportunities by the 1790s than earlier in the century. In Philadelphia, abolitionists even opened a school for girls who had been slaves because they would not have been able to attend a school for white children. Not surprisingly, female literacy rose.

Female academies provided more advanced learning. Many of these academies were founded in the North rather than in the South because the southern countryside had been so devastated by Revolutionary battles and recovery in the South was proceeding slowly. In small towns and large cities of Pennsylvania, New York, Connecticut, and Massachusetts, educated women such as Susanna Rowson and Sarah Pierce opened establishments that drew young women from great distances. While many of these schools taught music, dancing, and embroidery (the ornamental accomplishments), they also stressed reading, writing, and basic arithmetic, as well as offering lessons in history and geography.

Benjamin Rush, an important physician who argued that Pennsylvania needed public schools to educate both boys and girls for participation in the new nation, also helped to found the private Young Ladies' Academy in Philadelphia. He argued that girls needed to be educated to instill patriotism in their children and that women needed to learn good handwriting and basic mathematics to assist their husbands in their businesses.

Not everyone accepted the idea that girls needed to be educated or that they were even capable of learning traditionally male subjects such as history and mathematics. Thus, a debate developed about the intellectual capabilities of women, with some writers going far beyond the demands of those who supported republican womanhood, arguing instead that men and women were intellectual equals and that education was an important way to create independent women. Mary Wollstonecraft of England took this position in 1792 in her **A Vindication of the Rights of Woman**, which circulated widely in Europe and the United States. She claimed that while there were physical differences between men and women, female character had been shaped by environment rather than internal nature. Wollstonecraft argued that not only should boys and girls study the same subjects but that they should be educated together.

Judith Sargent Murray of Boston, an important essayist in the late eighteenth century, saw her essays as a complement to Wollstonecraft's. In her writings, she argued that women needed to be educated so that they would know how to best influence their families, but she also pointed out that educated women would have the ability to support their children if something happened to their husbands. In this way, Murray raised the possibility that education could lead to female independence. The radical implications of Murray's arguments became clear as she claimed that women were capable of such an education because they were "in *every respect* equal to men." Whether in fortitude or patriotism, governing or literary accomplishment, women were just as capable as men. Murray challenged the assumptions about female nature that underlay the gender philosophy of the Scottish Enlightenment and the status hierarchy of republican womanhood.

Although few women openly espoused Murray's arguments, Murray was not alone in discussing female equality. Some young women preferred the rights of men to those that had been allocated to women. When Priscilla Mason delivered an oration in 1794 at her graduation from the newly established Young Ladies'

A Vindication of the Rights of Woman Treatise by Mary Wollstonecraft published in 1792 in England arguing for the intellectual equality and rights of women.

Judith Sargent Murray penned the most cogent written arguments for the rights of woman in the new United States during the eighteenth century. Her essays appeared in the Massachusetts Magazine *and were later collected into a volume of essays called* The Gleaner. *This portrait was painted by John Singleton Copley in 1770–72. (John Singleton Copley (1738-1815), "Portrait of Mrs. John Stevens (Judith Sargent, later Mrs. John Murray)," 1770-72. Commissioned on the occasion of her first marriage, at age eighteen. Oil on canvas, 50 x 40 in. Daniel J. Terra Art Acquisition Endowment Fund, 2000.6. © Terra Foundation for American Art, Chicago/Art Resource, New York)*

Academy of Philadelphia, she not only celebrated her extraordinary education but also decried the "mighty Lords" who with "their arbitrary constitutions have denied us the means of knowledge, and then reproached us for the want of it." Turning to the broader political landscape, she further complained, "The Church, the Bar, and the Senate are shut against us. Who shut them? *Man*; despotic man." Ann Harker, another young graduate of the Young Ladies' Academy, was clearly in agreement, arguing, "In opposition to *your* immortal Paine, we will exalt *our* Wolstencraft."

A Limited Revolution

The celebration of the republican mother, virtuous wife, and educated daughter in the years following the Revolution suggests the ways in which ideas about the family had shifted along with ideals about the political order. The growing emphasis on companionship in marriage and equality in family relations also surfaced in some of the new laws that were drafted about divorce and inheritance. However, democracy in family and personal relationships was not always realized. New ideas about family may have provided elite women with status more than power and consigned poor women to an even more marginal position in society.

As each state rewrote their laws of inheritance after the Revolution, most changed the rules about how a father's property would be distributed if he died without writing a will. British law had stipulated that in such circumstances, the oldest son would receive twice as much as his brothers and sisters. In the new republic, ten of the thirteen new states rewrote these statutes to provide equal shares to all children in a family. While this legislation was meant to create more economic equality among siblings, fathers could easily ignore the law by simply writing their own wills. Those who did tended to continue the trend that had begun before the Revolution of trying to equalize the amount of property they willed to their sons by giving less to their daughters.

Most states (with the notable exception of South Carolina) also broke with British tradition by legalizing divorce, although only in very restricted circumstances. Puritans in New England had always recognized divorce, and Quakers in Pennsylvania also had been sympathetic to the idea because these religious groups viewed marriage as a civil contract, not a religious one. The English government had disagreed with this perspective, however, and had challenged the divorce statutes of these colonies while they were still under British rule. After the Revolution, more lenient divorce laws were finally enacted. Divorce was still a difficult process, however. Laws varied with each state, but in most cases women (and men) had to petition state legislatures to receive a divorce and usually only the most wealthy of women had the money and political connections to do so.

Regardless of whether or not legal divorces were within their reach, some women did continue to engage in a sexually expressive culture, at least in the first few years of the new republic. In Philadelphia, in particular, cases continued to proliferate of women who had had children out of wedlock with few consequences and others who had left their husbands when they found another who suited them better. However, arguments for sexual chastity began to increase in the newspapers and journals of the day as women, in particular, were urged to curb the licentious behavior of men. Female responsibilities for guarding republican virtue were extended from politics and education to encompass sexuality as well. As one gentleman wrote to the *Philadelphia Minerva*, "Ladies, much depends on you, towards a reformation in the morals of our sex. . . ."

This new approach to sexuality had important class implications because openly sexual behavior became associated with women of the lower classes. Servants, street hawkers, slaves, and poor women generally were excluded from the vision of virtuous womanhood. Men could engage in sexual relationships with these women because men were not charged with guarding the family virtue of the new republic as their wives and sisters were. A double standard emerged in which respectable women were expected to restrain their sexuality as a way of promoting the virtue of the nation in a way that men were not, another form of gender complementarity between the sexes of the respectable classes. As was true of gender complementarity generally, the sexual double standard was rooted in inequality. Men were allowed sexual freedoms that women were not, and poor women were further marginalized as unworthy of either respect or responsibility within society.

CONCLUSION

The eighteenth century truly had been an age of revolution for women. Consumer goods and a lively market economy had transformed their lives as both producers and consumers. Family life had changed as patriarchal authority was challenged on numerous levels, both small and grand, and a new republic of rights had been established. But the tradition of rights for men was different from the one established for women. For men, the tradition of natural rights had opened the door to political access and debates about equality. For women, however, rights were rooted in a very different tradition, one premised on inequality and the need for women to exercise their rights within their homes, not in public. This tradition of difference would define the debates about women's political status for the next two centuries.

REVIEW QUESTIONS

1. How did the market revolution change the ways women lived in the eighteenth century?
2. Why were challenges to patriarchal authority in British colonial families important?
3. What experiences influenced the growth of women's political consciousness during the Revolutionary period?
4. Did women gain power as a result of the Revolution?

WOMEN'S HISTORY		GLOBAL EVENTS
	1730	
		1738 George Whitefield first tours colonies
		1740s Great Awakening crests in New England
	1750	
		1756 Beginning of French and Indian War (Seven Years' War)
		1763 End of French and Indian War; Treaty of Paris
		1764 Sugar Act
		1767 Townshend Act
	1770	
1773 Phillis Wheatley gains her freedom		1773 Tea Act
1774 Ladies of Edenton, North Carolina, sign a petition to boycott imported goods		1775 Fighting begins at Lexington and Concord Second Continental Congress convenes Lord Dunmore promises freedom to slaves who fight against Patriots
1776 Women with property in New Jersey granted the right to vote		1776 Thomas Paine publishes *Common Sense* Declaration of Independence written
1777 Loyalist women driven from Newark		
	1780	
1780 Loyalist women driven from Philadelphia		
1783 Slaveholding widows in Charleston collectively sign a petition protesting legislation		
1790 Judith Sargent Murray publishes *On the Equality of the Sexes*		
1792 Mary Wollstonecraft publishes *Vindication of the Rights of Woman* Young Ladies' Academy in Philadelphia founded		

RECOMMENDED READING

Linda Kerber. *Women of the Republic: Intellect and Ideology in Revolutionary America.* New York: W. W. Norton, 1986. A classic interpretation of the meaning of the Revolution for women.

Cynthia A. Kierner. *Beyond the Household: Women's Place in the Early South, 1700–1835.* Ithaca, NY: Cornell University Press, 1998. Important study of the ways in which southern women's experience was distinct from that of northern women.

Clare A. Lyons. *Sex among the Rabble: An Intimate History of Gender and Power in the Age of Revolution,* *Philadelphia 1730–1830.* Chapel Hill: University of North Carolina Press, 2006. A lively and original interpretation of the sexual lives of women in an important commercial center during the eighteenth century.

Mary Beth Norton. *Liberty's Daughters: The Revolutionary Experience of American Women, 1750–1800.* Ithaca, NY: Cornell University Press, 1996 (1980). Still one of the most comprehensive surveys of women during the Revolutionary period.

ADDITIONAL BIBLIOGRAPHY

The Market Revolution

Ira Berlin. *Many Thousands Gone: The First Two Centuries of Slavery in North America.* Cambridge, MA: Harvard University Press, 1998.

Carl Bridenbaugh. *Cities in the Wilderness: The First Century of Urban Life in America, 1625–1742.* New York: Oxford University Press, 1966 (1938).

Elaine Forman Crane. *Ebb Tide in New England: Women, Seaports, and Social Change 1630–1800.* Boston: Northeastern University Press, 1998.

Christine Daniels. "Gresham's Laws: Labor Management on an Early-Eighteenth-Century Chesapeake Plantation." *Journal of Southern History* 62, no. 2 (May 1996): 205–38.

Cornelia Dayton. *Women Before the Bar: Gender, Law, and Society in Connecticut, 1639–1789.* Chapel Hill: University of North Carolina Press, 1995.

David R. Goldfield and Blaine A. Brownell. *Urban America: From Downtown to No Town.* Boston: Houghton Mifflin, 1979.

Joan R. Gunderson. *To Be Useful to the World: Women in Revolutionary America, 1740–1790.* New York: Twayne, 1996.

Cynthia M. Kennedy. *Braided Relations, Entwined Lives: The Women of Charleston's Urban Slave Society.* Bloomington: Indiana University Press, 2005.

Alan Kulikoff. *Tobacco and Slaves: The Development of Southern Cultures in the Chesapeake, 1680–1800.* Chapel Hill: University of North Carolina Press, 1986.

Gloria Main. "Gender, Work, and Wages in Colonial New England." *William and Mary Quarterly,* Third Series 51, no. 1 (January 1994): 39–66.

Sarah Hand Meacham. "Keeping the Trade: The Persistence of Tavernkeeping among Middling Women in Colonial Virginia." *Early American Studies* (Spring 2005): 140–63.

Philip D. Morgan, and Michael L. Nicholls. "Slaves in Piedmont Virginia, 1720–1790." *William and Mary Quarterly,* Third Series 46, no. 2 (April 1989): 211–51.

David E. Narrett. "Men's Wills and Women's Property Rights in Colonial New York." In *Women in the Age of the American Revolution,* edited by Ronald Hoffman and Peter J. Albert, 91–133. Charlottesville: University Press of Virginia, 1989.

Gary B. Nash. *The Urban Crucible: The Northern Seaports and the Origins of the American Revolution.* Cambridge, MA: Harvard University Press, 1986.

Edward A. Pearson. "'A Countryside Full of Flames': A Reconsideration of the Stono Rebellion and Slave Rebelliousness in the Early Eighteenth-Century South Carolina Lowcountry." *Slavery and Abolition* 17, no. 2 (August 1996): 22–50.

Deborah A. Rosen. *Courts and Commerce: Gender, Law, and the Market Economy in Colonial New York.* Columbus: Ohio State University Press, 1997.

Deborah A. Rosen. "Women and Property across Colonial America: A Comparison of Legal Systems in New Mexico and New York." *William and Mary Quarterly,* Third Series LX, no. 2 (April 2003): 355–82.

Sharon V. Salinger. *Taverns and Drinking in Early America.* Baltimore, MD: Johns Hopkins University Press, 2002.

Marylynn Salmon. *Women and the Law of Property in Early America.* Chapel Hill: University of North Carolina, 1986.

Carole Shammas, "The Female Social Structure of Philadelphia in 1775." *Pennsylvania Magazine of History and Biography* 107 (1983): 69–83.

Carole Shammas, Marylynn Salmon, and Michel Dahlin. *Inheritance in America: From Colonial Times to the Present.* New Brunswick, NJ: Rutgers University Press, 1987.

Laurel Thatcher Ulrich. *The Age of Homespun: Objects and Stories in the Creation of an American Myth.* New York: Alfred A. Knopf, 2001.

Stephanie Grauman Wolf. *As Various as Their Land: The Everyday Lives of Eighteenth-Century Americans.* New York: HarperCollins, 1993.

Betty Wood. "Some Aspects of Female Resistance to Chattel Slavery in Low Country Georgia, 1763–1815." *Historical Journal* 30, no. 3 (September 1987): 603–22.

Karen A. Wulf. *Not All Wives: Women of Colonial Philadelphia.* Ithaca, NY: Cornell University Press, 2000.

Family Relations and Social Responsibilities

Carol Berkin. *First Generations: Women in Colonial America.* New York: Hill & Wang, 1996.

Ruth Bloch. "Changing Conceptions of Sexuality and Romance in Eighteenth-Century America." *William and Mary Quarterly*, Third Series LX, no. 1 (January 2003): 13–42.

Catherine A. Brekkus. *Strangers and Pilgrims: Female Preaching in America, 1740–1845.* Chapel Hill: University of North Carolina Press, 1998.

Jay Fliegelman. *Prodigals and Pilgrims: The American Revolution against Patriarchal Authority, 1750–1800.* Cambridge: Cambridge University Press, 1989 (1982).

Robert Gross. *The Minutemen and Their World.* New York: Hill & Wang, 1976.

Susan Juster. *Disorderly Women: Sexual Politics and Evangelicalism in Revolutionary New England.* Ithaca, NY: Cornell University Press, 1994.

Catherine Kerrison. *Claiming the Pen: Women and Intellectual Life in the Early American South.* Ithaca, NY: Cornell University Press, 2006.

Thomas Laqueur. *Making Sex: Body and Gender from the Greeks to Freud.* Cambridge, MA: Harvard University Press, 1990.

Clare A. Lyons. "Mapping an Atlantic Sexual Culture: Homoeroticism in Eighteenth-Century Philadelphia." *William and Mary Quarterly*, Third Series LX, no. 1 (January 2003): 119–54.

Carole Shammas. "Early American Women and Control over Capital." In *Women in the Age of the American Revolution*, edited by Ronald Hoffman and Peter J. Albert, 134–54. Charlottesville: University Press of Virginia, 1989.

David Shields. *Civil Tongues and Polite Letters in British America.* Chapel Hill: University of North Carolina Press, 1997.

Daniel Scott Smith and Michael Hindus. "Premarital Pregnancy in America, 1640–1971: An Overview and an Interpretation." *Journal of Interdisciplinary History* 5 (1974–1975).

Declaring Independence

Carol Berkin. *Revolutionary Mothers: Women in the Struggle for America's Independence* New York: Random House, 2006.

Colin G. Calloway, *The American Revolution in Indian Country.* Cambridge: Cambridge University Press, 1995.

Judith Apter Klinghoffer and Lois Elkis. "'The Petticoat Electors': Women's Suffrage in New Jersey, 1776–1807." *Journal of the Early Republic* 12/2 (Summer 1992): 159–93.

Holly Mayer. *Belonging to the Army: Camp Followers and Community during the American Revolution.* Columbia: University of South Carolina Press, 1996.

Janice Potter-Mackinnon. *While the Women Only Wept.* Montreal: McGill-Queens University Press, 1993.

Barbara Clark Smith. "Food Rioters and the American Revolution." *William and Mary Quarterly*, Third Series 51, no. 1 (January 1994): 3–38.

A Virtuous Republic

Jan Lewis. "The Republican Wife: Virtue and Seduction in the Early Republic." *William and Mary Quarterly*, Third Series 44, no. 4 (October 1987): 689–721.

Margaret Nash. "Rethinking Republican Motherhood: Benjamin Rush and the Young Ladies' Academy of Philadelphia." *Journal of the Early Republic* 17 (Summer 1997): 172–91.

Kathryn Kish Sklar. "The Schooling of Girls and Changing Community Values in Massachusetts Towns, 1750–1820." *History of Education Quarterly* 33, no. 4 (Winter 1993): 511–42.

Rosemarie Zagarri. "Morals, Manners, and the Republican Mother." *American Quarterly* 44, no. 2 (June 1992): 192–215.

Rosemarie Zagarri. "The Rights of Man and Woman in Post-Revolutionary America." *William and Mary Quarterly*, Third Series (April 1998): 203–30.

Rosemarie Zagarri. *Revolutionary Backlash: Women and Politics in the Early Republic*. Philadelphia: University of Pennsylvania Press, 2007.

Biographies, Autobiographies, and Memoirs

Elaine Crane, ed. *The Diary of Elizabeth Drinker*. Boston: Northeaster University Press, 3 vol., c. 1991.

Barbara E. Lacey. *The World of Hannah Heaton: The Diary of an Eighteenth-Century New England Farm Woman*. DeKalb: Northern Illinois University Press, 2003.

Elise Pinckney, ed. *The Letterbook of Eliza Lucas Pinckey*, 1739–1762. Columbia: University of South Carolina Press, 1997.

William Henry Robinson. *Phillis Wheatley and Her Writings*. New York: Garland, 1984.

Jon F. Sensbach. *Rebecca's Revival: Creating Black Christianity in the Atlantic World*. Cambridge, MA: Harvard University Press, 2005.

Laurel Thatcher Ulrich. *A Midwife's Tale, The Life of Martha Ballard, Based on Her Diary*, 1785–1812. New York: Random House, 1991.

Rosemarie Zagarri. *A Woman's Dilemma: Mercy Otis Warren and the American Revolution*. Wheeling, IL: Harlan Davidson, 1995.

FRONTIERS OF TRADE AND EMPIRE, 1750-1860

HOW DID the power of women within their households change in different Indian groups as a result of trade with the British and Anglo-Americans?

HOW WERE women affected by changing laws of slavery and freedom as control of the Louisiana Territory shifted from France to Spain and then to the United States?

WHAT WERE the different ways that women created households in the western frontiers of Texas, New Mexico, and California?

CHAPTER 4

The duties of the housekeeper were many. In the first place, every day she handed out the rations for the mess hut. To do this, she had to count the unmarried women, bachelors, day-laborers, vaqueros [cowboys] . . . In short, she was responsible for the distribution of supplies to the Indian population and to the missionaries' kitchen. She was in charge of the key to the clothing storehouse where materials were given out for dresses for the unmarried and married women and children. . . .

They put under my charge everything having to do with clothing. I cut and fitted, and my five daughters sewed the pieces. When they could not handle everything, the

Comanche Village Women Dressing Robes and Drying Meat,
George Catlin, 1834–1835.

father was told, and then women from the town of Los Angeles were employed, and the father paid them. . . .

Besides this, I had to attend to the soap-house . . . to the wine-presses, and to the olive-crushers that produced oil, which I worked in myself . . .

In the Mission of San Gabriel there was a large number of neophytes [new converts]. The married ones lived on their rancherias with their small children. There were two divisions for the unmarried ones: one for the women, called the nunnery, and another for the men. They brought the girls from the ages of seven, eight or nine years to the nunnery, and they were brought up there. They left to get married. They were under the care of a mother in the nunnery, an Indian. During the time I was at the mission this matron was named Polonia—they called her "Mother Superior." The alcalde [an elected male leader] was in charge of the unmarried men's division. Every night both divisions were locked up . . . keys were delivered to me, and I handed them over to the missionaries.

A blind Indian girl named Andresillo stood at the door of the nunnery and called out each girl's name, telling her to come in. If any girl was missing at admission time, they looked for her the following day and brought her to the nunnery. Her mother, if she had one, was brought in and punished for having detained her, and the girl was locked up for having been careless in not coming in punctually.

Source: Eulalia Pérez, "Una vieja y sus recuerdos dictados," BANC Mss C-D 139, Bancroft Library, translated and reprinted in Carlos N. Hijar, Eulalia Perez, and Agustin Escobar, Three Memoirs of Mexican California (Berkeley, CA: Friends of the Bancroft Library, University of California at Berkeley, 1988), 78–81.

Eulalia Pérez was born in Baja California around 1768 but moved north to San Diego in the early nineteenth century when her husband, a soldier, was transferred to the fort there. After her husband died, she relocated to the San Gabriel Mission farther north, where her son worked as a guard and where she found work assisting the Spanish authorities in their attempts to convert and educate the Indians there. The mission where she worked operated as both an extended household and as a venue for promoting European ideas about domestic relations to Native Americans. The mission structure was peculiar to Spanish America; however, in frontier areas throughout the United States, household organization continued to be of central importance to the social order during the eighteenth and nineteenth centuries and thus of concern in struggles for dominance.

But market transactions throughout the North American frontier were transforming the meaning of household relationships, just at they had in the British colonies. As European countries vied for power with and among different Indian tribes during this period, competing structures of gender complementarity, property holding, freedom and slavery, and general principles of governance came into conflict around ideas of household organization. The status of women was constantly being rene-gotiated as Native Americans shifted their alliances with one another and faced successive challenges from different European powers and, eventually, the United States.

The British colonies of North America were the first to be incorporated as part of the United States, but by the middle of the nineteenth century, the territorial reach of the young nation extended to the Pacific Ocean. The "Indian Country" that stretched from the Appalachian Mountains to the Mississippi River was increasingly overrun by land-hungry settlers in the late eighteenth and early nineteenth centuries. Control of the Louisiana Territory had passed back and forth between France and Spain during the eighteenth century, but in 1803, the United States acquired rights from France to this vast expanse of land that extended from the Mississippi River to the Rocky Mountains. By the end of the Mexican War in 1848, the United States had not only annexed Texas but also acquired from Mexico the land stretching from Texas and the Rocky Mountains all the way to the Pacific Ocean. With each of these transitions, women faced new challenges to their households and their place in society amid a shifting legal terrain.

INDIAN COUNTRY

At the end of the French and Indian War, the British tried to slow Anglo settlement west of the Appalachian Mountains with the **Proclamation Line of 1763** that designated British territory west of

Eulalia Perez supervised a wide range of activities as a housekeeper in the San Gabriel Mission in California. She knew the importance of her work in not only feeding and clothing the residents of the mission, but in participating in the larger attempts to convert the Native peoples around her to Christianity.

OVERVIEW

Acquisition of Territories by British North America and the United States (1760–1860)

1763	**Treaty of Paris**	British claim control of North America east of the Mississippi River as a result of winning the French and Indian War
1803	**Louisiana Purchase**	The United States acquires territory extending westward from the Mississippi River to the Rocky Mountains from France
1845	**Annexation of Texas**	After eight years of lobbying to join the United States, the Republic of Texas was annexed by John Tyler in one of his last acts as President
1846	**Oregon Territory**	Oregon territory south of the 49th parallel added to the United States as the British give up their competing claims to the territory
1848	**Mexican Cession**	Southwest of the United States, including California, Arizona, New Mexico, and part of Texas acquired in Treaty of Guadalupe Hidalgo at the end of the Mexican War
1853	**Gadsden Purchase**	Purchase of additional Mexican land in the south of New Mexico

Proclamation Line of 1763 Boundary line designating British territory west of the Appalachian Mountains as Indian land.

Indian Country Land in British territory west of the Proclamation Line of 1763 reserved for Indians.

Indian Territory Unorganized territory west of the Mississippi River where Indians were forced to relocate in the 1830s.

the line as **Indian Country** and restricted entry by colonial settlers. Colonists were outraged, and within a few years, the British government was backpedaling on that issue. As the American Revolution unfolded, settlers such as Daniel Boone and his family continued to pour across the Appalachian Mountains, demanding that they not only be allowed to farm the land they found but also be allowed to purchase it. Indian conflicts—from the Cherokee War of 1761 to Pontiac's Uprising in 1763 to the resistance of Indians in the Ohio River Valley during the 1790s—only halted the pressure briefly. Native Americans, including the Iroquois in the North, the Shawnees in the Middle Atlantic, and the Cherokees in the South, were pushed farther westward. United States government representatives negotiated and renegotiated treaties demanding land forfeitures in exchange for both cash and goods that were supposed to acculturate Indians to western ideas of property and family. Protestant missionaries, including Quakers, Baptists, and Methodists, reinforced these ideals in the schools and churches they set up for Indians. This talk of acculturating Native Americans, however self-interested it might have been, collapsed by the 1830s. The government of President Andrew Jackson rejected the possibility of acculturation and demanded the removal of Indians to territories west of the Mississippi River in the newly created **Indian Territory.** As southeastern Indians were forced into Oklahoma during the 1830s, few Indians were left in the areas that had once been designated as Indian Country. For women in many of these tribes, European diplomatic, military, and market pressures changed their status within their households, while missionaries challenged their gender roles.

MAP 4-1 SOUTHERN INDIAN CESSIONS AND REMOVALS 1830S

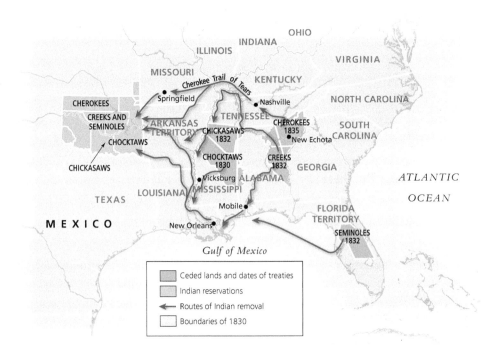

The Choctaws, Chickasaws, Creeks, Cherokees, and Seminoles were pushed off their lands in the southeastern United States during the 1830s and forced to move westward.

Multiple Meanings of Captivity

No women faced greater upheavals in their household status than those who were captured. Both colonial settlers and Indians faced this possibility, though their experiences were quite different.

European women who were captured by Indians during the eighteenth and nineteenth centuries faced terror, hardship, and sometimes death. But if they survived, their story could be published for all to read. Mary Rowlandson's was first (see chapter 2), but even more dramatic stories followed. Hannah Duston, captured by Indians in Haverhill, Massachusetts, in 1692, made her escape after killing ten of her captors while they slept. Her story was told by the famous minister Cotton Mather and retold in the nineteenth century by a succession of writers. Jemima Boone, who was captured by Indians on the Kentucky frontier in 1776, was rescued by her famous father, Daniel, and became a part of the widely read adventures of Daniel Boone written by different authors in later years. The story of Almira and Frances Hall's captivity was used to stir up support for the Black Hawk War in 1832. Other stories became even more sensationalistic in the nineteenth century, drawing on a growing market for popular entertainment.

Captivity narratives, such as this one about Frances and Almira Hall, were ubiquitous in the eighteenth and nineteenth centuries, and often focused on women. They not only provided exciting stories of adventure and spiritual challenges faced by women, but propaganda for various wars against the Indians.

While Rowlandson, Dustin, and Boone were all eager to return to their families, in fact, the outcome of other captivities was somewhat different. Many of the young women captured during the eighteenth century preferred to remain with their captors, even when offered the opportunity to return to the homes of their parents. Eunice Williams was only a child when she was carried off by Indians from her family in Deerfield, Massachusetts, in 1704 and adopted by a Mohawk family near Quebec. Although her family sought to purchase her release, her new Mohawk family refused. Williams eventually converted to Catholicism, married an Indian in the community, and reared her family there. In later years, she visited with her surviving siblings, but she refused to return to the society into which she had been born. Eunice Williams was not all that unusual. In early eighteenth-century New England, a majority of girls between the ages of twelve and twenty-one who were captured stayed with their captors, as did a sizable minority of girls who were under the age of twelve. Some married Indians or Frenchmen who lived nearby. Others converted to Catholicism and entered convents. In both cases, women such as these established households different from those of their mothers.

The outcome of these situations varied not only with the age and gender of the captives but also with the motives of the captors. In some cases, Indians took captives to replace individuals in their families who had died. These captives were often young women and children who were seen as more likely to adapt to their new circumstances than men would. In these cases, young captives often developed strong emotional bonds with their new Indian families and were reluctant to leave. In other cases, Indians took captives with the hope of obtaining ransom money. In those cases, men were as good as women, and the desire to remain with one's captors was much less likely.

Particularly in the South, captivity also began to blur into slavery. As European settlers experimented with different kinds of forced labor on their various plantations, they used the labor of not only African Americans and white indentured servants but also Indian slaves. Although slavery had existed among Indian tribes in the Southeast before the arrival of Europeans, it had generally been a by-product of war. Those captured

*Caroline Parker, a Christianized Seneca In-
dian woman, made the beaded-skirt she wears
in this photograph, taken about 1849. The
bead-work, in particular, distinguishes her
dress from that of other American women of
the time. (From the Arthur C. Parker Collection of Negatives, NYSM/RMSC)*

in battle either lost their freedom or their lives. However, as Indians began to realize that captives could be sold as commodities to Europeans,
some groups attacked others with the specific goal of obtaining captives
for trade—a practice their English clients encouraged. Indian captives
were traded by Europeans as slaves up and down the Atlantic coast and
often shipped to the Caribbean. As a result, far more Indians endured
captivity than did Europeans—and with far more dismal outcomes. Indian women who were sold as slaves into English households did not have
the same opportunities for marriage or religious commitment as did English women taken captive by Indians. They also left behind households
that were changing under the impact of trade and conflict.

Seneca Households: "A Perfect Equality"

Mary Jemison, a young teenager from western Pennsylvania who was
captured by the Shawnees in 1758 and later sold to the Senecas, quickly
came to realize that the power of Seneca women within their households and their communities was different from what she had experienced growing up with her Irish parents. "In the summer season, we
planted, tended and harvested our corn, and generally had all our children with us," she recalled, "but had no master to oversee or drive us, so
that we could work as leisurely as we pleased." Among the Senecas, who
lived in upstate New York as part of the Iroquois League, women continued to control use of the land in the eighteenth century, farming it
while their husbands and fathers hunted and traded animal skins with
the British. In their matrilineal clans, they elected a chief matron each
year who oversaw their farmwork, distributing parcels of land for women
to work and organizing assistance for those who were too sick to cultivate their own
crops. The women also organized their own ritual groups, known as Tonwisas, praying
to the "three sisters" of corn, beans, and squash for good harvests. They held their own
councils and continued to elect male speakers to represent their opinions at the councils held by men. It is little wonder that Henry Dearborn, the adjutant general of Massachusetts in the early nineteenth century, described the Seneca women as acting "on
a perfect equality" with the men in their community. The Seneca household structure,
which allowed women to control the land, provided a basis for their political power.

The world of the Senecas was changing dramatically, however, even as Dearborn
praised the gender equality in their society. The Patriot forces had burned their fields
and villages in 1779, and a smallpox epidemic the following year wreaked even greater
devastation. Trade with the British and Americans had flooded villages with alcohol,
and excessive consumption had undermined the social fabric of the Senecas. Their
population declined from ten thousand to two thousand within a few years.

The impact of this devastation was clear as women struggled to maintain control
of their land and the political voice that went with it. They had lost large amounts of
territory as a result of their support for the British during the Revolution. Even as they
found their territory shrinking, however, Seneca women continued to assert their political voice based on their control of the land. When they wanted their men to engage in peace negotiations with the U.S. government in 1791, they interrupted a
meeting between U.S. officials and the Seneca chiefs, arguing, "You ought to listen to

what we, women shall speak, as well as to the sachems; for we are the owners of this land—and it is ours. . . ." In 1797, faced with poverty, Seneca women agreed to sell even more land to Thomas Morris, who was acting for his wealthy father, the Revolutionary leader Robert Morris. The decision was a contentious one, but his promise that the money for the purchase would go to the women rather than the men carried the day.

While the loss of much of their land represented one threat to the household power exercised by Seneca women, the cultural values promoted by Quaker (and later Baptist) missionaries represented an even more potent challenge. The Quakers, who established a mission among the Senecas in 1789, promoted not only their religious beliefs but their ideas about gender as well. They encouraged men to take over the farming with the use of plows and urged women to devote their time to spinning, weaving, sewing, and house-keeping. They also encouraged men to spread out their farms, to fence off their lands, and to build individual dwellings for their nuclear families. To a certain extent, the move toward smaller dwellings had been under way for the preceding century because the Senecas and other Iroquois had decided that the large longhouses of the seventeenth century and before were too easily attacked. But the move to organize the family around a couple who lived separate from the larger clan of the woman's mother directly under-cut the power that women exercised through their matrilineal and matrilocal house-holds. The changes promoted by the Christian missionaries and government agents split the Senecas into bitter factions. Some families did set up separate houses. Age mattered in these disputes as younger women tended to be the ones most willing to try new ways while older women were at the heart of the resistance movement.

In the midst of these debates, Handsome Lake emerged as the leader of a powerful revitalization movement that directly challenged the power that women had derived from their households. A war leader who fought against the Americans during the Rev-olution, Handsome Lake had drowned his sorrows in alcohol in the years following his defeat in the war. But in 1799, he arose from a drunken stupor and began preaching to the Senecas that they should return to the traditional ways of the longhouse. Yet the longhouse he imagined was a far cry from the household structure that had underlay the power of women in Seneca society. His philosophy, which drew on moral tenets of Christianity, promoted a belief in frugality, temperance, and personal behavior. Most important, though, he attacked the traditional power of women in Seneca society. He urged men to give up hunting for farming, and he urged women to focus on their rela-tionships with their husbands rather than on their bonds with their mothers. Older women who challenged Handsome Lake's notion of "tradition" faced ruthless persecu-tion. Handsome Lake branded them witches, arguing that "The Creator is sad because of the tendency of old women to breed mischief." One older woman was murdered as she worked in her fields, and another was executed after a trial by the council.

As Seneca women entered the nineteenth century, they faced a new world of power relationships in which key aspects of their household authority were transformed. Quaker missionaries, who had promoted European-style households, helped the Senecas retain a small part of their lands in upstate New York during the 1830s and 1840s as most Indian tribes were ruthlessly pushed westward by government forces. The Senecas wrote a new constitution for a representative government in 1848, allowing women and men the right to elect judges and legislators and decreeing that all decisions had to be rati-fied by three quarters of the women as well as three quarters of the men. The Senecas also continued to recognize the economic importance of women's control of the land.

This new constitution limited the earlier power structure rooted in households, but it provided women with a direct vote in their government. The federal government had taken over payment of the annuities due to the Senecas as a result of their land sale to Thomas Morris in 1797, and the government insisted on paying the money to male chiefs. However, the chiefs usually distributed the money to the women, recognizing both the women's original land deal and their continued importance. It is not surprising the memory lived on because, regardless of the new political structure, many of the Seneca women continued to farm.

Shawnee Society and the Incorporation of Strangers

Shawnee women saw their household positions challenged in a somewhat different way from the Senecas as their territory in the Ohio River Valley switched from French to British and then American control. Like Seneca women, they faced criticism from men in their society as their tribe struggled for survival amidst an onslaught of Europeans. For Shawnee women, however, criticism focused on their role of incorporating European men into their households.

Shawnee women exercised their political voice both through the women who were their War Chiefs and the women who were their Peace (or civil) Chiefs. These political roles gave women who held them more status than anything they could have gained in marriage. The Peace Chiefs supervised the crops women grew, they counseled war parties against fighting, and they adopted prisoners of war to replace members of their villages who had died. The War Chiefs, on the other hand, prepared the meat that men hunted and welcomed war parties back into their villages, including the "good meat" men brought in the form of prisoners. Some of the prisoners were, in fact, burned to death and ritually consumed by the tribe.

Shawnee women not only adopted prisoners of war into their society but also incorporated European men into their households through marriage or more temporary relationships. This process of incorporation had worked well with French traders, who adopted Shawnee ways. The British gained control of Shawnee territory in 1763, after the French and Indian War, however, and the Shawnees had to shift their trade from the French to the English. British traders were not so easily incorporated. They would live with Shawnee women, but they were less likely than the French to use that relationship to enter into Indian culture. The gifts of reciprocity that were supposed to accompany these sexual relationships began to change. In earlier times, a piece of meat or a blanket that the woman could use would have been considered the appropriate gift; but British traders sometimes offered women rum, which the women resold to the men in their communities. This introduction of monetary profit into sexual relationships brought protests from Shawnee men and concerns about prostitution. Moreover, close on the heels of English traders were British settlers. These men came with their own wives and were anxious to own and farm Indian land rather than to set up networks of trade. The powers of incorporation that Shawnee women had exercised in earlier years faltered in the face of these new developments.

Compounding these problems, the Shawnees lost lands to the British and then Americans both before and after the Revolution. Their hunting lands were not only severely reduced in size but also depopulated of deer and beaver as a result of overkilling. White settlers who lived near the hunting grounds exacerbated the situation when they demanded that the Indians no longer burn the forests, a strategy necessary to create new growth that would draw deer for feeding. Shawnee villages divided over how to respond to these pressures, and village chiefs sometimes sold land to American settlers whether they had the right to or not because they feared another village chief would do so if they did not.

In the midst of this crisis, a revitalization movement developed among the Shawnees, just as it had among the Senecas. Visions of a return to earlier ways had begun with the dreams of several Indian women. One old woman bluntly told the hunters that their game had disappeared because they were imitating whites, and she commanded them: "You are to live again as you lived before the white people came into this land." Another woman had a vision that demanded an end to "evil, fornication, stealing, murder, and the like." But the most influential prophet was Tenskwatawa, brother of the powerful military leader Tecumseh and himself a failed shaman and alcoholic. In 1805, Tenskwatawa urged his followers to reject the culture they had created through exchange with Europeans: the alcohol, the clothing, the weapons, and the tools. He urged them to slaughter their cattle and other domesticated animals and to once again share the land in common.

Like Handsome Lake, however, Tenskwatawa deviated from his commitment to the past when it came to gender relationships and household structure. He demanded that men and women adopt new gender roles rather than adhering to the old. Men were to farm, not women, he explained. Even more important, women should be subordinate to men. Finally, women were to stop intermarrying with Europeans. Those "who were living with White Men was to be brought home to their friends and relatives, and their children to be left with their Fathers, so that nations might become genuine Indian." The role that women had played in incorporating European men into their societies through marriage was reviled rather than valued, and the significance of those households for female power was challenged as the Shawnees struggled to survive in the nineteenth century.

Inheritance and Power among the Cherokee

Cherokee women found their positions of power within their households challenged as they negotiated first with the British and then with the United States. Nancy Ward, a powerful Cherokee War Woman, traveled with men from her village to meet with officials of the United States in 1781 to negotiate a peace treaty. "You know that women are always looked upon as nothing," she told the startled commissioners; "but we are your mothers; you are our sons. Our cry is all for peace; let it continue. This peace must last forever. Let your women's sons be ours; our sons be yours. Let your women hear our words." Originally born Nan-ye-hi, Ward had first married a Cherokee warrior, and after his death, a British trader. Moving between the worlds of the Europeans and the Cherokees, she knew that motherhood was a powerful ideal for the Americans she was confronting; but Ward came from a world in which motherhood had different meanings. Inheritance passed through a mother's direct line, and women like Ward had acted as cultural go-betweens in their marriages to French and British traders. As was the case with other Indian groups, their powers in a matrilineal society were challenged by the demands they faced from Americans.

Cherokee women had experienced many changes in their world during the eighteenth century, changes that affected both their economic status and their political power. They had become the anchors of village life, as their men were gone for increasingly long periods of time hunting the animals they needed for trade with the British. Access to land and other goods continued to pass through the female line,

W**OMEN'S** V**OICES**

A CHEROKEE LEADER

Nancy Ward, a Cherokee War Woman whose life spanned the eighteenth and early nineteenth centuries, first married a Cherokee warrior and later a British trader. She was active in promoting interactions of the Cherokees with the British and later with their successors in the United States.

June 30, 1818

Beloved Children,

We have called a meeting among ourselves to consult on the different points now before the council, relating to our national affairs. We have heard with painful feelings that the bounds of the land we now possess are to be drawn into very narrow limits. The land was given to us by the Great Spirit above as our common right, to raise our children upon, & to make support for our rising generations. We therefore humbly petition our beloved children, the head men & warriors, to hold out to the last in support of our common rights, as the Cherokee nation have been the first settlers of this land; we therefore claim the right of the soil.

We well remember that our country was formerly very extensive, but by repeated sales it has become circumscribed to the very narrow limits we have at present. Our Father the President advised us to become farmers, to manufacture our own clothes, & to have our children instructed. To this advice we have attended in every thing as far as we were able. Now the thought of us being compelled to remove [to] the other side of the Mississippi is dreadful to us, because it appears to us that we, by this removal, shall be brought to a savage state again, for we have, by the endeavor of our Father the President, become too much enlightened to throw aside the privileges of a civilized life.

We therefore unanimously join in our meeting to hold our country in common as hitherto.

Some of our children have become Christians. We have missionary schools among us. We have heard the gospel in our nation. We have become civilized and enlightened, & are in hopes that in a few years our nation will be prepared for instruction in other branches of sciences & arts, which are both useful and necessary in civilized society.

There are some white men among us who have been raised in this country from their youth, are connected with us by marriage, & have considerable families, who are very active in encouraging the emigration of our nation. These ought to be our truest friends but prove our worst enemies. They seem to be only concerned how to increase their riches, but do not care what becomes of our Nation, nor even of their own wives and children.

Cherokee Women and Nancy Ward

Source: *Karen L. Kilcup, ed., "Petition of Nancy Ward and Other Cherokee Women to the United States Congress, 1818,"* Native American Women's Writing, 1800–1924: An Anthology, *(Malden, MA: Blackwell, 2000), 29–30.*

Questions

1. How do Nancy Ward and the other Indian women use the language of motherhood and family to make their case against Indian removal?

2. How do Nancy Ward and the other Indian women show a knowledge of American values in defending themselves and their lands?

though differences in individual wealth were not great. Indeed, in most cases of polygamy, a man married two sisters so that he was only part of one clan, and his wives had control of both the children and property produced in the marriage. Unlike women of other tribes who traveled with the hunt and who faced a growing burden of work in preparing the ever-increasing number of hides, Cherokee women did not significantly alter their workload. They continued to farm while the men hunted. However, because they were not directly engaged in the trade with the British, women also became increasingly dependent on the men of their villages for the goods that were acquired from Europe. By the end of the eighteenth century, for example, Cherokee women made their clothes almost exclusively from the manufactured fabrics acquired through trade.

Even more significant, Cherokee women lost political power as the British demanded that the Cherokees adopt a more centralized political structure. Cherokee politics had been rooted in villages where both men and women found it easy to express their opinions. The British, however, found it difficult to conduct negotiations with one village after another and pressured the Cherokees to hold their councils in one centralized spot. Men had to travel great distances to attend these political gatherings, and women, as guardians of the villages, were left behind, losing a crucial opportunity to debate important issues.

As the eighteenth century drew to a close, the U.S. government urged Cherokee men to farm individual plots of land and women to spin, joining the republic as independent yeoman farmers and virtuous housewives. Cherokee women welcomed the government agents and missionaries who taught them how to make cloth as many of them tried their hand at spinning. However, most women continued to farm as well, sharing land that was held in common by the village. This was just as well, because many men refused to take on what they considered "women's work." Some men did begin to herd domesticated animals. Others, however, either rented farmland to poor whites or used African American slaves to do the farmwork for them. Rather than becoming virtuous yeomen, these Cherokee men opted for a life as landlords or masters.

Many of the Cherokees who adopted these new roles were themselves the bicultural products of marriages between European traders and Cherokee women. Because their mothers were Cherokees, they were accepted as full members of the matrilineal clans, but their fathers conveyed to them both wealth and European cultural values that challenged traditional Cherokee mores. European fathers who had accumulated wealth in their trading activities not only had greater sums to convey to their heirs than did most Cherokees but also were unwilling to see their wealth passed on to their wives' families (as matrilineal customs dictated) rather than to their own children. Thus, in addition to introducing new cultural values, European men and their children provided an important constituency agitating for new laws that were more consistent with the republican form of government created and promoted by the United States. Christian missionaries, who had set up schools and churches among the Cherokees, provided further support for these changes.

As the state government of Georgia attempted to take over Cherokees lands, the Cherokees strove to establish their political legitimacy by creating their own republic. The Cherokees ratified a constitution in 1827, which resulted in a new political order that undermined the matrilineal organization of the Cherokees and attacked the power of women generally. Modeling their government on that of the United States in the hope that this proof of "civilization" would undercut attempts to seize Cherokee lands in Georgia and other parts of the Southeast, the new Cherokee government was divided into three branches, with courts, a legislature, and a chief. Cherokee men sat on the courts, replacing the leadership role women had exercised in determining the fate of captives or demanding vengeance. The National Council passed laws creating a social order that more closely conformed to that of the United States. The council outlawed polygamy and promoted nuclear families headed by a father. The children of Cherokee men who married non-Cherokee women were granted membership in the Cherokee Nation, opening up access to the community through the father as well as through the mother. These laws complemented the one that had been passed in 1825, dictating that if a man died without leaving a will, his property would be divided among his children and spouse rather than being directed to the wife's clan. The only laws that were passed protecting women's power came with the creation of several married women's property laws. In part to protect women (and the Cherokee Nation) from unscrupulous traders who sometimes married Cherokee women to gain access to their property, these laws recognized the right of married women to own their own property and shielded them from having to forfeit their property to pay their husbands' debts.

Probably no group went further than the Cherokees in their attempts to adopt the values of "civilization" promoted by the U.S. government. Yet, in the end, it gained them little as settlers from the East pressured them for their lands and the federal gov-

As this twentieth century painting makes clear, the Trail of Tears involved the massive uprooting of families throughout the southeastern United States.

ernment abandoned talk of acculturating Indians into the republic. Even women such as Nancy Ward, who had worked so hard to promote cultural as well as economic exchanges between Europeans and Cherokees, began to urge resistance. She and other Cherokee women signed a petition in 1817 urging the men of their council to not cede any more lands. Women submitted another petition in 1818. When the U.S. Congress passed the **Indian Removal Act** in 1830, Cherokee women again protested their loss of land. The Cherokees successfully challenged the Act in the Supreme Court, but Andrew Jackson refused to support the ruling. By 1838, sixteen thousand Cherokee women and men were forced westward to Oklahoma on the infamous **Trail of Tears.** Chin Deenawash lost her husband and all three of her children on the trip. Aggie Silk remembered the hardships of the long march and the frustrations that came with trying to survive. "When they got too sick to walk or ride, they were put in the wagons, and taken along until they died. The Indian Doctors couldn't find the herbs they were used to and didn't know the ones they did find, so they couldn't doctor them as they would have at home."

For Cherokee women, as for other Native American women, the demands of the American government that they adopt the gender roles of western culture cost them dearly. Those who did acculturate were still forced from their lands in most cases. More important, women had lost the power in their households that had given them a forceful voice in governance and in the creation of their societies.

SLAVERY AND FREEDOM IN LOUISIANA

The experiences of Seneca, Shawnee, and Cherokee women suggest the ways in which indigenous North American households were being transformed as a result of contact with Europeans. However, these were not the only kinds of changes that affected the status of women. In the Louisiana Territory, a growing European population that was predominantly male relied on slavery and the racial coding of inhabitants to create new kinds of households. As the Louisiana Territory shifted from French to Spanish to American control, African American and Indian women, in particular, recalculated their positions within households along with their opportunities for freedom in the shifting legal structure.

The Louisiana Territory was a vast expanse of land stretching from the Mississippi River to the Rocky Mountains, including New Orleans and St. Louis on its eastern end and brushing up against the outskirts of Santa Fe on its western end. France claimed much of the territory in the first half of the eighteenth century but ceded control to Spain in 1763 after losing the French and Indian War. The Spanish secretly returned the territory to France in 1800, and in 1803 France sold rights to the land to the United States. The following year, President Thomas Jefferson commissioned Captain Meriwether Lewis and Captain William Clark, both officers in the U.S. army, to explore this new acquisition. The famous expedition lasted for over two years and involved a trek from St. Louis to the Pacific Ocean. Guiding the men was a French trader, Toussaint Charbonneau, and one of his Indian wives, Sacagawea, a fifteen-year-old girl whom he had acquired as a slave. Sacagawea's status as both wife and slave suggests the kind of complicated household relationships that had evolved for some women in the Louisiana Territory.

Indian Removal Act
Act passed by both houses of Congress in 1830 allowing the president to negotiate treaties that would exchange Indian lands east of the Mississippi River for new territory west of the Mississippi.

Trail of Tears Westward journey of sixteen thousand Cherokee Indians from Georgia to Oklahoma in 1838.

MAP 4-2 LOUISIANA PURCHASE

The Louisiana Purchase more than doubled the size of the United States.

The Traffic in Women

French traders arrived in the Red River Valley, along the Texas and Louisiana border, early in the eighteenth century. Their trade centered on animal skins, horses, and slaves, for which they gave the Indians guns and other products manufactured in Europe. The French were happy to trade with any Native Americans who were willing, but the alliances of various Indian tribes in the region dictated that those trading partners would be Caddos, Comanches, and Wichitas but not the Lipan Apaches, whom these other tribes opposed.

As was the case farther north, French traders cemented their trading partnerships with Indian tribes through their relationships to women (see chapter 2). Thus Caddo women married to French traders gained status as go-betweens, facilitating deals made by the men. However, the French also sought Indian slave women for their households, both to satisfy their sexual desires and to do domestic work. The Caddos, the

WOMEN'S LIVES

SACAGAWEA

Sacagawea's life took her on one of the most famous journeys across the United States and embodied the ambiguities of status that many Indian women encountered in the trade that developed in the frontier regions of North America. Thus, Meriwether Lewis referred to her as both the wife and the slave of the French trapper Toussaint Charbonneau. Sacagawea had been born into a Shoshone Indian family toward the end of the eighteenth century, around 1790. As was the custom among the Shoshones, she was betrothed by her father to an older man when she was still a child. However, before Sacagawea could marry, she was captured by the Hidatsas at about the age of twelve. The Hidatsas sold her as a slave to a French trader, Charbonneau. In 1805, she bore Charbonneau a son, Jean Baptiste. By that time, Charbonneau had been hired as one of two interpreters for the expedition planned by Meriwether Lewis and William Clark from the Missouri River across the Continental Divide to the Pacific Ocean. Two months after the birth of her child, Sacagawea set off with Charbonneau as the only woman on the expedition. Charbonneau left behind his other teenage Shoshone slave, perhaps because it would be difficult for her to transport their son, who was a toddler, who would not be as easily carried as Sacagawea's new baby.

Sacagawea assisted with cooking and laundry on the trip; however, even more important were her abilities to find food and to translate. At times when the men were unable to find game from hunting, Sacagawea's ability to find roots and berries proved critical. As the expedition approached and reached Shoshone lands, Sacagawea provided important information about the terrain, served as the chief interpreter for Lewis and Clark,

and made sure they demonstrated their peaceful intentions by painting the cheeks of those they met with red paint.

Sacagawea's meeting with the Shoshones was a bittersweet experience for her, one that brought her back into contact with her family even as it underscored her distance from them. She was overjoyed to discover her brother, who by that time had become an important leader among the Shoshones. When she realized who he was, she "ran and embraced him, throwing over him her blanket, and weeping profusely." Her brother, while pleased to see her, was more circumspect. Sacagawea discovered from him that most of their family had died. The man she was supposed to marry had two other wives and once he realized she had a child by another man no longer wanted her. Although she had found her home after being gone for many years, there seemed to be no place

(continued)

for her and no move among her remaining family members to bring her back. She had little choice but to continue on with Lewis and Clark and Charbonneau. However, Sacagawea had also become engaged with the quest to push forward to the Pacific Ocean. Lewis and Clark had not planned to take her that far, but when she discovered she was to be left behind for the final trek Sacagawea spoke up. According to Lewis, "The poor woman stated very earnestly that she had traveled a great way with us to see the great water, yet she had never been down to the coast. . . . So reasonable a request could not be denied." Although her choices in life were limited, she directed where she could.

After returning from the trip across the West, Lewis and Clark parted from Charbonneau and Sacagawea, after paying Charbonneau five hundred dollars for his services and later wondering if they should have rewarded Sacagawea more as well. What happened to her after that point is less clear. She might have died six years later as a result of a "putrid fever." The clerk at Fort Manuel on the Missouri River reported that Charbonneau's Shoshone wife had died at the fort in 1812. Because Charbonneau had more than one Shoshone wife, it might not have been Sacagawea. Some Shoshones on the Wind River Indian Reservation claim she came to settle there in 1871 with her sons Bazil and Baptiste, dying in 1884. ■

Comanches, and the Wichitas captured slaves as part of their ongoing warfare with the Lipan Apaches in Texas. Realizing that slave women were a valuable commodity, these tribes increased their raids on the Lipan Apaches and solidified their trading relationships with the French through this exchange.

It was only after the Spanish began to govern the Louisiana Territory in 1769 that the fortunes of Apache women began to change. Indian slavery was not legal in New Spain. Although the Spanish government ignored the enslavement of Indian women elsewhere in its empire, Louisiana was a different story. These women were being exchanged for guns and ammunition that Indians used to fight the Spanish in Texas and New Mexico. Spanish authorities were eager to end this trade and so quickly reminded inhabitants that Spanish law prohibited the enslavement of Indians and requested that residents holding such slaves register them. Many Apache women who had been held in bondage were freed. In some cases, French owners married their slave women at the same time that they freed them. Ana Maria, an Apache woman who had been the slave of François Morvant, became his wife. Similarly, Françoise, another Indian captive, became the wife of her former owner, Pierre Raimond. While some of these women who were freed may have wanted to marry their former masters, it is not clear that all did. Some women may have simply been forced to exchange one form of legal servitude for another. One eighteen-year-old Apache woman, for example, did not marry her master after he freed her but, rather, signed an agreement that she would continue working for him.

Far fewer Indian women than African women were enslaved during the eighteenth century, and their percentage of the slave population declined even more dramatically after the Spanish took over the territory. However, even into the nineteenth century, some Indian women continued to be held as slaves in the Louisiana Territory. Sacagawea's experience, farther north, is a clear example of that continuing tradition.

New Orleans and Urban Slavery

Just as Indian women—both slave and free—were important participants in the French households of the Red River region, African women were important to the French households of New Orleans. African slaves had been brought to New Orleans beginning in 1719, shortly after the city was founded. By the time New Orleans was incorporated into the United States in 1803, slaves constituted 40 percent of the rapidly growing population of eight thousand people. More of these slaves were female than male precisely because so many slaves were used for domestic work.

Slave women were also laundresses and seamstresses, sometimes working directly for their owners but at other times hiring themselves out and remitting at least part of their earnings to their masters. Other slave women carried baskets of food or dry goods on their hips and heads as they went door-to-door with products from their owners' stores. They sold vegetables they had raised on their own plots, either keeping the profit or splitting it with their masters. These opportunities for wage work, combined with the widespread participation of slave women in the marketing of local goods, meant that slave women in cities were much more likely to accumulate capital than were slave women living on plantations.

Slave women in New Orleans sometimes used that money to set up their own households, independent from their masters; but even more important, they used it to buy their freedom. Purchasing freedom under French law had not been easy, but it was possible. A master had to initiate the process and agree to it, but it was possible for a slave to purchase her freedom. By 1769, when the Spanish officially began to govern, 7 percent of New Orleans was made up of these **libres.** Spanish law, however, offered far more opportunities for purchasing freedom. The Spanish practice of **coartacion** allowed slaves to purchase their freedom if they wished, even if their masters opposed the sale. The slave woman had to be assessed to determine her economic value, but once her price was agreed upon, she could gain her freedom if she produced the money for her purchase. Under Spanish law, slaves also had the right to own property. Thus, although it was difficult, some slaves were able to acquire enough capital to purchase themselves. Maria Luisa, for example, was able to purchase her own freedom and that of her four children in 1772 for a cost of five hundred pesos. When women could not muster enough resources to pay for the freedom of themselves and their children, they would remain in slavery while purchasing the freedom of their children; as Margarita did when she paid her master two hundred pesos to buy the freedom of her two-year-old son, Pedro. Thus, slave women in New Orleans constructed households that were complicated by a variety of different legal obligations between parent and child, but they had greater autonomy than slave women in the British colonies and in the new United States.

Once the United States took control of New Orleans, these self purchases became far more difficult. The Black Code of 1806 forbade the **manumission** of slaves under the age of thirty and required those who became emancipated after that time to leave the state. Some slaves still managed to become free, such as Marie, a slave of Jean Baptiste Laporte, who was guaranteed the right to purchase her freedom when she was sold to him in 1827. However, by then, slavery was becoming a much less important mode of labor, associated more with the plantation agriculture that lay outside of New Orleans than with the domestic service in city households. As the population of New Orleans boomed

libre Freed slaves and free persons of color in Louisiana Territory, particularly New Orleans.

coartacion Ability of a slave to purchase his or her freedom under Spanish law.

manumission Granting of freedom to a slave.

during the antebellum period, reaching over 100,000 by 1840 and 168,000 by 1860, the percentage of slaves living in New Orleans declined dramatically, constituting only 23 percent of the population in 1840 and 8 percent in 1860. Almost exclusively employed as servants, the slave population, which had always been predominantly female, became increasingly so. By 1850, there were three slave women for every two slave men living in New Orleans.

Gens de Couleur Libre

In large part because so many slaves were able to purchase their freedom during the period of Spanish control, these libres became a large and relatively prosperous part of the New Orleans population. By 1805, when the United States took over governing the territory, libres constituted one-third of the African American population in New Orleans and about 30 percent of the free population. As was the case with the slave population, this was also a group that was predominantly female, with approximately three women for every two men. While many of these women had purchased their freedom during the years of Spanish control, others had been freed by their masters as a result of long-standing sexual relationships. Among the white population, men had outnumbered women by a significant percentage, and men in the city turned to African women rather than Indian women to compensate for the dearth of European women. Indeed, although marriage between Europeans and Africans was forbidden, during the period of Spanish rule it was possible to petition for exemptions and some couples did. As a result, interracial households existed more openly in New Orleans than in other areas of North America.

Libres acquired not only freedom in New Orleans but also property, though usually not without hard work. At the end of the eighteenth century, most of the female libre household heads were either laundresses or seamstresses, though a few were shopkeepers or ran boarding houses and taverns. Carlota Derneville, for example, purchased her freedom from her father, Don Pedro Henrique Derneville, in 1773 and the freedom of her son Carlos from Santiago Landreau in 1775. During the last quarter of the eighteenth century, she not only ran a tavern but also owned several houses that she rented out. Prudencia Cheval, was even luckier. Although she worked as a seamstress, she acquired much of her property through inheritance when her father, Don Francisco Cheval, left her and her two children his entire estate, including a large house. Cheval was able to rent the top floor to a prominent city resident to supplement her income in dressmaking.

The growing number of libres in New Orleans began to create their own culture by the end of the eighteenth century, partially in response to growing discrimination by the white population. Libre women, many of whom were so light-skinned they could be mistaken for white, were required to wear a "tignon" beginning in 1786. These kerchiefs were often worn by slave women in the markets and thus were meant to identify libres with the slave rather than the free population of the city. Libre women responded by turning their tignons into fancy and fashionable headdresses, sometimes adorned by jewels and feathers. In the theaters, churches, and dance halls of the 1790s, nonwhites also were increasingly segregated from whites whether they were free or slave. Libres responded by creating their own public spaces and social events. Second- and third-generation libres also became increasingly more likely to intermarry and set up their own households, rather than forming unions (either formal or informal) with slaves or free whites. This movement was encouraged once the U.S. government took over New Orleans and libres were legally forbidden from marrying either free whites or slaves, a restriction on household formation that was meant to strengthen the racial hierarchy in the city, bringing it more in line with the rest of the United States.

These legal restrictions were particularly problematic for libre women, who outnumbered libre men. With this continuing imbalance in sex ratios, the custom of **plaçage** emerged among some families in the libre community. Plaçage was not a marriage, but it was a legal relationship. Young white men of means met fair-skinned libre women at cotillions such as the Bal de Cordon Bleu, where mothers carefully supervised their daughters' interactions with the young men. When a plaçage was arranged, the man was expected to provide both a house and financial support for the young woman. Such relationships could end when the young man married, though sometimes they did not, but in either case, the young woman gained some amount of financial independence as a result of her relationship. However, increasingly restrictive laws about racial mixing forced women into households that deviated from the socially respectable norms of legal marriage.

Although the Spanish government in New Orleans legally mandated that all African-American women wear tignons as a way of distinguishing them from the free white population in the late eighteenth century, the women made the headdresses a fashionable accessory that could convey beauty and dignity.

WESTERN FRONTIERS

Women farther west also had to face shifting laws as different countries vied for control of their lands. During the eighteenth century, the northern provinces of the Spanish Empire were both vast and weak. Inhabited by a few settlers, Texas, New Mexico, and California were valued primarily as buffers that protected the provinces farther south. This was a goal that was becoming increasingly difficult to achieve as nomadic Indian bands relying on horses and hunting pressed the Spanish outposts. The acquisition of Louisiana in the 1760s, however, reenergized the Spanish to expand their colonizing efforts in other areas of the North. They aggressively established missions in California and brokered peace treaties with the Comanches and (less successfully) with the Apaches in Texas. By the beginning of the nineteenth century, Spanish settlers had established large ranches in the Rio Grande River Valley of Texas, expanded trading networks in New Mexico, and created flourishing mission farmlands in California. Although each of these areas operated under Spanish and then Mexican law into the nineteenth century, their patterns of settlement and the kinds of households they established varied with each region. As a result, women in Texas, New Mexico, and California operated within very different systems of household power. Some of women's legal rights in these areas would be retained by the Anglo settlers who began moving westward in large numbers during the 1820s, even as Anglo women maintained a strong attachment to the domestic ideals they had brought with them.

plaçage Relationship in which a white man legally agreed to support a libre woman as part of an ongoing sexual relationship.

Texas: The Challenges of Settlement

Spanish settlement of Texas began early in the eighteenth century as an attempt to defend Spanish borders from French incursions but never surpassed a few thousand settlers. By the end of the eighteenth century, there were less than three thousand settlers

Tejanos/Tejanas Men and women of Spanish heritage who settled in Texas.

who spoke Spanish living in Texas (and this figure includes Christianized Indians). Many of these **Tejanos-Tejanas** lived on large cattle ranches around San Antonio or along the Rio Grande. Spanish women first came as wives of soldiers, who were granted land in recognition of their service. Some wives became quite active assisting their husbands in the ranching operations that developed, taking over for them if they died. Rosa Maria Hinojosa de Balli, for example, owned close to one-third of the lower Rio Grande Valley at the end of the eighteenth century.

presidio Spanish military garrison.

By 1720, the Spanish sought to expand their influence to the northeastern part of Texas, building both missions and **presidios** close to the same Red River Valley area that also attracted French traders. They sent a handful of missionaries, some soldiers, and a few women to these outposts, hoping to convert the Caddo Indians in the area to a life of Christianity under Spanish rule. The Spanish were far less successful than the French were in their overtures to the Indians, not only because they refused to trade guns but also because they refused to marry Caddo Indian women, whom they regarded as heathen. While Spanish soldiers had a long tradition of establishing relationships with indigenous women, most of those relationships were with Christianized Indians. Their lack of interaction with Caddo women was compounded by the failure of the Spanish men to bring enough of their own women to their settlements. The Caddos had little respect for Spanish men who engaged in what the Caddos viewed as the womanly tasks of farming. Moreover, without enough women, the Spanish were unable to maintain their household property or to extend hospitality to their Caddo neighbors.

While the Spanish did not establish successful alliances with Indians in Texas through intermarriage, female captivity did play into their diplomatic strategies. Throughout the eighteenth century, the Spanish struggled to broker alliances with the different Indian tribes who dominated Texas. Both the Indians and the Spanish recognized that the return of loved ones who had been captured by hostile forces could signal peaceful intentions in diplomatic negotiations and pave the way for a diplomatic alliance. In some cases, Indians offered to return Spanish women whom they had obtained through trade to provincial officers with whom they were negotiating. Spanish officials made similar offers of Indian women they had acquired.

Into the nineteenth century, however, the Indians continued to have the upper hand in Texas, as the Comanches, in particular, sought to protect their extensive buffalo territory from encroaching settlers. When Mexico gained independence from Spain in 1821, the fledgling government responded to the problem of the sparsely settled province of Texas—and the fear of Indian raids—by establishing formal agreements with **empressarios** from the United States who promised to bring settlers into the territory in exchange for large grants of land. The most famous of these agreements, but not the only one, was with Moses Austin and his son Stephen, providing a large tract of land between the Colorado and Brazos rivers. The settlers were supposed to become Catholics and citizens of Mexico, thus strengthening the newly established government of Mexico; but most of the new arrivals resisted these requirements. The terms of the land grants also strongly encouraged the immigration of families rather than individuals. Heads of household received 4,428 acres of pasture for ranching at a price of thirty dollars, four times the amount of land available to single men. In a move to promote cultural ties to Mexico, the laws gave men who married Tejana women additional allotments of land. Not surprisingly, by 1836, thirty thousand men and women, particularly from the southern states, left behind failed businesses, lost jobs,

empressarios Agents who brought parties of immigrant settlers from the United States to Texas.

and infertile land to seek new lives in Texas, overwhelming the population of Mexicans living in the province.

Some of the new arrivals pushed south in Texas, where Tejano settlements such as San Antonio were concentrated, and married into prosperous Tejano families, thus expanding both their political and economic opportunities through their new connections. Most others, however, settled farther north and had far less interaction with the Tejano community, regarding the Catholicism and mixed ethnic heritage of Tejano settlers with suspicion. Settlers to the north preserved a stronger Anglo culture, though with some significant variations. Single settlers usually came from Protestant backgrounds and felt little desire to be married by a Catholic priest, even if one could be found. Eager to gain the land grants that were available to household heads, however, many engaged in a substitute for marriage that had been created by Stephen Austin in 1824 as a response to the lack of priests available to perform marriages. Couples who signed a formal contract indicating their intention to marry, stipulating that they would pay a penalty if they reneged on their promise, were considered to be married. These **bond marriages,** which were usually accompanied by great festivities and a ceremony in front of the town commissioner, not only offered couples access to the larger land grants but also were easily dissolved if the relationship did not work out.

bond marriage Legal agreement to marry that was used as a substitute for marriage in the early days of settlement in Texas.

Anglo women who moved into Texas during the period of Mexican rule received the same property rights as Tejana women, and they used them. Under Spanish law, women were entitled to retain the property they brought into a marriage and also had the right to half the property acquired during the marriage. Married as well as single women ran shops and restaurants and hotels in towns, handling business accounts and banking transactions. They also supervised their ranches and negotiated contracts when their husbands were absent. Indeed, Anglo women were probably called upon to take over for their husbands more than Tejana women were because many of the Anglo men traveled for business purposes, leaving their wives to take care of their homesteads.

The huge Anglo influx from the United States quickly tipped the balance of power toward the newcomers, who fought for control of Texas in a war of independence from Mexico in 1836. Women's property rights were preserved after Texas became an independent republic. Recognizing the importance of the formation of households in the settlement process, legislators argued that given the blood and sweat women had poured into building their homesteads, they deserved to keep them. These property rights were important not only for married women and widows but for divorced women as well. In the new republic of Texas, judges routinely awarded wives half of the community property from their marriages and all of the property they had brought into their marriages, even if the wife was judged to be the guilty party in the divorce. Repeatedly, the judges indicated that the women had earned this property and they deserved to keep it. As Texas became first an independent republic in 1836 and then a U.S. state in 1845, community property laws were privileged over the British common-law traditions that would have transferred landholdings to the husband, creating an important variation in the kind of power U.S. women held within their households.

New Mexico Women and Trading Networks

Unlike the case in Texas, neither Spain nor Mexico needed Anglo women to gain control of New Mexico. The Spanish reasserted control over the province of New Mexico between 1692 and 1696, about a decade after the Pueblo Revolt (see chapter 2).

During the eighteenth century, the Pueblo Indian population dropped to almost half the size it had been in the seventeenth century, finally leveling off at between eight thousand and ten thousand people. Under Spanish domination, the Pueblo tribes increasingly shifted from matrilineal to patrilineal societies. While the Pueblo population stabilized during the eighteenth century, the Spanish population grew. By 1760, seventy-five hundred Spanish settlers were spread throughout New Mexico; and by 1800, the population had reached twenty thousand. This population grew particularly during the last two decades of the eighteenth century after the Spanish government abolished many of the trade and travel restrictions that had existed in the northern province, fueling an expansion of entrepreneurial activity and farming.

Spanish women who migrated to the area often showed the same entrepreneurial skills as their husbands. Gertrudis Barcelo became the owner of one of the most successful gambling operations in Santa Fe. When necessary, she used the courts to pursue her financial interests, as did other women such as Manuela Baca and Ursula Chavez. Often these women were in business with their husbands, but their economic independence was clear in the many legal transactions they carried out. Indeed, in some cases, they used the courts to remind their husbands of their legal rights in business deals. Francisca Romero sued her husband for using her burro to pay a gambling debt, and Gregoria Quintana hauled her husband into court for selling her grain mill without consulting her.

Spanish households on the New Mexican frontier also expanded with the widespread acquisition of Indian slaves. Although holding Indians as slaves was illegal in New Spain, rescuing them was not. In a thinly veiled set of laws that allowed Indian slavery to exist, the Spanish government urged its colonial settlers to redeem slaves by purchasing them, baptizing them, and then allowing them to work off their purchase price through years of servitude to their Spanish masters. Purchased at trade fairs or in individual exchanges, women were preferred over men and cost twice as much. Most of the Indian women who were acquired this way ended up as domestic servants, though definitions of household responsibility could be expansive. Certainly they possessed the abilities to farm, so that some of them may have taken on extensive agricultural chores. In other cases, women produced items for trade. Navajo slave women, in particular, became famous for producing woven blankets. Combining Mexican traditions with those of the Navajos, their watertight "slave blankets" were woven on an upright loom rather than on the horizontal type used by Mexicans but used Mexican dyes and a Mexican diamond pattern.

genizaros and genizaras Male and female Indian captives held as slaves in New Mexico.

As many as three thousand **genizaros and genizaras** (Indian slaves) entered New Mexican households through this strategy of rescue, creating what would eventually become a lower caste. As in so many other frontier societies, genizaras sometimes became concubines of their masters or were subjected to abuse by other Spanish men in their households. Their children, however, became an increasingly significant percentage of the Spanish population in New Mexico. As the children of genizaras gained independence from the families that had purchased their mothers, they often were encouraged to settle in outlying areas of the New Mexican frontier where they might create communities that would serve as military buffers between Mexican settlements and the Indian population. These communities were not only military buffers but also cultural ones in which New Mexican genizaros traded and intermarried with their Indian neighbors. The villages they created proved to be strongholds of resistance to both the Mexican government, when it tried to impose new taxes, and the U.S. government as

WOMEN'S LIVES

GERTRUDIS BARCELO

Gertrudis Barcelo, was born into a wealthy Mexican family in 1800 and moved to Albuquerque while still a child. A well-educated and independent woman, she married in 1823; soon after, she and her husband set up a gambling hall near the mining camps of Santa Fe. Clearly comfortable making contracts and managing her own property, Barcelo set up a more opulent operation in Santa Fe a few years later.

Gertrudis Barcelo's saloon brought together the cultures of New Mexico and the United States during the tumultuous time period when trade routes converged in Santa Fe and the Mexican War had resulted in the transfer of half of Mexico to the United States. The main room of her saloon was large and lined with folded mattresses that served as couches when the gambling tables were set up but that could easily be pushed out of the way to accommodate music and dancing as well. La Tules, as she was also known, usually presided over the central table, maintaining her reputation as the best monte dealer in the area. As one observer noted, "The cards fell from her fingers as steadily as though she were handling only a knitting needle." Merchants from St. Louis and American soldiers mingled with Mexican men and women at Barcelo's saloon during the 1840s.

During the Mexican War, Barcelo and her husband had sided with the United States. Barcelo had relayed critical information to the Americans and had even lent money to the troops so that they could provision themselves. However, Americans were not flattering in their descriptions of Barcelo. Her business abilities were viewed with suspicion. The dancing and gambling in her saloon were associated with immoral behavior, raising further rumors of prostitution.

Despite these criticisms, Americans patronized her establishment and left large amounts of silver on Barcelo's gaming tables. First and foremost, Gertrudis Barcelo was a successful businesswoman. In the tradition of other New Mexican businesswomen, she regularly used the courts to collect gambling debts from patrons who did not pay up. And as a result of her keen business sense, she amassed enough money to contribute to local charities and church activities. At the time of her death in 1852, she was able to pass on three houses and additional wealth to her heirs. She has been remembered in later years, as this twentieth century picture from a magazine makes clear. ■

it tried to govern the area during the Mexican War. New Mexican villagers joined with Pueblo Indians in 1847 to attack and kill Charles Bent, the U.S. governor in Taos.

California Missions

In California, more than in other Spanish regions, the mission system was used vigorously to draw Indian women into the Spanish plans for domination. Spain had shown little interest in California until the middle of the eighteenth century, when the Russians began setting up trading posts in the area just north of what is now San Francisco. Spain quickly retaliated by establishing several military garrisons to challenge the Russians and by authorizing the Franciscans to create a string of missions to convert and "civilize" local Indians. Beginning in 1769, Father Junipero Serra, a Franciscan monk, led an effort that would ultimately result in twenty-one missions along the coast of the California territory. As had been the case with mission attempts elsewhere in New Spain, the goal was to convert the local Indians to Christianity as well as to European methods of farming and norms of family structure. If the efforts were successful, the Indians would make good allies and good workers.

The first years of conquest were rocky, however, as soldiers sometimes attacked Indian women, undercutting efforts of the government to convert Indians to both Christianity and Spanish ways. One friar in California complained to his superiors that conversions had dropped because Indians were disappearing into the mountains so that "soldiers would not take their women." At the San Gabriel Mission, early attempts at conversion came to a screeching halt in 1771 when the rape of a young Indian girl sparked a revolt by the local Indian population.

In a move to civilize the soldiers as well as the Indians, Spain moved quickly to encourage the immigration of families and women to California. Christianized Indian families were recruited from Baja California in 1773 and from New Spain in 1774 to help run the missions and to provide a model of behavior that could entice local Indians to join in the mission endeavors. The families were few, at first. Only one family was placed at the San Diego Mission, for example, where it was hoped the woman of the family would "teach the Indians to sew and knit the wool which was beginning to come in from the sheep" of the mission. Most of the women who came from New Spain were married to the blacksmiths and storekeepers, and almost all of the women returned to New Spain when their husbands had served out their contracts. A larger group was enticed to make the arduous trek from Mexico in 1775 when promises were made of food, clothing, and pay to impoverished mestizos who had fallen on hard times. Women, for example, were promised skirts, blouses, petticoats, stockings, and shoes. The women included Feliciana Arballo, who had to cajole her way onto the expedition after her husband died. The authorities were reluctant to take a single woman, particularly one with two small children, but the impoverished widow prevailed and survived the overland journey of 165 days, which only stopped occasionally when women gave birth. Given these hardships, it is not surprising that by 1790 there were still less than one thousand settlers of Spanish descent in California and that almost two-thirds of them were men.

The Christianized women who came from Mexico and Baja California taught Indian women how to cook and sew as Europeans did, and they also worked as midwives and supervised the distribution of food to the Indians who lived there. Apolinaria Lorenzana, who had been brought to California from Mexico as a child, developed her medical skills to the point that she took care of the patients at the mission hospital despite the protests from a local priest. Lorenzana, like Eulalia Pérez, had broad powers at the San Diego Mission, where she taught sewing and oversaw the inventory of goods purchased for the mission.

The young Indian girls whom Lorenzana and Pérez instructed were brought to the mission as they approached adolescence and kept in a dormitory known as a *monjerio*, where they were locked in at night to protect their virginity. When they married, they would be allowed to leave with their new husbands to set up their own households. However, some of the young **neophytes** did not come willingly, according to foreign observers. Missionaries accompanied by bodyguards searched native villages for volunteers to join the mission, but when Indians refused the invitation, the friars took young female captives. Their expectation was that families would eventually follow the girls to the missions to be with them and that the Indians would be less likely to attack the missions if they knew their children were held inside. Reports of these strategies led church officials to urge greater restraint among its priests when searching for recruits.

neophytes Indian converts in California missions.

Some of the young Indian men and women of the missions embraced the Catholicism and the social mores of the Spanish. Marriage among Indians in California carried diplomatic consequences in building family alliances, so parents of Indian girls usually chose spouses for their daughters (albeit after consulting with them). The friars deferred more clearly to the wishes of young women, as long as they chose Christian spouses, an option that some girls preferred. Moreover, while the Spanish taught young women to be deferential to their husbands, the friars also stressed that women were the moral guardians of their households. Isadora Filomena de Solano was proud of her role in convincing her warrior husband not to slaughter the Indians he conquered but to turn them over to the mission where they would work. The young men and women who embraced Spanish ways were trained as farmers, artisans, and domestic workers, making the mission lands in California extremely productive. As they married, they were often given the opportunity to leave the mission and move into a whitewashed hut nearby, with their own chickens, creating the kinds of households the friars wished to promote.

Other Indian women, however, suffered from the regime of Christianity imposed on them. Many Christianized Indians did not fully embrace the Spanish ideal of monogamy and continued to have sexual relations with others besides their husbands and wives. Others practiced abortion or infanticide. Chumash women, for example, believed they had to kill their firstborn if they were to be successful bearing future children. The friars thus began to assume that most miscarriages were intentional and began a campaign of public shaming. Women who had miscarriages were forced to carry wooden dolls or logs about the size of a baby for several days after the incident.

Huge numbers of both male and female Indians died in the early nineteenth century as a result of epidemics that ranged from smallpox to syphilis, but women had higher death rates than men. Women had constituted about half of the Indian residents of missions in the late eighteenth century, but by the nineteenth century their proportion in the mission population was dropping. As a result, mission raids on Indian villages increased, and women were specifically targeted to replace the dying mission populations.

The mission period came to an end in the 1830s when the government in Mexico moved to secularize the lands held by the church. Some Christianized Indian households received small plots of land, and a few Christianized Indians with powerful ties to the government received larger landholdings. But most of the mission land was sold to **Californios/Californias,** as Mexican citizens living in California called themselves. About 13 percent of the land grants went directly to women. Daughters in these Californio families, however, inherited land equally with their brothers, creating large dowries

Californios/Californias Men and women of Spanish descent in California.

MAP 4-3 OVERLAND TRAILS 1840S

The Overland Trails started at the Missouri River and either headed south towards Santa Fe or north towards Portland. Those heading to California broke off early from the Oregon Trail and moved south to Sutter's Fort.

in land for many of these young women. New household structures quickly began to co-alesce as Anglo traders, particularly from the United States, began to move into the area and marry these land-wealthy Californias. The European household structure that the Spanish had hoped to use to control the land of California was firmly put in place, but the Indians whom they had tried to convert to this system did not benefit. Rather, American settlers from the East were integrated into Spanish households, providing an entrée for Anglo men and facilitating trade relationships with the United States.

The Overland Trails

Although the United States did not acquire territories in the far West until the 1840s, movement from the eastern United States had begun in earnest two decades before with immigration to Texas. By the 1830s, Americans had begun travel on overland trails that originated at the Missouri River, heading northward on the Oregon Trail all the way to the Oregon Territory or cutting off and heading south into California. Farther south, they followed the Santa Fe trade into New Mexico. By 1845, five thousand settlers had moved west to Oregon and almost three thousand had moved to California. As Anglo

WOMEN'S VOICES

A MISSIONARY'S PERSPECTIVE

Narcissa Whitman and her husband Marcus immigrated to the Walla Walla Valley in 1836 as missionaries. They wrote extensively of their work and kept missionary societies in the East appraised of their progress in spreading Christianity. They were murdered by Cayuse Indians in 1847, however, after the Indians blamed them for an outbreak of measles in the area.

Wailatpu, March 9, 1842

My Dear Jane and Edward,

. . . Attended maternal meeting this afternoon. Sister G. and I make all the effort our time and means will permit to edify ourselves in our responsible maternal duties. Read this P.M. the report of the New York for 1840, and what a feast it was to us! It is a comforting thought to us in a desert land to know that we are so kindly remembered by sister Associations in our beloved land. But the constant watch and care and anxiety of a missionary mother cannot be known by them except by experience. Sister G. has two of her own and I have three half-breeds. I believe I feel all the care and watchfulness over them that I should if they were my own. I am sure they are a double tax upon my patience and perseverance, particularly Helen; she wants to rule every one she sees. She keeps me on guard continually lest she should get the upper hand of me. The little boy appears to be of a pretty good disposition, and I think will be easy to govern. He proves to be younger than I first thought he was; he is not yet three years old—probably he is the same age Helen was when she came here. His old grandmother has been in to see him today, but appears to have no disposition to take him. She wanted I should give her something to eat every now and then, because I had got the child to live with me and take care of, also old clothes and shoes. So it is with them; the moment you do them a favour you place yourself under lasting obligations to them and must continue to give to keep their love strong towards you. I make such bungling work of writing the eve I believe I will stop, for I can scarcely keep my head up an eyes open. So good night, J., for you do not come to sleep with me, and I must content myself with Mary Ann [one of the Indian children the Whitmans had taken in].

Source: Narcissa Whitman to her sister and brother-in-law in The Letters of Narcissa Whitman, 1836–1847 *(Fairfield, WA: Ye Galleon Press, 1986), 128–31.*

Questions

1. What sort of maternal obligations does Narcissa Whitman feel toward the three Indian children that she and her husband have taken in?

2. What sorts of misunderstandings exist in Narcissa Whitman's perception of Native American customs?

women moved westward, they brought with them ideals of female behavior and family life that they found superior to those of Mexican and Indian women and that they hoped would triumph in a new western United States.

Leading the way were Narcissa and Marcus Whitman, two Presbyterian missionaries who pioneered travel on the Oregon Trail in 1836. They established a mission school for the Cayuse Indians in the Walla Walla Valley, hoping to convert local Indians and civilize them, though their efforts in this regard were not terribly successful. The Whitmans grew increasingly frustrated with the refusal of the Indians to change their religious

Jesse Benton Fremont was a high spirited and intelligent women who aided her husband's career in a variety of ways. She wrote much of John C. Fremont's report on the West in the middle of the 1840s, creating an image that encouraged readers to pack up and follow the Oregon Trail. (© National Portrait Gallery, Smithsonian Institution/ Art Resource)

Manifest Destiny Belief that the borders of the United States were destined to spread westward.

beliefs or their social relationships. The couple was more successful at promoting change by convincing other Americans to migrate west. Narcissa's letters back to her family and to missionary magazines fueled interest in the West, as did her husband's attempts to promote migration. In 1843, Marcus returned to the East and led a "Great Migration" of one thousand settlers westward. Unfortunately, the settlers brought diseases such as measles that killed many of the local Indians. In 1847, the Indians retaliated, killing Narcissa and Marcus, along with ten others.

Narcissa Whitman was not the only woman to promote westward movement. Even more influential was Jesse Benton Fremont. The headstrong daughter of the U.S. senator from Missouri, Thomas Hart Benton, she eloped with the impoverished John C. Fremont. With the patronage of his wife's powerful father, Fremont was given the opportunity to survey the Oregon Trail during 1843 and 1844. Jesse did not go with him, but she did write much of his report, using powerful language that provided not only a scientific description of the West but also an exciting and accessible image of a land ripe for settlement. Although the book acknowledged the dangers and difficulties of westward travel, it also described homey camp scenes of children frolicking and cows grazing. The best-selling book convinced thousands of Americans that they could make a new home in the West, with the kind of family life they recognized.

Both Narcissa Whitman and Jesse Benton Fremont promoted a vision of westward settlement that convinced Americans the West could and should be theirs. The two women wrote of a land that could be settled and farmed as well as Christianized and "civilized" with homesteads that closely resembled those found in the East. In promoting this vision, they helped to create a belief in what would soon be called **Manifest Destiny.** The term was coined by a Texas newspaper in 1845, suggesting that the United States had a divine mission to extend its democratic spirit and Christian principles as far west as the Pacific Ocean. As an ideology, Manifest Destiny became crucial in legitimating American conquests both on and beyond the North American continent. While it was a tool of war used by men, it was also a concept rooted in ideas of spreading American home life and setting up the American household as a model to be adopted by all. This was the part of the ideology that many women from the United States carried forward in the conquest of foreign territory.

CONCLUSION

By the early 1850s, the United States spread from the Atlantic Ocean to the Pacific Ocean. The process of incorporating territories that had been dominated by the French and Spanish, as well as many Indian tribes, was fought not only in battles but negotiated in households. The place of the household within the larger political order mattered, as did a woman's status within a family, her choice of marriage partners, and her ability to inherit and control property. Not surprising, then, was the fact that women in different frontier regions found their places within their homes shifting with the demands of trade and politics.

1690

1692
Hannah Duston captured by Indians

1704
Eunice Williams captured by Indians

1750

1758
Mary Jemison captured by Indians

1756
Seven Years' War begins in Europe

1763
Treaty of Paris ends Seven Years' War

Proclamation Line drawn separating
Indian Country from eastern colonies

France cedes Louisiana to Spain and territory
east of Mississippi to Britain

1769
Spain begins to govern Louisiana

1780

1781
Nancy Ward helps the Cherokees to negotiate
a treaty with the U.S. government

1786
Law passed in New Orleans requiring libre women
to wear a tignon on their heads

1797
Seneca women sell part of their land to Thomas Morris

1789
Quakers establish mission among the Senecas

1799
Handsome Lake has his first vision

1800

1803
Louisiana Purchase

1804–1806
Sacagawea assists Lewis and Clark
in their exploration of the Louisiana Territory

1817
Cherokee women petition their council not
to cede any more land to the United States

1804–1806
Voyage of Lewis and Clark

1805
Tenskwatawa has his first vision

1821
Mexico achieves independence from Spain

1827
Cherokees establish republic and ratify a constitution

1830

1836
Narcissa Whitman moves with her husband
to the Oregon Territory

1845
Jesse Benton Fremont helps her husband
to write his report on the West

1837
Texas becomes a republic

1845
Texas becomes a state

1846
Mexican War

1848
Treaty of Guadalupe Hidalgo approved
Mexican cession of land to United States

Household ideals were important not only on the frontier but also in the lives of all women in early nineteenth-century America. Women in the North and the South also had to confront key differences in their household structures. As the new government of the United States expanded, they also had to confront both the extent and the limits of their household authority in a world in which democratic political participation was becoming increasingly important.

REVIEW QUESTIONS

1. Compare the experiences of Seneca, Shawnee, and Cherokee women in confronting the changes to their households as a result of contact and trade with the British and the Americans.

2. Compare the ways in which African women and Indian women were affected by changing laws of slavery and freedom as control of the Louisiana Territory shifted from France to Spain and then to the United States.

3. How did Spanish laws of property affect women as they settled the frontiers of Texas, New Mexico, and California?

RECOMMENDED READING

Juliana Barr. *Peace Came in the Form of a Woman: Indians and Spaniards in the Texas Borderlands*. Chapel Hill: University of North Carolina Press, 2007. An important analysis of the ways in which tribal affiliation and diplomatic concerns resulted in different experiences for Indian women interacting with both the French and the Spanish.

Virginia Marie Bouvier. *Women and the Conquest of California, 1542–1840: Codes of Silence*. Tucson: The University of Arizona Press, 2001. Interesting study of the ways in which Native American women faced the challenges posed by Spanish colonization.

Kimberly S. Hanger. *Bounded Lives, Bounded Places: Free Black Society in Colonial New Orleans, 1769–1803*. Durham, NC: Duke University Press, 1997. A valuable scholarly analysis of how free black society in New Orleans emerged.

Theda Perdue. *Cherokee Women: Gender and Culture Change, 1700–1835*. Lincoln: University of Nebraska Press, 1998. Fascinating study that rewrites Cherokee history around the issue of the rights and status of women.

ADDITIONAL BIBLIOGRAPHY

Struggles for Survival

Judith Brown. "Economic Organization and the Position of Women among the Iroquois." *Ethnohistory* 17, no. 3/4 (Summer–Autumn 1970): 151–67.

Colin Calloway. "'We Have Always Been the Frontier': The American Revolution in Shawnee Country." *American Indian Quarterly* 16, no. 1 (Winter 1992): 39–52.

Alfred Cave. "The Failure of the Shawnee Prophet's Witch-hunt." *Ethnohistory* 42, no. 3 (Summer 1995): 445–75.

Wilma A. Dunaway, "Rethinking Cherokee Acculturation: Women's Resistance to Agrarian Capitalism and Cultural Change 1800–1883." *American Indian Culture and Research Journal* 21 (Spring 1997): 128–49.

Robert V. Hine and John Mack Faragher. *The American West: A New Interpretive History.* New Haven, CT: Yale University Press, 2000.

Joan Jensen. "Native American Women and Agriculture: A Seneca Case Study." *Sex Roles* 3, no. 5 (1977): 423–41.

Carolyn Ross Johnson. *Cherokee Women in Crisis: Trail of Tears, Civil War, and Allotment, 1838–1907.* Tuscaloosa: University of Alabama Press, 2003.

Slavery and Freedom in Louisiana

Virginia R. Dominguez. *White by Definition: Social Classification in Creole Louisiana.* New Brunswick, NJ: Rutgers University Press, 1986.

Virginia Meacham Gould. "'If I Can't Have My Rights, I Can Have My Pleasures, and If They Won't Give Me Wages, I Can Take Them': Gender and Slave Labor in Antebellum New Orleans." In *Discovering the Women in Slavery: Emancipating Perspectives on the American Past,* edited by Patricia Morton. Athens: University of Georgia Press,1996.

Kimberly S. Hanger. "'The Fortunes of Women in America': Spanish New Orleans's Free Women of African Descent and Their Relations with Slave Women." In *Discovering the Women in Slavery: Emancipating Perspectives on the American Past,* edited by Patricia Morton. Athens: University of Georgia Press, 1996.

Frances Karttunen. *Between Worlds: Interpreters, Guides, and Survivors.* New Brunswick, NJ: Rutgers University Press, 1994.

Joan M. Martin. "Plaçage and the Louisiana Gens de Couleur Libre: How Race and Sex Defined the Lifestyles of Free Women of Color." In *Creole: The History and Legacy of Louisiana's Free People of Color,* edited by Sybil Kein. Baton Rouge: Louisiana State University Press, 2000.

The Spanish Frontier

Teresa Palomo Acosta and Ruthe Winegarten. *Las Tejanas: 300 Years of History.* Austin: University of Texas Press, 2003.

Mark M. Carroll. *Homesteads Ungovernable: Families, Sex, Race, and the Law in Frontier Texas, 1823–1860.* Austin: University of Texas Press, 2001.

Antonia Castaneda. "Engendering the History of Alta California, 1769–1848: Gender, Sexuality, and the Family." In *Contested Eden: California Before the Gold Rush,* edited by Ramon A. Gutierrez and Richard J. Orsi. Berkeley: University of California Press, 1998.

Deena J. Gonzalez. *Refusing the Favor: The Spanish-Mexican Women of Santa Fe, 1820–1880.* New York: Oxford University Press, 1999.

Lisbeth Haas. *Conquests and Historical Identities in California, 1769–1936.* Berkeley: University of California Press, 1995.

Janet Lecompte. "The Independent Women of Hispanic New Mexico, 1821–1846." In *New Mexico Women: InterCultural Perspectives,* edited by Joan M. Jensen and Darlis A. Miller. Albuquerque: University of New Mexico Press, 1986.

Gloria Ricci Lothrop. "Rancheras and the Land: Women and Property Rights in Hispanic California." *Southern California Quarterly* 76 (1994): 59–84.

Deborah A. Rosen. "Women and Property across Colonial America: A Comparison of Legal Systems in New Mexico and New York." *William and Mary Quarterly,* Third Series LX, no. 2 (April 2003).

Richard White. *"It's Your Misfortune and None of My Own": A New History of the American West.* Norman: University of Oklahoma Press, 1991.

Biographies, Autobiographies, and Memoirs

John Demos. *The Unredeemed Captive: A Family Story from Early America.* New York: Vintage, 1995.

Kathryn Zabelle Derounian-Stodola, ed. *Women's Indian Captivity Narratives.* New York: Penguin Classics, 1998.

Carlos N. Hijar, Eulalia Perez, and Agustin Escobar. *Three Memoirs of Mexican California, 1877.* Berkeley: University of California, 1877.

Theda Perdue. *Sifters: Native American Women's Lives.* New York: Oxford University Press. 2001.

Daniel L. Schafer. *Anna Madgigine Jai Kingsley: African Princess, Florida Slave, Plantation Slaveowner.* Gainesville: University Press of Florida, 2003.

Lillian Schlissel. *Women's Diaries of the Western Journey.* New York: Random House, 2004.

Domestic Economies and Northern Lives, 1800-1860

HOW WERE women's lives affected by industrialization?

HOW DID the market create work for women in the cities and their hinterlands?

WHAT DID it mean to be a middle-class woman in the antebellum North?

HOW DID race and ethnicity affect a woman's home life?

WHAT WERE the domestic ideals expressed in popular plays and novels?

My dear sister,

. . . I will say to you that as to my work I get along very well indeed. Since I have wrote to you another payday has come around, I earned 14 dollars and a half, 9 and a half dollars besides my board. The folks think I get along just first rate, they say. I like it well as ever and Sarah don't I feel independent of every one! The thought that I am living on no one is a happy one indeed to me. . . . I tell you Sarah, it is grand to be a boarder. I leave my work at seven o'clock then I come home and I do what I please. . . . I [now] board with a Mr. Morse. . . . There is in all 17 boarders . . . I don't

"Shake Hands?" Lilly Martin Spencer, 1855

have even my bed to make. Quite a lady to be sure. . . . Aunt M. now thinks I better begin and put my money at interest. . . . I get up early, eat my breakfast, go to the shop, do my days work, come out any . . . hour I please, come home, then do anything I wish to. Grand thing, I tell you, so different from what I have been used to. . . .

Source: From Ann Swett, who left her poorly paid job shoe binding in Haverhill, Massachusetts, to work in one of the large textile factories in Manchester, New Hampshire. Reprinted from Mary H. Blewett, We Will Rise in Our Might: Workingwomen's Voices from Nineteenth-Century New England *(Ithaca, NY: Cornell University Press, 1991), 63–64.*

War of 1812 War between the United States and England over trade restrictions, fought between 1812 and 1815.

Erie Canal First canal built in the United States, connecting New York City with upstate New York.

Baltimore and Ohio Railroad First railroad built in the United States, opening in 1830.

*A*nn Swett, a young shoe binder in Haverhill, Massachusetts, felt trapped by the low paid work and domestic responsibilities that her life there entailed. Rather than submit to the dreary domesticity of stitching shoes and helping around the house, she decamped to Manchester, New Hampshire, in the 1840s, seeking a better life in the textile mills there. Manchester—along with other towns such as Lowell, Massachusetts, and Saco, Maine—was at the forefront of the transformation of American industry in the early nineteenth century. The first stages of the Industrial Revolution were unfolding in the United States as transportation, technology, and large concentrations of capital reorganized the way goods were made. The **War of 1812** had disrupted shipping routes to Europe, encouraging wealthy merchants to invest in production at home rather than abroad. The **Erie Canal** opened in 1825 and the **Baltimore and Ohio Railroad** in 1830, the first of many waterways and rail lines that efficiently moved goods between seaport cities and regions farther inland. Finally, new forms of machinery, from power looms to steam-run printing presses, were turning out products much faster and more cheaply than had been possible before.

As the United States slowly industrialized, the North also increasingly urbanized. Although most people in the United States continued to live on farms and in rural areas, the percentage of people living in cities increased from 7 percent in 1820 to 20 percent in 1860; and with a few exceptions, those cities were located in the North. Thus, the percentage of New Englanders living in cities during this time increased from 7 percent to 36 percent. The size of cities grew as banks and mercantile houses expanded to facilitate an explosion of economic activity and as immigrants, particularly from Ireland and Central Europe, began to flood American shores.

The fact that Ann Swett worked in both the new shoe industry and a textile factory is telling. Manufacturers in the United States often looked to young women as a desirable labor pool in their new industrial ventures. Factory owners knew that most male workers were committed to finding higher-paying jobs as skilled artisans. Instead, owners often looked to young, single women as an alternative workforce. Ironically, as women became ubiquitous in the new industrial workforce, the very idea that women should work for wages was challenged by an ideology that stressed the importance of domesticity and the home as woman's "separate sphere." Middle-class women, in particular, were urged to stay at home and care for their families. Stressing the emotional bonds between husband and wife as well as between parent and child, this new cult of domesticity ignored—and even disguised—the economic value of the housework done by women in middle-class homes.

INDUSTRIAL TRANSFORMATIONS

The nineteenth century was a difficult time for many of the young men who came of age. They had expected to train as apprentices in trades their parents helped them choose and then to establish their own shops and to experience the independence that came from being able to support themselves and their families. Indeed, the entire concept of citizenship in the new republic was tied to ownership of land, so owning one's shop meant political independence as well as economic independence. The **Industrial Revolution** made those goals more difficult to attain, as small shops gave way to large industry and ownership gave way to wage work. Many of these men faced the difficulty of living with a smaller income than they expected; and they had to come to terms with the work lives of their wives, daughters, and sisters who took on wage work of their own in these newly transformed industries. Women had to negotiate the meaning of their wages not only for themselves but also for the men in their families. They did so in different ways, depending on where they came from and what kind of work they did.

Industrial Revolution
Transformation from craft-based system to mass production of goods.

Factory Families

The earliest textile factories in the United States were not the massive structures that dominated towns such as Lowell, Massachusetts, or Manchester, New Hampshire. Rather, they were small spinning factories located along the rivers and streams of southern New England. Samuel Slater, an English machinist and textile entrepreneur, brought his knowledge of spinning technology to the United States at the end of the eighteenth century and set up some of the first of these mills in Pawtucket, Rhode Island. The factories were small and tended to employ poor families. Fathers made yearly contracts with owners such as Slater, promising that their children would work at particular jobs for a stipulated amount of pay.

Parents also made sure to negotiate time for schooling as well and, in the case of their sons, sometimes demanded training in one of the more skilled areas of millwork.

Traditional patterns of family authority were maintained in several ways through this arrangement. First of all, the children's wages were paid to their fathers. In addition, fathers and older brothers were more likely to work in the large farmlands owned by the mills rather than in the factory itself, perhaps to avoid conflicts with overseers over supervising their children in the mills. However, most men preferred to work in the fields as more gender-appropriate activity because factory work smacked of subservience. The mothers of these children were also scarce in the factories. Instead, they supplemented the family income by growing vegetables in their gardens, taking in boarders, or perhaps weaving cloth in their homes.

At Slater's Mill, children helped to support their families by spinning cotton thread under contracts that their fathers had negotiated. They were paid in scrip that was then used at the company store to purchase food and other goods.

Families were paid not in cash but in scrip, which was credit at the company store. Often the stores marked up their prices, diminishing the value of wages. Mill owners provided company housing for their employees and applied the wages of the children to the yearly rent. However, this practice also meant that families had a difficult time leaving the factories if they became dissatisfied with working conditions.

This fragile structure of family relations gradually crumbled as parents increasingly found themselves unable to control the terms of work for their children. If they objected to the way factory overseers treated their children, they could find their whole family turned out, as Peter Mayo's family discovered in the 1840s. Mill owners also began to insist on paying workers as individuals rather than as families. By the 1840s, children and teenagers were paid their wages directly, giving them more independence from the father's control. When they were eighteen and thirteen years old, Amanda and Amy Jepson were placed by their father in a mill in Webster, Massachusetts. Within a year, the girls made enough money to move to a nearby boardinghouse. Amanda and Amy thus experienced the new power in controlling their lives that wage work could give young women.

Independent Mill Girls

The move by these smaller factories to pay their workers as individuals rather than as families was inspired largely by their competition farther north. Places such as Lowell and Manchester were growing with huge, integrated factories that not only spun cotton thread but also wove it into cheap and cheerful fabrics. New technology, particularly the development of the power loom, had mechanized the manufacture of cloth by the early nineteenth century, and factory owners were eager to find unskilled workers to run the machinery. Eschewing the destitute families and child labor that staffed Slater's mills, they looked instead to young single women, ages fifteen to thirty, from farm fam-

Merrimack Mills and Boarding Houses. Boarding Houses were an important aspect of the mill experience in the nineteenth century. They provided young women (and their parents) with the assurance that female mill workers live in respectable circumstances while away from home.

MAP 5-1 LOWELL, MASSACHUSETTS IN 1832

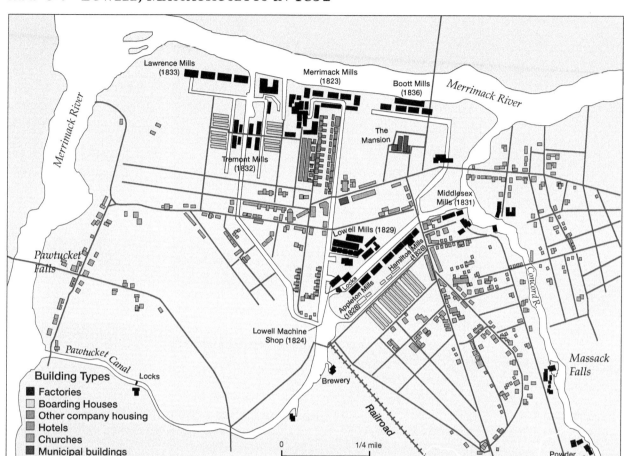

Boarding houses and factories were located close to one another in Lowell as part of one, large, comprehensive plan for living and working for young women.

ilies throughout New England. The daughters of these farmers often maintained a seasonal routine, working in Lowell for several months and then returning to their families for short visits. Many kept up this pattern—entering and leaving the payrolls of large companies such as the Hamilton, the Appleton, the Suffolk, and the Lawrence—until they married several years later. These patterns of employment were so successful that by 1860, the factories of New England employed over sixty thousand women.

For these young women, work in a large textile factory was a ticket to independence. In a factory town such as Lowell, for example, a newcomer could make only about forty-four cents per day, but more experienced workers made from sixty-six to seventy-eight cents per day. These were among the top wages a woman could make at this time, though they were still below what men were paid for similar labor. Some young women contributed their wages to family needs, such as a brother's education or their parents' mortgage, and all were responsible for paying for room and board at their dormitories; but most managed to save some of their wages for their own goals: education, dowries, and new clothes.

TABLE 5-1 Wages of Lowell Factory Workers

Men		Women	
Job	Mean Daily Pay	Job	Mean Daily Pay
Overseeer	$2.09	Speeder	$0.66
Second hand	1.20	Drawer	0.52
Operative	.85	Spinner	0.58
Machinist	1.27	Weaver	0.66
Watchman	1.10	Dresser	0.78
		Warper	0.73
		Drawing in	0.66
		Sparehand	0.44
Overall	$1.05	Overall	$0.66

(*Source: Thomas Dublin*, Women at Work, The Transformation of Work and Community in Lowell, Massachusetts, 1826–1860, *New York: Columbia University Press, 1979, p. 66*)

Although even the highest paid female workers in a factory did not make as much as the lowest paid male operatives, some women earned high wages for the time, particularly as warpers and dressers.

lyceums Lecture series or other forms of popular education.

Culture and education also drew young women to Lowell. The women patronized a wide variety of **lyceums**, churches, and clubs. Famous authors came from around the country and the world to see the factories and to lecture to rapt audiences. Many of these workers came from country towns where even good sermons were hard to come by, so the churches were equally exciting. Factory hands usually did not come from families that were able to afford the tuition of a female academy; but with the cultural riches surrounding them in towns such as Lowell, they still got an education. Cheap fabrics produced by their textile factories meant that fashionable clothes also were within their reach.

Still, criticisms were raised about the choices these young women were making. Women were not supposed to work for wages, nor were they supposed to be traipsing around the countryside on their own, so respectability was an issue. One of the ways factory owners in large towns such as Lowell and Manchester dealt with the issue of respectability was to provide company dormitories supervised by a matron. In Lowell boardinghouses, curfews were strictly enforced in an effort to make sure young women spent their nights under maternal supervision. Many young women also exerted peer pressure to make sure their friends behaved, and boardinghouse keepers intervened when they felt their charges were behaving improperly. When Delia Page, a Lowell factory worker, began seeing a married man, the matron refused to let him visit. Delia left the boardinghouse, but both the matron and a former roommate continued to pressure her about the relationship and within a couple of months Delia had given up the unsuitable gentleman.

Family Wage Economy

The young women in the factory towns of New England were not the only ones swept into the new world of industrialization. Other women found wage work in their own homes, particularly in the rapidly reconstituted trade of shoe making. This sort of industrialization relied not on machinery but, rather, on a division of labor. Sarah Trask, who lived at home with her widowed mother and brother in Beverly, Massachusetts, stitched shoes together in between household chores. If she was lucky, she made one dollar a week, money that probably contributed to her family's comfort as well as her own. Shoe binding was an activity Sarah shared with her female friends. In a new **putting-out system,** owners of large shoe companies paid skilled male shoemakers in a central shop to cut leather for premade shoes before handing it out to women across New England for stitching. Sometimes women worked alone, while at other times they worked together. Once their work was returned to the merchant, the shoes were shipped south and west to slave owners and farmers looking for cheap clothing.

putting-out system
Form of industrialization in which the owner of raw materials distributes the materials to workers who are paid by the piece to assemble them in their homes.

Women were not paid much for this work, usually from two to five cents a pair, depending on how crude or refined the product was supposed to be. This was approximately half of what a man would be paid for similar work, which is why shoe manufacturers were eager to recruit women into the trade. Indeed, women were at the center of a reorganization of shoe making, taking on the less-skilled tasks of shoe binding, while men were retained in the more skilled position of cutting the leather. Merchants who oversaw this process assumed women were not the sole support of their families and used that assumption to pay women less than men in order to increase their profit margins. Even the most productive of women shoe binders would not have been able to survive on the money she made from her work.

Many single women abandoned shoe binding for more lucrative opportunities in the mills, but others did not have that flexibility. Many of the women who worked as shoe binders were married and contributing to a **family-wage economy.** Their husbands were farmers or fishermen who were not making enough to support their families, or their husbands were shoemakers who had seen their incomes decrease as a result of this new industrialization of the shoe trade. So, in between housework and caring for their children, women stitched shoes to help make ends meet. It was not the most lucrative employment available for women, but for those who needed to be at home to care for their children and do their housework, the small amounts of money they made contributed to the economic stability of their families This family-wage economy was an adaptation of an earlier tradition in which wives and daughters had helped the men in the family making shoes. Binding had traditionally been women's work, but during the colonial era, they had done it for family members rather than for merchants. They had not been paid a wage, but that did not matter because the profits came to their families. In the new system, families lost most of that profit.

family-wage economy
Term for the situation in which all members of a family must earn wages and share them in order for the family to survive.

Town and Country

While industrialization was transforming the New England countryside, the financial backbone and trading networks that facilitated this new economic world lay in the rapidly growing cities. Here, too, young women arrived from rural areas and took many of the new jobs available. In cities such as New York, immigrants also poured in from England, Germany, and, most of all, Ireland after 1820, so that a housing crisis ensued. Old houses were broken up into apartments to squeeze in more families. Kitchens and parlors were combined in these newly created tenements, and if lucky, tenants would have a couple of cubicles in back for sleeping.

Seamstresses, Servants, and Shopgirls

In these crowded settings, working mothers struggled to provide a home for their children while trying to earn enough money to feed them. Most did so by taking in laundry or sewing for the rapidly expanding trade in ready-made clothing. During the first half of the nineteenth century, seamstresses in New York earned between $.75 and $1.50 per week. A single woman might get by on this amount, but a woman trying to support her family could not. As was the case with shoe binders, employers assumed that women were not family breadwinners in the wages they paid though in many cases women were trying to support their families without the assistance of a husband. Thus, many of the poorest women supervised their small children who scavenged for firewood and food to supplement their mothers' wages. The women also worked as informal tavern keepers, selling food and alcohol to neighbors, often from their kitchens. As a result, their homes were places of work and public socializing as well as places where their families lived.

Single women in New York found the opportunities provided by wage work to be more liberating than they were for mothers with children. Young single women found employment in book binderies and dress shops or in the other small manufactories that existed throughout the cities. However, domestic servitude was the most common form of employment. Although wages in 1835 averaged only $1.50 per week, servants were provided room and board so that they had an opportunity to save some of their

MAP 5-2 AMERICAN CITIES IN 1820

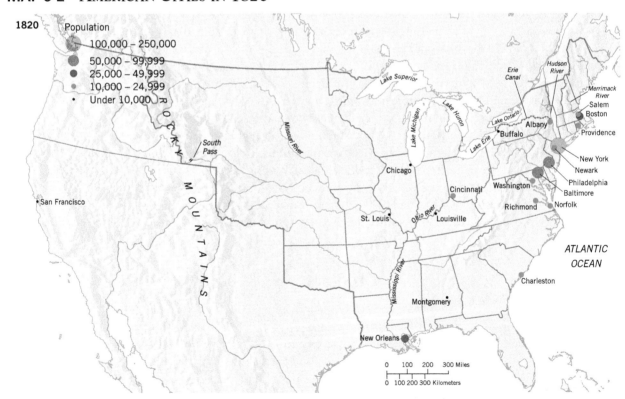

There were few cities in the United States in 1820, and those that existed were almost all located along the eastern seabord.

wages. Still, domestic work was an unpopular alternative as young women found their social independence curtailed by long hours and strict supervision.

Shopgirls and servants in New York City sometimes joined churches or attended lectures, but many found that the streets themselves offered entertainment. Sallying forth in groups, young women headed to the Bowery, where they encountered high-spirited young workingmen and opportunities for dancing and theatergoing. Young women and their beaux could see variety shows at Vauxhall Gardens or visit ice cream parlors, which had become a popular venue for socializing after a new method was developed for cheaply making the frozen delicacy. On summer evenings, they also took boat rides and on holidays, short trips to Staten Island. The young women of the Bowery used their money not only to venture out but also to buy brightly colored clothes that caught their fancy. The bold colors favored by working girls drew attention to their bodies, as did the tighter-fitting skirts they favored. Their hats revealed their faces rather than shielding them from public view. The dress of these workingwomen was fancy enough to show the independence they gained from their wages and revealing enough to signal a rejection of middle-class codes of modesty.

In cities such as New York, where young workingwomen were less supervised than in towns such as Lowell and where the streets were an accepted place of socializing, slight misunderstandings of body language could have severe consequences. A young woman out with her friends was understood to be respectable (and protected) whereas

MAP 5-3 AMERICAN CITIES IN 1860

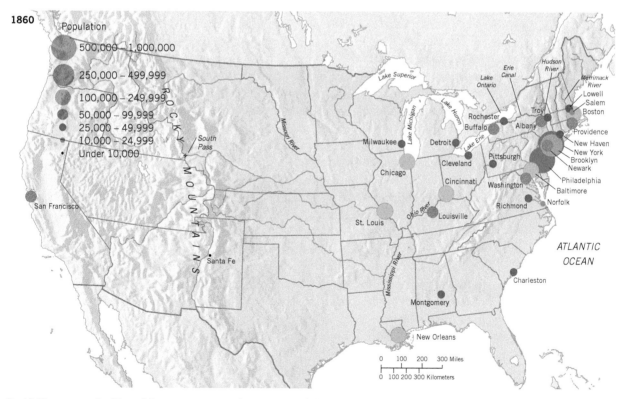

By 1860, cities in the United States were expanding in size and developing inland as well as along the coast. These rapidly growing urban centers were filled with immigrants and young people in search of employment, many of whom were women.

a young woman who ventured out alone faced the possibility of seduction or rape. She could be mistaken for a prostitute, or her solitary state could signal boldness and sexual interest. Court cases from that time reveal a number of women raped by one or more men who assumed them fair game.

Sex for Sale

antebellum period
Period in U.S. history extending roughly from 1830 to 1860.

The streets of large cities such as New York were dangerous for young women in part because the expanding commerce in sex rendered the behavior of young women ambiguous. In New York City, for example, several thousand prostitutes plied their trade during the **antebellum period,** probably somewhere between 5 and 10 percent of the young women in the city. The sex trade was one of the largest enterprises in New York, exceeded only by the clothing trade in terms of dollars spent. Prostitution flourished on the streets, in rowdy brothels, in more discreet parlor houses, and in furnished rooms rented by more independent young women. Prominent madams staged fancy masquerade balls, and theaters presented "tableaux vivants," living female paintings in which young women posed nude or in transparent clothing, imitating famous works of art such as *Venus Rising from the Sea* or *The Greek Slave.*

Perhaps the most visible combination of public culture and prostitution occurred in the notorious "third tier" of theaters. In these upper galleries, prostitutes enjoyed the evening's entertainment as they boldly advertised their charms to spectators below and dispensed sexual favors to men willing to pay the price. Occasionally, city marshals removed prostitutes and their clients for "outrageous, turbulent, and noisey" behavior, but in most cases, their activities were tolerated and even encouraged as part of the erotic excitement that drew patrons in.

Women were much more likely than men to run brothels during the antebellum period, when women exercised more control over prostitution than they would later. For some of New York's most successful prostitutes, sex was an important avenue to upward mobility. Maria Williamson owned and operated several whorehouses in New York that were valued at ten thousand dollars in the early 1820s. Julia Brown, nicknamed "Princess Julia," kept an elegant, expensive parlor house on Leonard Street and attended parties hosted by New York's upper crust. These madams also achieved success as they carved out specialized identities for their operations. Miss Mitchell provided "French love," while Rebecca Weyman's operation advertised "ropes and braces."

Most of the prostitutes operating in New York at the middle of the century had either been born in the Northeast or emigrated from Ireland. With the exception of madams, who tended to be older, prostitutes were teenagers or in their early twenties. Many had started out in trades such as sewing, shoe binding, or domestic service and found the wages too low for survival. Faced with poverty and deprivation, girls as young as twelve years old (and in one case, nine) contributed to a growing epidemic in child prostitution. Men were attracted to child prostitutes because they were thought to be free from venereal disease. Girls were attracted to prostitution because selling one's virginity could bring a high price: Ruth Hudspeth earned fifty dollars for hers from a Frenchman who paid her five dollars for each encounter thereafter. Some child prostitutes were the victims of rape or seduction; in fact, children under the age of twelve accounted for approximately one-third of the rape and attempted rape cases prosecuted in New York City during the early nineteenth century. In other cases, however, prostitution was a family-sanctioned activity. After her parents divorced, Charlotte Willis became a prostitute at

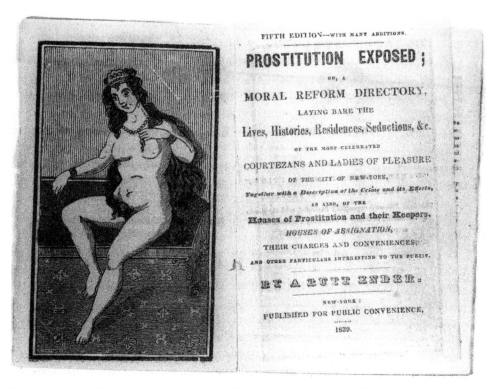

Prostitution was widespread in cities such as New York, and visitors could quickly locate brothels by purchasing books such as this, which claimed to be revealing and condemning prostitution, but which were actually promoting it.

age thirteen, along with her mother. Susan Brown's daughters both worked in her brothel, and William Shaw's daughters worked in his. When death or economic depression made times hard, sex was a vital commodity to sell for family or individual survival.

Prostitution was, without a doubt, the highest paying trade available to women, but it was also dangerous. In addition to the likelihood of contracting venereal diseases, prostitutes risked violence in their daily lives. Vigilantes would attack prostitutes and their brothels in moral outrage or, more likely, assault them during a drunken rampage. The three men who broke into Amanda Smith's house "destroyed her furniture" and "beat her on the face and head so as to blind her entirely" before they went after her son.

Butter and Eggs

While factory towns and cities were transforming the landscape of the North, most women still continued to live in rural households during the first half of the nineteenth century. As a result, their domestic lives were tied to farm chores as much as to their homes, giving their lives a different cast from that of their urban counterparts. Particularly in areas that were located near enough to cities to supply them with food, women became an important part of a network of commercial as well as subsistence agriculture.

In the farmland surrounding Philadelphia and Baltimore, for example, many women not only cared for their homes and their children, but also aggressively entered the dairy trade, producing milk, butter, eggs, and feathers for the local market. The income from butter could be a significant contribution to a family's income. In the

Brandywine Valley of Delaware, the 1850 census shows that the average farm produced $125.00 worth of butter over the year.

The active involvement of women in farming meant that the kitchen was the focus of their homes, a place of production that linked the interior spaces of the house with the exterior spaces of the garden, barn, and barnyard. A well-laid-out farm kitchen connected to a dairy room and coal house, had a separate sink for farmhands to wash up, and a large dining room to feed them. Rather than standing at the hearth, women were able to cook on a large stove, an invention that reduced the amount of wood they had to use tending the fire. A nice farmhouse had a parlor as well, but it received little attention. Family and farmhands used the kitchen door at the rear, while the front entrance was used only occasionally for village notables such as the preacher.

Women took their dairy products to market and returned with foods they could not grow such as sugar and coffee or some of the new textiles that were being produced farther north, providing their families with the new goods becoming available in the booming economy surrounding them. However, these women were entering the new market economy as producers as well as consumers, and their economic role was well recognized. Farmers' almanacs reminded their readers that a good wife must be both industrious and productive in her farmwork and that the economic well-being of the entire family was hinged to her efforts. Mothers trained their daughters to help with dairying, and if they had no daughters they relied on slaves or hired girls from poorer families. This recognition of the economic productivity of farm wives differed in some significant ways from the ways in which the roles of women in the rising middle class of the cities were being construed.

PRIVATE LIVES: DEFINING THE MIDDLE CLASS

In cities and towns throughout the North, the new industrial economy meant a change in the living and working arrangements for many who were caught up in it. In earlier years, artisans and merchants had lived above or near their shops, an arrangement that allowed their wives and children to easily help them. Home and workplace were closely associated, if not actually the same. As shops and stores became larger during the course of the nineteenth century, they were more likely to be located some distance from the homes of the owner and his employees. For women who stitched shoes or shirts, their homes were still clearly places of work as well as rest. But for women of the emerging middle class, whose husbands were clerks or shop owners or successful artisans, the workplace had moved and their homes were increasingly viewed as moral and emotional retreats. This did not mean that middle-class women did not work; it simply meant that their work was construed differently than it was for wage-earning women: it wasn't recognized as work.

Hidden Economy of Housework

Lydia Maria Child, a famous author and abolitionist, reviewed her domestic activities in 1864. She made afghans, towels, pillowcases, and curtains for her home. Almost every day, she cooked dinner and breakfast, swept out the kitchen and the rest of the house, and filled lamps. She also managed to write the literary pieces for women and children that supported her and her impecunious husband. Laundry was not on her list, so she was probably fortunate enough to have someone to help with this chore—an overwhelmingly exhausting activity that usually took two full days to complete. Not only was Child a loving wife; she was also the linchpin of what little financial security they had. In Utica, New York, Lavinia Johnson had her feet more firmly planted in the middle class than did Child, but her work was no less arduous. From doing laundry and ironing to washing windows and dusting, or tending her garden and preserving fruits and vegetables, Johnson kept busy year-round. She was a devoted mother, but she was also a workhorse.

The housework these women did carried an enormous but unacknowledged value. The cost of cooking meals, cleaning, and laundry was not insignificant. An unmarried man living in a boardinghouse could expect to pay seven hundred dollars per year for such services, a large sum given that the salary of many middle-class men at this time was about one thousand dollars per year. In addition to their unpaid housework, many middle-class women also brought in cash for their families or bartered for goods. Most women did not follow the lead of Lydia Maria Child and write for a living, but many engaged in the more prosaic activity of taking in boarders. Among Lavinia Johnson's neighbors in Utica, about one in five women cooked, washed, and cleaned for paying guests. In addition, women could earn cash selling kitchen fat, rags, berries, and eggs from their kitchen gardens.

Lydia Maria Child was a well-known writer of domestic literature for women and children as well as a fiery critic of slavery and other forms of injustice. She supported her husband and herself with the income from her writings.

The cash generated by these activities provided the family with important resources for gaining a foothold in the middle class. A mother who took in boarders relieved her teenage sons of the responsibility of working to contribute to the family well-being. As a result, teenage boys could stay in school longer and get the education they needed for the growing number of white-collar jobs. These young men pushed into the middle class aided by the work their mothers carried on at home.

Although a housewife's contribution to the family economy was quite significant, it was hard to recognize. The very houses families lived in muted the economic activity that was occurring there. Parlors grew in importance as the focal point of the new middle class. Furnished with soft carpets and upholstered furniture, these rooms allowed families to demonstrate their middle-class status through the purchase of consumer goods. The mother presided over family gatherings in the parlor, reading to her children or encouraging prayer. She also welcomed friends and hosted social events here, creating the impression that the home was a site of consumption rather than production, a site of leisure rather than work.

Cult of Domesticity

The middle-class home was invested with new significance by many of the leading authors of the day. The home was the place where mothers nurtured Christian consciences, trained young patriots, and fostered civilization. Such work was critical to the well-being of the nation, and it required careful training on the part of the women who were charged with this task.

No one spelled out the significance of domesticity more clearly than did Catharine Beecher, and she did so in clear practical terms in her best-selling *Treatise on Domestic Economy*. Beecher first published this book in 1841 and reissued it yearly for the next fifteen years. In 1869, she enlarged and revised the book with her sister, Harriett Beecher Stowe, into another best seller, *The American Woman's Home*. Beecher's book

WOMEN'S LIVES

LILLY MARTIN SPENCER

Lilly Martin Spencer, born Angelique Martin in London in 1822, immigrated to the United States with her parents in 1830 and settled with them in Marietta, Ohio. The Martins were utopian socialists and woman's rights activists, so that Lilly grew up in a family that consistently questioned the traditional organization of society. To help Lilly receive training as an artist, her father took her to Cincinnati in 1841, teaching French in order to earn money to pay for her art lessons. At the age of twenty-two, Lilly began her own unconventional family when she married Benjamin Rush Spencer, a tailor who never really held down a job. He did, however, help with the housework and child rearing, a demanding task because they eventually had thirteen children, seven of whom lived to be adults. The Spencers moved to New York in 1848, so that Lilly could pursue her career as an artist more aggressively.

Lilly Martin Spencer excelled in "genre paintings," a form of artwork that focused on the everyday activities of common people. Her portrayals of women in domestic settings were particularly striking. In *Domestic Happiness,* painted in 1849, the artist portrayed a young couple lovingly watching over their young sleeping children. In *Shake Hands?* painted in 1854, she focused on a smiling woman at work in her well-stocked kitchen. In both cases, these were women in charge of their sphere, women who clearly recognized the importance of the work they were doing. The young mother looking at her sleeping children stands slightly in front of her husband, her hand raised in a fashion that gently acknowledges her authority in the scene. The woman in the kitchen looks frankly at the viewer, her extended hand covered in flour. She is both engaged in the crucial work of cooking for her family and committed to the egalitarian values of democracy that were symbolized by shaking hands in the United States.

Lilly Martin Spencer became famous in both Europe and the United States as many of her paintings were turned into cheap, mass-produced prints that circulated through many of the types of homes she had painted. But these prints did little to pay her bills. Thus, during the 1850s, Lilly also took on work illustrating articles for *Godey's Lady's Book.* She continued to paint domestic scenes, particularly focusing on the image of the mother, but by the end of the 1860s the market for such artwork had disappeared and Lilly's reputation began to fade. She died in Poughkeepsie, New York, in 1902. ■

was filled with practical advice for young wives about how to make their homes run smoothly. She told them precisely how to set their tables, the kind of plumbing system they needed for a good kitchen, and the best kind of diet for a growing family. She gave women tips on how to save time when doing household chores if they could not afford a servant to help them. She showed women how the body functioned so that mothers could attend to sick family members.

Beecher did not simply offer practical advice in these works; she also argued for the larger significance of these household activities, championing what scholars have since called the **cult of domesticity**. She argued that a woman's home was an important complement to the democratic institutions of the new nation and that one could not function without the other. In the home, moral, religious, and civic values were fashioned. Ideals of civilization were upheld. Healthy bodies produced healthy minds.

Beecher believed that women should voluntarily take on the responsibilities of the home to bring order to their society. Others, such as Sarah Josepha Hale, believed that women had no choice. Hale, the powerful editor of *Godey's Lady's Book* from 1837 until 1877, believed that women were innately different from men and spiritually superior to them. Presiding over their homes was not simply a choice but, rather, the outgrowth of their different natures. Women were physically and psychologically suited to child rearing and housekeeping according to Hale, because they themselves were morally pure. Most important, this was a virtue that meant sexual purity. Women were increasingly imagined as both uninterested in sex and unaware of it. "I would have her as pure as the snow on the mount," claimed one author in *Godey's*, "as pure as the wave of the crystalline fount." The cult of domesticity marked an important turning point in the discourse of gender complementarity. The idea that women were not inferior to men but simply different had been growing during the eighteenth century. Now, this idea of complementarity became a cornerstone of middle-class formation. Women were expected to protect their virtue and provide a private refuge for their husbands in the **separate sphere** of their homes as a counterpoint to the public and morally compromised world of business and politics. The doctrine of separate spheres became an important ideology in the nineteenth century. Even though women engaged in both public and economic activities within and outside their homes, the doctrine of separate spheres argued that respectable women should not do so.

Writers such as Beecher and Hale imagined all women in the United States sharing in this mission. Beecher addressed not only the middle-class women who were busy rearing their families but also seamstresses and servants who had to support themselves; and Hale covered the struggles of wage-earning women in her periodical. Unfortunately, it was harder for wage-earning women to live up to their ideals. They had not the time to clean or the parlors to use for private moments of child rearing. Their homes were obviously places of work as well as refuge. As one farm woman noted, "If ever I had a sphere, I must have lost it long ago." This was one of the most problematic aspects of this ideology of domesticity. While democratic on the one hand in assuming that all women could and should live this way, it in fact reinforced distinctions of class

cult of domesticity ideology suggesting that women's work within the home was crucial to society, particularly because of its moral rather than economic value

separate spheres the idea that men and women operate in different worlds: women in the private world of the home and men in the public world of business and politics

"Domestic Happiness," painted by Lilly Martin Spencer in 1849, conveys the family ideals that were so central to middle class formation in the nineteenth century. Both parents share an intimate bond with the children pictured here, but the mother also shows her dominance within the family as she stands in front of her husband, positioned between him and the sleeping children. (Photograph © 1993 The Detroit Institute of Arts)

because some women due to economic circumstances would not be able to live up to these universal ideals. One of the most important characteristics and contradictions of the cult of domesticity was that while it purported to describe universal, natural characteristics of women, in fact, it described a condition most closely associated with white, middle-class women, particularly in the urban Northeast. The middle class, or bourgeoisie, was formed as a social group around a belief in this ideal. One of the ways the northern middle class became powerful was to argue that its ideals applied to all women, not just women of its own group.

Courtship and Marriage

Just as the middle-class home was no longer viewed as the locus of work in the nineteenth century, the middle-class marriage no longer centered on questions of inheritance and land. The emphasis on love that had been developing in the eighteenth century blossomed in the nineteenth century. While members of the new middle class were certainly aware of economic advantages that could derive from a strategic marriage, they had other avenues in acquiring capital, including their banks and credit ratings. When Mary Smith and Samuel Smith decided to get married in 1834, she wrote to her suitor, "As well as I love my parents—as well as I love my connections to friends—Yet *all* I could resign most willingly—most happily for your sake. . . ." Their romantic love trumped any other emotions she felt for family and friends.

The families that these couples formed were both smaller and more emotionally intense than those of the colonial period. At the beginning of the nineteenth century, American families had, on average, seven children. By 1850, they had only about five or six children, and by 1900 about three or four children. This decline in family size was most pronounced among native-born whites in the urban areas of the Northeast. Here, children were becoming more of an expense than an asset. Whereas children on farms contributed to their family's well-being by taking on a variety of chores, salaried families in the Northeast did not reap these benefits. Indeed, those who set their sights on white-collar work faced the opposite problem of having to pay for educating their sons to take a place in the new middle class.

As family size declined and emotional intensity grew, a new philosophy of child rearing dominated the middle-class home, a philosophy that eschewed colonial practices of corporal punishment in favor of strategies rooted in love and persuasion. Whereas the colonial father whipped a disobedient child, the nineteenth-century mother formed a child's conscience to make the right choice. A middle-class mother was expected to instill internalized controls that young men and women could rely on as they moved from one community to the next looking for work. The ability to display self-control and a strong conscience was critical in the ability to succeed in a business career and to gain access to credit. But these new forms of socialization also meant that women began to dominate their households during the nineteenth century. As a system of discipline emerged in which the internal restraints of conscience nurtured by the mother replaced the external constraints of physical punishment meted out by the father, women became the heart of family organization. The bonds of intimacy created by the parents were communicated to the children through their mothers.

WOMEN'S VOICES

MOTHERLY DISCIPLINE

Elizabeth Buffum Chace was the wife of a prosperous manufacturer and was an abolitionist and woman's rights activist from Rhode Island. She worked hard managing her lively family, as is clear in this letter to her husband, Samuel Chace.

Valley Falls [RI], 4th mo., 3rd, 1854

Yesterday I promised Eddie that I would buy a stick of molasses candy for him, but I forgot it until after supper tonight and then gave Lillie three cents to go and buy some. . . . She brought four sticks and, according to my promise, I gave Eddie one. I then broke one in two and gave it to Arnold, bidding him give one half to Sammy. He said he wanted a whole stick, and kept on fretting and scolding. Finally he threw the half stick in my lap and said he would not have it. I said he should not and arose with it. He screamed and endeavored to force it from me and finding he could not, he commenced striking me. I seized his hands and held them and bade Mary help me to undress him, but he kicked so we could not. . . Michael came and all three of us with the utmost difficulty divested him of his clothing, put on his nightgown, and then Michael laid him in bed. All this time I felt perfectly calm, without the slightest irritation. Something whispered encouragement in my spirit, saying, "Do it thoroughly; it will be the last time." . . . Arnold . . . took all his bedclothes and strewed them on the floor; pulled off the mattresses, pulled out the bed cord and then went to the bookcase, which stood in the room and took out every book and paper and threw it on the floor. The other children had gone to bed and nobody interfered with him. Then his angry passion seemed to

have spent itself. He lay down and wept. It grew pretty dark and he was alone. After a while he came out sobbing and said, "Mother, will thee get me a little stick to put the strings into my bedstead?" (meaning the bed cord. The bedstead has holes for the cord to go through). I gave him a fork and he went back. Sammy volunteered his assistance and by the dim twilight they put in the cord and put on the beds and then Sammy left him and he made up the bed. Then he went to the bookcase and commenced putting up the books and papers, in the dark. I let him work a while and then set a light in the room and he returned them all nicely to their places. Then he brought out the light, bade me farewell, and went to bed. I hoped he would come and acknowledge his fault, but did not think it best to draw this from him but to leave him entirely to his own thoughts. It was a crisis to which he had been for some time tending and I think it will do him good.

Should this record meet his eye in the future years, I doubt not that he will gratefully acknowledge that his mother did him no injustice and that her firmness helped him to overcome his obstinacy.

Source: Elizabeth Chace to Samuel Chace, 1854, in Virtuous Lives: Four Quaker Sisters Remember Family Life, Abolitionism, and Women's Suffrage, *edited by Lucille Salitan and Eve Lewis Perara. C 1994 and reprinted with the permission of the publisher, The Continuum International Publishing Group.*

Questions

1. How does Elizabeth Chace exercise power over her children?

2. Why does Elizabeth Chace wait for her son to "acknowledge his fault"?

Sexual Boundaries

By the middle of the nineteenth century, the idea that women were naturally lusty was long gone. A virtuous, middle-class white woman was expected to know little, if anything, about sex when she got married. Having said this, however, it is clear men and women continued to have sex in the nineteenth century—a lot. Indeed, as married couples sought to limit the size of their families in the nineteenth century, they increasingly associated sex with romantic love rather than procreation. A "Christian gentleman" was supposed to moderate his carnal passions for the woman he loved, but he was also expected to use sex to promote spiritual intimacy in his marriage.

Unmarried women also continued to have an interest in sex. Young women still developed erotic relationships with their fiancés as they built their romantic relationships. Mira Bigelow thus wrote to her suitor Elias Nason in 1831: "O! I do really want to kiss you. . . . How I should really like to be in that old parlor with you. . . . I hope there will be a carpet on the floor for it seems you intend to act worse than you ever did before. . . . but I shall humbly submit to my fate and willingly too, to speak candidly." What is important about the nineteenth century, however, is her fiancé's response. He made it clear to Mira that he expected her to draw limits when he embraced her. Couples such as Bigelow and Nason were far more careful about premarital sex than their parents or grandparents had been. The premarital pregnancy rate had begun a precipitous decline from its peak at the time of the American Revolution. About 20 percent of the women who married in the 1830s were pregnant; and by 1850, that number dropped to 10 percent. In the mobile society of the nineteenth century, young women could not count on their communities to force a marriage if they became pregnant.

In addition to the romantic relationships they formed with men, middle-class women also formed romantic relationships with other women, though of a very different type. At a time when men and women believed in separate spheres, intimate relationships within one's sphere were an accepted part of middle-class behavior. Young women formed intense relationships with one another at boarding schools and seminaries or in their normal course of socializing. In their letters to one another and in their diaries, they wrote of the electric excitement produced in such relationships, of rapture and pain, and of deeply felt emotions. Emily Dickinson, the famous poet, wrote to her dear friend Sue Gilbert in 1852 demanding, "Susie, will you indeed come home next Saturday, and be my own again, as you used to? . . . I . . . feel that I *cannot* wait, feel that now I *must* have you—that the expectation once more to see your face again, makes me feel hot and feverish, and my heart beats so fast."

Despite the passionate feelings between these two women, Gilbert married Dickinson's brother. Their relationship was not considered a substitute for marriage but, rather, intimacy of a different order. Indeed, friendships such as these often continued after the women married. Making visits to one another, they shared the same bed and each other's embraces. While this kind of physical intimacy would be considered "deviant" later in the century, it was considered quite acceptable for middle-class women during the antebellum period as long as codes of etiquette were followed. Advice books at the time reminded young ladies that their kissing and caressing should be done while they were alone and never in front of young men.

Controlling Family Size

Middle-class families in the North did not simply get smaller by accident. Men and women were clearly practicing contraception. Some practiced a version of the rhythm method, trying to have sex only when the women were not ovulating. However, until the 1840s, many believed that women were least likely to conceive a child halfway through their menstrual cycle, which was exactly when women were most likely to conceive. Men also could have practiced withdrawal, a method they could have learned about from lecturers on marital physiology, or they could purchase condoms. Until the 1830s, condoms had been fairly expensive, costing about one dollar a piece (close to a week's wages for a workingman); but by the 1860s, condoms could be purchased for half that price and by the 1870s were often only twenty-five cents. Women could use vaginal sponges, as well as metal or rubber shields and **pessaries** (glass shields) that were early versions of a diaphragm. Many of these devices were meant to stay in for long periods of time, though they were often painful and women had to remove them.

pessary Glass shield inserted in a woman's vagina to hold the uterus in place or for contraceptive purposes.

Knowledge of abortion as an alternative form of contraception was also widespread. Until the middle of the nineteenth century, most Americans believed that the fetus came to life about three months after conception in a process called "quickening," the point at which the fetus began to move. It was legal to induce an abortion before quickening, and a variety of potions were available to accomplish this task. Often these potions were advertised as regulating a woman's menstrual cycle, indicating that they could induce a woman's period. After the 1840s, abortion compounds were increasingly advertised in newspapers as "Female Regulator" or "Woman's Friend." Women could also consult local midwives, who not only delivered babies but also induced abortions for women who wanted them. Advertisements for abortion remedies were always coded and indirect. Some pills warned patients not to take them if they were pregnant because the pills would cause a miscarriage, an indirect way of indicating what the pills could actually do.

Regular medical doctors opposed the practice of abortion; and as the medical profession became stronger, doctors became increasingly critical of midwives and other "female doctors" who performed abortions. However, at the beginning of the nineteenth century, abortion before quickening was legal in all states and even if performed after quickening was seldom prosecuted with much vigor. During the 1830s and 1840s, however, a variety of states began to pass laws regulating who could perform an abortion and punishing those who performed illegal abortions. Some potions were also outlawed as abortion remedies because they were poisonous. Even so, juries were reluctant to convict people on abortion charges and self-induced abortions, in particular, were largely ignored. New York was the only state to pass more restrictive legislation in 1829 outlawing abortions of any type at any point in a pregnancy except to save a woman's life. In many of these debates, abortion was considered immoral because it was associated with licentious sex and with dangers to the mother's health rather than because it was considered an attack on the fetus. This view affected doctors' attitudes as well as those of lawmakers.

Types of Women's Work

Factory Families

Entire families, quite poor, were employed by small factories, usually in southern New England. Children, especially girls, worked in the factories, while their fathers farmed factory land. Wages were paid in scrip to a family account so that the father controlled the wages of the children.

Independent Mill Girls

Teenagers and young adults worked for cash wages in large factories that predominated in northern New England. They lived in boardinghouses supervised by a matron, using their money to support their families, buy clothes, pay for further education, or to create a dowry.

Putting Out System

Merchants with raw materials, such as shoe leather, distributed the materials to women, who worked in their homes to create finished products such as shoes. These products were then returned to the merchant for a set price. Many seamstresses also worked in this fashion to make shirts. Women earned less at these activities than they did working in factories that paid cash wages, but the putting out system allowed them to work at home if they needed to supervise their children.

Prostitution

Sometimes high paying, but very dangerous work selling sex that developed in large cities. It drew on particularly poor girls, some of whom were quite young.

Dairying

Women in rural areas, particularly if they were close to larger towns, produced excess butter, cheese, eggs, and milk for sale. In this way, they were able to provide important infusions of cash to purchase consumer goods for their families.

Laundress

Doing laundry was difficult and poorly paid. Sometimes African American women took in laundry as either a second job they did at home at night or as the job they did because they could find no other.

Domestic Service

Women who worked as household servants were often expected to live with the family they served and to work long hours. Because they received room and board as part of this arrangement, they could save their wages. However, the lack of independence that came with living in someone else's house made this job unpopular with native born white girls. Irish immigrants and African American women were more likely to be servants.

Housework

Most middle class women cooked, sewed, cleaned, and sometimes took in boarders. Even if they did not earn cash for their labor, the work they did was still of considerable economic value because their families did not have to pay for these services.

MULTIPLE IDENTITIES: RACE, ETHNICITY, AND THE FEMALE EXPERIENCE

A large number of immigrants who began to flood the country during these same years were drawn by the new industrial and commercial activities that were transforming the United States. While less than 2 percent of the population had immigrated to the country in 1820, by 1860 more than 10 percent had. The two largest groups came from Ireland and the Germanic states of Central Europe. German immigrants often headed for farmlands in the Midwest, though a sizable minority set up shops and stores in grow-ing cities. The Irish crowded into the cities along the Atlantic, so that in New York City, for example, almost half of the population in 1860 had been born abroad. Poor and uneducated, the Irish fought for jobs that none but African Americans had been willing to take in the past. The free blacks with whom they competed for employment were a much smaller community. About a quarter of a million African Americans lived in the North by the time of the Civil War, almost half of them in cities. However, dur-ing the first half of the nineteenth century, as cities exploded in size, the percentage of free blacks making up a part of that population actually declined. In Philadelphia, for example, although the actual number of the free black population increased from a lit-tle over four thousand in 1800 to almost eleven thousand in 1850, the percentage of free blacks in the population declined from 10 percent to 8 percent.

African American Independence

In the free black communities of this period, ideals of respectability circulated as a goal to be achieved by black women as well as white. *The Colored American,* a newspaper published by and for African Americans, repeatedly reminded women to be mindful of propriety. Thus, the newspaper urged its female readers to be sensible in dress and careful not "to seduce by her appearance, but only to please." Reminding women in another article to always welcome their husbands "with a smile," the paper also sug-gested attention to child care and cooking.

For many African American women, this responsibility for domestic life—along with the need that they work for wages—created a demanding schedule. Chloe Spear of Boston, for example, operated a boardinghouse and worked as a domestic servant for a local family. Her husband, Cesar, took care of the boardinghouse while Chloe worked as a servant, but when Chloe got home, she cooked dinner, cleaned, and washed laun-dry while Cesar "was taking his rest." Chloe's schedule was exhausting—more exhaust-ing than her husband's. But Chloe Spear also disposed of her money in a way that many white women did not. Although her husband legally held control over her earnings and her property, he did not exercise that right. When Chloe Spear decided to purchase a house for seven hundred dollars, her husband argued at first that they could not afford it. His wife, however, produced the necessary money and her husband acquiesced. Chloe Spear kept her own wages and determined their disposition, something her hus-band supported. It is not surprising that free African American women constituted a significant percentage of the property holders in the free black community.

Free women of color needed to be independent. In most cities of the North (and of the South), women outnumbered men among the free black population. This may have been one reason they were less likely to marry than white women were, but it was not the only reason. Even where black women did not outnumber men, they were still less likely than whites to marry. Single parent families became increasingly common among free African Americans during the first half of the nineteenth century. In Cincinnati, black families headed by women increased from 11 percent in 1830 to 22 percent in 1850. This imbalance may have been caused by high rates of mortality among black men as well as their difficulty in finding employment in the cities. Many black women were widows by the time they reached their forties.

African American women such as Chloe Spear often created extended families in the boardinghouses they ran. Men and women who migrated to the cities found not only food and shelter in their boarding houses but also contacts for work, opportunities for socializing, and a helping hand if economic disaster struck. In several instances in Boston, members of boardinghouses joined together to rescue fugitive slaves. Lydia Potter provided a more informal boarding arrangement for Sarah Hall, an African American newcomer, when she arrived in Boston during the 1850s. Potter employed Hall as a servant in her house in exchange for her bed and board, but she also provided Hall with access to the social networks of African Americans in Boston. Most African American women, however, worked as servants for white families, not for black ones. Though lowly and demanding, even these opportunities were threatened in the 1850s as large numbers of Irish women increasingly competed for domestic work.

Irish Domesticity

Before the great famine in the mid-1840s, women seldom immigrated to the United States from Ireland. Ireland had few jobs, so families often chose which child should emigrate as part of a larger financial investment, and boys were considered more likely to find employment and send their wages home to the rest of the family. As a result, about two-thirds of the Irish who immigrated to the United States in the first half of the nineteenth century were men. That proportion changed, however, after the potato famine struck Ireland in 1845, when more and more women left Ireland to seek their fortunes abroad. Still, immigration continued to be a family decision, even if individuals migrated alone. With footholds established by brothers and uncles, young women began migrating in large numbers to the factory towns and cities where their relatives lived and worked. Like their male relatives, women often sent home part of their wages as they could. "I am sending ye two pounds," Eliza Quin wrote to her parents in 1848, adding, "I will not forget to send ye some assistance as soon as I can." While some of these women began working as seamstresses or in textile factories, most of the Irish women who came to the United States—both before and after the famine—found jobs as servants.

Native-born women usually scorned domestic service, but these jobs represented an attractive option for young Irish women who found virtually no paid employment in Ireland. Domestic work was demanding, because servants often lived in their employers' homes and were at their beck and call night and day. But domestic workers earned more than seamstresses. And servants could change households, as their mistresses never failed to bemoan, abandoning a tyrant in the hope of finding a more compliant mistress. Domestic service was an important, if brief, activity in the life cycle of young Irish women. Even if living with their parents, Irish girls began work as domestic servants when they were as young as eleven years old. In Buffalo, New York, over half of the young Irish women who were age seventeen were working as domestic servants and by age twenty-one most of them were. In New York City, young immigrant girls were quickly absorbed into the world of domestic service when they were sent over. While Irish men, like other male immigrants, tended to drift away to other cities and regions in search of work, women did not do so until they married, at which point they were influenced by the inclinations of their husbands. As a result, by 1850, almost two-thirds (58 percent) of the Irish immigrants living in New York City were female.

Because most of these young women were working in households of middle-class, native-born whites, they were exposed to ideals of domesticity and middle-class gentility that their brothers and future husbands knew little about. These young women carried their ideals of gentility into their own households when they married. Marriage

𝒲OMEN'S 𝒱OICES

AN IRISH IMMIGRANT

Margaret McCarthy immigrated to the United States in the late 1840s. Scholars do not know what happened to her or her family in later years.

New York September 22nd, 1850

My Dr. Father and Mother Brothers and Sisters,

I write these few lines to you hopeing That these few lines may find you all in as good State of health as I am at present thank God. . . . Come you all Together Couragiously and bid adieu to that lovely place the land of our Birth. that place where the young and old joined Together in one Common Union, both night and day Engaged in Innocent Amusement, But alas. I am now Told it's the Gulf of Misersry oppression Degradetion and Ruin of evry Discription which I am Sorry to hear. . . . This my Dr. Father induces me to Remit to you in this Letter 20 Dollars. . . . I could not Express how great would be my joy at seeing you all here Together where you would never want or be at a loss for a good Breakfast and Dinner. So prepare as soon as possible for this will be my last Remittince until I see you all here. Bring with you as much Tools as you can as it will cost you nothing to Bring them And as for Mary She need not mind much as I will have for her A Silk Dress A Bonnet and Viel. . . .

Dan Keliher Tells me that you Knew more of the House Carpentery than he did himself and he can earn from twelve to fourteen Shilling a day that is seven Shilling British and he also tells me that Florence will do very well and that Michl can get a place Right off. . . . I am sure its not for Slavery I

want you to Come here no its for affording My Brothers and Sisters And I an oppertunity of Showing our Kindness and Gratitude and Comeing on your Seniour days that we would be placed in that possession that you my Dr. Father and Mother could walk about Lesuirly and Indepenly without Requireing your Labour. . . .

I am proud and happy to Be away from where the County Charges man or the poor Rates man or any other Rates man would have the Satisfaction of once Inpounding my cow or any other article of mine Oh how happy I feel and am sure to have look as The Lord had not it destined for me to get married to Some Loammun or another at home. . . . So my Dr. Father according as I have State to you I hope that whilst you are at home I hope that you will give my Sister Mary that privelage of Injoying herself Innocently and as for my Dr. Ellen I am in Raptures of joy when I think of one day Seeing her and you all at the dock in New York. . . .

Margaret McCarthy

Source: *Margaret McCarthy to her family in Lisa Grunwald and Stephen J. Adler, eds.,* Women's Letters: America from the Revolutionary War to the Present *(New York: Dial Press, 2005) 202–5. Reprinted from Diarmaid O. Muirithe, A Seat Behind the Coachman: Travellers in Ireland, 1800–1900 (Dublin: Grill and Macmillan Ltd., 1972) 138–142.*

Questions

1. What sort of responsibilities does Margaret McCarthy feel toward her family?

2. How is Margaret's life better in the United States than it was in Ireland?

often provided a welcome end to days of service. Catharine Ann McFarland had tired of her life as a servant and eagerly accepted the proposal of a young Irish carpenter. As she explained to her mother back in Ireland, "i never had mutch plesur in my young days' sow I hope to have some now." The ability to create a domestic environment in which the woman was the moral center of the household offered many young Irish women a much more desirable alternative to the patriarchal controls exercised by their fathers in their Irish homeland. By the time they married, young Irish women shared many of the domestic ideals of their native-born counterparts, but not all. Most important, they did not share the same commitment to limiting family size.

German Guardians of Tradition

Catholic, Protestant, and Jewish immigrants from the Germanic states in Central Europe also poured into the United States during the antebellum period. The United States offered jobs in growing cities to peddlers and artisans as well as land in the Midwest to poor farmers who faced the same potato famine as the Irish. Immigrants also came to escape discrimination. Both poor peasants and Jews faced difficulties marrying in some German states where they had to wait years for permission to marry and had to pay high fees for the privilege. In the United States, no such restrictions existed.

Men were the primary immigrants in the early decades of the nineteenth century, though women soon began to follow as part of family groups. Catholic and Protestant women, like their male family members, were most likely to end up on farms. Some of these women worked first as servants, trying to save money for a dowry that would contribute to the purchase of a family farm. Jewish immigrants were more likely to head for cities, seeking work as skilled artisans and, most important, as peddlers, a job many had left behind in Europe as their trade routes disappeared.

Like many of their native-born neighbors, German women also ran boardinghouses. Jewish women took in young Jewish peddlers who traveled from town to town and needed a place to live. For those who kept kosher (following strict dietary rules about what to eat), the ability to live in such a household was highly valued. Catholic and Protestant women also catered to German boarders who were new to the country, offering food from the old country and a shared language for socializing.

German girls who migrated to the United States found their opportunities to marry expanded given the large number of German men in their new communities. Throughout the nineteenth century, 60 percent of the immigrants from the German states were men. As a result, German women were more likely to marry German men than vice versa. German women nourished ethnic traditions in their cooking and their celebration of traditional holidays. They prided themselves in keeping their houses cleaner than their native-born counterparts.

However, there were other ways in which some immigrants quickly adopted American ways. The Jewish women who came to America, for example, had expected their parents to arrange their marriages. They had little knowledge of the world of romantic love that was becoming so important to many of their native-born neighbors. They expected to grow closer to their husbands as their lives became intertwined, but they viewed marriage as a practical matter. In the United States, though, these attitudes began to change. Hannah Marks, a young orphan from Philadelphia, for example, caused a family crisis in the 1850s when she jilted her suitor from California. He had paid for her passage west, but when she met him, he was not to her liking. Hannah instead took a job teaching school for the next decade and eventually married a man she preferred. Like other young immigrants, she had embraced the culture of sentiment flourishing around her.

The Culture of Sentiment

The urbanizing and industrializing world of the urban Northeast spawned a varied and wide-reaching cultural market. Theaters sprang up in cities large and small, though by mid-century, New York was the capital of drama. Perhaps most influential and widespread, however, was the revolution in publishing that unleashed an unprecedented number of books and periodicals on the public. Important technological innovations made printing both cheaper and faster.

As in most forms of business, men maintained control but women participated extensively in this cultural revolution. In all cases, women had to proceed cautiously. The world of culture was essentially a public world and, thus, the realm of men. Women who spoke in public, whether on stage or in print, risked their respectability and their status as ladies. Moving carefully, many of these women addressed their performances to the domestic world of women, not only creating a cultural interpretation of domesticity but also, ironically, turning domesticity into a commodity. Although conceived as a separate sphere, a world apart from that of business and even antithetical to it, domesticity circulated as an economic product just as shoes, cloth, and teapots did.

Women on Stage

Theaters proliferated in the new urban atmosphere, and with them came jobs for women. The time had long since passed when young boys played female parts, so theater managers paid handsomely for women with good memories and strong elocution skills who were willing to tread the boards. Early in the nineteenth century, one actress earned one hundred dollars per week while another, Agnes Gilfert, earned two hundred dollars per night. Often, these were women who took to the stage in the company (and protection) of their husbands. Susanna Rowson, for example, worked as an actress for five years with her husband William before she quit the stage in 1791 to open a girls' school.

The fact that Rowson could open a successful girls' school suggests that she was able to retain her reputation despite her association with the theater. Other famous actresses of the period also worked hard to preserve their reputations. Fanny Kemble, one of the most famous actresses of the nineteenth century, drew admirers from the most respectable quarters of society when she arrived in the United States from London in the 1830s. She abandoned her career for what turned out to be a disastrous marriage to a southern wastrel, Pierce Butler, who lived off the work of his slaves and squandered his fortune. Kemble was horrified with both aspects of his life and finally left him. When her husband sued her for divorce, Kemble deftly defended herself in the press as the injured party: an honest and hardworking woman who had been deceived and abused by an unfaithful, irresponsible husband. With her reputation intact, Kemble embarked on a new and lucrative career reading Shakespeare to audiences around the country.

Charlotte Cushman also guarded her reputation as she came to dominate the stage in the 1840s and 1850s. Cushman, who never married, took to the stage to support her mother and various other relatives after the bankruptcy of her father left them destitute. Early on, Cushman wrote for *Godey's Lady's Book*; and, as she dragged her sister Susan

Charlotte Cushman was one of the most successful actresses of the antebellum period. She often portrayed powerful women, or even men, onstage.

onto the stage with her, she made sure Susan joined an appropriate female benevolent society in order to shore up her reputation. Cushman not only played powerful women on stage such as Lady Macbeth, she also played men: most notably Romeo opposite her sister's Juliet. Such "breeches" roles were popular for several conflicting reasons. When women played men, they often wore tights and revealed their legs to a titillated audience. But the audience also associated purity of purpose in the relationship between characters such as Romeo and Juliet when they knew both roles were being played by women. Charlotte Cushman herself may have enjoyed these roles because she was strongly attracted to women and shared two successive relationships with women: Mathilda Hays, to whom she pledged "celibacy and eternal attachment," and later, when that relationship disintegrated, Emma Stebbins. In a world in which such relationships had not yet been labeled "perverse lesbianism," Charlotte Cushman lived a respectable life.

Respectability had become a predominant concern of many theater owners by the middle of the nineteenth century as they decided middle-class women constituted an important part of the audience they wanted to draw. By the 1850s, most theater owners had barred prostitutes and many had also outlawed the sale of alcoholic beverages. They also created afternoon matinees, knowing that middle-class women would be the ones most likely to have the flexibility in their schedules that would allow them to attend. Finally, theater owners encouraged moralistic presentations such as the successful temperance play, *The Drunkard,* which enjoyed a long run in Boston as well as other cities.

To be sure, not all theaters carried these marks of middle-class respectability. In the Olympic Theater in New York, working-class audiences cheered their Bowery B'hoi hero Mose and his girlfriend Lize. Model artist shows and various other productions in which women revealed parts of their bodies also occupied a well-defined niche. But these were shows that defined the boundaries rather than the center of nineteenth-century theater. By the middle of the nineteenth century, a variety of women had found ways to use notions of domesticity and female virtue to promote their dramatic activities.

Scribbling Women

Novel reading continued to be just as scandalous in the early nineteenth century as it had been in the eighteenth century: a peculiar female folly bemoaned by ministers and educators who feared that the young women of the country had lost what little good sense they might have had. The hand wringing did no good, however. Novels exploded as a literary genre in the nineteenth century, overwhelmingly produced and consumed by women. Nathaniel Hawthorne, who viewed himself as a more serious contender in the literary arena, famously complained that "America is now wholly given over to a d--ned mob of scribbling women, and I should have no chance of success while the public taste is occupied with their trash—and should be ashamed of myself if I did succeed. . . ." Despite this carping, female novelists sold more books than most of their male colleagues and, in doing so, shaped this literary form around the concerns of middle-class women: their families, their love lives, and their homes.

Catherine Maria Sedgwick was one of the first of these writers, capturing public attention in the 1820s with the publication of *A New England Tale; Or, Sketches of New England Character and Manners*. Like many of her female contemporaries, she worried about the respectability of appearing in print and only did so after being nudged by supportive family members. Many of the other women who took up professional writing abandoned their reservations only when faced with economic hardship. Some were widows, others deserted by their husbands, and still others faced with supporting their families because their husbands for reasons of health or temperament were unable to command the salaries they needed for survival. Calvin Stowe fretted endlessly about his ability (or rather, inability) to support his family. Trying to calm him at one point, his wife, Harriet Beecher Stowe reassured him that God would watch out for them; but better yet, she would "bring things right." E.D.E.N. Southworth had to support herself and her daughter after her husband deserted her. Sara Parton lost her first husband to death and her second to divorce before beginning her writing career in her forties under the pen name "Fanny Fern" to support herself and her two children.

Many women writers concentrated on issues of home and heart in sentimental novels. They created dramas of love, often fraught with misunderstandings between a heroine and her lover, not to mention conflicts with parents who could never seem to understand who was the appropriate mate for their daughters. Susan Warner spun a story of female submission in her popular novel *The Wide, Wide World*, with a heroine who faced a series of trials after the deaths of her mother and her close friend. Most stories, however, ended in marriage, anchoring women in the place they were expected to occupy.

Despite their heavy emphasis on personal feelings, some of these stories also raised larger political and social issues. Lydia Maria Child's early novel, *Hobomok*, depicted the marriage of a white woman to an Indian man. More famous, however, was Harriet Beecher Stowe's *Uncle Tom's Cabin*, which when it was published in 1852 kindled a storm of sympathy for the antislavery movement. Writing a story of domestic disarray, Stowe adapted the conventional themes of the nineteenth-century novel to argue that slavery perverted family relations by denying slaves the ability to form their own families and by encouraging cruelty and sloth among the white families who owned the slaves. In a less well-known but equally hard-hitting novel, the African American writer Harriet Wilson condemned the racism found in northern society in her 1859 novel, *Our Nig; or, Sketches from the Life of a Free Black*. Wilson explored the abuse suffered by Frado, an African American servant, at the hands of her heartless northern employer, Mrs. Bellmont. As both Wilson and Stowe recognized, the injustices and hierarchies of society were easily replicated in the home and could be explored symbolically in the context of sentimental fiction.

Earnest Readers

Female authors and their novels found a large, eager, and increasingly literate audience in the nineteenth century in part because the structure of society was changing. Publishers in Boston, New York, and Philadelphia used newly available technology to print books more cheaply than before and distributed them along the canal and railroad lines that became available in the 1830s. During the eighteenth century, only

WOMEN'S LIVES

SARA PARTON (FANNY FERN)

Fanny Fern, the pen name of Sara Willis Parton, was one of the most famous and well-paid writers of the nineteenth century. Like most of the women who entered that profession, she did so out of financial need after the death of her first husband and her divorce from her second husband. Born in 1811, she grew up in Boston and attended Catharine Beecher's Female Seminary in Hartford during 1828 and 1829, where she was taught by both Catharine and Catharine's sister, Harriet Beecher Stowe, who later remembered her fondly as "a certain naughty girl."

Like most women of her class, Sara married a promising young man, Charles Harrington Eldredge, who died of typhoid fever in 1846, leaving his wife penniless. Sara's father pressured her into a second marriage with Samuel Farrington three years later, in hopes of shoring up her financial security. Farrington turned out to be so intensely jealous and controlling that a couple of years later she fled with her children to a hotel. Attempting to begin a career as a writer, she sent several pieces to her brother Nathaniel Parker Willis, editor of the *Home Journal*. He peevishly rejected her work, complaining, "You overstrain the pathetic, and your humor runs into dreadful vulgarity sometimes."

Sara persevered. She found other newspapers, such as the *Olive Branch,* willing to take her writings and she soon published a collection of her works in the wildly successful and very sentimental *Fern Leaves from Fanny's Portfolio* in 1853. Over one hundred thousand copies sold within a year, providing the young author with a solid return based on her royalties of ten cents per copy. Her newfound fame also brought her to the attention of the publisher of the *Musical World and*

Times, who offered to double her salary if she would move to New York and write for his newspaper exclusively. With her newfound wealth, she was able to purchase a house in Brooklyn, support her family, and continue her writing career. She also met and married her third husband, James Parton, in 1856. Much shrewder about business matters by this time, the new Mrs. Parton made sure that her husband signed a prenuptial agreement before their marriage, giving her ownership and control over all of her property and the royalties from her writing.

Parton's writing became more interesting as her career matured. *Ruth Hall,* published in 1854, depicted the difficulties faced by a woman who was forced to work to support her children after her husband died and who successfully met the challenge as a writer. Because *Ruth Hall* was based on Sara Willis's life, celebrating the professional triumph she had achieved and pillorying the male relatives who had deserted her, a storm of controversy arose over what some critics claimed were her pride and her vindictiveness. But Nathaniel Hawthorne, never one to coddle female writers, disagreed. Praising the controversial novel, he argued that when women writers "throw off the restraints of decency, and come before the public stark naked, as it were—then their books are sure to possess character and value." Fanny Fern knew well the dilemmas women faced as they struggled to survive in a world that expected them to be cared for and adored but in which such a scenario was often derailed. She died in 1872. ■

about 50 percent of the women in the North could read. By the time of the Civil War, the figure was closer to 90 percent. No doubt this increase was due in large part to increasing opportunities for women to receive at least a rudimentary education at local town schools.

In big cities and small towns, lending libraries proliferated, bringing books within the reach of the masses. Almost all of these lending libraries were private, and membership in some of the most well-known athenaeums was quite expensive. Fortunately, more modest libraries were also available. A shopkeeper would have a room above his store where he kept popular novels, for example, charging a membership fee of a dollar a year that could be paid in monthly installments.

Women formed reading societies to discuss and debate the issues raised by new books in towns and villages that were large enough. Sometimes the reading societies were composed of men as well as women so that chairs were pushed aside after some quick discussion to facilitate dancing and games. In other instances, women preferred to talk among themselves. They not only discussed published works but also shared their own poetry and essays. As a result, literary societies became a kind of public space for women to discuss a wide range of ideas.

While many of the literary societies established in the North were composed of white (and middle-class) women, African American women also formed some of these organizations. African American women not only shared their readings but, like most of their white counterparts, wrote for their societies as well. However, literary societies took on additional levels of meaning for African American women, in part because many of these women faced widespread discrimination. Literary societies provided a way for African American women to show that they could generate the same levels of intellectual engagement and cultural refinement as their white counterparts. With this recognition of the way in which a consciousness of racism influenced their approach to literature, it is not surprising that some of these societies devoted a good part of their time to reading and writing about issues related to slavery.

CONCLUSION

The early stages of the Industrial Revolution, along with the growth of transportation networks and urban centers, opened up a new world of material goods in the United States. It also changed the way men and women in the North worked and, consequently, the way in which they related to one another. The family relationships of the colonial period, rooted in shared economic as well as social activities, steadily crumbled in the new world of market relations. Employers looked to women wageworkers for cheap labor that would boost their profit margins. In some cases, this brought economic opportunity to young women who had few alternatives on their family farms. For other women, their earnings were far from sufficient to feed their children without additional

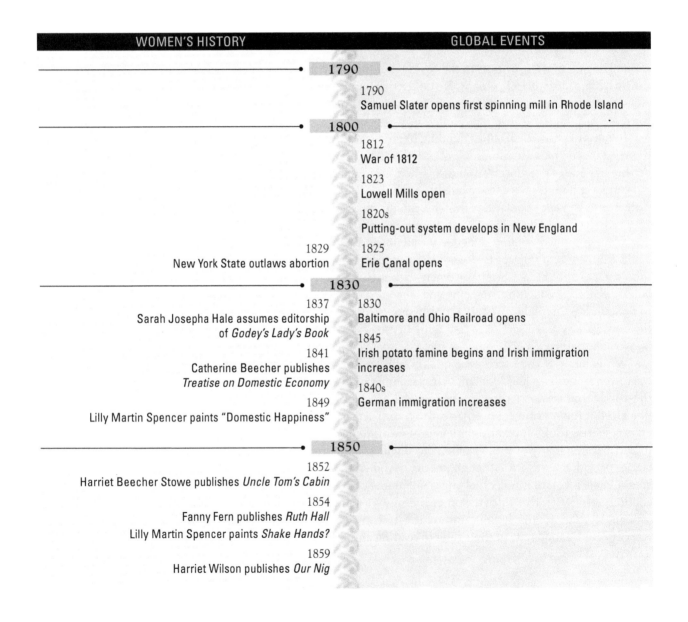

WOMEN'S HISTORY		GLOBAL EVENTS
	1790	
		1790 Samuel Slater opens first spinning mill in Rhode Island
	1800	
		1812 War of 1812
		1823 Lowell Mills open
		1820s Putting-out system develops in New England
1829 New York State outlaws abortion		1825 Erie Canal opens
	1830	
1837 Sarah Josepha Hale assumes editorship of *Godey's Lady's Book*		1830 Baltimore and Ohio Railroad opens
1841 Catherine Beecher publishes *Treatise on Domestic Economy*		1845 Irish potato famine begins and Irish immigration increases
1849 Lilly Martin Spencer paints "Domestic Happiness"		1840s German immigration increases
	1850	
1852 Harriet Beecher Stowe publishes *Uncle Tom's Cabin*		
1854 Fanny Fern publishes *Ruth Hall* Lilly Martin Spencer paints *Shake Hands?*		
1859 Harriet Wilson publishes *Our Nig*		

income from other family members. Yet, even as women took on these new forms of wage work, the very idea of women working came under attack in the domestic literature that circulated, particularly among the new middle class. The cult of domesticity increasingly associated women's virtue with the emotional work of rearing their children. This ideology of a separate sphere, which was celebrated in the literature of the day, masked the economic value of the work that many middle-class women did at the same time that it cast suspicion on the morals of the many women who took on wage work to support themselves or their families. Yet, the middle-class home and the factory were products of the same economic transformation that was changing the place of women in northern society; and in both places women often were asserting themselves, either morally or economically, in new ways. Some women found independence in their wages while other women found new power in the moral influence they wielded in their homes.

REVIEW QUESTIONS

1. When women worked for wages, how was their independence limited?

2. How did the Industrial Revolution shape the notion of separate spheres?

3. How did the cult of domesticity shape the middle class?

4. How would you assess the control that women exerted over their bodies in the antebellum North? How would you compare the way a prostitute controlled her body to the way a middle-class married woman controlled hers?

5. How did a woman's race or ethnic background affect her ability to be middle class?

6. Did literature create a domestic ideal or merely reflect it?

RECOMMENDED READING

Jeanne Boydston. *Home and Work: Housework, Wages, and the Ideology of Labor in the Early Republic.* New York: Oxford University Press, 1994. An important study that examines how, during the nineteenth century, housework ceased to be recognized as a valuable economic contribution to a family's well-being.

Hasia Diner, and Beryl Lieff Benderly. *Her Works Praise Her: A History of Jewish Women in America from Colonial Times to the Present.* New York: Basic Books, 2002. Lively account of the ways in which Jewish women lived and worked as well as the ways in which they adapted their cultural traditions to the demands of American life.

Thomas Dublin. *Women at Work: The Transformation of Work and Community in Lowell, Massachusetts, 1826–1860.* New York: Columbia University Press, 1980. A highly readable statistical study that analyzes the backgrounds and life trajectories of young women who worked in the Lowell mills and shows how they responded to deteriorating conditions of labor.

Timothy Gilfoyle. *City of Eros: New York City, Prostitution, and the Commercialization of Sex, 1790–1920.* New York: Norton, 1994. A careful study of how women's lives were shaped by prostitution and how prostitution was deeply entrenched in the culture of New York City.

Kathryn Sklar. *Catharine Beecher: A Study in Domesticity.* New York: Norton, 1973. A classic study of Beecher and of the cult of domesticity, which she did so much to articulate and popularize through her writings.

ADDITIONAL BIBLIOGRAPHY

The Market Economy

Mary Blewett. *Men, Women, and Work: Class, Gender, and Protest in the New England Shoe Industry, 1780–1910*. Champaign: University of Illinois Press, 1988.

Mary Blewett. *We Will Rise in Our Might: Workingmen's Voices from Nineteenth-Century New England*. Ithaca, NY: Cornell University Press, 1991.

Thomas Dublin. *Farm to Factory: Women's Letters, 1800–1860*. New York: Columbia University Press, 1981.

Joan Jensen. *Loosening the Bonds: Mid-Atlantic Farm Women, 1750–1850*. New Haven, CT: Yale University Press, 1988.

Sally McMurry. *Families and Farmhouses in Nineteenth-Century America: Vernacular Design and Social Change*. New York: Oxford University Press, 1988.

Jonathan Prude. *The Coming of the Industrial Order: Town and Factory Life in Rural Massachusetts, 1810–1860*. Cambridge: Cambridge University Press, 1983.

Christine Stansell. *City of Women: Sex and Class in New York, 1789–1860*. Champaign: University of Illinois Press, 1987.

Barbara Tucker. *Samuel Slater and the Origins of the American Textile Industry, 1790–1860*. New York: Cornell University Press, 1984.

Private Lives: Defining the Middle Class

Janet Brodie. *Contraception and Abortion in Nineteenth-Century America*. Ithaca, NY: Cornell University Press, 1994.

John D. Emilio, and Estelle B. Freedman. *Intimate Matters: A History of Sexuality in America*. New York: Harper & Row, 1988.

Katherine Grier. *Culture and Comfort: Parlor Making and Middle-Class Identity, 1850–1930*. Washington, DC: Smithsonian Institution Press, 1997.

Karen Halttunen. *Confidence Men and Painted Women: A Study of Middle-Class Culture in America, 1830–1970*. New Haven, CT: Yale University Press, 1982.

Helen Lefkowitz Horowitz. *Rereading Sex: Battles of Sexual Knowledge and Suppression in Nineteenth-Century America*. New York: Alfred A. Knopf, 2002.

Karen Lystra. *Searching the Heart: Women, Men, and Romantic Love in Nineteenth-Century America*. New York: Oxford University Press, 1992.

April F. Masten. "Shake Hands? Lilly Martin Spencer and the Politics of Art." *American Quarterly* 56.2 (2004): 348–94.

Ellen Rothman. *Hands and Hearts: A History of Courtship in America*. Cambridge, MA: Harvard University Press, 1984.

Mary Ryan. *Cradle of the Middle Class: The Family in Oneida County, New York, 1790–1860*. Cambridge: Cambridge University Press, 1983.

Carroll Smith-Rosenberg. *Disorderly Conduct: Visions of Gender in Victorian America*. New York: Oxford University Press, 1986.

Barbara Welter. "The Cult of True Womanhood: 1820–1860." *American Quarterly* 18 (1966): 151–74.

Multiple Identities: Race, Ethnicity, and the Female Experience

Leonard P. Curry. *The Free Black in Urban America 1800–1850*. Chicago: University of Chicago Press, 1981.

Carol Groneman. "Working-class Immigrant Women in Mid-nineteenth Century New York: The Irish Women's Experience." *Journal of Urban History* 4 (3): 255–73.

James Oliver Horton. *Free People of Color: Inside the African American Community*. Washington, DC: Smithsonian Institution Press, 1993.

Kerby Miller. *Emigrants and Exiles: Ireland and the Irish Exodus to North America*. New York: Oxford University Press, 1985.

Kerby Miller with David N. Doyle and Patricia Kelleher. "'For Love and Liberty': Irish Women, Migration and Domesticity in Ireland and America." *In Irish Women and Irish Migration*, edited by Patrick O'Sullivan. London: Leicester University Press, 1995.

Richard Stott. *Workers in the Metropolis: Class, Ethnicity, and Youth in Antebellum New York City*. New York: Cornell University Press, 1990.

The Culture of Sentiment

Cathy N. Davidson. *Revolution and the Word: The Rise of the Novel in America*. New York: Oxford University Press, 1986.

Ann Douglas. *The Feminization of American Culture*. New York: Alfred A. Knopf, 1978.

Faye Dudden. *Women in the American Theatre: Actresses and Audiences, 1790–1870*. New Haven, CT: Yale University Press, 1997.

Mary Kelley. *Private Woman, Public Stage: Literary Domesticity in Nineteenth-Century America*. New York: Oxford University Press, 1984.

Elizabeth McHenry. *Forgotten Readers: Recovering the Lost History of African American Literary Societies*. Durham, NC: Duke University Press, 2002.

Patricia Okker. *Our Sister Editors: Sarah J. Hale and the Tradition of Nineteenth-Century American Women Writers*. Athens: University of Georgia Press, 1995.

Shirley Samuels, ed. *The Culture of Sentiment: Race, Gender, and Sentimentality in Nineteenth-Century America*. New York: Oxford University Press, 1992.

Jane Tompkins. *Sensational Designs: The Cultural Work of American Fiction, 1790–1860*. New York: Oxford University Press, 1986.

Nancy A. Walker. *Fanny Fern*. New York: Twayne, 1993.

Ronald J. Zboray. *A Fictive People: Antebellum Economic Development and the American Reading Public*. New York: Oxford University Press, 1993.

Biographies, Autobiographies, and Memoirs

Deirdre David. *Fanny Kemble: A Performed Life*, Philadelphia: University of Pennsylvania Press, 2007.

Lucy Larcom. *A New England Girlhood Outlined from Memory*. 1889. Project Gutenberg E-text 2293. August, 2000. http://www.gutenberg.org/etext/2293.

Harriett Hanson Robinson. *Loom and Spindle or Life Among the Early Mill Girls*. New York: Thomas Y. Crowell & Co., 1898.

Joyce Warren. *Fanny Fern: An Independent Woman*. New Brunswick, NJ: Rutgers University Press, 1992.

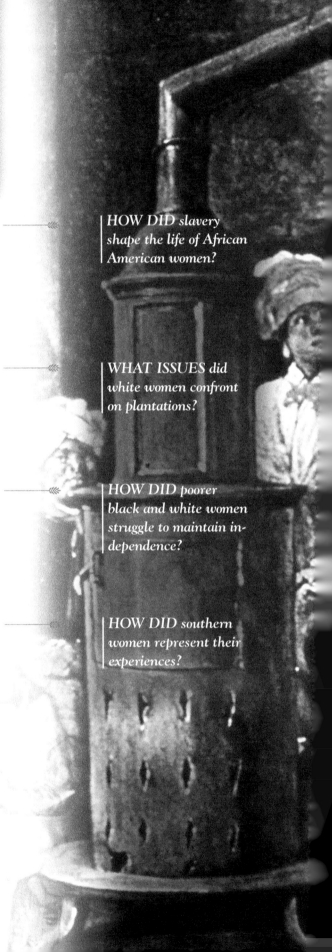

FAMILY BUSINESS: SLAVERY AND PATRIARCHY, 1800–1860

HOW DID slavery shape the life of African American women?

WHAT ISSUES did white women confront on plantations?

HOW DID poorer black and white women struggle to maintain independence?

HOW DID southern women represent their experiences?

CHAPTER 6

Once massa goes to Baton Rouge and brung back a yaller [light-skinned] girl dressed in fine style. She was a seamster nigger. He builds her a house way from the quarters and she done fine sewin' for the whites. Us niggers knowed the doctor took a black woman quick as he did a white and took any on his place he wanted, and he took them often. But mostly the chillun born on the place looked like niggers. Aunt Cheyney allus say four of hers were massas, but he didn't give them no mind. But this yaller gal breeds so fast and gits a mess of white young'uns. She larnt them fine manners and combs out they hair.

"Slave Auction in Richmond," Eyre Crowe, 1852.

Once two of them goes down the hill to the doll house where the Kilpatrick chillun am playin'. They wants to go in the dollhouse and one the Kilpatrick boys say, "That's for white chillun." They say, "We ain't no niggers, cause we got the same daddy you has, and he comes to see us near every day and fotches us clothes and things from town." . . .

When massa come home that evenin' his wife hardly say nothin' to him, and he ask her what the matter and she tells him, "Since you asks me, I'm studyin' in my mind bout them white young'uns of that yaller nigger wench from Baton Rouge." He say, "Now, honey, I fotches that gal jus' for you, cause she a fine seamster." She say, "It look kind of funny they got the same kind of hair and eyes as my chillun and they got a nose looks like yours." He say, "Honey, you jus' payin' tention to talk of li'l chillun that ain't got no mind to what they say." She say, "Over in Mississippi I got a home and plenty with my daddy and I got that in my mind."

Well, she didn't never leave and massa bought her a fine new span of surrey hosses. But she don't never have no more chillun and she ain't so cordial with the massa.

—Mary Reynolds

Source: Mary Reynolds, ex-slave from Dallas, Texas. Retrieved from http://xroads.virginia.edu/~hyper/wpa/reynold1.html

*M*ary Reynolds was born a slave on the Kilpatrick plantation in Louisiana. Her father was a free man from the North who gave up his job fixing pianos to work in the fields with Reynolds's mother after Kilpatrick refused to sell her. Like so many African Americans, Mary Reynolds had personal experience with the roadblocks that slavery created for both her family life and that of her owner.

While northern middle-class ideals of family narrowed in the antebellum period to focus on intense emotional bonds among parents and their children, southern ideals of family remained much broader and became increasingly complex. Even the wealthiest plantations were sites of production rather than refuge. Family ties were far-reaching and complicated. Women cherished their relationships with distant cousins as well as those with siblings. Yet, as the situation on the Kilpatrick plantation made clear, another layer of kinship relationships tied white and black residents together. Slaveholders argued that they viewed slaves as part of their extended families, but the sexual activities of masters created blood relationships white southerners preferred to ignore. Even more problematic was the family life of slaves, who were denied the legal rights to marry or control their children. If the family was the arena in which women were most likely to exercise power, then southern women, whether slave or free, would have to do so in very different ways from northern women.

Slavery withered in the North during the years following the American Revolution, and all the northern states abolished slavery by the 1820s. However, the invention of the cotton gin in 1793 gave new life to the slave system in the South. Cotton quickly became the South's most important crop, drawing farmers more deeply into a system of commercial agriculture that eclipsed significant interest in developing industry or trade routes. Agriculture provided surer profits than industry, though the two were inextricably linked. Cotton produced in the southern United States was shipped to textile factories in the North and even more commonly to England, making slave labor an integral part of the transatlantic Industrial Revolution. As a result of the commercial demand for cotton and, to a lesser extent, other crops such as rice and tobacco, the slave population in the South expanded dramatically during the antebellum period. In 1820, about 1.5 million slaves lived in the United States, but by 1850 that number had expanded to over 3 million. Unlike other slave societies in the New World, this increase was largely the result of natural reproduction because Congress had outlawed the international slave trade in 1808.

Fear of this expanding slave population had led to successive battles in Congress over whether slavery would be legal in new states joining the Union. The **Missouri Compromise** of 1820 was meant to ensure an equal number of slave and free states by prohibiting slavery north of the 36° 30' parallel. Acquisition of territory farther west in the 1840s upset that balance, leading to the **Compromise of 1850**, which allowed states in the new territories to choose whether they would be slave or free. The **Kansas-Nebraska Act** of 1854 further fanned antagonisms by stipulating that states still to be carved out of the Louisiana Territory could disregard the old rules of the Missouri Compromise that they had been operating under for twenty-four years and that they, too, could vote whether to be slave or free.

These struggles about whether to allow slavery or not were about more than controlling Congress. The North had developed as a society that increasingly championed industrial production, individualism, and contractual relationships in the workplace, while the South had developed as a society that was more clearly based in commercial agriculture, patriarchal control, and the extended household as the model of both production and interaction. Women in the South were regarded as nurturers, but they were also more closely and clearly tied to activities of production. While many embraced growing notions of romantic love, the power that white men held over both white and black women wreaked havoc in such relationships. For African American slave women, the situation was particularly brutal. Aside from the personal tragedies created by slavery, different notions of family and hierarchy that were central to the South's embrace of slavery meant that the status of women was closely tied to the ways in which the South increasingly defined itself as a distinct society from the North in the years leading up to the Civil War.

Missouri Compromise
Agreement admitting Maine as a free state and Missouri as a slave state and stipulating that slavery not exist north of the 36° 30' parallel in the states created out of the Louisiana Territory.

Compromise of 1850
Congressional act allowing New Mexico and Utah to decide if they will be free or slave but also allowing California to be admitted to the Union as a free state.

Kansas-Nebraska Act
Act of that repealed the Missouri Compromise by allowing the residents of Kansas and Nebraska to choose whether to be slave or free.

ANTEBELLUM SLAVERY

Women as well as men experienced slavery in many different ways in the South. Living as the only slave of a white family on a dilapidated farm was far different from living on a large plantation with many slaves. Region mattered also. Rice farming in the Carolinas demanded different kinds of work from cotton farming in Alabama. And because cotton depleted the soil quickly, slavery was a system that was expanding rapidly in the newly opened fields of the Lower South and Southwest rather than on the overworked plantations of the Upper South. The slave population was increasingly concentrated in the Lower South so that by the time of the Civil War, slaves made up 47 percent of the population in those states but only 29 percent of the population in the Upper South and 13 percent of the population in the Border States.

MAP 6-1 POPULATION OF THE SOUTH IN 1850

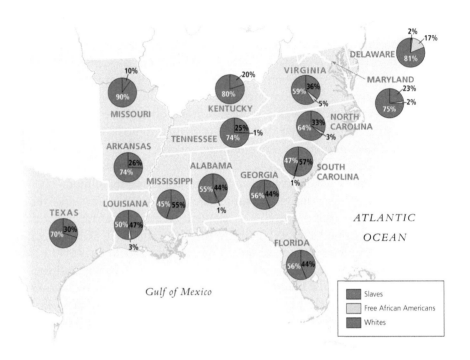

By 1850, slaves were a large percentage of the population in states of the deep South, even constituting a majority of the population in South Carolina and Mississippi. Slaves were a much smaller percentage of the population in states of the upper South.

Strong as Any Man: Slave Women's Work

In an 1859 broadside advertising the sale of Luther McGowan's slaves in Savannah, Georgia, Minda, a twenty-seven-year-old cotton hand was priced at twelve hundred dollars, slightly more than Adam, a twenty-eight-year-old cotton hand. Callie May, a twenty-seven-year-old rice hand cost one thousand dollars, just like twenty-six-year-old Deacon. As prices in the slave markets made clear, women were valued as much as men. Slave women made up a substantial proportion of the field hands on large plantations and were flexible enough to help indoors as well on smaller farms. Most slave women spent at least part of their lives in the fields doing the same work as male slaves. In some areas, this meant tending tobacco; in other areas, it meant picking cotton; while in the lowlands of Georgia and the Carolinas, it meant cultivating and harvesting rice. Slave women cut down trees, hauling the logs away using leather straps; they plowed the land when needed. Although slave owners often argued that they adjusted the workload of their slaves to accommodate their age, physical condition, and gender, this was not always the case. When Fanny Kemble arrived at the Georgia plantation of her new husband, Pierce Butler, she quickly noted that despite claims to the contrary, men and women did the same labor in the fields. It was, Kemble sarcastically observed, "a noble admission of female equality." Despite these demands, slave women were able to carve out small areas of autonomy for themselves.

Those slaves who grew rice in Georgia and the Carolinas, for example, had much more autonomy than slaves on cotton plantations. As part of a negotiated practice that had evolved during the colonial period, masters continued the **task system** for rice cultivation. Each slave, male or female, was responsible for tending a specific plot of rice. The work was extremely dangerous because slaves stood in disease-infested swamplands to tend their crops, facing the dangers of malaria, alligators, and poisonous snakes. However, once a slave had tended her crop, she was free to focus the rest of the day on her own work, including the cultivation of her vegetable garden and chickens. Some of these slaves produced not only enough food for their own subsistence but also enough to trade at market. Slave women continued their eighteenth-century traditions of hawking their wares in cities such as Savannah, Georgia, and Charleston, South Carolina. In Savannah, slave women elbowed out competition from most free white and black women by cutting their prices to the bone when necessary. With control over the street markets, these women began to charge white shoppers a higher price than black shoppers, leading to ugly words with some of the poor whites who bought their groceries there. Although selling independently, these slave women had clearly formed a female network strong enough to affect prices.

On large cotton plantations, female slaves used their work activities to develop social networks that provided a significant underpinning for the stability of their communities. Work in the cotton fields was organized around the **gang system** rather than tasks, and women often worked in gangs that were separated from men even if they were doing similar kinds of labor. Women also formed the backbone of the **trash gangs**, which were composed of women who were pregnant, nursing, or old, as well as boys and girls in their early teens. Working in groups, they cleared fields, weeded, picked up trash, and lightly hoed. These women also ate, sang, and gossiped together for most of the day as they worked and cared for their babies.

While slave women did not always face a gendered division of labor during the day when working for their masters, they did face one at night when working for their families. In slave families as in white ones, women were responsible for most of the domestic work such as cooking, cleaning, and sewing. Fannie Moore remembered that her mother would work in the fields during the day, then "piece and quilt all night." Betty Brown's mother made not only her children's clothes but moccasins for their feet. As with the trash gangs, however, women tried to do these activities together when they could, thus providing an opportunity to socialize while they worked. Mary Frances Webb remembered how women on her Missouri plantation enjoyed talking to one another on Saturday afternoons when they did their laundry.

Sale of Slaves and Stock.

The Negroes and Stock listed below, are a Prime Lot, and belong to the ESTATE OF THE LATE LUTHER McGOWAN, and will be sold on Monday, Sept. 22nd, 1852, at the Fair Grounds, in Savannah, Georgia, at 1:00 P. M. The Negroes will be taken to the grounds two days previous to the Sale, so that they may be inspected by prospective buyers.

On account of the low prices listed below, they will be sold for cash only, and must be taken into custody within two hours after sale.

No.	Name	Age	Remarks.	Price.
1	Lunesta	27	Prime Rice Planter,	$1,275.00
2	Violet	16	Housework and Nursemaid,	900.00
3	Lizzie	30	Rice, Unsound,	300.00
4	Minda	27	Cotton, Prime Woman,	1,200.00
5	Adam	28	Cotton, Prime Young Man,	1,100.00
6	Abel	41	Rice Hand, Eyesight Poor,	675.00
7	Tanney	22	Prime Cotton Hand,	950.00
8	Flementina	39	Good Cook, Stiff Knee,	400.00
9	Lanney	34	Prime Cottom Man,	1,000.00
10	Sally	10	Handy in Kitchen,	675.00
11	Maccabey	35	Prime Man, Fair Carpenter,	980.00
12	Dorcas Judy	25	Seamstress, Handy in House,	800.00
13	Happy	69	Blacksmith,	575.00
14	Mowden	15	Prime Cotton Boy,	700.00
15	Bills	21	Handy with Mules,	900.00
16	Theopolis	39	Rice Hand, Gets Fits,	575.00
17	Coolidge	29	Rice Hand and Blacksmith,	1,275.00
18	Bessie	69	Infirm, Sews,	250.00
19	Infant	1	Strong Likely Boy	400.00
20	Samson	41	Prime Man, Good with Stock,	975.00
21	Callie May	27	Prime Woman, Rice,	1,000.00
22	Honey	14	Prime Girl, Hearing Poor,	850.00
23	Angelina	16	Prime Girl, House or Field,	1,000.00
24	Virgil	21	Prime Field Hand,	1,100.00
25	Tom	40	Rice Hand, Lame Leg,	750.00
26	Noble	11	Handy Boy,	900.00
27	Judge Lesh	55	Prime Blacksmith,	800.00
28	Booster	43	Fair Mason, Unsound,	600.00
29	Big Kate	37	Housekeeper and Nurse,	950.00
30	Melie Ann	19	Housework, Smart Yellow Girl,	1,250.00
31	Deacon	26	Prime Rice Hand,	1,000.00
32	Coming	19	Prime Cotton Hand,	1,000.00
33	Mabel	47	Prime Cotton Hand,	800.00
34	Uncle Tim	60	Fair Hand with Mules,	600.00
35	Abe	27	Prime Cotton Hand,	1,000.00
36	Tennes	29	Prime Rice Hand and Coachman,	1,250.00

There will also be offered at this sale, twenty head of Horses and Mules with harness, along with thirty head of Prime Cattle. Slaves will be sold separate, or in lots, as best suits the purchaser. Sale will be held rain or shine.

As the bill of sale indicates, slave women were often valued as much as men because they could not only work in the fields, but they could also bear children, thus increasing the value of the master's property.

task system System for organizing slave labor that delegates to an individual slave entire responsibility for production of a crop, such as rice, on a particular plot of land.

gang system System for organizing slave labor that groups slaves together to work on successive tasks.

trash gang Gang of slaves composed of pregnant and older women as well as children, delegated to do lighter field tasks such as weeding and collecting trash.

SCENE ON A COTTON PLANTATION. GATHERING COTTON.

Big House African American description of the house on the plantation where the master lived.

On large cotton plantations, slaves often worked in gangs divided by gender. As this drawings shows, women on this plantation were responsible for picking the cotton, while men were responsible for transporting it.

Slave women not only tended rice crops in disease-infested swamps, they also harvested the rice and winnowed it to prepare it to prepare it for consumption. Fanner baskets were originally used in Africa and were part of the technology that slaves introduced in the New World as they taught Europeans how to cultivate rice.

Status and Special Skills

Not all slave women worked in the fields. On large plantations, some worked in the "**Big House**" as domestic servants while others cooked in the kitchen or tended the young and the sick. Such jobs bore a mark of distinction because not all slaves had the requisite skills. As Lucy McCullough noted, "De house servants hold that dey is uh step better den de field niggers. House servants wuz hiyyah quality folks." However, the distinctions were not always welcomed, because domestic servants were at the mistress's beck and call twenty-four hours a day and close enough to the white folks that they could be easily struck when they made mistakes.

Plantation mistresses felt that the best way to get good house servants was to begin training them when they were young. Many slave girls between the ages of six and twelve were separated from their families in the slave quarters and moved into the master's house. Assigned simple tasks such as shooing away flies or running errands, young slave girls were kept busy and assessed. At night, they usually slept at the foot of the bed of their mistress and master or one of the white children so that they could respond to any needs and prepare the morning fire. Those with promise were trained in more difficult tasks of housekeeping as they entered their teenage years, while less likely prospects were returned to the trash gang and slave quarters.

Cooks, who operated away from the main house in separate kitchen buildings, had more autonomy than other servants. While sometimes men were cooks, usually women did this job, many of them trained by their mothers in the craft. Cooking not only provided more autonomy but also provided a better diet, because cooks could help themselves surreptitiously to the food they were preparing for their owners.

Other slaves took on the job of nursing both free and slave members of a plantation household. Some slave nurses developed skills as midwives or "root doctors." These slave practitioners who used herbal remedies to treat a wide variety of complaints provided important medical care to slaves on plantations and, sometimes, to whites. Slaves also took on child care. Though some slave owners worried about the irresponsible habits of slave girls, they still put them to work tending both white and black toddlers. Older slave women with babies of their own were called upon to share their breast milk with the mistress's babies as well. A woman particularly apt in caring for children would rise in status within the household to care for successive generations of white children. Achieving a kind of revered status in a household, these nurses provided the basis for the **mammy** figure that many southern whites celebrated in their depictions of their extended households. An aristocrat among both whites and slaves on a plantation, the mammy maintained standards of deportment as well as health. Susan Eppes recalled how her mammy would scold her, saying "you ain't got no call to say dat—you ain't no pore white trash— nor no nigger nuther—take yer finger out of yore mouth—held your hed an' don't forgit your manners."

D.L. Kernion with nurse maid "Marguerite." Some slave women were trained to be nurses and nannies for the children of their masters. Southern families viewed these slaves as privileged and began to commemorate the relationship between nurses and their children with photographs, once photography was invented. Not all slave women, however, viewed their charges with the same degree of attachment. (From the Collection of the Louisiana State Museum)

The status of mammy, like that of other privileged slaves, was neither as secure nor as uncomplicated as white southerners wanted to believe. White mistresses, in most cases, still maintained control of the plantation. Slave nurses were also challenged by white doctors who dismissed their work as either ineffective or dangerous. And as mammies grew too old to work, the white families they had nurtured did not always care for them. Frederick Douglass recalled how his grandmother was moved to a cabin in the woods and left to die.

mammy Stereotype of southern female slave who identified with the interests of her white charges and exercised great authority in their lives.

Family Life

Slave women in the antebellum United States constructed their families in ways that had to differ from their free counterparts. After all, they were not legally allowed to marry their husbands and they had no legal right to control their children; worse yet, their loved ones could be sold from them at any time. The breakup of families through sale was a growing problem in the nineteenth century as fields became depleted in the East and slavery expanded farther west and south. Between half a million and a million slaves were carried by slave traders into the new states of Alabama, Mississippi, and Louisiana between 1820 and 1860, in many cases causing the breakup of family units. Despite these hardships, however, slaves continued to marry and have families, even though their marriages and family units were not legally recognized. Indeed, because slaves could not control property and slave men had no legal authority to exert over their wives, more gender equality was possible in slave marriages than among those who were free.

Types of Slave Labor

Task System	The slave, male or female, took control of a plot of land and was responsible for raising the entire crop. This system was used particularly in rice cultivation. Slaves had more control over their time in this system of work, though the rice fields were dangerous.
Gang Systems	Slaves worked in gangs, usually segregated by sex. This form of labor was often used on large cotton plantations. Supervised by overseers, slaves had little control over their time.
House Servants	Slaves who worked in the house were often women who had been chosen in childhood for training as cooks, nurses, and maids. Housework carried more status than fieldwork, but the hours were long and autonomy was difficult because demands were made on the time of servants from early morning to late at night.

fictive kin People with strong emotional ties similar to those of family members but not related to each other through marriage or birth.

abroad marriage Marriage of slaves who live on two different plantations.

Particularly in areas of the Upper South, where slaves were more likely to be sold away due to soil depletion, slaves faced challenges in creating strong nuclear families. Slave owners were often reluctant to separate a mother from her small children, but they did not have the same reservations about selling the father, creating a situation in which families were matrifocal. Extended kin and even **fictive kin** became particularly important in these situations. Slave children were taught to address their elders as "aunt" or "uncle" regardless of their blood relationships. In the absence of blood kin, these relationships created an alternative family structure for many slaves. Matrifocal relations were also encouraged when slaves married abroad. An **abroad marriage** meant that husband and wife lived on different plantations and the husband would only be able to visit his wife once or twice a week. Some slaves preferred abroad marriages because it meant they did not have to witness the abuse of their partners. Slaves were particularly upset to see their spouses beaten, whipped, or raped, because there was little they could do to stop it. Regardless of the motives, women who lived in abroad marriages took on the traditional responsibilities of men as well as women in raising their families. This could involve stealing pigs to feed her family, as Eliza Overton's mother did, or hunting raccoons and deer, as Betty Brown's mother did. In raising children without their husbands' help, albeit with strong support from their slave communities, these women were also continuing West African traditions in which husband and wife often lived in separate dwellings.

Many slave girls had their first child by the time they were nineteen. While they could end up married to the father of their first child, slave girls seemed to have more leeway to experiment in their choice of partners than free white girls did. Some slave girls chose a mate other than the father of their first child, settling down with him to have the rest of their children. Because no legal marriages were recognized among slaves and no inheritances were at stake, this flexibility was possible. Moreover, young women were eager to prove as soon as possible that they were not barren so that they could avoid being sold away as a bad investment. But by embracing motherhood early,

A SLAVE'S PLEA

Virginia Boyd was pregnant, probably by her master Judge Samuel Boyd, when he turned her over to the slave trader Rice Carter Ballard with instructions to sell her. In this letter to Ballard, Virginia Boyd begged that she not be sold. However, by August, both she and one of her children had been sold.

May 6, 1853

I am at present in the city of Houston in a Negro traders yard, for sale, by your orders. I was present at the Post Office when Doctor Ewing took your letter out through mistake and red it a loud, not knowing I was the person the letter alluded to. I hope that if I have ever done or said any thing that has offended you that you will for give me, for I have suffered enough Cince in mind to repay all that I have ever done, to anyone, you wrote for them to sell me in thrity days, do you think after all that has transpired between me & the old man, (I don't call names) that its treating me well to send me off among strangers in my situation to be sold without even my having an opportunity of choosing for my self; its hard indeed and what is still harder for the father of my children to sell his own offspring Yes his own flesh & blood. My God is it possible that any free born American would brand his character with such a stigma as that, but I hope before this he will relent & see his error for I still beleave that he is possest of more honer than that. I no too that you have influence and can assist me in some measure

from out of this dilemma and if you will God will be sure to reward you, you have a family of children & no how to sympathize with others in distress. . . .

Is it possible that such a change could ever come over the spirit of any living man as to sell his child that is his image. I dont wish to return to harras or protest his peace of mind & shall never try [to] get back if I am dealt with fairly. . . .

I have written to the Old Man in such a way that the letter cant fail to fall in his hands and none others I use every precaution to prevent others from knowing or suspecting any think I have my letters written & folded put into envelope & get it directed by those that don't know the Contents of it for I shall not seek ever to let any thing be exposed, unless I am forced from bad treatment &c.

Virginia Boyd

Source: *Virginia Boyd to Rice Carter Ballard, 1853, in Lisa Grunwald and Stephen J. Adler, eds.,* Women's Letters: America from the Revolutionary War to the Present *(New York: Dial Press, 2005), 226–27. Also reprinted and described in* Africans in America, *PBS Web site. Retrieved on 15 January, 2008 http://www.pbs.org/wgbh/aia/part4/4h3436.html*

Questions

1. How does Virginia Boyd express her outrage at being sold?

2. What does her use of the term *Old Man* tell us about her relationship with Judge Boyd?

they continued West African traditions that regarded motherhood as critical to the continuation of the genealogical line.

Sometimes masters intervened to choose a mate for their slaves, but they also knew that having slaves choose their own spouses could produce even better results in terms of both production and reproduction. Slaves who were happy in their home lives would work better and be more likely to reproduce. Young slaves thus carried on a lively courtship leading up to marriage. Although the marriages were not legal, a ceremony still occurred. Sometimes it involved jumping over a broomstick—a tradition similar to the one employed by free couples engaging in informal marriage practices. Caroline Johnson of Virginia remembered that an old slave named Aunt Sue married her. Aunt Sue prayed: "we stay together an' have lots of chillum an' none of 'em git sol' away from de parents." Then Aunt Sue laid the broomstick in front of the house that the couple was going to occupy and the couple stepped over it. "When we step 'cross de broomstick, we was married, Was bad luck to tech de broomstick," Johnson recalled.

Because slaves were not legally married, they did not have to face any legal hurdles in getting divorced. A woman could just give up her husband or request that her master move her to a more distant plantation if it was possible. Marriages disintegrated for slaves for many of the same reasons they did for whites, though in some cases it was because women found themselves unhappily married to men who had been chosen by their masters. Regardless of these issues, however, many marriages among slaves were quite long lasting. After the Civil War, when freed slaves registered their marriages throughout the South, a large number indicated that they had been together many years. In North Carolina, for example, 49 percent of the slaves registering their marriages in 1866 had been together for ten years or more.

Sexual Demands of Slavery

While slave women may have experienced more gender equality with slave men than free women were likely to experience in their relationships, slave women faced another situation altogether in their dealings with white men. Many slave women recalled being sexually assaulted by white men or fighting off their advances. Others entered into quiet and even long-lasting relationships with their owners. Either way, however, the details of these encounters highlight the specific ways in which African American women experienced their loss of freedom and power in antebellum slavery.

Annie Wallace recalled how a plantation overseer hanged her mother by her arms from the barn rafters and "would start beating her naked until the blood ran down her back to her heels," because her mother refused his sexual advances. Fannie Berry remembered brawling with a white master who wanted her body. Whether they successfully resisted or not, slave women were considered fair game by many of the white men who lived in their households or nearby. Sometimes they were even purchased to satisfy the sexual cravings of their masters. A particularly attractive and light-skinned young woman would sell for a high price as "a fancy," a code word that indicated her sexual desirability. Celia, a young slave in Missouri, was only fourteen when purchased by Robert Newsom, a sixty-year-old widower, in 1850. She quickly learned what her role in his household would be when he raped her soon after buying her.

In many other cases, the pressures placed on slave women for sex resulted in hard choices. Cynthia, a slave in Saint Louis, was given "the choice" of being the mistress of her white master, where she would live as his housekeeper, or being sold to a plantation in Mississippi where she would face a grueling life as a field hand. Her survival dictated her response more than her sexual inclinations did. Harriet Jacobs also had to make a difficult choice. Faced with the unwelcome advances of her master, and despised rather than protected by her jealous mistress, Jacobs forsook the free black carpenter she wanted to marry. Instead, Jacobs, at age fifteen, turned to an unmarried white man for protection. He pleased her more than her master and she hoped he would be able to buy her. She also preferred a lover she had chosen to one who forced himself on her. They had two children, but only after a protracted struggle with her owner did Jacobs and her children gain their freedom. In both cases, it is clear that the choices slave women made about many of their sexual relationships with white men were really quite limited.

Many of the masters who engaged in these relationships viewed themselves as quite considerate. James Henry Hammond, for example, wrote to his son Harry in 1856 urging him to take good care of his slave mistress. "I cannot free these people and send them North. It would be a cruelty to them. Nor would I like that any but my own blood should own as Slaves my own blood or Louisa. I leave them in your charge," he said, "believing that you will best appreciate and most independently carry out my wishes in regard to them. Do not let Louisa or any of my children or possible children be slaves of Strangers. Slavery *in the family* will be their happiest earthly condition. . . . " Hammond had purchased both Louisa and her mother Sally in 1839. Sally was his mistress first, but by the time Louisa turned twelve in 1850, Hammond had turned his attention to her. The fact that he was not quite sure exactly which of the children on his plantation were his suggests the extent to which he had had sexual relations with his slaves.

In part to justify this sort of sexual exploitation of slave women, southerners constructed the stereotype of the **jezebel**. Young slave women, described as jezebels, were an extension of the image of the black wench that had emerged in the colonial period. The jezebel was lascivious and particularly attracted to white men. This idea of an oversexed black slave, eager to have intercourse with white men, not only justified the activities of masters but also made sense of many of the other indignities slave women suffered. Whether their bodies were being physically examined in a slave market or they were forced to pull up their skirts to work in the fields, slave women had to reveal their bodies in ways that white women did not. Moreover, there were no laws in the antebellum period to protect the bodies of slave women. Even children were unprotected. When a slave named George raped a ten-year-old girl in Mississippi in 1859, the judge refused to uphold his conviction, pointing out that it was not against the law for anyone to rape a female slave. The Mississippi legislature passed a law the following year making it illegal for a black man to rape a slave under twelve years of age, but the limits of the law are as striking as its effect. Slave women over twelve years of age were still fair game, and nothing was said about white men attacking female slaves of any age.

jezebel White southern stereotype of young slave woman who was thought to seek out sexual relationships with white men.

Violence and Resistance

Slave women, like slave men, were well aware of the injustices they faced by being enslaved, and they too tried to defend themselves. However, they were not able to respond in quite the same ways. Slave men, for example, were much more likely to run away than slave women were, in large part because slave women did not feel they could leave their children. In Huntsville, Alabama, less than 20 percent of the fugitive slave advertisements placed during the antebellum period were looking for women. Most slaves who ran away were young adults between the ages of sixteen and thirty-five, but that was precisely the time when women were likely to have small children who needed care. There were exceptions, of course. Ellen Craft successfully ran away with her husband in the 1840s, but she did so before they had children. Women who tried to escape with their children were more likely to be caught; children simply could not run as fast—nor did they have the stamina to survive without food for as long as adults.

As a result, many slave women engaged in **truancy** rather than escape. After a severe beating, a slave woman would hide in nearby woods for several days or even several months. Celeste, a slave in Louisiana who had been severely beaten by her overseer, built a hut in a nearby swamp where she hid for most of a summer, sneaking back to her plantation at night for food in order to survive. Harriet Jacobs, who eventually escaped to freedom in the North, began her flight as a truant, hiding for seven long years in the attic of her grandmother's house.

Jacobs' story represents the triumph of resistance, but there were more tragic forms of resistance as well. Although slaves had children at a higher rate than whites and worked hard to nurture and protect their children from the abuses of the slave system, some slave mothers could not bear to see their children enslaved. A few chose instead to kill their children. While infanticide was not widespread on plantations, it did occur. One woman who had seen her first three children sold away from her determined that this would not happen with her fourth child. "I'm not going to let Old Master sell this baby," she told another slave. Having made up her mind, she poisoned the newborn. Margaret Garner, whose story became the basis for

truancy Process of a slave absenting himself or herself from a plantation for days or months as a form of protest.

When escaped slave Margaret Garner killed her daughter in 1856 after slave-catchers cornered her family, the story became known throughout the country and continued to be re-told in later decades. This etching was based on the 1867 painting by Thomas Satterwhite Noble, The Modern Medea.

Toni Morrison's novel *Beloved*, fled with her husband and four children from their slave owners in Kentucky. When slave catchers cornered them in Cincinnati in 1856, Garner claimed she would kill herself and her children rather than go back into slavery. Her husband tried to fight off their assailants, but as his efforts failed, Garner slit the throat of one of her daughters and tried to kill herself before they were captured.

Other slaves used physical violence to protect themselves. When Ellen Cragin's mother was whipped by her young master for falling asleep at the loom, her mother hit back hard. As he backed away and begged for mercy, she moved to a verbal assault, telling him, "I'm going to kill you. These black titties suckled you, and then you come out here to beat me." Celia, who for five years was repeatedly raped by her master, Robert Newsom, finally killed him as he tried to have sex with her yet again. Newsom had ignored her demands that he leave her alone, so Celia struck him with a heavy stick and burned his body in the fireplace of her cabin. Although Celia's lawyers argued that she was acting in self-defense to protect her honor, the white, all-male jury who heard the case declared her guilty and Celia was executed.

PLANTATION HOUSEHOLDS

Only about one-third of the southern population owned slaves when the Civil War broke out. Of those who did own slaves, most owned only a few. The large plantation owners who lived in luxury with more than fifty slaves never constituted more than 2 to 3 percent of the population in the South. However, this small group was extremely influential in shaping southern politics and ideology. Supervising the lives of slaves on these plantations were mistresses of the elite planter class. They considered the home their sphere, but their homes were quite different from those in urban, commercial areas of the North. Like rural households everywhere, their homes continued to be a center of production rather than consumption. Moreover, their social relations with their husbands, their children, and their slaves were structured by a commitment to the kind of patriarchal control that was dissipating in the North. Thus, while they were extremely privileged on the one hand, plantation mistresses worked hard and operated in a world that was more explicitly hierarchal than the one occupied by their northern counterparts.

Keeper of the Keys

Plantations were more than homes; they were small communities, far more self-sufficient than comparable households in the North. Whereas the homes of the wealthy and middle class of the North tended to exist under one roof, plantation households were spread among out buildings for smoking meats, housing livestock, and sheltering slaves. Although the main house contained some of the luxuries found in the North, such as carpets, it was not necessarily palatial. Large southern plantations displayed their wealth through the purchase of slaves as much as through the purchase of consumer goods. Four large rooms on a main floor and two above, perhaps covered with uneven clapboards, were not uncommon. In part, this was because southern households often moved with the seasons to town or to the seaside—and sometimes moved altogether as soil became depleted.

The plantation mistress supervised many of the activities on these plantations. She held the keys to various storerooms, which were usually locked to keep slaves from stealing supplies. It was she who released hams and flour and sugar from the storerooms to the cook. While some fancy clothes were bought ready-made or fine fabrics purchased from abroad, much was still made at home, including slave clothing. Slave women sewed most of the clothing for the slave community, but the mistress would do fancywork for her own family or take on delicate tasks of cleaning crystal and china. It was also the mistress who oversaw the nursing of both her own family and slaves—a job that reflected not only her "nurturing" abilities but also the economic value of the slaves she tended—losing one was a costly expense. Because plantations were such large enterprises, the domestic responsibilities of the plantation mistress were far more extensive than those of her northern counterparts.

Management of slave labor was probably the most challenging task the plantation mistress faced. Young brides, with little experience in housekeeping, were particularly intimidated when faced with an experienced cook or housekeeper. Mistresses complicated matters by assuming that slaves identified with the interests of their owners and simply needed proper direction. Mary Henderson saw little choice but to maintain constant vigilance. "I arose earlier than usual," she noted at one point, "as I find nothing goes on properly if I lie abed, it is therefore not a privilege that I can indulge."

The work of the plantation mistress also took place in a very different context from that existing in the North. Middle-class and elite women in the North were assuming control of their domestic sphere, a sphere that was considered complementary to that of men. Southern women, by way of contrast, operated in a more clearly defined hierarchy. The plantation mistress often supervised the labor of slaves rather than doing the work herself. Her slaves beat the carpets, cooked the food, and walked the crying baby. But just as white women dominated slaves on their plantation, their husbands dominated them. While the household was considered the woman's sphere, the plantation mistress did not have the same autonomy as her northern counterpart. Her sphere was not separate from her husband's because the plantation was also a place of business, ruled by the male owner who expected obedience from all dependents including his wife and children as well as his slaves. The wife who challenged the authority of her husband knew she was setting a bad example for slaves.

Defense of Patriarchy

Planters saw themselves as guardians of weak women and even weaker slaves—or "servants," as many masters preferred to call them. All were a part of their extended households. "Foby," writing for the *Southern Cultivator*, admonished his readers that "All living on the plantation, whether colored or not, are members of the same family and to be treated as such." Planters saw themselves as benevolent rulers and maintained the ideal that the family, with its relations of power, provided the basis for government. They were horrified at ideals in the North that relied on a growing belief in individual rights and direct relationships between individuals and the state. Slaves, they argued, were unable to carry such a responsibility. Both family and slavery were benevolent despotisms that created stability among individuals born to different ranks in society.

The men who saw themselves as protecting their extended households did not shy away from physical violence. They valued their physical prowess in hunting, and they

WOMEN'S LIVES

MARY RANDOLPH RANDOLPH

Mary Randolph, born to a prominent Virginia family in 1762, married her cousin David Randolph in 1780 and settled with him on the 750-acre Presquile. While her husband worked assiduously to farm the land and dabbled in science on the side, Mary gained a reputation as a successful hostess. As the farm began to falter, the couple moved to Richmond with their four sons, where David became a leading political figure as the U.S. marshal of Virginia. Mary entertained lavishly in their Richmond home, assisting her husband in his political ambitions. However, once Thomas Jefferson became president in 1800, her husband's opposing political views ended his political career, the beginning of a decline in fortune that led to the sale of their house in Richmond.

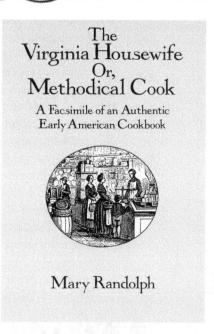

The
Virginia Housewife
Or,
Methodical Cook

A Facsimile of an Authentic
Early American Cookbook

Mary Randolph

Within a few years, Mary became the main breadwinner in her family, gamely trading on the skills she had acquired in running a successful household to set up one of the most successful boardinghouses in Richmond. Offering "comfortable chambers, and a stable well supplied for a few Horses," Mary Randolph's boardinghouse quickly became one of the most fashionable addresses in town. She supervised this enterprise for over a decade, only giving it up in 1819 when the couple moved to Washington to live with one of their children.

Mary did not abandon her love of housekeeping in Washington. Instead, she turned her attention to producing one of the first and most influential cookbooks in the United States, *The Virginia Housewife*. The cookbook was an immediate success, going through numerous editions (it is still in press). Filled with recipes for everything from catfish soup to chicken pudding to walnut ice cream, the book was read widely, particularly by women in the South. Al-

though Mary Randolph addressed her readers with the assumption that they had servants or slaves performing much of their actual labor, she was quite clear about the need for the mistress of the household to know exactly how food needed to be prepared and served, as well as the need to run a household methodically. As she explained, "We have no right to expect slaves or hired servants to be more attentive to our interest than we ourselves are." Yet, the book reached (and was intended) for a much larger audience. Women who could not afford servants could cook these recipes themselves and use Randolph's housekeeping advice just as successfully. Although nothing in *The Virginia Housewife* suggested that women lived lives without slaves or servants, Mary Randolph's own life history demonstrated the ways in which a talented woman could adapt that role to changing circumstances. She died in Washington, D.C., in 1828. ■

preserved traditions of dueling as an important means to defend personal and family honor. Their gender identity as men was tied to their ability to render justice (as well as corporal punishment) both within their families and in defense of them. They expected to discipline their slaves by beating them, if necessary, and some extended that logic to their wives. Marion Singleton Converse actually jumped from a bedroom window in fear of her husband, Augustus Converse, after he loaded his gun. While she escaped that time, she did not the next, when he beat her severely.

The privileges that white women had gained, many of these theorists contended, came with their acceptance of a subordinate position in this hierarchy. Southern writers such as Thomas Dew argued that it was the labor of slaves that had freed white women to advance from a state of savagery to one of civilization. Like slaves, they were part of a larger hierarchy that underlay the advance of civilization. Men were their protectors and rulers; but in exchange for accepting their own subordination and the subordination of slaves below them, white women were rewarded with comfortable and fulfilling lives. As George Fitzhugh summed up, "A husband, a lord and master, whom she should love, honor and obey, nature designed for every woman."

This belief in the benevolent rule of male patriarchs over their extended families, white and black, carried with it some enormous contradictions. Selling one's kin, as slave owners did with their slaves, challenged all conventional definitions of family relationships. Abolitionists repeatedly pointed this out, and slave owners had to scramble in defense. Sometimes a slave had to be sold for financial reasons, they argued, but this was for the greater good of the remaining family members. Slave owners argued that the relationship between master and slave was one of affection and respect, yet in the law, it was a relationship of property above all else. Plantation mistresses as well as masters confronted a complicated and contradictory system in the extended household of the patriarchal plantation.

Family Networks

belles Wealthy young southern women of marriageable age presented to society in a series of balls.

When elite young women in southern society reached their late teenage years, they entered an exciting period of balls and parties. No longer girls, they became **belles**, making their debuts to society in cities such as Richmond, Charleston, and Washington, D.C. With ball gowns that may have come from as far away as New York or Paris, belles were expected to draw a bevy of admirers. The dinner parties and long nights of dancing were not simply for fun, however. As they engaged in their whirl of social activities, southern belles were announcing that they were of marriageable age, and it was fully expected that within a couple of years of they would have made a suitable match. The guest lists of the parties they attended were carefully supervised so that they would meet young men whom their parents would find socially acceptable.

Like their counterparts in the North, elite white women in the South looked for love and companionship in their spouses. Gertrude Clanton of Augusta, Georgia, found her "beau ideal" in Jefferson Thomas when they met in the fall of 1851. Although her father had reservations about the match, Gertrude prevailed and married her suitor the following year. However, despite this growing commitment to companionate ideals in marriage, southern courtship and marriage differed in some subtle ways from patterns in the North. Marriage in the South tended to be more of a family matter, in the broadest sense of the term. Elite young women expected their parents to intervene in their deliberations about choosing a mate, and they expected to be supervised in their courtships. They expected that the landholdings and financial re-sources of both bride and groom would be carefully considered.

Extended family ties were further solidified as cousins often intermarried. While in some instances marriages among cousins solidified landholdings, many of these mar-riages may have also been the product of rural settings where few other options were available. Sometimes families disapproved of the practice, but it was commonly ac-cepted in many others. Such marriages provided another way in which southern women continued to operate in densely constructed kin networks. These women were likely to see themselves operating not as independent individuals but as part of a larger family.

Southern elite women did their fair share to create these kin networks as they con-tinued to have more children than did their counterparts in the North. Although deeply committed to their children, the dangers of childbirth and the high mortality rates of youngsters made motherhood a bittersweet experience for many. Slowly, elite women in the South began to limit their childbearing as their counterparts in the North had already begun to do. In Virginia, some plantation mistresses began to limit their childbearing once they reached their mid-thirties. They were more likely to have six children than the eight their mothers would have born in the previous century. Like women in the North, they feared the dangers of childbirth, a perception that be-came clearer as they and their husbands began to speak of pregnancy as an illness.

The strong sense of family and elaborate kin networks of elite southern women were complicated by the unacknowledged family ties that extended to the slave quar-ters. As plantation mistress Mary Chesnut famously noted in her diary, "Every lady tells you who is the father of all the mulatto children in everybody's household, but those in her own she seems to think drop from the clouds." Elite women were well aware that men in their households sexually exploited slave women, though usually they tried to ignore the situation. However, when the relationship between a master and a slave became common knowledge, wives and their husbands battled. When Catherine Hammond had to confront the fact that her husband James had a long-standing relationship with their slave Louisa, she left him for several years. White women who could not influence their husbands sometimes took out their anger on the slave women or their children. One slave remembered a white mistress angry about her husband's infidelity. She "slipped in a colored gal's room and cut her baby's head clean off 'cause it belonged to her husband." Mistresses blamed the slaves as much as their menfolk for sexual improprieties and used their authority over slave women to punish and torment them for their husbands' misbehavior.

Breaking Ties

In part because kinship ties were so important in the South, migration farther west-ward posed a particularly bitter challenge for women in planter families. Yet many men, faced with limited inheritances or concerned that their farms in the East were not productive enough, struck out for lands in newly created southwestern states such as Alabama, Mississippi, and Texas. Their wives usually had little input into the deci-sion, though their dismay with the situation was clear. Israel Pickens ignored his wife's fears about moving from North Carolina to Alabama, while Sarah Gordon Brown's husband refused to even discuss their impending move with her. "He sais he is going to move but makes no farthere preparation and none of us know what he is going to do," she told her son.

For young men, such moves represented an opportunity for independence, which they relished, and an opportunity to gain wealth that would not have been available to them in the East. Their wives, however, usually found themselves without family support just at the time they most needed it: during their childbearing years. They lost the support of their sisters and mothers who would have otherwise been present to help them with pregnancy, childbirth, and child rearing. It is not surprising, therefore, that women, unlike men, thought of their moves as a kind of death. One woman cried bitterly as her daughter left, saying "Oh, Mary, I will never see you again on earth."

The rough surroundings they confronted did little to ease their concerns. While the "big house" of eastern plantations was not necessarily opulent, it was certainly more luxurious than the log cabins that planters threw up on their land when they first arrived. Women in these circumstances found it difficult, if not impossible, to re-create the lives they had known in the East when confronted with homes composed of one or two rooms and a dirt floor, crawling with bugs and poorly lit. Even if family members had been able or willing to visit, it was hard for a woman to imagine how she would have the room to accommodate them if they came.

With few relatives surrounding them, planter households in these frontier areas of the South tended to be slightly smaller than those in the East and were usually confined to the nuclear family. For the women on these plantations, life without kin was lonely. Fanny Polk described herself as "depressed" in her new home in Tennessee. Ann Finley wished desperately for "a good talk" with her family, and Adelaide Crain reread

MAP 6-2 EXPANSION OF SLAVE STATES DURING THE ANTEBELLUM PERIOD

Slavery expanded dramatically into the deep South and Southwest during the antebellum period as planters moved their wives and children in search of more fertile land. Many slaves were sold from the upper South to planters in these newly developing regions, also breaking up an increasing number of slave families.

letters from her relatives so often that she had them memorized. For these women, whatever their husbands earned in wealth was not worth the loss of their loved ones.

STRUGGLES FOR INDEPENDENCE

Most southerners lived on the margins of plantation society with few or no slaves, drawing on the physical labor of all family members to eke out a living on their farms. These **yeoman farmers** valued their independence and counted on the work done by their wives and children to help them achieve economic self-sufficiency. While the vast majority of these farmers were white, a few were black. Independence was the watchword in all of these households, white and black, as those who were free struggled to distinguish their lives from those who were enslaved.

yeoman farmer
Independent farmer who owns a small plot of land that he works himself.

By the Sweat of Their Brow: White Yeoman Households

At the end of the Civil War, when federal officials asked Nancy Beard of Alabama exactly what kind of work she had done on her farm that year, she answered without hesitation that she had killed thirteen hogs, and they "weighed about 125 or 130 lbs. each." Like other southern women who lived without the help of slaves, Nancy Beard's labor was central to the productivity of her family. Yeoman wives milked cows, slaughtered animals, spun and wove the fabric to make clothing for their families, and often produced enough excess to trade at country stores. In the entries recorded in store ledgers, women brought in eggs and butter, feathers, and tallow, along with a few bushels of cotton. These commodities not only gave their families access to market products but also gave the women a sense of independence that came from producing goods that could lead to self-sufficiency.

Many yeoman wives not only labored in their gardens and dairies but also labored in the fields. Their labor was particularly important at harvest time or if their husbands were not wealthy enough to own a slave or two. Those families who put their women to work hoeing or harvesting cotton, though, were usually making a public admission of poverty.

Women in these yeoman households had little time and no money for the domestic niceties that plantation mistresses and the middle class of the North could increasingly afford; they often settled for rough furniture, bare floors, and straw mattresses. For many wives of the yeoman class, an addiction to nice things was dangerous. If families had any money to spare, they preferred to plow it back into their farms as a way of guaranteeing their independence rather than succumbing to the temptations of worldly goods.

Some white families who were unable to support themselves on the land tried textile production. There were few factory opportunities in the South before the Civil War, but by 1860, about three thousand people were employed in mills that were mostly located in Georgia. Women outnumbered men in these factories by about three to two, sometimes living in boardinghouses as single workers but more often living with their families in company housing. Both working and living conditions in these factories were so wretched that New England mill girls hired to work in the factories quickly departed. Families with few economic options put their children, usually girls, to work in the mills when they were as young as ten years old. This child labor purchased a kind of yeomanly independence for destitute families. Mothers stayed home with small children while fathers farmed on company land and collected the wages of their daughters. Parents were able to at least imagine themselves in traditional gender roles as independent farmers and housewives, even though they were, in fact, dependent on the mills for their livelihood.

Although urbanization was taking place much more slowly in the South than in the North, some white women also found wage work as baby nurses in cities of the Upper South. Plantation families put their slaves to work tending children, but city families were more reluctant to trust their children to African American women. Perhaps because popular ideals of domesticity and motherhood were increasingly associated with white women, they were deemed a more appropriate choice for child care. In cities such as Louisville, Kentucky, and Baltimore, Maryland, over half the advertisements placed for nurses in the antebellum period specified that the applicant be white. One advertisement requested, for example, "a middle-aged white woman who understands the management of small children." In addition to nursing, white women also took in boarders, another form of work that still conformed to domestic ideals of white womanhood. A few were shopkeepers, but in those cases, they clearly faced a more public world of exchange than would be evident in either nursing or keeping a boardinghouse.

Freedom in the Midst of Slavery: The Free African American Community

During the antebellum period, free black families who struggled to maintain their independence not only faced the crushing demands of work but also faced increasing legal discrimination, particularly after Nat Turner's Rebellion in 1831. Turner, an educated and deeply religious slave in Virginia, led a revolt in which fifty-five white southerners were killed. Slave owners feared that the free black community raised the hopes of freedom among slaves such as Turner to dangerous levels. They increasingly restricted the abilities of free blacks to get an education and practice their trades, leading many to head north. They also made it increasingly difficult for slaves to purchase their freedom or even for slave owners to manumit their slaves. By the 1850s, only Delaware, Missouri, and Arkansas still allowed masters to free their slaves. Not surprisingly, the growth of the free African American community in the South slowed dramatically during the antebellum period. Although the number of free African Americans in the South increased from about 134,000 to 262,000, they made up a smaller proportion of the overall population.

As manumissions decreased during the nineteenth century, the percentage of free blacks that were female grew. This growing gender imbalance was probably due to several factors. First of all, as the general sympathy for emancipation that existed in the years after the Revolution dissipated, slaveholders were less likely to free their slaves for ideological reasons and more likely to do so for personal reasons. They freed slaves whom they knew well and cared about, usually slaves who worked in their homes. Because women were more likely to be domestic workers, they would have benefited from these personal feelings. Moreover, women were seen as less of a threat than men in causing rebellions. Finally, masters were most likely to free slave women who had been their mistresses as well as the children they had had together.

Once free, African American women usually lived lives of poverty as they struggled to secure a living for themselves and their families. Jobs they had done as slaves, such as nursing and child care, were often unavailable to them as free women, so most turned to laundry or sewing. But just as was the case in the North, these jobs were among the worst paid. Free African American women had to work to support their families and were much more likely to do so than white women. In Savannah, Georgia, for example, 80 percent of the free black women between the ages of twenty and sixty worked, as compared with a little over 30 percent of the white women. If fortunate, some African American women could acquire enough capital to open their own bakeries, taverns, or boardinghouses, but such opportunities were rare.

Although poor, some free African American women did acquire property, and they did so at almost the same rate as African American men. In Petersburg, Virginia, for example, 46 percent of the free blacks who owned property were women. This was a much higher percentage than was found among white women, who constituted 24 percent of the white real estate owners. In many other towns throughout the South, similarly high rates of female real estate holding occurred among free blacks.

Property holding extended not only to land but to slave owning as well. A few free black men and women owned slaves in the South, but their numbers were quite limited. In some cases, the slaves they owned were their spouses or children. Restrictive slave laws made it difficult to free one's own kin. In Virginia, for example, any slave freed after 1806 was required to leave the state. Free persons living in Virginia often preferred to keep their families in bondage rather than sending them away. Others, however, held slaves for the same kind of economic advantages that white people held them. Milly Swan was a free black woman who built successful businesses as a washerwoman and a farmer in Memphis, Tennessee, beginning in the 1840s. In building her businesses, she managed to purchase and free her husband, Bob Price, who worked with her, and Price's daughter from an earlier relationship. But Swan acquired other slaves as well, slaves she did not free. These were probably slaves who were not related to her but crucial to her business ventures in laundering and farming.

Living with the Law

Both poor white and poor black women struggled to create families in ways that differed markedly from their more affluent neighbors. In the South, for example, the practice of informal marriages continued more strongly than in the North, particularly among couples for which property was not at stake or for which an interracial union made an official marriage illegal. State courts throughout the country recognized these unions as legal, as long as the couple had lived as man and wife. Virginia was the first state to pass a law allowing children born of such unions to inherit property from their mothers, though other states soon followed suit. North Carolina did not officially recognize informal marriages, but courts nonetheless acknowledged them in a variety of contexts, particularly if the couple had lived together and if their neighbors accepted them as a married couple. Informal marriages occurred because of problems finding local officials, because interracial unions were illegal, and also because of the great difficulty couples faced in getting a legal divorce. Couples who married informally could just as easily divorce informally—usually with the husband moving away.

A variety of complicated reasons brought free black women, in particular, to informal marriages. One issue was cost. In states such as Virginia, free blacks were prohibited from becoming ministers in 1832, after Nat Turner's Rebellion. Black ministers had charged less than white ministers to perform a wedding ceremony, and the fees a white minister charged overwhelmed many African Americans. Moreover, because of manumission practices in the antebellum period, free black women outnumbered free black men, particularly in cities. This meant that some of these free women, if they wanted to have children, formed relationships with slaves whom they

WOMEN'S LIVES

ELIZABETH KECKLEY

Elizabeth Hobbs Keckley was born a slave in Virginia in 1818. At the age of fourteen, she was separated from her mother, Agnes, and sent to live with her master's oldest son, a Presbyterian minister, who eventually moved to North Carolina. As the only slave in a relatively poor household, Keckley faced a demanding schedule. She also faced sexual abuse, which resulted in the birth of her only child, George.

As Keckley grew into young womanhood, she and her mother were sent to live with another of her master's children in St. Louis, Missouri. Keckley established a successful dressmaking business as a way of supporting the family when it became clear her new master was penniless. Eventually, she convinced her owners to allow her to purchase the freedom of herself and her son for twelve hundred dollars.

Once free, Keckley moved to Baltimore and then to Washington, D.C., where her dressmaking shop catered to the wives of prominent politicians in the years leading up to the Civil War. It was in this context that she met Mary Todd Lincoln and became her dressmaker and confidante. Keckley provided moral support and advice as the family faced tragedies in the death of their son Willie and in Lincoln's assassination. Keckley, too, faced tragedy during the Civil War years when she lost her only son, who was fighting with the Union army, in 1861. Her high status within the free black community was clear as she headed the Contraband Relief Society in Washington, D.C., which provided money and clothing to emancipated slaves.

Keckley's successful career came to a halt when she published her autobiography, *Behind the Scenes: Thirty Years a Slave and Four Years in the White House*. It was one thing for her to reveal, as other slaves had done, the humiliations she had personally experienced in slavery. It was quite another matter to reveal the huge debts that Mary Todd Lincoln had incurred in purchasing her wardrobe. Faced with poverty, Mrs. Lincoln had requested Keckley's aid in trying to secretly sell the clothes to pay off her debts, a plan that failed miserably. Mrs. Lincoln's embarrassment only deepened as the details of her situation and letters documenting the debacle were printed in Keckley's autobiography. Robert Lincoln, the president's oldest son, had the book recalled by the publishers. Many fashionable ladies stopped patronizing Keckley's shop. Eventually, Keckley found work teaching sewing at Wilberforce College in Ohio, an institution to which she had provided support in earlier years. Her final years were spent at the Home for Destitute Women and Children, living on a Civil War pension for survivors of Civil War soldiers until her death in 1907. ∎

legally could not marry. In the eyes of the state, therefore, these women headed their own households, their husbands hidden from census takers by the legal restrictions of their times. Jane Cook considered herself married to Peter Mathews. Because Jane was free, however, and Peter was a slave, no legal marriage existed. Jane handled the property in the family, including two boats that she had bought for Peter, apparently with money he had earned, and property that she had independently acquired. When she wrote her will, Jane appointed an independent guardian to look after their daughter and the property their daughter would inherit. Peter, as a slave, was allowed no place in these legal proceedings.

Other African American women formed relationships with white men and faced similar bars to marriage. During the antebellum period, states throughout the Union passed laws prohibiting marriage between blacks and whites. Of the twenty-three states and/or territorial legislatures passing such legislation, three were in the North, seven in the Midwest, four in the West, and nine in the South. South Carolina, Alabama, Mississippi, and Georgia did not have such laws before the Civil War, though they did after. The absence of legislation in these states of the Lower South, where most free blacks were mulattos, may have grown out of West Indian traditions that gave mulattos a special status. It was clear, though, that even in frontier areas where such relationships were often tolerated, public acceptance of interracial marriage was declining as slavery expanded.

In the frontier setting of Memphis, Tennessee, for example, Mary Loiselle married Marcus Winchester during the 1820s; over the next couple of decades, the Winchesters had eight children. Loiselle was a free black woman from Louisiana while Winchester was a white man of some status. He was the first mayor of Memphis and managed to govern successfully into the 1830s. By that time, however, the community was becoming more settled and free African Americans were under attack in the state. The Whigs successfully attacked Winchester, a Democrat, in the 1836 election because of his interracial family. Winchester continued on as an alderman and as postmaster but never again as mayor. Community disapproval was voiced in a new ordinance passed by the city council that forbade citizens from "keeping colored wives."

Free white women who lived with black men also faced discrimination, though their interracial relationships were more easily tolerated in the antebellum period than in the years after the Civil War, when such behavior could have led to a lynching. In 1860, the federal census for South Carolina revealed sixty-one interracial couples. More than two-thirds, forty-four of those couples, were African American men living with white women. In other states, where interracial marriages were illegal, such relationships surfaced indirectly. When John Weaver, a free mulatto in North Carolina, got into a dispute over a cattle sale in 1827, the court had to confront the fact that he lived in an informal marriage with a white woman. Records of these relationships usually came to light when one or both of the individuals entered the court system for other reasons. They were not usually brought to court for their interracial relationships, and it is clear from the court records that in many cases, their relationships had existed for some time and had been tolerated by their communities.

It is also clear that white women who engaged in interracial relationships could run into trouble, not simply because of the nature of their relationships with black men but because of their class status, which was usually low. The courts did not hesitate to discipline them and their families. Susan Williford, a white woman, lost custody of the children she had with Peter Curtis, a free black man. The North Carolina court placed the children in apprenticeships, as it did other children who were "illegitimate." Williford and Curtis also faced recurring court charges of fornication. For women who lost control of their children to the courts, the limits of their freedom were clear. Crossing the color line in creating sexual relationships would not necessarily lead to a lynching, but it could still carry significant penalties, particularly for those who were without property and family ties to protect them.

REPRESENTING THE SOUTH

Although their family structures differed from those in the North, southern women wrote avidly about their own vision of domesticity. Southern domestic writers, aiming for a national audience, addressed the same issues of sentiment and family that held their northern counterparts in such good stead. However, southern writers often addressed these issues with slavery in mind. As a result, domestic writing often became the occasion of political commentary.

Constructing Virtue: Slave Women

The few slave women who wrote about their experiences did so for northern audiences. Because they could address the abuses of slavery to both their families and their bodies, the narratives they produced engaged the conventions of domestic writing in powerful ways. Their stories also embodied an extra layer of complexity as the authors negotiated the treacherous terrain of trying to convey the degradation they endured in slavery at the same time that they conveyed the feminine virtue they had managed to preserve.

Harriet Jacobs produced *Incidents in the Life of a Slave Girl* under the pseudonym "Linda Brent" in 1861, just as the Civil War was breaking out. Vividly describing the abuse she suffered from her lecherous master and jealous mistress, Jacobs was faced with the challenge of arousing northern sympathies in spite of the fact that she had voluntarily had an affair with another white man in her town. Jacobs was careful to describe why she needed her lover's protection and to modestly express embarrassment at her behavior. She urged her northern readers to recognize that slave women sometimes had to live by different rules of morality than did free women in the North. This was an extremely powerful argument, given that the general sentiment of domestic writers in the North was to assume that all women could live by the same code of morality and domesticity and that those who did not were morally corrupt rather than legally deprived.

Elizabeth Keckley, who published her autobiography, *Behind the Scenes, or Thirty Years a Slave and Four Years in the White House*, in 1868, faced a similar dilemma. She described vividly how the village schoolmaster in Hillsboro, North Carolina, beat her brutally and repeatedly. Suggesting the sexual overtones of his abuse, she noted, "I was eighteen years of age, was a woman fully developed, and yet this man coolly bade me take down my dress." Keckley was far more circumspect, however, in describing the scenes of rape committed by another white man in her community. Speaking of the pain her child could suffer from being born of such a union, Keckley suggested that her son "must blame the edicts of that society which deemed it no crime to undermine the virtue of girls in my then position." Equally important, Keckley's response to both these sexual and physical attacks was to survive and come back stronger. She recognized her own worth as a seamstress and eventually convinced her master to let her buy her freedom.

The strong element of female independence that characterizes Keckley's autobiography is also clear in an 1850s manuscript, *The Bondswoman's Narrative*, a novel that was probably written by an escaped slave who adopted the pseudonym "Hannah Crafts." The heroine, also named Hannah, escaped several times from slavery, finally achieving domestic bliss in the North, where she kept a school and lived in a small cottage with her husband and two children. Her independence was her salvation in a world in which marriages were repeatedly undermined by slavery. As the heroine observed, "in a state of servitude marriage must be at best of doubtful advantage."

The kind of domestic independence demanded of African American women in slavery was clear in their stories of bondage. They celebrated the domestic values that were cherished by their northern audiences. Yet, in each case, as women who were denied conventional domestic lives, they provided alternative models of virtuous female behavior that were rooted in their own self-reliance as their source of salvation.

Plantation Novels

Not surprisingly, many of the white women writing in the South produced a much more celebratory vision of the southern household and plantation society. Their stories were often a variation of the plantation novels, which had developed during the first decades of the nineteenth century. Originally written by male authors such as William Gilmore Simms and espousing values of agrarian harmony rather than northern competition, these novels portrayed an idealized version of plantation life in which benevolent masters presided over a harmonious extended family. Their wives were both virtuous and submissive, while their slaves were well treated and grateful. Female writers such as Caroline Gilman, Caroline Hentz, Mary Terhune, Augusta Evans, and Maria McIntosh combined the ideology of the plantation novel with the sentimental novel popular in the North.

While their novels stressed the harmonious relationship between master and slave, they also highlighted the responsibilities of the plantation mistress. The heroine of Martha Hunter's "Sketches of Southern Life," for example, had a busy day working with her seamstresses, cooks, gardeners, and housemaids before turning her attention to her male cousin who needed help writing a political speech. Heroines such as these were both more politically informed and more independent than the typical woman portrayed in the southern novels pioneered by male writers. The same could be said about the authors of these novels. Although they identified with the wealthy planter class, many of these women supported their families with the money they earned, just as female authors did in the North. Caroline Hentz was the sole support of her family after her husband became ill. Caroline Gilman and Mary Terhune supplemented the salaries of their clergymen husbands, and Augusta Evans provided her parents with financial stability before she married relatively late in life.

While focusing on plantation life, female novelists in the South saw their projects as national ones. Northern presses generally published their books, and these presses sought a northern as well as a southern audience. By writing of southern slavery in a favorable light, women writers hoped to ease tensions between the North and the South, countering a conflict they saw as rooted in partisan politics. In these novels, writers used marriages across the Mason-Dixon line to explore the differences between northern and southern society, critiquing not only the acquisitiveness of northern businessmen, for instance, but also the indolence of southern planters. As cousins from the North and South married one another, their interactions worked metaphorically to mitigate the faults of both regions.

Many of these writers abandoned that hope, however, when Harriet Beecher Stowe published *Uncle Tom's Cabin*. Stowe had thrown down the gauntlet with her indictment of southern plantation life; and for many southern writers, a strong response was necessary. Both male and female southern writers penned a large number of "anti-Tom" novels. Caroline Hentz attacked northern hypocrisy in *The Planter's Northern Bride*, published in 1854; while Mary Eastman, in *Aunt Phillis's Cabin*, described a woman who was so content living as a slave that she refused freedom when it was offered her.

Fighting for the South

Most women who wrote in the South, like those in the North, confined their literary expressions to novels and poetry. A few, however, went further and took up nonfiction writing. Most often they expressed their opinions in diaries and journals; but in a few cases, they wrote essays on politics or economics—literary genres generally reserved for men. Many of these writings showed a subtle understanding of the social hierarchy in which the writers lived, including the meaning of a patriarchal society both for elite white women and the slaves who served them.

Mary Chesnut became the most famous diarist of the South, though her journal was not published until much later in the nineteenth century. Her descriptions of plantation life in South Carolina, mostly recorded during the Civil War, provide some of the most important commentary on life among planters and their slaves. She had married James Chesnut in 1840 when she was still a teenager. Life on his parents' well-staffed plantation and the couple's inability to have children left her with plenty of time for reading and writing, in addition to the assistance she provided her husband in his expanding political career beginning in the 1850s.

Although deeply committed to the southern cause and unable to imagine a world other than the one she inhabited, Chesnut's diary is compelling because of the way it demonstrates her ambivalence about the system of slavery and patriarchy that characterized the antebellum South. She bemoaned the sight of a slave woman being sold at a slave market even as she commented on the silks in which the young slave was dressed and the way in which she ogled her potential buyers. She acknowledged that slavery was a flawed system doomed to disappear, but she despised abolitionists and she saw the wage labor of northern factory workers as a brutal substitute. Most famously, perhaps, Chesnut critiqued the system of patriarchy that subordinated both women and slaves to men who abused their power. Comparing planters to "patriarchs of old" who added more wives to their households by taking slave mistresses, thereby humiliating their legal wives, Chesnut deftly highlighted the power relations of the South. Yet, Chesnut felt little empathy for the slave women engaged in these relationships, asserting instead the purity of white southern women as her point of contrast.

Mary Chesnut's diary provides one of the most vivid and incisive accounts of social life in the South during the Civil War. Although Chesnut recognized many of the problems that existed in the slave system of the South, she was ultimately unable to imagine life without it. (© National Portrait Gallery, Smithsonian Institution/Art Resource)

Chesnut's friend Louisa McCord expressed none of Chesnut's ambivalence as she defended the power relations and economy of the South. McCord did, however, have to reconcile her enthusiasm for arguing about political ideas normally considered the province of men with her deep commitment to a social hierarchy in which women were both subordinate and retiring. Penning essays on slavery and labor for the *Southern Literary Messenger* during the early 1850s, McCord resolved this conflict by signing her essays with her initials only, letting her readers believe that she was a man rather than a woman. Her ability to live with this contradiction was no doubt due in part to the larger social argument she saw for women's subordination: the need to maintain social order. Although McCord championed the principles of a free-market economy, she argued that such an economy operated best with a social order that was hierarchical and based on a recognition of racial differences. African Americans, in her view, were racially fit for manual labor while white Americans were not; and white Americans were racially fit for freedom, while African Americans were not. Thus, slavery offered the best solution for the different racial abilities in the United States. White women were the equal of men intellectually but not physically, so this hierarchical system demanded that women take their place in the private world of the home rather than in the public world of politics—unless they were willing to sign their initials.

Although Chesnut was more ambivalent about slavery than McCord, both recognized that their own privileges rested on its existence. They imagined their lives as women not as separate from their social status but as part of it. Just as ideals of northern domesticity were strengthening the power of a growing middle class, ideals of elite southern womanhood reinforced the power of the planters.

Louisa McCord was one of the few women in either the North or the South to write essays on politics and economy for publication. Although she stressed the need for women to recognize their domestic responsibilities and their subordinate positions in the social hierarchy, she herself ventured into male territory on a regular basis with her writings. (Library Company of Philadelphia)

CONCLUSION

Women in the antebellum South experienced the early Industrial Revolution and growing market economy in the United States primarily through agricultural activities rather than through industrial production and commercial transactions. With their homes continuing and sometimes expanding traditions of household industry, even elite women engaged the cult of domesticity differently than did their counterparts in the North. While celebrating their roles as nurturers, they did not fully embrace their homes as "separate spheres." A planter's wife needed to recognize her husband as master of a household that extended beyond the big house and into the slave quarters. Women in the more modest dwellings of yeoman farmers believed the well-being of their families lay in economic independence and the productivity of their land, so this was where they focused their energies. Slave women, of course, provided the antithesis: lives without land; without legal control of their bodies, children, or families; and without the same protection of the law that was afforded white women. Working within these constraints, slave women constructed social networks to protect their families as best they could and, in fashioning their domestic worlds, demonstrated both resourcefulness and independence. Whether slave or free, black or white, southern women experienced gender in ways that were different from women in the North and these differences were central to

WOMEN'S VOICES

A DEFENSE OF THE SOUTH

Louisa McCord wrote extensively during the antebellum period defending the southern way of life. In this letter, written from Columbia, South Carolina, she carries that defense into the postscript of a letter to her cousin, Mary Cheves Dulles.

Columbia, Oct 9th, 1852

Dear Mary

. . . . The girls would have answered your kind epistle to them, but I have been too busy to rule paper etc. for the poor little things who have been rather neglected by me, owing to my having my hands full with Mr. McCord who has been seriously sick ever since I wrote to you. I do not know what has been the matter with him. He has been bothered and plagued by numbers of things and people of late and all sorts of disagreeable affairs (I don't mean anything of our own at home) and in truth I believe it just broke him down. He is doing better now; indeed has improved very much in the last 36 hours and I believe is going to get pretty well again. He is a regular spoiled one though and wants a deal of nursing. . . .

Please any time, if not too troublesome, get me some gloves a size larger for the girls. Those sent are very pretty but rather tight. 2 pair each will do, and 2 or 3 pair more for *me* will last for six months. I am a terrible glove-consumer.

Goodbye—Love to all—Write to me soon.

Your's affectionately

Louisa S. McCord

Oh! Mrs. Stowe! One word of that abominable woman's abominable book,—I have read it lately and am quite shocked at *you*, my dear Cousin, Miss Mary C. Dulles, for thinking it as if I remember right, you said you did, a strong exposition against slavery. It is one mass of fanatical bitterness and foul misrepresentation wrapped in the garb of Christian Charity. She quotes the Scriptures only to curse by them. Why! Have you not been at the South enough to know, that our gentlemen don't keep mulatto wives, nor whip negroes to death nor commit all the various other enormities that she describes? She does not know what a gentleman or a lady is, at least according to our Southern notions any more than I do a Laplander. Just look at her real benevolent gentleman (as she means him to be) her Mr. St. Clare, or her sensible woman Mrs. Shelby and two more distressing fools and hypocrites I never met with. The woman (Mrs. Stowe I mean) has certainly never been in any Southern State further than across the Kentucky line at most, and there in a very doubtful society. All her Southern ladies and gentleman talk coarse Yankee. But I must stop. The thought of Mrs. Stowe doubles my infliction of horses heels. Read the book over again my dear child and you will wonder that you ever took it for anything but what it is, i.e. as malicious and gross an abolitionist production (though I confess a cunning one) as ever dis-graced the press. Encore adieu—

Yours always

L.S. Mc

Source: Louisa McCord. Letter to Mary Dulles. October 9, 1852. In Richard C. Lounsbury, ed. Louisa S. McCord: Poems, Drama, Biography, Letters. *Charlottesville: University Press of Virginia. 1996. Reprinted in: Lisa Grunwald and Stephen J. Adler, eds., Women's Letters: America from the Revolutionary War to the Present (New York: Dial Press, 2005), 222–23.*

Questions

1. What are Louisa McCord's primary objections to *Uncle Tom's Cabin*?

2. How is McCord's life different from the one portrayed by Stowe?

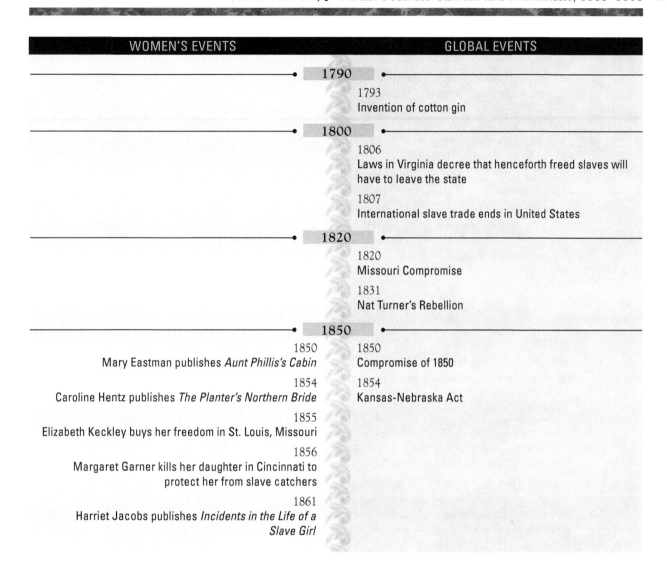

WOMEN'S EVENTS	GLOBAL EVENTS
	1790
	1793 Invention of cotton gin
	1800
	1806 Laws in Virginia decree that henceforth freed slaves will have to leave the state
	1807 International slave trade ends in United States
	1820
	1820 Missouri Compromise
	1831 Nat Turner's Rebellion
	1850
1850 Mary Eastman publishes *Aunt Phillis's Cabin*	1850 Compromise of 1850
1854 Caroline Hentz publishes *The Planter's Northern Bride*	1854 Kansas-Nebraska Act
1855 Elizabeth Keckley buys her freedom in St. Louis, Missouri	
1856 Margaret Garner kills her daughter in Cincinnati to protect her from slave catchers	
1861 Harriet Jacobs publishes *Incidents in the Life of a Slave Girl*	

the ways in which the two regions increasingly defined their societies as different from one another.

REVIEW QUESTIONS

1. What were the most important ways that slavery affected ideals of womanhood in the South?

2. How did patriarchy operate as a system of both racial control and sexual control?

RECOMMENDED READING

Elizabeth Fox-Genovese. *Within the Plantation Household: Black and White Women of the Old South.* Chapel Hill: University of North Carolina Press, 1988. A wide-ranging book that argues powerfully for the importance of class in determining the attitudes of southern women, both slave and mistress.

Stephanie McCurry. *Masters of Small Worlds: Yeoman Households, Gender Relations, and the Political Culture of the Antebellum South Carolina Low Country.* New York: Oxford University Press, 1995. Innovative study of the lives and values of white women who lived without slaves.

Melton A. McLaurin. *Celia, A Slave.* New York: Avon Books, 1993. Engaging narrative of a slave woman who killed her master and the trial that followed, situating the story in the larger context of conflicts over slavery and contradictions in slave law.

Deborah Gray White. *Ar'n't I a Woman? Female Slaves in the Plantation South.* New York: W. W. Norton, 1985. Concise and important argument, based primarily on narratives of ex-slaves, about the ways in which slave women worked and lived in the antebellum South.

ADDITIONAL BIBLIOGRAPHY

Overviews

Peter W. Bardaglio. *Reconstructing the Household: Families, Sex, and the Law in the Nineteenth-Century South.* Chapel Hill: University of North Carolina Press, 1995.

Victoria E. Bynum. *Unruly Women: The Politics of Social and Sexual Control in the Old South.* Chapel Hill: University of North Carolina Press, 1992.

Janet Coryell, Thomas Appleton Jr., Anastatia Sims, and Sandra Gioia Treadway. *Negotiating the Boundaries of Southern Womanhood.* Columbia: University of Missouri Press, 2000.

Susanna Delafino, and Michele Gillespie. *Neither Lady Nor Slave: Working Women of the Old South.* Chapel Hill: University of North Carolina Press, 2002.

Laura Edwards. *Scarlett Doesn't Live Here Anymore: Southern Women in the Civil War Era.* Urbana: University of Illinois Press, 2000.

Michele Gillespie, and Catherine Clinton, eds. *Taking Off the White Gloves: Southern Women and Women Historians.* Columbia: University of Missouri Press, 1998.

Martha Hodes. *White Women, Black Men: Illicit Sex in the Nineteenth-Century South.* New Haven, CT: Yale University Press, 1997.

Suzanne Lebsock. *The Free Women of Petersburg: Status and Culture in a Southern Town, 1784–1860.* New York: W. W. Norton, 1984.

James Oakes. *The Ruling Race: A History of American Slaveholders.* New York: Vintage Books, 1982.

Brenda E. Stevenson. *Life in Black and White: Family and Community in the Slave South.* New York: Oxford University Press, 1996.

African Americans, Free and Slave

Ira Berlin. *Slaves Without Masters: The Free Negro in the Antebellum South.* New York: New Press, 1974.

Leonard P. Curry. *The Free Black in Urban America 1800–1850.* Chicago: University of Chicago Press, 1981.

Herbert Gutman. *The Black Family in Slavery and Freedom.* New York: Pantheon Books, 1976.

Darlene Clark Hine, and Kathleen Thompson. *A Shining Thread of Hope: The History of Black Women in America.* New York: Broadway Books, 1998.

Walter Johnson. *Soul by Soul: Life Inside the Antebellum Slave Market.* Cambridge, MA: Harvard University Press, 1999.

Marie Jenkins Schwartz. *Birthing A Slave: Motherhood and Medicine in the Antebellum South.* Cambridge, Harvard University Press, 2006.

Betty Wood. *Women's Work, Men's Work: The Informal Slave Economies of Lowcountry Georgia.* Athens: University of Georgia Press, 1995.

Plantation Mistress and Yeoman Wife

Joan E. Cashin. *A Family Venture: Men and Women on the Southern Frontier.* New York: Oxford University Press, 1991.

Joan E. Cashin. *Our Common Affairs: Texts from Women in the Old South*. Baltimore, MD: Johns Hopkins University Press, 1996.

Catherine Clinton. *The Plantation Mistress: Woman's World in the Old South*. New York: Pantheon Books, 1982.

Jan Lewis, and Kenneth Lockridge. "'Sally Has Been Sick: Pregnancy and Family Limitation among Virginia Gentry Women, 1780–1830." *Journal of Social History* 22 (Fall 1988): 5–19.

Ann Firor Scott. *The Southern Lady: From Pedestal to Politics 1830–1930*. Charlottesville: The University Press of Virginia, 1995 (1970).

Elizabeth Varon. *We Mean to Be Counted: White Women and Politics in Antebellum Virginia*. Chapel Hill: University of North Carolina Press, 1998.

Bertram Wyatt-Brown. *Honor and Violence in the Old South*. New York: Oxford University Press, 1986.

Representing Southern Culture

Hazel Carby. *Reconstructing Womanhood: The Emergence of the Afro-American Woman Novelist*. New York: Oxford University Press, 1987.

Hannah Crafts. *The Bondswoman's Narrative*. Edited by Henry Louis Gates. New York: Warner Books, 2002.

August Jane Evans. *Macaria; or, Altars of Sacrifice*. Edited by Drew Gilpin Faust. Baton Rouge: Louisiana State University Press, 1992.

Elizabeth Moss. *Domestic Novelists in the Old South: Defenders of Southern Culture*. Baton Rouge: Louisiana State University Press, 1992.

Rebecca Grant Sexton, ed. *A Southern Woman of Letters: The Correspondence of August Jane Evans Wilson*. Columbia: University of South Carolina Press, 2002.

Biographies, Autobiographies, and Memoirs

Mary Chesnut. *Mary Chesnut's Civil War*. Edited by C. Vann Woodward. New Haven: Yale University Press, 1993.

Leigh Fought. *Southern Womanhood and Slavery: a Biography of Louisa S. McCord, 1810–1879*. Columbia: University of Missouri Press, 2003.

Harriet Jacobs. *Incidents in the Life of a Slave Girl, Written by Herself*. New York: Signet Classics, 2000 (1861).

Elizabeth Keckley. *Behind the Scenes: Thirty Years a Slave and Four Years in the White House*. New York: Arno Press, 1968.

RELIGION AND REFORM, 1800-1860

HOW DID women participate in religious activities during the antebellum period?

HOW WERE different religious practices related to different ideas about women's authority?

WHAT WERE the different ways that women worked to control their bodies and those of their families?

IN WHAT ways did women begin to participate in movements for social and political reforms?

CHAPTER 7

Philadelphia, 8th month, 30th, 1835

Respected Friend:

I can hardly express to thee the deep and solemn interest with which I have viewed the violent proceedings of the last few weeks. …

Religious persecution always begins with <u>mobs</u>: it is always unprecedented in the age or country in which it <u>commences</u>, and therefore there are <u>no laws</u>, by which Reformers can be punished; consequently, a lawless band of unprincipled men determine to take the matter into their hands, and act out in <u>mobs</u>, what they know are the <u>principles</u> of a large majority of those who are too high in <u>Church</u> and State

"Shakers, Their Mode of Worship," *D.W. Kellog, ca. 1830 - 1840.*

to <u>condescend</u> to mingle with them, though they <u>secretly</u> approve and rejoice over their violent measures. The first martyr who ever died, was stoned by a <u>lawless mob</u>; and if we look at the rise of various sects—Methodists, Friends, &c.—we shall find that <u>mobs began</u> the persecution against them, and that it was not until <u>after</u> the people had thus spoken out their wishes, that laws were framed to fine, imprison, or destroy them. Let us, then, be prepared for the enactment of laws even in our <u>Free</u> States, against Abolitionists. And how ardently has the prayer been breathed, that God would prepare us for all he is preparing for us; that he would strengthen us in the hour of conflict, and cover our heads (if consistent with his holy will) in the day of battle! But O! how earnestly have I desired, <u>not</u> that we may escape suffering, but that we may be willing to endure unto the end. If we call upon the slave-holder to suffer the loss of what he calls property, then let us show him we make this demand from a deep sense of duty, by being ourselves willing to suffer the loss of character, property—yea, and life itself, in what we believe to be the cause of bleeding humanity. . . .

A. E. Grimke

Source: Angelina Grimke to William Lloyd Garrison. Reprinted in American Memory Website, *Library of Congress, "Slavery and the Boston Riot," Printed Ephemera Collection, Retrieved January 11, 2008 at http://memory.loc.gov/cgi-bin/query.*

Angelina Grimke was shocked by the riot that broke out in Boston in 1835 when a mob attacked an abolitionist meeting and put a noose around the neck of William Lloyd Garrison, one of the most prominent abolitionists of the time. For Grimke, the cause was a religious one: there was a clear line from her deep Quaker faith to her opposition to slavery. Grimke's path from religious commitment to abolitionism was a radical one that few women chose. However, there were many other reform efforts that women, particularly in the North, supported with enthusiasm during the antebellum period.

Free women of the United States engaged in unprecedented activism during the nineteenth century. They were at the forefront of the religious revivals of the Second Great Awakening, and they also played a central role in most of the reform movements of the time. Many women prayed, while a few even preached. Some attacked brothels, others went on strike, and thousands signed petitions protesting slavery. Although they viewed themselves as the guardians of traditional family values, female activism posed significant challenges to traditional patterns of male authority. Women were divided as to whether they should confine their activities to churchgoing or attempt broader reforms in society. They also disagreed about how far they should carry their concerns into the public and political world normally considered the province of men. Despite these concerns, women began to create new social identities for themselves as they moved beyond their households to form female organizations. Some even began to engage political and economic issues collectively—as women.

Not surprisingly, the racism and ethnocentrism that underlay slavery and western expansion also infected these movements for reform. Women usually organized themselves along class, racial, and religious lines, unintentionally replicating—and in some cases exacerbating—the hierarchies of the larger society. But for better or for worse, in both their demands for change and the relations of power they created, these women were reshaping civil society in the United States.

REVIVALS AND RELIGIOUS VIRTUE

In the aftermath of the American Revolution, urban women, in particular, had demonstrated their civic consciousness not only through their commitment to republican womanhood but also in their creation of benevolent societies to assist the poor. That notion of virtue was transformed during the first decades of the nineteenth century as women adopted a central role in promoting the religious messages of the Second Great Awakening. Working to protect and convert their families and those of others, women expanded their female networks and in some cases began to challenge the authority of men in their society.

Gendered Revivals in the North

Religion was at a low point at the end of the eighteenth century. Churches were scrambling to reorganize in the wake of the Revolution, and their congregations had diminished. However, by the 1790s, faint glimmerings of religious fervor began to appear in scattered revivals, foreshadowing the dramatic outbreak in religious enthusiasm spanning the first half of the nineteenth century that became known as the **Second Great Awakening.** As women became caught up in this spiritual upheaval, they encountered a new world of religious inspiration and reorganized their social worlds.

The evangelicalism of the Second Great Awakening swept through many denominations including Baptists, Methodists, and Presbyterians. It was characterized most forcefully by a conversion experience in which the convert came to the belief that he or she had been saved and was therefore ready to join a church. Many people experienced their conversion during a **revival**. Some revivals occurred in a particular town as ministers from local congregations along with visiting preachers hosted frequent and intensive religious gatherings in their respective churches over the period of a few months. Other revivals occurred at **camp meetings** that were held in open fields, usually in the summer, attracting campers from throughout the region for days or even weeks of religious activity. In either case, followers left their homes and their jobs for days on end to hear powerful and emotional preaching. Sometimes they collapsed in anguish as they confronted their sinful pasts and tearfully sought a new path to salvation. Regardless of their exact form, revivals occurred everywhere in the United States from New England mill towns to southern agricultural communities to western frontier settlements, and they echoed similar religious enthusiasm across the Atlantic in England. Indeed, itinerant preachers crossed the Atlantic both ways, connecting England and the United States in an evangelical awakening.

Wherever revivals occurred, women were far more predominant than men. In Oneida County, New York, for example, the percentage of female converts in varying revivals ranged from a low of 52 percent to a high of 72 percent (1981). Female participants came from all walks of life. Believers could be found among women of

Second Great Awakening Series of religious revivals throughout the United States that spanned the first half of the nineteenth century.

revival An intense religious awakening taking place in a series of evangelical services meant to promote conversion.

camp meetings Religious revival meetings held in open fields, usually during the summer.

Negro Methodists Holding a Revival Meeting *by John Lewis Krimmel. Revival meetings took place in both town and country, transforming the everyday world of work into scenes of religious torment and ecstasy. Women were key participants in revivals, which drew in African American as well as white Protestants.*

the emerging middle class or those who worked in factories, as well as farmwomen on the frontier. Evangelical religion provided these women with a strong internal moral compass as they confronted the vicissitudes of a new market economy or life in a new factory town. Evangelicalism, with its emphasis on a religious understanding of the heart rather than the mind, meant that adherents did not have to be highly educated to feel a mastery of its principles. In addition, evangelical churches offered female adherents a space of sociability beyond the home that they could attend with propriety.

As women joined evangelical churches in greater numbers than men, many women necessarily declared a kind of spiritual independence from their husbands and fathers. They not only asserted their right to choose their own beliefs and achieve their own salvation, they brought these beliefs back into their homes in child-rearing activities, because evangelicals of the nineteenth century believed that individuals could improve their chances of being saved by improving their moral behavior. Mothers took on increasing responsibilities in supervising the spiritual welfare of their children. In most cases, this new assumption of religious authority went smoothly, reinforcing a trend begun during the colonial period that associated women with spirituality. However, it is also clear that female religious independence could be disruptive within families. Revival meetings, held at all times of day and night, could mean that meals were not cooked, clothes were not washed, or sleep was disrupted as a result of midnight meetings. At camp meetings, young women mingled with young men under relatively lax supervision, leading to charges of licentious behavior. Equally disturbing were the close relationships women developed with their ministers as their new sources of spiritual and moral guidance. Not surprisingly, ministers sometimes faced charges of seduction or lewd behavior in their relationships with female converts. Elder Ray Potter was run out of Pawtucket, Rhode Island, in 1820 after his affair with a young follower was revealed; he was also burned in effigy.

Regardless of the spiritual independence exercised by women, there were still important limits to their power. While women made up the vast majority of congregants, for example, their access to leadership was severely constrained. Women did find a voice in some of the new nontraditional evangelical churches in the North or on the frontier, for example, among the Freewill Baptists and Christians; but by and large, their participation in church governance continued to be limited.

Evangelical Commitments in the South

In the South, women were also more likely than men to join evangelical churches. In Edenton, North Carolina, for example, approximately three-fourths of the Methodist converts in the early nineteenth century were women. In Baptist churches, the gender ratio was more balanced, but women still made up about 60 percent of white membership.

As was the case in the North, religion provided an important refuge for many women. Slave women on large plantations sometimes slipped away for private prayer meetings that reinforced their collective will to survive. One such woman, a slave named Elizabeth, found solace in her prayers. "I betook myself to prayer, and in every lonely place I found an altar," she claimed.

Southern women also took it upon themselves to exhort as well as pray. Arriving in a new settlement where there was no religious leadership, for example, women in the backwoods of Georgia felt empowered to take on preaching duties. On a plantation in Mississippi, Aunt Sylvia led services for her fellow slaves. Plantation mistresses sometimes extended their responsibilities for the well-being of their slaves into the realm of religious instruction through exhortations on occasion. One exuberant mistress moved from one house to another in the slave quarters on Sundays. One of her ex-slaves recalled that "Sometime she git so happy she git to shoutin."

However, even more than in the North, women in the South faced strong opposition when they pushed too far in assuming positions of religious leadership. Some southern denominations tolerated female exhorting, but they drew the line at more formal preaching. Indeed, although southern men had not been initially swept up in the earliest revivals of the nineteenth century, they moved quickly to join these churches and assert their leadership once it became clear that female participation in evangelicalism could challenge their authority as the heads of their households. Women (and African Americans) in southern congregations were universally excluded from voting on church business. In religion, as in household matters, patriarchal authority in the South remained strong.

Mothers and Missionaries

Women who were barred from church governance found alternative outlets for spiritual leadership in maternal associations and missionary societies, organizations that added a new religious layer to the traditions of organized benevolence begun in the 1790s. In maternal associations, women met regularly to share strategies for raising their children in a godly manner and to pray for their salvation. More than any other voluntary organizations, maternal associations focused the attention of the participants on their child-rearing responsibilities. These groups did not challenge social hierarchies, but they highlighted the growing spiritual leadership of women within the domestic sanctuary.

In missionary societies, women supported efforts to spread Christianity abroad and increasingly focused their attention on religious issues closer to home. As a result, many poor relief efforts that had been more secularly oriented in the late eighteenth century took on an increasingly evangelical cast. These organizations often made and collected clothing for the poor at the same time they distributed Bibles and paid missionaries to bring salvation to the downtrodden of their cities. Many of these efforts were rooted in a particular denomination so that Catholics and Jews were often careful to maintain separate organizations. In this new tradition of religious benevolence, a more spiritually based ideal of womanhood began to emerge, subtly transforming the more secular definition of the late eighteenth century. Republican mothers of the eighteenth century, who had proven their capacity for civic virtue, were being replaced by the new ideal of the religiously inspired women who were expanding their domestic capabilities to help those in need. This spiritual ideal was linked to a powerful drive to "civilize" as well as convert large parts of the world, a zeal that was clear in the activities of Marcus and Narcissa Whitman on the Oregon frontier (see chapter 4). As a result, religious commitment was freighted with powerful social consequences.

Missionary activities of women who traveled overseas usually occurred in the context of their status as wives; it was not considered appropriate for female missionaries to travel overseas alone. Missionary wives, however, played an explicit and important role in efforts to convert others. They not only were expected to run their husbands' households but also were expected to set an important example of civilized values for those who were considered unenlightened. One of the most famous of the missionary wives was Ann Haseltine Judson, who traveled to Burma with her husband, Adoniram, and threw herself into the business of trying to convert Burmese women to Christianity and Western values. Women throughout the United States read her letters to missionary journals detailing her triumphs and concerns. When Ann Judson died at the age of thirty-seven, her biography became a best seller, ensuring her continued fame in the nineteenth century.

Other women traveled with their husbands to Hawaii. In 1819, when the first companies of missionaries sailed from Boston Harbor to Hawaii, the adventurous group included seven very recently married couples. By 1848, when the final company landed, more than 153 missionaries had taken up active service on the distant island. The missionary wives, much like their husbands, considered the local population "uncivilized." Hawaiian women labored in the fields and devoted little time to child care, they complained, yet spent much of their day at leisure. Equally offensive to their Christian sensibilities was the propensity of native women to indulge freely in sexual behavior. "The sight of these nearly naked heathen is disgusting but at the same time," one missionary wife wrote, "increases our pity and desire for their salvation."

To illustrate the virtues of "civilization," that is, domesticity, the missionary wives did their utmost to set an example through their contrasting style of dress and child-rearing practices. They went to great lengths to abide the principles of "separate spheres," a prime indicator of "civilization," and took pride in their clean, orderly houses and "ladylike"—if impractical—clothing. Indeed, if they fell short in converting Hawaiian

Ann Haseltine Judson was one of the most famous missionaries of her time. She traveled to Burma with her husband Adoniram Judson during the 1830s and wrote letters to a wide variety of missionary journals in the United States detailing her efforts to convert Burmese women.

women to Christianity, missionary wives could measure their success by how well they themselves became exemplars of "civilization" under "primitive" conditions.

The missionaries had a particularly large impact on native life in Hawaii. By 1853, one-fourth of the islanders were at least nominally Protestant. Within just three decades, missionaries had written down the local language, printed primers and hymn books, and translated the Bible. They also built schools and medical dispensaries and set the Hawaiians on the track of constitutional government, helping years later to plan the 1893 coup that dislodged the monarchy of Queen Liliuokalani, who herself had been educated by missionaries.

Preaching the Word

While most women found their religious enthusiasm channeled into maternal associations and missionary societies, a few women actually became preachers within their denominations. Quakers and Shakers had always allowed female leaders, but new evangelical sects that were growing in prominence during the early nineteenth century, such as the Freewill Baptists, Christians, African Methodists, and Methodists, also began to welcome female preachers. This was one way in which they demonstrated their differences from the established churches, such as the Congregationalists and Presbyterians. Because these evangelical sects opened themselves to the poor and uneducated and because they preached a religion of the heart, conceivably anyone could be a preacher—slave, day laborer, or woman.

Female preaching began, in part, because upstart evangelical churches in both the North and the South had allowed women to speak about their religious experiences in church or in informal social gatherings. This practice of exhorting could (quite literally) give women a very powerful voice within their congregations. They called on God to guide them, shared their struggles with temptations, and looked to fellow believers for support. In addition, they tried to draw sinners to God, warning of the damnation that awaited those who ignored his rule. Most female preachers were itinerants, traveling from town to town and from one camp meeting to the next. They recounted powerful conversion experiences and "calls" from God that drew them away from family and work to carry their religious beliefs to potential converts. Female preachers lacked formal theological training, so that they spoke from the heart, rooting their preaching in their own everyday experiences that resonated with their audiences. Camp meetings were a particularly inviting spot for women to try their preaching. They did not have to rely on an invitation from a potentially hostile minister to occupy his pulpit, and normal social rules were suspended. Women who took on these roles compared themselves to prophetesses of the Old Testament who had a special mission to preach the word of God.

This independent lifestyle left female preachers open to criticism and led them into conflicts with church superiors. Nancy Towle, an itinerant preacher from New Hampshire, refused to join any particular denomination because she feared that church leaders would seize the opportunity to silence her. She traversed the eastern seaboard several times and crossed the Atlantic to Ireland and England during the 1820s and 1830s before finally abandoning her ministry. Jarena Lee, a free black woman in Bishop Richard Allen's African Methodist Episcopal Church in Philadelphia struggled for eight years to receive permission to preach. Allen insisted at first that Lee confine her activities to exhorting and leading prayer meetings. Only after

WOMEN'S VOICES

RECEIVING THE CALL TO PREACH

In 1836, Jarena Lee, the famous African American preacher, recalled how she finally received recognition to take up her calling.

. . . [T]he Rev. Richard Williams was to preach at Bethel Church, where I with others were assembled. . . . The text he took is in Jonah, 2d chap., 9th verse,—"Salvation if of the Lord." But as he proceeded to explain, he seemed to have lost the spirit; when in the same instant, I sprang, as by an altogether supernatural impulse, to my feet, when I was aided from above to give an exhortation on the very text which my brother Williams had taken.

I told them that I was like Jonah; for it had been then nearly eight years since the Lord had called me to preach his gospel to the fallen sons and daughters of Adam's race, but that I had lingered like him and delayed to go at the bidding of the Lord, and warn those who are as deeply guilty as were the people of Ninevah.

During the exhortation, God made manifest his power in a manner sufficient to show the world that I was called to labor according to my ability, and the grace given unto me, in the vineyard of the good husbandman.

I now sat down, scarcely knowing what I had done, being frightened. I imagined, that for this indecorum, as I feared it might be called, I should be expelled from the church. But instead of this, the Bishop rose up in the assembly, and related that I had called upon him eight years before, asking to be permitted to preach, and that he had put me off; but that he now as much believed that I was called to that work, as any of the preachers present. These remarks greatly strengthened me. . . .

Source: Jarena Lee, "The Life and Religious Experience of Jarena Lee, A Coloured Lady, Giving an Account of Her Call to Preach the Gospel. Revised and Corrected from the Original Manuscript, Written by Herself," Philadelphia, 1836, Reprinted in Digital Schomburg African American Women Writers of the 19th Century, Retrieved January 11, 2008, from http://digilib.nypl.org/dynaweb/digs/wwm9716/@Generic_BookView

Questions

1. How does Jarena Lee use the authority of God to justify her call to preaching?

2. How did Jarena Lee demonstrate to the Bishop that she had been called to preach?

Lee became a widow did Allen relent and allow her to travel through New England and the Middle Atlantic states as an itinerant preacher. Lee had to combat frequent innuendo that she was sexually promiscuous or mannish, charges that dogged African American women more than their white counterparts. Lee was careful of her dress and deportment when she traveled, and she also took great care to present an image of respectability in the portrait of herself that she included in her memoirs.

While Lee, Towle, and other female preachers took great pains to assert their respectability, they did not encase themselves in the trappings of domesticity. Carrying the word of God from one town to another, they lived in a spiritual but public world in which housekeeping and child rearing were of minor importance at most. Without addressing the gender hierarchy that came with a commitment to domesticity, they nonetheless challenged it in their daily lives, a trend that continued until the 1840s, when many of the denominations that had previously tolerated female preaching began to silence those voices. This change may have occurred for a variety of reasons. Some churches may have feared being associated with the more radical female speakers in the burgeoning antislavery movement. In other cases, upstart denominations that had once welcomed female preaching were becoming more settled, stocked with a growing pool of male converts eager to assume the reins of leadership.

RELIGION AND FAMILY AUTHORITY

The explosion in religious activities during the early nineteenth century extended far beyond the confines of the Second Great Awakening. In a variety of nonevangelical contexts, women engaged in religious practices that challenged or complicated the dominant ideals of gender hierarchy. Small sects such as the Shakers challenged the institution of marriage and divided worshippers into separate groups of men and women. Spiritualists championed female autonomy. Immigrant Jewish women who participated in the growing Reform Tradition in their religion asserted themselves in new ways within their synagogues while Catholic women, particularly those who took the veil and entered convents, confronted nativist mobs and domineering bishops. Intentionally or not, they contested patterns of authority that were rooted in a model of the male-headed household.

Quakers, Spiritualists, and Female Autonomy

During the nineteenth century, Quakers continued their belief in the importance of an **inner light,** which had been so important in encouraging a female as well as male ministry. However, as a growing number of Quakers achieved financial success, some Quakers criticized the growing worldliness of their religion, including the participation of some members in the slave trade, and important splits occurred. Controversy over these issues waxed and waned for decades, but came to a head most pointedly in a bitter split between critics of worldliness and slavery led by Elias Hicks (known as the Hicksite Quakers) and the Orthodox Quakers. Many Quaker women who would later emerge in more radical antislavery and women's rights activities followed the Hicksites in this split.

> **inner light** Quaker belief that Jesus is a guiding light within each person.

Some of these Quakers who had been cut off from their religious base formed the core constituency of early **Spiritualism,** a movement of people who believed they could communicate with the dead. The movement began in 1848 when Kate and Margaret Fox, ages twelve and fourteen, heard unexplained rappings at their home in upstate New York and soon after began to convey messages to their friends and neighbors from the spirit world that they heard in these rappings. Spiritualism soon spread from upstate New York to California, offering those who were living the hope of contacting those who had died. Others stepped forward claiming that they too had received messages from the spirit world. Eschewing any formal religious structure, Spiritualists met in each other's homes, often circled around a table in which at least one individual acted as the **medium** and relayed messages between the world of the living and the world of the dead. This connection to loved ones who had died was particularly meaningful to women, who were traditionally the caregivers for children and other relatives in the time leading up to death. Mediums could be either men or women, but frequently they were female because women were seen as more spiritually sensitive than

> **Spiritualism** A loosely organized movement around the belief that the living can communicate with the dead.

> **medium** A person who facilitates communication between the living and the dead.

men and thus more receptive to communications from the spirit world. Moreover, because mediums were constructed as passive vehicles of communication between the living and the dead, their role as mediums was viewed as feminine, even if the medium was a man. Spirits sought them out; they did not act as agents in choosing this role. These characteristics were evident among female trance speakers as well. As Spiritualism spread throughout the country, mediums addressed audiences that could be as large as several thousand. Usually men called the meetings to order and presided over the proceedings. Women, as passive mediums, spoke in a trance, unconscious of their surroundings. As a result, they were able to speak in public while still maintaining some commitment to gendered notions of propriety.

Unlike other religions, Spiritualism fostered the public speaking of women and also fostered an explicit commitment to woman's rights. Spiritualism eschewed all institutional conventions, such as churches and ministers, in the communications that took place between the living and the dead. Both male and female Spiritualists repeatedly indicated their strong support for the individual rights of women as part of a larger move to challenge the institutional constraints of organized religion. Spiritualists argued that women who sought the truth needed an education equal to men's, for example, and that women did not deserve to be subjugated to men in either marriage or employment. Not all advocates of women's rights became Spiritualists, but it is understandable why some did given these positions on female autonomy.

Reform Judaism and Gender Hierarchies

Challenges to patterns of male authority took place in more established religions as well, as became clear in the Reform Tradition of Judaism. In the years immediately following the Revolution, there were very few Jews living in the United States—no more than a few thousand—who mostly congregated in cities from Charleston, South Carolina, to Philadelphia, Pennsylvania, and Newport, Rhode Island. Many were merchants who thrived economically and moved in elite circles. While maintaining their own religious practices, their wives and daughters were as well educated as their Protestant counterparts and engaged in shared cultural and benevolent concerns. Elite Jewish women such as Rebecca Gratz of Philadelphia shared leadership positions with Protestant women in the running of the city's Female Association for the Relief of Women and Children in Reduced Circumstances and the Philadelphia Orphan Society. Gratz also read the Bible with her non-Jewish sisters-in-law, suggesting the extent of religious tolerance between Protestants and Jews in this early period, when there were few Jews in the United States and class affinities often trumped religious commitments.

Rebecca Gratz was an elite Jewish woman in Philadelphia who worked with Protestant women during the early nineteenth century in shared benevolent activities to assist poor women and children. She was celebrated for her learning, her beauty, and her good works.

However, between 1840 and 1860, approximately 250,000 German Jews migrated to the United States as a result of religious persecution in their home country (see chapter 5). As a result of these growing numbers and in response to the more clearly defined Protestant identities of women participating in the Second Great Awakening, Jewish women began setting up educational and benevolent organizations, such as the Hebrew Benevolent Society of New York, which were comparable to those run by Protestant women.

To a certain extent, female participation in Jewish benevolent organizations was the result of widespread changes among a segment of the Jewish community that sought to modernize their religious practices in a movement known as Reform Judaism. Jewish religion, as it had been practiced in Europe during earlier centuries, had separated the religious activities of women from men, and female religious duties were oriented toward aiding men in the fulfillment of their religious responsibilities. This subordination came under scrutiny during the eighteenth century, particularly in countries such as Germany and France where Enlightenment principles were widespread.

In the United States, women of the Jewish Reform tradition set up benevolent organizations and also began to participate more in their synagogues. By the 1840s, the Reform tradition deemed women to be equal to their male counterparts. They were counted as full members of their congregations and sat with men during services just as women in evangelical congregations often did—and sang on occasion. The previously male realm of the synagogue became increasingly feminized as the scope of women's activities expanded.

Power and Danger in Catholic Convents

Roman Catholicism grew during the antebellum period to become the largest denomination in the United States. While periodic revivals or "renewals" of religion contributed a small amount to this growth, the real reasons for this stunning transformation lay in the massive migration of Catholics, particularly from Ireland and Germany, during the 1840s and in the acquisition of vast amounts of Spanish territory in the West, particularly after the Mexican War (see chapter 4 and chapter 5).

Catholicism was not an evangelical religion, but women still outnumbered men in Catholic churches. This gender imbalance became more pronounced as the century progressed because, increasingly, female immigrants outnumbered male immigrants from Ireland. Among Catholic families, as among Protestant families, women provided the active religious instruction of children. Unlike their Protestant counterparts, however, Catholic women generally ceded more institutional efforts at benevolence to religious orders of sisters. Convents brought to the United States a distinctive form of female benevolence and spirituality because they consisted of women who defined their lives outside of the traditional boundaries of the family structure.

During the nineteenth century, nuns migrated from Europe to set up convents and native-born women established religious orders, in both cases creating communities that had more freedom than existed for their counterparts in Europe. In part, the nuns were able to operate with more flexibility because during the nineteenth century the United States was still considered a mission territory and the sisters were unlikely to lead the cloistered lives that existed among some orders in Europe. Indeed, nuns in the United States often did not have the financial endowments or dowries that made a truly cloistered life possible; they needed to engage in some kind of work to support themselves.

Most commonly, religious orders took on the work of education. The Ursulines established the first convent in New Orleans in 1727, and the Visitation nuns established a school at Georgetown in 1799. In some cases, schools took in both paying students who covered the bills and charity students who benefited. This was the pattern established by Elizabeth Seton, who founded the Sisters of Charity and established a school in Emmitsburg, Maryland, in 1809. In addition to schools, nuns also ran hospitals and orphanages throughout the country. In many of the religious orders established in southern states

Sister Mary Elizabeth Lange, a refugee from Saint Domingue, founded the order of the Oblate Sisters of Providence in Baltimore in 1828 for women of African descent. The order provided the sisters with protection and status in a world that was often hostile to free black women.

during the early nineteenth century, the nuns relied on slave labor to do their farmwork or household chores while they took on the more skilled activities of nursing and educating. Slaves were an important form of wealth that new sisters from the South brought with them when they entered convents and that wealthy southern donors supplied.

In addition to the religious orders being created by white European and American women, women of African descent, migrating from the Caribbean, established the Oblate Sisters of Providence in Baltimore in 1828. Led by Sister Mary Elizabeth Lange, who migrated from Saint Domingue as a relatively privileged mulatto with both property and status, the Oblates opened a school for the education of black girls. Convent life in Baltimore may have offered Lange and other mulatto women more of the status and autonomy they had enjoyed in the Caribbean than they found in Baltimore. The Oblate sisters did not own slaves, but they largely kept silent on the issue of slavery. Women entering the order were (with one possible exception) free blacks, though some had begun their lives as slaves. With a large and growing free black population in Baltimore, including refugees from Saint Domingue (Haiti), the school founded by the sisters was an important resource.

Nuns who ran schools, hospitals, and orphanages in some ways lived far more independently than most American or European women at the time. They held managerial positions normally closed to women, supported themselves, and acquired and managed property for their religious orders. However, they were still subject to a male religious hierarchy, which resulted in conflicts on numerous occasions. Elizabeth Seton, although now recognized as a saint by the Catholic Church, was almost expelled from the Catholic Church as a result of conflict with her male superiors. Rose Philippine Duchesne, who founded the Society of the Sacred Heart in America, was refused communion by her bishop in the Louisiana Territory because she tried to resist his control of convent affairs. Struggles involved everything from the specific teaching and nursing activities nuns were to undertake to the disposition of the money they raised.

Distrust of convents extended far beyond the male leadership of the Catholic Church. The influential writer and editor Sarah Josepha Hale urged the creation of Protestant schools to counter the effects of Catholic schools. Anti-immigrant sentiment, which began to flourish in the 1830s as more foreigners arrived, sometimes focused violently on convent schools. In 1834, the Ursuline Convent in Charlestown, Massachusetts, was burned to the ground while other convents were threatened.

Equally as sensational was the salacious literature printed by the anti-Catholic press claiming to expose convents as little more than bordellos kept for corrupt priests. The most famous example of this kind of attack came from Maria Monk, whose claims of sexual intrigue were laid out in the *Awful Disclosures of the Hotel Dieu Nunnery of Montreal* (1836). Maria described in graphic detail how she (like all nuns) was forced to have sex with priests in a nearby rectory and how babies born of these sinful practices were baptized then strangled at birth. Although her allegations were proven false, her books continued to sell well to a Protestant public fearful of both the Catholic Church and women who lived beyond the controls of a male household head.

The pornography that flourished about the sex lives of nuns revealed the deep skepticism harbored by many Protestants about the viability of celibacy as a respectable and realistic sexual choice. Many Protestants saw celibacy as a sure road to moral corruption in its denial of natural impulses. Even if nuns were imagined to be sexually passionless (as other white women were), priests were not; and there were no husbands, brothers, or fathers to protect nuns from these male predators. A community of women, unprotected by family ties, posed a dangerous challenge to the social order embodied by Protestant families. This pornography provided a vivid and expanded portrayal of the fate that awaited any woman who declared her independence from her family, whether she was a factory girl, a convert at a camp meeting, or a Catholic nun.

CONTROLLING THE BODY, PERFECTING THE SOUL

The religious enthusiasm that brought women into churches in the nineteenth century infused their voluntary associations as well. Spiritual beliefs were manifested in bodily behavior, and salvation was increasingly tied to worldly activities. Not surprisingly, movements aimed at perfecting the soul by controlling the body gained prominence during this period. However, approaches to bodily control varied dramatically. The Shakers rejected all sexual contact. Members of the Oneida community outraged the nation by attacking sexual monogamy, while other reformers drew attention to the dangers of masturbation. More commonly, though, reformers took aim at sexual promiscuity, the consumption of alcohol, and the family violence that accompanied drunkenness.

Female reformers who attacked family violence, drinking, and prostitution sometimes adopted controversial techniques in their crusades against immorality, and they engaged in public behavior that many of their critics found unladylike. As was the case with evangelical women, these reformers were not social revolutionaries. They took up their causes as the spiritual guardians of their homes, not as secular critics asserting political rights. Yet, their activities were deeply enmeshed in a dual revolution in power relations in American society: the creation of a bourgeois ethic of self-control that was fundamental to the creation of a middle class and a critique of marriage for unfairly allowing men to physically dominate or even abuse their wives. As women moved to defend their homes, in various ways they also undermined the structures of authority that lay at the heart of household relations.

Celibacy of Shakers

The Shakers, who had established themselves as a small sect during the First Great Awakening under the leadership of Mother Ann Lee, expanded in concert with the rhythms of the Second Great Awakening (see chapter 3). With communities in New England, New York, Kentucky, and Ohio, Shakers created an alternative family structure rooted in their belief that sexual intercourse—even between a married couple— was sinful. This meant that they could not expand through the procreation of their members and were thus a sect of converts that had largely died out by the end of the nineteenth century. In the antebellum period, however, Shakers were not worried about this problem because they believed the end of the world was at hand. They continued their beliefs in celibacy throughtout the nineteenth century and institutionalized roles of religious leadership for women, two factors that may explain the appeal Shakers held for many women. Women who were worried about the dangers of childbirth and the demands of traditional family life found Shaker communities an attractive alternative.

The commitment of Shakers to celibacy and their belief in the strict separation of men from women meant that women needed their own leaders. For this reason, Lucy Wright became the spiritual leader for female Shakers after Ann Lee died in the late eighteenth century. Wright struggled valiantly to organize women into a religious group independent of male control, and by 1796 she had become a powerful enough figure within the movement to become its new leader. However, while female leadership was central to the Shaker religion, this does not mean the Shakers were intent on attacking all gender distinctions or forms of gender hierarchy.

With leaders chosen from each sex, large families of anywhere from thirty to one hundred members were established. Husbands, wives, and their children who converted to Shakerism were reconstituted as part of this larger communal order in which religious leadership, child rearing, and labor were divided broadly along gendered lines. While duties of religious leadership were shared equally, conventional gender distinctions dictated other allocations of labor. Men, for example, worked in the fields and shops while women cooked, cleaned, and cared for children. Yet, for women who felt isolated on individual farms or who chafed at the spiritual domination of their husbands or who wished to limit their family size, Shaker communities offered an important alternative to traditional social patterns.

As in other religious movements, women were predominant. By 1800, in all Shaker communities in the East, women outnumbered men. As the sect grew, the philosophy of separate but equal gender segregation that was so crucial to Shaker beliefs was ritualized. One of the most potent forms of expression came in the Shaker dance during religious services. Men and women lined up in separate rows facing one another, singing, clapping, and jumping. In some cases, believers stood in place while in others they engaged in a circular movement in which four concentric circles were formed to symbolize the four great periods in religious history.

Bible Communism: Complex Marriage in the Oneida Community

The Oneida community established one of the most radical experiments in bodily control by incorporating sexual intercourse into their religious practices. Founded by John Humphrey Noyes in 1848, members of this community in upstate New York practiced **complex marriage,** a system in which every man and woman were married to one another and available to one another as sexual partners. In its critique of marriage, the Oneida community undermined traditional sources of male household authority, though in other ways, new forms of gender inequality were instituted.

Noyes was converted during the revivals of the Second Great Awakening and after his theological training began to incorporate ideas of perfectionism into his theology and preaching. He eventually established communities, first at Putney, Vermont, and later at Oneida, New York, where he and his followers attempted to achieve spiritual perfection in the living of their lives. By 1851, they had just over two hundred members. They opposed not only monogamous marriage but also private property, so that adults pooled their resources to support their communal lifestyle. Children were raised communally in the Children's House, which they entered when they were fifteen months old. Men and women shared the responsibilities of rearing each other's children as well as the more mundane chores of housework. The rearrangement of child rearing and housework meant that women had more time to pursue other activities of self-improvement—and

complex marriage
Form of marriage promoted in the Oneida community in which every man and every woman in the community were considered married to one another.

they were encouraged to do so. However, not all women were comfortable surrendering their children to community control.

The most controversial aspect of the Oneida community was its practice of complex marriage, a practice intended to liberate women from slavery to their husbands and to promote a more highly developed form of communal relations. Promoting "male continence," Noyes argued that orgasms were desirable for women but not for men, because male orgasm resulted in the ejaculation of semen and the possible creation of children. Men were expected to practice male continence, which meant they did not ejaculate during intercourse. In that way, sexual pleasure could be separated from procreation and shared by community members as a form of spiritual bonding that would not result in dangerous or debilitating pregnancies for women.

Although the Oneida Community was never very large, as this photograph from 1863 makes clear, its commitment to complex marriage gave it a national reputation. While the community sought to improve the status of women by protecting them from unnecessary childbirth and limiting their housework, some women still found the sexual regime oppressive.

While complex marriage was meant to be liberating for women, women still did not maintain full control over their sex lives. Shortly after young women began to menstruate, they were initiated into the sex life of the community by older men, who were chosen by Noyes and a small group of male and female advisors. Young women were not allowed to have sex with men their own age until they could prove they would not engage in a monogamous relationship. Young women often received many requests for sex, and while in theory they were free to reject some, in practice this was not always possible. Thus, although the Oneida community sought to free women from domestic drudgery and recognized women's interest in sexual pleasure, it did not grant women full autonomy. In 1879, the community voted to abandon complex marriage in favor of more traditional monogamous relationships, thus dramatically changing the character of the group.

Moral Reform Societies: Combating the Sex Trade

A more widespread approach to bodily control came from the women's societies set up to combat prostitution. Evangelical women in New York City established the New York Magdalen Society in the early 1830s and opened the House of Refuge for prostitutes wishing to repent. They were supporters of Rev. John McDowell, who began his crusade against prostitution during the spring of 1830. By 1834, the women had also founded the New York Female Moral Reform Society, which was particularly rooted in the Third Free Presbyterian Church, a hotbed of evangelicalism.

Although legal charges of prostitution tended to occur in larger cities such as Boston and New York, where there were many brothels, smaller towns in the Northeast and Midwest with very few cases of prostitution also established moral reform societies. Women

WOMEN'S VOICES

REFORMING THE MEN

Emily Porter, of Windham, Ohio, wrote this letter to the New York Female Moral Reform Society in April of 1838 reporting on the growth of their moral reform society and the measures being taken in her small town to promote sexual morality.

At our annual meeting in 1837, the Society numbered 32. Since then it has gained 23. Two have been called at a distance from us, but we trust they are laborers with us still in this important cause.

It will hardly be worth while to inform you, that it is our lot to share with others in the usual opposition which the espousel of the cause of Moral Reform has called forth. We have many friends, and also many foes. The young gentlemen of this place have very decidedly come out against us. They say, "You have raised your sacrilegious hands against a custom both ancient and honorable." I will state an article in our Constitution. It is called by them "The 9 o'clock Article."

"Believing that the prolonging of visits with any gentleman after the usual hour of retirement, is one of the first steps towards licentiousness, we pledge ourselves to discountenance such practices by precepts and example."

Had not this article become binding upon us, they say, "We would not notice you." As it is, they have formed a society, and pledged themselves not to associate with us, because we are bringing into disrepute an innocent practice, handed down to them by their venerable forefathers, and which has been to them a source of great pleasure and enjoyment.

There are quite a number of ladies with whom they associate, who do not belong to a Moral Reform Society. They are told to "remain firm," and in so doing they are assured of receiving "the respect and attentions of all" "gentlemen of honor," which is the title they have taken to themselves, and those who countenance them are called "ladies of respectability." We are sorry to have offended the gentlemen, but our Master said, "This is the way, walk ye in it"; and if they do not like our Society and principles, we will cherish a spirit of kindness, and pray that their minds may be enlightened from on high.

On behalf of the Society,

Affectionately yours,

E.E.

Porter

Source: *E. E. Porter to the New York Female Moral Reform Society Corresponding Secretary, April 21, 1838; printed in* Advocate of Moral Reform, *June 15, 1838. Reprinted in Daniel S. Wright and Kathryn Kish Sklar, "What Was the Appeal of Moral Reform to Antebellum Northern Women, 1835–1841?"* Women and Social Movements *Web site, Alexander Street Press.*

Questions

1. Why did the women of the Windham Moral Reform Society believe that late night visiting was morally problematic?

2. Why were men in Windham so angry about the "9 o'clock article"?

in these towns did not have to contend with widespread prostitution, but they were very concerned about the sexuality of young people who had become increasingly mobile in the nineteenth century. Young, single men showed up in any number of small towns as college students, and young people of both sexes were migrating to jobs in factories and businesses at far-flung locations. Mothers wanted to make sure that new men in their towns would not seduce their daughters and that their daughters would be safe if they went to work in another location.

The women who joined these moral reform societies supported antiprostitution journals such as the *Friend of Virtue* and *McDowell's Journal*, which became the *Advocate of Moral Reform*. The Female Moral Reform Society put the onus of illicit sex on the men. In graphic terms, these newspapers described scenes of seduction and the dreadful consequences wreaked by brutal male libertines. Even more controversial, the newspapers listed the names of men who had been reported to visit a brothel. Indeed, in New York City, members not only paid missionaries to visit brothels to stage prayer meetings of repentance, they eventually visited the brothels themselves. The women who engaged in this behavior opened themselves to public ridicule and censure for venturing where true ladies did not belong. Yet, they created a powerful critique of a sexual double standard in which men usually escaped censure while women were singled out for punishment in an illicit act.

Many of the issues raised by the Female Moral Reform Societies surfaced again in the Rosine Societies of the 1840s, which also opposed prostitution. The Rosine Society, however, moved one step further in trying to establish a sense of community among reformers and the prostitutes they were trying to reform. Members of the Rosine Society noted that economic circumstances rather than lax morals could push women into prostitution. Moreover, they made a biting connection in noting it was the same lack of economic opportunity that forced other women into marriage.

Bodily Purification and the Dangers of Drink

Concerns about prostitution were part of a wider range of concerns about sexuality that became particularly clear in the early health movements, which many women supported. Sylvester Graham, who began his career as a temperance lecturer, articulated a philosophy for regulating food as well as alcohol, insisting on strict vegetarianism and homemade bread. During the 1830s, thousands of people flocked to his lectures. Graham and his followers argued that debilitating diseases and insanity were often caused by sexual stimulation, particularly masturbation. A bland diet would not only nourish the body but also control unhealthy sexual impulses that Graham attributed to the consumption of alcohol, caffeine, meat, and sugar. Although he was dismissed as a quack by a growing medical profession and attacked by mobs in several instances when he attempted to lecture on chastity, Graham still developed a following. Boardinghouses that served a Graham diet were established by his followers, including Mary Gove Nichols.

Although the control of sexual behavior received widespread attention during the antebellum period, the temperance movement dominated the reform efforts of nineteenth-century Americans and became the most visible attribute of middle-class respectability in cities and villages where commerce flourished and workshops hummed with activity. The consumption of alcohol became a concern early in the nineteenth century for two reasons. First of all, drinking did increase dramatically after the American Revolution, particularly as whiskey became a popular product of grain. Secondly, an increasingly regimented workplace demanded workers who were sober and industrious while they were at work. As a result, temperance organizations, led originally by members of the new middle class, began to spring up in the 1820s.

Throughout the 1820s and into the 1830s, temperance organizations led by men formed an important counterpart to the maternal associations and benevolent groups

WOMEN'S LIVES

MARY GOVE NICHOLS

Mary Gove, born in 1810, ran not only a Graham boardinghouse but also a Graham boarding school in Lynn, Massachusetts, during the antebellum period. Like Graham, she began to write and lecture on health issues, directing her attention particularly to women, though her lectures drew mixed audiences. Although Mary tried to distinguish herself from Graham, she too stressed the importance of diet and the dangers of masturbation, arguing in her 1839 pamphlet *Solitary Vice,* that the dangers of self-pollution extended to females as well as males. Mary soon began lecturing on the topic and joined Graham in initiating an unusually frank discussion on sexuality. While Mary focused on the dangers of masturbation and the importance of chastity, her writings and lectures brought to women detailed information on their bodies, sources of sexual pleasure, the nature of passion, and the mechanics of reproduction. Her lectures were well attended and her writings sold well, but her behavior was nonetheless considered scandalous enough that her Quaker meeting expelled her.

Mary's concern for regulating the body evolved into a philosophy of a woman's right to control her body. By the early 1840s, she was speaking more broadly on gender issues and attacking marriage as the "annihilation of woman." And while Mary deplored masturbation as dangerous, she began to advocate passion rooted in true love as a desirable goal for women. A woman's control of her body, rather than the state's control of it through marriage, became her guiding principle. Given her Quaker background and emphasis on female autonomy, it is not surprising that Mary found a new religious home in the Spiritualist movement where she became a well known medium as well as a health practitioner.

Working with her second husband, Thomas Low Nichols, Mary set up a variety of water cure establishments, attending to sick patients with a strict regimen of bathing and vegetarian diets. While her

(Library Company of Philadelphia)

attacks on marriage and her celebration of passion had branded her a scandalous woman and partisan of the radical free love cause, in fact, Mary and her husband began moving toward an emphasis on chastity and Catholicism by the end of the 1850s. Contacted by several dead Jesuit priests during her Spiritualist seances, Mary and Thomas Nichols were persuaded to convert. Mary recanted any earlier positions she had espoused that violated church doctrine and spent several years traveling among different Catholic convents, aiding the nuns with their medical responsibilities. Although the teachings of the Catholic Church flatly contradicted Mary's critique of marriage, the alternative of celibacy offered by convent life did not. As Mary had explored avenues of sexual liberation and autonomy, chastity had always been an important alternative. Convents presented her with a long-lived tradition of bodily control that she felt comfortable embracing until she died in 1884. ■

headed by women. Men dominated these groups, in part, because drinking was construed as a male problem. There are numerous examples to suggest that women drank, but they were not usually targeted in temperance campaigns. Women were more often depicted as the victims of a drunken husband rather than the perpetrators of alcohol abuse. Women did not lead the temperance organizations, but they did join them and constituted between one-third and two-thirds of the membership of temperance organizations in the 1820s and the early 1830s. They were important advocates for the movement, attending meetings and encouraging their family members to limit their consumption of alcohol. This subordinate role within the temperance movement reinforced ideals of domesticity central to the temperance literature that described women as victims of alcoholic husbands in a disintegrating family.

As this certificate for membership in a temperance society makes clear, temperance was considered a central value for family stability. Excessive drinking was viewed as one of the causes for spousal abuse and family collapse.

By the end of the 1830s, however, women began to play a more active role in temperance reform through the creation of their own independent or auxiliary organizations. While most of these organizations were composed of middle-class white women, working women and African American women also formed temperance associations. Among the most important female temperance societies to be created were those of the Martha Washingtonians, founded as part of the larger Washingtonian movement. Washingtonians, whose members often came from the ranks of the working classes, represented a new phase in the temperance movement as reformed drunkards took over leadership of the temperance movement from more respectable businessmen and shopkeepers to preach a philosophy of total abstinence. Many Martha Washingtonian members were related to the male members. The Martha Washingtonians were particularly important because they broke the taboo of talking about female drinking. They visited women who drank and worked to reform them. Although many were not middle class, they still shared in some of the fundamental tenets of middle-class domesticity, including a belief in the centrality of women to family morality and cohesiveness, as well as a sense of the extent to which alcohol could make an already tenuous economic existence unbearable.

The defense of a virtuous home life, which made temperance the most respectable of reform movements, could develop a more radical edge. By the 1840s, some female temperance supporters were demanding the legal right of women to divorce husbands who were habitual drunkards; and by 1850 they had achieved that goal in fourteen states. As women were repeatedly portrayed as victims of abuse from drunken spouses, more radical temperance advocates began to urge women to fight back. From fictional portrayals of women who forced their husbands to sign a temperance pledge at knifepoint to actual attacks on local saloons, this more assertive wing of the temperance movement pushed women to reimagine the nature of marriage and their roles as guardians of their homes, creating warriors at the gates rather than angels of the hearth.

Curbing Domestic Violence

Temperance reformers who raised the issue of physically abusive spouses were challenging older ideas of bodily discipline that accepted corporal punishment as a legitimate way for a man to maintain order in his home. Wife beating was not legal in most states in the Union during the antebellum period. In fact, as early as 1650, it had been outlawed in Massachusetts Bay Colony. But common law did allow husbands the right of "modest chastisement" of their wives.

"Modest chastisement" referred to a husband's right to inflict physical punishment on his wife to keep order in his household. During the 1840s, when two women on a wagon train headed for Oregon began pulling each other's hair in a dispute, the captain ordered their husbands to administer corporal punishment: "a good licking that nite not over the Back But not far from the ass and all wod bee well." In North Carolina, the court ruled that husbands were allowed to strike their wives in order to maintain discipline but not out of "mere wantonness & wickedness." Both of these cases reflected a patriarchal order in which fathers were expected to keep charge of their households, and one in which external forms of punishment, such as a beating, were a bedrock of the social order. As families began to organize around nurture and conscience, however, corporal punishment became increasingly controversial.

In addition to the question of corporal punishment, there was another side of wife beating that also drew attention: vicious and even life-threatening attacks on spouses. Hester Bishop, for example, had been beaten more than once by her husband James before he finally killed her at their home in New Jersey on November 12, 1842. Their neighbor, William Hayes, heard the mayhem that night and assumed Bishop was whipping his wife; but as the noise quickly died down, he did not intervene. He did recollect, however, a previous incident in which James had "bruised her up once before so badly that I did not think she would live twenty-four hours." James's sister-in-law, with whom the couple shared a house, also recalled earlier beatings. None of these beatings had been reported.

This sort of wife beating had always been illegal, but it was also tolerated in many communities. Some courts were reluctant to interfere unless it could be proven that a wife's life was in danger. Neighbors could ridicule a brutal husband, but that did not always stop him. In other cases, wives held back from calling for help because the financial burdens resulting from court intervention were also distressing. When Patrick Cook was fined forty dollars and sentenced to forty days in jail for beating his wife Betsy in 1846, his whole family suffered the financial consequences. A woman whose husband was jailed or fined for beating her lost the income he would have provided had he been working or not paying the fine. Either way, she suffered.

During the first half of the nineteenth century, the threat of serious spousal abuse was real and it was on the rise. In jurisdictions throughout the country, the courts began to handle more and more cases of domestic violence, even as the number of other kinds of criminal cases began to decline. The reasons for this development varied with the region. In the West, many men lived with violence as part of frontier conditions; in the South, white men cultivated a sense of patriarchy that was rooted in the ability to physically abuse their slaves; but even in the Northeast, more men were killing their wives than had been true in the colonial period. The number was never very high, but in Vermont and New Hampshire, for example, the percentage of women killed by their husbands more than tripled during the middle years of the nineteenth century. Some of these men faced the frustrations of poverty, but many others were part of the new middle class. In beating their wives, they rejected the codes of sentiment and moral suasion that were at the core of the bourgeois household, reverting instead to an exaggerated enactment of the patriarchal privilege that was under attack.

As temperance advocates noted, many of the men who beat their wives were drunk. Husbands regularly defended themselves against spousal abuse charges by claiming that they were drunk. Indeed, when Alvin Preslar was convicted of murdering his wife in North Carolina in 1856, over three hundred petitioners pleaded with the governor to overturn his death sentence, arguing that he had beaten her as "the result of a drunken frolic." Not surprisingly, female temperance reformers took up the issue, arguing that women should be protected from their drunken spouses and allowed to divorce them if necessary.

CONTESTING THE NATION: SOCIAL AND POLITICAL REFORMS

While most women focused their efforts on moral reform, smaller groups of women carried their moral concerns into women's movements that collectively addressed employers and legislatures. They often used a language of sin and morality in their campaigns; but unlike moral reformers, they sought to change government policies and laws about work, slavery, and Indian removal through their direct intervention. Thus, their activities were controversial because of the challenges they posed to economic elites and government leaders and because they ventured the farthest beyond traditional definitions of women's separate spheres.

Working Women and Labor Protests

Women in industrial towns and cities throughout the North organized during the 1830s and 1840s. In all areas of wage work, pay was declining and working conditions deteriorating as employers sought to maintain profits in an increasingly competitive marketplace and through a series of recessions. As women engaged in their collective labor protests, they moved into territory that men had been defining since the 1790s.

In 1825, the seamstresses of New York went on strike, the first all-female labor protest on record in the United States. A few years later, in 1831, the tailoresses of New York turned out to protest the lowering of prices they were to be paid for their work. New York was not the only place where women staged protests. In Lowell, Massachusetts, factory workers began to protest as well. When mill owners reduced wages by 25 percent in 1835, female factory workers signed petitions and eight hundred of them turned out and paraded through the streets. They stressed the importance of their independence from both their families and their employers, claiming their rightful heritage as "daughters of freemen." To those who witnessed the turnout, this expression of independence was clear; one newspaper reported a "flaming Mary Woolstonecroft speech on the rights of women," and a mill agent described the strikers as Amazons. In 1836, they turned out again when mill owners tried to raise the rates at boardinghouses, a move that just as effectively reduced the earnings of the factory operatives as a wage cut would have.

Seamstresses faced some of the lowest wages and most difficult working conditions of any female workers in the nineteenth century.

Smaller industrial towns such as Lynn, Massachusetts, also experienced unrest in 1834 from the women who worked as shoe binders, because they too faced a reduction in their wages. Many of the women who formed the Female Society to protest the wage cuts, were the wives and daughters of male shoemakers, living in family units different from the boardinghouses of the young women in Lowell or the seamstresses in New York. Thus, they justified their demands not only in terms of independence and economic fairness but also in relationship to the cost of the housework they would otherwise be performing. These women made it clear that their labor should not be bought cheaply because many of them were contributing to a family income, providing a necessary supplement to the wages of their husbands and children.

During the 1840s, workers began to argue that their working conditions undermined the commitments to spiritual salvation and moral reform that they had pledged in the revivals and temperance meetings that spread through factory towns. This commitment to moral reform infused the ten-hour movement begun among male carpenters in the shipbuilding and construction trades, as the men demanded that their workday extend only from 6:00 A.M. to 6:00 P.M. with two hours off for lunch. Female factory workers, who faced equally long hours in the summer, adopted this demand in the 1840s, creating a powerful and organizationally sophisticated movement. Their interest was propelled not only by the length of their workdays but also by the rapidly increasing amounts of work they faced in speedups and stretch-outs. **Speedups** meant that operatives had to tend machinery operating at a faster speed, and **stretch-outs** meant that operatives were being required to operate more pieces of machinery. While operatives saw their pay increase slightly as a result of these changes, most of the resulting profit went to the mill owners and many operatives found themselves exhausted.

By the end of 1844, a few factory women in Lowell had joined together to form the Lowell Female Labor Reform Association (LFLRA). They spearheaded a massive petition drive in 1845, garnering signatures from over one thousand individuals, three quarters of whom were women. The LFLRA, under the leadership of Sarah Bagley, also went on to purchase *The Voice of Industry,* an important labor newspaper, in 1846.

Bagley and other female factory workers used the newspaper to challenge the Christian principles of mill owners who left their workers little time to read the Bible at night and too exhausted to attend church on Sunday. Another female operative described the participation of women in the ten-hour struggle as consistent with the moral mission of women. Factory women argued they were trying to protect their own virtue and that of others.

Women in Lowell and other factory towns did not succeed in gaining a ten-hour workday. While the state legislature in Massachusetts agreed that abuses existed, it refused to act. However, the women who had pushed for the legislation did demonstrate how the ideals of moral reform that were being used to legitimate the goals of an expanding middle class could be used by working-class women to defend their goals as well.

Protesting Indian Removal

The labor petitions submitted by workingwomen in the 1840s continued an important political tradition begun by women opposed to President Andrew Jackson's Indian removal policies. As debate heated up on this issue, leaders from the American Board of Commissioners for Foreign Missions, a group that had been actively working to convert Indians, joined a gathering storm of criticism, claiming that Indian removal was

speedup Increase in the speed of machinery in a factory to produce greater output.

stretch-out Increase in the number of machines a factory worker tends in order to increase output.

WOMEN'S LIVES

SARAH BAGLEY

Sarah Bagley was born in 1806. When she began work in the Hamilton Company at Lowell in 1837, she embraced the town's rich cultural life, joining the First Universalist Church and writing articles for the *Lowell Offering* about the benefits of millwork. However, within a few years, she began to feel the stress that came from lengthy, demanding workdays, and her view of factory life became more critical. She joined with other operatives to form the Lowell Female Labor Reform Association (LFLRA) in the winter of 1844, working with mechanics, artisans, and factory workers throughout New England to enact a ten-hour day. As president of the organization, Sarah not only led several petitioning campaigns to the state legislature demanding shorter hours but also entered a broader world of social reform movements that were sweeping the country.

Sarah corresponded with Thomas Dorr, who had led a rebellion of propertyless workers in Rhode Island seeking the right to vote, and she made friends with Albert Brisbane who led the Fourierist movement, which sought to create societies organized along communal principles. Sarah also corresponded with Angelique Martin, a member of a utopian community in Ohio, who urged the factory girls to view their struggles in terms of labor inequality as well as gender inequality.

However, as the labor reform movement sputtered, Sarah left both the mills and the labor move-

ment in frustration. Her anger grew as she faced wage discrimination at her new job in the telegraph office. "I am a woman and it is not worth so much to a company for <u>me</u> to write a letter as it would be for a man," she wrote to Martin. Soon after, Sarah left Lowell for Philadelphia where she joined the Rosine society, which was dedicated to rehabilitating prostitutes. She possibly met her future husband there and acquired some medical training. By the middle of the 1850s, she was living in Albany as a doctor, tending to women and children with the patent medicines made by her husband, James Durno. Although this new career was a far cry from the social activism of her factory days, it demonstrated her continuing disregard for the traditional expectations society held for women. She probably died in the 1880s. ◼

not only illegal but sinful. Cherokee Indian women, as early as 1817, had submitted petitions to their National Council urging the Council not to cede Cherokee lands to the United States government (see chapter 4).

White women, who had been supportive of missionary work among the Cherokees, joined in the protests. Catharine Beecher, who was running her Hartford Female Seminary at the time, was so troubled by Indian removal that she called a meeting and initiated a petitioning campaign among women in 1829 to protest Jackson's policies.

This was the first mass petitioning movement of its kind. Beecher, who would later become famous for her *Treatise on Domestic Economy* (see chapter 5) knew she was pushing far beyond the bounds of normal propriety and moving women into a sphere of political activism, so she kept her participation in the movement a secret. Indeed, she later wrote that her conflicted feelings about her political activities had led her to the point of a breakdown.

Beecher sent her circular to women's benevolent groups throughout the United States urging them to petition Congress. Hundreds of them did, from Hallowell, Maine, to Steubenville, Ohio. In at least some cases, female signers were tied to missionary efforts among the Indians, an effort they referenced in their petitions. Many of them were also prominent women in their communities, carefully chosen by Beecher because of their elite status. Cherokee women also submitted some petitions as part of this campaign. The women who submitted these petitions did so carefully, wording their pleas in a manner quite distinct from that found in male petitions. Female petitioners described their activities as moral rather than political (by which they meant partisan). They couched their concern for Indians as part of their expressions of domesticity and benevolence—expressing concern for both the spiritual and domestic well-being of Indians forced to move and legitimating their interests as an extension of their missionary concerns. Finally, these women used very submissive language, prostrating themselves before Congress to influence debate rather than assert a right of participation.

Despite the supplicating posture, members of Congress attacked the female petitioners for wasting their time. Proremoval senators, such as Thomas Hart Benton, criticized the women for failing to understand their appropriate gender roles. Others criticized men for failing to keep their women under control. Most of the petitions to Congress were tabled by opponents, but they did at least have the effect of stimulating further debate on the issue.

Even though female petitioners were unable to stop the removal of Indians, they did provide an important impetus for further organizing against injustice. Many activists who went on to lead antislavery movements began their criticisms of social injustice in their defense of Indians. William Lloyd Garrison and James Birney, important leaders in the antislavery movement, learned the strategy of petitioning through the Indian removal campaign. Lydia Maria Child and Angelina Grimke also expanded their opposition to Indian removal into opposition against slavery.

Hiram Powers' 1846 statue, The Greek Slave, received widespread attention in Europe and the United States. Although it portrayed a Greek Christian woman captured by Moslem Turks, the statue also encouraged viewers to contemplate the horrors of African American slavery. (Hiram Powers, "The Greek Slave." 1846. Marble. H: 65" W: 19 1/2". The Corcoran Gallery of Art, Washington, DC)

Race, Hierarchy, and the Critique of Slavery

During the early nineteenth century, organized opposition to slavery began in 1817 with the American Colonization Society (ACS). The ACS founded the African colony of Liberia that year and began to purchase the freedom of American slaves, paying their passage to Liberia and promoting emigration among free blacks as well. Although this movement received some support from African Americans, it was condemned by others. During the 1820s, free blacks began setting up societies throughout the North that argued slavery was immoral and sinful and demanding an immediate end to slavery instead of gradual emancipation. In 1832, the white abolitionist William Lloyd Garrison introduced this radical critique of slavery to the white community, spawning a powerful but contentious abolition movement.

In 1832, black women in Salem, Massachusetts, organized the first female antislavery society in the United States. Maria Stewart, an African American woman in Boston, became the first female antislavery lecturer. During the 1830s, she became well known for her fiery speeches attacking slavery and her challenge to other African Americans that they rise up against the brutal institution. Eventually, however, her verbal attacks on African American men for not doing enough to combat slavery led to bitter retaliation from her audience. Stewart argued that she was being attacked because as a woman she had dared to speak, and she left for New York.

The antislavery societies created by African American women continued a broader tradition of racial uplift that was central to traditions of organizing among free black women. Whether providing loans to members of their benevolent societies or supporting schools for African American children or asylums for orphans, the tradition of mutual aid societies begun by African American women had burgeoned during the antebellum period and inspired the activities of antislavery activists. Opposition to slavery was never an end in itself for the African American organizations; rather, it was part of a broader commitment to achieving racial equality, opportunity, and mutual aid. African American antislavery advocates struggled to keep these broader issues alive in the antislavery movement.

White women quickly followed the lead of these African American women, establishing antislavery societies in cities such as Boston, New York, and Philadelphia. Some of the associations were integrated—but not all, and African American women continued to maintain all black associations as well, sometimes participating in both. In part, this was due to the reluctance of white women to share positions of leadership with African Americans. In New York City, for example, white antislavery women refused to allow African American women to hold any positions of leadership, and few African American women joined. White women were often more narrowly focused on antislavery issues, which frustrated the broader goals of African American women who were concerned with issues of equality and the well-being of free blacks, as well as with the goal of emancipation.

Assumptions about racial hierarchy were also encoded in the literature and visual symbols of the antislavery movement. Hiram Powers' statue *The Greek Slave* (1841–1843) was widely viewed in Europe and the United States. Depicting a Christian Greek woman sold in a Muslim Turkish slave market, it encouraged white women to empathize with the indignity of slavery. But it did not necessarily lead them to identify with the travails of black American slaves, who were portrayed differently, as was clear in the image of *The Virginia Slave* that appeared in the British humor magazine *Punch*. In another case, one of the most popular emblems of female antislavery societies depicted a female slave, half-clothed and in chains, kneeling before her white female liberator who was standing. Although they shared their identities as women, it was the white woman who was viewed as powerful. Similarly, in antislavery stories by authors such as Lydia Maria Child, "the tragic mulatta" was often the central character in the narrative depicting the evils of slavery. This mulatto figure was white rather than black in appearance, a racial characterization that would lead northern whites to identify

The cartoon of the Virginia Slave, published in the British humor magazine, Punch, *made the comparison of African American slavery with the Turkish slavery explicit. The image of the Virginia slave, which is considerably more sassy than that of the Greek Slave, captured some of the stereotypical characteristics associated with African American women.*

with the sufferings of slaves. However, such descriptions also undermined sympathy for real African Americans and effectively denied them the same feelings as whites in antislavery literature.

Politics and Gender in the Antislavery Movement

The women who became involved in abolition during the early years of the 1830s did so in part because they believed slavery was a sin. William Lloyd Garrison's abolitionist crusade was a moral and spiritual one in which adherents borrowed ideas and strategies from the revival movement to provoke an awakening of conscience. Literature that stressed the immorality of slavery and its attack on the family also made slavery a women's issue. It was part of their moral responsibility as women, therefore, to eliminate that sin from the world. But antislavery activists struck at both the heart of the U.S. government, whose Constitution legalized slavery, and at the basis of millions of dollars of wealth held by white southerners in their slaves. Female antislavery activists undertook their crusade with a firm conviction that they were fighting sin, but their experience was a radicalizing one. They emerged from their struggle with a much broader sense of the structural inequalities that permeated society.

Women who joined antislavery societies drew on skills they had developed in other benevolent organizations. Although their numbers were comparatively small, probably no more than 1 percent of the population, antislavery women used their organizing skills to maximize the impact of their efforts. They sponsored antislavery fairs as fund-raising activities in cities and towns throughout the North and newly settled Midwest. They sold articles that they had sewn or that had been donated, sometimes from abroad. British women, for example, showed support for the American cause by shipping goods to the antislavery fairs in the United States once emancipation had been achieved for slaves in the British territories of the Caribbean in 1833. These fairs raised impressive sums of money to keep antislavery associations and presses afloat. Over a period of about a quarter of a century, the Boston Female Anti-Slavery society raised sixty-five thousand dollars. In addition, these fairs were important public rituals aimed at celebrating freedom and ending slavery.

As antislavery women pushed forward in their attack on slavery, they found themselves increasingly drawn into public and political activities that previously had been reserved for men. They drew on the experience of activists who opposed Indian removal to stage massive and repeated petitioning campaigns. Thousands of women in the North and Midwest signed antislavery petitions on a variety of questions, from abolishing slavery in the District of Columbia to opposing the annexation of Texas (because it would enter as a slave state). Antislavery women also supported and contributed to antislavery newspapers such as *The Liberator* and *The National Anti-Slavery Standard*. Sometimes they went door-to-door in their communities, looking for readers and/or subscribers. Their public speaking, however, was their most controversial behavior. Sarah and Angelina Grimke of South Carolina, for example, had grown up as slaveholders and could speak powerfully from firsthand experience about the evils of the system. Although they had originally expected to speak only to women in domestic settings, they had to change their speaking venues to more public spaces to accommodate large audiences, which soon included men as well as women. Such gatherings ignited mob violence on more than one occasion.

As the antislavery movement evolved during the 1830s, however, the very radicalism of the cause provoked intense self-scrutiny among the women and growing fissures developed. The entire antislavery movement split in 1840, in large part over the "woman question." Many of the participants in the antislavery movement (women as well as men) were uncomfortable with the public speaking of women and their leadership role in antislavery activities at the national level. However, Garrison and his followers argued that the inequality that women faced should be included in a broader antislavery agenda. This was the minority wing within the organization, but it retained control of the name, the **American Anti-Slavery Society.** The other group formed the **American and Foreign Anti-Slavery Society,** advocating a more traditional role for women, a focus on the single issue of slavery, and entry into politics as a legitimate way to abolish slavery.

Despite the split, women on both sides continued their antislavery activities and found themselves inexorably drawn into the political controversies their agitation created. Lydia Maria Child, an avid abolitionist who had eschewed political topics in the 1830s, admitted to a growing interest during the following decade. More than with any other voluntary group, antislavery pushed the women involved toward a political culture. Not surprisingly, many of the antislavery activists became leaders in the woman's movement that was starting to form.

American Anti-Slavery Society Organization founded by William Lloyd Garrison in 1833 committed to an immediate end to slavery.

American and Foreign Anti-Slavery Society Organization created in 1840 to oppose slavery through political channels but to ignore other issues such as the right of women to lead the reform movement.

OVERVIEW

Antebellum Reform Movements

Moral Reform Societies	Antiprostitution societies were founded in the 1830s. Originally centered in New York City, these societies spread throughout the Northeast and Midwest. Societies broadened their focus to support a variety of reforms in sexual behavior.
Temperance Societies	Beginning in the 1820s, temperance societies promoted moderate drinking. By the 1840s, they were promoting total abstinence. While men originally led these movements, women eventually began to create their own, arguing they needed to protect women from drunken spouses and, in some cases, reaching out to female drunks.
Diet	Beginning in the 1830s, several reformers, including Sylvester Graham and Mary Gove Nichols, argued for dietary reforms to promote sexual restraint. Health food reformers encouraged followers to give up alcohol, coffee, meat, sugar, and spices.
Indian Removal Opposition	Campaigns were initiated beginning in 1829 to petition against legislation in Congress that would forcibly divest Indians of their lands and push them westward across the Mississippi River. Led by Catharine Beecher, women as well as men submitted petitions to Congress opposing this legislation.
Labor Protests	Beginning in 1825, wage-earning women in cities and industrial towns began to organize strikes, public demonstrations, and petition campaigns to protest low wages and/or long hours.
Antislavery	Beginning in the 1830s, black and white women began to organize their own local antislavery societies and to participate in a broader national movement with men demanding an immediate end to slavery. The movement split in 1840, in part over the question of whether women should assume positions of leadership in the movement.

WOMEN'S EVENTS	GLOBAL EVENTS

1790

1796
Lucy Wright becomes leader of Shakers

1790s
Beginnings of the Second Great Awakening

1800

1817
Cherokee women petition their National Council not to cede Cherokee land to the U.S. government

1825
Seamstresses in New York City start first strike by women

1828
Oblate Sisters of Providence established in Baltimore for Catholic African American women

1829
Catharine Beecher secretly spearheads women's petitioning campaign against Indian removal

1817
American Colonization Society formed

1819
First missionaries sail to Hawaii

1826
American Temperance Society founded

1830

1832
African American women form first female antislavery society in Salem, Massachusetts

1834
Ursuline Convent in Charlestown, Massachusetts burned
New York Female Reform Society founded to combat prostitution
Shoe binders in Lynn form Female Society to protest wage cuts

1835
Female workers in Lowell mills go on strike

1836
Awful Disclosures of Maria Monk published

1839
Mary Gove publishes *Solitary Vice*

1830
Congress passes Indian Removal Act

1830s
High point of Second Great Awakening

1833
William Lloyd Garrison founds American Anti-Slavery Society

1835
Rioters attack William Lloyd Garrison in Boston during an antislavery meeting

1840

1840
Washingtonian Temperance Society formed in Baltimore
American Anti-Slavery Society splits over issue of women's leadership in the movement; those opposed form American and Foreign Anti-slavery Society

1848
Fox sisters hear rapping that will begin Spiritualist religious movement

1848
Oneida community founded by John Humphrey Noyes

CONCLUSION

Many of the different strands of social activism that had been created in the 1830s and 1840s would reconfigure around demands for women's rights in the 1850s. While many women had taken up moral reform activities with the intention of saving souls and maintaining a stable family life, they, like other activist women, created a variety of public roles for themselves. The ideals of republican womanhood that developed in the wake of the Revolution had assumed that women would demonstrate their civic consciousness within their homes by influencing their sons and husbands, and the cult of domesticity had reinforced that belief. However, through their participation in a wide variety of religious and reform movements in the antebellum period, women had begun to directly and collectively address a wide range of social, political, and economic issues. These activities necessarily provoked questions and debates about their "natural sphere," debates that were central to the emerging women's movement.

REVIEW QUESTIONS

1. Did religion empower women?
2. How would you compare the power exercised by Catholic women, Jewish women, and Protestant women?
3. How did the movements to reshape sexual practices, drinking, and eating affect family structure and household authority?
4. What is the significance of women's involvement in social and political movements?

RECOMMENDED READING

Catherine A. Brekkus. *Strangers and Pilgrims: Female Preaching in America, 1740–1845.* Chapel Hill: University of North Carolina Press, 1998. A study of the female preachers who traveled up and down the East Coast preaching during the Second Great Awakening.

Thomas Dublin. *Women at Work: The Transformation of Work and Community in Lowell, Massachusetts, 1826–1860.* New York: Columbia University Press, 1979. A classic study of the lives of women who worked in the Lowell mills during the early nineteenth century.

Lori Ginzberg. *Women and the Work of Benevolence: Morality, Politics, and Class in the 19th-Century United States.* New Haven, CT: Yale University Press, 1990. Important study of the ways in which women's benevolence and social activism evolved

during the nineteenth century, responding in different ways to changes in the political and economic conditions of the country.

Christine Leigh Heyrman. *Southern Cross: The Beginnings of the Bible Belt.* Chapel Hill: University of North Carolina Press, 1997. Analysis of religious practices in the South during the antebellum period, which challenges the idea that revivals opened up opportunities for women and democratized social relationships.

Shirley Yee. *Black Women Abolitionists: A Study in Activism, 1828–1860.* Knoxville: University of Tennessee Press, 1992. A study of the ways in which African American women led the antislavery movement and the ways in which their goals sometimes diverged from those of white women.

ADDITIONAL BIBLIOGRAPHY

Revivals and Religious Virtue

Anne M. Boylan. *The Origins of Women's Activism: New York and Boston, 1797–1840*. Chapel Hill: University of North Carolina Press, 2002.

Ann Braude. *Radical Spirits: Spiritualism and Women's Rights in Nineteenth-Century America*. Boston: Beacon Press, 1989.

Bruce Dorsey. *Reforming Men and Women: Gender in the Antebellum City*. Ithaca, NY: Cornell University Press, 2002.

Janet Wilson James. *Women in American Religion*. Philadelphia: University of Pennsylvania Press, 1980.

Jane H. Pease, and William H. Pease. *Ladies, Women, and Wenches: Choice and Constraint in Antebellum Charleston & Boston*. Chapel Hill: University of North Carolina Press, 1990.

Religion and Family Authority

Ann Braude. "The Jewish Woman's Encounter with American Culture." In *Women and Religion in America*. Vol 1, *The Nineteenth Century*, edited by Rosemary Radford Ruether and Rosemary Skinner Keller. San Francisco: Harper & Row, 1981.

Carol K. Coburn, and Martha Smith. *Spirited Lives: How Nuns Shaped Catholic Culture and American Life, 1836–1920*. Chapel Hill: University of North Carolina Press, 1999.

Jennifer Cubic, and Heather Rogan (under the direction of Kathryn Sklar). "Bible Communism and Women of the Oneida Community." Web site of *Women and Social Movements in the United States, 1775–2000*. Available from http://womhist.alexanderstreet.com.

Lawrence Foster. *Women, Family, and Utopia: Communal Experiments of the Shakers, the Oneida Community, and the Mormons*. Syracuse, NY: University of Syracuse Press, 1991.

Peter Gardella. *Innocent Ecstasy: How Christianity Gave America an Ethic of Sexual Pleasure*. New York: Oxford University Press, 1985.

James J. Kenneally. *The History of American Catholic Women*. New York: Crossroad, 1990.

Louis J. Kern. *An Ordered Love: Sex Roles and Sexuality in Victorian Utopias—the Shakers, the Mormons,* and the Oneida Community. Chapel Hill: University of North Carolina Press, 1981.

Cynthia Lyerly. *Methodism and the Southern Mind, 1770–1810*. New York: Oxford University Press, 1998.

Diane Batts Morrow. *Persons of Color and Religious at the Same Time: The Oblate Sisters of Providence, 1828–1860*. Chapel Hill: University of North Carolina Press, 2002.

Pamela S. Nadel, and Jonathan D. Sarna, eds. *Women and American Judaism: Historical Perspectives*. Hanover, NH: University Press of New England, 2001.

Mary Ryan. *Cradle of the Middle Class: The Family in Oneida County, New York, 1790–1865*. Cambridge: Cambridge University Press, 1981.

Nancy Schultz. *Fire and Roses: The Burning of the Charlestown Convent*. Boston: Northeastern University Press, 2000.

Stephen J. Stein, *The Shaker Experience in America: A History of the United Society of Believers*. New Haven, CT: Yale University Press, 1992.

Controlling the Body, Perfecting the Soul

Ruth Borden. *Women and Temperance: The Quest for Power and Liberty, 1873–1900*. Philadelphia: Temple University Press, 1981.

Barbara Epstein. *The Politics of Domesticity: Women, Evangelism, and Temperance in Nineteenth-Century America*. Middletown, CT: Wesleyan University Press, 1981.

Barbara Meil Hobson. *Uneasy Virtue: The Politics of Prostitution and the American Reform Tradition*. New York: Basic Books, 1987.

Stephen Nissenbaum. *Sex, Diet, and Debility in Jacksonian America*. Westport, CT: Greenwood Press, 1980.

Carroll Smith Rosenberg. *Religion and the Rise of the American City: The New York City Mission Movement, 1812–1870*. New York: Cornell University Press, 1971.

Contesting the Nation

Mary Blewett. *Men, Women, and Work: Class, Gender, and Protest in the New England Shoe Industry, 1780–1910*. Urbana: University of Illinois Press, 1988.

Debra Gold Hansen. *Strained Sisterhood: Gender and Class in the Boston Female Anti-Slavery Society*. Amherst: University of Massachusetts Press, 1993.

Blanche Glassman Hersh. *The Slavery of Sex: Feminist-Abolitionists in America*. Urbana: University of Illinois Press, 1978.

Mary Hershberger. "Mobilizing Women, Anticipating Abolition: The Struggle against Indian Removal in the 1830s." *Journal of American History* 86 (June 1999): 15–40.

Nancy Hewitt. *Women's Activism and Social Change: Rochester, New York, 1822–1872*. Ithaca, NY: Cornell University Press, 1984.

Julie Roy Jeffrey. *The Great Silent Army of Abolitionism: Ordinary Women in the Antislavery Movement*. Chapel Hill: University of North Carolina Press, 1998.

Teresa Murphy. *Ten Hours' Labor: Religion, Reform, and Gender in Early New England*. Ithaca NY: Cornell University Press, 1992.

Christine Stansell. *City of Women: Sex and Class in New York, 1789–1860*. Urbana: University of Illinois Press, 1987.

Jean Fagan Yellin. *Women and Sisters: The Antislavery Feminists in American Culture*. New Haven, CT: Yale University Press, 1989.

Jean Fagan Yellin, and John C. Van Horne. *The Abolitionist Sisterhood: Women's Political Culture in Antebellum America*. (Ithaca, NY: Cornell University Press, 1994.

Biographies, Autobiographies, and Memoirs

William Andrews. *Sisters of the Spirit: Three Black Women's Autobiographies of the Nineteenth Century*. Bloomington: Indiana University Press, 1986.

Carolyn Karcher. *The First Woman in the Republic: A Cultural Biography of Lydia Maria Child*. Durham, NC: Duke University Press, 1995.

Gerda Lerner. *The Grimke Sisters from South Carolina: Pioneers for Woman's Rights and Abolition*. New York: Oxford University Press, 1998.

Jean L. Silver-Isenstadt. *Shameless: The Visionary Life of Mary Gove Nichols*. Baltimore, MD: Johns Hopkins University Press, 2002.

POLITICS AND POWER: THE MOVEMENT FOR WOMAN'S RIGHTS, 1800–1860

WHAT WERE the debates about the relationship of women to property in the antebellum period?

HOW WAS "woman's sphere" expanding in the antebellum period?

WHAT WERE the different ways women approached questions of influence and political participation in the antebellum period?

WHAT WAS the nature of the woman's rights movement in the 1850s?

CHAPTER 8

Walnut Hills [*Ohio*]—July 11 [1855]

Dear Nettee

. . . I expect to be at Saratoga, tho only for one day. But I do not think it is *any* sense good economy to have a meeting *there*—The people who congregate at Saratoga are not reformers, not workers and will *never* help forward our ideas. I would give more for a patient hearing in some country school-house. The rich and fashionable, move only when the masses that are behind and under them move. So that our real work is with the mass, who have no reputation to lose, no ambition

Women's Rights Meeting in Europe

to gratify, and who, as they do not depend upon the Public, need not smother their convictions for its favor—. . . .

Paulina Davis has written me, that she wants the marriage question to come up at the National Convention (I hope she won't be here, with her vanity and her jealousy.) It seems to me that we are not ready for it. I saw that at Philadelphia, by private conversations. No two of us think alike about it. And yet it is clear to me, that question underlies, this whole movement and all our little skirmishing for better laws, and the right to vote, will yet be swallowed up, in the real question, viz, has woman, as wife, a right to herself? It is very little to me to have the right to vote, to own property &c. if I may not keep my body, and its uses, in my absolute right. Not one wife in a thousand can do that now, & so long as she suffers this bondage, all other rights will not help her to her true position—This question will *force* itself upon us some day, but it seems to me it is *untimely* now—. . . .

ever lovingly

Lucy

Source: Women's rights activist Lucy Stone to her sister in law, Antoinette Brown Blackwell. In Carol Lasser and Marlene Deahl Merrill, eds., Friends and Sisters: Letters between Lucy Stone and Antoinette Brown Blackwell, 1846–93 (Urbana: University of Illinois Press, 1987) 143–144.

In writing to her dear friend and sister-in-law, Antoinette Brown Blackwell, woman's rights activist Lucy Stone succinctly captured the dynamic and conflicting impulses that animated the woman's rights movement in the 1850s. Personality clashes among participants, such as that between Davis and Stone, had to be managed. But more important, an array of issues had surfaced about the political rights of women that ranged from voting to property holding to divorce. As Stone indicated in her letter, there was not a broad consensus, even among the leaders of the woman's rights movement, whether all of these issues should be supported and divorce was the most contentious issue of all. What precisely was the meaning of marriage? Should it be classified as one of the many contracts that individuals entered into (and ended for good cause) or isolated as a spiritually privileged union never to be torn asunder? Marriage, and the households constructed around it, had been promoted for so long as fundamental to the political and moral order, what would happen if its contours were redefined as more of a contractual relationship between individuals?

Stone's references to the masses and to voting rights were also telling. The government formed after the Revolution had assumed a hierarchical system in which male property holders were expected to represent the best interests of society. Women did not vote in this system, but neither did many men. During the first decades of the nineteenth century, this view was dramatically refashioned as state after state rewrote their constitutions and, in almost all cases, gave the right to vote to white men without property. Andrew Jackson, as president of the United States from 1828 to 1836, symbolized this new political spirit, as did the new **Democratic Party** that formed around him. The **Whig Party** emerged a few years later in opposition to Jackson's policies but with a keen appreciation for building a mass base of political support that could successfully challenge the Democrats. Both political parties courted votes with barbeques and torchlight parades, leading to a boisterous new democracy that invited broader scrutiny about how political representation should be constructed. How were women to be represented in this new kind of government? Imagining the household as the basic political unit was an increasingly anachronistic concept. The many reform movements in which women were participating during this period had already raised questions about the extent to which they could extend their "sphere," and these questions began to converge with new ones about whether or not successful reform would require the same political tools that had heretofore been the province of men. Thus, from many different directions, questions about how women would participate in their rapidly changing world necessarily arose. From questions of property holding to marriage to political participation, the rights of woman as well as the rights of man demanded debate.

LIFE, LIBERTY, AND PROPERTY

The control of property was closely tied to the exercise of power in the new United States. Many believed that one of the main reasons to have a government was to protect property and in the early years of the government, property was a necessary prerequisite for voting. These beliefs meshed well with a civil code that folded the legal identity of a wife into that of her husband and a political system in which families were represented politically by the father, who was the head of the household. In this world of household representation, a husband's right to control his wife's property made perfect sense. However, this world of property ownership became the focus of reform efforts during the early nineteenth century as both wealth and poverty exploded and the economic risks faced by an emerging middle class threatened the stability of many families. Reforms in property laws, however, struck at the relations of power existing between men and women.

Communitarian Experiments in Family and Property

The ideals of equality that had been raised in the revolutions of France and the United States were effectively channeled into narrow debates on political representation during the early nineteenth century. Radical proponents of early **communitarian** experiments decried this limitation, as they forcefully argued that true equality also demanded a more equitable distribution of wealth and an end to male dominance over women. Thinking about these issues emerged most clearly among the **Owenites** of England and the **Fourierists** of France, both of whom eventually established and inspired utopian communities in the United States. Robert Owen, leader of the Owenites, purchased an Indiana town of thirty thousand acres of land and buildings in 1825 to showcase his ideas. Changing the name to New Harmony, Owen recruited residents to his model community. A decade later, followers of Charles Fourier established communities known as **phalanxes** in towns throughout New England and the Midwest.

Fourierists and Owenites criticized the competitive spirit and physically degrading work regimes of early industrial capitalism, substituting instead a collective work

Democratic Party Political party that formed around Andrew Jackson in the 1820s, supporting his policies of limited federal government.

Whig Party Political party formed in opposition to the Democrats supporting an active role for the federal government in economic development.

communitarian Referring to experimental collective communities meant to demonstrate how societies could be constructed around shared property and social responsibilities rather than around individual property.

Owenites Followers of Robert Owen who participated in his communitarian experiment in England and the United States.

Fourierists Followers of Charles Fourier who participated in his communitarian experiment in France and the United States.

phalanx A Fouierist community.

During the 1820s, Robert Owen established New Harmony in Indiana as a socialist community that promoted economic and gender equality. Some women found their experience at New Harmony liberating, though others were overwhelmed by the amount of work expected of them.

ethic in which members of their communities pooled their resources and supported one another. They also viewed marriage and capitalism as parallel systems of oppression in which financial profits and women were both greedily sought as forms of property. The wealthy unfairly exercised power over the poor and men unfairly exercised power over women. True equality demanded an attack on marriage as well as property, because, as Robert Owen argued, it was in marriage and through the family that men dominated the women who were their daughters and wives.

socialist In the antebellum period, a belief in collective sharing of wealth and work rather than a reliance on individual property holding as a basis of society and government.

New Harmony and dozens of other **socialist** communities experimented with a variety of ways to promote economic and gender equality. The attack on property meant that everyone at New Harmony received the same small allowance each week to spend at the company store. The minimal wages paid at Fourierist phalanxes even extended to payment for domestic chores, a revolutionary concept that recognized the economic value of housework. Attempts to create gender equality surfaced in ideas about clothing, property, and living arrangements. Women and men in New Harmony, for example, were encouraged to adopt an almost unisex clothing style that included trousers under a knee-length tunic for women. In many Fourierist phalanxes, where members bought into the community by purchasing stock, women as well as men were allowed to buy shares. Both Owenite and Fourierist communities also allowed women to vote on community matters; and in an attempt to limit the power of patriarchy in nuclear families, many communities constructed large structures to house most members of their groups, only reluctantly giving separate quarters to families who wished to live together. Indeed, both Robert Owen and Charles Fourier had originally suggested that their communities would promote a liberated sexual life in which the constraints of marriage would be eased. Fourier actually imagined a variety of sexual relationships that ranged from monogamy to polygamy to homosexuality and even to incest. However, in actual practice, the sex life in most of these communities was considerably more staid, as followers focused instead on issues of sociability, work, and governance.

Many of the women who came to these communities, particularly single women, enjoyed the conviviality of communal households and the opportunities for independence they found. However, it was also clear that these communities were far from achieving the kind of gender equality they espoused, in part because communal leaders were still trapped by conventional expectations of male and female behavior. Although women in Fourierist phalanxes were supposed to be free to choose the work they did, most ended up doing traditionally female domestic work. It was revolutionary for phalanxes to pay women for their housework, but those who did housework received lower wages than those who did traditionally male work such as blacksmithing or farming. The jobs apportioned to women in many Owenite communities were those traditionally associated with the domestic sphere. And in some communities, as wages became attached to labor, the work of men was valued at a significantly higher wage than that of women. This was particularly problematic because the activities of the women, particularly cooking and child rearing, were necessary and unrelenting, leading to a much harder workload for women than for men.

Sarah Pears, for example, had come to New Harmony in 1825 with her husband and seven children, hoping to find new opportunities after their gristmill in Kentucky had failed. She was unimpressed with the voting rights she was offered and appalled by the idea of wearing trousers, but she was most disappointed by the workload that she and her daughters faced in their new community. As she watched her older daughter, Maria, take on the heavy duties of washing laundry for the community, Sarah complained, "[A]ll the hard work falls on [Maria] and it is more than she can bear. We had hoped she would have been rather relieved from her heavy labor than otherwise by coming here, but at present it is far from the case." For Sarah Pears, New Harmony brought not an escape from domestic tyranny but an expansion of it.

Unable to solve problems of either class or gender inequality and unable to sustain themselves economically, these communal experiments were fleeting. However, their attempts to link questions of gender inequality with economic inequality and their attempts to reformulate their structure of governance to include direct rights for all raised important possibilities for future thought.

Family Assets: Married Women's Property Laws

While communitarians tried to restructure both property and gender relations, many other Americans confronted questions about women and property in a more prosaic way: through the passage of married women's property laws. During the antebellum period, one legislature after another passed laws that increasingly gave married women ownership of the property they had brought into marriage. While this legislation would eventually become a rallying point for woman's rights activists, the roots of this movement had far more to do with protecting family legacies in a volatile market economy than it did with woman's rights.

The movement for married women's property laws was rooted in a legal loophole that wealthy families had exploited for years: families could establish a "separate estate" for a married woman that her husband could not control. This was a particularly useful instrument if a son-in-law or potential son-in-law was viewed as a ne'er-do-well of some sort. When Agnes Ruffin of Virginia hitched herself to T. Stanly Beckwith in 1838, for example, her father, Edmund Ruffin watched with dismay and anger as his son-in-law contracted debts to cover his failing medical practice and patent medicine ventures. Ruffin had no intention of letting a man he considered shiftless and lazy get

WOMEN'S LIVES

FRANCES (FANNY) WRIGHT

Branded "The Red Harlot of Infidelity" by the *New York Commercial Advertiser* in 1829, Fanny Wright's name was synonymous with scandal in the antebellum period. A wealthy young orphan from Scotland, who had been born in 1795, Fanny Wright enthusiastically embraced the United States as a republican ideal in need of improvement. Joining the economic theories of the socialist reformer Robert Owen, who had founded the community of New Harmony, Indiana, to her own trenchant critique of slavery, Wright set out to reform the problems of the United States (and the world) by devoting a considerable part of her inherited fortune to the establishment of an interracial community in Nashoba, Tennessee.

The experiment at Nashoba began in 1825 when she paid $480 for 320 acres of Tennessee wilderness. Hoping to create a community of interracial harmony, Wright expected to welcome whites and free blacks, as well as slaves who would be manumitted after earning their freedom and learning the skills of personal responsibility. Wright looked to sex as well as work to promote equality, arguing that the best way to end slavery and racism was through interracial unions. As one race evolved, she believed, ideas of racial superiority and inferiority would die. The explosive potential of these beliefs became clear when James Richardson, one of the white trustees at Nashoba, revealed in the widely read antislavery newspaper *The Genius of Universal Emancipation* that he was living with a young quadroon woman named Josephine. Wright stoked public criticism when she wrote a blistering defense of her community, not only attacking slavery and the economic injustices of capitalism but also attacking marriage. It was not public outrage, however, but financial failure that finally killed Nashoba, and Wright reluctantly took her slaves to Haiti, where slavery no longer existed.

As Nashoba floundered, Wright turned to writing and lecturing. Her lecture topics were wide-ranging; she attacked military glory and religious superstition. Preaching most passionately for education (and the need for tax-supported, national schools) as well as equality, Wright fearlessly argued for women's education and their right to control their own property. Thousands of men and women packed lecture halls to hear her speak, and thousands more clucked over her behavior as they read of it in local newspapers.

Fanny Wright shocked society on both sides of the Atlantic not only with her experimental community and her public lecturing but also with her life. Traveling with only her younger sister as chaperone, Fanny Wright developed intense and public relationships with men such as General Lafayette and Robert Dale Owen. While some of these relationships were platonic, others were not, and the truth was that no one could tell.

Even more shocking, Fanny Wright did not care. Her example, as well as her words, set a bold standard for what gender equality should mean. By the end of the decade, however, Wright was exhausted from the demands of her public life and the brutality of public criticism. She retired briefly to France, where she married her lover, Phiquepal d'Arusmont, the father of her newborn daughter. Fanny Wright settled into a quiet and dispirited life that became even more painful as her marriage disintegrated and she fought with her husband over control of her inheritance. Returning to the United States after a few years to quietly support reform activities, Fanny Wright continued her battles with her husband until her death in 1852. ■

his hands on Agnes's inheritance; so when he divided his property among his children, he left Agnes a farm, ten slaves, and railroad stock in a separate estate that her brother controlled for her. Agnes's inheritance was safe from her husband's clutches, but she was hardly financially independent as a result. Her financial fortunes were simply controlled by two different men rather than simply one.

Of course, the goal was not to promote female independence but to protect family property (and by extension, the well-being of the family). Given the volatility of the antebellum economy, even husbands found the creation of separate estates for their wives to be desirable in many cases, realizing that should disaster strike their businesses, assets that were held in their wives' names would be beyond the reach of creditors. The married women's property laws that began to be passed by state legislatures in the 1830s were originally meant to eliminate the complicated legal proceedings that were required to set up such estates and to make the benefits of separate estates available to all women with property. In many cases, they also were part of a more widespread movement to enact bankruptcy legislation after the **Panic of 1837.** During the Panic, the banking system of the United States collapsed, leaving many businessmen and farmers in debt with little recourse to pay their creditors and no ability to protect their families. Legislatures scrambled to pass laws that set up bankruptcy proceedings and abolished imprisonment for debts.

Panic of 1837 Economic depression in 1837 tied to the widespread failure of banks and businesses in the United States.

The first married women's property law was passed in Mississippi in 1839, allowing women to keep both the property they brought to their marriages and property they individually inherited after their marriages, including slaves. Women were not allowed to keep any money they earned, however, nor did they have the right to control their property. Their husbands were expected to make all management decisions concerning the use of their wives' property. A Michigan law passed in 1844 simply stated that creditors could not seize a wife's property to pay her husband's debts. As state constitutions were formed in the newly organized territories of the West, protections of women's properties were included there as well. Married women received protection from the California Constitution in 1849, the Oregon Constitution in 1857, and the Kansas Constitution in 1859. Most states offered some form of a married women's property law by the end of the Civil War.

The need to pass married women's property acts derived not only from concerns about a more volatile market economy but also in response to conquest and acquisition of vast amounts of territory previously held by France and Spain. Under Spanish law, a woman did not merge her legal identity with that of her husband. She was allowed to own her own property, prosecute her financial interests in court, and shield her assets from her husband's creditors (see chapter 4). As territories from the Spanish Empire were incorporated into the United States, many of these property arrangements were preserved. Territorial legislatures in Arkansas and Florida passed laws in 1835 continuing earlier policies that protected a woman's property from debts her husband had incurred prior to marriage. Shortly after Texas declared its independence from Mexico in 1836, the Lone Star legislature incorporated Spanish law on women's property holding into their new constitution.

Probably the most famous set of women's property laws emerged in New York State, where debate focused early and often on woman's rights as well as family protection. Thomas Herttell, an assemblyman in the New York legislature, introduced a bill in 1837 arguing that the French example allowing married women to own their own property was far superior to what existed in the United States and a source of greater stability in marriage. Herttell defended his bill not only as a boon to marriage but also as a natural right of women, leading him to support not only a woman's right to own property but also, by logical extension, her right to vote. Herttell's bill did not receive an outpouring of public support. Ernestine Rose, recently arrived from Poland, managed to garner six signatures on a petition from Utica, New York, supporting Herttell's effort, and another small petition of women was also submitted. But Herttell had clearly identified why married women's property rights could be so powerful—they linked women directly to the political tradition of property holding and the natural rights that were supposed to be tied to that ownership. Property rights involved more than simply preserving family assets.

While some activists seized on this connection as an entering wedge in debating women's equality with men, others studiously avoided connecting the question of property with the question of rights. Sarah Josepha Hale, editor of *Godey's Lady's Book*, ignored Herttell's arguments about voting, even as she lent support to his goals of female property holding in the pages of her magazine. Hale would never support voting rights for women, and she eschewed any notion that women deserved equality to men. Instead, Hale legitimized her support for property laws by arguing that women needed this legislation to protect their separate sphere. Marriage without property protection for wives was slavery in Hale's view. Herttell's bill did not pass; but over the next decade, the issue surfaced repeatedly in the New York legislature, receiving support both from advocates for women like Hale, who emphasized their separate sphere, and from those like Ernestine Rose, who emphasized their shared rights with men.

Ernestine Rose, a Polish émigré to the United States, became involved in the movement for woman's rights in the 1830s when she collected signatures on a petition supporting property rights for married women. During the following decades, she became one of the most vocal and well-known supporters of the woman's movement.

Work and Wages

While legislatures scrambled to pass legislation to protect the property that women brought into marriages, they were far less enthusiastic about recognizing a woman's right to another form of her property: her labor. In most states, husbands retained the legal right to their wives' wages before the Civil War. Only Massachusetts passed an earnings act in 1855. In part, this lack of agitation may have been due to the fact that widespread wage earning was a fairly recent phenomenon, not only for women but also for men. Moreover, many married women who were paid a wage, such as shoe binders in Lynn, Massachusetts, saw themselves as contributing to a family economy and thus did not see themselves as independent wage earners. Their earnings, like those of their husbands and children, were meant to be shared.

This new world of female wage work meant that women also had to contend with another form of discrimination: they were paid less than men. Workingmen who criticized the lower wages paid to women saw this more as an injustice to men than to women. They argued that women were dragging down wages for men by working for so little. Employers, of course, exploited the fact that they could pay women less than men for the same work, and some women, in order to find employment, took what they could get. Workingwomen began to challenge this injustice as early as the 1830s. When the tailoresses in New York City went on strike in the spring of 1831, the secretary of their society, Louise Mitchell, demanded to know why women were paid less than men. "When we complain to our employers and others, of the inequality of our wages with that of the men's, the excuse is, they have families to support, from which females are exempt." As Mitchell pointed out though, this was poor reasoning. "How many females are there who have families to support, and how many single men who have none, and who, having no other use for the fruits of their employers' generosity, they child like, waste it." Some of these seamstresses may well have been inspired by Fanny Wright, the socialist and reformer who had lectured to large audiences during this period. At one point, Wright had argued that women were an economic underclass in society, forced to depend on the larger salaries of men for survival—either as housewives or prostitutes.

A decade later, Ellen Munroe made a similar criticism in the *Boston Bee*, with stinging prose that was reprinted in the labor newspaper of Lowell, the *Voice of Industry*. Mocking the claims of men that they were the general protectors of women, Munroe directed their attention to "the thousands of women, doomed to lives of miserable drudgery, and receiving 'a compensation which if quadrupled, would be rejected by the man-laborer, with scorn.'" The factory workers in Lowell may have been particularly interested in Munroe's argument. Inspired by their correspondence with French immigrant Angelique Martin, a strong woman's rights advocate and communitarian reformer from Marietta, Ohio, the workingwomen of Lowell had hired a lecturer on women's rights.

The sporadic complaints voiced by workingwomen about inequitable wages converged with similar concerns raised by antiprostitution reformers in the 1840s. Female moral reform societies had begun to link prostitution with economic distress rather than moral depravity. Like many middle-class reformers, they criticized the pitiful wages of seamstresses and tailoresses and demanded to know how these women could support themselves. Groups as far away as Oregon began to demand better compensation for female wageworkers.

Those who fought against wage discrimination, like those who fought for a married woman's right to own property, did so for many different reasons. They were not part of a unified women's movement. They were, however, all part of a dynamic and volatile capitalist economy in which economic relations were being radically transformed. Businesses could easily go bankrupt, and employers looked for every opportunity to cut wages in order to make a profit. Regardless of what their ideals of domesticity were, women were a part of this new economic world. Whether as wage earners or wives, they were increasingly economic individuals in need of legal protections independent of their husbands or fathers.

CHALLENGING THE DOCTRINE OF SEPARATE SPHERES

While controlling property and wages represented one set of issues confronted by women in the antebellum period, defining the nature of the domestic sphere represented another. This was an issue that struck at the heart of the contemporary organization of power, for it was the husband who represented his family to the state on the one hand and who ruled his wife and children on the other. Redefining the relations of power within that sphere thus carried tremendous implications. The educational responsibilities of women, tied to their roles as mothers, were promoted in a growing number of ambitious educational ventures. At the same time, the legal bonds of matrimony were reexamined as the grounds for divorce in many states were broadened. While women continued to be legally incorporated within their husbands' identities, the extent of their domestic sphere was expanding and the relations of power within their domestic world were being challenged.

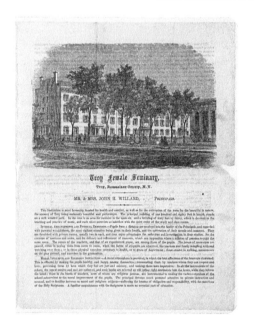

Troy Female Seminary was established by Emma Willard in 1821, promoting a rigorous education for young women in mathematics, science, and history. Although Emma Willard was careful to distance herself from political issues, some of her students were not. Elizabeth Cady Stanton, who became a leader of the early woman's movement, was one of the most famous graduates of the Troy Female Seminary.

Promoting Female Seminaries

The seminary movement that began after the Revolution blossomed during the nineteenth century. Emma Willard became a particularly powerful leader with the Troy Female Seminary in upstate New York where students studied algebra, geometry, physics, history, and geography. Lucy Larcom, who had worked in the Lowell mills, traveled west to Illinois to attend Monticello Seminary. "It was worth while for me to go to those Western prairies, if only for the broader mental view that opened upon me there," she recalled. Describing her trepidation at facing demanding mathematics courses and the rigor of her history and philosophy classes, Lucy credited the "Lady Principal" who taught many of these subjects with getting her through. She "was surely one of my strong guiding angels, sent to meet me as I went to meet her upon my life-road," Lucy concluded.

Female academies and colleges proliferated in the South even more than in the North during the antebellum period. The elite young women who attended these schools sometimes studied classical languages such as Greek that were more commonly the province of men's colleges. They also took on science, mathematics, and history. For southern women, the mastery of such subjects was a mark of class distinction, evidence of their family's wealth and status. Parents thus embraced the opportunity to provide their daughters with a higher education if they could afford it because they felt it would make their daughters more desirable when the time came for them to marry.

In the North, women were educated not only to mark their status but more often to provide them with training in case they needed to support themselves. Emma Willard had always imagined her students could become teachers, even though men dominated the teaching profession at the time. Catharine Beecher raised the stakes by arguing that teaching should become a woman's profession. After running her Hartford Female Seminary during the 1820s, Beecher began to formulate an argument that this kind of rigorous education fitted women to properly extend their sphere from teaching their own children to teaching others as well. Mary Lyon, who founded Mount Holyoke Female Seminary in 1837, focused on the creation of Christian missionaries who would use their training to both convert and civilize the world.

These northern seminaries produced a more independent woman than the southern seminaries did, but almost all of the leaders of this movement were at great pains to avoid pushing too far beyond the bounds of "woman's sphere." Emma Willard was adamant about avoiding direct involvement in political affairs, as was Mary Lyon. Catharine Beecher anguished over the problem—becoming perhaps the most vociferous opponent of political activism at the same time that she secretly engaged in it with the campaign against Indian removal (see chapter 7). Overall, these schools worked hard to create an expanded woman's sphere rather than a challenge to woman's sphere, though some of their students used their educations for more radical purposes. Elizabeth Cady Stanton, one of the most famous of women's rights activists, graduated from Emma Willard's seminary. Moreover, despite the commitment to motherhood, women who graduated from Troy Female Seminary and Mt. Holyoke in the antebellum period were less likely to marry than their peers—evidence of independence their teachers had not anticipated.

Confronting Educational Barriers

Students in female academies demonstrated the intellectual capabilities of women, and their successes encouraged women to seek higher degrees that challenged traditional boundaries between male and female education. As colleges experimented with coeducation and as women demanded postgraduate training, the boundaries of woman's sphere were repeatedly questioned. One of the first places women confronted these barriers was at Oberlin College in Ohio. Oberlin opened in 1833 with a revolutionary commitment to educating not only men and women together but also black and white students together. Inspired by the fires of the Second Great Awakening, Oberlin was the first great experiment in coeducation, though many other small private institutions and public colleges set up by the states would soon follow suit. However, while Oberlin was coeducational, women there soon encountered—and challenged—some of the assumptions about separate spheres built into its curriculum.

Men and women at Oberlin attended the same classes and ate together in the dining halls, where the ideal of civilized discourse between the sexes was enshrined. However, men and women used the library at different times and, more problematic, women were expected to receive a different college degree. The "Ladies' Course," which was eventually renamed "the literary course," did not demand the same level of competence in classical languages as did the "bachelor degree" that men received. Women at Oberlin who entered with training in classical languages quickly complained, and within a decade of its founding, Oberlin was awarding its A. B. degrees to women who qualified while continuing to offer the Ladies' Course to most of the women at the school.

WOMEN'S VOICES

THE IMPORTANCE OF COLLEGE

Sally Rudd was the housekeeper for Asa Mahan, the president of Oberlin College, when she wrote to her niece Mary Caroline Rudd. She encouraged her to attend and offered assistance, recognizing that Caroline's father would scoff at the idea of a girl attending college. Her niece accepted the offer, entering Oberlin as one of the first female candidates for the bachelor degree, graduating from Oberlin in 1841 and eventually marrying George Nelson Allen, a professor of music at the college.

Oberlin March 26 1836

My dear Mary,

. . . I am quite sanguine in my belief that you will come. I think after he [Mary's father] has considered the thing long enough, his judgement will preponderate, & he will say you may come, on this belief, I act. I have kept the ground for you altho at times I have trembled, there has been such a rush in here you say you should like to be where you could wait on me that would indeed be very grateful to me, specialy when I have those distressing fainting turns which I continue to have, although not very frequent, but much as I should want you, to smoth the down hill of life to me, it is not my object in pressing you to come; here my dear Mary you could have an opportunity to obtain a complete education & with my assistance could sustain yourself. I know it must be painfull for your friends to part with you but parents do part with there children to have them educated & hundreds of Parents would rejoice to have there daughters situated as you would be here, & give them up cheerfully. Perhaps you will wonder what you would have to do.

. . . [W]e have a girl that does the washing & kitchen work. You would have the parlers and Mr Mahan's study to keep in order, & what little chamber work there will be to do, but our chambers will all be occupied by boarders, that take care of there own rooms. . . . Mrs Mahan would want you to see to the children, & probably teach them & be ready (when not occupied with your studys) to wait on company & be a kind of minute man. She has three children two little girls one seven & the other coming 5 & a little Oberlin boy ten months old. I give you these particulars, thinking you Father might wish to know something about what your place would be. I shall be with you to release you any time, for your study, & recitations. . . .

Well Mary I will go upon the supposition that you will come. I tell you it would be a new card in your short life & you might start with the impression that now I will get instruction from all that passes before me, & I would advise you to keep a sketch book to note down the various scenes that you pass all through from day to day. . . . This is a place that the intellect is called into exercise & knowledge that is gathered little & little may always be brought into requisition. if you should come I hope you would go through a thourough course of study & be prepared for usefulness.

Your Affect Aunt Sally Rudd

Source: *Sally Rudd to Mary Caroline Rudd, March 26, 1836, Oberlin College Archives, reprinted in Carol Lasser and the students of History 266 at Oberlin College, "How Did Oberlin Women Students Draw on Their College Experience to Participate in Antebellum Social Movements, 1831–1861?" in* Women and Social Movements *Web site, Alexander Street Press.*

Questions

1. What value does Sally Rudd see in her niece receiving a college education?

2. Why did Mary Caroline Rudd's father object to her going to college?

Even more troubling was the demand one early graduate, Antoinette Brown, made to become an ordained minister. Women at Oberlin received theological training to become the wives of ministers, not ministers themselves, and Brown's dogged pursuit of her own pulpit raised hackles around campus. The Ladies Board, which was responsible for the education of women at Oberlin, tried to dissuade Brown. Brown persevered; but when she completed her studies and asked to be licensed as a preacher, the college committee refused. Brown became an active speaker on behalf of religious and reform causes, but ordination was an elusive and difficult goal. She was finally called in 1853 to a small parish in upstate New York; but even then, local Congregational ministers refused to participate in the ordination ceremony. Women could function as informal traveling preachers, but Brown's challenge made it clear that recognition among the "regulars" was a different matter.

Brown's challenge to the theological establishment and the schools it controlled was echoed in the attempts of women to become doctors. This was particularly clear in the experience of Brown's sister-in-law, Elizabeth Blackwell. Blackwell applied for admission to Geneva Medical College in New York in 1847 after having attended a course of medical lectures in Cincinnati. It was the only medical college that would take her, and that occurred in part because the male students, viewing the possibility more as a joke than a real possibility, voted to let her in. Soon after she received her medical degree, Geneva instituted a new policy that forbade the admission of women. Most other medical schools followed the lead. Keeping the regular medical profession male was one of the ways doctors sought to establish their legitimacy and to distinguish themselves amidst the broad array of midwives, botanists, and irregularly trained doctors in the country.

The medical education of women, however, attracted support from a variety of quarters for different reasons. Most women, including Blackwell, argued that providing medical relief had long been the province of women and that women needed female doctors to attend them. Sarah Josepha Hale argued that it was part of woman's sphere to attend to the sick and that no one but a woman should be examining another woman's body. With such issues as female propriety and tradition to back them up, medical study could well be argued to be a natural extension of woman's sphere. Formal medical training had been the province of men, however, and it was hard to avoid the egalitarian implications of offering women this sort of training. Because medical schools were slamming their doors shut to women, supporters of regularly trained female doctors began to organize medical schools for women. The Female Medical College of Pennsylvania was established by the Quakers in Philadelphia in 1850, and the New England Female Medical College in Boston was chartered in 1856. Blackwell herself, along with her sister Emily, who also became a doctor, opened the Women's Medical College of the New York Infirmary in 1868.

Demands for Divorce

Divorce laws had been liberalized in the early republic following the Revolution; however, divorce was still difficult to obtain and women in particular felt that burden. A person had to petition the

Elizabeth Blackwell was educated at Geneva Medical College in New York and later went on to establish the Women's Medical College of the New York Infirmary in 1868. Blackwell's move to establish a medical college was driven by the refusal of established medical schools to admit women.

state legislature for a divorce, a process that required both money and influence. Given the difficulty of such proceedings, many unhappy couples found that a more informal tactic worked better: one of the partners just moved. This was a solution that only worked, however, when there was no property at stake or one of the partners was willing to relinquish his or her claim to it. Frontier areas such as Texas were filled with men (and women) who had left behind unhappy marriages to make a fresh start—a situation that led to a surprisingly casual tolerance of bigamy. William Smith abandoned his wife and three children in Missouri in 1826, moving to Texas where he married Maria Jesusa Delgado of San Antonio in 1830. Smith's first wife divorced him a few years later, but Smith's reputation appears to have suffered little from his complicated marital situation: he was repeatedly elected mayor of San Antonio in the 1830s. After his death in 1845, his first wife and her children sued for control of his estate, arguing that Smith could not have legally married Delgado in 1830 and that she had no right to his estate. The courts thought differently, however, upholding Maria Delgado's claims and the claims of her children.

During the antebellum period, states in both the North and the South increasingly moved divorce proceedings out of the legislatures and into the courts, making them more routine and more accessible to residents. Pennsylvania began this trend in 1816. Even in the South, where colonial divorce laws had been stricter than in the North, all states except South Carolina had passed divorce laws that allowed courts to end marriages in particular circumstances. As a result of these changes, divorce became more common in the United States. In New Jersey, for example, only thirteen divorces were granted between 1788 and 1799 (roughly one per year), whereas in 1860 alone, eighty-six divorces occurred.

Divorce became more accessible not only because it had become a matter for the courts rather than the legislature but also because the grounds for divorce were expanded in most states. One of the most important new criteria for divorce was that of mental cruelty. In a variety of states, legislators accepted the idea that a marriage could be intolerable as a result of not only physical abuse but also mental abuse. However, the courts had to give teeth to these laws, and many justices maintained a very high standard in judging mental cruelty. When Huldah Barber sued her husband Hiram for divorce in Ohio in 1846, the court accepted her contention of mental cruelty because not only had her husband humiliated her by charging her with sexual incapacity and forcing her to have a medical examination to prove it, but he had repeatedly tried to have sex with her daughter. The courts in Connecticut were considerably less open to the mental cruelty plea in a divorce case in which the wife claimed she had been forced by her husband to have sex repeatedly against her will. Describing the husband's actions as "harsh," the court dismissed any notion of mental cruelty and argued that he was exercising his marital rights. In North Carolina, where local justices usually gave plaintiffs a sympathetic hearing, the superior court was far more stringent and seldom granted divorce. As Judge Pearson explained when he overturned the divorce decree from a lower court of a woman whose husband had committed forgery, "She agreed to take him for better or worse."

In addition to the problems associated with actually obtaining a divorce, women also faced hurdles in maintaining their relationships with their children after divorce. Courts in the nineteenth century did increasingly recognize the rights of mothers to custody rather than necessarily giving children to fathers, as they would have done in the colonial period. This was due not to ideas of woman's rights but to woman's nurture—that women were the more "natural" protectors of children. In one case, a New Jersey court even awarded custody to a woman in 1813 who had left her husband for her lover. The court cited the need of the children for their mother's nurture and pointed out that while the mother had behaved badly toward her husband, she had been exemplary in her treatment of her children. However, the courts were much less likely to recognize women's ability to control the legal or financial aspects of their children's lives. Fathers were the ones who were expected to control the property of children, even if their former wives were the nurturers.

WOMAN'S INFLUENCE VERSUS WOMAN'S RIGHTS

These debates about women's property rights, women's education, and what constituted legitimate grounds for divorce took on heightened significance in the volatile world of reform and democratic politics. In a variety of forums, from temperance to antislavery, women were working to shape public policy in a political world that was rapidly changing. One state after another held constitutional conventions in the antebellum period to ratify new documents defining the precise nature of their polity. Old patterns of political hierarchy and deference were being swept away as voting rights were extended to the masses. How would the views of women be represented in this new democratic world? As these questions were debated, two broad lines of reasoning about woman's rights emerged. One focused on the difference between men and women, stressing their separate spheres and complementary roles, while the other focused on the shared characteristics of the two sexes and egalitarianism in their relationships. Those who focused on difference saw women exercising power in society through influence—advising their husbands, educating their children, and providing an exemplary model of virtue in their behavior. They continued the tradition that underlay the celebration of republican womanhood at the end of the eighteenth century. Those who focused on egalitarianism stressed rights over influence. They began to articulate a philosophy that stressed direct relationships between women and the state, women and their property, and women and their employers. In doing so, they laid claim to the tradition of natural rights that had been claimed by men during the Revolution. While continuing to champion the value of woman's sphere, they nonetheless discounted it as the route to power, arguing instead that women needed to exercise power as men did, through political and economic rights. This philosophy would become most clearly articulated in the woman's rights movement of the 1850s, but the outlines were becoming clear by the 1830s.

The Beecher-Grimke Debate

The different philosophies inherent in the influence versus rights approaches crystallized in the mid-1830s as Catharine Beecher conducted a two-year-long pamphlet debate with the Grimke sisters about their antislavery activities and more broadly, the proper relationship of women to political questions. Although Beecher opposed slavery, she was outraged by the *Appeal to the Women of the Nominally Free States* penned by Angelina Grimke in 1836, which not only attacked the religious and legal defenses of slavery but also urged women to combat it by petitioning the government. "Are we aliens because we are women?" Angelina Grimke demanded. "Are we bereft of citizenship because we are the *mothers, wives,* and *daughters* of a mighty people? Have *women* no country . . . ?" Although Grimke did not demand the right to vote for

Angelina Grimke was a powerful anti-slavery advocate in the antebellum period. Her Appeal to the Women of the Nominally Free States *in 1836 provoked a debate in the press with Catharine Beecher about whether or not women should become involved in political conflicts.*

women, she pointedly noted that the American Revolution had been fought over the problem of taxation without representation, and that single women in the nineteenth century faced exactly the same problem: they had to pay taxes on their property but had no voice in the government.

As Angelina Grimke embarked on a speaking tour of northern cities in 1837 to rouse women to the cause of abolition, Beecher penned her first volley in the attack on the Grimke sisters' public speaking and political agitating: *An Essay on Slavery and Abolitionism with Reference to the Duty of American Females.* Beecher saw little hope in the factionalism, patronage, and torch light parade politics that the Democrats and Whigs had created. Ignoring her own role a few years earlier in the petitioning campaigns against Indian removal (see chapter 7), she argued instead that women needed to hold themselves above the fray, promoting their political ideals through the influence they wielded in their homes. Beecher's view was a hierarchical one in which women were subordinate to men but also powerful within this hierarchy. She did not feel that women should divorce themselves from all knowledge of politics but that they should engage it within their homes.

In their counter to Beecher's attack, Angelina and Sarah Grimke stressed the importance of women responding the same way as men to the world's problems because both were endowed with the same souls and moral capacities. The Grimke sisters thus advanced a kind of natural rights argument, one that stressed the shared spiritual characteristics of men and women. However, their natural rights theory was legitimated not by reference to a social contract (which was commonly imagined to have been made by men) but by reference to God. The natural rights of woman were both "sacredly and inalienably hers." Angelina Grimke published her response in *Letters to Catharine Beecher,* which focused mostly on the immorality of slavery. Even more famous, however, was Sarah Grimke's defense in a series of essays for the New England *Spectator* and *The Liberator,* which were gathered together and reprinted as *Letters on the Equality of the Sexes.*

Sarah Grimke argued powerfully for the equality of women and men before God, challenging biblical translations that suggested women were inferior to men. Grimke also drew extensively on history, specifically Lydia Maria Child's *History of Women,* to argue that men had repeatedly abused and dominated the very creatures they were supposed to love. Although Sarah Grimke shied away from suggesting women should vote or serve in the military, she made it clear they were just as capable as men in doing both. She also took on issues of inequality that had been simmering in other venues, pointing out that married women faced injustices as their husbands squandered their inheritances and wages even as women received far less pay than men for performing the same jobs. Property, wages, rights, and religion were joined together in Sarah Grimke's plea for equality.

Sarah Grimke, the sister of Angelina, carried her defense of women's right to participate in the anti-slavery movement into a broader argument about the rights of women in her Letters on the Equality of the Sexes.

Political Participation

The debate over rights versus influence and equality versus difference was inspired not only by the activities women were undertaking but also by changes in the larger political system around them. By the 1840s, only Rhode Island

and South Carolina still restricted the franchise to property owners. Two political parties, the Whigs and the Democrats, emerged during this period to compete for the votes of the newly enfranchised masses. The number of white men participating in elections skyrocketed. In 1824, only 30 percent of adult white men voted in the presidential election, whereas by 1840, the figure was closer to 80 percent. While this new democracy has led some historians to characterize this period as the "Age of the Common Man," it is important to remember that not everyone benefited equally. Even as many propertyless white men were gaining voting rights, free African American men were losing theirs because state conventions often inserted new and higher property qualifications for black men who wanted to vote. Women, whether they had property or not, were universally excluded from direct participation in the new democracy.

However, many American women still participated in the new mass political order. Particularly within the Whig Party, and eventually within the Democratic Party as well, women attended political rallies and parades. In cities from New York to New Orleans to San Francisco, women filled the balconies on political parade routes, waving their handkerchiefs. Some even rode in parades, dressed in white to symbolize purity or to symbolize liberty or the larger body politic. They cooked food for the rallies and made banners in support of their candidates. Politicians for a variety of reasons welcomed their presence. First of all, women symbolized a kind of disinterested virtue that rose above the grimy competition of political campaigns. Women, presumably, were interested not so much in winning but in creating a virtuous society. Somehow, politicians could feel ennobled by female presence. In this sense, women were passive spectators and symbols, meant to be protected but hardly active agents.

However, some of the women who participated in these political events embraced the partisanship of their selected parties. One of the most forceful female supporters of the Whig Party was Lucy Kenney of Fredericksburg, Virginia. An aspiring writer and originally a Democrat, she had written pamphlets supporting Andrew Jackson during the 1830s and was willing to continue writing for presidential candidate Martin Van Buren if he would pay her. Van Buren offered her a dollar for her services; and Kenney, insulted by the offer, switched her allegiances to the Whigs (who paid her considerably more). During the 1840 election, Kenney criticized Van Buren in a pamphlet attack that escalated when Eliza Runnells, defending the honor of the Democrats, accused Kenney of having been "transfigured from an angel of peace, to a political bully." On a more popular level, women joined with men at times in cheering on their candidates, particularly in the frontier regions of the South and Midwest. Mary Ann Inman of Tennessee addressed a crowd of five thousand when she introduced the chief speaker at a Whig rally. Jane Field whipped up her Illinois convention in support of William Henry Harrison's candidacy for president by reminding her audience, "When the war whoop on our prairies was the infant's lullaby, our mothers reposed in security for Harrison was their protector."

Some of the most politically active women in the United States were those who campaigned for the support of private military adventures aimed at taking over foreign countries, some of the most flamboyant expressions of the belief in Manifest Destiny (see chapter 5). **Filibustering,** as the activity was known, occurred most famously when William Walker of the United States overthrew the government of Nicaragua in 1855. Anna Ella Carroll, daughter of one of Maryland's governors, attacked President Franklin Pierce in print for refusing to recognize Walker's ambassador to the

filibustering Private military adventures to take over foreign governments with whom the United States is not at war.

WOMEN'S LIVES

JANE CAZNEAU

Jane McManus Cazneau was one of the most prominent advocates of U.S. expansion during the nineteenth century. She was born into a wealthy New
York family in 1807 and married by the age of eighteen. She divorced her husband six years later and
faced further scandal when rumors circulated that
she was former Vice President Aaron Burr's mistress.
Soon after her divorce, she began to look for property in Texas, applying to Stephen Austin for land
in his colony and petitioning the Mexican government for additional lands farther south on which
she hoped to establish a colony of German settlers.
She and her brother Robert bought and sold property in Texas during the 1830s and 1840s, moving
their parents there in an attempt to shore up family
finances. As a result, McManus became one of the
most prominent early Anglo settlers in Texas.

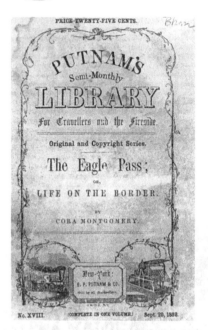

McManus established a powerful political presence in both Texas and the United States as a
writer for newspapers such as the *New York Sun* and
the *New York Tribune*, as well as the *Democratic Review*. Sometimes she wrote as Cora Montgomery,
Corinne Montgomery, or just plain Montgomery. In
the pages of these journals, she championed the independence of Texas from Mexico during the 1830s
and the annexation of Texas in the 1840s. During
the Mexican War, she traveled to Mexico City with
Moses Beach, editor of the *Sun*, on a secret peace
mission at the same time that she took advantage of
her position behind enemy lines to report on the
war. Beginning in 1847, she began campaigning for
the annexation of Cuba, carrying her advocacy into
her column "The Truth," which was published between 1848 and 1853 in the newspaper *La Verdad*.
She also became a supporter of William Walker in

his attempts to take over Nicaragua during the
1850s. She lobbied Jeremiah Black, the attorney
general of the United States, in an attempt to get
the U.S. government to recognize Walker's regime.

In 1849, Jane married the wealthy Texas entrepreneur William Cazneau. The Cazneaus set up
housekeeping at Eagle Pass on the Mexican Border,
where Jane claimed that Mexicans kidnapped
Texas residents and forced them to work in Mexico. The state department took her claims seriously
enough that they investigated them, but no evidence was found to sustain her charges. She and
her husband subsequently moved to the Domini-
can Republic, where he was both a government
commissioner and secret agent. In 1878, she died
when the ship she was traveling on from New York
to Santo Domingo sunk. ■

United States. Jane McManus Cazneau of Texas pressured the *New York Sun* to promote Walker's adventures and dragged her husband to Nicaragua for Walker's inauguration as president. Sarah Pellet lectured on behalf of Walker in New Orleans after visiting him in Nicaragua. Using the press and the podium, women such as these pushed the belief in Manifest Destiny to new heights.

Even women who followed the more traditional route of "influencing" their husbands rather than participating directly in politics could be quite forceful in expressing their political views. Margaret Randolph, a Democrat and a descendent of Thomas Jefferson, was outraged by her husband's Whig leanings. "You have no idea what a source of vexation it is to me," she wrote to her sister. "We had several hot quarrels about it and determined not to mention the subject again however I took advantage of Williams being stretched on the bed with a mustard plaster on . . . and we got in such a rage that he wanted me to come to the side of the bed & take it out in a fisty cuff. . . . "

From Moral Suasion to Political Action

By the 1850s, many moral reform causes were moving out of the realm of moral suasion and into the realm of legislative initiative. Whether fighting for temperance or chastity or even more explosively, an end to slavery, reformers began to seek political solutions to problems that had been the target of their moral reform concerns during the 1830s and 1840s. Women who wanted to continue pushing for those reforms had to come to terms with this new political world and figure out how they were going to be a part of it.

The beginnings of this move toward political involvement lay in the petition campaigns of the antebellum period (see chapter 7). In protesting Indian removal, slavery, and labor conditions, women had affixed their names as individuals to political causes and sought political solutions to these problems. They passed petitions among their friends, and they also knocked on the doors of strangers and submitted their petitions in the impersonal halls of the legislature. The petition campaigns continued to expand to other reform efforts, and reformers increasingly sought legislative solutions.

Of course, elite women had always had informal access to political leaders. If they were not married to them, they socialized with them. Sitting at dinner, contributing financially to their campaigns, and facilitating introductions, these women effectively utilized informal networks to lobby effectively for their benevolent causes: local orphanages, schools, or other worthy ventures. Many of the women who became involved in more radical and national causes, however, did not have this kind of access. They usually did not have the same social connections and their causes were far more controversial. If they wanted to reach politicians, they had to rely on more public methods.

By the end of the 1840s, as moral reform stalled and political participation was defined increasingly in terms of the vote, it was difficult to ignore politics as an arena of potential change. The **Liberty Party,** which was established in 1840, established an antislavery beachhead in the political system. The **Free Soil Party,** established in 1848 and largely incorporated into the Republican Party in 1854, continued this trend. Temperance also became more of a political issue in the 1850s as laws against the sale and consumption of alcohol were debated. If women wanted to continue to

Liberty Party Political party created in 1840 around opposition to slavery in the United States.

Free Soil Party Political party created in the 1840s around a belief that slavery should not be allowed in the territories acquired by the United States.

Different Approaches to Women's Exercise of Power

Influence   Built on ideals of separate spheres and the cult of domesticity, this approach argued that women should exercise power in society by influencing the men in their families through prayer, education, example, and persuasion. This approach accepted participation in reform societies and the education of women as part of women's separate sphere. Championed by Sarah Josepha Hale and Catharine Beecher, this view of women's role in society was widely accepted by the middle class.

Rights   Although accepting the idea of separate spheres, this approach argued that women should receive the same rights as men in society and government, including the right to vote. Led by women such as Susan B. Anthony and Elizabeth Cady Stanton, this movement was championed by a small group of men and women, many of whom had participated in the antislavery movement.

provide leadership in these movements, they would have to come to terms with the political world in which their causes were now being agitated.

FORGING A MOVEMENT

Dred Scott decision
Decision by the Supreme Court that Dred Scott could not sue for his freedom even though he lived in a free state because slaves were not citizens.

The movement for woman's rights emerged in the 1850s as Americans of all stripes debated ideas of citizenship and worried about the protection of their rights. Not only were established states rewriting their constitutions, new states were conceiving of theirs as they sought entry into the union. The **Dred Scott decision** focused national attention on the Supreme Court decision in 1857 that a slave could not be a citizen. Both northerners and southerners were increasingly suspicious that their rights were being trampled by each other's demands. The woman's movement, however, focused attention on how rights were affected by gender rather than by race or region. Composed of a very small group of devoted supporters, the movement was a regional one in some important respects—it never gained any support in the South, for example. Yet, because it took on the issues of what a government should be, it had national implications; and as correspondence with supporters abroad made clear, the woman's movement in the United States was part of a larger set of concerns about the shape of governments of western Europe as well.

Seneca Falls and Other Conventions

The debate over woman's rights versus woman's influence took an important turn in July of 1848. Approximately three hundred women and men packed the Wesleyan Methodist Chapel in Seneca Falls, New York, to self-consciously proclaim a long list of women's rights. They were northerners, many of them tied together by shared struggles in the abolitionist movement. The New York legislature had finally passed a Married Woman's Property Act in 1848, inspiring Lucretia Mott, Elizabeth Cady Stanton, Martha C. Wright, Mary Ann McClintock, and Jane Hunt to plan a meeting to discuss additional issues related to women. Stanton drafted eleven resolutions for debate in a **Declaration of Sentiments,** a document that bore more than passing resemblance to the Declaration of Independence. The convention and its resolutions signaled the way in which the organizers hoped to reconstitute the government of the United States around issues that would include women rather than exclude them. The audacity of such a move was clear. Although Mott and Stanton were veteran reformers, they still hesitated to chair the meeting, so that James Mott, Lucretia's husband, presided over the event.

The issues that had been swirling around the civic identity of women for the past several decades finally came to a boil. Stanton's Declaration of Sentiments and Resolutions asserted that "all men and women had been created equal" as its most basic principle and then articulated eighteen ways in which men had injured women and usurped their rights, including their property, their wages, and their civil identity in marriage; the imposition of a double standard of morality; discrimination in marriage and divorce; and taxing women without allowing them a voice in the government. Arguing that women had a natural right to equality with men, the convention debated eleven resolutions attached to the Declaration of Sentiments that asserted the equality of women with men, the right of women to speak in church and in public, and the right to equal participation in trade and commerce. The most controversial of these resolutions by far was the one that stated, "[I]t is the duty of the women of this country to secure to themselves their sacred right to the elective franchise." While Stanton's convictions on this score had been clear for several years, many of her fellow reformers were still shocked. Some were personally opposed to the idea of women voting; others felt that such a radical demand would undermine the movement. Debate on the issue was overheating when the abolitionist and reformer Frederick Douglass rose to speak passionately in defense of woman's suffrage. The balance tipped and the resolution passed. From that time forward, suffrage became a defining issue of the woman's rights movement, though it was far from the only concern.

Another small convention was held a few weeks later in Rochester, and soon plans were afoot for a national convention. Throughout the 1850s, national conventions were held yearly in locations that ranged from Philadelphia, Worcester and New York to Akron and Cincinnati, Ohio. These meetings often drew thousands of participants in rather boisterous circumstances as reformers of all stripes took the floor and as rowdies and hecklers sought to disrupt debate. Rising above the pandemonium, however, was the sense that just as an earlier convention had legitimated the U.S. Constitution, and just as many states were convening conventions to debate revisions to their own constitutions, a new voice of the people would be heard in the National Woman's Rights Conventions. How could the legitimacy of rule be established, after all, without the consent of the people?

The women's rights movement during the 1850s was neither tightly organized nor unified. Supporters struggled and differed over a variety of issues that tried to reconcile the problem of what it meant to be both a woman and a citizen at the same time. Convention debates, rather than a clearly structured platform, provided the intellectual core to the movement. Both within these conventions and in response to them, woman's rights advocates explored a variety of issues that were specific to confronting how a *woman* should go about being a citizen.

Declaration of Sentiments Statement produced at the Seneca Falls convention in 1848 listing injustices faced by women and rights they deserved.

WOMEN'S VOICES

A RELIGIOUS DEFENSE OF WOMAN'S RIGHTS

Jane Cowen of Indiana sent this letter of support to the organizers of the National Woman's Rights Convention held in Worcester in 1850. Although the letter was not read at the convention, it was published in the proceedings.

Dear Sister:—

. . . After studying on woman's position for fifteen years, without divulging my thought to any person, taking the Bible for my guide, I have come to the conclusion that this great evil has its original root in the Church of God. I do not mean a particular church, but all the different denominations, (Quakers excepted,) taken as a body. I am of the opinion, that if the Church would allow woman the privileges that God has given her, in both the Old and New Testaments, an education equal with the male sex, and every right that belongs to her, would follow.

Let us go to the Bible and examine for ourselves whether God had forbidden woman from reading the Law, either in public or in private. It was Moses's mother who instructed him and formed his character; the law being written in her heart, for the law was not written at that time. We read in Exodus, 15 chapter, 20th verse, of Miriam leading the choir, to celebrate on the banks of the Red Sea, the overthrow of Pharaoh, 1491, B.C.; and in Micah, 6th chapter, 14th verse, God says to the Israelites, by the mouth of the prophet, "I sent before thee Moses, Aaron, and Miriam." Their mission was to rule, instruct, and guide the people in piety and virtue. In Judges, 4th chapter, 14th verse, we read of Huldah, the Prophetess, who lived contemporaneously with Jeremiah and Zephaniah, 624, B.C. I heard an intelligent, and I believe, a pious clergyman, say, not long since, that there were instances recorded in the Old Testament of females being chosen to fill the important station of a prophet; Judge G. saying that, in New Testament dispensation, females were not allowed this privilege, but are commanded to keep silence in the churches, etc. There is a possibility of even good men being mistaken, owing to the prejudice of education.

Let us go now to the New Testament, and see if he be correct. If I mistake not, Joel prophesied, 726 years B.C.—Joel, 2nd chapter, 28th and 29th verses—"And it shall come to pass afterward, that I will pour out my spirit upon all flesh; and your sons and your daughters shall prophecy. . . . "

Jane Cowen

Source: *Jane Cowen to National Woman's Rights Convention, Worcester, 1850, reprinted by The Women's History Workshop. Available from http://www.assumption.edu/WHW*

Questions

1. How does Jane Cowen use the Bible to justify a belief in women's rights?

2. Why does Jane Cowen criticize churches?

The Female Citizen

The woman's rights conventions that took place during the 1850s repeatedly called for access to education and stressed the importance of women controlling their own property. They demanded citizenship, and they demanded the vote. In doing so, they still maintained a belief in the importance of a woman's separate sphere and upheld her responsibilities to domesticity. Their view of rights, by and large, still accepted a belief in gender difference. They wanted equality with men but not sameness. They wanted a state that recognized the issues that had been raised during the previous half century about women's place in the public and political sphere. In raising these issues, they distinguished themselves from those who saw the route to women's power in influence rather than rights. But they also had to think about gender inequality in relationship to problems that women, in particular, faced.

One of the earliest questions many reformers tackled was that of dress. The heavy skirts that middle-class women were expected to wear were expensive, uncomfortable, and unhealthy, with waists tightly cinched by constricting corsets. Thus, women's rights activists took notice when the famous actress Fanny Kemble donned "male attire" in 1849. Amelia Bloomer, editor of the temperance journal *The Lily* championed the loose-fitting trousers and long tunic. Although a variety of woman's rights activists, including Elizabeth Cady Stanton, adopted the new style, the publicity generated by *The Lily's* editor led to the outfit being called "bloomers." Proponents of bloomers pointed out that women would be able to conduct household chores and take vigorous, healthy walks far more easily with the new style. Although the outfits were quite different from what men wore at the time, they did more closely approximate male dress and provide many of the physical freedoms associated with male clothing. This challenge to gender distinctions, however, brought down a hailstorm of criticism on women who tried to wear the outfits. Newspapers across the country ridiculed the women for their manly costume. Children followed them in the streets, harassing them and calling them names. The symbolism of dress was so powerful and so volatile, it was impossible for women to adopt it, even if it was more comfortable and healthy. By the middle of the 1850s, dress reform advocates were ready to give up. The criticisms from the press and conflicts within the movement over appropriate attire were too exhausting. Their decision to abandon dress reform, however, was not without consequences. Gerritt Smith, a wealthy abolitionist, was so dismayed over the loss of dress reform as a cause that he ceased funding the national conventions. This is one of the reasons a national convention was not held in 1857.

Women also had to confront the long-standing tradition that associated female public speaking with moral turpitude. Most woman's rights activists had thrown aside their reservations about public speaking by the middle of the 1850s, but that did not mean they were comfortable with speaking or that they were particularly good at it. At the Syracuse Convention, Elizabeth Cady Stanton objected to the leadership of Elizabeth Oakes Smith because she lacked a powerful speaking voice. Stanton argued that a woman should not be allowed to address the audience unless her voice was loud enough to be heard by everyone in the hall. Paulina Wright Davis was outraged by Stanton's motion and urged the convention not to "gag" any of the women present. Davis also went further in 1852, using her wealth to establish a newspaper, the *Una*, that would provide an alternative public sphere to the boisterous conventions that were the focus of organizing.

Elizabeth Cady Stanton and Susan B. Anthony developed a life-long friendship and working relationship in their struggle for woman's rights, beginning with the woman's rights conventions that took place yearly during the 1850s.

Women who participated in the woman's rights movement were lampooned in the press, with cartoons that portrayed them as abondoning the womanly qualities for mannish and vulgar behavior. The bloomers that many woman's rights activists adopted were seen as particularly threatening to the gendered order of society.

Aren't I a Woman?

The issues of the woman's rights movement grew not only from the potent convergence of questions of citizenship and difference but also from issues articulated in debates over slavery. Many of the men and women who participated in the woman's rights movement came out of the abolitionist movement. Lucy Stone and Lucretia Mott, for example, were important antislavery lecturers; Susan B. Anthony helped slaves escape on the Underground Railroad. Their consciousness about discrimination against women had been raised through their antislavery experiences, as they increasingly compared the condition of women to the condition of slaves. Elizabeth Cady Stanton and Lucretia Mott had famously formed their friendship—and begun to contemplate the issue of woman's rights—at the 1840 World Anti-Slavery Convention in London when female delegates such as Mott were rejected from participation and speaking. The issue of women's leadership had precipitated the split in the American antislavery movement.

Just as antislavery activists had debated whether to support woman's rights, woman's rights activists debated whether to support antislavery. Jane Swisshelm, in particular, provoked controversy by arguing that the woman's rights movement was not strong enough to bear the burden of antislavery agitation as well. She criticized participants of the 1850 Worcester convention for introducing slavery into their debate. As she put the question bluntly in an article for the *Saturday Visitor*, "There are many of both sexes who are, or would be, anxious for the elevation of woman, as such, who nevertheless hate 'the niggers' most sovereignly." Parker Pillsbury, an ardent abolitionist, was appalled by Swisshelm's argument, and most woman's rights supporters distanced themselves from her point of view.

Despite Swisshelm's comments, African American women did cross over from abolitionism to support woman's rights. Harriet Forten Purvis and Margaretta Forten were two of the lead organizers of the Fifth National Woman's Rights Convention in Philadelphia in 1854. Nancy Prince, one of the first African American authors, attended the convention, where she addressed the audience on the way slavery degraded African American women. Sarah and Charles Remond, a brother and sister from Boston, also took up the cause, as did Mary Ann Shadd Cary. Many of the African American activists were particularly prominent in pushing women not only to demand rights but also to disregard ideas about "woman's sphere" that essentially limited the ability of women. As Mary Ann Shadd Cary and her sister Amelia Shadd argued in their newspaper, "[W]oman's work was anything she put her mind or her hand to."

Sojourner Truth, the most famous African American woman to participate in the woman's rights movement, continued the arguments of these African American activists about disregarding "woman's sphere." Truth, whose real name was Isabella van

Wagenen, had been born a slave in New York and freed when slavery was abolished in 1825. Her white colleagues worried at first about having her speak at their conventions, fearing both her illiteracy and her commitment to abolitionism. However, Truth was a powerful orator whose speeches brought audiences to their feet cheering. Her most famous speech, at the Woman's Rights Convention in Akron, Ohio, in 1851, has been the subject of some debate. Not all of those who reported it remembered her saying, "Aren't I a Woman?" as Frances Gage claimed she had. But they do agree on the gist of her message: she could do as much as any man. As Marius Robinson reported at the time, Truth argued, "I have as much muscle as any man, and can do as much work as any man. I have plowed and reaped and husked and chopped and mowed, and can any man do more than that? I have heard much about the sexes being equal; I can carry as much as any man, and can eat as much too."

Sojourner Truth was a committed abolitionist and woman's rights activist. Having been born a slave, Truth was illiterate, but she was one of the most powerful speakers in antebellum reform circles.

African American women understood the importance of separate spheres in definitions of respectability, but they had had to violate its terms much more obviously and regularly than middle-class white women. Whether in wage earning, in property holding, or in heading their own households, African American women had shouldered burdens as great as their menfolk, and they brought that understanding with them into the struggle for woman's rights.

Reaching Out

The woman's rights conventions that were held throughout the 1850s took place in the Northeast and the Midwest, reflecting the home base of their constituents. Even within these regions, the woman's rights movement was a small one. Few women or men (and men often numbered close to half the audience at these conventions) were willing to commit themselves to ideals of gender equality at this time. However, the movement was widely recognized, hailed by some and criticized by many.

Support came early from several women in Europe. 1848 was not only the year of the woman's rights convention at Seneca Falls; it was also the year in which revolutions erupted in Europe, ending conservative monarchies that had been engineered by Austria's powerful foreign minister, Metternich, and leading to democratic upsurges in France and Germany, among other places. Participants in the revolutions included women who moved quickly to place women's issues on the broad agendas at hand. In France, socialist Jeanne Deroin assisted in organizing a variety of groups dedicated to improving the condition of women and to supporting the rights of workers while Louise Otto made sure the minister of the interior in Saxony heard her demand that women be involved in the reorganization of labor. These revolutions were quickly undermined by conservatives, who squelched demands for woman's rights as well as workers' rights. But into the mid-1850s, agitation continued—from jail cells if need be.

Jeanne Deroin and Pauline Roland, who had both been jailed for their socialist activities, wrote to the Worcester Woman's Rights convention in 1851 to offer their support. When Harriet Taylor Mill published her essay on the "Enfranchisement of Women," in England, she began by telling her readers about the convention in

Worcester. Mill's son took copies of the essay to Lucretia Mott in Philadelphia, who made sure that her compatriots in the United States read it. Louise Otto in Germany also wrote about the woman's rights conventions in the United States in her *Women's Newspaper*. Thus, the women who participated in the woman's movement in the United States were part of a larger transatlantic debate about the place of women in the rapidly shifting political order of both the Old World and the New.

Despite this worldwide recognition, most Americans (as well as Europeans) remained skeptical of the demands for woman's rights. *Harper's Magazine* published cartoons of women trying to act like men, lounging about, dressed in pants, and smoking cigars. *Godey's Lady's Book* published stories on woman's rights that recast the very notion, suggesting that women felt most rewarded when exercising their "rights" to feed the poor and clean the dirty faces of children. Even many of the women active in reform movements were reluctant to add woman's rights to their list of causes.

Women in the South remained unanimously hostile to the movement for woman's rights. To a certain extent, this may have been because there was such a strong overlap in the supporters of woman's rights with participants in the abolition movement. It may also have been that the issues raised by the more contractual economy of the North had less meaning in the South. Whatever the reason, newspapers in the South lambasted supporters of the woman's rights movement as "cackling geese." Rebecca Hicks, writing for her journal *The Kaleidoscope*, argued, "[I]t is absolutely necessary that we should please the men, before we can ever hope to conquer them. This important truth has been entirely overlooked by the Woman's Rights women." Thus, as the woman's rights movement rose in the North, those southern women who had been actively involved in politics, speaking in public to support their political candidates, became a little quieter. Women from Virginia did not speak as frequently in the 1856 presidential election as they had in the 1852 election, preferring to make their remarks known through male representatives instead. Although woman's rights was not a terribly popular cause anywhere, southern women made it clear that woman's rights was a northern issue.

Marriage and Divorce

The most contentious conflict among woman's rights activists was over divorce. Some of the more radical supporters of the temperance movement had been pushing to liberalize divorce laws for over a decade, arguing that women and children should not have to live in a house with a drunkard. In this sense, divorce legislation was very much a "woman's issue," tied to her distinctive position within the home as both a dependent of her husband and nurturer of her children. But marriage was also a legal contract between two freely consenting individuals. In this sense, it was a question of citizenship. Framing marriage as a contract, however, moved it into a category of business relationships that scandalized even the most dedicated of women's rights activists.

Elizabeth Cady Stanton had been one of the most ardent supporters of liberalizing divorce laws for the wives of drunkards, but as she argued for changing divorce laws, her arguments moved beyond protecting wives from drunken husbands to a more dramatic revisioning of marriage as a contract between two individuals rather than a sacred bond. Marriage reform, she argued, was of central importance in creating a society based on equality; for in marriage, men had the right to dominate their wives.

The issue came to a head at the 1860 Woman's Rights Convention. Brushing aside the concerns of Lucy Stone that her goals were premature, Stanton demanded in her address, "How can she [woman] endure our present marriage relations by which woman's life, health, and happiness are held so cheap that she herself feels that God has given her no charter of rights, no individuality of her own?" Stanton's speech sparked a wrenching controversy at the convention. Ernestine Rose, who stood shoulder to shoulder with Stanton on the divorce issue, argued that it was a question of rights. The state had an obligation to protect its citizens, even if it meant abrogating a marriage contract. Antoinette Brown Blackwell struck back, defending marriage as a sacred institution. Even if a woman had to protect herself from a drunken husband by obtaining a divorce, Blackwell argued that the man and woman would still be married in the eyes of God and that the divorced wife should still recognize the spiritual connection. Wendell Phillips, a famous abolitionist and supporter of woman's rights, was so appalled by Stanton's position that he wanted the entire discussion struck from the convention proceedings. Phillips argued that men and women were treated equally under laws of marriage, so that marriage reform was not really a proper topic for the woman's movement. The focus, he argued, should be on areas such as political rights where women were truly discriminated against.

The debate over divorce was the last big debate to take place in the woman's rights movement of the 1850s. Woman's rights activists were almost all deeply committed antislavery activists as well. Sectional tensions between the North and the South had been growing during this time period. With the outbreak of the Civil War in 1860, reformers turned their attention wholeheartedly to the conflict that was tearing the nation apart.

CONCLUSION

The woman's rights movement of the 1850s challenged fundamental beliefs about the household as the basic political unit of government, stirring bitter debate about how women could be citizens in the democratic government that had developed in the United States. Proponents of woman's influence had pushed the limits of the domestic sphere to encompass a broad range of educational and economic demands, even as they shunned agitation for the vote. Proponents of woman's rights, although acknowledging the differences between men and women, had struggled with a more radical agenda that would allow women autonomy in the control of their property, their education, and their political representation. But even among woman's rights activists, there were differences, most particularly around the issue of marriage and divorce. With the coming of the Civil War, woman's rights activists postponed these pressing discussions about the legal rights of women in both the state and the family.

WOMEN'S EVENTS	GLOBAL EVENTS

1800

1816
Pennsylvania moves divorce proceedings from legislature to courts

1821
Troy Female Seminary founded

1820s
Democratic Party formed

1825
Robert Owen establishes New Harmony in Indiana

1828
Andrew Jackson elected president

1830

1835
Florida and Arkansas pass laws continuing Spanish practices protecting women's property

1836
Angelina Grimke publishes *Appeal to the Women of the Nominally Free States*

1837
Mount Holyoke Female Seminary founded
Catharine Beecher pens *An Essay on Slavery and Abolitionism with Reference to the Duty of American Females*

1838
Sarah Grimke writes *Letters on the Equality of the Sexes*
Moral Reform Society begins campaign against seduction

1839
Mississippi passes married women's property law

1830s
Whig Party formed

1833
Oberlin College founded

1839
Liberty Party established

1840

1847
Elizabeth Blackwell enters Geneva Medical College

1848
Woman's Rights convention in Seneca Falla
Declaration of Sentiments
Fanny Kemble wears new fashion that will be called "Bloomers"

1847
Free Soil Party established

1848
Revolutions sweep Europe

1850

1850
Female Medical College of Pennsylvania established

1851
Sojouner Truth delivers "Aren't I a Woman" speech

1852
Paulina Wright Davis establishes the *Una*

1856
Massachusetts passes earnings act

1857
New England Female Medical College chartered

1855
Dred Scott decision

1860

1869
Women's Medical College opened

REVIEW QUESTIONS

1. How were demands for woman's rights tied to a changing economy?
2. Why was education tied to debates about woman's rights?
3. Which of the demands of the woman's rights movement would most significantly affect women's ability to exercise power?
4. Why was divorce a more controversial issue than suffrage in the woman's rights debates?

RECOMMENDED READING

Nancy Isenberg. *Sex and Citizenship in Antebellum America.* Chapel Hill: University of North Carolina Press, 1998. Close examination of the ways in which questions of citizenship and women's rights were analyzed in light of gender differences.

Nell Painter. *Sojourner Truth: A Life, a Symbol.* New York: W. W. Norton, 1996. Fascinating and detailed study of one of the most important African American activists of the nineteenth century.

Elizabeth Varon. *We Mean to Be Counted: White Women and Politics in Antebellum Virginia.* Chapel Hill: University of North Carolina Press, 1998. Study of the surprisisng extent to which women in a southern state engaged the growing democratic politics of the antebellum period.

Susan Zaeske. *Signatures of Citizenship: Petitioning, Antislavery, and Women's Political Identity.* Chapel Hill: University of North Carolina Press, 2003. Detailed study of the ways in which early petitioning activities of women developed political meanings.

ADDITIONAL BIBLIOGRAPHY

Life, Liberty, and Property

Norma Basch. *In the Eyes of the Law: Women, Marriage, and Property in Nineteenth-Century New York.* Ithaca, NY: Cornell University Press, 1982.

Carl J. Guarnari. *The Utopian Alternative: Fourierism in Nineteenth-Century America.* Ithaca, NY: Cornell University Press, 1991.

Carol A. Kolmerton. *Women in Utopia: The Ideology of Gender in the American Owenite Communities.* Bloomington: Indiana University Press, 1990.

Barbara Taylor. *Eve and the New Jerusalem: Socialism and Feminism in the Nineteenth Century.* New York: Pantheon Books, 1983.

Challenging the Doctrine of Separate Spheres

Elizabeth Ann Bartlett. *Sarah Grimke: Letters on the Equality of the Sexes and Other Essays.* New Haven, CT: Yale University Press, 1988.

Barbara Berg. *The Remembered Gate: Origins of American Feminism.* New York: Oxford University Press, 1978.

Richard Chused. *Private Acts in Public Places: A Social History of Divorce in the Formative Years of American Family Law.* Philadelphia: University of Pennsylvania Press, 1994.

Nancy Cott. *Public Vows: A History of Marriage and the Nation*. Cambridge, MA: Harvard University Press, 2000.

Christine Daniels, and Michael V. Kennedy, eds. *Over the Threshold: Violence in Early America*. New York: Routledge, 1999.

David Peterson Del Mar. *What Trouble I Have Seen: A History of Violence against Wives*. Cambridge, MA: Harvard University Press, 1996.

Christie Anne Farnham. *The Education of the Southern Belle: Higher Education and Student Socialization in the Antebellum South*. New York: New York University Press, 1994.

Myra C. Glenn. *Campaigns against Corporal Punishment*. Albany: State University of New York Press, 1984.

Willystine Goodsell. *Pioneers of Women's Education in the United States: Emma Willard, Catherine Beecher, Mary Lyon*. New York: McGraw-Hill, 1931.

Michael Grossberg. *Governing the Hearth: Law and the Family in Nineteenth-Century America*. Chapel Hill: University of North Carolina Press, 1985.

Carol Lasser. *Educating Men and Women Together: Co-education in a Changing World*. Urbana: University of Illinois Press, 1987.

Regina Morantz-Sanchez. *Sympathy and Science: Women Physicians in American Medicine*. Chapel Hill: University of North Carolina Press, 1985.

Elizabeth Pleck. *Domestic Tyranny: The Making of American Social Policy against Family Violence from Colonial Times to the Present*. New York: Oxford University Press, 1987.

Amanda Porterfield. *Mary Lyon and the Mount Holyoke Missionaries*. New York: Oxford University Press, 1997.

Anne Firor Scott. "The Ever-Widening Circle: The Diffusing of Feminist Values from the Troy Female Seminary." *History of Education Quarterly* 19 (Spring 1979): 3–25.

Barbara Miller Solomon. *In the Company of Educated Women: A History of Women and Higher Education in America*. New Haven, CT: Yale University Press, 1985.

Woman's Influence versus Woman's Rights

Joe L. Kincheloe Jr., "Transcending Role Restrictions: Women at Camp Meetings and Political Rallies," *Tennessee Historical Quarterly* 40 (Summer 1981): 158–169.

Robert E. May. "Reconsidering Antebellum U.S. Women's History: Gender, Filibustering, and America's Quest for Empire," *American Quarterly* 57.4 (2005): 1155–88.

Michael McGerr. "Political Style and Women's Power, 1830–1930." *Journal of American History* 77 (1990): 864–85.

Mary Ryan. *Women in Public: Between Banners and Ballots, 1825–1880*. Baltimore, MD: Johns Hopkins University Press, 1990.

Forging a Movement

Bonnie S. Anderson, *Joyous Greetings: The First International Women's Movement, 1830–1860*. New York: Oxford University Press, 2001.

Mari Jo Buhle, and Paul Buhle, eds. *The Concise History of Woman Suffrage: Selections for the Classic Work of Stanton, Anthony, Gage and Harper*. Urbana: University of Illinois Press, 1978.

Rosalyn Terborg-Penn. *African American Women in the Struggle for the Vote, 1850–1920*. Bloomington: Indiana University Press, 1998.

Web Site

U.S. Women's History Workshop at http://www.assumption.edu/whw.

Biographies, Autobiographies, and Memoirs

Lois Banner. *Elizabeth Cady Stanton. A Radical for Women's Rights*. Boston: Little, Brown, & Company, 1980.

Elizabeth Cazden. *Antoinette Brown Blackwell: A Biography*. New York: Feminist Press, 1983.

Janet Coryell. *Neither Heroine Nor Fool: Anna Ella Carroll of Maryland*. Kent, OH: Kent State University Press, 1990.

Cecilia Morris Eckhardt. *Fanny Wright: Rebel in America*. Cambridge, MA: Harvard University Press, 1984.

Elisabeth Griffith. *In Her Own Right: The Life of Elizabeth Cady Stanton*. New York: Oxford University Press, 1984.

Alma Lutz. *Emma Willard: Pionner Educator of American Women*. Boston: Beacon Press, 1964.

THE CIVIL WAR, 1861–1865

HOW DID women in the North respond to the outbreak of the Civil War?

ON THE battlefront, in what ways did women transgress the bounds of femininity?

WHAT WERE the particular hardships endured by Confederate women?

HOW DID women help to shape the memory of the Civil War and its place in American history?

CHAPTER 9

We got into an ambulance and rode to the hospital tents of the Second Corps. We were driven by a pleasant fellow from Vermont, who told us many interesting things about the battle-ground, which we crossed. We saw the rifle-pits, the dead horses, the shattered windows and the stone walls, all scattered and many soldiers' graves. But who shall describe the horrible atmosphere which meets us almost continually? . . .

We dispensed buckets of milk punch and quantities of corn-starch, nicely prepared with condensed milk and brandy, besides sundry cups of tea, an unwonted luxury and broth

A Ride for Liberty- The Fugitive Slaves, 1862. Eastman Johnson (American, 1824–1906). Oil on wood; 21½ by 26 inches. Virginia Museum of Fine Arts, The Paul Mellon Collection, 85.644.

made of beef jelly condensed, with many other services and a little chat occasionally with some poor fellow. I found a great many Maine boys; many from Wisconsin and Minnesota; scarcely one who had not lost an arm or a leg. I felt as if I could hardly wait upon the rebels; but the first call almost upon my sympathies, was to see a young Mississippian, and all day long we found the Union soldiers side by side with the rebels. Death is very busy with these poor fellows on both sides. It seems hard for no kind voice to speak a word of cheer to the parting spirit and yet there are many laborers in the vineyard; but the work is great. There are perpetual calls for "something for a wounded soldier who can't eat anything hard,"—"milk punch," "a cup of tea," or "a cup of coffee with milk." Two or three desperately wounded men begged for *ice*, with an earnestness of agonized entreaty which could brook no denial. I promised, if possible, to obtain it; but found that the surgeon had absolutely forbidden that the ice should be touched, as the lives of many men depended upon their having it. You may judge how painful it was to carry this message in lieu of the cooling morsel of which I hoped to be the bearer.

But it is getting late and I am keeping the ladies awake. We all occupy one room and enjoy each other's society highly. Good night.

Source: Letter from Emily Bliss Thacher Souder, July 15, 1863, in Leaves from the Battlefield of Gettysburg: A Series of Letters from a Field Hospital. and National Poems *(Philadelphia, PA: C. Sherman, Son & Co., 1864) 15–19.*

riting to her husband of nearly thirty years, Emily Bliss Thacher Souder described her experiences as a volunteer nurse for the Union army during the Civil War. It was July 1863, a little more than two years since President Abraham Lincoln, just one month after he took the oath of office, faced the secession crisis as eleven southern states withdrew from the Union to form the Confederate States of America. Although Lincoln had been hoping for a peaceful resolution, an attack on federal troops stationed at Fort Sumter prompted him to prepare for war. He called for the immediate enlistment of seventy-five thousand troops to preserve the Union. By the time the war ended in May 1865, more than two million men had served in the union army, making the Civil War the largest mobilization of armed forces in U.S. history. Women loyal to the Union like Souder were determined to do more than merely keep the home fires burning.

Emily Souder volunteered to serve as a nurse at the military encampments. She experienced her own baptism of fire at Gettysburg, where in early July 1863, the largest battle of the war took place and more men fell to their death than in any other battle fought within the United States. In writing to her "dear husband," she hoped to provide a "truthful picture of a portion of the field of labor." She decided to publish her letters within the year, well before the war ended, in order to inspire other women to join her in providing crucial support services to the Union army.

Not all volunteers rushed to the battlefields as Souder did. The majority of Union women stayed in their communities, building on decades of work in voluntary associations to organize the procurement and distribution of supplies for the regiments from

MAP 9-1 UNION AND CONFEDERATE STATES

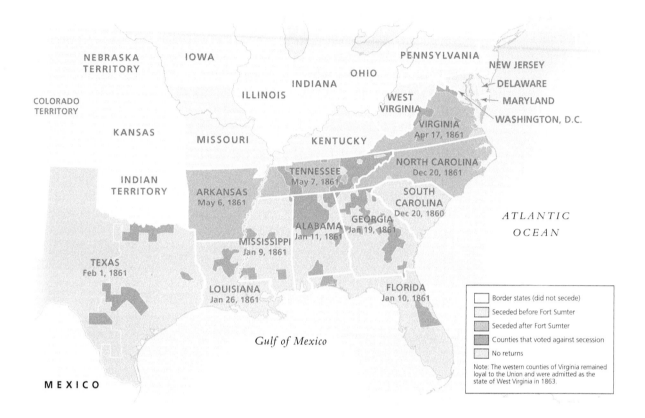

Seven southern states seceded before Lincoln's inauguration; four more seceded after the Civil War began. The United States of America, known as "The Union," viewed secession as illegal and never recognized the new Confederate States of America, also known as the Confederacy.

their area. For their part, Confederate women literally lived with the war, for the fighting took place primarily on their own soil. Most dramatic of all were the changes experienced by southern black women: they secured their emancipation from slavery. Writing early in 1862, the popular writer Fanny Fern accurately predicted that "there's one thing certain. This war won't leave women where it found them, whatever may be said of men."

THE NORTHERN HOME FRONT

For many northern women, the call of duty did not overcome the anxiety provoked by war. Ann Dexter, writing to her husband who had enlisted as an army surgeon, expressed herself without reservation. "I am more a wife than a patriot," she acknowledged, "& although I do care for my country, I care for you much more."

Although many women, perhaps the majority, shared Dexter's feelings, large numbers by either necessity or desire stepped into new roles. By the end of the war in May 1865, nearly 40 percent of all men of military age had served in the Union army, leaving much of the work on the home front in women's hands. For thousands upon thousands of middle-class women, decades of experience in organized benevolence charted a clear path into relief activities, including nursing. For those women who lost the family breadwinner, wage-earning jobs in wartime industries often kept them and their children from the brink of starvation. Attuned to local and national politics, many women demonstrated their capacity for citizenship; and a sizable number emerged from the war ready to test the limits of power that these new roles seemed to offer.

Woman's National Loyal League

The advocates of woman's rights had contemplated the coming of the Civil War with mixed feelings. For a long time they had rallied with fellow abolitionists and insisted on "No Union with Slaveholders!" Yet, with so many Quakers and peace activists among them, a large sector detested the idea of war and greeted with trepidation Abraham Lincoln's election to the presidency in November 1860 and the secessionist fever it provoked in the South. In December, after South Carolina became the first state to secede from the Union, abolitionist Maria Weston Chapman resigned herself to accept what now seemed inevitable and "not so bad as Slavery."

Elizabeth Cady Stanton and Susan B. Anthony viewed the outbreak of military conflict as a signal to push for the emancipation. They set themselves on a grand tour of New York State, calling upon women to prepare for war by taking a public stand against slavery. Indeed, if the Union were restored with slavery intact, Anthony wrote to a member of Congress, "[O]ur terrible struggle will be invested with no moral dignity, and it will have no moral value as a historical lesson for the human race."

Anthony did not see her wish granted with the speed she desired. In April 1862, Congress abolished slavery in the nation's capital while compensating slaveholders for their loss of property. In July, the Second Confiscation Act allowed the Union army to grant freedom to all slaves who escaped behind their lines. But only after the war had raged for nearly two years did Lincoln issue the **Emancipation Proclamation**. Even then, in January 1863, he made "forever free" only those slaves in areas held by the Confederacy while specifically exempting the border states.

Emancipation Proclamation Issued by President Lincoln on January 1, 1863, freeing slaves in the Confederate states.

Having declared "a temporary moratorium" of conventions for the duration of the war, woman's rights advocates increased the pressure for a comprehensive and absolute abolition of slavery. Stanton and Anthony issued a bulletin to the "Loyal Women of the Nation," calling them to a meeting in New York City on May 14, 1863. The meeting attracted, among others, seasoned activists Lucy Stone, Martha Wright, Amy Post, Angelina Grimke Weld, Ernestine Rose, and Antoinette Brown Blackwell. Commending President Lincoln for granting partial emancipation, they pledged their loyalty to his administration and to the Union and underscored their faith that "freedom to the slaves was the only way to victory."

Stanton, the new president of the Woman's National Loyal League (WNLL), and her coworker Anthony hoped to give northern women a broad purpose for their war work—to "labor for a principle," as Matilda Joslyn Gage put it, rather than merely carry on the benevolent activities that for decades had been women's avocation. They set their sights on a Constitutional amendment prohibiting slavery. By 1864, members had gathered four hundred thousand signatures on a petition requesting Congress to pass an amendment to the Constitution "emancipating all persons of African descent held to involuntary service or labor in the United States." Two African American men carried the first installment of one hundred thousand signatures into the Senate and turned it over to the abolitionist senator, Charles Sumner, who presented the Emancipation Petition to his colleagues on February 9, 1864. Lincoln endorsed the amendment, which was passed by the House of Representatives in January 1865. Ratified in December 1865, the **Thirteenth Amendment** forever prohibits slavery and involuntary servitude.

The activism of the WNLL marked a further departure from the moral suasion that drove the majority of antebellum women's organizations. Whether campaigning for the Thirteenth Amendment or producing uniforms for the troops, women were looking beyond their local communities and toward the state and federal governments to redress injustices and to solve the nation's problems. Nevertheless, the WNNL, which ultimately claimed a membership of five thousand, did not become a vehicle for woman's rights. Stanton and Anthony could not convince the members to endorse unanimously their bold resolution that declared that "true peace in this Republic" cannot be established "until the civil and political rights of all citizens of African descent and all women are practically established." The majority of Northern women chose more conventional means to support the Union cause.

This lithograph, produced in 1888, includes the full text of the Emancipation Proclamation issued on January 1, 1863. Lincoln's proclamation declared "that all persons held as slaves" within the states that had seceded and not yet under Union control "are, and henceforward shall be free."

Bonnet Brigades

Throughout the northern states, middle-class white women upgraded a long tradition of female benevolence to support their menfolk as they marched off to war. The same day that President Lincoln called for volunteers to serve in the Union army, the women of Bridgeport, Connecticut, organized the first society to assist the soldiers from their area. Within a week, women in hundreds of northern communities had rushed to form similar organizations.

Many organizers of **soldiers' aid societies** had for years provided for the poor and now redirected their energies toward very needy soldiers. The state governments supplied the volunteer army with little in terms of equipment, clothing, or food provisions; the federal government did even less. The Union army therefore relied on women to assume responsibility for their hometown regiments.

In great numbers, women gathered into bandage-rolling teams, collected handcrafted items of clothing, and expressed boxes of prepared foods to the military encampments of local regiments. One upstate New Yorker challenged anyone to match her personal record of one hundred hand-knit mittens. The Ladies' Springfield

Thirteenth Amendment Extended the terms of the Emancipation Proclamation to free slaves throughout the United States; ratified in 1865.

Soldiers' Aid Societies Woman's voluntary associations organized to assist the troops from their communities.

(Illinois) Soldiers' Aid Society reported that during their first year of the war they had supplied:

50 cotton shirts . . . 522 pairs of cotton drawers . . . 122 pairs of cotton socks, 259 pairs of woolen socks, 155 pairs of slippers . . . 213 handkerchiefs, 2,234 towels . . . 154 pillow ticks . . . 676 pillow cases . . . 2,492 bandages, and large quantities of cornstarch, barley, tea, crackers, soap, jars, jellies, pickles, fruits . . .

Local committees also raised money to purchase supplies by canvassing their neighborhoods and staging fairs, dinners, and entertainments. Although often enjoyable, this was serious work. One member of a soldiers' aid society in Rochester, New York, explained that "the service required is something more than the result of occasional spasms of patriotism; that it is work, undisguised, continuous work, that we must render."

After 1863, African American women rallied to support the Colored Troops. Although many African American men had rushed to enlist with the outbreak of war, they were turned away. Only in July 1862 did Congress repeal a law dating to 1792 that prohibited African American men from serving in the military. Then, after President Lincoln issued the Emancipation Proclamation in January 1863, black men swamped the recruiting offices, and within six months more than thirty black regiments had formed. In response, African American women, usually in conjunction with their churches, took on the work of supplying their troops, fearing that the soldiers would be ignored by white-led societies.

The leaders of local societies soon acted to bring greater efficiency to scattered efforts and proposed plans for statewide or regional coordination. Annie Wittenmyer of Keokuk, Iowa, a center of military activity, decided to transform the city's soldiers' aid society into a clearinghouse for the entire state. Advertisements appeared in newspapers throughout Iowa advising local societies to send all contributions to Keokuk, and Wittenmyer herself took responsibility for distributing supplies to all Iowa troops.

In New York, Dr. Elizabeth Blackwell and her sister Dr. Emily Blackwell, founders of the New York Infirmary for Women and Children, nurtured even greater aspirations. They outlined a plan to "organize the whole benevolence of the women of the country into a general and central association." Nearly four thousand enthusiastic women responded to their call and gathered in the great hall of Cooper Union in April 1861 to form the **Woman's Central Relief Association** (WCRA).

Woman's Central Relief Association
Served as the foundation for the United States Sanitary Commission.

Managed by "Ninety-Two Respected Ladies," the WCRA invited local societies in New York State and throughout southern New England to forward their donations to the central office in New York City. "The response made to our appeals is grand," wrote Louisa Lee Schuyler, the recording secretary of the WCRA, "and it is a privilege to know and feel the noble spirit that animates the women of the loyal states." However, despite their ambitions, the WCRA and local soldiers' aid societies soon became auxiliaries to a yet more powerful organization, the United States Sanitary Commission, which was presided over by equally dedicated men.

United States Sanitary Commission

In June 1861, President Lincoln approved the establishment of the United States Sanitary Commission (USSC) as a quasi-official organization funded and managed entirely by civilians. The USSC took charge of military hospitals and eventually laid claim to the network of more than twelve thousand local soldiers' aid societies. The

Shortly after war was declared, northern women organized to provide vital services to the Union troops. This photograph shows members of the Michigan Soldiers' Relief Society outside a field hospital.

USSC became, according to activist Mary Livermore, "the great channel, through which the patriotic beneficence of the nation flowed to the army."

Although officiated by men, the USSC made it possible for a cadre of middle-class women to play major roles in a vast, centralized organization of war relief. Women served as directors of all twelve regional branches. In addition to coordinating the relief work of local soldiers' aid societies, the regional branches established scores of additional programs and maintained soldiers' homes and lodges for men separated from their regiments; claims agencies to secure bounties, back pay, or pensions for soldiers and their widows; and a directory of the names and locations of injured and deceased soldiers. After African American men began to serve in the army, a group of well-to-do women in Philadelphia formed the Colored Women's Sanitary Commission, which performed similar services.

In 1863 and 1864, regional directors organized their most noteworthy contribution to the war effort, **sanitary fairs**. Held in Chicago in October 1863, the first great fair drew crowds estimated at six thousand daily for two weeks and raised more than one hundred thousand dollars. The Metropolitan Fair in New York City, held in April 1864, was even more successful, attracting up to thirty thousand visitors and raising a million dollars for the USSC treasury.

sanitary fairs
Extravaganzas organized mainly by women to raise funds for the Union troops during the Civil War.

WOMEN'S VOICES

WORKING FOR THE U.S. SANITARY COMMISSION

Mary Rice Livermore (1820–1905) discusses her experiences as regional director of the northwestern branch of the U.S. Sanitary Commission, which she believed prepared her for a future life of activism in the woman's movement. Before the Civil War, Livermore had been involved in temperance, antislavery, and benevolent reform activities but had kept her distance from the nascent woman's rights movement. After the war, she shook off all reservations and organized the woman's suffrage movement in Illinois.

I was reluctant to enter upon the work of the Commission in an official capacity, for I saw that it would take me from home, break up my habits of study and literary work, and take me altogether too much from my husband and children. But the need of relief work for the sick and wounded men of the army became more and more imperative,—the necessity of a better organization and wise methods were more keenly felt,—and the government was preparing for a more vigorous prosecution of the war than it had yet ventured upon,—and I felt compelled to withdraw all objections and obey the call of my country. My husband was very desirous that I should enroll myself regularly in the work of the Commission, and aided me in finding a suitable housekeeper, and governess for the children, so that home interests should not suffer because of my absences. And when Dr. Bellows, president of the United States Sanitary Commission, proposed that my friend, Mrs. Jane C. Hoge, and myself should become associate members of the Commission, with headquarters at Chicago, we consented, and remained at our posts until the October after the war closed. . . .

The work of the next three or four years was severe in the extreme. Many women broke down

under the incessant strain, and some of them died. I resigned all positions save that on my husband's paper, and subordinated all demands on my time to those of the Commission. I organized Soldiers' Aid Societies, delivered public addresses, to stimulate supplies and donations of money in the principal cities and towns of the Northwest; wrote letters by the thousand, personally and by amanuenses; answered all that I received, wrote the circulars, bulletins, and monthly reports of the Commission; made trips to the front with sanitary stores, to the distribution of which I gave personal attention; brought back large numbers of invalid soldiers, who were discharged that they might die at home, and accompanied them in person, or by proxy, to their several destination; assisted to plan, organize, and conduct colossal sanitary fairs, the histories of which I wrote at their close; detailed women nurses for the hospitals by order of Secretary [of War] Stanton, and accompanied them to their posts; in short, the story of women's work during the war has never been fully told, and can never be understand save by those connected with it. . . .

All through the war I was buoyed up by the sympathy of my co-workers, and by demonstrations of gratitude from the brave men for whom I labored. At one time three somewhat decimated regiments, returning from the front to Minnesota, with one to Wisconsin, reached Chicago, completely exhausted by their long comfortless ride and lack of food. For them to go farther in their weary and famished condition was hardly possible. Their arrival was unexpected, and the members of the Sanitary Commission and Soldiers' Home were all engaged elsewhere on important duties, except Mrs. Hoge and myself. It devolved upon us to provide a dinner for the men, and to furnish the lunch which they must take with them for the last stage of their journey. It was a very simple and easy thing to do, only requiring us to give orders to subordinates in the Soldiers' Home near our headquarters, where there was always an abundance of food, cooked and uncooked, in every variety, and to supervise the work.

But the hungry fellows were overwhelmed with gratitude, and magnified this little service into a generous deed of great importance. When they departed, they left with one of the clergymen of Chicago a contribution from their hard-earned and scanty savings, for the purchase of a testimonial to Mrs. Hoge and myself. We were each presented with a gold-lined silver goblet, and a verd-antique

table bell of rare shape. . . . But the most highly prized gifts I have received have been the comparatively inexpensive souvenirs of every sort and variety, made by individual soldiers, to whom I have ministered, manufactured from all kinds of material, with scanty and imperfect tools.

Source: *Mary A. Livermore,* The Story of My Life; or the Sunshine and Shadow of Seventy Years *(Hartford, CT: A. D. Worthington and Company, 1899), 471–78.*

Questions

1. How and why does Mary Livermore present herself as a woman new to activism?

Despite the apparent success of the USSC, some activists hesitated to turn over control of local soldiers' aid societies to a seemingly impersonal national organization. Such was the case in Keokuk where Annie Wittenmyer balked at the idea of relinquishing her authority to the group of men who headed the Iowa branch of the USSC. Ignoring their entreaties, she continued to solicit supplies from local societies and distributed the provisions herself to her "boys" in the Union army. Many of her coworkers supported her decision. They viewed the work of the male "honorables" as self-aggrandizing and insisted that women's long tradition as caretakers made them the "natural" overseers of relief work. Moreover, they wanted their contributions to go directly to their own loved ones, not to a regional organization.

By 1863, the honeymoon between local societies and the national organization had ended. The flow of donations slowed considerably, and fewer and fewer women volunteered their services. Toward the end of the war, relationships had become so strained that local women accused USSC agents of fraud and corruption. Then, too, by this time, heavy tax burdens and inflation made it nearly impossible for many women to handle more than the responsibility of caring for themselves and their children at home or, at best, in their own neighborhood. As before the war, they put the welfare of their own communities first, looked with suspicion on national organizations, and concerned themselves primarily with providing a decent homecoming for injured and indigent soldiers.

Freedmen's Aid Societies

With the outbreak of war, northern African American women organized to assist fugitive slaves who sought protection behind Union lines. Dubbed **"contrabands of war"** by the abolitionist general Benjamin F. Butler, these displaced people received only minimal help from either Union troops or the federal government. To ease their suffering, African American women organized a small network of local societies that became the basis of a national commission. Toward the end of the war, in March 1865,

"contrabands of war" Term for escaped slaves who sought refuge behind Union lines during the Civil War.

Freedmen's Bureau Established by Congress in March, 1865 to provide assistance to Civil War refugees.

Contraband Relief Association Formed in August 1862 to provide food and relief to destitute former slaves.

the U.S. Congress provided official sanction and federal coordination by establishing the Bureau of Refugees, Freedmen and Abandoned Lands, better known as the **Freedmen's Bureau**.

The women who spearheaded this movement drew on networks that extended across antislavery and urban philanthropy. For example, in February 1862, New York organizers staged the Grand Calico Dress Ball to raise money so that the fugitives "know that they have friends of their own race at the North, who are proud to aid them." In 1863, a group of wealthy Chicagoans established the Colored Ladies Freedmen's Aid Society for the purpose of gathering household supplies for refugees and supporting the agents who worked full time to raise money for the cause.

One of the most active societies was the **Contraband Relief Association** (CRA), which had formed in August 1862. Its president was Elizabeth Keckley, a former slave who worked in the White House as a confidante and seamstress for Mary Todd Lincoln (see chapter 7). The CRA provided food and clothing to destitute African Americans and, after enlarging its field of activities, became the Ladies' Freedman and Soldiers' Relief Association.

Women affiliated with the Baptist and African Methodist Episcopal (AME) churches were the mainstays of these organizations. They organized first to assist the growing number of fugitive slaves in their communities and eventually extended their range to provide assistance to freedpeople in the regions of the South occupied by federal troops.

The writer Harriet Jacobs proved especially effective as a fund-raiser, partly as a result of her renown as the author of *Incidents in the Life of a Slave Girl*, which was published during the first year of the war (see chapter 7). She used some of the money to sponsor a school for the children of refugees at Freedmen's Village in Alexandria, Virginia, and to help African Americans manage it. "I do not object to white teachers," she explained, "but I think it has a good effect on the freedpeople to convince them their own race can do something for their elevation." After the war, the Freedmen's Bureau devoted much of its resources to the educational needs of southern black communities.

Wartime Employments

With so many men serving in the army and as industry geared up to meet the increased demands of wartime production, many women took jobs outside the home. In 1861, the U.S. Treasury Department hired women to trim notes and continued to employ them as clerks and copyists despite intermittent expressions of concern about the propriety of men and women working together in close quarters. Several branches of the printing trades, retail sales, and light manufacturing for the first time admitted women to their ranks. War-related manufacturing, such as shoe making, provided the largest number of new jobs, while teaching offered the best wages. Overall, an estimated three hundred thousand women became wage earners during the Civil War.

Despite increased opportunities, the majority of workingwomen lived on the margins of subsistence during the war. With inflation soaring from the effects of war production, their wages remained steady at about half the amount paid to men. Congress helped to stabilize this disparity by setting the salaries of women clerks at approximately one-half of men's. Women's wages lagged far behind the rising prices of food and shelter, which, because of shortages, nearly doubled during the war years. As a sign of the times, the *New York Times* reported a raucous demonstration of "half-starved . . . wives,

In 1862 the head of the U.S. treasury explained the reasons behind his new employment policy: "A woman can use scissors better than a man, and she will do it cheaper. I want to employ women to cut Treasury notes." This engraving, published in Harper's Weekly, *February 18, 1865, depicts "lady clerks" leaving the Treasury Department at Washington, D.C.*

mothers, and relatives of volunteers" who demanded "bread, bread, bread" and who shouted "maledictions" on those who sent "their male protectors" to war.

As the news of these hardships traveled to the battlefront, desertions among common soldiers began to increase while the rate of enlistment fell so low that Congress passed a conscription law, requiring all men ages twenty to forty-five to register for the draft. However, the weight of service fell hardest on working-class men because the new law allowed the wealthy to pay a three-hundred-dollar fee to send a substitute. Antidraft riots broke out in several cities, the most violent in New York City, which in July 1863 took the lives of more than one hundred people.

As the war dragged on, working conditions only worsened, especially within the garment industry. To keep up with orders for army uniforms, commercial manufacturers hired masses of women to sew, often in their own homes, while they sold the finished articles of clothing to the U.S. government at a considerable profit. Working by hand, a needlewoman could make six pair of drawers in a day and receive an income of thirty-four cents, scarcely subsistence. The Civil War, it could be said, served as midwife to the increasing widespread practice of subcontracting known as the *sweating system*. Nevertheless, women, especially "war widows," were desperate to earn whatever they could.

Many local aid societies began to sponsor relief programs for soldiers' families and hired impoverished women to sew garments for Union troops. The organizers procured government contracts and, vowing to shun the exploitative practices of commercial manufacturers, pledged to pay a living wage. For example, a group of prominent Boston

Ladies Industrial Aid Association of Union Hall Organized to provide aid to soldiers and their families in the Boston area only.

women organized the **Ladies Industrial Aid Association of Union Hall** and employed approximately one thousand women, who produced nearly 350,000 garments for soldiers. The association also maintained emergency funds to help families in dire need. By 1864, many soldiers' aid societies were just as concerned with the welfare of soldiers' families as they were with the work of supplying the army. Many soldiers wrote letters thanking the societies for sending provisions to the front lines but closed by begging them to pay greater attention to the needs of their wives and sweethearts. "Succor them," one solider pleaded, "and withhold your charity from us."

In several cities, workingwomen organized to protest low wages and long hours. Groups of seamstresses in Philadelphia and New York sent petitions to Washington, D.C., complaining against their employers and demanding a living wage. In 1863, New York workingwomen began to strike for higher wages; the following year, they invited wealthy philanthropists to help them form a mutual-benefit society. The **Working Women's Protective Union** soon began to maintain a registry of jobs that met wage standards and placed women, many of whom were soldiers' wives or widows, in these positions. The new organization also supported numerous claims against fraudulent employers.

Working Women's Protective Union Organized in New York to assist wage-earning women during the Civil War.

ON THE BATTLEFIELDS

In April 1861, the famed Lowell textile operative Lucy Larcom wrote in her diary: "I have felt a solider-spirit rising within me, when I saw the men of my native town armed and going to risk their lives for their country's sake." A small minority of women acted on this impulse. They put away their skirts and crinolines, resized military uniforms to fit their figures, cropped their hair, and once disguised as men headed for the battlefields. Others took an opposite tack and engaged in espionage. More than a few women became international celebrities for strategically deploying their feminine charms to ferret military secrets from officers on the other side.

With far less fanfare, a much larger number of women volunteered as nurses in the bloodiest war in U.S. history. In the end, it was not the glory of battle— the "red badge of courage," in the words of novelist Stephen Crane—that made heroes of men and saviors of these women. "Camp diseases" such as smallpox, dysentery, typhoid, pneumonia, malaria, and infected wounds killed more soldiers than combat injuries and sent many frontline nurses to an early grave.

Army Nurses

At the outbreak of the Civil War, nursing was not a profession but a womanly obligation, for the most part work performed at home and without formal training. However, many American women had heard of Florence Nightingale, the British reformer who had just recently transformed this familiar household chore into a major public enterprise. Nightingale had trained British nurses for overseas duty during the Crimean War, 1853 to 1856, and she now encouraged American women to follow in her steps. In New York, Dr. Elizabeth Blackwell did just that and set out to recruit nursing volunteers under the auspices of the Woman's Central Relief Association. Meanwhile, in Massachusetts, Dorothea L. Dix acted on the same impulse but took her case directly to the War Department. Well known for her campaigns to improve the asy-

This 1868 portrait by the American artist Samuel Bell Waugh depicts Dorothea Lynde Dix (1802–1887). Well known for her work on behalf of the mentally ill, Dix volunteered to organize a nursing corps during the war. She was appointed Superintendent of Nurses for the Union Army and was dubbed "Dragon Dix" for her stern manner.

lum conditions of the mentally ill, Dix immediately received an official commission as superintendent of nursing for the War Department. At age fifty-nine, Dix began to organize military hospitals.

Despite Dix's appointment, neither the government nor the medical profession was eager to employ women as nurses. Public opinion also ran against them, underscoring a commonplace notion that women were too frail to cope with the sight of blood and too delicate to handle naked male bodies. Even Dix herself harbored reservations. She recruited only middle-class white women who were between thirty and fifty years old, in good health, and "matronly" and "plain" in appearance. To promote propriety in the hospital wards, she additionally imposed a strict dress code of dark skirts without hoops or frills. However, as casualties mounted, resistance weakened, and white women began to serve in large numbers as nurses in military hospitals and on the front lines. It was not until January 1864 that the U.S. War Department officially allowed hospitals under its jurisdiction to employ African American women and, then, primarily as chambermaids and cooks.

Most volunteers defied predictions and simply refused to "shrink from the sights of misery," as reformer Mary Livermore put it. Livermore, a member of the U.S. Sanitary Commission, later recounted her first visit to a hospital when the sight of a soldier's ghastly facial wound threw her into a faint. "Three times I returned," she confessed, "and each time some new horror smote my vision, some more sickening

Organized in the fall of 1861, the United States Christian Commission sent volunteers to the camps and hospitals to aid the Union troops. Women acted as nurses to care for the wounded on the battlefields and also staffed the kitchens in the hospitals.

odor nauseated me, and I was led out fainting." Livermore soon developed the fortitude to cope with such sights as, in the words of another determined nurse, amputated
arms and legs "thrown out of one of the windows [of an operating room] until they
made a pile *five feet high just as they fell.*"

After adjusting to the horrors and rigors of war, hospital nurses tried their best to
alleviate suffering and to provide comfort. They dressed wounds and assisted surgeons
in the grisly tasks of amputations. They cared for their patients by serving them meals,
delivering medicines, combing their hair and bathing them, changing their bedding,
and providing companionship.

Women accompanying regiments handled a greater variety of tasks and even
tended to the livestock. Because they often performed under fire, their risks were far
greater, their experiences more gruesome. A famous Civil War nurse, Mary Ann Bickerdyke, for example, routinely searched the fields in the aftermath of battle, shoving
corpses aside in the hope of recovering one live soldier.

It was said that nurses often ignored the rules of military discipline and even tried
to temper the surgeon's impulse to amputate. Mary Newcomb, a nurse for the 11th Illinois Regiment, remembered confronting a group of doctors. "I don't care who sent you
nor what authority you work under," she charged. "I wear no shoulder-straps, but that
boy's arm shall not come off while I'm here." However, such bravado did not stop the
War Department from ultimately acceding to the wishes of surgeons and allowing
them, beginning in October 1963, to terminate Superintendent of Nursing Dorothea
Dix's right to appoint nurses and to create their own staffs of more compliant assistants.

United States pension records, compiled in 1890, indicate that more than twenty
thousand women received pay for the medical support services they performed for the
Union. Many more women worked as volunteers and earned only subsistence. Twelve
Catholic women's religious orders, such as the Sisters of Mercy and the Sisters of Charity, which were experienced in caring for the sick, served in army hospitals. Soldiers'
wives and daughters often bypassed all authorities and simply attached themselves to
regiments. Two nurses, deservedly recognized for their contributions, Clara Barton and
"Mother" Mary Ann Bickerdyke, worked independently of the government and volunteer agencies and without compensation.

**Hospital Act of
September 1862**
Legislation by the Con-
federacy that allowed
women to serve as nurses
in hospitals.

In the Confederacy, the **Hospital Act of September 1862** legislated positions for
women in military hospitals. When the fighting reached their doorsteps, southern
women made makeshift hospitals of local churches and schools and even their own
homes and barns. Still, the number of volunteers like Kate Cumming proved inade-
quate to demand, especially as casualties escalated. It was "only a few, a very few," one
dedicated nurse reported, who accepted the responsibilities of steadfast commitment
to hospital work. Women of the gentry brought food and occasionally visited the wards
to read the Bible to the bedridden and write letters for illiterate soldiers. For the drudgery of patient care, they sent their slaves or relied on immigrant and working-class
women to do the work.

The Civil War brought women into the public eye as nurses, affording them training, salaries, and titles. In the North, a sizable number emerged from the experience ready
to take their place as professionals. A few, such as Barton, Dix, and Bickerdyke, achieved
a public prominence more typical of men and continued their reform work after the war.
Clara Barton founded and for many years headed the American Red Cross; Mary Ann
Bickerdyke, who helped build three hundred hospitals during the war, organized charita-

WOMEN'S VOICES

A CONFEDERATE NURSE'S STORY

Inspired by the work of Florence Nightingale, who had organized nurses during the British Crimean War, Kate Cumming (1835–1909) volunteered to help in Confederate hospitals. Over the objections of her wealthy parents, who insisted that nursing was not suitable for "refined" ladies, Cumming joined a brigade of forty women who left for the battlefield of Shiloh in northern Mississippi in April 1862 to care for the wounded and the dying. She later traveled to various hospitals in Alabama, Tennessee, and Mississippi and spent the last years of the war working in field hospitals established along the path of Sherman's famous March to the Sea, which left much of the South in ruins. After the war ended, Cumming returned to Mobile, where she published the journal she had kept of her day-to-day activities as a Confederate nurse.

September 8, 1862

—A very warm day. Mrs. Williamson and myself went out to try to get some sweet potatoes for some of the men in the Buckner Hospital. They are very scarce here at present, as the season is a dry one. We got some from a lady who would not take up any for her own use, but as soon as we told her who they were for she gave them to us, and would take no money for them. This lady had two young daughters, who were busy weaving and spinning. They had on dresses spun and woven by themselves. This ancient work is all the fashion now, as we are blockaded and can get no other kind of goods. . . .

There is a good deal of trouble about the ladies in some of the hospitals of this department. Our friends here have advised us to go home, as they say it is not considered respectable to go into one. I must confess, from all I had heard and seen, for awhile I wavered about the propriety of it; but when I remembered the suffering I had witnessed,

and the relief I had given, my mind was made up to go into one if allowed to do so. . . .

It seems strange that the aristocratic women of Great Britain have done with honor what is a disgrace for their sisters on this side of the Atlantic to do. This is not the first time I have heard these remarks. Not respectable! And who has made it so? If the Christian, hightoned, and educated women of our land shirk their duty, why others have to do it for them. It is useless to say the surgeons will not allow us; we have our rights, and if asserted properly will get them. This is our right, and ours alone.

In a book called the "Sunny South," written by the lamented Rev. J. H. Ingraham, are the following words: "Soldiers fight the battles of our country, and the least we can do is to cherish them in their helplessness, and bind up their wounds, and all *true* women will do it, who love their country." Who among us does not echo his sentiments? Women of the South, let us remember that our fathers, husbands, brothers, and sons are giving up all that mortals can for us; that they are exposed hourly to the deadly missiles of the enemy; the fatigues of hard marching, through burning suns, frost, and sleet; pressed by hunger and thirst; subject to diseases of all kinds from exposure; and last, though by no means least, the evil influences that are common in a large army. Are we aware of all this, and unwilling to nurse these brave heroes who are sacrificing so much for us? What, in the name of common sense, are we to do? Sit calmly down, knowing that there is many a parched lip which would bless us for a drop of water, and many a wound to be bound up? These things are not to be done, because it is not considered respectable! Heaven help the future of our country, for nothing but God's special aid can save any country where such doctrines are inculcated. . . .

I know there are hundreds of our women who look on this subject in the proper light, having

(continued)

household duties to attend to, which they can not leave; but have we not thousands who, at this moment, do not know what to do to pass the time that is hanging heavily on their hands? I mean the young: the old are not able for the work. If it will hurt a young girl to do what, in all ages, has been the special duty of woman—to relieve the suffering—it is high time the youth of our land were kept from the camp and field. If one is a disgrace, so is the other.

Source: Kate Cumming, A Journal of Hospital Life in the Confederate Army of Tennessee from the Battle of Shiloh to the End of the War *(Louisville, KY: John P. Morton & Co., 1866), 44–45.*

Questions

1. What kind of work did Kate Cumming do as a southern case nurse during the Civil War?

2. Why were there so many objections to women volunteering for this service?

Best remembered as the founder of the American Red Cross in 1881, Clara Barton (1821–1912) worked closely with the Union army in providing relief services, including medical care behind enemy lines in Virginia and South Carolina. In 1865 she was appointed by President Lincoln to organize efforts to find missing Union soldiers.

ble homes for those dislodged by wartime poverty. A few Civil War nurses entered medical school. For their part, many doctors who had initially resisted women's service in military hospitals now supported the new profession. In 1868, the American Medical Association passed a resolution recommending the establishment of hospital-based training schools for women nurses.

Soldiers

Conventions of womanhood at midcentury dictated a supportive wartime role for women. Nevertheless, patriotism did not always obey the rules of gender. One southern woman complained that it was only her birthright as a woman that compelled her to "stay home and pray with heart and soul." In letters and diary entries, more than a few writers exclaimed: "If only I was a man!"

Some women toyed with temptation. Sarah Morgan Dawson of Baton Rouge, Louisiana, musing on the prospect of Confederate troops recapturing her city in 1862, considered the idea of putting on "the breeches, and joining the assailants." After further reflection, she decided she was not quite ready for such a bold move: "How do breeches and coats feel, I wonder? I'm actually afraid of them. . . . I have heard so many girls boast of having worn men's clothes; I wonder where they get the courage."

Other women showed far less restraint. An Ohio woman, writing to Lincoln, insisted that she "could get up a Regt. in one day of young Ladies of high rank." Although the president refused all such offers, hundreds of women managed to slip through the ranks. It is known that at least eight women fought at Antietam and five at Gettysburg. Mary Livermore claimed that more than four hundred women served as Union soldiers, although the actual number remains unknown. What records do exist relate primarily the activities of white women. African American women had their own, compelling reasons to support Union military campaigns, but they rarely did so as soldiers. However, at least one former slave, Maria Lewis, fought valiantly. Serving with the 8th New York Cavalry, Lewis traveled with the troops to Washington, D.C., to deliver seventeen captured Rebel flags to the War Department.

Many women became soldiers primarily to stay close to their husbands. Rather than challenging the rules of gender, these women adapted a centuries-old tradition to modern warfare and quartered with their husbands, not to join them in combat but to cook meals and do laundry. Their actual roles proved far more extensive and more often than not extended to nursing the "boys" of their regiment.

Occasionally, women served in a paramilitary capacity. Katy Brownell, for example, accompanied her new husband into the sharpshooter division of the 1st Rhode Island Infantry Volunteers. After commanded to leave by General Burnside, she appealed to the governor of Rhode Island who granted her petition and appointed her "daughter" of the regiment. Wearing a modified military uniform, a knee-length skirt covering her trousers, Brownell occasionally served as color-bearer, an honor usually reserved for men. At the Battle of Bull Run, she proved steadfast in guarding the regimental flag. She later received a government pension for her wartime service.

However, the Union army afforded few opportunities for women to serve in even limited capacities. In 1802, Congress had passed an act restricting the number of women who could accompany the troops to no more than four per company. As a consequence, only the most determined women accompanied their husbands or brothers into combat. Disguised as men and often enlisted as regular soldiers, they managed to stay close to their male companions, sleeping beside them in the makeshift tents and fighting alongside them on the battlefield. Lucy Thompson Gauss, for example, served for nearly a year and a half with her husband Bryant in the 18th North Carolina Infantry before returning home to give birth to their daughter.

Passing as a man was certainly a challenge, but many women succeeded for years at a time, the average for documented women soldiers being sixteen months. The preinduction medical examinations were often hurried, and the loose-fitting military uniforms worked well to conceal the female figure. The battlefield custom of infrequent bathing also worked in their favor. Moreover, many of the women who enlisted hailed from working-class or farm backgrounds and were exceptionally fit as well as intimately familiar with hard work and rough living conditions. Especially in the Civil War army of citizen-soldiers, many of them but beardless youths, these women were scarcely at a disadvantage. The majority of soldiers, men and women alike, had to learn how to drill, dig trenches, and handle muskets. Not poor performance but combat injuries and death were the primary causes of a woman's discovery in the ranks.

Spies

Other women who were attracted to adventure or moved by patriotism did not hide their femininity but, to the contrary, exploited it in the work of espionage. More often middle and upper class than were their soldier counterparts, women spies could more easily gain access to the officer ranks of the army. As well-heeled ladies, they could also take full advantage of the fashionable clothing popular during the era. A lot of secret and coded messages could be hidden in hoop skirts, parasols, and even corsets. The

A theatrical performer, Pauline Cushman (1833–1893) used her acting talents to serve as a spy for the Union army. She traveled with the Confederates in Kentucky and Tennessee before she was caught and then tried by a military court. Barely escaping death by hanging, she received an honorary commission from President Lincoln. Too famous to resume spying, "Miss Major Cushman" returned to the stage in 1864, donning her new uniform to lecture about her exploits.

greatest asset of the southern spy in particular was femininity itself. Contemporary northern newspapers, which printed many stories about their escapades, commonly branded them as "loose women" or "secesh harlots."

One of the most infamous was Maria Isabella ("Belle") Boyd, a graduate of Mount Washington Female College. Early during the war, she shot a Union soldier who broke into her family home in Martinsburg, Virginia, and insulted her mother. Vindicated at a military hearing, she turned to nursing injured soldiers before discovering her true calling. She became an intrepid spy for the Confederacy. Celebrated for her late-night horseback rides through Union camps, Boyd perfected the art of flirtation to the point that federal officers commonly leaked precious secrets to her, which she delivered to Confederate commanders. General Thomas "Stonewall" Jackson commended Belle Boyd for her "immense service" to the Confederacy by providing him the crucial information about the position of Union troops that gave him an important victory in the Shenandoah Valley in June 1862.

The Union, too, inspired some women to take on the risky business of espionage. Pauline Cushman, for example, successfully gathered information about Confederate operations by posing as a secessionist. She also used a variety of disguises, occasionally wearing men's clothes. In 1864, "Major" Cushman was awarded an honorary military commission for her wartime service.

PLANTATION SOCIETY IN TURMOIL

Fought mainly on southern soil, the Civil War disrupted nearly every aspect of Confederate society. The war brought freedom to between three and four million African Americans—40 percent of the population of the South—and destroyed much of the wealth and political power of the planter elite. Of the 1,064,000 men who fought for the Confederacy, 250,000 died and more than 137,000 were wounded. In addition to bringing a fundamental change in race and class relations, the Civil War also posed an immense challenge to the prevailing gender system. As one woman from Virginia remarked: "We shall never any of us be the same...."

Unflinching Loyalty to the Cause

High-ranking Confederates flaunted the loyalty and dedication of their women. Indeed, women of the planter elite had cheered wildly from the balconies at state assemblies where secession was declared. On February 18, 1861, when representatives from the secessionist states met in Montgomery, Alabama, to ratify the formation of the **Confederate States of America**, women of slave-owning families dressed in their best finery and lined the halls to celebrate their new president, Jefferson Davis.

Confederate States of America The union of the eleven southern states that seceded to preserve slavery and protect states rights.

After the declaration of war, the Confederate government and local newspapers alike extolled the patriotism of those white women who put aside their private feelings and joyfully sent their men into battle. "Better a widow than married to a craven," a popular motto read. "When you write to soldiers, speak words of encouragement; cheer their hearts, fire their souls, and arouse their patriotism," one counselor wrote. "Say nothing that will embitter their thoughts or swerve them from the path of patriotic duty." Stories abounded of southern women refusing to consort with any man not wearing the gray uniform of the Confederacy and even sending frilly underwear to those who refused to enlist.

Love of the Confederacy went hand in hand with hatred of the Yankees. "If all the words of hatred in every language under heaven were summed up together into one huge epithet of detestation," one young woman wrote, "they could not tell how I hate Yankees. They thwart all my plans, murder my friends, and make my life miserable." Southern women showed their disrespect of Union soldiers so forcefully that the commander of Union occupation forces in New Orleans, Benjamin F. Butler, issued a proclamation to quell all jeering, spitting, and otherwise insolent behavior. Should a woman violate this ruling, the general warned, "she shall be regarded and held liable to be treated as a woman of the town plying her avocation," that is, as a prostitute. Most women demonstrated their loyalty in more reserved ways, such as by pinning small Confederate flags to their bodices.

Despite early displays of enthusiasm for the war, Confederate women lagged behind Yankee women in providing support services for the troops. Women of the planter and mercantile elite lacked a strong tradition of female benevolence and organized more slowly to assist the war effort. However, within a few months, more than one thousand voluntary associations formed and pledged, like their northern counterparts, to keep soldiers outfitted. "Our needles are now our weapons," one Charlottesville woman proclaimed, "and we have a part to perform as well as the rest. . . . Yes, Yes, we women have mighty work to perform for which we will be responsible." Relieved to assist "the great cause, in the way best suited to the sphere of woman," one soldiers' aid society observed, they learned quickly and produced thousands of flags, uniforms, tents, and sandbags. However, elite women, in line with the customs of a regional aristocracy, preferred fundraising to sewing and served the Confederacy primarily by sponsoring elaborate dinner parties and extravagant bazaars and entertainments.

Throughout the war, white women's loyalty and self-sacrifice remained central elements in public oratory and newspaper editorials. In April 1862, the Confederate Congress passed a declaration of gratitude; in 1863, the Mississippi legislature expressed appreciation to the "mothers, wives, sisters and daughters of this State" for their "ardent devotion . . . unremitting labors and sacrifices."

With much of the South cut off from supplies by the Union blockade, women's contributions were indeed crucial to the Confederate conduct of the war. Yet, as the number of injured soldiers mounted, many women discarded their needles and moved beyond their sewing circles and into the hospitals where they attended to the wounded and dying. Eventually, the wreckage of war forced many Confederate women to abandon both voluntary societies and hospital work altogether. On the brink of destitution if not already displaced from their homes, they did what they could to protect their children and merely survive.

Plantations without Patriarchs

In the absence of men, the Civil War plantation became a woman's world. Three of every four white men of military age had left their homes to fight for the Confederacy. By 1862, the Confederate government had began to impress male slaves to do manual labor, such as hauling supplies, constructing and fortifying the camps, digging ditches on the battlefront, and working in military hospitals. In regions of the South occupied by the Union troops, those male slaves still on the plantation usually fled to fight for the Union.

Women, black and white, remained on plantations that had been, in the words of one South Carolinian woman, "thinned of men." Many female slaves, especially the mothers of young children, chose to stay, less from loyalty to their mistress than from determination to keep their families together and to maintain the ties of kinship during insecure times. Although some planter wives followed their husbands to military camps or took refuge with relatives, the majority tried to hold fast. And with the odds of experiencing the death of a husband or son three times that of their northern counterparts, many white women saw their new roles become permanent. What did it mean to them personally as well as to the plantation system at large for white men to vacate their roles as heads of household, that is, as slave-owning patriarchs, and turn over the whole enterprise to women?

Many planter women faced a great challenge in not only overseeing the entire plantation but also taking responsibility for increasingly restless and insubordinate slaves. As the Union troops moved ever deeper into Confederate territory, many slaves were willing to continue working but only if recognized as free laborers. They could not readily demand wages because money was in short supply for everyone, but they did try to negotiate working conditions with their mistresses. According to reports by Union soldiers serving in occupied territories, slaves felt free to make demands because "there was nobody on the plantations but women and they were not afraid of them." The disciplinary rules that had defined slavery during the antebellum period no longer held the same power.

Harper's Weekly Magazine *and* Frank Leslie's Illustrated Newspaper *published engravings of Civil War scenes, providing an increasing number of news-hungry readers their only images of the war. This engraving, entitled "Sowing and reaping," appeared in Frank Leslie's in May 1863 and depicts southern women egging on their husbands at the beginning of the war and later rioting for bread in the face of deepening hardships.*

Some plantation mistresses embraced the challenge, being accustomed to taking charge during the frequent absences of their planter husbands. But, given the uncertainties of wartime, they more commonly expressed doubt and fear. They wrote complaining letters to their husbands and occasionally sent petitions to state and Confederate governments. "I fear the blacks more than I do the Yankees," a Mississippi woman explained. Ironically, the absence of the master forced his wife to become more dependent on her slaves than before the war. The anxiety created by this situation caused a few mistresses to express their disillusionment with the institution of slavery, if only in the privacy of their diaries. More commonly, they became more assertive in their racial animosity and more aggressive in wielding their power as white women.

The Union blockade and the Confederate military mobilization combined to create more work for everyone in the household. For the plantation mistress, unfamiliar domestic chores—cleaning, cooking, and sewing, as well as child care—became routine. But even more untried were the tasks associated with running a plantation in wartime. To feed the army, the Confederate government had encouraged the growth of staples like corn and grains instead of the usual crops of cotton and indigo. The plantation mistress also took over her husband's responsibility of balancing the books as well as finding the money to pay the high taxes levied by the wartime government. Enslaved women found their work becoming even more burdensome. With consumer goods such as textiles in short supply or prohibitively expensive, even field hands were forced to spin and weave.

And during planting and harvest seasons, many slave women who had previously worked solely as servants within the confines of the big house found themselves tending the crops. Overall, slaves worked harder than before the war, often because their mistresses refused to endure shortages or bear the humiliation of wearing calico dresses.

As the war dragged on, even elite women could not find the resources to maintain the plantation. The most adventurous—or the most desperate—sent their daughters to the relative safety of boarding school and ventured outside the household for the first time in their lives. They hoped to earn a livelihood as school teachers or as clerks in the Confederate government.

Not a few white women flourished in such unfamiliar roles. An exceptionally bold group in Virginia even mobilized to defend themselves and their property against the invading Yankees by forming small drill teams and asking the governor of Virginia to send them some pistols. Others, however, could not help feeling that, by assuming such independent roles, they had violated the sacred principles of southern womanhood.

During the last years of the conflict, when the Union army adopted tactics designed specifically to demoralize Confederate soldiers and citizens alike, looting and burning houses and arming slaves against their former masters, many Confederate women felt they could no longer bear the burdens. "Yankees stripped us bare of everything to eat; drove off all the cattle, mules, horses; killed chickens; and turned their horses into a wheat field so that what the horses could not eat was destroyed by trampling," a Georgian woman reported. Fearing for their own safety, on the brink of starvation, and virtual paupers, many gentry women left their homes and joined the growing ranks of refugees who traveled the countryside, staying temporarily in camps, and often headed for towns and cities. Not a few withdrew their support from the patriotic endeavor. White women of yeoman and propertyless families, who were typically poor before the outbreak of the war, suffered far more deprivation. These women often became vocal opponents of the war and helped men who deserted.

Confederate women, rich as well as poor, began to petition the government to return the men who had not yet died in battle. But for many, as one in three white southern men lay dead, there would be no return.

Camp Followers and Contrabands

After the Emancipation Proclamation, large numbers of slaves began to follow the Union army as it reached farther into the South. Men and women alike—perhaps as many as 15 percent of the slave population—fled the plantations, choosing to taste the first fruits of freedom by securing themselves behind the new Union lines. In Mississippi alone, nearly one-half of the slave population, estimated as more than one hundred thousand, set up camps near the Union troops or worked on plantations seized by the U.S. army and transferred to Yankee management. Although many officers regarded fugitives, especially women and children, as a nuisance, the soldiers themselves often encouraged former slaves to accompany them. Sally Dixon of Mississippi later recounted that when "the Union cavalry came past our plantation [and] told us to quit work, and follow them, we were all too glad to do so." Former slaves who crossed Union lines were often designated *contrabands*, that is, as confiscated property or the spoils of war.

The experiences of freedmen and freedwomen differed considerably. African American men at first did manual labor for the Union army and later became soldiers.

Women, however, had less clearly defined roles. One observer reported that after Grant took Vicksburg on July 4, 1863, freedwomen could be seen "following the army, carrying all their possessions on their heads, great feather beds tied up in sheets and holding their few belongings." Where African American soldiers were encamped, their wives and children sometimes lived in tents provided for them or in shantytowns on the edge of cities occupied by Union troops. Some women became nurses, cooks, or launderers for the colored troops and lived in barracks. Harriet Tubman, who had helped slaves escape through the Underground Railroad, offered assistance to contrabands. Susie King Taylor, for example, traveled with her husband's regiment, working as needed as a laundress or nurse. "My services were given at all times for the comfort of [the] men," she later recalled. "I was on hand to assist whenever needed." She also made certain that she could handle a musket and assisted the soldiers by cleaning and reloading their guns.

In December 1862, General Grant ordered the exclusion of women and children from the field and encouraged the organization of contraband camps near the cities where the U.S. Colored Troops were quartered. In these camps, freedwomen worked to support themselves and their families but also to provide supplies to the troops. Overcrowding and outbreaks of infectious disease were typical of these camps. Freedmen's Village in Alexandria, Virginia, for example, grew from three thousand people in 1863 to seven thousand a year later. Plagued by measles, smallpox, and whooping cough, these camps registered far more deaths than births. Partly in response to the high infectious disease and death rate, Union officials preferred to relocate African American women to abandoned or confiscated plantations.

Union officials also aimed to create a distance between African American women and the troops for the purpose of reducing the sexual commerce that flourished near the garrisons. Although the ranks of prostitutes were filled with both white women and black women, the officers singled out African Americans as "women of bad character" and viewed them as more licentious by nature than their white counterparts. And whereas they merely scolded white soldiers for inappropriate dalliances, Union officials induced black soldiers to marry their lovers. In fact, a large number of the women who engaged in sexual relations with black soldiers were already their wives, unrecognized as such by the white officials who did not recognize slave marriages as legal unions. Proof of a legal marriage became a requirement for the right of many black women to live in many camps or towns controlled by the Union army. As Colonel John Eaton Jr., who oversaw the camp at Corinth, Mississippi, explained, "untold evils resulted from the presence of lewd women; to meet this, marriage was started on the basis of the laws of the U.S., [and] regular registration [was] established."

But even a certificate of legal marriage and paid employment did not guarantee a freedwoman the right to keep her family intact. In Mississippi toward the end of the war, for example, military officials allowed African Americans who worked for the Union army to remain in Natchez but forced others to leave the city. Although many African American soldiers and their wives protested this policy, the general in charge of the Mississippi Valley insisted that freedpeople "should be put into a position to make their own living. The men should . . . be mustered into the service as soldiers, and the others with the women and children placed on abandoned plantations to till the ground."

WOMEN'S LIVES

HARRIET TUBMAN

The abolitionist Samuel J. May wrote that Harriet Tubman "must be regarded as the first heroine of the conflict." After the Civil War began, she refused to be deterred by the Lincoln administration's policy of calling only white men into the union army. She traveled alongside Massachusetts troops heading for Fort Monroe in Maryland, where she began the work of helping slaves—"contrabands"—secure refuge behind Union lines. She acted as nurse, cook, and laundress to those fleeing the Confederacy.

Tubman had prepared well to take on this important work. Born into slavery on the eastern shore of Maryland in the early 1820s, she had managed to escape from her abusive master in 1849. She settled in Philadelphia, where she lived as a freewoman. Drawn into antislavery circles, she embraced the role of conductor on the Underground Railroad that helped and protected runaway slaves. In nineteen rescue missions, she brought out of bondage between three hundred to four hundred people, including her sister and her aged parents. After southerners offered a ten-thousand-dollar bounty for her capture, Tubman, celebrated as the "Moses" of her people, sought refuge for a time in Canada. She followed her own counsel: "If you are tired, keep going; if you are scared, keep going; if you are hungry, keep going; if you want to taste freedom, keep going."

Shortly after the Emancipation Proclamation of January 1863, Tubman agreed to serve as an espionage agent for the federal government. Now situated in Beaufort, South Carolina, she worked as a spy and trained scouts. Familiar with this area, which was occupied by union troops, she often traveled around the countryside posing as an old trembling and deranged slave and under this guise organized slaves and former slaves to serve the Union cause.

Well known to abolitionist circles and former slaves, Tubman achieved international fame for her heroic role in the military operation known as the Combahee River Raid in June 1863. With her careful maneuvering, 756 slaves from the Tidewater rice plan-

tations, some of the richest in the South, escaped from their masters and crossed over to Union lines. Tubman led the sneak attack, guiding upriver the gunboats piloted by fifty black soldiers and picking up fugitives along the way. The escaped men, about four hundred in number, eagerly enlisted in the United States Colored Troops. With Tubman's instruction, the women formed a colony to sustain both themselves and the troops. They made clothing, grew crops, and built a washhouse to handle the soldiers' laundry.

As a scout, Tubman continued to work closely with Union officers, helping them to conduct several major raids on Confederate supply and ammunition depots. She accompanied the black 54th Regiment from Massachusetts to Fort Wagner, where more than three hundred African American soldiers were killed. By the fall of 1863, Tubman felt her health giving out, and by the following spring she headed North to recuperate. After the Civil War, she joined the lecture circuit, often speaking for woman's suffrage. Known far and wide as a war hero, Tubman petitioned for nearly thirty years before she received a federal pension for her work for the Union army. At her death in 1913, Tubman was awarded a funeral with full military honors. ∎

In rural areas controlled by the Union army, freedwomen became field laborers on reorganized plantations, which the federal government leased to white northerners or to white southerners who took an oath of loyalty to the United States. Working now for wages, these women and their children performed many of the same tasks that had been theirs under slavery and did so under the direction of and for the profit of whites. They picked and baled the cotton that, unattended, would have gone to seed. Although the federal government emphasized the humanitarian goals of this system, the actual conditions on badly managed plantations rivaled those of the contraband camps, producing in some cases even higher mortality rates. Moreover, the common practice of irregular payments of wages and in some cases outright fraud denied many field-workers their rightful compensation. Poorly paid, their mobility restricted, freedwomen were forced to endure conditions of labor little better than slavery. As early as 1862, the *Weekly Anglo-African* newspaper condemned this system as "but another name for Government slavery."

By 1864, the African American women and children who constituted the majority of refugees suffered the deprivations that accompanied the final battles of the war. Eager to flee the plantations, they attached themselves to Union troops. Thousands of African American women braved General William Tecumseh Sherman's destructive 285-mile march through Georgia. "Babies tumbled from the backs of mules to which they had been told to cling, and were drowned in the swamps, while mothers stood by the roadside crying for their lost children," one Union officer reported. By the time

In November and December 1864, General William Tecumseh Sherman led one of the most devastating campaigns against the Confederacy. His troops marched through Georgia, terrorizing the civilian population, leveling buildings, and destroying food supplies. Along the way, former slaves fled the plantations and sought refuge by marching with the Union troops.

Sherman's army reached the sea, less than seven thousand of the estimated twenty-five thousand African Americans who attempted the journey were still alive.

A Woman's War

"I have never studied the art of paying compliments to women," President Lincoln confessed toward the end of the war, "but I must say, that if all that has been said by orators and poets since the creation of the world were applied to the women of America, it would not do them justice for their conduct during this war." Quite a few women, such as Elizabeth Stuart Phelps, were eager to write and publish their own assessments. They filled the pages of popular magazines and illustrated weekly newspapers with their commentary on women's contributions to both the home and battlefronts. However, for the most prolific, writing itself served as a form of war work. "I thank God that instead of giving me a wash-tub, or a needle, or a broom to work my work with," Mary Dodge, a popular writer better known as Gail Hamilton, wrote in 1864, "he has given me a pen, and a whole country for my family."

A Moral Crusade to End Slavery

Even before the attack at Fort Sumter, several prominent abolitionists had accepted the inevitability of a bloody conflict and pledged themselves to make the eradication of slavery the principal goal of the war. To this end, Lydia Maria Child set herself to editing *Incidents in the Life of a Slave Girl*, Harriet Jacobs's semiautobiographical narrative that is unremitting in its documentation of slavery. As if by design, Jacobs's novel was published on the eve of the war in April 1861 and soon became one of the most important abolitionist missives of the decade. Published in 1863 as a timely complement to the Emancipation Proclamation, Fanny Kemble's *Journal of a Residence on a Georgian Plantation* added to Jacobs's revelations about the horror of slavery. The book by the well-known British actress, which had been written nearly a quarter-century earlier, told the world, in the words of a sympathetic reviewer, "what the black women of the South have so long endured."

The longtime abolitionist Julia Ward Howe wrote the most popular and enduring tract of the war years. In November 1862, after a White House reception with President Lincoln, she and her husband, Samuel Gridley Howe, attended a military review a few miles away, and along the way their party sang patriotic songs. Someone urged Howe, who was already well known for her poetry, to update the abolitionist hymn they all loved so well. That night, she woke up feeling inspired and drafted new lyrics to the tune of "John Brown's body lies a-mouldering in the ground;/ His soul is marching on." The next month, the *Atlantic Monthly* published her poem, which included the moving stanza,

In the beauty of the lilies Christ was born across the sea,

With a glory in his bosom that transfigures you and me:

As he died to make men holy, let us die to make men free,

While God is marching on.

Reprinted in newspapers and magazines throughout the North, Howe's stirring lyrics called upon Americans to view the war as retribution for the sins of their nation and to seek redemption by freeing the slaves. Union troops soon began to sing the "Battle Hymn of the Republic" while they headed into battle.

WOMEN'S LIVES

ELIZABETH STUART PHELPS

The writer Elizabeth Stuart Phelps was one of the many women who helped create the myth of the Civil War as a "woman's war." Born in Boston in 1844, she followed in her mother's footsteps as a writer of children's stories and religious works. It was her memorial to the war widows, however, that turned her into an author of international renown.

Still in her teens when the war began, Phelps lost her fiancé at Antietam, Maryland, on September 17, 1862, the single bloodiest day of the conflict. When the long, brutal war finally ended, she later remembered, "[T]he country was dark with sorrowing women" like herself. Even the joyous celebrations that greeted the returning regiments could not dispel so much grief.

Phelps decided to do what she could to provide solace to these women and wrote a novel of consolation. Putting aside the emotional and physical trauma endured by men, she addressed herself mainly to "the helpless, outnumbering, unconsulted women; they whom the war trampled down, without a choice or protest; the patient, limited, domestic women, who thought little, but loved much, and loving had lost all." *The Gates Ajar* became a best seller and in less than twenty years was reprinted more than fifty times.

The Gates Ajar tells the story of a young woman suffering the loss of her much beloved brother. At first she turns for comfort to the deacon of the local Congregational Church. However, his vision of the afterlife is so cold and sterile that it fails to raise her spirits. Fortunately, she crosses paths with two women who offer an entirely different vision of heaven and assure her that she and her brother will eventually be reunited. Moreover, they offer a vivid depiction of an afterlife imbued with all the merits and pleasures of domesticity. Phelps demolishes the prevailing vision of heaven, as one of her admirers described it, as "seas of glass and cherubim and seraphim . . . dim, monotonous, and narrow." In its place, she offers a distinctly feminine retreat, a home replete with parlors, pianos, and even window

boxes with geraniums—in short, the accoutrements of domesticity that many women lost forever with the death of their fathers, husbands, and lovers.

"At the time, be it said, I had no interest at all in any especial movement for the peculiar needs of women as a class," Phelps later recalled. "I was reared in circles which did not concern themselves with those whom we should probably have called agitators." Yet, there is no doubt that she succeeded in reminding her readers that the impact of the Civil War extended far beyond the battlefield. Men had declared the war, planned the military strategy, and sacrificed their lives in battle. But women, too, with little choice, had been drawn into the conflict. They, too, had experienced danger, faced new challenges and unfamiliar responsibilities, and endured deprivations. The "unconsulted" women, Phelps suggested, emerged from the Civil War with a new perspective on their rights and duties.

Before she died in 1911, Elizabeth Stuart Phelps produced nearly sixty volumes of fiction, poetry, and essays. ∎

Other women excelled as orators. Born free and raised as an abolitionist, Frances Ellen Watkins Harper wrote poetry and lectured to raise funds for the war effort and became an extraordinarily popular speaker for the African American community. "The Union of the past, thank God, is gone," she proclaimed in 1864. "Darkened by the shadow of a million crimes, it has sunk beneath the weight of its own guilt, and now we stand upon the threshold of a new era—an era whose horizon is gilded with promise, and flushed with hope."

Harper's rhetorical flourish found its equal in the impassioned oratory of the youthful white abolitionist Anna Dickinson of Philadelphia. Just nineteen years old when the war broke out, Dickinson had been raised in the Quaker tradition of female preaching. "While the flag of freedom waves merely for the white man," she warned, "God will be against us." Huge crowd's listened in awe as she rebuked President Lincoln for hesitating to emancipate all slaves.

Memoirs and Memories

In mid-1863 Louisa May Alcott began to serialize several short stories based on her nursing experiences at the makeshift Union Hotel Hospital in the Georgetown area of Washington, D.C. She served there for only two months before typhoid fever nearly took her life. Yet, even this short stint provided the thirty-year-old aspiring writer with enough material to make heroes of both injured soldiers and the female nurses who cared for them. Her main character, Nurse Tribulation Periwinkle, draws on conventional notions of womanhood while continuously enlarging her realm of responsibility in the hospital. She showers her wards with the affection a mother would give to her sons and, at the same time, proves herself a competent and skilled nurse. Alcott went on to write the perennial children's classic *Little Women* but achieved her first moment of fame with the publication of her wartime nursing tales.

Alcott was far from alone in developing this important genre. By the end of the war, more than two dozen stories or books had already appeared in print, and after the war several hundred more nurses wrote their memoirs. Unlike their fictional counterparts, they offered more pointed criticism of male physicians and described their relationships with them as contests over authority. Still, both the tragedy and romance of the war remained fixed elements, as indicated by the subtitle of Sophronia Bucklin's engaging memoir, *In Hospital and Camp: A Woman's Record of Thrilling Incidents among the Wounded in the Late War*, published in 1869. Writers, northern and southern alike, determinedly illustrated women's capacity to be as heroic in their roles as soldiers were in theirs.

Yet no nursing memoir rivaled the exciting tales written by former spies. Rose O'Neil Greenhow, for example, was one of the first women to exploit her adventures in print. The Washington socialite had served the South by transmitting vital information and became instantly famous for contributing to the Confederate victory at Bull Run in July 1861. She was soon captured and, with her small daughter, detained in a federal prison. After her release, Greenhow traveled to England and France where she wrote about her espionage activities. *My Imprisonment, and the First Year of Abolition Rule at Washington*, which was published in 1863, ensured her fame. However, fate cut short her promising career as a writer. On her return trip in 1864, Greenhow drowned off the shore of North Carolina.

The Confederate spy Belle Boyd met with longer-lasting acclaim. After the war, she capitalized on her fame by narrating her adventures as a spy for audiences across the country. Boyd was especially popular with veterans' groups who, according to lore, remembered her fondly as "the most daring woman in the Confederacy."

The first official histories of the U.S. Sanitary Commission, written shortly after the war by the men who spearheaded the venture, played down the friction between the regional branches and the local soldiers' aid societies and instead duly praised the women who contributed so much to the war effort. They erred primarily on the side of excessive flattery, deploying such familiar gender phrases as "self-sacrifice" and "motherly devotion" to praise individual women. Although many women basked in the glow of such adulation, the majority who served in the leadership ranks did not.

The regional directors of the USSC countered the official histories with their own interpretation of the significance of women's role in the USSC. In charge of the northwestern region, Mary Livermore and Jane Hoge understood quite clearly that they had transformed volunteer charity work, a staple of antebellum female activism, into a salaried profession. As directors, they had not only set their own agenda but demanded pay for their work. In New York, the youthful Louisa Lee Schuyler ran the branch on a voluntary basis but nevertheless launched herself on a lifelong career in charity organization. Such was also the case with Boston activist Abby May, who envisioned the USSC as the mechanism for creating a "sisterhood of states" of the local relief organizations.

By building a bridge between community activism and the exigencies of the growing nation-state, regional leaders of the USSC fostered a new civic culture for women and created a network of activists comfortable with national organizational goals. Moreover, before the war, these middle-class women had enlarged their domestic sphere by undertaking philanthropic endeavors; but after the war, a sizable number put aside domesticity altogether for public service and careers.

CONCLUSION

Shortly after the beginning of the Civil War, Julia Le Grand pined: "I wish I had a field for my energies. I hate common life, a life of visiting, dressing and tattling, which seems to devolve on women, and now that there is better work to do, real tragedy, real romance and history weaving every day, I suffer, suffer, leading the life I do." Ultimately, the war that emancipated four million slaves put new demands on this otherwise privileged southern woman as well as nearly everyone living in its path. Barred from combat, women took on untried roles, availed themselves of new opportunities, and gained unprecedented access to power.

At the same time, for both Northern and Southern women, the specter of suffering and death hung over them—for good reason. The Civil War was the most devastating war in American history. At least 50,000 civilians died, and military casualties topped 500,000. Approximately 360,000 Union soldiers lost their lives. The toll was proportionately greater in the South, where an estimated one in four Confederate soldiers— approximately 258,000—were killed. Of the men who managed to survive the carnage, a large number returned home maimed or psychologically scarred.

Despite bearing the weight of personal tragedy, many men and women emerged from their wartime experiences with new perspectives on the roles of men and women. "During the war, and as a result of my own observations," Mary Livermore wrote, "I became aware that a large portion of the nation's work was badly done, or not done at all, because woman

WOMEN'S HISTORY	GLOBAL EVENTS

1860

	1860
	Abraham Lincoln wins presidential election
	South Carolina secedes from the Union
1861	1861
Harriet Jacobs's *Incidents in the Life of a Slave Girl* published	Confederate States of America form
Soldiers' Aid Societies form in North and South	Lincoln inaugurated
Woman's Central Relief Association forms	Attack on Fort Sumter, war begins
Dorothea Dix appointed Superintendent of Women Nurses for the Union Army	United States Sanitary Commission established
	First Battle of Bull Run
1862	1862
Confederate Hospital Act places women nurses in military hospitals	Congress repeals law prohibiting African American men from serving in military
Julia Ward Howe writes "The Battle Hymn of the Republic"	Contraband Relief Association forms
	Preliminary Emancipation Proclamation
	Battles of Antietam and Fredericksburg

1863

1863	1863
Woman's National Loyal League forms	Lincoln issues Emancipation Proclamation
Louisa May Alcott publishes *Hospital Sketches*	55th Massachusetts Regiment begins to form
Harriet Tubman foments Combahee River slave rebellion	Federal Conscription Act
	Battle of Gettysburg
	Surrender of Vicksburg
	New York City draft Riots
	Great Sanitary Fair, Chicago
1864	1864
U.S. War Department allows military hospitals to employ African American women	Metropolitan Sanitary Fair, New York
Working Women's Protection Union forms	General Sherman's march to the sea
Woman's National Loyal League petition presented to U.S. Senate	Lincoln reelected president
	1865
	House of Representatives passes Thirteenth Amendment
	Freedmen's Bureau established
	Richmond falls
	Lee surrenders to Grant at Appomattox
	Lincoln assassinated
	Thirteenth Amendment ratified

was not recognized as a factor in the political world." She nevertheless anticipated that with the return of peace women would eagerly resume their domestic roles. Such was not to be because, she later noted, "during those days of hardship and struggle, the ordinary tenor of woman's life had changed. She had developed potencies and possibilities of whose existence she had not been aware, and which surprised her, as it did those who witnessed her marvelous achievements." Like so many women of her generation, Livermore believed that the Civil War had wrought revolutionary changes, perhaps not least in a "great awakening of women." Those women involved in the woman's rights movement came to a similar conclusion, claiming that the Civil War "created a revolution in woman herself, as important in its results as the changed condition of the former slaves."

REVIEW QUESTIONS

1. In what ways did notions of womanliness affect the ways women responded to the Civil War?

2. What were the major regional differences in the ways women experienced the Civil War?

3. How did women's experience in antebellum voluntary societies prepare them for a new role in the Civil War?

4. How did enslaved women respond to the outbreak of the war?

5. Why did many women writers view the Civil War as a turning point in American women's history?

RECOMMENDED READING

DeAnne Blanton, and Lauren M. Cook. *They Fought Like Demons: Women Soldiers in the American Civil War*. Baton Rouge: Louisiana State University Press, 2002. A study of women who cross-dressed to disguise themselves as men and fought as soldiers in both Union and Confederate armies.

Catherine Clinton and Nina Silber, eds. *Divided Houses: Gender and the Civil War*. New York: Oxford University Press, 1992. A collection of essays illustrating the impact of social history on recent scholarship of the Civil War. Includes several essays about men and masculinity.

Laura F. Edwards. *Scarlett Doesn't Live Here Anymore: Southern Women in the Civil War Era*. Urbana and Chicago: University of Illinois Press, 2000. Making the household the center of her narrative, Edwards charts the relationship between the private and public spheres for African American women and white women of both planter and yeoman families.

Judith Ann Giesberg. *Civil War Sisterhood: The U.S. Sanitary Commission and Women's Politics in Transition*. Boston: Northeastern University Press, 2000. Examines the network constructed by women in the USSC as a transition between the local activism of the antebellum period and the wider postwar reform endeavors and political movements. Giesberg's study also covers the commission's program to employ women as nurses in Civil War hospitals and on the battle front.

Drew Gilpin Faust. *Mothers of Invention: Women of the Slaveholding South in the American Civil War*. Chapel Hill: University of North Carolina Press, 1996. Based on the writings of more than 500 Confederate women, Faust's book examined the ways Confederate elite women negotiated their womanhood amid the turmoil of the Civil War.

Ella Forbes. *African American Women during the Civil War*. New York: Garland, 1998. Documents the role of both free black women and those emerging from slavery in making the Civil War a struggle for liberation.

Elizabeth D. Leonard. *Yankee Women: Gender Battles in the Civil War.* New York: W. W. Norton & Co., 1994. Stories of three Union women—Sophronia Bucklin, Annie Wittenmyer, and Mary Edwards Walker—who pushed the boundaries of woman's role through their wartime activism.

Nina Silber. *Daughters of the Union: Northern Women Fight the Civil War.* Cambridge, MA: Harvard University Press, 2005. Provides a compelling argument that the Civil War was not a transforming moment for many Northern women, that it instead in many ways reaffirmed their subordination to men.

Lyde Cullen Sizer. *The Political Work of Northern Women Writers and the Civil War, 1850–1872.* Chapel Hill: University of North Carolina Press, 2000. Focusing on the work and lives of nine writers, including Louisa May Alcott and Elizabeth Stuart Phelps, Sizer provides a rich context for examining their fictional works about the Civil War.

Wendy Hamand Venet. *Neither Ballots Nor Bullets: Women Abolitionists and the Civil War.* Charlottesville: University Press of Virginia, 1991. About the women, such as Anna Dickinson, who worked for abolition during the civil war and organized to secure a political and constitutional end to slavery with major emphasis on the activities of the Woman's National Loyal League.

ADDITIONAL BIBLIOGRAPHY

Home Fronts, North and South

Steven V. Ash. *When the Yankees Came: Conflict and Chaos in the Occupied South 1861–1965.* Chapel Hill: University of North Carolina Press, 1995.

Jeanie Attie. *Patriotic Toil: Northern Women and the American Civil War.* Ithaca: Cornell University Press, 1998.

Edward D.C. Campbell, et. al., eds. *A Woman's War: Southern Women, Civil War, and the Confederate Legacy.* Richmond: Museum of the Confederacy, 1996.

Jacqueline Glass Campbell. *When Sherman Marched North from the Sea: Resistance on the Confederate Home Front.* Chapel Hill: University of North Carolina, 2003.

Catherine Clinton. *Tara Revisited: Women, War, and the Plantation Legend.* New York: Abbeville Press, 1995.

Marilyn Mayer Culpepper. *Trials and Triumphs: Women of the American Civil War.* East Lansing: Michigan State University Press, 1991.

Mauriel Phillips Joslyn, ed. *Confederate Women.* Gretna: Pelican Publishing Company, 2005.

Mary Elizabeth Massey. *Women in the Civil War.* Lincoln: University of Nebraska Press 1994, 1966.

Thomas H. O'Connor. *Civil War Boston: Homefront and Battlefield.* Boston: Northeastern University Press, 1997.

George Rable. *Civil Wars: Women and the Crisis of Southern Nationalism.* Urbana: University of Illinois Press, 1989.

LeeAnn Whites. *The Civil War as a Crisis in Gender: Augusta, Georgia 1860–1890.* Athens: University of Georgia Press, 1995.

On the Battlefront

Carol K. Bleser and Lesley J. Gordon, eds. *Intimate Strategies of the Civil War: Military Commanders and Their Wives.* New York: Oxford University Press, 2002.

Nancy Scripture Garrison. *With Courage and Delicacy: Civil War on the Peninsula: Women and the U.S. Sanitary Commission.* Mason City, IA: Savas Publishing, 1999.

Richard Hall. *Women on the Civil War Battlefront.* Lawrence: University Press of Kansas, 2006.

Elizabeth D. Leonard. *All the Daring of the Soldier: Women of the Civil War Armies.* New York: W.W. Norton & Company, 1999.

Gerald F. Linderman. *Embattled Courage: The Experience of Combat in the American Civil War.* New York: Free Press; London: Collier Macmillan Publishers, 1987.

Sister Mary Denis Maher. *To Bind Up the Wounds: Catholic Sister Nurses in the U.S. Civil War.* Baton Rouge: Louisiana State University Press, 1989.

Reid Mitchell. *The Vacant Chair: The Northern Soldier Leaves Home.* New York: Oxford University Press, 1993.

Jane E. Schultz. *Women at the Front: Hospital Workers in Civil War America.* Chapel Hill: University of North Carolina Press, 2004.

Memoirs, Diaries, and Biographies

Elizabeth Frances Andrews. *The War-Time Journal of a Georgia Girl, 1864–1865.* Cambridge, MA: Harvard University Press, 1997.

Elizabeth R. Baer, ed. *Shadows on My Heart: The Civil War Diary of Lucy Rebecca Buck of Virginia.* Athens: University of Georgia Press, 1997.

Melba Joyce Boyd. *Discarded Legacy: Politics and Poetics in the Life of Frances E. W. Harper 1825–1911.* Detroit: Wayne State University Press, 1994.

Joan E. Cashin. *First Lady of the Confederacy: Varina Davis's Civil War.* Cambridge, MA: Harvard University Press, 2006.

Catherine Clinton. *Harriet Tubman: The Road to Freedom.* New York: Little, Brown 2004.

Kate Cumming. *Kate: The Journal of a Confederate Nurse.* Baton Rouge: Louisiana State University Press, 1987.

Curtis Carroll Davis, ed. *Belle Boyd in Camp and Prison, Written by Herself.* New York: Thomas Yoseloff, 1968.

S. Emma E. Edmonds. *Nurse and Spy in the Union Army: Comprising the Adventures and Experiences of a Woman in Hospitals, Camps, and Battlefields.* Boston: De Wolfe, Fiske, B64.

Elizabeth Keckley. *Behind the Scenes: Or Thirty Years a Slave and Four Years in the White House.* New York: G. W. Carleton & Co., 1968.

Peg A. Lamphier. *Kate Chase and William Sprague: Politics and Gender in a Civil War Marriage.* Lincoln and London: University of Nebraska Press, 2003.

Mary Livermore. *My Story of the War.* Hartford: A. D. Worthington & Co., 1888.

Stephen B. Oates. *A Woman of Valour: Clara Barton and the Civil War.* New York: Free Press, 1994.

Phoebe Yates Pember. *A Southern Woman's Story.* Marietta, GA: Mockingbird Books, 1959.

Susie King Taylor. *Reminiscenes of My Life in Camp with the 33rd U.S. Colored Troops, Late 1st South Carolina Volunteers: A Black Woman's Civil War Memoirs.* New York: Arno Press, 1988f, 1902.

Loreta Janeta Velazquez. *The Woman in Battle.* Madison: University of Wisconsin Press, 1876.

Wendy Hamand Venet. *A Strong-Minded Woman: The Life of Mary A. Livermore.* Amherst, Mass., and London: University of Massachusetts Press, 2005.

C. Van Woodward, ed. *Mary Chesnut's Civil War.* New Haven: Yale University Press, 1981.

In the Age of Slave Emancipation, 1865–1877

HOW DID Reconstruction policies affect black and white households in the South?

WHAT WERE the major issues facing the postbellum woman's rights movement?

HOW DID the debates about women's wage earning intersect with discussions of marriage?

IN WHAT ways did the temperance campaign challenge male authority within the family?

CHAPTER 10

Salvisa, Kentucky, April 7, 1866

Dear Husband

I received your letter the 5 of this month and was very glad to hear from you. You wish me to come to Virginia. I had much rather you would come after me but if you cannot make it convenient you will have to make some arrangement for me and family. I have 3 little fatherless girls. My husband went off under Burbridge's command and was killed at Richmond Virginia. If you can pay my passage I will come the first of May. I have nothing much to sell as I have had my things all

The women of St. John's Guild for the Destitute Sick Children of New York City, at their Monday evening sewing circle, making garments for the poor. Wood engraving. Frank Leslie's Illustrated Newspaper, December 12, 1874.

burnt. You must not think my family to large and get out of heart for if you love me you will love my children and you have to promise me that you will provide for them as well as if they were your own. I heard that you spoke of coming for Maria [their daughter] but were not coming for me. I know that I have lived with you and loved you then and I love you still. I was very low spirited when I heard you was not coming for me. My heart sank within me in an instant. You will have to write and give me directions how to come.

Maria sends her love to you but seems to be low spirited for fear that you will come for her and not for me. No more at present but remain your true wife. (I hope to be with you soon.)

Willie Ann Grey

Source: Bureau of Refugees, Freedmen and Abandoned Lands, Record Group 105, Richmond, Virginia, National Archives; reprinted in Dorothy Sterling, ed., We Are Your Sisters: Black Women in the Nineteenth Century (New York: W.W. Norton, 1984), 316.

illie Ann Grey had experienced the Civil War as a great victory—she had won her freedom. Like the majority of former slaves, she undoubtedly hoped to live out her life with little interference from whites. Having been sold out from her first husband during slavery and remarried, she now hoped to reunite with him and to gather all her children into a stable family.

The recipient of Grey's letter had not been, in all probability, her legal husband; nor had her children been her "own." According to the laws that had prevailed in the antebellum South, slave families did not exist. Each person, regardless of his or her biological relationship to other slaves, existed in the law solely as the property of the master. The master, who claimed the fruits of all labor, denied the enslaved man responsibility for the welfare of his wife and children. The master also claimed control over the enslaved woman's body and the disposition of her children. In essence, law and custom denied slaves the basic rights of citizenship, including the benefits of civil marriage.

The Thirteenth Amendment, which banned slavery and involuntary servitude in the United States, also extended, as one senator put it, to "the hapless bondman . . . the sacred rights of human nature, the hallowed family relations of husband and wife." In the aftermath of emancipation, many former slaves like Grey embraced the right to marry as an emblem of their freedom. "The Marriage Covenant," one African American soldier explained, "is the foundation of all our rights."

While Willie Ann Grey hoped to secure the family that slavery had denied her, the prospects for reaching this goal depended not merely on the sentiments of her husband or even their financial resources. Much rested on the policies implemented by the government to rebuild the nation, that is, the terms for readmitting the former Confederate states to the Union and the parameters of freedom of the recently emancipated slaves.

Plans for **Reconstruction**—reconstructing the nation—had begun well before the end of the Civil War, but the assassination of Abraham Lincoln on April 14, 1865, made these matters even more urgent. His successor, President Andrew Johnson, pardoned all white southerners except Confederate leaders and left the status of freedpeople under the jurisdiction of the former Rebel states. Southern legislatures took this opportunity to draft the highly discriminatory **Black Codes**, which granted some civil

Reconstruction The period 1865–1877 that reintegrated the former Confederate states into the Union and established the terms of freedom for former slaves.

Black Codes Legislation enacted by former Confederate states, 1865–1866, to define the rights and limits of freedom of former slaves.

rights to African Americans, such as the right to own property and make contracts, but at the same time severely limited their freedom.

In December 1865, Congress reconvened and condemned the Black Codes, repudiated Johnson's plans, and moved to secure for African Americans the full rights of citizenship. In 1866, Congress passed a civil rights act that for the first time clearly designated all persons born in the United States as citizens and denoted their rights without regard to race. To give Constitutional backing to these provisions, legislators proposed the **Fourteenth Amendment** and the **Fifteenth Amendment,** which prohibit racial distinctions in the law and introduce additional measures to guarantee African Americans the same civil and political rights enjoyed by whites.

These measures did more than redefine race relations in the United States. By specifying the rights and responsibilities of citizenship, legislation enacted in the decade after the Civil War had a profound impact on the laws governing marriage and the family, including the relationship between husband and wife and both to the state. The new legislation gave more power to the state to govern the affairs of the household, such as establishing the terms of marriage, the ownership of property, and custody over children.

In the decade following the Civil War, then, the government cast new light on the status of women and the power of men within marriage and the family. For this reason, the woman's rights movement, which had suspended its activities during the war, revived and asked a new series of questions. As persons "born or naturalized in the

Fourteenth Amendment Confers national citizenship on all persons born or naturalized in the United States and introduces the word "male" into the Constitution.

Fifteenth Amendment Prohibits the denial of suffrage because of race, color, or previous condition of servitude and leaves out "sex."

TABLE 10-1 African-American Population during Reconstruction in the States Subject to Congressional Reconstruction

	African-American Population in 1870	African Americans as Percentage of Total Population
South Carolina	415,814	58.9
Mississippi	444,201	53.6
Louisiana	364,210	50.1
North Carolina	391,650	36.5
Alabama	475,510	47.6
Georgia	545,142	46.0
Virginia	512,841	41.8
Florida	91,689	48.7
Arkansas	122,169	25.2
Texas	253,475	30.9
Tennessee	322,331	25.6

(*Source: Eric Foner*, Freedom's Lawmakers: A Directory of Black Officeholders during Reconstruction (1993), xiv; The statistics of the Population of the United States, Ninth Census (1873), xvii.)

In several states in the Deep South, such as South Carolina and Louisiana, African Americans represented a slight majority of the population.

MAP 10-1   DATES OF FORMER CONFEDERATE STATES READMITTED TO THE UNION

1868 Date of readmission to the Union

In 1867, Congress enacted the First Reconstruction Act, creating five military districts in the former Confederacy. To be readmitted to the Union, ex-Confederate states had to ratify the Fourteenth Amendment which barred former Confederates the right to hold public office, and guarantee the right to vote to all men.

Freedmen's Bureau
The federal agency that coordinated relief efforts for former slaves and established schools for black children.

United States" and defined as citizens, could women enjoy all the rights and privileges now ostensibly assured to freedmen? Did the Fourteenth and Fifteenth amendments, which guaranteed political rights to freedmen, advance or hinder women's own claim to the ballot? Could women who worked outside the home expect to receive the same guarantee to the fruits of their labor as men did? What were the limits of women's power within marriage and the family?

RECONSTRUCTING SOUTHERN HOUSEHOLDS

In the aftermath of the Civil War, four million black men and women claimed their freedom in a variety of ways. One elderly woman, a former slave from South Carolina, aspired to be "settin' at de white folks' table, a eating off de white folks' table, and a rocking in de big rocking chair." Another, more spunky woman confronted her former mistress saying, "I expect the white folks to be waiting on me before long!" More realistic, the majority of freed slaves sought to reunite as families and establish their own households at a location of their choice.

The Civil War, however, had effected major changes in the dynamics of the households of both large plantations and small farms and for both blacks and whites. By necessity, many white women had taken on a greater number of responsibilities while their husbands were away fighting for the Confederacy and emerged from the war with a greater feeling of self-respect. After the war, while their husbands were trying to piece together the fragments of their former lives, many of these women continued to gain power within the sphere of domesticity. In contrast, many African American women sought to build a new life with men, impoverished but "free" and eager to occupy a new position of authority within their families.

The Meaning of Freedom

African American women throughout the South welcomed the end of the war as an opportunity to realize their dream of freedom and, foremost, to come together with their families. "In their eyes," an agent of the Freedmen's Bureau observed, "the work of emancipation was incomplete until the families which had been dispersed by slavery were reunited."

To find their husbands, many women turned first to the **Freedmen's Bureau**, which had been established by Congress in the last month of the war to provide relief to the refugees from slavery and to assist their transition to freedom. The agents eagerly encouraged former slaves to marry, believing that marriage ensured a degree of family stability and sexual self-discipline that slavery had denied. As a legal arrangement, state-sanctioned marriage forced freedmen and freedwomen to be accountable

At the close of the Civil War, former slaves were encouraged to make their marriages legal. This engraving, which appeared in Harper's Weekly, *June 30, 1866, depicts Chaplain Joseph Warren of the Freedmen's Bureau marrying an African American soldier and his bride.*

for the welfare of their children and, in effect, released former slave owners as well as the state from such obligations. This responsibility, the agents noted, was to be borne primarily by men, thereby encouraging manhood and preparing freedmen for the rights and privileges of citizenship. Many former slaves therefore followed the advice of the Freedmen's Bureau and renewed the vows they had made under slavery.

But the new state laws enabling freedpeople to marry did not necessarily overcome old customs. A large number of men and women chose to make do with familiar arrangements. For example, older freedpeople usually accepted their slave marriages as adequate and simply ignored the new legislation. War widows, who risked losing their pensions upon remarrying, perpetuated informal practices and "took up" or "sweethearted" with men without the benefit of legal marriage. Other women found common-law marriage preferable to the more cumbersome state-sanctioned relationship. Frances Long recalled that she "took up with Dallas Miles . . . and lived with him" for nine years. They had three children together and "were recognized as husband/wife" by everyone. Legal marriage, she implied, seemed more like a form of discipline or coercion than a source of power.

Still, the fluidity that characterized family life during slavery persisted into the new era. Households continued to incorporate kin, biological and fictive, especially in the case of children, many of whom were orphaned by the war. Women in particular benefited from extended families because they could turn to kin for assistance if they chose to "quit" a relationship with an abusive or unsupportive spouse. Moreover, the community continued to sanction premarital or occasional extramarital sexual relationships, although men or women who were repeatedly unfaithful to their spouse risked censure by friends and neighbors. To be sure, both men and women valued fidelity in their partners, but adultery did not necessarily spell disaster.

WOMEN'S VOICES

A SLAVE'S CHILD REMEMBERS THEIR QUEST FOR FREEDOM

Annie L. Burton was born in Clayton, Alabama, around 1858 to a white planter and an enslaved mother who worked on a nearby plantation as a cook. When Annie was little more than a toddler, her mother suffered a whipping at the hands of her mistress and ran away. Annie and her two siblings stayed behind to live through the harsh years of the Civil War. At the end of the war, her mother, like so many former slaves, returned to re-claim their children and other kin. Annie married at age thirty and moved with her husband to the Boston area where she worked in domestic service. In 1909, she published Memories of Childhood's Slavery Days.

My mother came for us at the end of the year 1865, and demanded that her children be given up to her. This, mistress refused to do, and threatened to set the dogs on my mother if she did not at once leave the place. My mother went away, and remained with some of the neighbors until supper time. Then she got a boy to tell Caroline [her older half-sister] to come down to the fence. When she came, my mother told her to go back and get Henry [her younger half-brother] and myself and bring us down to the gap in the fence as quick as she could. Then my mother took Henry in her arms, and my sister carried me on her back. We climbed fences and crossed fields, and after several hours came to a little hut which my mother had secured on a plantation. We had no more than reached the place, and made a little fire, when master's two sons rode up and de-manded that the children be returned. My mother refused to give us up. Upon her offering to go with them to the Yankee headquarters to find out if it were really true that all negroes had been made free, the young men left and troubled us no more.

The cabin that was now our home was made of logs. It had one door, and an opening in one wall, with an inside shutter, was the only window. The door was fastened with a latch. Our beds were some straw.

There were six in our little family: my mother, Caroline, Henry, two other children that my mother had brought with her upon her return, and myself.

The man on whose plantation this cabin stood, hired my mother as a cook, and give us this little home. We children used to sell blueberries and plums that we picked. One day the man on whom we depended for our home and support, left. Then my mother did washing by the day, for whatever she could get. We were sent to get cold victuals from hotels and such places. A man wanting hands to pick cotton, my mother Henry and I were set to help in this work. We had to go to the cotton field very early every morning. For this work, we re-ceived forty cents for every hundred pounds of cot-ton we picked.

Caroline was hired out to take care of a baby.

In 1866, another man hired the plantation on which our hut stood, and we moved into Clayton, to a little house my mother secured there. A rich lady came to our house one day, looking for some one to take care of her little daughter. I was taken, and adopted into this family. This rich lady was Mrs. E. M. Williams, a music teacher, and wife of a lawyer. We called her "Mis' Mary."

Some rich people in Clayton who had owned slaves, opened the Methodist Church on Sundays, and began the work of teaching the negroes. My new mistress sent me to Sunday school every Sun-day morning, and I soon got so that I could read. Mis' Mary taught me every day at her knee. I soon could read nicely, and went through Sterling's Second Reader, and then into McGuthrie's Third Reader. The first piece of poetry I recited in Sunday school was taught to me by Mis' Mary during the week. . . . As I grew older, she taught me to cook and how to do housework. During this time Mis' Mary had given my mother one dollar a month in return for my services. . . .

Source: Annie Louise Burton, Memories of Childhood's Slavery Days *(Boston: Ross Publishing, 1909), 11–14.*

Questions

1. How does Annie Louise Burton describe the quality of her life after slavery?

2. How did emancipation affect the ability of her mother to keep her family together?

Nevertheless, by investing freedmen with the right to support and protect their wives and children and designating the latter as their dependents, the new legislation reaffirmed the gender hierarchies idealized in middle-class households. As one proponent intoned: "No monarch upon his throne is more secure in the enjoyment of his rights than he . . . What he has is his own. His wife is his, . . . the sweet voices that call him father are the voices of his own." In short, the new legislation governing marriage granted African American husbands with a source of power within the family that had long been denied to them under slavery. For her part, a wife could expect support and protection while she fulfilled her primary obligation to maintain the home and care for children and elders. She could in addition work outside the home, but the law required her to turn over all earnings to her husband and, in essence, subordinate her personal identity to his. In slavery, a woman and her children bore the surname of her master; in freedom, they carried the surname of her husband.

Despite these new restrictions, freedwomen married for love as well as for practical reasons. For example, male-headed households afforded them some protection against harassment by white employers. Able to earn only one-half to two-thirds of the wages paid to men, most women simply could not afford to live and provide for their children by themselves. Whether inside or outside the law, adult men and women tended to live as married couples. By 1870, for example, 80 percent of black households in the populous region of the Cotton Belt included both a husband and a wife, a proportion equal to that of the nearby white population.

Negotiating Free Labor

During the last year of the war, the Freedmen's Bureau began to distribute forty-acre plots of abandoned or confiscated property to former slaves; and in some regions, such as the South Carolina and Georgia low country, freedpeople farmed the land with the expectation that they would some day become its lawful owners. However, in May 1865, Lincoln's successor, President Andrew Johnson, restored the property rights of the original white owners, and within one year the planter class had recovered virtually all its land. The dream of acquiring land from the government—"forty acres and a mule"—

nevertheless died hard. As one observer remarked at the time, freedpeople had no greater ambition than "to have little homes of their own and to work for themselves."

By 1868, most former slaves had returned to the countryside, which remained the focal point of the southern agricultural economy, and were working as tenant farmers or sharecroppers. Conditions varied across the South depending on the local geography and the choice of crops—cotton, rice, or indigo—but, as free laborers, former slaves contracted to work for white planters, sometimes for their former masters and often as entire families. A typical contract lasted for one year, and black families received one-third to one-half share of the harvest plus rations. At first, white planters had tried to organize former slaves to work in gangs on the big plantations and even to live in the old slave quarters, but freedpeople overwhelmingly resisted the centralized plantation system. Setting up their own households in small homes spread out on the plantation, they worked as much as possible without white supervision. Equally important, they now made a clear distinction between the work they did for their landlord and the work they did for their own household and aimed to achieve a suitable balance between them.

Married women often chose to leave fieldwork to men and to devote themselves as much as possible to their own households. As an African American man from Georgia put it in the late 1870s: "The able-bodied men cultivate, the women raise chickens and take in washing; and one way and another they manage to get along." Many women found themselves devoting more time to the household chores because white planters no longer supplied food and clothing, as they did during the days of slavery. Freedpeople had to produce all such items themselves or purchase them from local merchants. Black women did the bulk of this work and often bartered among friends for items they did not make themselves.

As much as possible, African American women avoided working for white employers, especially as servants on plantations situated in the remote countryside, a situation that was too reminiscent of slavery. But because their families needed cash, many former slave women did hire out as servants, cooks, or laundresses, although the majority refused to live in. Moreover, if the mistress overstepped the bounds of their agreement, black women held back their labor, refusing, for example, to cook the dinner if they had been hired specifically to clean the house. Nor would they tolerate the behavior of those white women who were unable to tell the difference between slaves and servants, particularly when it came to meddling in their private affairs. African American women avoided domestic service whenever possible.

Freedpeople, both men and women, took satisfaction in managing their own household economies. Although few prospered, their families grew stronger than slavery had ever allowed.

White Women on the Old Plantation

For their part, elite white women often continued to perform many of the domestic tasks that had been forced upon them during the war, and they were mostly unhappy about it. "[W]e have most of the housework to do all the time," Amanda Worthington wrote in her diary, "and one thing certain, it does not make me like the Yankees any better. . . ." Still, some formerly wealthy mistresses surprised themselves. They expressed relief and even joy in the departure of their "servants" and embraced their new responsibilities. "To be without them [black servants] is a misery," one vexed white employer complained, "and to have them is just as bad."

The most strong-willed women discovered a source of satisfaction in many of the tasks and took pride in the independence they achieved during wartime. Rarely, however, did they relish the arduous work of laundry. Kate Foster complained that handling the washing by herself for six weeks nearly ruined her because she had been "too delicately raised for such hard work." In contrast, the younger women who had come of age during the wartime emergency were more likely to accept general housekeeping as woman's lot in life and ultimately came to regard domesticity—even without servants—as a measure of their womanhood. Cooking, cleaning, and generally caring for husband and children became the principal avocation of many postbellum elite women.

Some elite white women embraced domesticity with a fervor if only to help their husbands to cope with their public defeat and economic reversal. It was as if, one editorial writer suggested, "the mighty oak" had been "hit by lightning" and only the "clinging vine now kept it erect." The men of the former Confederacy, now stripped of the right to hold another human being in bondage, viewed the domestic sphere as the sole remaining source of their power to dominate. These husbands undoubtedly found some satisfaction knowing, as one newspaper writer put it, that "there is still a little world at home of which he is monarch." And their wives often went along. "I console myself with the idea," one Georgian woman wrote, "that I am what every good woman should be—his friend and counselor, never loving him better than when the day seems darkest and the duty hardest." Indeed, such willing subordination to the needs of her husband became the signature of the southern lady.

In contrast, poor white women found far fewer sources of pride or satisfaction in their postwar roles. Many had lost both their husbands and their land and found themselves trapped in a cycle of debt from which they would never escape. Lacking money to buy the necessary supplies, they tried, often in vain, to tame their overgrown fields and to plant for the next harvest. By 1880, one-third of all white southerners were sharecroppers or tenant farmers, and wives found themselves spending their days in the field rather than in the home, hoping to maintain their households amid the grinding poverty of the postwar South.

"Freedom Was Free-er" in Towns and Cities

During the summer and fall of 1865, when freedpeople fled the plantations in huge numbers, a sizable number headed for nearby towns and cities. With the countryside devastated, food and shelter were in short supply. The towns, which housed the local offices of the Freedmen's Bureau, seemed to offer not only the prospect of relief but also employment. However, freedpeople rarely found either. "Sometimes I gits along tolerable," a widow in Atlanta reported, "sometimes right slim; but dat's de way wid everybody;—time is powerful hard right now."

Agents of the Freedmen's Bureau, overwhelmed by refugees, encouraged freedpeople to return to the countryside. Also, the Black Codes adopted by several state governments included harsh vagrancy and curfew laws that virtually forced any African American without a labor contract or a place to live to leave the city or face arrest. Local authorities did whatever they could to discourage former slaves from settling in their towns. They imposed licensing fees and taxes on jobs that freedpeople could seek and directed landlords to rent only to whites. Formed in 1866, the Ku Klux Klan burned down the shantytowns that served as the first black settlements and murdered their residents. Under such duress, freedpeople returned to the countryside in such numbers that by 1870 only one in ten southern African Americans lived in towns with populations greater than twenty-five hundred.

Yet, a sizable minority persevered. In the decade following the outbreak of the Civil War, southern towns and cities experienced a huge rise in the proportion of black residents, as much as 75 percent in some places. The black population of Vicksburg, Mississippi, for example, tripled. By 1870, Atlanta, Richmond, Norfolk, Montgomery, and Raleigh all had become home to nearly an equal number of blacks and whites.

Women played a disproportionate role in the upsurge of the black urban population. A large number were widows or single women with children in tow who had realized that the countryside offered few possibilities for supporting themselves and their families. In towns and cities, they could earn wages primarily as housekeepers and, in smaller numbers, as seamstresses, nurses, cooks, and laundry workers. Especially with the added benefit of a military pension, they could begin to imagine a new life for themselves. In several postbellum southern cities, women came to outnumber men by a ratio of ten to eight; in Atlanta and Wilmington, North Carolina, women outnumbered men by a ratio of four to three.

Although the absolute number of women living in southern towns and cities remained small compared to the countryside, this first sizable generation of urban dwellers set trends that would become apparent decades later in both the North and the South. For example, women headed more households in the city—according to some estimates, as much as twice as many as they did in the countryside. Even when men were present, opportunities for black male employment were so restricted by discriminatory ordinances that few men could earn enough to support a household. Thus, black families became increasingly reliant on the wages women brought in.

Towns and cities, more than the countryside, also offered opportunities for education. Believing that ignorance and bondage went hand in hand, freedwomen urgently desired education for both themselves and their children. When a former slave heard that a school would soon open in her vicinity, she pledged to "work her fingers off" so her children could enroll. With a 90 percent illiteracy rate in 1860, freedpeople pursued the basics of reading and writing, even if it meant taking evening classes after a long day at work.

Many black women eventually served as teachers in these new schools. The Freedmen's Bureau, in cooperation with the American Missionary Association, set up schools as quickly as possible, and by 1869 nearly thirty-three hundred teachers had staffed nearly as many schools and about half were African American, many of them volunteers from the North. A large number were northern white women, commonly known as "Yankee schoolmarms" for their strict disciplinary habits and, too often, their condescending attitude. Whenever possible, freedpeople preferred to support their own schools and hire teachers of their own race. Young women, scarcely out of their teens, sought these positions as soon as they learned how to read and write. To train these teachers, four universities were established: Howard University in Washington, D.C.; Hampton Institute in Hampton, Virginia; Morehouse College in Atlanta, Georgia; and Fisk University in Nashville, Tennessee.

The streets of the city also afforded young women, black and white, opportunities for new pastimes. Young white women indulged themselves in rounds of dances and seemingly endless flirtations with young men. Young black women also tasted the enjoyments of urban life, spending a considerable portion of their wages in defining their

The Freedmen's Bureau opened more than one thousand schools during the Reconstruction Era. This engraving, which appeared in Frank Leslie's Illustrated Newspaper *in September 1866, shows a sewing class at the industrial school in Richmond, Virginia.*

womanhood through hair style, clothing, and jewelry. White southerners commented profusely on freedwomen's fashion, in particular their preference for bright fabrics, colored ribbons, and large earrings, as well as what they perceived as infringements on white women's own sense of style. Black women were "putting on airs," they complained, by presuming the right to wear veils and carry parasols and handkerchiefs. Moreover, such outrageous dress, in their perspective, was often accompanied by "impudent" behavior. One white woman described freedpeople as "very insolent in the streets," refusing to step aside for her or lowering their eyes when passing, and even daring to make such rude remarks as "'look at dat rebel.'"

Although black women rarely rose out of poverty in towns or cities, they often found the pleasure of camaraderie and friendship with other African Americans. The majority of the eighty thousand black occupation troops were stationed in towns and cities, thus increasing a woman's chances of finding a mate. Also, the city became the site of a growing black community and its institutions. Schools, churches, benevolent societies, and political groups all sprang up and gave women as well as men additional purposes for congregating with other members of their race.

WOMAN'S RIGHTS REEMERGE

Antebellum woman's rights activists had viewed the right to vote as only one of many demands. Property rights; educational opportunities; equal wages for equal work; and changes in the laws governing marriage, divorce, and child custody had all figured prominently in their agitation. The Civil War shattered this constellation and, at the same time, linked the prospects for a democratic nation to broader participation in the political process. "Now in the reconstruction is the opportunity, perhaps for the century," Elizabeth Cady Stanton announced, "to base our government on the broad principle of equal rights to all." As national attention turned toward assuring freedmen of their rights as citizens, woman's rights activists began to reconsider women's changing status within the institutions of marriage and family and to demand their rights as citizens, foremost the right to vote.

"The Negro's Hour"

Woman's rights activists emerged from the Civil War ready for action. Having set aside their own demands for the duration of the conflict, they had successfully enlisted women to support the Union cause, including the Thirteenth Amendment. Republican congressmen and even Union army officers praised the Woman's National Loyal League for its leadership in the campaign that helped to abolish slavery forever. Now, with the war over and the WNLL disbanded, woman's rights activists anticipated more than rhetorical bouquets: they wanted the nation to acknowledge women's contribution to the war by granting them the full rights of citizenship, foremost the right to vote.

Their longtime abolitionist allies disagreed. Taking advantage of their new prominence in government circles, they targeted black manhood suffrage as a priority and, furthermore, warned that linking woman suffrage to their proposed legislation would doom the black man's chances. As early as December 1865, Elizabeth Cady Stanton commented with profound displeasure that many abolitionists were already designating this as **"the Negro's hour."**

Prospects for women's voting rights grew dimmer when in June 1866 Congress passed the Fourteenth Amendment, which conferred national citizenship on all persons born or naturalized in the United States and at the same time, in a section of the bill dealing with state representation, introduced the word "male" into the Constitution. Many woman's rights advocates who in principle stood for universal suffrage endorsed the Fourteenth Amendment as a matter of expediency. Stanton, however, refused to compromise and taunted her opponents: "Do you believe the African race is composed entirely of males?"

Stanton distanced herself even farther from her longtime allies during the summer of 1866 when she and Susan B. Anthony intervened in a campaign against a state referendum in Kansas that would restrict the right to vote to white males. In touring the state, they shared the platform with George Francis Train, a virulent racist who implored Kansas voters to place the "Woman first, and the Negro last." They also accepted Train's financial backing in order to publish a new weekly magazine, *The Revolution*, which debuted in January 1868. Meanwhile, the Kansas campaign ended in defeat, and Stanton and Anthony paid dearly for their opportunism by losing many of their friends.

Finally, during the winter of 1869, the rift widened nearly to the breaking point. The Fifteenth Amendment to the Constitution, which aimed to guarantee the right to vote without regard to "race, color, or previous condition of servitude," contained,

"the Negro's hour"
Phrase used to describe the subordination of woman's rights to the campaign to advance the political rights of African American men.

OVERVIEW

Amendments to the Constitution and Federal Legislation during Reconstruction, 1865–1875

Thirteenth Amendment	*Passed by Congress January 1865; ratified December 1865* Prohibited slavery in the United States
Freedmen's Bureau Act	*Passed by Congress March 1865* Established the Bureau of Refugees, Freedmen, and Abandoned Land within the Department of War to provide social services such as food, housing, education, and employment to former slaves making the transition to freedom. Disbanded in December 1868.
Civil Rights Act of 1866	*Passed by Congress March 1866; presidential veto overrode April 1866* In reaction to the Black Codes, the act defined rights of national citizenship for all persons born or naturalized in the United States and granted African American citizens equal rights to make contracts, own property, and marry.
Fourteenth Amendment	*Passed by Congress June 1866; ratified July 1868* Strengthened the Civil Rights Act by prohibiting states from violating the rights of their citizens Reduced state representation in Congress proportionally for any state disfranchising male citizens Denied former Confederates the right to hold state or national office Repudiated Confederate debt
Fifteenth Amendment	*Passed by Congress February 1869; ratified March 1870* Prohibited denial of suffrage because of race, color, or previous condition of servitude
The Civil Rights Act of 1871	*Passed by Congress April 1871* Known as the Ku Klux Klan Act, the act was enacted to enforce the Fourteenth Amendment, particularly to protect African American citizens from intimidation by illegal action, such as by the KKK, in cases where states could not, or would not, secure their safety or protect their rights.
The Civil Rights Act of 1875	*Passed by Congress February 1875* Entitled all the "full and equal enjoyment" of "public accommodations," such as hotels, restaurants, transportation, and amusements The Act was generally unenforced and was declared unconstitutional by the Supreme Court in 1883.

The center image of this lithograph depicts the grand parade held in Baltimore, Maryland, in 1870, to celebrate the passage of the amendment granting African American men the right to vote. The surrounding images depict prominent abolitionists, African Americans, and ordinary black citizens partaking in the economic and social life of the nation.

in Stanton's opinion, a glaring omission, the word "sex." The passage of this amendment, she insisted, would ensure the establishment of an "aristocracy of sex on this continent." Anthony shared Stanton's opinion, pledging: "I will cut off this right arm of mine before I will work for or demand the ballot for the negro and not the woman." However, a sizable contingent of woman's rights activists, loyal to their abolitionist heritage, threw their support behind the Fifteenth Amendment. Hoping to bridge the differences, Stanton and Anthony proposed a Sixteenth Amendment to the Constitution that would secure the vote specifically for women.

Several of Stanton's erstwhile allies called her up short because she had, in the words of Stephen Foster, "ridiculed the Negro and pronounced the 15th Amendment infamous." The esteemed black abolitionist and longtime supporter of woman's rights, Frederick Douglass, also criticized Stanton for her use of derogatory epithets against black men, referring explicitly to her common practice of referring to the freedman as "Sambo." Douglass expressed his regret that women had not been included in the Fifteenth Amendment but offered an impassioned plea for "The Negro's hour": "When women, because they are women, are hunted down through the cities of New York and New Orleans; when they are dragged from their houses and hung upon lamp-posts; when their children are torn from their arms, and their brains dashed out upon the pavement; . . . then they will have an urgency to obtain the ballot equal to our own."

A person from the audience asked if what he said was not true for black women. "Yes, yes, yes," Douglass responded, "but not because she is a woman, but because she is black." By May 1869, the woman's rights movement had divided into two camps.

Organizing for Woman Suffrage

With the fault line clear, the two factions proceeded to organize into rival associations. The **National Woman Suffrage Association (NWSA)**, led by Stanton and Anthony and headquartered in New York City, introduced itself by speaking out against the Fifteenth Amendment and, equally important, by pushing a sixteenth amendment that would guarantee women the right to vote. This strategy—campaigning for a federal amendment—would remain its signature. But despite its focus on the ballot, the NWSA did not limit its agitation to political rights. The association energetically revived topics that had been the staples of the antebellum woman's rights conventions, most prominently marriage and divorce reform, education, and equal wages for work.

The **American Woman Suffrage Association (AWSA)**, which viewed NWSA as little more than a small clique, formed in Cleveland in November 1869. Its leaders, including Lucy Stone and Henry Blackwell, had laid the foundation a year earlier when they formed a regional network of woman suffrage societies, the New England Woman Suffrage Association. Headquartered in Boston, the AWSA pledged to work for the ratification of the Fifteenth Amendment. As Julia Ward Howe stated simply: "I am willing that the negro shall get [the ballot] before me."

On the question of strategy, the AWSA chose to work at the local level, primarily by initiating referenda to remove the word "male" from articles covering voting rights in state constitutions and also by supporting such "limited" voting rights as the right to participate in school board elections. The AWSA also published its own paper, the *Woman's Journal*, "Devoted to the Interests of Woman, to her Education, Industrial, Legal and Political Equality and especially her right to Suffrage." With solid financial backing, the weekly paper championed the campaign for woman suffrage to its conclusion in 1920.

What was striking about the AWSA was its success in attracting recent converts to the suffrage cause, including men as well as women and a large number of Midwesterners. Like the NWSA, the AWSA rarely reached beyond the circles of the middle class, but it did manage to recruit a coterie of women who had achieved prominence during the Civil War. The list was impressive, headed by Julia Ward Howe, Louisa May Alcott, Mary Livermore, and other longtime abolitionists such as Abby Kelley Foster, Frances Dana Gage, and Lydia Maria Child. A larger number of prominent African American suffragists, such as Charlotte Forten and Frances Ellen Watkins Harper, chose to affiliate with the AWSA.

The Notorious Victoria C. Woodhull

On March 30, 1870, President Ulysses S. Grant announced the adoption of the Fifteenth Amendment and, unwittingly, opened yet another chapter in the woman suffrage saga. Acting alone, Victoria C. Woodhull decided to test the limits of the new amendments. In December, she presented a memorial to Congress in the form of an elegant argument that the Fourteenth and Fifteenth amendments, by guaranteeing civil

National Woman Suffrage Association (NWSA) Formed in 1869 in New York City and led by Elizabeth Cady Stanton and Susan B. Anthony to advance a strategy to introduce a federal amendment to grant women the right to vote.

American Woman Suffrage Association (AWSA) Formed in 1869 in Cleveland and led by Lucy Stone and Henry Blackwell to work for woman suffrage at all levels.

WOMEN'S VOICES

LECTURING ON WOMAN'S RIGHTS

After the Civil War, Elizabeth Cady Stanton embarked on a grand lecture tour under the sponsorship of the Lyceum Bureau. She spoke on behalf of woman's rights, providing herself with a source of income and her audiences with a strong political message. She spoke frequently on woman suffrage and also managed, when she could, to engage women alone in conversations concerning family limitation and reproductive health. Mostly she advocated higher education for women.

In 1869 I gave my name, for the first time, to the New York [Lyceum] Bureau, and on November 14 began the long, weary pilgrimages from Maine to Texas, that lasted twelve years; speaking steadily for eight months—from October to June—every season. That was the heyday of the lecturing period, when a long list of bright men and women were constantly on the wing. Anna Dickinson, Olive Logan, Kate Field—later, Mrs. Livermore and Mrs. Howe, Alcott, Phillips, Douglass, Tilton, Curtis, Beecher . . .; these and many others were stars of the lecture platform.

Some of us occasionally managed to spend Sunday together, at a good hotel in some city, to rest and feast and talk over our joys and sorrows, the long journeys, the hard fare in the country hotels, the rainy nights when committees felt blue and tried to cut down our fees; the overheated, badly ventilated cares; the halls, sometimes too warm, sometimes too cold; babies crying in our audiences; the rain pattering on the roof overhead or leaking on the platform—these were common experiences. In the West, women with babies uniformly occupied the front seats so that the little ones, not understanding what you said, might be amused with your gestures and changing facial expression. . . . It was the testimony of all the bureaus that the women could endure more fatigue and were more conscientious than the men in filling their appointments.

The pleasant feature of these trips was the great educational work accomplished for the people through their listening to lectures on all the vital questions of the hour. Wherever any of us chanced to be on Sunday, we preached in some church; and wherever I had a spare afternoon, I talked to women alone, on marriage, maternity, and the laws of life and health. We made many most charming acquaintances, too, scattered all over our Western World, and saw how comfortable and happy sensible people could be, living in most straitened circumstances, with none of the luxuries of life....

While in Ann Arbor I gave my lecture on "Our Girls" in the new Methodist church—a large building well lighted, and filled with a brilliant audience. The students, in large numbers, were there, and strengthened the threads of my discourse with frequent and generous applause; especially when I urged on the Regents of the University the duty of opening its doors to the daughters of the state. There were several splendid girls in Michigan, at that time, preparing themselves for admission to the law department. Some said the chief difficulty in the way of the girls being admitted to the university was the want of room. That could have been easily obviated by telling the young men from abroad to betake themselves to the colleges in their respective states, that Michigan might educate her daughters. As the women owned a good share of the property of the state, and had been heavily taxed to build and endow that institution, it was but fair that they should share in its advantages. . . .

Mt. Vernon was distinguished for a very flourishing Methodist college, open to boys and girls alike. The president and his wife were liberal and progressive people. I dined with them in their home, and met some young ladies from Massachusetts, who were teachers in the institution. All who gathered round the social board on that occasion were of one mind on the woman question. I gave "Our Girls" in the Methodist church, and took the opportunity to compliment them for taking the word "obey" out of their marriage ceremony. I heard the most encouraging reports of the experiment of educating the sexes together. It was the rule in all the Methodist institutions in Iowa, and I found that the young gentlemen fully approved of it.

Source: Elizabeth Cady Stanton, As Revealed in Her Letters, Diary, and Reminiscences, Vol. I, edited by Theodore Stanton and Harriot Stanton Blatch (New York: Harper & Brothers, 1922), 218–236.

Questions

1. Judging from Stanton's report, what was it like to campaign for woman suffrage in the era after the Civil War?

2. Why did people attend Stanton's lectures?

and political rights to all citizens, had in effect enfranchised women. The Reconstruction amendments, she concluded, had rendered "void and of no effect" all previously enacted state laws prohibiting woman suffrage. Woodhull advised Congress to devise the "necessary and proper" legislation so that all citizens "without regard to sex" could exercise their right to vote. A month later, she appeared before the House Judiciary Committee, the first woman to do so, and restated her argument at greater length.

Victoria Woodhull appeared before the House Judiciary Committee in January, 1871 to argue for woman suffrage. She contended that because the Fifteenth Amendment guarantees the right to vote to all citizens "women are the equals of men before the law, and are equal in all their rights," including suffrage.

Woman suffrage leaders were both taken off guard by Woodhull's actions and very curious about this newcomer to the cause. Although born into humble circumstances, the thirty-three-year-old Woodhull and her younger sister Tennessee had managed to befriend the railway capitalist Cornelius Vanderbilt and, with his assistance, establish their own brokerage firm on Wall Street. The two sisters also found sufficient financial backing to put out a newspaper, *Woodhull & Claflin's Weekly*, which ranged widely and boldly across the spectrum of reform. Stanton and Anthony hoped to make the most of Woodhull's celebrity and invited her to speak at the NWSA's convention in May 1871.

Woodhull did indeed put woman suffrage in the spotlight. At the meeting, she went so far as to advise voteless women to break away from the Union and form their own government. "We mean treason! We mean secession, and on a thousand times greater scale than that of the South!" she warned. "We are plotting Revolution! We will overthrow this bogus republic and plant a government of righteousness in its stead."

But Woodhull gained even more attention as an unrelenting critic of the institution of marriage. She soon delivered a yet more infamous speech. Speaking in New York to a crowd of three thousand, she announced: "Yes, I am a Free Lover. I have an inalienable, constitutional and natural right to love whom I may, to love as long or as short a period as I can; to change that love every day if I please, and with that right neither you nor any law you can frame have any right to interfere." Rather than dissociating themselves from such flamboyant rhetoric and radical ideas, Stanton and Anthony saw in Woodhull an opportunity to broaden the discussion of woman's rights well beyond suffrage.

Woodhull, however, had not yet revealed all her cards. She decided to run for president of the United States, and in May 1872 she transformed *Woodhull & Claflin's Weekly* into a publicity sheet for her campaign. The mainstream news media began to caricature Woodhull and her sister as the "Famous Family of Free Lovers."

Woodhull retaliated by making an object lesson of Henry Ward Beecher, a pastor of a wealthy congregation, a presumed pillar of society, and a former AWSA president. *Woodhull & Claflin's Weekly* reported that Beecher was involved in an illicit sexual relationship with one of his parishioners, Elizabeth Tilton, a married woman and mother of four, and went on to condemn the popular preacher not for his actions but for hypocritically shrouding his affair in secrecy. Woodhull and her sister were then arrested under the provisions of the newly enacted federal antiobscenity legislation, the **Comstock Act**, which carried the name of its proponent, Anthony Comstock. The two sisters spent four weeks in jail for using the U.S. Postal Service to send "obscene" literature.

Woodhull's persistent attack on the institution of marriage reopened old wounds among suffragists. At the last convention before the Civil War, in 1860, the fledgling woman's rights movement nearly split apart when the discussions on marriage went, in the opinion of some, too far (see chapter 8). The debate had become so heated that the participants agreed to hold to a "narrow platform" that excluded marriage as a subject for discussion, and the Civil War moratorium kept the opponents at bay.

Now, as questions of citizenship became more pressing, Woodhull took the lead in reviving the discussion of marriage as, in her words, an "*insidious* form of slavery." Stanton shocked many of her coworkers when she endorsed Woodhull's proposition, similarly describing marriage as an institution that designated "one to command and one to obey." She reaffirmed what she had the prescience to write to Anthony in 1853: "This whole question of woman's rights turns on the pivot of the marriage relation."

Woodhull, however, proved to be an unreliable ally. In the wake of the **Beecher-Tilton scandal**, her presidential candidacy collapsed. Several years later,

Comstock Act The 1873 law that forbade the use of the U.S. Postal Service to mail "obscene" materials, which included contraceptive information and devices.

Beecher-Tilton scandal The furor created by the revelation of the Rev. Henry Ward Beecher's affair with Elizabeth Tilton, one of his parishioners.

she and her sister headed to England, where they both married into wealthy families.

Woodhull's attack on the institution of marriage widened the divide between the rival suffragists. By siding with the mercurial Woodhull, the NWSA suffered a loss of credibility, and a disheartened Stanton soon withdrew from the organization. In contrast, the AWSA remained relatively unscathed. The association had treated Woodhull as they had George Francis Train: as a political oddity who mirrored the opportunism of the NWSA leaders. The AWSA gained status as the premier suffrage organization and won additional support from the Republican Party, which included a mildly prosuffrage plank in its platform of 1872.

The New Departure

Despite her misadventures, Victoria Woodhull did help to shape a strategy that she herself termed "a new direction" for the woman suffrage movement. She claimed that the Reconstruction amendments ensured the right to vote to *all* citizens. She now invited women to act on their citizenship and join her in testing the provisions in practice.

In November 1871, Woodhull headed a contingent of women who went to the polls and attempted to cast their ballots. They were turned away but nevertheless encouraged other women to keep the pressure on. Mary Ann Shadd Cary, the first woman to study law at the newly opened Howard University Law School, and sixty-three other women tried to register to vote in Washington, D.C. Like Woodhull, Cary made her case before the House Judiciary Committee in 1872, arguing that black women like herself required the same degree of protection that black men enjoyed from the provisions of the Reconstruction amendments. At the same time, Sojourner Truth was turned away from the polling booth in Battle Creek, Michigan. More celebrated was the case of Susan B. Anthony. Anthony had hoped that if she were turned away from the polls she would be in a position to carry a civil suit all the way to the Supreme Court. Instead, she was allowed to vote and then arrested and later convicted of violating a federal law. At her highly publicized trial, the presiding judge fined her one hundred dollars, refusing a jail sentence to prevent her from appealing his decision and bringing yet more attention to her cause.

Where Anthony failed, Virginia L. Minor succeeded. She, too, decided to test the provisions of the Fourteenth Amendment, reasoning that "the power to regulate is one thing, the power to prevent is an entirely different thing." When the St. Louis registrar, Reese Happersett, refused to let her register to vote, she and her husband Francis Minor—married women could not initiate legal action on their own—brought suit against him for abridging her rights as a citizen. In 1874 the U.S. Supreme Court unanimously ruled against her appeal for protection, declaring that the Constitution does not define the privileges of citizenship and, therefore, that individual states enjoy the right to restrict voting rights to male citizens. In effect, the **Minor v. Happersett** decision established that citizenship and the right to vote were not synonymous and thereby put to rest all cases for woman suffrage made in the name of the Reconstruction amendments.

In the wake of these cases, the NWSA returned to its former strategy, campaigning for a sixteenth amendment. In January 1878, the **"Susan B. Anthony" amendment** was introduced into Congress. It read: "The right of citizens of the United States to vote

Born to a prominent free black and abolitionist family, Mary Ann Shadd Cary (1823–1893) became an activist for woman suffrage during the Reconstruction Era. She is often described as the first black woman lawyer in the United States and the first black woman to vote in a national election.

Minor v. Happersett U.S. Supreme Court ruling in 1784 that allowed states to restrict the right to vote to male citizens.

Susan B. Anthony amendment Introduced in January 1886, the amendment specifies that the right to vote shall not be "denied or abridged" on account of sex.

In the aftermath of Susan B. Anthony's arrest for voting in the 1872, the New York Daily Graphic *published this caricature of "The Woman Who Dared." The accompanying text nevertheless noted the significance of her bold activism: "Whenever women rule the hour, they must acknowledge the person of Miss Anthony, the pioneer who first pursued the way they sought."*

family wage The idea that a man should earn sufficient wages to provide the sole support of his family.

shall not be denied or abridged by the United States or by any State on account of sex," which was the wording adopted in the Nineteenth Amendment (1920). The AWSA meanwhile supported the petition for the new amendment and simultaneously restated its preference to appeal first to state legislatures to extend voting rights to women.

In the short run, neither the AWSA nor the NWSA made much headway. When the Sixteenth Amendment finally reached the Senate floor in 1886, only forty of seventy-six senators bothered to vote, and those who did voted it down, thirty-four to six. Before 1890, only eight states held referenda on woman suffrage, and all went down in defeat. The only victories suffragists could tally were in the nineteen states that granted women the right to vote in local school board elections and, in a few locations, municipal elections.

WOMAN'S RIGHT TO LABOR

In 1860, Caroline Healey Dall issued a critique of marriage from yet another direction. The prominent abolitionist and woman's rights advocate called into question the concept of the **family wage**, the idea that honored the man as a family's sole breadwinner. Under the provocative title *Woman's Right to Labor*, Dall published a series of lectures that amply demonstrated that more women—including married women—were supporting themselves than most people cared to admit. "The old idea, that all men support all women" was, she insisted, "an absurd fiction." Dall and many other woman's rights advocates rallied under the catchphrase of "equal wages for equal work" and sought to realize this goal both for themselves as salaried professional workers and for those women who could find only menial jobs in the growing postwar marketplace.

Women's Clubs

With antislavery agitation in the past, many activists shifted their attention to the difficulties women endured in trying to support themselves and their families. The Civil War, they reported, had whetted their appetites for useful endeavors outside the home, and they organized clubs and various societies specifically to sustain the activist life that had filled the years of the conflict. Now, in middle age, they also sought the companionship of other women as well as the means to advance themselves professionally. This idea was for its time radical enough to generate mounds of complaints and ridicule. "Better women should organize to distribute handkerchiefs to the natives of Timbuctoo," one exasperated woman complained, "than to gather together for their own self-improvement and pleasure."

In 1868, the first women's clubs formed in New York and Boston and soon served as beacons for similar clubs in large cities such as Chicago and most small towns. The

Women's Organizations Formed 1868–1876

1868	New England Women's Club	Organized to promote self-improvement and to reform philanthropic endeavors of women activists in the Boston area
	Sorosis	Organized for women's self-improvement at the same time as the NEWC by mostly professional women in New York City
	Working Women's Association	Organized in New York City and aided by Elizabeth Cady Stanton and Susan B. Anthony to link labor and suffrage
1869	Troy Collar Laundry Union	Short-lived union of women laundresses led by Kate Mullaney in up-state New York
	National Woman Suffrage Association	Formed to promote woman suffrage and led by Elizabeth Cady Stanton and Susan B. Anthony, with headquarters in New York City
	American Woman Suffrage Association	Formed to promote woman suffrage and led by Julia Ward Howe, Lucy Stone, and Josephine Ruffin with headquarters in Boston
	Working Women's League	Organized in Boston with assistance of suffragists
	Daughters of St. Crispin	Organized as an international union of mainly women shoeworkers, centered in Massachusetts
1873	Association for the Advancement of Women	Organized by Sorosis members as a series of congresses to showcase women's achievements
	Chicago Fortnightly	Formed by a group of women for the purpose of "intellectual and social culture"
1874	National Woman's Christian Temperance Union	Growing out of the Woman's Crusade, founded in Cleveland to organize women's protest against the sale and consumption of alcohol
1876	Chicago Woman's Club	Organized to provide members with "mutual sympathy and counsel" and to assist them in the work of social reform

New England Women's Club (NEWC), headquartered in Boston, and Sorosis of New York gathered seasoned activists and aspiring professional women and developed a philosophy and program for what would become, twenty years later, a mass movement.

Although the constitutions of the first two clubs specified companionship as their primary purpose, the founders all vowed to campaign for woman's right to labor. As the first president of Sorosis explained, the purpose of the club was "to open out new avenues of employment for women, to make them less dependent and less burdensome, to lift women out of unwomanly self-distrust, disqualifying diffidence, into womanly self-respect and self-knowledge." The right to vote was, for the

The dress reform movement revived in the 1870s, putting aside a critique of fashion for an emphasis on health and hygiene. Lecturers spoke mainly about the physical limitations created by restrictive undergarments, such as corsets and cumbersome petticoats, and used dolls to demonstrate simpler fashions.

Association for the Advancement of Women (AAW) Formed in October 1873 to promote the formation of women's clubs and to showcase women's accomplishments.

majority, a secondary concern compared to the necessity to achieve equality in the marketplace.

A sizable portion of the women who formed these clubs were white and middle class, advanced in age, and married or widowed. They were also aspiring professionals. The founder of Sorosis, for example, was Jane Cunningham Croly, a pioneering journalist who wrote the first syndicated column by a woman under the name "Jennie June." The roster of Sorosis, which by its first year listed more than eighty names, included artists, writers, editors, teachers, lecturers, philanthropists, and physicians. Some of these women were working outside the home by necessity, others by choice. They met biweekly to discuss such questions as: "In which profession can a woman do the most good: that of the ministry, the law, pedagogy, or medicine?"

The Civil War had prepared many of these women for work outside the home. Such was the case with Julia Ward Howe, the NEWC president from 1871 until her death in 1910. Howe had served as a volunteer to the U.S. Sanitary Commission despite her husband's strenuous objections to her extradomestic activities. When Samuel Gridley Howe died in the mid-1870s, he bequeathed his sizable fortune to their daughters, leaving his financially strapped widow with a compelling reason to work outside the home. With the encouragement of the NEWC members, Julia Ward Howe supported herself through her writing and public speaking while leading the postbellum suffrage and peace movements.

The NEWC developed a series of programs to help young women work outside the home. Club members supported the Girls' Latin School to prepare female students for college and founded a small horticultural school to train women for vocational work.

To promote the formation of women's clubs in other localities, Sorosis and the NEWC founded the **Association for the Advancement of Women (AAW)** in October 1873. The AAW held an annual "congress" in a different city each year with programs adapted from the format of women's club meetings. Leading lights of the movement presented papers on a vast array of topics, including woman's right to the ballot. These programs were so successful that it was not unknown for local schools to close so that teachers and students could attend the sessions and hear the papers.

The membership of the AAW, never more than five hundred in its twenty-five-year history, constituted a national network of the most prominent and steadfast "lady agitators," as the mainstream press described them—or, according to its own assessment, "The First Who's Who of Women." Ambitious career women and reformers such as Mary Livermore, Catharine Beecher, Harriet Beecher Stowe, Elizabeth Cady Stanton, Emily Blackwell, Clara Barton, and Elizabeth Stuart Phelps all used its platform to disseminate their ideas. President Julia Ward Howe expressed their collective aspirations. "The cruel kindness of the old doctrine that women should be worked for,

WOMEN'S LIVES

MYRA COLBY BRADWELL

On August 2, 1869, having passed the bar exam with honors, Myra Colby Bradwell applied to practice law in the state of Illinois and included with her application a brief summarizing her one concern: "The only question involved in this case is—Does being a woman disqualify [me] under the law of Illinois from receiving a license to practice law?"

The Illinois Supreme Court rejected Bradwell's petition but not on the grounds that she had anticipated. The court decided that the fact of her womanhood alone did not make her unsuited for the practice of law. Rather, as the communication from the court read, it was "the DISABILITY IMPOSED BY YOUR MARRIED CONDITION." Bradwell, married since 1852 and the mother of four children, could neither retain her earnings in her own name nor enter into contracts. Even if admitted to the bar, she could not, in effect, practice law.

In her own mind, marriage had not deterred her but had actually stimulated her interest in the law. As a young wife, Myra had been determined to "work side by side and think side by side" her husband, James, who was then an ambitious young law student. By 1869, when she submitted her application to the Illinois bar, Bradwell was thirty-eight years old and possessed a commanding knowledge of the law, so much so that she published and edited the *Chicago Legal News*, one of the most powerful and respected legal journals in the nation.

Bradwell decided to pursue her case, characterizing the court's negative decision as "a blow at the rights of every married woman in the great State of Illinois who is dependent on her labor for support." Resolute, she retained a sharp constitutional lawyer to take her case to the U.S. Supreme Court.

In *Bradwell v. Illinois*, Bradwell's lawyer argued that under the terms of the Fourteenth Amendment all employments were open to all citizens, regardless of race, sex, or marital status. In their ruling of April 15, 1873, the chief justices did not concur. They explained: "[C]ivil law, as well as nature herself, has always recognized a wide difference in the respective spheres and destinies of man and woman. Man is, or should be, woman's protector and defender. The natural and proper timidity and delicacy which belongs to the female sex evidently unfits it for many of the occupations of civil life. . . . The paramount destiny and mission of woman are to fulfill the noble and benign offices of wife and mother. *This is the law of the Creator*." The U.S. Supreme Court, in essence, told Myra Bradwell to go home.

Bradwell did not retreat. She continued to press for greater civil rights for married women. In 1880, the Illinois Bar Association invited her to become a member. Finally, in 1890, the Illinois Supreme Court granted Bradwell a license to practice law based on her original application filed in 1869. A few months before she died of cancer, she cast her only ballot, in the elections for the Chicago school board. ∎

and should not work, that their influence should be felt, but not recognized, that they should hear and see but neither appear nor speak," she predicted, will soon be exposed as a sham and pummeled into retreat.

Associations for Working Women

In August 1866, delegates representing labor unions from thirteen states met to create the first national labor federation in the United States, the National Labor Union (NLU). Although no women were among the delegates, the new president, William Sylvis, asked the assembly to pledge to support the "daughters of toil in this land." Woman's rights advocates took heart in Sylvis's words and expected NLU members not only to welcome wage-earning women to their ranks but also to reciprocate by endorsing woman suffrage. As one enthusiast explained, woman is the "NATURAL ALLY of the laborer, because she was the worst paid, and most degraded laborer of all." However, the majority of male trade unionists shared little of Sylvis's enthusiasm for organizing women wage earners and preferred to keep their distance from controversies generated by women's claim to the ballot.

Undaunted, Stanton and Anthony invited a group of women typesetters to the office of the *Revolution* to organize an association "to elevate women and raise the value of their labor." Stanton proposed naming the new organization the "Working Women's Suffrage Association," but one of the typesetters protested on the grounds that the word *suffrage* would couple the organization with the idea of women "with short hair and bloomers and other vagaries." Stanton and Anthony gave in, and the

This wood engraving, published in 1875, depicts women working under male supervision in the sewing room of A.T. Stewart's, one of the first department stores in New York City.

Working Women's Association formed in 1868 with the goal of improving the condition of wage-earning women.

The alliance proved short-lived. A few months later, when an all-male typographical union called a strike in the New York printing industry, the Women's Typographical Union chose to honor it. In contrast, Anthony saw the strike as an opportunity for women to replace the male strikers and get hands-on experience in the trade. The male strikers condemned Anthony's maneuver, and the members of the Women's Typographical Union, refusing to become "scabs," pulled out of the Working Women's Association. In the aftermath of this debacle, Anthony retreated, urging working women to devote themselves to campaigning for suffrage. "[T]he one and only question in our catechism," she concluded, "is, Do you believe women should vote?"

Like Stanton and Anthony, clubwomen did not wish to restrict their activism to programs that benefited only middle-class women like themselves. For this reason, during their first year, both Sorosis and the New England Women's Club set up committees to advance the cause of working women, first by investigating working conditions in their respective cities. The NEWC's Committee on Work concluded their survey by calling for the creation of day nurseries for working mothers and temporary lodgings for women who came to the city to search for jobs.

Wage-earning women often welcomed such support from middle-class allies but more readily acknowledged that class differences could not be easily overcome. For their part, they tended to guard their independence. In April 1869, for example, several NEWC members attended the founding meeting of the Boston Working Women's League, and Julia Ward Howe addressed the assembly. They all agreed that the idea that "the only true sphere of woman is at the head of a household" was a "silly flippancy," especially when half of all women have no homes. Nevertheless, the short-lived Working Women's League did not seek an alliance with its middle-class peers and instead restricted membership to "any working-woman of Boston, dependent upon the daily labor of her own hands for her daily bread."

Trade Unions

During the Civil War, to protest paltry wages and harsh working conditions, wage-earning women had organized several trade unions in the laundry and needle trades. Although most of these small unions dissolved after the war ended, prospects appeared to brighten with the appointment of Kate Mullaney as assistant secretary of the new **National Labor Union**.

Mullaney, who had been the chief breadwinner in her immigrant family since her teens, took a major step in bringing women into the burgeoning trade union movement. In May 1869, she led a strike of the mainly Irish workers who washed, starched, and ironed the detachable collars for the men's shirts manufactured in the "Collar City" of Troy, New York. The local male unionists supported the striking women, but the business community set out to crush the union. Mullaney responded by enlarging her base of support, touring the state to raise funds and to stage mass rallies. At one point, she traveled to New York City and appealed to the members of the Working Women's Association to support their sister workers in Troy. When she netted a meager thirty dollars, Mullaney concluded that the organization sponsored by Stanton and Anthony was not a "real" association of working women. After the strike petered out,

National Labor Union A federation of trade assemblies formed in 1866 that supported woman's right to labor.

WOMEN'S LIVES

JENNIE COLLINS

Born into humble conditions in Amoskeag, New Hampshire, Jennie Collins spent a lifetime exploring the many dimensions of women's work and, in her later years, trying to forge an alliance between middle-class activists and hard-pressed wage earners. She began her journey at age fourteen, working first as a textile mill operative in the mills of Lawrence and Lowell, Massachusetts. Like many other young women, she sought greater opportunities in the big city and moved to Boston in the 1840s. There she found work as a domestic servant and, a little later, as a seamstress. The local abolitionist movement of the 1850s drew her in, and the ferment surrounding the Civil War swept her away. She organized the seamstresses in her shop to work after hours to make supplies for soldiers and helped to raise money to fund the new hospitals for the returning injured. By the end of the war, she had become a determined activist and, like others in her milieu, turned her attention from chattel slavery to wage slavery. In 1869, Collins organized one of the nine short-lived workingwomen's associations that sprang up in the Boston area and lectured to groups of workingwomen, including the Daughters of St. Crispin, throughout the states of Massachusetts and New Hampshire.

In October 1870, Collins opened Boffin's Bower as a downtown headquarters for Boston's workingwomen. The peculiar name of the establishment came from Charles Dickens's novel *Our Mutual Friend*, but the inspiration, according to Collins, came from workingwomen themselves. Over the years, she had attended many of their meetings and had heard workingwomen express their desire for self-improvement. They longed to establish reading rooms and even debating clubs, she recounted. Boffin's Bower would do just that, "collect in the warm, well-lighted bower all the over-taxed, weary working girls, and with entertainments of music, lectures, and readings . . . advance them morally and intellectually by giving them opportunities for improvement."

To fund her model enterprise, Collins sought assistance from prominent women reformers. Mary Livermore, for example, proved so dedicated to her effort that the prominent suffragist's portrait hung on the parlor wall. With Livermore's help, occasional contributions from the New England Women's Club, and publicity from the *Woman's Journal*, Collins offered a range of programs. She kept a guest chamber for women coming to the city in search of work, ran a job registry and a workroom to train women for the dressmaking and tailoring trades, and dispensed free meals during the depressions and hard winter months. In the aftermath of the great fire of 1872, which swept through Boston's commercial district, she offered food and shelter to women who lost their jobs.

Jennie Collins ran Boffin's Bower for seventeen years, not to offer charity, she believed, but to help workingwomen help themselves. "I have seen women exult in triumphs in drama, literature, music, on the rostrum, and in the drawing-room," she wrote, "but—NEVER MORE PROUDLY THAN IN THE WORKSHOP OR THE HOUSEHOLD." Collins never waivered in her dedication to working-class women and in her respect for their labors. ∎

she switched tactics and invited the striking workers to join her in establishing a laundry workers' cooperative.

Women shoeworkers embarked on a similar uphill struggle. In Lynn, Massachusetts, the Knights of St. Crispin, the nation's largest trade union, encouraged the organization of an all-women's branch; and by 1869, sister locals of the **Daughters of St. Crispin** had formed in ten other cities. Although the shoe-producing state of Massachusetts enjoyed the largest membership, nine states in the East, Midwest, and West, including California, and Canada helped to make the Daughters of St. Crispin the first international trade union of women. The union resolved to demand equal pay for equal work and warned the factory owners that "American Ladies Will Not Be Slaves."

By 1872, all the women's unions and workingwomen's associations had vanished. Employers had successfully hired strikebreakers and blacklisted union members to destroy the unions. Meanwhile, the leaders of the National Labor Union, despite Sylvis's early support, tightened their ranks against women workers. Prospects dimmed even further when the nation entered into a severe economic depression, in 1873, which sent the nation reeling for the next six years. Unemployment was massive. "There never was a period at which working women were in more need of help than now," the *New York Times* reported, but little help was forthcoming.

Daughters of St. Crispin Formed in 1869 as the woman's branch of the all-male Knights of St. Crispin, which supported the principle of equal pay for equal work.

THE WOMAN'S CRUSADE

In 1873, the bankruptcy of a major Philadelphia bank caused a financial panic that precipitated a severe depression that soon spread across the nation. The Panic of 1873, as it was called, forced many workingwomen into destitution and took an especially heavy toll on women whose livelihoods depended on men who, even in the best of times, squandered their wages on liquor. Concerned for the welfare of her family, what could the wife of a drunkard do? To answer this question, women by the thousands joined a crusade against the demon rum. Unlike the antebellum agitation, which was led by men (see chapter 7), the temperance movement that formed in the mid-1870s was led by women who challenged their subordination within marriage and, ultimately, within the broader society.

In the name of temperance, women became involved in direct action as well as political lobbying and soon formed permanent organizations with an all-female leadership and rank and file. "The seal of silence is moved from Woman's Lips by this crusade," one activist attested, "and can never be replaced."

"Baptism of Power and Liberty"

Beginning in the late 1860s and swelling during the hard winter of 1873 and 1874, groups of Protestant women took to the streets and barged into saloons where they implored men to give up drink and sign a pledge of abstinence. They sang hymns as they marched through the streets and staged all-night prayer vigils, kneeling on the sawdust floors or, if denied entrance, on the snow-covered ground outside the taverns. They were soon holding mass meetings, organizing societies, and vowing to carry out this agitation until they closed every tavern in the nation. With the press covering the events in extravagant detail, the agitation that first concentrated in Ohio spread like wildfire throughout the Midwest and into cities and towns in New England.

woman's crusade The grassroots component of the temperance campaign that erupted in 1873–1874 that brought thousands of women into activism.

Hillsboro, Ohio, became known as the birthplace of the **woman's crusade**. It was there that the popular reformer, Dio Lewis, delivered a lecture at Music Hall on December 23, 1873. He repeated a story that he had told many, many times, how his own mother, who was distraught about her husband's habitual drinking, invited several of her friends to pray in the saloon until they succeeded in closing down the business. This time, according to local lore, women in Ohio outdid Lewis's mother. They issued a call to women in other communities; and within fifty days, the newly formed temperance leagues had driven the liquor traffic—"horse, foot, and dragoons"—out of 250 communities. Six months later, the crusade took credit for closing more than three thousand saloons. The following summer, several crusaders, working mainly through their church networks, put out a call for a national convention in Cleveland.

Woman's Christian Temperance Union (WCTU) Founded in November 1874 to curtail the use of alcohol and became the largest organization of women in the nineteenth century.

In November 1874, approximately two hundred women representing seventeen states gathered to form the **Woman's Christian Temperance Union (WCTU).** The first president was Annie Wittenmyer, who had headed up soldiers' relief work in Iowa during the Civil War and served as editor of the *Christian Woman*, an enormously popular magazine. While the initial movers in Ohio and the regional leaders were the wives of mainly professional men, the women who came to fill the ranks in the nation's heartland described themselves proudly as "farmers' wives."

The WCTU, drawing on the remarkable energy of the woman's crusade, made temperance the premier issue of the late 1870s. The new organization also capitalized on a shift in strategy from moral suasion to direct political action. Activists continued to implore their menfolk to abstain from drink, but they also made targets of the brewers and distillers of beer and liquor and especially to the distributors who encouraged men to drink.

Equally important, the WCTU promoted the crusade as a means to empower women. As Mary Livermore later reflected, the value of the woman's crusade could not be measured merely by its accomplishments in the realm of temperance alone. Rather, "that phenomenal and exceptional uprising of women . . . lifted them out of a subject condition where they had suffered immitigable woe . . . to a plateau where they saw that it had ceased to be a virtue!"

Frances E. Willard

Under the brilliant leadership of Frances E. Willard, the WCTU developed into the largest, most powerful organization of American women in the nineteenth century. Born in 1839, considerably younger than the luminaries of either the NWSA or the AWSA, Willard had grown up on a Wisconsin farm and, with great determination, had become in 1873 the first dean of women and professor at Northwestern University. When the woman's crusade was at its peak, she had been too busy with her administrative duties to give it her full attention. However, by the fall of 1874, Willard had decided to quit her position at Northwestern and dedicate herself wholly to the WCTU. She began to push for the "temperance ballot" as president of the Chicago WCTU and then carried her message far and wide as corresponding secretary of the national organization.

In 1879, Willard began in earnest to exploit the principle upon which the WCTU was founded, that "much of the evil by which this country is cursed" is the fault of "the men in power whose duty is to make and administer the laws." Having succeeded Wittenmyer as president, she became within a few years the most prominent woman in the United States. During her own lifetime, she was esteemed as the "Woman of the Century," canonized "Saint Frances" by her admirers, and known as just "Frank" to her friends. Possessing nothing less than an uncanny talent for leadership, Willard soon transformed the WCTU from a holy crusade against drink to a mass movement with wide-ranging goals.

Almost immediately, Willard pled with WCTU members to consider the ballot as a means to advance their cause. As a member of the Illinois Woman Suffrage Association, she believed simply that women deserved the right to vote; as a temperance organizer, she promoted woman suffrage on the grounds that decisions concerning the sale of liquor would be determined mainly by local elections and legislative initiatives. A spellbinding speaker, Willard was extraordinarily effective in making these arguments appealing to her constituents. Although several of the founding members of the WCTU held back and discouraged her from introducing a suffrage resolution at the 1876 national convention, Willard persevered.

Frances E. Willard (1839–1898) joined the Woman's Christian Temperance Union in 1874, the year of its founding. In 1879 she became the president of the national union, a position she held until her death.

Home Protection

Willard paved the way to equal rights by developing a rationale for women's political activities under the banner of **"home protection."** The phrase at once challenged male authority and upheld for women all the conventional responsibilities associated with woman's sphere, such as devotion to family. For many women who were either unprepared to demand the ballot or alienated by recent turns in the woman suffrage movement, this argument was persuasive. Drinking was, they already knew, mainly a male prerogative that endangered the home: the drunkard harmed his family by throwing away his money on liquor and, moreover, often by beating his wife and abusing his children. Armed with the ballot, Willard explained, women could protect themselves and their families against the violence perpetrated by drunken men.

Even Lucy Stone recognized the brilliance of Willard's strategy. The main objection to woman suffrage, she noted, centered on the contention that the woman who was truly attentive to the home had no time for politics. The WCTU refuted this argument by affirming that "the home is the special care of woman" and then demanding the ballot in order to protect it.

Willard tested this strategy in 1877 when she and other members of the Illinois WCTU petitioned the state legislature to allow cities and towns to establish bans on the sale of liquor and demanded additionally that women be allowed to vote in these decisions. The bill was turned down, but the determined agitators set out to gather yet more signatures. They returned two years later with a petition with the name of 180,000 people. Although the legislators once again voted against the bill, the following year a majority of Illinois towns responded to the WCTU campaign by adopting local option rules. Equally important, the bill, which carried the title of "home protection," justified for many women their right to assume a greater degree of responsibility for public affairs.

"home protection"
The slogan promoted by WCTU president Frances E. Willard to secure the organization's endorsement of woman suffrage.

This 1870 Currier and Ives lithograph depicts a scene that temperance activists would frequently describe in their arguments for prohibition: husbands and fathers too frequently spent their wages on drink, bringing misery to their blameless wives and vulnerable children.

At first, WCTU members, under the banner of *"Home Protection,"* demanded the right to vote on referenda related directly to the liquor traffic, such as licensing and prohibition. With Willard's encouragement, they soon began to enlarge the number of issues that claimed their attention. The WCTU began to denounce the disproportionate power that state laws allowed men to exercise in both family and civil society. Not only did women lack the right to vote; in most states, they could not control their own property or wages or claim custody of their children in case of divorce. For the most part, women and children lacked legal protection. Rape was rarely prosecuted, and the "age of consent" in some states was as low as seven years of age.

The WCTU tackled all these issues, in effect exposing what Willard and other woman's rights advocates knew to be a sham, the presumption of male protection. Willard's slogan of "home protection" inspired her followers to demand the vote as part of a grander mission to reconstruct the nation from the evil that men in particular perpetuated. The ballot, she claimed, would serve to counter women's defenselessness against men's abuse of the power.

Willard quickly brought the Illinois WCTU into a major force for woman suffrage, followed closely by state unions in Iowa, Indiana, Nebraska, North and South Dakota, and Colorado. Women in the western states and territories seemed especially eager to abide Willard's advice. Just three years into her presidency, Willard had secured the national WCTU's endorsement of equal voting rights for men and women. "We must first show power," Willard insisted, "for power is always respected whether it comes in the form of a cyclone or a dewdrop." Over the next two decades, the WCTU would continue to pick up speed and storm the nation.

CONCLUSION

The era between 1865 and 1877, when federal troops withdrew from the South and Reconstruction formally ended, defined the civil rights of African Americans, although not with absolute clarity or with the genuine force of law. Nevertheless, for the first time, former slaves gained the right to own their own person, including the right to sell their labor on the free market and to marry and establish a household. The Reconstruction amendments to the Constitution, along with other legislation, marked out the meaning of freedom and the privileges of citizenship.

At the same time, Reconstruction also provided a new context for the struggle for woman's rights. The woman's rights movement, which had suspended its activities during the Civil War, revived in its aftermath and immediately began to demand the rights and privileges of citizenship as guaranteed to former male slaves. Women demanded the right to sell their labor and own property on the same terms as men; to preserve their autonomy as individuals even when married; and to participate in the affairs of government on the same basis as men. Woman's rights activists such as Victoria Woodhull thus protested the laws governing the marriage relationship and at the same time tested the provisions of the Reconstruction amendments by insisting on the right to vote. Other activists demanded "equal wages for equal work" and promoted programs to assist women who aspired to support themselves by their own labors. They disputed the principle of the "family wage" and demanded the right to negotiate labor contracts in their own names. They also organized to protect their families from men's abuse of their privileges, particularly in the realm of alcohol consumption.

Victories were few. By the mid-1870s, the Supreme Court had ruled in *Minor v. Happersett* that voting is a privilege and not a right of citizenship; and that woman's "natural" sphere was the home. Despite these setbacks, groups of women had formed scores of organizations to struggle for their rights as citizens. They had created a nascent woman suffrage movement, numerous clubs and associations to advance women's interest in the labor market, and a network of organizations—the powerful WCTU—that would increase women's power within the home and over the family.

REVIEW QUESTIONS

1. How did the politics of Reconstruction affect the dynamics within African American households in the South? What kinds of work did black women perform during this era?

2. Why did the woman's rights movement focus on the ballot in the years following the Civil War? How did the Fourteenth and Fifteenth amendments affect women's strategy for gaining women's political rights?

3. What kinds of organizations did women create to ease their entry into wage labor? How did marriage affect women's right to earn a livelihood?

4. Why did the temperance movement revive in 1873 and 1874? What role did Frances Willard play within the revived movement? How did temperance agitation challenge men's authority within the household?

WOMEN'S HISTORY	GLOBAL EVENTS

1865

	1865 Freedmen's Bureau established Civil War ends President Abraham Lincoln assassinated Andrew Johnson begins presidential Reconstruction Black Codes introduced in southern states Thirteenth Amendment ratified
	1866 Civil Rights Act of 1866 enacted by Congress Congress passes Fourteenth Amendment Kansas Campaign to secure universal equal rights in state constitution Congress readmits seven Southern states National Labor Union forms Ku Klux Klan formed
	1867 Reconstruction acts passed over presidential veto
1868 *The Revolution*, edited by Stanton and Anthony, debuts Workingwomen's associations form in New York and Boston Sorosis forms in New York City New England Women's Club forms in Boston	1868 Fourteenth Amendment ratified Most southern states readmitted to Union Freedmen's Bureau ends
1869 Troy Collar Laundry Union strikes Daughters of St. Crispin organize National Woman Suffrage Association forms American Woman Suffrage Association forms	1869 Fifteenth Amendment passed by Congress

1870

1870 *Woman's Journal* begins publication Victoria C. Woodhull announces her candidacy for president Woodhull memorial presented to Congress	1870 Congress readmits Mississippi, Texas, and Virginia Fifteenth Amendment ratified
1871 Woodhull speaks before House Judiciary Committee Woodhull attempts to vote Mary Ann Shadd Cary attempts to register to vote	1871 Ku Klux Klan Act passed
1872 Woodhull exposes Beecher-Tilton affair Woodhull and Claflin arrested under the Comstock Law Susan B. Anthony, Sojourner Truth, and Virginia Minor attempt to vote The NWSA abandons "new departure" strategy	

WOMEN'S HISTORY	GLOBAL EVENTS
	1865

1873	1873
Bradwell v. Illinois turns down Bradwell's petition to practice law	Financial panic begins long depression
Fortnightly forms in Chicago	
Association for the Advancement of Women forms	
Woman's Crusade begins in Hillsboro, Ohio	
1874	
Woman's Christian Temperance Union organizes	
U.S. Supreme Court, in *Minor v. Happersett,* rules that voting is not a right of citizenship	
1876	1875
Chicago Woman's Club forms	Civil Rights Act of 1875 enacted
1877	1877
"Susan B. Anthony amendment" introduced in Congress	Federal troops pulled out of South; Reconstruction ends
1879	
Frances Willard elected president of WCTU	

RECOMMENDED READING

Karen J. Blair. *The Clubwoman as Feminist: True Womanhood Redefined, 1868–1914.* New York: Holmes and Meier, 1980. A comprehensive overview of the history of the woman club movement with detailed coverage of the founding of Sororsis and the New England Women's Club as well as the Association for the Advancement of Women.

Jack Blocker, Jr. *"Give To the Winds Thy Fears": The Women's Temperance Crusade, 1873–1874.* Westport, Conn. Greenwood Pub, 1985. Analyzes the woman's crusade as a function of the suffering women experienced as a consequence of the excessive drinking of their male relatives.

Ruth Bordin. *Woman and Temperance: The Quest for Power and Liberty, 1873–1900.* Philadelphia: Temple University Press, 1981, 1990. Offers insightful chapters on the founding of the Woman's Christian Temperance Union in the 1870s and the role of Frances Willard in broadening its agenda beyond the prohibition of alcohol.

Jane Turner Censer. *The Reconstruction of White Southern Womanhood 1865–1895.* Baton Rouge: Louisiana State University Press, 2003. Focuses on elite white women utilizing evidence from the postwar historians of women in Virginia and North Carolina. Censer argues that the end of slavery allowed Southern women's lives to resemble more closely those of their northern counterparts.

Nancy F. Cott. *Public Vows: A History of Marriage and the Nation.* Cambridge, MA: Harvard University Press, 2000. Includes a chapter delineating the changes affecting marriage during the Civil War and Reconstruction especially with regard to freedpeople.

Ellen Carol DuBois. *Feminism and Suffrage: the Emergence of an Independent Women's Movement in America, 1848–1869.* Ithaca: Cornell University Press, 1978. Argues for the importance of the Reconstruction Era in establishing woman's rights as a movement separate from the abolitionist movement.

Laura P. Edwards. *Gendered Strife and Confusion: The Political Culture of Reconstruction.* Urbana and Chicago: University of Illinois Press, 1997. Makes a forceful argument for the importance marriage and particularly the household as key to the meaning of emancipation.

Suzanne M. Marilley. *Woman Suffrage and the Origins of Liberal Feminism in the United States, 1820–1920.* Cambridge, MA: Harvard University Press, 1996. Examines various expressions of the demand for equal rights for women, including the right of women to defend themselves and their children from injury caused by drunken men.

Amy Dru Stanley. *From Bondage to Contract: Wage Labor, Marriage, and the Market in the Age of Slave Emancipation.* New York: Cambridge University Press, 1998. Offers a brilliant interpretation of contract law as the link between the abolition of slavery and a married woman's right to labor.

Leslie A. Schwalm. *A Hard Fight For We: Women's Transition from Slavery to Freedom in South Carolina.* Urbana: University of Illinois Press, 1997. A close study of African American women on South Carolinian rice plantations and their efforts to define the meaning of freedom in the aftermath of the Civil War.

ADDITIONAL BIBLIOGRAPHY

Reconstructing Southern Households

Peter Winthrop Bardaglio. *Reconstructing the Household: Families, Sex, and the Law in the Nineteenth-Century South.* Chapel Hill: University of North Carolina Press, 1995.

Nancy Bercaw. *Gendered Freedoms: Race, Rights, and the Politics of Household in the Delta 1861–1875.* Gainesville: University Press of Florida, 2003.

Marilyn Mayer Culpepper. *All Things Altered: Women in the Wake of Civil War and Reconstruction.* Jefferson, North Carolina: McFarland & Company, Publishers, 2002.

Wilma A. Dunaway. *The African-American Family in Slavery and Emancipation.* New York: Cambridge University Press, 2003.

Carol Faulkner. *Women's Radical Reconstruction: The Freedmen's Aid Movement.* Philadelphia: University of Pennsylvania Press, 2004.

Eric Foner. *Reconstruction: America's Unfinished Revolution, 1863–1877.* New York: Harper & Row, Publishers, 1988.

Noralee Frankel. *Freedom's Women: Black Women and Families in Civil War Era Mississippi.* Bloomington: Indiana University Press, 1999.

Sharon Ann Holt. *Making Freedom Pay: North Carolina Freedpeople Working for Themselves, 1865–1900.* Athens, GA: University of Georgia Press, 2000.

Jacqueline Jones. *Soldiers of Light and Love: Northern Teachers and Georgia Blacks, 1865–1873.* Chapel Hill: University of North Carolina Press, 1980.

Leon F. Litwack. *Been in the Storm So Long: The Aftermath of Slavery.* New York: Alfred A. Knopf, 1979.

Elizabeth Regosin. *Freedom's Promise: Ex-Slave Families and Citizenship in the Age of Emancipation.* Charlottesville: University Press of Virginia, 2002.

Nina Silber. *The Romance of Reunion: Northerners and the South, 1865–1900.* Chapel Hill: University of North Carolina Press, 1993.

Marli F. Weiner. *Mistresses and Slaves: Plantation Women in South Carolina, 1830–1880.* Urbana: University of Illinois Press, 1998.

Woman's Rights Re-emerge

Steven M. Buechler. *The Transformation of the Woman Suffrage Movement: The Case of Illinois, 1850–1920.* New Brunswick: Rutgers University Press, 1986.

Philip S. Foner, ed. *Frederick Douglass on Women's Rights.* Westport: Greenwood Publishing Group, 1976.

Amanda Frisken. *Victoria Woodhull's Sexual Revolution: Political Theater and the Popular Press in Nineteenth-Century America.* Philadelphia: University of Pennsylvania Press, 2004.

Anne Firor Scott and Andrew MacKay Scott, eds. *One Half the People: The Fight for Woman Suffrage.* Urbana: University of Illinois Press, 1975, 1982.

Madeleine B. Stern. ed. *The Victoria Woodhull Reader.* Weston, Mass: M & S Press, 1974.

Rosalyn Terborg-Penn. *African American Women in the Struggle for the Vote, 1850–1920.* Bloomington: Indiana University Press, 1998.

Wendy Hamand Venet. "The Emergence of a Suffragist: Mary Livermore, "Civil War Activism, and the

Moral Power of Women," *Civil War History*, 48.2 (June 2002), 143–164.

Employment for Women

Mary Blewett. *We Will Rise in Our Might: Working-women's Voices from Nineteenth-Century New England.* Ithaca: Cornell University Press, 1991.

Carol Turbin. *Working Women of Collar City: Gender, Class and Community in Troy, New York, 1864–86.* Urbana: University of Illinois Press, 1992.

Howard M. Wach. "A Boston Feminist in the Victorian Public Sphere: The Social Criticism of Caroline Healey Dall," *New England Quarterly*, 68.3 (September 1995), 429–450.

Biographies and Memoirs

Jean J. Baker. *Sisters: The Lives of America's Suffragists.* New York: Hill and Wang, 2005.

Lois W. Banner. *Elizabeth Cady Stanton: A Radical for Women's Rights.* New York: Longman, 1997, 1980.

Kathleen Barry. *Susan B. Anthony: A Biography of a Singular Feminist.* New York: New York University Press, 1988.

Jim Bearden and Linda Jean Butler. *Shadd: The Life and Times of Mary Shadd Cary.* Toronto: NC Press Ltd., 1977.

Jane M. Friedman. *America's First Woman Lawyer: The Biography of Myra Bradwell.* Buffalo: Prometheus, 1993.

Mary Gabriel. *Notorious Victoria: The Life of Victoria Woodhull.* Chapel Hill: Algonquin Books of Chapel Hill, 1998.

Barbara Goldsmith. *Other Powers: The Age of Suffrage, Spiritualism, and the Scandalous Victoria Woodhull.* New York: Alfred A. Knopf, 1998.

Elisabeth Griffith. *In Her Own Right: The Life of Elizabeth Cady Stanton.* New York: Oxford University Press, 1984.

Julia Ward Howe. *Reminiscences, 1818–1899.* Boston: Houghton, Mifflin and Company, 1899, 1969.

Andrea Moore Kerr. *Lucy Stone: Speaking Out for Equality.* New Brunswick, NJ: Rutgers University Press, 1992.

Mary A. Livermore. *The Story of My Life.* New York: Arno Press, 1899, 1974.

Elizabeth Cady Stanton. *Eighty Years and More: Reminiscences 1815–1897.* Boston: Northeastern University Press, 1993.

Frances E. Willard. *Glimpses of Fifty Years: The Autobiography of an American Woman.* Chicago: Women's Temperance Publication Association, 1889, 1997.

THE TRANS-MISSISSIPPI WEST, 1860–1900

HOW DID the skewed sex ratio on the range and mining frontier affect the position of women?

HOW DID gender relations among Mormons differ from those of other settlers?

WHAT WERE the effects of incorporation on Spanish-speaking women?

HOW DID men and women distribute the work of managing a household on the plains?

WHAT WAS the impact of the Dawes Severalty Act on the status of Indian women?

CHAPTER 11

When courage to look around had at last been mustered, I found that my new home was formed of two wall tents pitched together so the inner one could be used as a sleeping and the outer one as a sitting room. A calico curtain divided them, and a carpet made of barley sacks covered the floor. In my weary state of mind and body the effect produced was far from pleasant. The wall tents were only eight feet square, and when windowless and doorless except for the one entrance, as were those, they seemed from the inside much like a prison.

As I lay in bed that night, feeling decidedly homesick, familiar airs, played upon a

Oglala Sioux performing the Ghost Dance at Pine Ridge, South Dakota, illustration by Frederic Remington, Harper's Weekly, December 6, 1890. (The Granger Collection, New York)

very good piano, suddenly sounded in my ears. It seemed impossible that there could be a fine musical instrument such a distance from civilization, particularly when I remembered the roads over which we had come, and the cluster of tents that alone represented human habitation. The piano, which I soon learned belonged to our captain's wife, added greatly to her happiness, and also the pleasure of us all, though its first strains only intensified my homesick longings.

This lady and myself were the only women at the post, which also included, besides our respective husbands, the doctor and an unmarried first lieutenant. The latter, as quartermaster and commissary, controlled all supplies, could make us either comfortable or the reverse, as he chose. . . .

My housekeeping was simplified by absolute lack of materials. I had, as a basis of supplies, during the succeeding two years, nothing but soldiers' rations, which consisted entirely of bacon, flour, beans, coffee, tea, rice, sugar, soap, and condiments. Our only luxury was dried apples, and with these I experimented in every imaginable way until toward the last my efforts to disguise them utterly failed, and we returned to our simple rations.

Source: Mrs. Orsemus Boyd. Cavalry Life in Tent and Field (New York: J. Selwin Tait & Sons, 1894), as reprinted in Christiane Fischer, ed., Let Them Speak for Themselves: Women in the American West, 1849–1900 (New York: E. P. Dutton, 1978), 11–12, 16.

Frances Mullen Boyd (1848–1926) was one of many Euro-American women who left their childhood homes to journey to the western states and territories in the decades after the Civil War. Just a few months after marrying in October 1867, she joined her husband, a recent graduate of West Point, at Camp Halleck, Nevada, where they set up housekeeping.

Fannie Boyd was just one woman in what was, up until that time, the largest mass migration in history. The discovery of gold in California in 1849 sparked a movement of thousands of people from all parts of the world, making the West the most ethnically diverse region of the United States. Moreover, new communities formed at such an unprecedented rate that by the end of the century nearly one-quarter of the U.S. population lived west of the Mississippi River. The new settlers carved a niche for themselves in the expanding western industries—mining, cattle ranching, and agriculture—and helped to make the western states and territories a crucial element in the growing national economy by furnishing both capital and raw materials.

But contrary to the image of the West popular among some easterners, the trans-Mississippi West was not an unsettled wilderness. The newcomers interrupted and often displaced established communities and helped to destroy centuries-old ways of life. They sparked warfare, brought poverty and disease, and altered the natural environment at the same time that they helped to make the United States the leading industrial nation in the world.

After the completion of the transcontinental railroad in 1869, the trip westward became easier than the one Fannie Boyd endured. Nevertheless, the challenge of making a home in unfamiliar, often harsh surroundings persisted. Some women never adjusted. Other Euro-American women, like Boyd, who had grown up in New York City, demonstrated courage and resourcefulness and adapted to the new setting. Whether they found themselves living, as Boyd did, in the primitive dwellings of an army camp, the complex households of a ranching community, or the hurriedly constructed houses that dotted the plains and prairie, most of these women tried to create and maintain their homes in the wilderness. The doctrine of separate spheres became a prime marker of not only a stable community but "civilization," as measured by their own precepts (see chapter 5). However, their domestic ideals often conflicted with those of other women who were struggling to hold on to their own households amid the aggressive westward expansion of the United States.

On the Range and in Mining Communities

The industries that flourished in the trans-Mississippi West—cattle driving, mining, freighting, and lumbering—attracted a disproportionate number of men and encouraged the growth of towns and cities that appeared virtually overnight to cater to their needs and interests. Dodge City, Kansas, and Butte, Montana, for example, were "wide-open" towns where gambling, drinking, and prostitution prospered and where "respectable" women were in short supply. The few women who settled in the region often found fault with its "masculine" character. "The more I see of men," one complainer wrote, "the more I am disgusted with them . . . this is the Paradise of men—I wonder if a Paradise for poor *Women*, will ever be discovered—I wish they would get up an exploring expedition, to seek for one." However, some women relished the opportunity to take on the challenge of a rough and often rowdy environment. Through a combination of luck and hard work, they achieved a degree of financial independence and status rare among their contemporaries back East.

Home on the Range

The two decades after the Civil War witnessed the creation of a spectacular cattle market that produced not only a steady supply of beef for eastern consumers but the legendary Wild West. The muscular cowboy dressed in leather chaps and a broad-brimmed Stetson hat, with a pair of silver-handled pistols strapped to his narrow hips, played the starring role. A few women tapped into this imagery: Annie Oakley was the most famous. Born in 1860 in a log cabin on the Ohio frontier, Oakley was such a skilled sharpshooter by age nine that she was supporting her entire family. In 1885, she joined "Buffalo Bill's Wild West" touring company; and, billed as "Little Sure Shot," she soon became the main attraction. Oakley, like Buffalo Bill himself and his troop of fancy-dressed cowboys, had little to do with cowpunching. They found their niche as well-paid entertainers.

The popular image of cowboys and cowgirls obscured the reality of an exhausting and tedious job that only men performed. Driving a herd several hundred miles from Texas to the stockyards of Wichita or Abilene, Kansas, took a toll on even the strongest young men who made up the workforce. Most cowboys hung up their spurs after only one run. Except for the prostitutes who worked in trailside "hoghouses," very few women made the long drive. Sally Redus once accompanied her cattleman husband, riding side saddle and carrying her baby on her lap all the way from Texas to Kansas. In 1871, Mrs. A. Burks made the journey in a little buggy while her

In this 1900 photograph, Annie Oakley (1860–1926) is shown with some of the many medals she won for sharp-shooting. At the time, she was traveling with Buffalo Bill Cody's Wild West show. Women flocked to see her perform.

husband led a group of Mexican vaqueros. Despite the dangers of stampedes and confrontations with rustlers, she relished both the excitement and her special status as the only woman in camp. "The men rivaled each other in attentiveness to me," she reported, "always on the lookout for something to please me, a surprise of some delicacy of the wild fruit, or prairie chicken, or antelope tongue." Wives of prosperous ranchers, Redus and Burks were in no danger of becoming one of "the fellers."

Back on the ranch, a familiar division of labor prevailed, although most wives crossed over to do men's work when necessary. "The heavy work of the ranch naturally falls to men," a Wyoming woman explained in 1899, "but I think most ranch women will bear me out in saying that unless the women . . . be always ready to do anything that comes along, . . . the ranch is not a success." Not infrequently, husband and wife worked as a team. After her husband died, Elizabeth Collins turned their ranch into such a prosperous business that she became known as the "Cattle Queen of Montana."

For the majority of ranch wives, the daily routine was far more conventional and often very demanding. Women handled the "inside work," that is, the usual domestic chores of housekeeping and tending children. However, if their ranch was large, so too was their household, encompassing perhaps dozens of servants, hired hands and their wives, and perhaps a tutor or schoolteacher for the children, as well as a stream of visitors.

Not all women, especially those who were recent migrants to the West, possessed the emotional or physical stamina for this work. Angie Mitchell, who lived on a ranch near Prescott, Arizona, kept a pistol on the trunk near her bed in response to the regular nocturnal invasion of skunks. More frightening, however, were the bands of stampeding cattle that threatened her insubstantial homestead. "We took a firm hold of our sheets flapped them up & down & ran forward yelling as loud as we could," she reported, while her friends beat a tin pan with a stick and waved their aprons. The cattle, which had been startled by coyotes, swerved just past their flimsy shack before crossing the creek to safety. Two nights later, the cattle panicked again, this time in response to the screaming of mountain lions. Once again, the women rallied and diverted the stampede. "A few more nights of this sort of business," Mitchell concluded, "& we'll all be crazy."

Their daughters, however, often thrived in the wide-open spaces. Rejecting sunbonnets and petticoats for wide-brimmed hats and split skirts, they worked alongside their fathers and brothers, riding horses "clothespin style," roping calves and branding cattle, and shooting guns. One young woman reported that her grandmother, after visiting their ranch near Laramie, Wyoming, complained that her father was "making a boy out of me." However, such fears did not hold back the many young women who relished "outside work."

The Sporting Life

As many as fifty thousand women in the trans-Mississippi West sold companionship as well as sex in burgeoning cities like San Francisco and Denver and in the many small, makeshift towns and mining camps. Although few conformed to the myth of the racy madam who made a fortune or the dance-hall girl with a heart of gold, prostitutes did play important parts in shaping the culture and institutions of western cities. A vivid example of the division of labor by gender, their trade nevertheless undermined some of the treasured tenets of the doctrine of separate spheres by making certain behaviors usually associated with marriage major items of commerce.

With men far outnumbering women in mining camps, on the range, at military forts, and in the towns that sprang up along the freight routes, prostitution supplied women with the largest source of employment outside the home. Prostitutes traveled first from Mexico, Brazil, and Peru and later from other regions of the United States and from Europe, Australia, and China. As the lyrics of a mining song from Butte, Montana, where the first hurdy-gurdy house opened in 1878, attested: "First came the miners to work in the mine./ Then came the ladies to live on the line."

Chinese prostitutes, often kidnapped as girls or sold by their impoverished fathers to procurers, served the nearly thirty-five thousand Chinese men who had immigrated to the American West in search of the "Gold Mountain." Called "Chiney ladies" or "she-heathens" by their white patrons, and "wives to a hundred men" by their Chinese patrons, these women worked in big cities like San Francisco but also in the remote mining towns. The Page Law of 1875, implemented by the federal government in response to rising anti-Chinese prejudice, targeted prostitutes and effectively halted the immigration of all Chinese women. Nevertheless, as late as 1880, nearly half of the prostitutes in the mining town of Helena, Montana, were Chinese.

In general, prostitutes represented a stratified, ethnically diverse, and youthful population. The most impoverished Indian women turned to prostitution after mining operations encroached on their settlements and drove them to the brink of starvation. However, the majority of prostitutes were native-born white women. Prostitutes ranged in status from the lowest, the women who plied their trade on the street, to the higher-class ladies who worked in brothels. Yet, the majority of prostitutes remained flexible, picking up paying customers wherever they could. Having grown up in poverty, many accepted hard work, even servitude, as their fate.

Although prostitutes routinely practiced some form of birth control, such as the use of pessaries and douches, and frequently terminated pregnancies by abortion, many gave birth. However, motherhood was rare. Local authorities would not allow children to live in the red-light districts, even if it meant sending them to the county poor farm.

A few "soiled doves" managed to become rich as well as notorious by running profitable bordellos. A successful Denver madam explained, "I went into the sporting life for business reasons and for no other. It was a way for a woman in those days to make money and I made it." In addition, the "summer women," the prostitutes who moved into the mining camps or cattle towns during the busy season, could earn wages in just a few months that far exceeded the annual income of local retail clerks or domestic servants.

Although highly publicized, such success stories were rare and became increasingly so by the turn of the century. By that time, town officials had responded to the demands of the "respectable" citizenry and forced many prostitutes out of business. The majority of prostitutes responded to diminishing opportunities and increasing threats of arrest by quitting. Those who chose to persevere often turned for protection to men who, for a large cut of their earnings, acted as pimps and solicitors. Addicted to drugs or alcohol, often infected with syphilis or tuberculosis, many had little choice but to live out their lives in the trade. Prostitutes commonly lived in destitution and faced an early, sometimes violent death. Suicide rates were especially high.

Domesticity on the Mining Frontier

The discovery of gold in California in 1848 encouraged a huge number of men and very few "respectable" women to seek their fortune in the West. Women and children made up less than 5 percent of the newcomers to the region. Most wives, known as "gold rush widows," stayed home waiting for their husbands' case of "gold fever" to run its course. Some wives, however, refused to be left behind. In the 1860s and 1870s, when reports of new rushes in Colorado, Montana, and Idaho spread eastward as far as Europe, these women decided to brave the harsh conditions of the mining frontier. They risked arrest by putting on men's trousers, grabbed a pick or a drill, and joined their husbands in the pursuit of Eldorado.

However, the majority of these adventurers were neither prospectors nor prostitutes but housekeepers, although distinctions were not sharply drawn. In the central Arizona mining district, for instance, where in the 1860s small towns sprang up around the goldfields, Mexican women adapted a long-standing folk custom and became the temporary companions of either Mexican or Anglo miners. In contrast, the Anglo women who lacked a tradition of informal unions rarely cohabited with men who were not their husbands and even more rarely crossed racial lines to do so. However, in either case, transgressions were easily overlooked. "We never ask women where they come from or what they did before they came to live in our neck of the woods," one Montana woman explained. "If they wore a wedding band and were good wives, mothers, and neighbors that was enough for us to know."

In the early days of settlement, mining camps and towns afforded women opportunities to bridge the customary division of labor by gender. In Helena, Montana, for example, one of every five adult women in 1870 worked for wages outside the home. Many took advantage of their domestic skills to run boardinghouses and restaurants, to work as shopkeepers, and to teach school. In many communities, they often competed with the Chinese men who had gained a toehold in the laundry business. "True there are not many comforts and one must work all the time and work hard but [there] is plenty to do and good pay," one woman wrote home from Nevada City. "It is the only country that I ever was in where a woman received anything like a just compensation for work." But even on the mining frontier, the overwhelming majority of married women preferred the familiar role and "kept house."

Housework, however, rarely provided the satisfaction of a job well done. The dirt and grime of makeshift towns proved implacable enemies, and even basic supplies like soap and butter were often in short supply. Equally important, in towns where nine of every ten residents moved within a decade, and where men outnumbered women five to one, many housewives found it very difficult to recreate the circle of female friends and family that in other regions made domesticity a social enterprise. "I never was so lonely and homesick in all my life," a young wife of a Denver prospector complained. However, most housewives eventually learned to cope with such unfavorable conditions, often by becoming more inventive and self-reliant.

On the mining frontier, as throughout the trans-Mississippi West, marriages dissolved at a higher rate than in other parts of the United States. Hard-rock miners faced both erratic employment and extremely dangerous conditions, and many women were abandoned by restless husbands or widowed early. Contemporaries routinely commented on the "very liberal" divorce laws in the new states and territories, noting that men and women rarely stayed married against their wills. In 1867, in one county in Montana, divorces actually outnumbered marriages.

In the face of such uncertainties, women looked outward to their communities and established various civic institutions to protect their families. In the 1880s, in Candelaria, Nevada, known as a "good sporting town," the miners supported thirteen saloons and not a single church. Fistfights and even murders were common. No wonder that women organized themselves to impose some semblance of order. In Helena,

The discovery of gold in 1897 in the Yukon region of Canada prompted as many as 100,000 fortune-seekers to head for the region. One in ten participants in the Klondike Gold Rush, as this movement was called, was a woman. As one adventurer reported: "when our fathers, husbands and brothers decided to go, so did we, and our wills are strong and courage unfailing. We will not be drawbacks nor hindrances, and they won't have to return on our account."

Montana, for example, at least half of the pioneering generation of women supported some kind of reform society. They campaigned vigorously for temperance and against prostitution, sponsored schools and libraries, and formed religious and benevolent societies. One woman reporting from Virginia City in 1869 claimed that "the entire religious and social life of Nevada is conducted by the ladies." "The lords of creation," she insisted, were "mere money-making machines, with apparently no other human attributes than a hasty appreciation of a good dinner, the hope of a fortune, and a home 'at the bay' [San Francisco], or in the dimly remembered East." The second generation of women advanced even more rapidly to leadership positions in their communities, often forsaking marriage and family to work full time for civic betterment.

Greatly outnumbered during the early days of settlement, women eventually made an impact on their communities and often explored opportunities for self-support that would have been unavailable to them in other regions of the country. Western expansion fostered such possibilities for some women, but it also placed new restrictions on established communities, especially those with households that varied from the emerging norms.

MORMON SETTLEMENTS

In the 1840s, Joseph Smith, the founder of the Church of Jesus Christ of Latter-day Saints, claimed an angel had told him that it is "the will of Heaven that a man have more than one wife." After newspapers exposed and ridiculed this revelation, Mormons became the targets of persecution and violent physical attacks. Forced to abandon their prosperous settlement in Nauvoo, Illinois, a group led by Brigham Young migrated to the Great Salt Lake Basin in 1846. In the Utah wilderness, they rebuilt their exclusive community. By 1870, Mormon missionaries had recruited settlers from the East and from as far away as Scandinavia, and their population exceeded eighty-seven thousand. And unlike other western territories, Utah could boast a sex ratio that was nearly equal.

plural marriage The Mormon custom of taking more than one wife in order to maximize the number of children.

Plural marriage quickly became one of the defining characteristics of the Mormon community. Brigham Young, the first territorial governor and president of the Church of Jesus Christ of Latter-day Saints, wedded twenty-seven women and fathered fifty-six children. However, even at its peak, polygamy was practiced by no more than 15 percent of Mormon families, and the majority of male practitioners took only two wives. Nevertheless, plural marriages affected all members of the community, always remaining a possibility and serving as an important symbol of their spiritually unique way of life.

The Doctrine of Plural Marriage

As sanctioned by their faith, Mormon families were strictly patriarchal, and a woman's spiritual salvation depended on her relation to her husband. If their marriage were "sealed" as a "celestial marriage," it would last through eternity and qualify both husband and wife for the highest degree of spiritual glory, exaltation. However, all Mormons bore a unique responsibility: to serve the needs of the ethereal spirits who required a mortal body to prove themselves worthy of salvation. Brigham Young proclaimed it "the duty of every righteous man and every woman to prepare tabernacles for all the spirits they can." Thus, a woman's spiritual destiny was determined in part by the number of "tabernacles"—that is, children—she brought into this world. In turn, men aspired to take at least two wives, each ideally bearing between seven and eight children.

Among the minority of Mormons who practiced polygamy (more precisely, polygyny, for only men were allowed more than one spouse), families functioned much like families in other regions of the West. Wives sometimes shared a single home, each keeping her own bedroom and together sharing common household chores and child rearing. Occasionally, if the husband were sufficiently wealthy, his wives lived in separate homes and even in different towns. Plural wives sometimes formed strong bonds, although it was not unknown for jealousy to figure into these relationships, especially if their husband favored one wife over others. However, in other aspects of family life, such as fertility and divorce rates, Mormons deviated little from the average.

Like other newcomers to the western territories, women expected to work hard. Women spun and wove cloth, made clothing, and tended household gardens. In the face of the enormous challenge of growing crops in the semiarid land, women joined men in planting and harvesting and often in the vital work of irrigation. It was not uncommon for a wife, particularly a first wife, to manage the household in her husband's absence and often for long periods. Church leaders explicitly encouraged women to be competent and to teach their daughters to be self-reliant.

The church invited women to work outside the home as a means to strengthen the local economy. By the late 1860s, women were running cooperative stores for the sale of homemade products; eventually, they were overseeing a successful silk manufacturing industry. Women also formed female relief societies, which sponsored religious programs, such as Bible readings and lectures, and administered local charities.

"The Mormon Question"

By the time of the Civil War, the population of the Utah territory was growing quickly enough to warrant a bid for statehood; from the perspective of the Christian Northeast, the prospect of a new state that promoted polygamy—allegedly a "relic of barbarism"—was intolerable. The popular press and government officials likened polygamy to slavery and portrayed plural wives as hapless victims of male lust. In 1862, Congress passed the **Morrill Anti-Bigamy Act**, which made plural marriage a federal crime. Nevertheless, because Mormons did not publicly record second or subsequent marriages, and because juries in Utah typically refused to enforce the new law, the Morrill Act had little impact on Mormon communities.

Morrill Anti-Bigamy Act Passed by Congress in 1862, this legislation made plural marriage a federal crime.

With the completion of the transcontinental railroad in 1869, which brought new settlers to the territory, Mormon marriage practices once again attracted national attention. President Ulysses S. Grant pledged to eradicate polygamy; and his successors—Hayes, Garfield, and Arthur—concurred, all taking up the "Mormon Question" in their annual messages to Congress.

The bulk of the commentary focused on Mormon women. The former abolitionist Harriet Beecher Stowe equated polygamy and slavery and waged a new campaign "to loose the bonds of a cruel slavery whose chains have cut into the hearts of thousand of our sisters." The popular Civil War orator Anna Dickinson, who visited Salt Lake City in 1869, returned to the East with a new lecture in her repertoire, "White Sepulchers," in which she described the debasement of plural wives by sexually craven men. Like many other critics, she alleged that Mormon women had been either seduced or tricked into a relationship no better than prostitution.

Mormon women refuted these charges. In 1870, when Senator Shelby M. Cullom of Illinois introduced a bill in Congress that would strip Mormon men of the bulk of their rights as citizens should polygamy continue to prevail in Utah, Mormon women staged mass demonstrations to protest this "mean, foul" legislation. One spokeswoman praised the outpouring of women for giving "lie to the popular clamour [sic] that the women of Utah are oppressed and held in bondage." To those who would abolish the Mormon way of life, she charged: "[W]herever monogamy reigns, adultery, prostitution, free-love and foeticide [abortion], directly or indirectly, are its concomitants. . . ." Mormon women, she insisted, look upon polygamy as a "safeguard" to these common evils.

The Woman's Vote in Utah

The protest by Mormon women had also undermined a novel plan to curtail the practice of polygamy. Several members of Congress proposed enfranchising Utah's women, assuming that Mormon women, if given a chance, would use their votes to eradicate polygamy. The "great indignation meeting" of five thousand angry women protesting the **Cullom Bill** quickly put this plan to rest. However, for their own purposes, the Mormon-controlled territorial legislature gave the ballot to the women of Utah in February 1870.

Cullom Bill Introduced into Congress in 1870 to strengthen the provisions of the Morrill Anti-Bigamy Act, which had been largely ignored during the Civil War.

Within the week, according to Brigham Young, twenty-five women voted in municipal elections in Salt Lake City, proving to the world that Mormon women were no slaves to a religious patriarchy. Moreover, these women wielded their new political power primarily to show themselves as willing participants in plural marriage. Equally significant, by placing women on the roster of eligible voters, Mormons had increased their representation in territorial elections to more than 95 percent.

A leading suffragist and longtime friend of Susan B. Anthony, Emmeline Blanch Wells (1828–1921), front and center, poses with five sister wives. Wells played a prominent role in the Salt Lake City Relief Society and served as editor of the Women's Exponent, *a journal that vigorously defended the practice of plural marriage.*

These events took the national woman suffrage movement off guard. The leaders greeted the enfranchisement of Utah women as a major victory for their side. Elizabeth Cady Stanton and Susan B. Anthony made a long journey to Utah in 1871 to celebrate; a representative of the American Woman Suffrage Association likewise visited Salt Lake City. Yet, all this goodwill could not obscure the fact that most suffrage leaders detested the association of their cause with plural marriage. With Victoria Woodhull whipping up controversy by advocating free love, neither the NWSA nor the AWSA could afford to be linked to yet another heterodox position on marriage.

In 1882, after Congress passed the Edmunds Act outlawing "bigamous cohabitation," a major movement for the disfranchisement of Utah women gained force. Antisuffragists insisted that Mormon women, in casting their votes, simply obeyed their husbands' dictates, thus proving that women in general were unprepared to take on responsibilities of citizenship. Meanwhile, several Mormon women who had abandoned their faith and former plural wives—including a woman known as "The Rebel of the Harem," an estranged plural wife of Brigham Young—added fuel to the fire by publishing shocking accounts of sexual bondage. Finally, in 1887, Congress passed the **Edmunds-Tucker Act,** simultaneously disincorporating the Mormon church and disenfranchising the women of Utah.

Although suffragists formally protested the antisuffrage clause of the Edmunds-Tucker Act, they did so only halfheartedly. The *Woman's Journal* called woman suffrage in Utah a "sham of freedom." Moreover, suffragists adamantly refused the requests of Mor-

Edmunds-Tucker Act
Legislation disincorporating the Mormon church and disenfranchising supporters of polygamy, including women.

WOMEN'S VOICES

AN ANONYMOUS MORMON SPEAKS HER MIND

The editor of the Anti-Polygamy Standard, *Jennie Anderson Froiseth, collected stories by apostate Mormon women, that is, by women who had abandoned their faith to illustrate the abuse and degradation they allegedly endured under the system of plural marriage. "If the wives and mothers of America could only be made aware of the extent and character of this degradation of their sex . . ."* she explained, *"the onrushing tide of public sentiment, once set in motion, would sweep away the curse of polygamy in a single year."*

My husband and self became converted to Mormonism in the Eastern State through the preaching of a traveling missionary. We were both enthusiastic converts, and speedily removed to Zion, bringing with us two little ones and a fair share of this world's goods. While on the plains, we heard of the doctrine of polygamy; but I was in such an abnormal state of mind, being so completely infatuated with the new religion, that I received the announcement of the revelation with comparatively little astonishment. . . .

Of course, after we had been in Zion for awhile my husband was admonished to "live his religion." When I found the cross likely to come home to me, although I began to feel very different about it, I had still sufficient faith in the system as a divine principle, not to violently oppose my husband. I told him it would break my heart to see another supersede me in his affections; but that I loved him too well to peril his future glory, and prevent his exaltation in the next world, consequently I would sacrifice my own feelings, and not oppose him, if he would promise me solemnly that I should always be first in his esteem and regard. . . .

The young bride was brought home to my house, and became one of our family, no provision for separate housekeeping being made for her. I tried to feel kindly toward her; for after I had consented to the marriage, I was woman enough to try and treat her well; although, at times, the very sight of her at my table, or sitting in my little sewing-room with my husband at her side, almost drove me wild with jealousy, even before I perceived that she was using all her arts, and every means at her command, to win his affections from me. She was a true daughter of her father, a man who stepped on hearts as if they were stones, and little by little, I discovered how she was ensnaring my husband, getting him so completely in her power, and under her control, that he seemed to have no thoughts for any one but her. In less than six months, her influence over him became so strong that he did her bidding as if he were a mere child, while wife and little ones were totally neglected. When he entered the house, he would rush off to her apartment, unmindful of me, or the children whom he had always met with a smile and a kiss. I cannot describe the change that came over our home in those few months; and when I found that I, his true and loyal wife, who had left home, friends, and kindred to follow him to the promised land, was being neglected and almost totally discarded for a girl whose name we did not even know one short year before, I became nearly insane with grief and remorse. I suffered the bitterest kind of remorse, for in reality I was more to blame in the outset than he; and I could not disguise from myself the fact that I had dug a grave, and buried my happiness with my own hands.

Source: *Jennie Anderson Froiseth, ed.,* The Women of Mormonism: Or, The Story of Polygamy as Told by the Victims Themselves *(Detroit: C. G. G. Paine, 1882), 77–78.*

Questions

1. How does the selection of the "second wife" take place, according to this report?

2. How do we interpret this document given its purpose to expose the evils of plural marriage?

mon women to defend plural marriage. By this time, the woman's vote in Utah had become a liability to the suffrage movement—just as polygamy had become a liability to the Mormon Church. In 1887, the Mormon leadership announced that the church would no longer sanction plural marriage, thus clearing the way for admission of Utah to statehood.

After enjoying voting rights for seventeen years, Utah women would not give up the ballot graciously. The most militant formed the Utah Territory Woman Suffrage Association and spearheaded a vigorous campaign. When the state was finally admitted to the Union in 1896, Utah women regained the right to vote and won the right to hold public office.

SPANISH-SPEAKING WOMEN OF THE SOUTHWEST

"My life is only for my family," wrote Adina de Zavala in 1882. "My whole life shall be worth while [sic] if I can render happy and comfortable the declining years of my parents and see my brothers safely launched on life's troubled seas." This San Antonio matron paid tribute

MAP 11-1 LAND ACCESSION, TREATY OF GUADALUPE HIDALGO

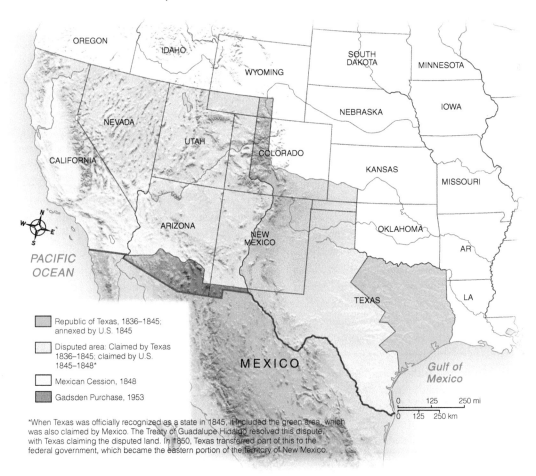

By the terms of the Treaty of Guadalupe Hidalgo, which marked the end of the war between the United States and Mexico in 1848, Mexico ceded large parts of its land to the United States.

to **la familia,** that is, the enduring bonds of affection and duty extending from biological kin to close friends that characterized Mexicano settlements in the region that came to be known as the American Southwest. They respected the authority of their husbands—*machismo*—and revered marriage and motherhood as the primary source of a woman's self-affirmation and esteem. However, in daily life, the actual behavior of Spanish-speaking women often diverged from these ideals. Moreover, by the 1880s, Anglos were settling in the Southwest in such great numbers that old mores could not survive intact.

la familia Spanish expression denoting the enduring bonds of affection and duty extending from biological kin to close friends.

During the last half of the nineteenth century, Spanish-speaking women were drawn into the processes of incorporation into the United States (see chapter 4). In 1848, the Treaty of Guadalupe Hidalgo, which marked the end of a war between the United States and Mexico, granted to the United States half of all Mexican territory—what would become the states of California, Arizona, Nevada, and Utah, most of New Mexico, and parts of Colorado and Wyoming. In 1853, the United States purchased an additional strip of land between El Paso and the Colorado River that rounded off the accession of all the land north of the Rio Grande River. The Mexicanos who lived in this region were formally guaranteed the "free enjoyment of their liberty and property" as citizens of the United States, although Anglo developers and land speculators soon took over the local economy. By the 1880s, Anglo-owned industries, including rairoads, lumber mills, and mines, and the transformation of subsistence agriculture into a thriving commercial enterprise had effected dramatic changes that encompassed *la familia* and women's role within the Mexicano household.

Landowning Elite

Through the 1870s, elite Spanish-speaking women continued to benefit from the well-established practice of intermarriage with Anglos as well as from the customary right to accumulate property jointly with their husbands and to inherit and maintain property in their own names (see chapter 4). Following the United States–Mexican War, this long-standing Spanish tradition was incorporated into the legal system of several southwestern states, including Texas, where big cattle ranches flourished. Several wealthy Texan widows took their place among the largest landowners in the state, registering their own cattle brands as well as filing homestead claims with the county courts.

One Texan woman profited immensely from these customs and stood out among the wealthiest citizens of the state. Salome Balli had come from a large landowning family, and during the years of her marriage to an ambitious Anglo, John Young, she expanded her holdings many times over. In 1860, newly widowed but still a young woman of twenty-nine, Balli owned the title to land worth more than one hundred thousand dollars, a veritable fortune at the time.

However, only the wealthiest women benefited from this system. The majority of women, like their male contemporaries, fared less well with the rise of Anglo-owned commercial ranching and agriculture. In the Lower Rio Grande Valley, for example, where Mexicanos outnumbered Anglos, they lost the bulk of their property to Anglos who were better equipped to manipulate the new court system. While their husbands and sons found themselves herding cattle or tending sheep and goats for Anglo landowners,

A woman of the Mexican upper class, as this portrait indicates, had access to fine clothing and expensive jewelry. Her personal finery marked her family's status in the community.

Mexicanas worked as domestic servants, cooks, gardeners, or field hands. It was not uncommon for whole families to join the ranks of migrant workers, finding a meager source of income as pickers in the cotton fields of South Texas.

Communal Villagers

Well before the United States–Mexican War, in an effort to encourage settlement in what had then been the northern outpost of the nation, the Mexican government had conferred communal property rights to groups that petitioned for land. After the accession of this region by the United States, thousands of Mexican families continued to live and work in villages scattered throughout the mountains and deserts of northern New Mexico and part of Colorado. The women who lived in these communal villages of small-scale cattle and sheep herders enjoyed similar benefits of inheritance and property rights but nevertheless lived very different lives from those of the elite landowners.

As in other agricultural communities, Mexicanas cared for the home and maintained nearby a small garden plot and perhaps a patch of land reserved for a few grazing sheep and goats. Their husbands in turn took responsibility for the heavy outdoor labor, such as herding sheep and cattle and plowing the fields. The community as a whole shared the principal resources, including the large pastures and water supply, and took collective responsibility for their maintenance. Men and women also pooled their labor. Women often worked in groups to prepare foodstuffs, spin wool, and plaster their adobe homes, an annual chore; and men worked together in the physical and seasonal labor typical of agricultural economies. Men also managed the external trade, selling grain and livestock on the open market.

By the 1880s, the transcontinental railroads that passed through this region served as a catalyst of change in the work of men and women. Anglos came in great numbers, bringing new commercial opportunities for men. Mexicanos took advantage of a growing cash economy, finding jobs on the railroads and in the mines. They also worked for Anglo ranchers, digging irrigation ditches and herding sheep and cattle. While the actual tasks were often familiar, the location and exchange of labor for cash were not. Men now left their villages for long stretches of time, hoping to earn enough money to keep up with rising taxes and household expenses. Left behind, women assumed more responsibilities.

Although religious and ethnic traditions continued to support the patriarchal authority invested in *machismo*, the new economic arrangements worked against old customs. With men absent for months at a time, women gained power in their family and community. Women took on the work of herding sheep or tending the communal fields. Equally important, they strengthened their own networks.

Women's networks, which were rooted in kin relationships, extended far into the tightly knit neighborhoods. For example, most married women maintained very strong ties with parents and in-laws. Grandparents customarily served as godparents for a family's first- and second-born children; they were called *comadres* and *copadres*, and their responsibilities often included child rearing. Godparents not only officiated at christening services, a common Catholic custom, but also acted as surrogate guardians. Maternal grandparents usually served as godparents for the first child, paternal grandparents for the second, and then other relatives and friends assumed these important roles. In this fashion, kin and kith became links in a network of reciprocal obligations, which in the absence of men became women's sole domain.

While men were away, women also took responsibility for the physical and spiritual well-being of the village. Some older women whose children were grown served as midwives, delivering babies, caring for new mothers, and acting as counselors to the whole village. Even within the male-dominated Roman Catholic Church, the locus of spiritual life from baptism, feast days, weddings, and burial, village women played unusually prominent roles. Although men sustained the *Penitentes*, a religious and mutual aid society known for its flagellant practices, women carried out their own rituals and formed auxiliaries to men's societies. They prevailed in religious ceremonies during May, the month devoted to the Blessed Virgin Mary. In general, **Mariolatry** muted the masculine character of many rituals and legitimated women's participation in church affairs. So, too, did the chronic shortage of priests.

Mariolatry Worship of the Virgin Mary as religious practice within the Roman Catholic Church.

As Anglos encroached on their land and drew more and more villagers into the market economy, even the determination of women could not save the community. Whole families began to pull up stakes, heading for the burgeoning towns and cities where women joined men in the expanding system of wage labor.

Urban Householders

In the decades following the United States–Mexican War, the new Anglo settlers drove out many longtime Mexican residents, reducing the Hispanic population by as much as half in southwestern cities such as San Antonio, Texas. However, by the end of the century, this trend had reversed. Expanding trade and industry worked like a magnet, attracting not only Mexicanos from the communal villages but also many immigrants from Mexico. Single women and widows in particular took advantage of expanding opportunities for wage work, flocking to Texas cities as well as to well-established urban enclaves such as Santa Fe, Albuquerque, Tucson, and Denver. They moved in such numbers that before the century ended, the majority of Mexican Americans had become urban dwellers.

Upper-class Spanish-speaking women often came from families that had lived in these cities for generations; they considered themselves distinct from the growing populations of *mestizos*, Mexicans of mixed Spanish and Indian blood; and they tended to identify with Spain rather than Mexico (see chapter 4). They maintained their high status by spearheading the emerging consumer culture, although by the 1880s even women in the communal villages had access to sewing machines, cook stoves, and manufactured furniture. Wealthy women, however, ordered their furnishings and fashions from prominent retailers, such as Bloomingdale's in New York. If they enjoyed a status comparable to that of the Amadors family in Las Cruces, New Mexico, they sent their children to English-language schools and perhaps traveled to Chicago to take in the World's Fair of 1893.

At the other end of the social scale were the women who had fled rural poverty to build a better life for themselves and their family in the city. They lacked the means to enjoy the new consumer goods and instead found themselves barely able to scrape by on the wages they could earn as cooks, domestic servants, seamstresses, or laundresses for wealthy Anglo or Hispanic families. Old customs died hard, however, and many of the newcomers supplemented their wages by maintaining small backyard gardens. Mexicanas staffed the open markets, selling produce, bowls of chili, baked goods, and handicraft. Overall, though, few women earned more than subsistence and, as a group, far less than men. The move to the city usually made Mexicanas dependent on their husbands for support, unraveled the networks that had sustained them in the communal village, and ultimately reduced their power within both the family and community.

Despite such setbacks, Mexicanas continued to play important roles in preserving old traditions, including their allegiance to the Roman Catholic Church. Their families continued to baptize their children, celebrate the feast day of their patron saints, mark the transition from girlhood to womanhood at age fifteen by the *Quinceañera*, and marry according to prescripts of the church. National holidays of Mexico, such as *Cinco de Mayo*, which marked the Mexican victory over French invaders in 1862, continued to give the community distinctive reasons to celebrate its heritage.

BUILDING COMMUNITIES IN THE HEARTLAND

"The average farmer's wife is one of the most patient and overworked women of the time," one writer proclaimed in 1884 in *The American Farmer*. Many European-born and Euro-American women who settled the western territories, including the nation's heartland, may have agreed with this sentiment. They tended to put aside the drudgery and tedium that often characterized life in the wilderness and instead took pride in their contribution to the welfare of their family and community. Women worked hard to create a home and sought to reestablish old ways, including familiar patterns of love and labor. In the 1880s, for the three of every four people who lived in rural areas, the most enduring element was the household, the primary site of production that required the labor of all able-bodied members.

Homestead Act of 1862 Legislation allowing a household head, male or female, to obtain land in the public domain to establish a family farm.

The Homestead Act and Immigration

The **Homestead Act of 1862** made landowning a possibility for adventurous, free-spirited Euro-American women. The Act allowed a household head, male or female, to file for a quarter section (160 acres) of the public domain with the option of buying it at a bargain price at the end of six months' residence or owning it outright after five years of improving the land. Legally subordinate to her husband, a married woman could not qualify as a household head.

Unmarried women, however, were eligible to file claims. Wyoming homesteader Elinore Pruitt Stewart insisted that "any woman who can stand her own company, can see the beauty of the sunset, loves growing things, and is willing to put in as much time and careful labor as she does over the washtub, will have independence, plenty to eat all the time and a home of her own in the end." Few women accepted Stewart's invitation. Women filed less than 15 percent of all claims, and those who did file were more often than not acting as proxies for sons or brothers who for some reason failed to meet the terms of the Homestead Act. Only rarely did women homesteaders farm or ranch on their own. Stewart herself fudged on the details of her own, highly publicized success story: one week after filing her claim, she married the rancher who lived on the adjacent lot, thus securing for the newlyweds enough acreage to support a household.

Although land speculators took the greatest advantage of the Homestead Act, the completion of the transconti-

South Dakota, which became a state in 1889, advertised free land for homesteading in this poster prepared for the Columbian Exposition, held in Chicago in 1893. Although the early days of settlement were over, the state continued to encourage the formation of new communities.

nental railroad in 1869 encouraged many prospective farmers and ranchers to head west in droves. At the same time, marketing campaigns describing the rich bounties to be had in the American West targeted Europeans, many of whom lacked access to land in their home countries. Promotional literature often emphasized the opportunities available to women in particular, underscoring the possibility of attending school, earning a living, and holding property. By the end of the century, more than two million Europeans—from Germany, Scandinavia, Poland, Ireland, Russia, and many smaller countries—had relocated to the Great Plains, remapping the region as a potpourri of tightly knit ethnic communities.

A few African American families took advantage of the Homestead Act and left the South in the hope of becoming farmers. At the close of Reconstruction, as many as fifteen thousand black people, known as **Exodusters**, moved to Kansas, where they formed a handful of distinct communities. A smaller number moved to Indian Territory, which later became Oklahoma, while others scattered throughout the Great Plains and Rocky Mountains. Meanwhile, white farming families—known as "Yankees" to both European immigrants and African Americans—created a steady stream of migrants from states bordering the Mississippi River.

The Homestead Act helped to bring ethnic diversity to most regions of the nation's heartland. It was not unusual for neighbors to lack even a common language. Nevertheless, despite such diversity, the basic patterns of women's lives varied little from group to group.

Exodusters A term for the nearly 15,000 African Americans who moved to Kansas at the close of Reconstruction.

Woman's Work, Never Done

A familiar division of labor governed most farm households. Men tended the fields and outbuildings; women performed their customary tasks, such as sewing and knitting, preserving and preparing food, and cleaning the house, as well as the especially burdensome chore of laundering clothes. Although these everyday jobs fell to married women nationwide, housekeeping could prove especially challenging to even the most dedicated farm wife. For instance, because so few trees grew on the plains, settlers typically used bricks of compacted soil instead of lumber to build their houses. "Soddies," as they were called, provided sufficient protection from most elements of nature, although not the bugs and snakes that made their own home in the walls. Moreover, the walls of sod houses continuously shed bits of dirt while the ceilings let in rain, and the mud that formed eventually ruined most carpets and furniture. In addition to the Herculean chores of housekeeping, women took responsibility for several outdoor tasks. They tended chickens and gathered eggs, milked cows, and maintained a vegetable garden to keep their household supplied with produce.

Although farm communities readily acknowledged the importance of women's labor in the family economy, it is unclear if women's status was commensurate with their contribution. For example, rural isolation forced husbands and wives to rely on one another for companionship, but this situation could either foster a more egalitarian marriage or make a woman more vulnerable to domestic violence. However, men continued to enjoy the privilege of both custom and law in making major decisions, such as buying more property and equipment or pulling up stakes altogether. Also, the seasonal nature of men's work gave them an advantage. Men enjoyed enough leisure to make trips to town, where politics and fraternal activities eased the tedium of their routine. In contrast, women's work was unremitting, especially when it came to the care of children.

Children grew up with these role models before them, working alongside their mothers and fathers at gender-specific chores. "I assist Mother in household duties which are various," one young woman wrote. "She is preparing me for a Farmer's wife," that is, for a life of hard work.

Farm wives did find ways to contribute to the family economy that were often more satisfying than the ceaseless rounds of cooking, cleaning, and washing. Many women ran small-scale businesses. By selling baked goods such as breads, pies, and cookies, they could earn a small amount of cash; or they could barter for needed supplies, such as trading eggs and butter for household items like soap, linens, and clothing produced by neighboring women.

There were times, however, when the customary division of labor broke down. Men pitched in to help with the housework and child care, typically when their wives were recovering from illness or childbirth. In turn, women were prepared to take over when their husbands were called away to scout out new land, herd cattle, or take crops to market and, in such cases, assumed responsibility for the entire farming enterprise for weeks or months at a time. It was not unknown for farm wives to take on outdoor work, such as helping with the planting and harvesting, digging cellars, and building barns and sheds. However, as soon as cash could be spared to hire male helpers, most wives retreated to the home. The U.S. Department of Agriculture, in its 1872 annual report, affirmed the status quo, specifically advising farmers to encourage their wives to stick to the occupations "essentially feminine," such as the "household arts in which women are qualified by nature to excel" and not to "hold the plow or dig ditches, or build fences."

The Chrisman sisters are shown in front of their sod house in 1886, a year before Lizzie, the eldest, filed her homestead claim in Custer County, Nebraska. Eventually, all but the youngest acquired land under the provisions of the Homestead Act.

WOMEN'S LIVES

LAURA INGALLS WILDER

Laura Ingalls Wilder grew up in a pioneering family constantly on the move. Her father, Charles Ingalls, loved the open space of the prairie, and convinced his wife, Caroline Ingalls, and their four daughters to try homesteading in various locations throughout the Midwest and Plains states. When Laura was thirteen, the family settled in De Smet, a market town in the Dakota Territory with a population not much more than eighty. In later life, at age sixty-five, Laura began to use her memories of these small towns, such as Pepin, Wisconsin, where she was born, and Independence, Kansas, as settings for seven historical novels, the "Little House" books that have been read and savored by children across the generations.

Based in part on childhood memories, her stories capture the joys and hardships of rural life. *The Long Winter*, for example, dramatically depicts a winter of extremely harsh temperatures and ferocious snowstorms that brought her family to the brink of starvation because trains could not cut a passage to bring the needed provisions. In contrast, *These Happy Golden Years* offers a joyful conclusion to her series of stories, recounting her own stint as a young schoolteacher and, finally, her engagement and marriage.

The youthful Laura's imagination did not, however, preclude a childhood that was typical for girls growing up in the nation's heartland. Necessity often compelled Laura to assist her father in outdoor chores, serving, as she later recalled, as his "right-hand man." Nevertheless, her stories feature the heroic role of her otherwise stoic mother, who worked relentlessly to create for her family a comfortable home in the wilderness. The "Little House" books, with their tender details of domestic life, exalt the contribution of women to community building and family preservation, even under the most adverse circumstances. Indeed, whatever success Pa achieved could be attributed to the perseverance and talent of Ma, as he knew all too well. These were the lessons that Ma passed on to her daughters, depicted by Laura in careful and loving detail: making cheese and butter, preserving fruits and meats, and cooking meals over an open fire; knitting socks and gloves, sewing shirts and dresses by hand, and weaving straw into hats; cleaning house, lugging buckets of water for laundry, and carrying in wood for the fireplace.

These skills served the adult Laura Ingalls, who became a homesteader herself. In 1885, she married Almanzo Wilder, who shared her love of the rural life, and they soon had a baby daughter, Rose. However, misfortune followed this happy beginning. A son died shortly after birth, and a fire destroyed their home and barn. Laura and her husband nearly succumbed to diphtheria, and Almanzo never fully recovered. After a series of moves to escape drought and debt, they created a new home for themselves in a log cabin in Mansfield, Missouri, in 1894. A decade of hard work ended in prosperity, and the couple enjoyed a good life in the farming of poultry, dairy products, and fruit.

At the prompting of her daughter, Rose Wilder Lane, who herself became a successful writer and fled the rural life as soon as she was able, Laura began to fashion her childhood experiences into memorable and best-selling works of fiction. *Little House on the Prairie* appeared in 1935. ■

Immigrant women, in comparison to native-born farm wives, were more likely to pitch in whenever and wherever needed. "Among us Yankees," one Iowan observed, "the German habit of working women in the field was the sure mark of the 'Old Countryman," Whereas many such "Yankees" viewed immigrant farm wives as they did the women of many Indian tribes, as victims of lazy men, most immigrants considered the absence of Anglo women in the fields a sign of degeneracy. Coming from the European peasantry and accustomed to farm labor, most immigrant women simply assumed they would tend the fields and dairies and then, when time and energy allowed, tackle housekeeping. For similar reasons, immigrant farm families tended to be larger than those among the native-born families because they viewed children as an asset, as essential components of the household labor pool and insurance to parents in old age.

Turning Wilderness into "Civilization"

"I feel quite lonesome & solitary," one woman complained to in her diary. "My spirits are depressed. I have very little female society." Frequent moves made friendships fragile, and many women new to the region yearned for the friends and family left behind. To ease the isolation, settlers often built their homes on the adjacent corners of their allotments. Even strongly held prejudices did not keep some women from seeking female companionship from neighbors of different ethnicities or races from themselves. Mothers and daughters often found their relationship develop into an enduring friendship. While sons moved on to greener pastures, daughters were more likely to stay close to their mothers, often marrying local farmers and remaining in the community.

Farm wives typically turned to their neighbors and friends as much for help with chores as for companionship. Planting and harvesting brought neighbors together as did the occasional work of building new houses or barns. Quilting bees were popular forms of amusement for women, while county fairs attracted whole families. Childbirth summoned neighboring women to serve as midwives and supporters.

After the initial period of settlement, men and women broadened their range of social contacts beyond their families and neighbors and began to build the basic institutions of the small town or village. First came the school, which was built by men and staffed by women. The church was not far behind. As in other regions, western women formed auxiliaries and involved themselves in missionary activities. They organized Sunday schools and carried the gospel to nearby Indian reservations. Men and women alike joined clubs, although usually along gender-exclusive lines. Men organized themselves into fraternal associations and sporting clubs; women constructed a network of voluntary associations and benevolent societies as well as clubs devoted to education and culture.

Men and women often nurtured diverging aspirations for their communities. Men looked to the town to provide services relevant to both their business and their leisure. They promoted the establishment of banks, saloons, and brothels. Women more typically sought to impose order and morality, favoring Sunday-closing laws for retail establishments and financial institutions and the abolition of drinking, gambling, and prostitution altogether. As in other regions of the country, women assumed their role as moral guardians, an ideal that was affirmed in print media, church sermons, and public lectures.

Temperance rallied the largest number of women. The Woman's Crusade of 1873–74 recruited women across the West, from the mining frontier as well as from numerous towns of the plains and prairie. The first president of the national WCTU, Annie Turner Wittenmyer, hailed from the farming state of Iowa. Although native-born women provided the bulk of WCTU membership, some immigrant groups, Swedes in particular, formed their own chapters and sponsored a variety of programs to discourage the use of alcohol.

The Patrons of Husbandry

The household basis of the farm economy was reflected in the region's largest organization, the Patrons of Husbandry, better known as the Grange (a word for "farm"). The **Grange** began as a secret fraternal society in 1867 and grew in the 1870s to some 1.5 million members. For men and women alike, the Grange became the center of social life, the chief sponsor of picnics in the summer and holiday dances in the winter. The Grange organized cooperatives to sell grain and to buy equipment and household items and promoted state legislation to regulate shipping rates.

Grange The popular term for the Patrons of Husbandry, an organization of family farmers that formed in 1867.

From its inception, the Grange set itself apart from most other fraternal societies by inviting both women and men to join. "The Grange door swings inward as readily at the gentle knock of woman," one Granger announced, "as to the ruder knock of man." Grangers thus emphasized the distinctive and complementary roles of farm husbands and wives. One woman explained that the Grange resembled a healthy family, with the husband supplying "rude and vigorous force" and the wife adding "the refinement of her more sympathetic impulses to his energy." Only men served on the committees dealing with cooperatives or lobbying legislatures, while women managed the educational, charitable, and social activities of the order.

The order's 1874 Declaration of Purposes called for a "proper appreciation of the abilities and sphere of woman." In their newspapers and at their meetings, Grangers thoroughly addressed issues of rural domesticity, exchanging tips on housework and cooking as well as child rearing. They also acknowledged the repetitive, exhausting nature of these tasks and identified the farm woman's plight as one of drudgery. The Patrons of Husbandry emerged as one of the few national organizations to endorse woman's suffrage and saluted the WCTU as a kindred organization and required all members to take a vow of abstinence.

INDIAN WOMEN, CONQUEST, AND SURVIVAL

Ravaged by disease and pressured by the onslaught of Euro-American traders, prospectors, and homesteaders, Native American tribes nevertheless survived in far greater numbers than they did east of the Mississippi (see chapter 7). At the close of the Civil War, approximately 360,000 Indian people lived in this region, the majority on eight reservations where white Christian missionaries taught them to speak English, convert to Christianity, and become farmers. Greater changes lay ahead. In response to lobbying by white settlers and corporate interests, the federal government drastically reduced the land allotments that had earlier been promised to native peoples "for as long as the grass grows and the water runs." Large-scale war broke out, marked by intermittent bloody conflicts that lasted until 1886, when the Apache warrior Geronimo surrendered in Skeleton Canyon, Arizona, to the U.S. Army.

All the while, groups of Christian reformers were lobbying the federal government to implement more humane assimilationist policies on the reservations. The noted author Helen Hunt Jackson was one of the most influential. Her book, *A Century of Dishonor* (1881), exposed the cruelties that had been inflicted on Indian peoples and became to Indian reformers what Harriet Beecher Stowe's *Uncle Tom's Cabin* was to

Women's National Indian Association
Founded in 1879 to promote assimilationist policies among Native American women.

Dawes Severalty Act
Also called the Indian Allotment Act, this 1887 legislation divided reservation land in an effort to assimilate tribal members into the general American population as "responsible farmers."

abolitionists. Jackson was also active in various reform organizations, including a branch of the **Women's National Indian Association** (WNIA), which had formed in 1879. The WNIA raised money to promote assimilationist programs, sponsoring teachers, missionaries, and physicians to work among various Indian tribes. It also staged a massive petition campaign, urging Congress to phase out the reservation system, to make homesteaders of individual Indian families, and to establish a school system for children.

The WNIA was the chief force behind the **Dawes Severalty Act** (1887), named after the senator who sponsored it, which allowed the United States to convert communal tribal lands to individual ownership. The government distributed allotments of 160 acres to heads of households, that is, to Indian men who agreed to be "severed" legally from their tribes and to become farmers; in return, they could petition to become citizens of the United States. Indian women were to relinquish their roles as producers to become farm wives and care primarily for home and children. In sum, the Dawes Severalty Act strengthened the authority of the federal government to prescribe a nuclear family system and to proselytize the doctrine of separate spheres as the chief means to assimilate Indian men and women into "civilization."

The Nez Perce

According to tribal lore, it was a woman who facilitated the first friendly contact between white explorers and her tribe. Wet-khoo-weis was so grateful to a white woman for rescuing her from captivity by rival Indians that when the Lewis and Clark Expedition arrived in Nez Perce territory in 1806 she persuaded tribal leaders to "do them no harm." From this point on, the Nez Perce regarded themselves as friends to white traders and settlers.

Living on the plateau where Idaho, Washington, and Oregon now meet, the Nez Perce remained on good terms with the U.S. government until the 1860s, when, following the discovery of gold, they were forced to cede nearly nine-tenths of their land. A substantial portion of the tribe refused assignment to a reservation and, in 1877, followed Chief Joseph to search for sanctuary in Canada. During the long journey, Nez Perce women performed the essential tasks of setting up and dismantling the camps and caring for the wounded warriors. When their husbands were killed in battle, women occasionally retrieved the guns, mounted their horses, and joined the fight. United States troops finally forced Chief Joseph's band to surrender in northern Montana, just thirty miles from the Canadian border.

Meanwhile, those Nez Perce women who had accepted reservation status became enmeshed in assimilationist programs based on the doctrine of separate spheres. In 1869, President Ulysses S. Grant put Christian missionaries in charge of reservations, and the Presbyterians who volunteered to work among the Nez Perce did more than instruct the tribe in the tenets of their religion. The missionaries pleaded with tribal members to abide by the sexual division of labor deemed appropriate to "civilization." For example, they advised the Nez Perce to replace their tipis with the wooden-frame houses typical of sedentary American farmers. Such houses, which could comfortably accommodate only a few people, would undermine the prevailing extended-family living arrangements and induce the Nez Perce to live as nuclear families, or so the missionaries believed. Moreover, the missionaries insisted that men construct the new homes, thereby displacing the women who customarily built the tipis and thereby served as the chief providers of housing.

The missionaries had less success, however, in pursuading women to reject traditional clothing styles and functions. Used to fashioning buffalo skins into ornately beaded garments, Nez Perce women welcomed the sewing machine and woven textiles traded by the Euro-Americans. Even in the building of tipis, they readily switched from buffalo hides to canvas. However, they were reluctant to follow the advice of missionaries to forsake highly decorated clothing, which the Protestants denounced as "heathen" and wasteful. Viewing clothing as an important marker of identity and status, most Nez Perce women continued to savor beaded leggings, feathered hats, and shell jewelry.

However, Nez Perce women did adapt to farming as a way of life, although in ways that undoubtedly surprised their Protestant instructors. Men resisted the role of farmer because, traditionally, gardening among the Nez Perce was "women's work." In contrast, women readily accepted basic farm chores as routine. But contrary to the missionaries' wishes, Nez Perce women also took on the heavy outdoor work of cultivating, threshing, and harvesting. At first, they used horses to drag the equipment; later they drove tractors. The women also refused to stay put on their own farms and instead continued the customary practice of working in groups, even pitching tents in the field and spending the night together. In the few instances when the missionaries convinced men to farm, their wives still refused to retreat to the home and instead hired out, earning wages by sifting and winnowing wheat.

Plains Indians

The role and status of Plains women underwent similarly dramatic changes as a result of the U.S. government's determination to turn Indians into self-sufficient farmers. By the 1870s, the buffalo, which had inhabited the plains for thousands of years, were on the verge of extinction, a consequence of reckless slaughter by white overland traders wielding powerful new weapons. Various tribes, with the mainstay of their livelihood disappearing, agreed to cede large portions of their land in return for the right to live in security in Indian Territory or on a reservation. Believing that the prospects for "civilizing" these tribes lay in the hands of women, federal agents and missionaries then began to implement vigorous programs to transform Indian women into homemakers.

Such was the case of the Sioux women who lived on the Devil's Lake Reservation in North Dakota, which had been established in 1867. More quickly than the Nez Perce, it seemed, Sioux men accepted responsibility for agricultural production. Federal agents persuaded them to take up what had traditionally been "women's work" by offering such incentives as kerosene,

The 1891 photograph by the J.C. H. Grabill shows the wife of the Lakota Sioux chief American Horse with several other Indian women sitting in an encampment tipi, probably at the Pine Ridge Reservation, South Dakota.

WOMEN'S VOICES

LEAVING FOR THE MISSION SCHOOL

Gertrude Simmons Bonnin, *who wrote under her chosen name* **Zitkala-Sa** *(Red Bird), trained as a musician and devoted much of her life to pan-Indian activism. She was born and raised on the Yankton Sioux Reservation in South Dakota until she enrolled, at age eight, in the Quaker mission school in Wabash, Indiana. In this autobiographical piece, she recalls her mother, Ellen Simmons, whose Yankton-Lakota name was Taté Iyòhiwin (Every Wind or Reaches for the Wind).*

My Mother

A wigwam of weather-stained canvas stood at the base of some irregularly ascending hills. A footpath wound its way gently down the sloping land till it reached the broad river bottom; creeping through the long swamp grasses that bent over it on either side, it came out on the edge of the Missouri.

Here, morning, noon, and evening, my mother came to draw water from the muddy stream for our household use. Always, when my mother started for the river, I stopped my play to run along with her. She was only of medium height. Often she was sad and silent, at which times her full arched lips were compressed into hard and bitter lines, and shadows fell under her black eyes. Then I clung to her hand and begged to know what made the tears fall.

"Hush; my little daughter must never talk about my tears"; and smiling through them, she patted my head and said, "Now let me see how fast you can run today." Whereupon I tore away at my highest possible speed, with my long black hair blowing in the breeze.

I was a wild little girl of seven. Loosely clad in a slip of brown buckskin, and light-footed with a pair of soft moccasins on my feet, I was as free as the wind that blew my hair, and no less spirited than a bounding deer. These were my mother's pride,—my wild freedom and overflowing spirits. She taught me no fear save that of intruding myself upon others. . . .

Setting the pail of water on the ground, my mother stooped, and stretching her left hand out on the level with my eyes, she placed her other arm about me; she pointed to the hill where my uncle and my only sister lay buried.

"There is what the paleface has done! Since then your father too has been buried in a hill nearer the rising sun. We were once very happy. But the paleface has stolen our lands and driven us hither. Having defrauded us of our land, the paleface forced us away."

"Well, it happened on the day we moved camp that your sister and uncle were both very sick. Many others were ailing, but there seemed to be no help. We traveled many days and nights; not in the grand happy way that we moved camp when I was a little girl, but we were driven, my child, driven like a herd of buffalo. With every step, your sister, who was not as large as you are now, shrieked with the painful jar until she was hoarse with crying. She grew more and more feverish. Her little hands and cheeks were burning hot. Her little lips were parched and dry, but she would not drink the water I gave her. Then I discovered that her throat was swollen and red. My poor child, how I cried with her because the Great Spirit had forgotten us!"

"At last, when we reached this western country, on the first weary night your sister died. And soon your uncle died also, leaving a widow and an orphan daughter, your cousin Warca-Ziwin. Both your sister and uncle might have been happy with us today, had it not been for the heartless paleface."

My mother was silent the rest of the way to our wigwam. Though I saw no tears in her eyes, I knew that was because I was with her. She seldom wept before me.

Source: *Zitkala-Sa (Gertrude Bonnin), American Indian Stories (Washington, DC: Hayworth Publishing House, 1921), 7–11.*

Questions

1. How does Zitkala-Sa, who left the reservation when she was a young child, describe her relationship with her mother?

2. In this work of fiction, how much do you think Zitkala-Sa draws from her own experiences?

tools, and clothing and even plots of land for the most adept farmers. Eventually, some Sioux men became very successful wheat farmers. With their husbands now acting as chief breadwinners of the family, women left the fields and tended only small gardens for domestic consumption.

The reservation boarding schools, established in the 1870s to "uplift" the Indians, reinforced this arrangement. Immediately upon arrival, children had their long, straight hair shorn and their distinctive tribal clothing stripped away, while their Christian teachers attempted to refashion them in the style of Anglo boys and girls. The teachers promoted acculturation by establishing curricula clearly delineated by gender. They taught Sioux boys agricultural methods, as well as other vocational skills such as carpentry and blacksmithing with the expectation that as adults they would take on the role of chief breadwinner of the family. In contrast, girls prepared for a life of economy dependency. They studied and practiced the homemaking arts, including cooking and baking; housecleaning; and quilting, crocheting, and knitting. In addition, Sioux girls received a heavy dose of moral training to prepare for their future role in sustaining a Christian home. However, a small number of girls flourished in the new educational setting and went on to become doctors, writers, and teachers themselves.

Ultimately, the majority of Sioux women lost considerable status as tribal members. At one time highly skilled in tailoring and decorating buffalo hides, tribal women adapted readily to the new forms of needlework; and quilting soon emerged as major decorative art on the reservations, and quilts were important items for sale or exchange. However, women's handicraft and homemaking activities did not carry the same weight as men's contribution to the livelihood of family and tribe alike. Women retained some traditional prerogatives, such as the right to dissolve a marriage and to participate in ceremonies and rituals. However, women were no longer consulted about intertribal dealings; nor could they negotiate with federal agents who recognized only men as heads of household.

A small group of Sioux women faced their greatest trial in 1890. Their land area reduced by the federal government, the Sioux could no longer sustain their tribes and suffered for want of food and other necessities. Many believed that the day of judgment was near, and they joined an ecstatic spiritual movement, the Ghost Dance, which swept the plains and simultaneously provoked federal officials who interpreted it as a war dance. In December, representatives of various Sioux tribes gathered at the Wounded Knee Creek near the Pine Ridge and Rosebud reservations in South Dakota and on December 19 were massacred by the 7th U.S. Cavalry. At least forty-four women and eighteen babies died in the **Wounded Knee Massacre** considered the final armed conflict between Native Americans and the federal government.

> **Wounded Knee Massacre** The attack by the US 7th Calvary on December 29, 1890 that resulted in the deaths of nearly 190 Indians, the majority of whom were women and children.

The Southern Ute

At one time, the Southern Ute lived by hunting and foraging in a wide region spanning the Rocky Mountains and the Great Basin; and by the early nineteenth century, they had become powerful actors in a flourishing trade economy among other Indians, Mexicans, and Anglos. However, when the land they occupied became part of the United States in 1848, the Ute started down a path that ultimately led to reservation status. By the terms of the Dawes Severalty Act, the reservation became an administrative unit of the Office of Indian Affairs (OIA), which, along with missionary and reform organizations, acted to undermine the remaining vestiges of the Ute's collectivist society and egalitarian gender system.

WOMEN'S LIVES

SUSAN LA FLESCHE PICOTTE, M.D. AND SUSETTE LA FLESCHE TIBBLES

A few remarkable Indian women took on important roles as cultural mediators. Such was the case of two Omaha sisters, Susan and Susette La Flesche. Both their parents were children of intermarriage with French traders, but the family's identity as Omaha was secure across the generations. Their father, Joseph La Flesche, also known as Iron Eye, had served as tribal chief until shortly after Susan's birth, a time when the Omaha, like other Plains Indians, were up against the era of the reservation. Disease and malnourishment plagued the small tribe, and their father represented the faction promoting partial acculturation over its likely alternative, extinction. He himself had given up the lodge home and traditional clothing and had converted to Christianity.

Susan and Susette, who was older by eleven years, from early childhood acquired traditional skills by working beside their mother, and they learned English and other academic subjects from the teachers at the mission boarding school. The Presbyterian-run school closed in 1869, and both Susette and Susan continued their formal education at the Elizabeth Institute for Young Ladies in New Jersey. In 1884, Susan joined, as she put it, other "happy seekers after knowledge" at an industrial boarding school, the Hampton Institute in Virginia, where she was trained to teach "civilization" and bring Christianity back to the reservation. However, both Susan and her sister wanted to do more, and they used their education to become cultural brokers or mediators.

Susette returned to the reservation and taught for a short time before emerging as a prominent activist for Indian rights. In 1878, she and her future husband, Thomas Henry Tibbles, became forceful advocates for the destitute Ponca tribe, which had been forcibly re-moved from Dakota Territory to the increasingly crowded Indian Territory. Acting as a translator for Ponca chief Standing Bear, Susette conducted a dramatic speaking tour of the eastern states. Until her death, she offered a counterpart to those reformers who aspired to "civilize" the Indians, arguing forcefully instead for citizenship rights and protection of the law.

Susan, in contrast, took to heart the lessons she had learned at school and pledged herself to help the Indians progress toward "civilization." However, like her sister, she herself refused to embrace the idealized role of homemaker and continued her education at the Woman's Medical College in Philadelphia. The first Indian woman to receive a medical degree, she accepted an appointment from the Office of Indian Affairs and in 1889 returned to Omaha as physician to the students who attended the government-run boarding school. Within a short time, she was supplying medical services to the entire tribe. Although she took a few years off to recuperate from her challenging and time-consuming responsibilities to marry and to give birth to two sons, until her death Susan La Flesche Picotte, M.D., practiced medicine among her people. ■

The Carlisle Indian School in Pennsylvania opened in October 1879 to assimilate Indian children to white ways. This photograph, taken at the turn of the century, shows young women attending the "breakfast lesson" in home economics. More than 10,000 Indian children were educated at Carlisle before the school closed in 1918.

Prior to the reservation, Ute men achieved status in the highly masculine role of raider and warrior, while women derived their authority from the responsibility of guarding the camp and protecting the children. On occasion, when the fighting neared their home territory, armed women joined the men in battle, scalping their enemies and carrying back the spoils. In the victory ceremonies, women received their share of the honor.

Like other Indian women, Ute women found it increasingly difficult to hold on to their customary roles in the aftermath of the Dawes Severalty Act. The terms of the Act decreed their husbands the head of the household, and the Office of Indian Affairs similarly assumed that political leadership on the reservation belonged to men alone. Government agents therefore dealt only with all-male councils on matters ranging from allotments to educational programs.

Ute women resisted these changes in governance and continued to participate in tribal-sponsored forums about various aspects of reservation policy. For example, Ute women, reluctant to send their children to boarding schools that had high rates of contagious disease, forced the OIA to open a day school in 1886. Four years later, 150 women presented their opinions at a major meeting about tribal finances. Within their families, they preserved their authority to make decisions about the care of their children and the welfare of their household. They also served as liaisons with Ute families in other jurisdictions, thereby helping to maintain the regional tribal community. And given the stringencies on the reservation, especially the prevalence of disease, the tribe had little choice but to value women's contributions.

CONCLUSION

In 1890, the director of the U.S. Census declared that the nation's "unsettled area has been so broken into by isolated bodies of settlement that there can hardly be said to be a frontier line." The trans-Mississippi West had been incorporated into the United States. Americans had brought to this region their political, legal, and economic systems, as well as their cultural and social institutions. For women, this transformation had pivoted on the doctrine of separate spheres, foremost the tenets of domesticity.

WOMEN'S HISTORY	GLOBAL EVENTS
	1840
	1846 Mormons settle in Great Salt Lake Basin, Utah
	1848 California gold rush begins
	1848 United States–Mexican War ends
	1860
	1860s Texas cattle drives begin
	1862 Homestead Act passes in Congress
	1862 Morrill Anti-Bigamy Act passes in Congress
	1867 Patrons of Husbandry (the Grange) organizes
	1869 Transcontinental railroad completed
	1870
1870 Women in Utah gain the right to vote	1877 Defeat of the Nez Perce
1873 Woman's Crusade begins	
1875 Page Law restricts Chinese women's immigration	
1879 Women's Indian Reform Association organizes	1879 "Exodusters" migrate to Kansas
	1880
1881 Helen Hunt Jackson publishes *A Century of Dishonor*	1882 Edmunds Act passes Congress
1885 Annie Oakley joins "Buffalo Bill's Wild West" company	1887 Dawes Severalty Act passes Congress
	1890 Wounded Knee Massacre

Even as the federal government marked the closing of the frontier, the trans-Mississippi West served as home to more and more women whose cultures intersected, often clashed, and encouraged new meanings for traditional practices. They found themselves enmeshed in a continuous struggle that would define ethnic, racial, and class hierarchies in this region while they simultaneously reconsidered established practices of women's work and markers of women's status within their families and their communities. In other words, domesticity served as a major site of contest, an arena for asserting power and establishing identity, and a measure of civilization over wilderness.

REVIEW QUESTIONS

1. What factors promoted the imbalanced sex ratio in the states and territories west of the Mississippi?

2. Why did woman suffrage come first to the western territories and states?

3. How did the incorporation of Mexican lands into the United States affect the lives of Spanish-speaking women?

4. How did men and women manage their households on the plains and prairies?

5. How did Indian women respond to the assimilationist programs sponsored by the U.S. government and carried out by missionaries?

RECOMMENDED READING

Kathryn M. Daynes. *More Wives Than One: Transformation of the Mormon Marriage System.* Urbana: University of Illinois Press, 2001. A 150-year study of polygamy in Manti, Utah, this book provides an especially vivid portrait of plural marriage in this locality during the last half of the nineteenth century.

Sarah Deutsch. *No Separate Refuge: Culture, Class, and Gender on an Anglo-Hispanic Frontier in the American Southwest 1880–1940.* New York: Oxford University Press, 1987. Traces and analyzes the increasing marginality of Hispanic women as their communities moved into Anglo areas to the north of their original communal villages of New Mexico.

Deborah Fink. *Agrarian Women: Wives and Mothers in Rural Nebraska, 1880–1940.* Chapel Hill: University of North Carolina Press, 1992. Centered on Boone County, Nebraska, this well-researched book explores the lives of farm wives and mothers with an eye on their roles in a family economy dominated by their husbands.

Dee Garceau. *The Important Things of Life: Women, Work, and Family in Sweetwater County, Wyoming, 1880–1929.* Lincoln: University of Nebraska Press,
1997. Emphasizes ethnic diversity and studies in close detail the roles of women in both mining and ranching communities across two generations.

Caroline James. *Nez Perce Women in Transition, 1877–1900.* Moscow: University of Idaho Press. 1996. Based in part on forty-six interviews with Nez Perce women, this book covers many facets of reservation life in the process of acculturation and supplements a rich narrative with extraordinary photographs.

Elizabeth Jameson and Susan Armitage, eds. *Writing the Range: Race, Class, and Culture in the Women's West.* Norman: University of Oklahoma Press, 1997. A collection of essays emphasizing the cultural diversity of the American West and highlighting the interconnections of gender, class, race and ethnicity in four centuries of history in this region.

Katherine Osburn. M.B., *Southern Ute Women: Autonomy and Assimilation on the Reservation, 1887–1934.* Albuquerque: University of New Mexico Press, 1998. Provides compelling evidence that Southern Ute women resisted many of the assimilationist programs imposed by the Dawes Severalty Act and continued to participate in tribal affairs well into the twentieth century.

Benson Tong. *Unsubmissive Women: Chinese Prostitutes in Nineteenth-Century San Francisco*. Norman: University of Oklahoma Press, 1994. Tells a complicated story of the women who came from China to work in the burgeoning commercial sex industry. Less a study of victimization than one of survival in a new land.

ADDITIONAL BIBLIOGRAPHY

General Histories and Historiography

Susan Armitage and Elizabeth Jameson, eds. *The Women's West*. Norman: University of Oklahoma Press. 1987.

Elizabeth Jameson. "Toward a Multicultural History of Women in the Western United States," *Signs* 13 Summer 1988, 761–91.

Julie Roy Jeffrey. *Frontier Women: "Civilizing the West? 1840–1880.* New York: Hill and Wang, Revised Edition 1998.

Sandra L. Myres. *Westering Women and the Frontier Experience, 1800–1915*. Albuquerque: University of New Mexico Press, 1982.

Glenda Riley. *Women and Indians on the Frontier, 1825–1915*. Albuquerque: University of New Mexico Press, 1984.

Lillian Schlissel, Vicki L. Ruiz, and Janice Monk, eds. *Western Women: Their Land, Their Lives*. Albuquerque: University of New Mexico Press, 1988.

Quintard Taylor and Shirley Ann Wilson Moore, eds. *African American Women Confront the West*. Norman: University of Oklahoma Press, 2003.

On the Range and in Mining Communities

Anne M. Butler. *Daughters of Joy, Sisters of Mercy: Prostitutes in the American West, 1865–90*. Chicago: University of Illinois Press, 1985.

Marion S. Goldman. *Gold Diggers and Silver Miners: Prostitution and Social Life on the Comstock*. Ann Arbor: University of Michigan Press, 1981.

Lucie Cheng Hirata. "Free, Indentured, Enslaves: Chinese Prostitutes in Nineteenth-Century American," *Signs*, 5 Autumn 1979, 3–29.

Ruth B. Moynihan, Susan Armitage, and Christiane Fischer Dichamp, eds. *So Much to Be Done: Women Settlers on the Mining and Ranching Frontier*, 2d ed., New Haven: Yale University Press, 1983, 1998.

Paula Petrik. *No Step Backward: Women and Family on the Rocky Mountain Mining Frontier, Helena, Montana, 1865–1900*. Helena: Montana Historical Society, 1990.

Sally Zanjani. *A Mine of Her Own: Women Prospectors in the American West, 1850–1950*. Lincoln: University of Nebraska Press, 1997.

Mormon Communities

Maureen Ursenbach Beecher, and Lavina Fielding Anderson, eds. *Sisters in Spirit: Mormon Women in Historical and Cultural Perspective*. Urbana: University of Illinois Press, 1987.

Jessie L. Embry. "Effects of Polygamy on Mormon Women," *Frontiers*, 7, #3. 1984, 56–61.

Sarah Barringer Gordon. *The Mormon Question: Polygamy and Constitutional Conflict in Nineteenth-Century America*. Chapel Hill: University of North Carolina Press, 2002.

Jeffrey Nichols. *Prostitution, Polygamy, and Power: Salt Lake City, 1847–1918*. Urbana: University of Illinois Press, 2002.

Spanish-Speaking Women of the New Southwest

Teresa Palomo Acosta, and Ruthe Winegarten. *Las Tejanas: 300 Years of History*. Austin: University of Texas Press, 2003.

Darlis A. Miller. "Cross-Cultural Marriages in the Southwest: The New Mexico Experience, 1846–1900, *New Mexico Historical Review*, 57 October 1982, 335–59.

Vicki Ruiz, and Susan Tiano, eds. *Women on the United States-Mexico Border: Responses to Change*. Westminster, Mass.: Allen and Unwin, 1987.

Building Communities in the Heartland

Sheryll Black-Patterson. "Women Homesteaders on the Great Plains Frontier, *Frontiers: A Journal of Women Studies*, Vol. 1, No. 2 (Spring, 1976), pp. 67–88.

Katherine Harris. *Long Vistas: Women and Families on Colorado Homesteads.* Niwot, Co.: University of Colorado Press, 1993.

Norman Juster. *So Sweet to Labor: Rural Women in America, 1865–1895.* Norman: University of Oklahoma Press, 1979.

H. Elaine Lindgren. "Ethnic Women Homesteading on the Plains of North Dakota," *Great Plains Quarterly,* 9, 1989, 157–73.

Sally McMurry. *Families and Farmhouses in Nineteenth Century America.* New York: Oxford University Press, 1988.

Donald B, Marti. *Women of the Grange: Mutuality and Sisterhood in Rural America, 1866–1920.* Westport: Greenwood Press. 1991.

Indian Women

Patricia Albers. and Beatrice Medicine. *The Hidden Half: Studies of Plains Indian Women.* Washington, DC: University Presses of America, 1983.

Evelyn Blackwood. "Sexuality and Gender in Certain Native American Tribes: The Case of Cross-Gendered Females," *Signs,* 10 Autumn 1984, 27–42.

Lisa Emmerich. "Right in the Midst of My Own People': Native American Women and the Field Matron Program," *American Indian Quarterly,* 15 Summer 1991, 201–16.

Margaret D. Jacobs. *Engendered Encounters: Feminism and Pueblo Cultures, 1879–1934.* Lincoln: University of Nebraska Press, 1999.

Devon Abbott Mihesuah. *Cultivating the Rosebuds: The Education of Women at the Cherokee Female Seminary, 1851–1909.* Urbana: University of Illinois Press, 1997.

Theda Purdue, ed. *Sifters: Native American Women's Lives.* New York: Oxford University Press, 2001.

Jane E., Simonsen. *Making Home Work: Domesticity and Native American Assimilation in the American West, 1860–1919.* Chapel Hill: University of North Carolina Press, 2006.

Mary C. Wright. "The Woman's Lodge: Constructing Gender on the Nineteenth-Century Pacific Northwest Plateau," *Frontiers,* 24, #12003, 1–18.

Memoirs, Diaries, Autobiographies and Biographies

Maureen Ursenbach Beecher. *Life Writings of Frontier Women,* 5 vol. Salt Lake City: University of Utah Press.

Isabella Bird. *A Lady's Life in the Rocky Mountains.* Norman: University of Oklahoma Press, 1883, 1971.

Rachel Calof and J. Sanford Rikoon. *Rachel Calof's Story: Jewish Homesteader on the Northern Plains.* Bloomington: Indiana University Press, 1995.

Cheryl J. Foote. *Women of the New Mexico Frontier, 1846–1912.* Niwot: University Press of Colorado, 1990.

Kay Graber, ed. *Sister to the Sioux: The Memoirs of Elaine Goodale Eastman, 1885–1891.* Lincoln: University of Nebraska Press, 2004.

Elizabeth Hampsten. *Read This Only to Yourself: The Private Writings of Midwestern Women, 1880–1910.* Bloomington: Indiana University Press, 1982.

Joan Mark. *A Stranger in Her Native Land: Alice Fletcher and the American Indians.* Lincoln: University of Nebraska Press, 1988.

Valerie Mathes. *Helen Hunt Jackson and Her Indian Reform Legacy.* Austin: University of Texas Press, 1990.

Darlis A. Miller. *Mary Hallock Foote: Author-Illustrator of the American West.* Norman: University of Oklahoma Press, 2002.

Lillian Schlissel. *Women's Diaries of the Westward Journey.* New York: Schocken Books. 1982, 1992.

Lillian Schlissel and Catherine Lavender, eds. *The Western Women's Reader: The Remarkable Writings of Women Who Shaped the American West, Spanning 300 Years.* New York. HarperPerennial, 2000.

Patty Barlett Sessions. *Mormon Midwife: The 1846–1888 Diaries of Patty Barlett Sessions.* Logan: Utah State Univesity Press, 1997.

Elinor Pruitt Stewart. *Letters of a Woman Homesteader.* Boston: Houghton Mifflin Co., 1914.

Benson Tong. *Susan La Flesche Picotte, M.D.: Omaha Indian Leader and Reformer.* Norman: University of Oklahoma, 1999.

Sally Zanjani. *Sarah Winnemucca.* Lincoln: University of Nebraska Press, 2001.

Appendix

The Declaration of Independence (1776)

When in the course of human events it becomes necessary for one people to dissolve the political bands which have connected them with another and to assume, among the powers of the earth, the separate and equal station to which the laws of nature and of nature's God entitle them, a decent respect to the opinions of mankind requires that they should declare the causes which impel them to the separation.

We hold these truths to be self-evident, that all men are created equal; that they are endowed by their Creator with certain unalienable rights; that among these are life, liberty, and the pursuit of happiness. That, to secure these rights, governments are instituted among men, deriving their just powers from the consent of the governed; that, whenever any form of government becomes destructive of these ends, it is the right of the people to alter or to abolish it, and to institute a new government, laying its foundation on such principles, and organizing its powers in such form, as to them shall seem most likely to effect their safety and happiness. Prudence, indeed, will dictate that governments long established should not be changed for light and transient causes; and, accordingly, all experience hath shown that mankind are more disposed to suffer, while evils are sufferable, than to right themselves by abolishing the forms to which they are accustomed. But when a long train of abuses and usurpations, pursuing invariably the same object, evinces a design to reduce them under absolute despotism, it is their right, it is their duty, to throw off such government and to provide new guards for their future security. Such has been the patient sufferance of these colonies, and such is now the necessity which constrains them to alter their former systems of government. The history of the present King of Great Britain is a history of repeated injuries and usurpations, all having, in direct object, the establishment of an absolute tyranny over these States. To prove this, let facts be submitted to a candid world.

He has refused his assent to laws the most wholesome and necessary for the public good.

He has forbidden his governors to pass laws of immediate and pressing importance, unless suspended in their operation till his assent should be obtained; and, when so suspended, he has utterly neglected to attend to them.

He has refused to pass other laws for the accommodation of large districts of people, unless those people would relinquish the right of representation in the legislature, a right inestimable to them and formidable to tyrants only.

He has called together legislative bodies at places unusual, uncomfortable, and distant from the depository of their public records, for the sole purpose of fatiguing them into compliance with his measures.

He has dissolved representative houses, repeatedly for opposing, with manly firmness, his invasions on the rights of the people.

He has refused, for a long time after such dissolutions, to cause others to be elected; whereby the legislative powers, incapable of annihilation, have returned to the people at large for their exercise; the state remaining, in the meantime, exposed to all the danger of invasion from without and convulsions within.

He has endeavored to prevent the population of these States; for that purpose, obstructing the laws for naturalization of foreigners, refusing to pass others to encourage their migration hither, and raising the conditions of new appropriations of lands.

He has obstructed the administration of justice by refusing his assent to laws for establishing judiciary powers.

He has made judges dependent on his will alone for the tenure of their offices and the amount and payment of their salaries.

He has erected a multitude of new offices and sent hither swarms of officers to harass our people and eat out their substance.

He has kept among us, in time of peace, standing armies, without the consent of our legislatures.

He has affected to render the military independent of, and superior to, the civil power.

He has combined with others to subject us to a jurisdiction foreign to our Constitution and unacknowledged by our laws, giving his assent to their acts of pretended legislation—

For quartering large bodies of armed troops among us;

For protecting them, by mock trial, from punishment for any murders which they should commit on the inhabitants of these States;

For cutting off our trade with all parts of the world;

For imposing taxes on us without our consent;

For depriving us, in many cases, of the benefit of trial by jury;

For transporting us beyond seas to be tried for pretended offences;

For abolishing the free system of English laws in a neighboring province, establishing therein an arbitrary government, and enlarging its boundaries, so as to render it at once an example and fit instrument for introducing the same absolute rule into these colonies;

For taking away our charters, abolishing our most valuable laws, and altering, fundamentally, the powers of our governments.

For suspending our own legislatures and declaring themselves invested with power to legislate for us in all cases whatsoever.

He has abdicated government here by declaring us out of his protection and waging war against us.

He has plundered our seas, ravaged our coasts, burnt our towns, and destroyed the lives of our people.

He is, at this time, transporting large armies of foreign mercenaries to complete the works of death, desolation, and tyranny already begun with circumstances of cruelty and perfidy scarcely paralleled in the most barbarous ages, and totally unworthy the head of a civilized nation.

He has constrained our fellow citizens, taken captive on the high seas, to bear arms against their country, to become the executioners of their friends and brethren, or to fall themselves by their hands.

He has excited domestic insurrections amongst us and has endeavored to bring on the inhabitants of our frontiers, the merciless Indian savages, whose known rule of warfare is an undistinguished destruction of all ages, sexes, and conditions.

In every stage of these oppressions, we have petitioned for redress in the most humble terms; our repeated petitions have been answered only by repeated injury. A prince whose character is thus marked by every act which may define a tyrant is unfit to be the ruler of a free people.

Nor have we been wanting in attention to our British brethren. We have warned them, from time to time, of attempts made by their legislature to extend an unwarrantable jurisdiction over us. We have reminded them of the circumstances of our emigration and settlement here. We have appealed to their native justice and magnanimity, and we have conjured them, by the ties of our common kindred, to disavow these usurpations, which would inevitably interrupt our connections and correspondence. They, too, have been deaf to the voice of justice and consanguinity. We must, therefore, acquiesce in the necessity which denounces our separation, and hold them, as we hold the rest of mankind, enemies in war, in peace, friends.

We, therefore, the representatives of the United States of America, in general Congress assembled, appealing to the Supreme Judge of the world for the rectitude of our intentions, do, in the name and by the authority of the good people of these colonies, solemnly publish and declare, that these united colonies are, and of right ought to be, free and independent states: that they are absolved from all allegiance to the British Crown, and that all political connection between them and the state of Great Britain is, and ought to be, totally dissolved; and that, as free and independent states, they have full power to levy war, conclude peace, contract alliances, establish commerce, and to do all other acts and things which independent states may of right do. And, for the support of this declaration, with a firm reliance on the protection of Divine Providence, we mutually pledge to each other our lives, our fortunes, and our sacred honor.

Declaration of Sentiments and Resolutions Woman's Rights Convention, Seneca Falls, New York (1848)

We hold these truths to be self-evident: that all men and women are created equal; that they are endowed by their Creator with certain inalienable rights; that among these are life, liberty, and the pursuit of happiness; that to secure these rights governments are instituted, deriving their just powers from the consent of the governed . . . But when a long train of abuses and usurpations, pursuing invariably the same object evinces a design to reduce them under absolute despotism, it is their duty to throw off such government, and to provide new guards for their future security. Such has been the patient sufferance of the women under this government, and such is now the necessity which constrains them to demand the equal station to which they are entitled.

The history of mankind is a history of repeated injuries and usurpations on the part of man toward woman, having in direct object the establishment of an absolute tyranny over her. To prove this, let facts be submitted to a candid world.

He has never permitted her to exercise her inalienable right to the elective franchise.

He has compelled her to submit to laws, in the formation of which she had no voice.

He has withheld from her rights which are given to the most ignorant and degraded men—both natives and foreigners.

Having deprived her of this first right of a citizen, the elective franchise, thereby leaving her without representation in the halls of legislation, he has oppressed her on all sides.

He has made her, if married, in the eye of the law, civilly dead.

He has taken from her all right in property, even to the wages she earns.

He has made her, morally, an irresponsible being, as she can commit many crimes with impunity, provided they be done in the presence of her husband. In the covenant of marriage, she is compelled to promise obedience to her husband, he becoming, to all intents and purposes, her master—the law giving him power to deprive her of her liberty, and to administer chastisement.

He has so framed the laws of divorce, as to what shall be the proper causes, and in case of separation, to whom the guardianship of the children shall be given, as to be wholly regardless of the happiness of women—the law, in all cases, going upon a false supposition of the supremacy of man, and giving all power into his hands.

After depriving her of all rights as a married woman, if single, and the owner of property, he has taxed her to support a government which recognizes her only when her property can be made profitable to it.

He has monopolized nearly all the profitable employments, and from those she is permitted to follow, she receives but a scanty remuneration. He closes against her all the avenues to wealth and distinction which he considers most honorable to himself. As a teacher of theology, medicine, or law, she is not known.

He has denied her the facilities for obtaining a thorough education, all colleges being closed against her.

He allows her in Church, as well as State, but a subordinate position, claiming Apostolic authority for her exclusion from the ministry, and, with some exceptions, from any public participation in the affairs of the Church.

He has created a false public sentiment by giving to the world a different code of morals for men and women, by which moral delinquencies which exclude women from society, are not only tolerated, but deemed of little account in man.

He has usurped the prerogative of Jehovah himself, claiming it as his right to assign for her a sphere of action, when that belongs to her conscience and to her God.

He has endeavored, in every way that he could, to destroy her confidence in her own powers, to lessen her self respect, and to make her willing to lead a dependent and abject life.

Now, in view of this entire disfranchisement of one-half the people of this country, their social and religious degradation—in view of the unjust laws above mentioned, and because women do feel themselves aggrieved, oppressed, and fraudulently deprived of their most sacred rights, we insist that they have immediate admission to all the rights and privileges which belong to them as citizens of the United States.

In entering upon the great work before us, we anticipate no small amount of misconception, misrepresentation, and ridicule; but we shall use every instrumentality within our power to effect our object. We shall employ agents, circulate tracts, petition the State and National legislatures, and endeavor to enlist the pulpit and the press in our behalf. We hope this Convention will be followed by a series of Conventions embracing every part of the country.

The following resolutions were adopted:

Resolved, That such laws as conflict, in any way, with the true and substantial happiness of woman, are contrary to the great precept of nature and of no validity, for this is "superior in obligation to any other."

Resolved, That all laws which prevent woman from occupying such a station in society as her conscience shall dictate, or which place her in a position inferior to that of man, are contrary to the great precept of nature, and therefore of no force or authority.

Resolved, That woman is man's equal—was intended to be so by the Creator, and the highest good of the race demands that she should be recognized as such.

Resolved, That the women of this country ought to be enlightened in regard to the laws under which they live, that they may no longer publish their degradation by declaring themselves satisfied with their present position, nor their ignorance, by asserting that they have all the rights they want.

Resolved, That inasmuch as man, while claiming for himself intellectual superiority, does accord to woman moral superiority, it is pre-eminently his duty to encourage her to speak and teach, as she has an opportunity, in all religious assemblies.

Resolved, That the same amount of virtue, delicacy, and refinement of behavior that is required of woman in the social state, should also be required of man, and the same transgressions should be visited with equal severity on both man and woman.

Resolved, That the objection of indelicacy and impropriety, which is so often brought against woman when she addresses a public audience, comes with a very ill-grace from those who encourage, by their attendance, her appearance on the stage, in the concert, or in feats of the circus.

Resolved, That woman has too long rested satisfied in the circumscribed limits which corrupt customs and a perverted application of the Scriptures have marked out for her, and that it is time she should move in the enlarged sphere which her great Creator has assigned her.

Resolved, That it is the duty of the women of this country to secure to themselves their sacred right to the elective franchise.

Resolved, That the equality of human rights results necessarily from the fact of the identity of the race in capabilities and responsibilities.

Resolved, therefore, That, being invested by the Creator with the same capabilities, and the same consciousness of responsibility for their exercise, it is demonstrably the right and duty of woman, equally with man, to promote every righteous cause by every righteous means; and especially in regard to the great subjects of morals and religion, it is self-evidently her right to participate with her brother in teaching them, both in private and in public, by writing and by speaking, by any instrumentalities proper to be used, and in any assemblies proper to be held; and this being a self-evident truth growing out of the divinely implanted principles of human nature, any custom or authority adverse to it, whether modern or wearing the hoary sanction of antiquity, is to be regarded as a self-evident falsehood, and at war with mankind.

Resolved, That the speedy success of our cause depends upon the zealous and untiring efforts of both men and women, for the overthrow of the monopoly of the pulpit, and for the securing to woman an equal participation with men in the various trades, professions, and commerce.

Constitution of the Woman's National Council of the United States (1888)

Preamble

We, women of the United States, sincerely believing that the best good of our homes and nation will be advanced by our own greater unity of thought, sympathy and purpose, and that an organized movement of women will best conserve the highest good of the family and the State, do hereby band ourselves together in a confederation of workers committed to the overthrow of all forms of ignorance and injustice, and to the application of the Golden Rule to society, custom and law.

That we may more successfully prosecute the work, we adopt the following

CONSTITUTION.

Article I.

Name.

This federation shall be called the Woman's National Council of the United States.

Article II.

General Policy.

This Council is organized in the interest of no one propaganda, and has no power over its auxiliaries beyond that of suggestion and sympathy; therefore, no society voting to become auxiliary to this Council, shall thereby render itself liable to be interfered with in respect to its complete organic unity, independence or methods of work, or be committed to any principle or method of any other society or to any utterance or act of the Council itself, beyond compliance with the terms of this Constitution.

Article III.

Officers.

The officers shall be a President, Vice-President at Large, Corresponding Secretary, Recording Secretary and Treasurer. Each president of an auxiliary society shall be *ex officio* Vice-President of the National Council and the President of the National Council shall be *ex officio* Vice-President of the International Council.

The five general officers, with the Vice-Presidents, shall constitute an Executive Committee, of which seven members shall make a quorum, to control and provide for the general interests of the Council.

Article IV.

Auxiliaries.

Any society of women, the nature of whose work is satisfactory to the Executive Committee, either as to its undoubtedly national character or national value, may become auxiliary to this Council by its own vote and by the payment of a sum amounting to half a cent yearly per member, in addition to a payment of twenty-five dollars, into the treasury of the National Council not later than three months prior to its triennial meetings.

Article V.

Meetings.

The National Council shall hold triennial meetings. The Committee of Arrangements shall be composed of the Executive Committee and one delegate chosen by each auxiliary society as its representative.

Article VI.

This Constitution may be altered or amended by a majority vote of the Council at any triennial meeting, printed notice thereof having been sent to each member of the Executive Committee at least three months prior to such meeting.

Nineteenth Amendment to the Constitution of the United States of America (August 26, 1920)

SECTION 1. The right of citizens of the United States to vote shall not be denied or abridged by the United States or by any State on account of sex.

SECTION 2. Congress shall have the power to enforce this article by appropriate legislation.

The National Organization for Women's 1966 Statement of Purpose

This Statement of Purpose was written by Betty Friedan, author of "The Feminine Mystique."

We, men and women who hereby constitute ourselves as the National Organization for Women, believe that the time has come for a new movement toward true equality for all women in America, and toward a fully equal partnership of the sexes, as part of the world-wide revolution of human rights now taking place within and beyond our national borders.

The purpose of NOW is to take action to bring women into full participation in the mainstream of American society now, exercising all the privileges and responsibilities thereof in truly equal partnership with men.

We believe the time has come to move beyond the abstract argument, discussion and symposia over the status and special nature of women which has raged in America in recent years; the time has come to confront, with concrete action, the conditions that now prevent women from enjoying the equality of opportunity and freedom of choice which is their right, as individual Americans, and as human beings.

NOW is dedicated to the proposition that women, first and foremost, are human beings, who, like all other people in our society, must have the chance to develop their fullest human potential. We believe that women can achieve such equality only by accepting to the full the challenges and responsibilities they share with all other people in our society, as part of the decision-making mainstream of American political, economic and social life.

We organize to initiate or support action, nationally, or in any part of this nation, by individuals or organizations, to break through the silken curtain of prejudice and discrimination against women in government, industry, the professions, the churches, the political parties, the judiciary, the labor unions, in education, science, medicine, law, religion and every other field of importance in American society.

Enormous changes taking place in our society make it both possible and urgently necessary to advance the unfinished revolution of women toward true equality, now. With a life span lengthened to nearly 75 years it is no longer either necessary or possible for women to devote the greater part of their lives to child- rearing; yet childbearing and rearing which continues to be a most important part of most women's lives—still is used to justify barring women from equal professional and economic participation and advance.

Today's technology has reduced most of the productive chores which women once performed in the home and in mass-production industries based upon routine un-skilled labor. This same technology has virtually eliminated the quality of muscular strength as a criterion for filling most jobs, while intensifying American industry's need for creative intelligence. In view of this new industrial revolution created by au-tomation in the mid-twentieth century, women can and must participate in old and new fields of society in full equality—or become permanent outsiders.

Despite all the talk about the status of American women in recent years, the ac-tual position of women in the United States has declined, and is declining, to an alarming degree throughout the 1950's and 60's. Although 46.4% of all American women between the ages of 18 and 65 now work outside the home, the overwhelming majority—75%—are in routine clerical, sales, or factory jobs, or they are household workers, cleaning women, hospital attendants. About two-thirds of Negro women workers are in the lowest paid service occupations. Working women are becoming in-creasingly—not less—concentrated on the bottom of the job ladder. As a consequence full-time women workers today earn on the average only 60% of what men earn, and that wage gap has been increasing over the past twenty-five years in every major in-dustry group. In 1964, of all women with a yearly income, 89% earned under $5,000 a year; half of all full-time year round women workers earned less than $3,690; only 1.4% of full-time year round women workers had an annual income of $10,000 or more.

Further, with higher education increasingly essential in today's society, too few women are entering and finishing college or going on to graduate or professional school. Today, women earn only one in three of the B.A.'s and M.A.'s granted, and one in ten of the Ph.D.'s. In all the professions considered of importance to society, and in the executive ranks of industry and government, women are losing ground. Where they are present it is only a token handful. Women comprise less than 1% of federal judges; less than 4% of all lawyers; 7% of doctors. Yet women represent 51% of the U.S. population. And, increasingly, men are replacing women in the top positions in secondary and elementary schools, in social work, and in libraries—once thought to be women's fields.

Official pronouncements of the advance in the status of women hide not only the reality of this dangerous decline, but the fact that nothing is being done to stop it. The excellent reports of the President's Commission on the Status of Women and of the State Commissions have not been fully implemented. Such Commissions have power only to advise. They have no power to enforce their recommendation; nor have they the freedom to organize American women and men to press for action on them. The reports of these commissions have, however, created a basis upon which it is now pos-sible to build. Discrimination in employment on the basis of sex is now prohibited by federal law, in Title VII of the Civil Rights Act of 1964. But although nearly one-third of the cases brought before the Equal Employment Opportunity Commission during the first year dealt with sex discrimination and the proportion is increasing dramati-cally, the Commission has not made clear its intention to enforce the law with the same seriousness on behalf of women as of other victims of discrimination. Many of these cases were Negro women, who are the victims of double discrimination of race and sex. Until now, too few women's organizations and official spokesmen have been willing to speak out against these dangers facing women. Too many women have been restrained by the fear of being called "feminist." There is no civil rights movement to speak for women, as there has been for Negroes and other victims of discrimination. The National Organization for Women must therefore begin to speak.

We believe that the power of American law, and the protection guaranteed by the U.S. Constitution to the civil rights of all individuals, must be effectively applied and enforced to isolate and remove patterns of sex discrimination, to ensure equality of opportunity in employment and education, and equality of civil and political rights and responsibilities on behalf of women, as well as for Negroes and other deprived groups.

We realize that women's problems are linked to many broader questions of social justice; their solution will require concerted action by many groups. Therefore, convinced that human rights for all are indivisible, we expect to give active support to the common cause of equal rights for all those who suffer discrimination and deprivation, and we call upon other organizations committed to such goals to support our efforts toward equality for women.

We do not accept the token appointment of a few women to high-level positions in government and industry as a substitute for serious continuing effort to recruit and advance women according to their individual abilities. To this end, we urge American government and industry to mobilize the same resources of ingenuity and command with which they have solved problems of far greater difficulty than those now impeding the progress of women.

We believe that this nation has a capacity at least as great as other nations, to innovate new social institutions which will enable women to enjoy the true equality of opportunity and responsibility in society, without conflict with their responsibilities as mothers and homemakers. In such innovations, America does not lead the Western world, but lags by decades behind many European countries. We do not accept the traditional assumption that a woman has to choose between marriage and motherhood, on the one hand, and serious participation in industry or the professions on the other. We question the present expectation that all normal women will retire from job or profession for 10 or 15 years, to devote their full time to raising children, only to reenter the job market at a relatively minor level. This, in itself, is a deterrent to the aspirations of women, to their acceptance into management or professional training courses, and to the very possibility of equality of opportunity or real choice, for all but a few women. Above all, we reject the assumption that these problems are the unique responsibility of each individual woman, rather than a basic social dilemma which society must solve. True equality of opportunity and freedom of choice for women requires such practical, and possible innovations as a nationwide network of child-care centers, which will make it unnecessary for women to retire completely from society until their children are grown, and national programs to provide retraining for women who have chosen to care for their children full-time.

We believe that it is as essential for every girl to be educated to her full potential of human ability as it is for every boy—with the knowledge that such education is the key to effective participation in today's economy and that, for a girl as for a boy, education can only be serious where there is expectation that it will be used in society. We believe that American educators are capable of devising means of imparting such expectations to girl students. Moreover, we consider the decline in the proportion of women receiving higher and professional education to be evidence of discrimination. This discrimination may take the form of quotas against the admission of women to colleges, and professional schools; lack of encouragement by parents, counselors and educators; denial of loans or fellowships; or the traditional or arbitrary procedures in graduate and professional training geared in terms of men, which inadvertently discriminate against women. We believe that the same serious attention must be given to high school dropouts who are girls as to boys.

We reject the current assumptions that a man must carry the sole burden of supporting himself, his wife, and family, and that a woman is automatically entitled to life-long support by a man upon her marriage, or that marriage, home and family are primarily woman's world and responsibility—hers, to dominate—his to support. We believe that a true partnership between the sexes demands a different concept of marriage, an equitable sharing of the responsibilities of home and children and of the economic burdens of their support. We believe that proper recognition should be given to the economic and social value of homemaking and child-care. To these ends, we will seek to open a reexamination of laws and mores governing marriage and divorce, for we believe that the current state of "half-equity" between the sexes discriminates against both men and women, and is the cause of much unnecessary hostility between the sexes.

We believe that women must now exercise their political rights and responsibilities as American citizens. They must refuse to be segregated on the basis of sex into separate-and-not-equal ladies' auxiliaries in the political parties, and they must demand representation according to their numbers in the regularly constituted party committees—at local, state, and national levels—and in the informal power structure, participating fully in the selection of candidates and political decision-making, and running for office themselves.

In the interests of the human dignity of women, we will protest, and endeavor to change, the false image of women now prevalent in the mass media, and in the texts, ceremonies, laws, and practices of our major social institutions. Such images perpetuate contempt for women by society and by women for themselves. We are similarly opposed to all policies and practices—in church, state, college, factory, or office—which, in the guise of protectiveness, not only deny opportunities but also foster in women self-denigration, dependence, and evasion of responsibility, undermine their confidence in their own abilities and foster contempt for women.

NOW will hold itself Independent of any political party in order to mobilize the political power of all women and men intent on our goals. We will strive to ensure that no party, candidate, president, senator, governor, congressman, or any public official who betrays or ignores the principle of full equality between the sexes is elected or appointed to office. If it is necessary to mobilize the votes of men and women who believe in our cause, in order to win for women the final right to be fully free and equal human beings, we so commit ourselves.

We believe that women will do most to create a new image of women by acting now, and by speaking out in behalf of their own equality, freedom, and human dignity—not in pleas for special privilege, nor in enmity toward men, who are also victims of the current, half-equality between the sexes—but in an active, self-respecting partnership with men. By so doing, women will develop confidence in their own ability to determine actively, in partnership with men, the conditions of their life, their choices, their future and their society.

Equal Rights Amendment

SECTION 1. Equality of Rights under the law shall not be denied or abridged by the United States or any state on account of sex.

SECTION 2. The Congress shall have the power to enforce, by appropriate legislation, the provisions of this article.

SECTION 3. This amendment shall take effect two years after the date of ratification.

Title IX of The Education Amendments (1972)

SEC. 1681. SEX **(a) Prohibition against discrimination; exceptions**
No person in the United States shall, on the basis of sex, be excluded from participation in, be denied the benefits of, or be subjected to discrimination under any education program or activity receiving Federal financial assistance, except that:
(1) Classes of educational institutions subject to prohibition in regard to admissions to educational institutions, this section shall apply only to institutions of vocational education, professional education, and graduate higher education, and to public institutions of undergraduate higher education;
(2) Educational institutions commencing planned change in admissions in regard to admissions to educational institutions, this section shall not apply
(A) for one year from June 23, 1972, nor for six years after June 23, 1972, in the case of an educational institution which has begun the process of changing from being an institution which admits only students of one sex to being an institution which admits students of both sexes, but only if it is carrying out a plan for such a change which is approved by the Secretary of Education
or
(B) for seven years from the date an educational institution begins the process of changing from being an institution which admits only students of only one sex to being an institution which admits students of both sexes, but only if it is carrying out a plan for such a change which is approved by the Secretary of Education, whichever is the later;
(3) Educational institutions of religious organizations with contrary religious tenets this section shall not apply to an educational institution which is controlled by a religious organization if the application of this subsection would not be consistent with the religious tenets of such organization;
(4) Educational institutions training individuals for military services or merchant marine this section shall not apply to an educational institution whose primary purpose is the training of individuals for the military services of the United States, or the merchant marine;
(5) Public educational institutions with traditional and continuing admissions policy in regard to admissions this section shall not apply to any public institution of undergraduate higher education which is an institution that traditionally and continually from its establishment has had a policy of admitting only students of one sex;
(6) Social fraternities or sororities; voluntary youth service organizations this section shall not apply to membership practices

(A) of a social fraternity or social sorority which is exempt from taxation under section 501(a) of title 26, the active membership of which consists primarily of students in attendance at an institution of higher education, or

(B) of the Young Men's Christian Association, Young Women's Christian Association, Girl Scouts, Boy Scouts, Camp Fire Girls, and voluntary youth service organizations which are so exempt, the membership of which has traditionally been limited to persons of one sex and principally to persons of less than nineteen years of age;

(7) Boy or Girl conferences this section shall not apply to

(A) any program or activity of the American Legion undertaken in connection with the organization or operation of any Boys State conference, Boys Nation conference, Girls State conference, or Girls Nation conference; or

(B) any program or activity of any secondary school or educational institution specifically for—

(i) the promotion of any Boys State conference, Boys Nation conference, Girls State conference, or Girls Nation conference; or

(ii) the selection of students to attend any such conference;

(8) Father-son or mother-daughter activities at educational institutions this section shall not preclude father-son or mother-daughter activities at an educational institution, but if such activities are provided for students of one sex, opportunities for reasonably comparable activities shall be provided for students of the other sex; and

(9) Institution of higher education scholarship awards in "beauty" pageants this section shall not apply with respect to any scholarship or other financial assistance awarded by an institution of higher education to any individual because such individual has received such award in any pageant in which the attainment of such award is based upon a combination of factors related to the personal appearance, poise, and talent of such individual and in which participation is limited to individuals of one sex only, so long as such pageant is in compliance with other nondiscrimination provisions of Federal law.

(b) Preferential or disparate treatment because of imbalance in participation or receipt of Federal benefits; statistical evidence of imbalance

Nothing contained in subsection (a) of this section shall be interpreted to require any educational institution to grant preferential or disparate treatment to the members of one sex on account of an imbalance which may exist with respect to the total number or percentage of persons of that sex participating in or receiving the benefits of any federally supported program or activity, in comparison with the total number or percentage of persons of that sex in any community, State, section, or other area: *Provided*, That this subsection shall not be construed to prevent the consideration in any hearing or proceeding under this chapter of statistical evidence tending to show that such an imbalance exists with respect to the participation in, or receipt of the benefits of, any such program or activity by the members of one sex.

(c) "Educational institution" defined

For purposes of this chapter an educational institution means any public or private preschool, elementary, or secondary school, or any institution of vocational, professional, or higher education, except that in the case of an educational institution composed of more than one school, college, or department which are administratively separate units, such term means each such school, college, or department.

GLOSSARY

A Vindication of the Rights of Woman Treatise by Mary Wollstonecraft published in 1792 in England arguing for the intellectual equality and rights of women.

abroad marriage Marriage of slaves who live on two different plantations.

age of consent Phrase referring the minimum age at which a person is considered capable of giving informed consent to any contract or behavior, with particular reference to sexual acts.

Aid to Dependent Children (ADC) A program that gave grants to states to use for the support of dependent children.

All American Girls Baseball League (AAGBL) Women's professional baseball league that began as a response to the lack of young male athletes who had joined the armed services.

American and Foreign Anti-Slavery Society Organization created in 1840 to oppose slavery through political channels but to ignore other issues such as the right of women to lead the reform movement.

American Anti-Slavery Society Organization founded by William Lloyd Garrison in 1833 committed to an immediate end to slavery.

American Birth Control League Founded in 1921 to provide services to women in need; later became Planned Parenthood.

American Woman Suffrage Association (AWSA) Formed in 1869 in Cleveland and led by Lucy Stone and Henry Blackwell to work for woman suffrage at all levels.

antebellum period Period in U.S. history extending roughly from 1830 to 1860.

antimiscegenation laws State legislation enacted to prevent interracial marriage.

Articles of Confederation Document adopted by Second Continental Congress in 1777 to create first government of the United States as a loose confederation of states.

Association for the Advancement of Women (AAW) Formed in October 1873 to promote the formation of women's clubs and to showcase women's accomplishments.

Association of Southern Women to Prevent Lynching (ASWPL) Founded by Jessie Daniel Ames in 1930 to mobilze white southern women to oppose lynching.

baby boom The cohort of babies born in the United States between 1946–1964.

back-alley abortions Illegal abortions, done in unsanitary and often dangerous nonmedical settings.

Baltimore and Ohio Railroad First railroad built in the United States, opening in 1830.

Beats A group of mostly male writers and poets centered in Greenwich, who rebelled against 1950s social and sexual conventions.

Beecher-Tilton scandal The furor created by the revelation of the Rev. Henry Ward Beecher's affair with Elizabeth Tilton, one of his parishioners.

belles Wealthy young southern women of marriageable age presented to society in a series of balls.

Big House African American description of the house on the plantation where the master lived.

Black Codes Legislation enacted by former Confederate states, 1865–1866, to define the rights and limits of freedom of former slaves.

Black Death Bubonic plague that swept Europe beginning in the 1340s and continuing particularly through the seventeenth century.

Black Power movement A younger and more militant phase of the civil rights movement that highlighted the importance of black masculinity.

bond marriage Legal agreement to marry that was used as a substitute for marriage in the early days of settlement in Texas.

Boston marriage A term popular in the late nineteenth century that referred to women who set up housekeeping together and lived in a marriage-like relationship.

Brown v. Board of Education of Topeka The 1954 Supreme Court case overturning the "separate but equal" doctrine established in *Plessy v. Ferguson*.

Californios/Californias Men and women of Spanish descent in California.

camp meetings Religious revival meetings held in open fields, usually during the summer.

casta Person of mixed heritage.

Chamberlain-Kahn Act Passed in July 1819, this legislation established federal grants for state venereal disease programs aimed to protect men serving in the armed forces.

charity girls A reference used in the early twentieth century for young women who traded sexual favors for treats and amusements.

Child Support Enforcement Amendments Act This act strengthened child support agencies' abilities to get money from the nonresidential parent of children on Aid to Families with Dependent Children (AFDC) for medical expenses and cost of living.

children's crusade Plan to send the children of the textile strikers to temporary homes outside Lawrence.

Christian Coalition A group formed by Roman Catholic and Evangelical Protestants to influence Republican party politics.

Civilian Conservation Corps (CCC) Program was designed to tackle the problem of unemployed young men from ages 18 to 25.

coartacion Ability of a slave to purchase his or her freedom under Spanish law.

cold war The foreign policy of containment directed at Communist Soviet Union and includes the alignments between foreign policy abroad and the expression of anti-Communism throughout U.S. culture.

Commission on Interracial Cooperation (CIC) Established in Atlanta in 1921 the Commission worked with white and black leaders to bring an end to lynching and improve the conditions of poor African Americans.

communitarian Referring to experimental collective communities meant to demonstrate how societies could be constructed around shared property and social responsibilities rather than around individual property.

companionate marriage A new style of marriage that emphasized companionship and compatability between spouses, as well as sex education, birth control, and easier access to divorce.

complementarity Idea that men and women have different characteristics that complement one another.

complex marriage Form of marriage promoted in the Oneida community in which every man and every woman in the community were considered married to one another.

Compromise of 1850 Congressional act allowing New Mexico and Utah to decide if they will be free or slave but also allowing California to be admitted to the Union as a free state.

Comstock Act The 1873 law that forbade the use of the U.S. Postal Service to mail "obscene" materials, which included contraceptive information and devices.

Confederate States of America The union of the eleven southern states that seceded to preserve slavery and protect states rights.

Congress of Industrial Organizations (CIO) The labor union formed in 1935 by John L. Lewis as the result of a dispute with the American Federation of Labor.

consciousness raising A popular practice of groups of women sharing intimate details of their lives to study them for the effects of sexism and gender oppression.

consumption The purchasing of consumer goods.

Contraband Relief Association Formed in August 1862 to provide food and relief to destitute former slaves.

contrabands of war Term for escaped slaves who sought refuge behind Union lines during the Civil War.

Council of National Defense Created by the U.S. Congress during World War I to manage the domestic aspects of the nation's war effort.

counterculture The youth culture of the mid-1960s that grew out of the student protest movements, with a focus on lifestyle liberation.

coureurs de bois French trappers.

coverture Legal status of a woman upon marriage under common law, in which her legal identity is merged with that of her husband.

crillo Person of Spanish heritage born in a colony.

cross-class alliance A concept referring to the joint projects of middle- and upper-class women and working-class women based on the assumption of "sisterhood."

Cullom Bill Introduced into Congress in 1870 to strengthen the provisions of the Morrill Anti-Bigamy Act, which had been largely ignored during the Civil War.

cult of domesticity Ideology suggesting that women's work within the home was crucial to society, particularly because of its moral rather than economic value

culture wars A set of clashes between conservative and liberal Americans over issues pertaining to private life.

Daughters of Bilitis A political group formed by lesbians to promote greater tolerance of homosexuality.

Daughters of Liberty Women who organized to support the Patriot cause.

Daughters of St. Crispin Formed in 1869 as the woman's branch of the all-male Knights of St. Crispin, which supported the principle of equal pay for equal work.

Dawes Severalty Act Also called the Indian Allotment Act, this 1887 legislation divided reservation land in an effort to assimilate tribal members into the general American population as "responsible farmers."

de facto segregation Racial segregation based on social practice, not enforced by law.

de jure segregation Racial segregation based on law.

Declaration of Independence Written by the Second Continental Congress in 1776 rejecting the King of England as the leader of the British colonies and asserting the right of men to form their own government.

Declaration of Sentiments Statement produced at the Seneca Falls convention in 1848 listing injustices faced by women and rights they deserved.

Democratic Party Political party that formed around Andrew Jackson in the 1820s, supporting his policies of limited federal government.

deputy husband Position assumed by a woman who took on the responsibilities of her husband while he was gone.

do-everything policy This policy provided an umbrella for the promotion of a multitude of programs beyond temperance.

domestic feminism Coined by historian Daniel Scott Smith, refers to the increasing power of married women to control reproduction.

double V campaign Winning the fight against racial segregation, or Jim Crow, and against fascism.

Dred Scott decision Decision by the Supreme Court that Dred Scott could not sue for his freedom even though he lived in a free state because slaves were not citizens.

Eagle Forum Pro-family organization founded by Phyllis Schlafly in 1972.

Edmunds-Tucker Act Legislation disincorporating the Mormon church and disenfranchising supporters of polygamy, including women.

elect People chosen by God to be saved.

Ellis Island Located in the New York Harbor, the main port of entry for immigrants in the late nineteenth and early twentieth centuries.

Emancipation Proclamation Issued by President Lincoln on January 1, 1863, freeing slaves in the Confederate states.

empressarios Agents who brought parties of immigrant settlers from the United States to Texas.

Enlightenment Intellectual movement stressing human reason and the ability to achieve progress by applying reason to problems of science and society.

Equal Employment Opportunity Commission (EEOC) The federal agency charged with enforcing employment antidiscrimination laws.

Equal Opportunity Act This act legislated a broader jurisdiction for the EEOC and strengthened its ability to enforce its rulings.

Equal Pay Act of 1963 Federal legislation that prohibited pay differentials based on sex.

Equal Rights Amendment (ERA) A proposed constitutional amendment outlawing discrimination "on account of sex."

Erie Canal First canal built in the United States, connecting New York City with upstate New York.

Executive Order 8802 This order prohibited government contractors from engaging in employment discrimination based on race, color, or national origin.

Exodusters A term for the nearly 15,000 African Americans who moved to Kansas at the close of Reconstruction.

Fair Labor Standards Act of 1938 The federal law establishing minimum wages, standards for overtime work and pay, and restrictions on child labor.

Family and Medical Leave Act (FMLA) Passed in 1993, the Act provided twelve weeks of unpaid family leave for workers.

family system of labor The practice of employing entire families, including young children, common in the production of textiles.

Family Violence Prevention and Services Act The 1984 Act provided funds for shelters and family violence programs.

family wage The idea that a man should earn sufficient wages to provide the sole support of his family.

family-wage economy Term for the situation in which all members of a family must earn wages and share them in order for the family to survive.

Farm Security Administration (FSA) Created to assist poor farmers during the dust bowl and the Great Depression.

Farmers' Alliance Organized in the 1880s as the political wing of the Granger movement and became the backbone of Populism by the end of the decade.

Federal Emergency Relief Administration (FERA) Passed in 1933, the agency gave direct aid to the states, which funneled funds through such local agencies as home relief bureaus and departments of welfare for poor relief.

Federalists Political faction that supported the Constitution and a strong central government.

feme covert Status of married woman under common law in which her legal identity is merged with that of her husband.

feme sole Status of a single woman under common law in which her legal identity is independent of a man.

feminism A term introduced into the United States around 1910 to augment the demands for voting rights and economic equality with a psychological dimension akin to "self-realization."

feminist art movement A movement in the 1970s to redefine women's art and women's place in the art world.

feminization of poverty The gradual and proportionate increase of women living in poverty in the 1970s.

fictive kin People with strong emotional ties similar to those of family members but not related to each other through marriage or birth.

Fifteenth Amendment Prohibits the denial of suffrage because of race, color, or previous condition of servitude and leaves out "sex."

filibustering Private military adventures to take over foreign governments with whom the United States is not at war.

Florence Crittenton Mission A refuge for prostitutes and safe haven for women without homes named for the recently-deceased daughter of founder Charles Crittenton.

Fourierists Followers of Charles Fourier who participated in his communitarian experiment in France and the United States.

Fourteenth Amendment Confers national citizenship on all persons born or naturalized in the United States and introduces the word "male" into the Constitution.

Free Soil Party Political party created in the 1840s around a belief that slavery should not be allowed in the territories acquired by the United States.

Freedmen's Bureau Established by Congress in March, 1865 to provide assistance to Civil War refugees; the federal agency that coordinated relief efforts for former slaves and established schools for black children.

French and Indian War Also known as the Seven Years' War in Europe, it was fought between France and England from 1754 to 1763 in both Europe and North America.

gang system System for organizing slave labor that groups slaves together to work on successive tasks.

General Federation of Women's Clubs Formed in 1890 as a federation of local women's clubs.

genizaros and genizaras Male and female Indian captives held as slaves in New Mexico.

GI Bill or the Servicemen's Readjustment Act of 1944 Provided college or vocational education, one year of unemployment compensation, and loans for returning veterans.

glass ceiling A term that refers to situations in which the advancement of a qualified person stops at a particular level because of some form of discrimination, most commonly sexism or racism.

Grange The popular term for the Patrons of Husbandry, an organization of family farmers that formed in 1867.

Great Awakening Series of religious revivals that swept the colonies in the middle of the eighteenth century.

Great Migration Movement of Puritans from England to New England between the 1620s and 1650s as a result of religious persecution.

Great Migration The migration of thousands of African Americans from the rural South to the urban North, which was especially pronounced during World War I when job opportunities opened up.

Henry Street Settlement Founded in New York City in 1893 by Lillian Wald to provide social and health services to mainly immigrant families.

Heterodoxy A club of "unorthodox women" formed by Marie Jenny Howe in 1912 that included the cream of New York's literary, artistic, and political activists.

heterosociality When women and men socialize together, as opposed to single-sex or homosocial settings.

Hollywood Production Code "Morality" codes imposed on Hollywood films in between 1930 and 1960.

home economics Originated in the 1880s as an academic discipline devoted to the care of home and family.

home protection The slogan promoted by WCTU president Frances E. Willard to secure the organization's endorsement of woman suffrage.

Homestead Act of 1862 Legislation allowing a household head, male or female, to obtain land in the public domain to establish a family farm.

Hospital Act of September 1862 Legislation by the Confederacy that allowed women to serve as nurses in hospitals.

Hull-House One of the first settlement houses in the United States, founded in Chicago in 1889 by Jane Addams and Ellen Gates Starr.

Hyde Amendment A 1976 law that reframed the government's responsibility to offer abortion services and restricted abortion from the health care provided by Medicaid.

identity politics Political action to advance the interests of members of groups that share a marginalized identity, such as race or gender.

Illinois Factory Inspection Act Passed in 1893, this landmark act specified conditions of labor in sweatshops in the state of Illinois; it was declared unconstitutional the following year.

Illinois Woman's Alliance Formed in 1888 to assist working women and their children.

indentured servant Person bound to work for a master for four to seven years as payment for transportation to the New World.

Indian Country Land in British territory west of the Proclamation Line of 1763 reserved for Indians.

Indian Removal Act Act passed by both houses of Congress in 1830 allowing the president to negotiate treaties that would exchange Indian lands east of the Mississippi River for new territory west of the Mississippi.

Indian Territory Unorganized territory west of the Mississippi River where Indians were forced to relocate in the 1830s.

Industrial Revolution Transformation from craft-based system to mass production of goods.

Industrial Workers of the World Founded in Chicago in 1905, represented the radical wing of the labor movement and organized workers into "one big union" without regard to skill.

inner light Quaker belief that Jesus is a guiding light within each person.

International Council of Women Formed in 1888 as a counterpart to the National Council of Women with delegates representing women activists from nine nations.

International Council of Women of the Darker Races of the World Founded by African American Mary Talbert in 1922 to promote Pan-African activism.

International Ladies' Garment Workers' Union Founded in Chicago in 1905, the "Wobblies" represented the radical wing of the labor movement and organized workers into "one big union" without regard to skill.

Jane Club The Chicago cooperative housekeeping arrangement for a group of working women who wished to avoid boarding-houses.

Jeffersonian Republicans Political faction that opposed the Federalists and favored limited government and an agrarian republic.

jezebel White southern stereotype of young slave woman who was thought to seek out sexual relationships with white men.

juvenile court system Special courts established to handle children under the age of 18 who commit acts that would be crimes if committed by adults as well as children who run away from home or engage in behaviors dangerous to themselves or others.

juvenile delinquency Antisocial or criminal acts performed by juveniles.

Kansas-Nebraska Act Act that repealed the Missouri Compromise by allowing the residents of Kansas and Nebraska to choose whether to be slave or free.

la familia Spanish expression denoting the enduring bonds of affection and duty extending from biological kin to close friends.

labor segmentation A practice by employers that governs the corporate labor market, opening up jobs to only specific groups by race, ethnicity, or gender.

Ladies' Federal Labor Union Chicago union of women working in several trades that did much of the campaigning for the passage of the Illinois Factory Inspection Act of 1893.

Ladies Industrial Aid Association of Union Hall Organized to provide aid to soldiers and their families in the Boston area only.

Liberty Party Political party created in 1840 around opposition to slavery in the United States.

libre Freed slaves and free persons of color in Louisiana Territory, particularly New Orleans.

Loyalists Colonists who sided with Britain during the American Revolution.

lyceums Lecture series or other forms of popular education.

mammy Stereotype of southern female slave who identified with the interests of her white charges and exercised great authority in their lives.

Manifest Destiny Belief that the borders of the United States were destined to spread westward.

Mann Act Also known as the White-Slave Traffic Act of 1910, banned the interstate transport of women for "immoral purposes."

manumission Granting of freedom to a slave.

Mariolatry Worship of the Virgin Mary as religious practice within the Roman Catholic Church.

maternalism A term used by historians to describe the emphasis of Progressive Era reformers on the health and welfare of women and children.

matrilineal Tracing inheritance and descent through the female line.

matrilocal Living with the wife's family.

medium A person who facilitates communication between the living and the dead.

mestizo Person of mixed Spanish and Indian heritage.

metis Mixture of French and Indian cultures.

Minor v. Happersett U.S. Supreme Court ruling in 1784 that allowed states to restrict the right to vote to male citizens.

miscegenation A term introduced into the United States in 1863, refers to an alleged mixing of "races" through sexual relations and provided the basis for laws prohibiting interracial marriage and cohabitation.

Missouri Compromise Agreement admitting Maine as a free state and Missouri as a slave state and stipulating that slavery not exist north of the 36° 30' parallel in the states created out of the Louisiana Territory.

modern welfare state Federal and state programs that offer working populations protections against unemployment, sickness, old-age insecurity, and the loss of a family breadwinner. FDR hoped the New Deal would create cradle-to-grave security against "the hazards and vicissitudes of life."

momism The tendency in the 1950s to blame all social ails and psychological problems on bad mothers and failed mothering.

monogamous Marriage to one spouse.

Morrill Anti-Bigamy Act Passed by Congress in 1862, this legislation made plural marriage a federal crime.

mothers' pensions State legislation established to subsidize the domestic work of poor women with dependent children.

Muller v. Oregon The landmark U.S. Supreme Court ruling that upheld Oregon state law restricting the hours a woman may work on the grounds that the state has an interest in protecting a woman's health.

municipal housekeeping A phrase popular during the Progressive Era to connote the extension of women's domestic skills to urban affairs.

National American Woman Suffrage Association Formed in 1890 to promote the ballot for women.

National Association of Colored Women Established in 1896 as the merger of the National Federation of Afro-American Women and the National League of Colored Women.

National Association Opposed to Woman Suffrage Formed in New York City in 1911 as a federation of state antisuffrage groups, which included both men and women.

National Birth Control League Founded in 1916 to advocate changes in legislation that restricted the dissemination of birth control information and devices.

National Congress of Mothers Founded in 1897, the organization promoted education for child-rearing and infant health; later became the Parent-Teaching Association.

National Consumer's League Founded in 1899 by a group of women affiliated with Hull-House to lobby for improved conditions in the manufacture of consumer goods.

National Council of Negro Women (NCNW) Founded to bring together many different national and local organizations serving or representing African American women.

National Council of Women Formed in 1888 in commemoration of the fortieth anniversary of the woman's rights meeting at Seneca Falls, New York, as a representative body of women's reform organizations.

National Labor Union A federation of trade assemblies formed in 1866 that supported woman's right to labor.

National League for the Protection of Colored Women Formed in 1906 as a federation of organizations established to assist young African American women migrating to northern cities.

National Organization for Women (NOW) The feminist organization founded in 1966 to promote women's equality.

National Recovery Administration (NRA) The government agency established to coordinate businesses who voluntarily drew up "codes of fair competition" to enhance economic recovery. These codes were intended to help workers by setting minimum wages and maximum hours, and help consumers by setting fair prices.

National Urban League A nonpartisan civil rights organization formed to give support to newly arrived migrants from the South to northern cities.

National Woman Suffrage Association (NWSA) Formed in 1869 in New York City and led by Elizabeth Cady Stanton and Susan B. Anthony to advance a strategy to introduce a federal amendment to grant women the right to vote.

National Woman's Alliance A short-lived organization led by Populist women and their allies in the temperance and suffrage movements.

National Woman's Party Succeeded the Congressional Union as the militant wing of the woman suffrage movement and focused on amending the Constitution.

National Women's Political Caucus Founded as a bipartisan organization whose goal was to increase the number of women in politics.

National Women's Trade Union League Founded in Boston in 1903 to "assist in the organization of women wage workers into trade unions."

National Youth Administration A program to devise useful work for young people who were on relief in 1935.

nativist A person who supports the interest of native inhabitants against those of immigrants.

Neighborhood Union A social settlement founded in Atlanta in 1908 by Lugenia Burns Hope in response to the impoverished conditions of African Americans.

neophytes Indian converts in California missions.

New Left A loosely connected network of campus groups that sought an immediate end to the Vietnam War and broad and wide-reaching reforms of U.S. society.

New Lights People converted to evangelical religious beliefs in the Great Awakening.

Nineteenth Amendment The so-called "Susan B. Anthony Amendment," which granted women the right to vote, was endorsed by the Senate on June 4, 1919 and became law on August 26, 1920.

Office of War Information (OWI) Created in 1942 and served as an important U.S. government propaganda agency during World War II.

Old Lights People who supported the status quo in churches and opposed the religious changes promoted by New Lights.

open marriage Refers to an agreement that recognizes the right of husbands and wives to engage in extramarital sexual relationships without the stigma of infidelity.

Operation Wetback A 1954 federal program to close the border between Mexico and Texas, California, and Arizona.

Owenites Followers of Robert Owen who participated in his communitarian experiment in England and the United States.

Page Act of 1875 Enacted by the U.S. Congress to restrict immigration from Asian countries, especially women identified as prostitutes.

Pan-African movement An international movement to promote unity among people of African nations and of African descent.

Panic of 1837 Economic depression in 1837 tied to the widespread failure of banks and businesses in the United States.

patriarchal order Society in which the father is the head of the family and the rest of the society is based on this hierarchy.

patrilineal Tracing inheritance and descent through the male line.

patrilocal Living with the husband's family.

Patriots Colonists who opposed Britain during the American Revolution.

pawn A person who is held as security for a debt.

Personal Responsibility and Work Opportunity Act Passed in 1996, the Act ended welfare as an entitlement program.

pessary Glass shield inserted in a woman's vagina to hold the uterus in place or for contraceptive purposes.

phalanx A Fourierist community.

Phyllis Wheatley Home Named after the famous African American poet, homes that were established to assist African American working women searching for work and residences.

pink-collar job A type of employment traditionally held by women, especially relatively low-paying office work.

plaçage Relationship in which a white man legally agreed to support a libre woman as part of an ongoing sexual relationship.

Plessy v. Ferguson The 1896 Supreme Court decision that established "Jim Crow" as the law of the land by condoning "separate but equal" facilities for black and white people.

plural marriage The Mormon custom of taking more than one wife in order to maximize the number of children.

polygamy Marriage to more than one spouse.

Populism Radical agrarians who sought political office in the 1890s to challenge corporate control.

President's Commission on the Status of Women (PCSW) A committee established by President John F. Kennedy to advise him on pending legislative issues concerning women.

presidio Spanish military garrison.

Proclamation Line of 1763 Boundary line designating British territory west of the Appalachian Mountains as Indian land.

Progressive movement A broad coalition of reformers who advocated efficiency in government and various legislative measures to alleviate the social injustices that accompanied the second industrial revolution.

public work A common phrase for wage labor in the postbellum South.

putting-out system Form of industrialization in which the owner of raw materials distributes the materials to workers who are paid by the piece to assemble them in their homes.

race suicide A phrase attributed to President Theodore Roosevelt heralding the demise of "civilization" caused by the dropping birth rate among Americans of Anglo-Saxon ancestry.

race women A term that denoted politically active African American women.

Reconstruction The period 1865–1877 that reintegrated the former Confederate states into the Union and established the terms of freedom for former slaves.

regent Person who rules when a king or monarch is too young or enfeebled to do so.

Retirement Equity Act Attempted to meet the needs of women in the work force and those women married to, or divorced from, working men by providing more benefits for surviving spouses, lowering the age for participation to 55, and granting the divorce spouse rights to retirement pension if stipulated in the separation papers.

revival An intense religious awakening taking place in a series of evangelical services meant to promote conversion.

Roe v. Wade The 1973 Supreme Court case that established women's right to have an abortion.

Salon Regular reception, usually held in the home of a wealthy woman, where social, intellectual, and political leaders mixed.

sanitary fairs Extravaganzas organized mainly by women to raise funds for the Union troops during the Civil War.

Scottish Enlightenment Intellectual movement centered in Scotland that assumed inequalities and hierarchies were natural and necessary in society.

Second Continental Congress Representatives of the thirteen colonies in rebellion against England, meeting as a government body from 1775 to 1781 to direct the Patriot cause.

Second Great Awakening Series of religious revivals throughout the United States that spanned the first half of the nineteenth century.

second industrial revolution The major advances in the technical aspects of industrial production, including consumer goods, that occurred in the last half of the nineteenth century.

second shift The full-time and unpaid domestic work women did when they came home from work.

second-wave feminism The surge of feminist activism that took place in the late 1960s and early 1970s.

sectarian medicine Originated as an alternative to the harsh or "heroic" practices of mainstream or "allopathic" medicine and included such movements as homeopathy, hydrotherapy, and eclecticism.

separate spheres the idea that men and women operate in different worlds: women in the private world of the home and men in the public world of business and politics

sex-segregated labor market The division of job classification along gender lines.

sexual inversion An early sexological term for same-sex desire.

sexual revolution The liberalization of U.S. attitudes toward sexuality that took place in the 1960s and 1970s.

shaman Spiritual leader, often with the power to heal.

social purity The ideal of a single standard of sexual morality for both men and women, advocating abstinence before marriage and restrained behavior after.

Social Security Act of 1935 A governmental program that created pensions for the elderly.

socialist In the antebellum period, a belief in collective sharing of wealth and work rather than a reliance on individual property holding as a basis of society and government.

Sojourner Truth Home for Working Girls Formed in 1895 for African American working women.

Soldiers' Aid Societies Woman's voluntary associations organized to assist the troops from their communities.

Sons of Liberty Organization of Patriots opposed to British taxes.

soral polygamy Marriage to two sisters by the same man.

Southern Christian Leadership Conference (SCLC) A principal organization of the civil rights movement that formed out of the Montgomery bus boycott of 1955–1956; led by Martin Luther King Jr.

sovereign Autonomous ruler or chief of state.

Spanish American War A short war between Spain and the United States in 1898 that liberated Cuba and the Philippines from Spanish rule.

specie Coin rather than paper money.

speedup Increase in the speed of machinery in a factory to produce greater output.

Spiritualism A loosely organized movement around the belief that the living can communicate with the dead.

State Children's Health Insurance Program (SCHIP) Established in 1997 to provide health insurance for families who earned too much to qualify for Medicare.

stretch-out Increase in the number of machines a factory worker tends in order to increase output.

Student Nonviolent Coordinating Committee (SNCC) A principal organization of the civil rights movement that formed in 1960 from student meetings led by Ella Baker.

Students for a Democratic Society (SDS) The main organization of the New Left.

Susan B. Anthony amendment Introduced in January 1886, the amendment specifies that the right to vote shall not be "denied or abridged" on account of sex.

sweatshop A workshop is supervised by a middleman, the sweater, whose employees produce mainly clothing under harsh conditions.

task system System for organizing slave labor that delegates to an individual slave entire responsibility for production of a crop, such as rice, on a particular plot of land.

Tejanos/Tejanas Men and women of Spanish heritage who settled in Texas.

The International Ladies Garment Workers Union (ILGWU) Formed in 1900 by the amalgamation of seven local unions.

the Negro's hour Phrase used to describe the subordination of woman's rights to the campaign to advance the political rights of African American men.

the personal is political One of the founding principles of second-wave feminism; the phrase captured feminists' attention to the psychological, sexual, and privately experienced aspects of women's oppression.

Thirteenth Amendment Extended the terms of the Emancipation Proclamation to free slaves throughout the United States; ratified in 1865.

Title IX of the Education Amendments of 1972 Passed on June 23, 1972, the law forbid sex discrimination in any educational program or activity funded by the federal government, including athletics.

tobacco brides Young women brought to Virginia in the 1620s who promised to marry men who would pay for their passage.

Trail of Tears Westward journey of sixteen thousand Cherokee Indians from Georgia to Oklahoma in 1838.

trash gang Gang of slaves composed of pregnant and older women as well as children, delegated to do lighter field tasks such as weeding and collecting trash.

Treaty of Paris Treaty that ended the French and Indian War between France and England.

truancy Process of a slave absenting himself or herself from a plantation for days or months as a form of protest.

U.S. Children's Bureau Created in 1912 within the federal government to investigate and report *"upon all matters pertaining to the welfare of children and child life among all classes of our people."*

United Cannery, Agricultural, Packing and Allied Workers of America A labor union that made the greatest inroads with Mexican cannery workers and African American tobacco workers, many of whom were women.

United Electrical, Radio and Machine Workers of America One of the first unions to affiliate with the Congress of Industrial Organization in 1936.

United Packinghouse Workers of America A union was committed to organize all workers in the meatpacking industry, regardless of skill or trade.

United States Constitution Document adopted by Constitutional Convention in 1787 to replace Articles of Confederation and to provide for a stronger centralized government of the United States.

United States v. One Package of Japanese Pessaries This case challenged the Comstock Act and made it legal for medical professionals to ship and receive contraceptives.

Uprising of 30,000 Popular name for the strike of the shirtwaist makers who shut down the New York garment industry for several months beginning in November 1909.

War Advertising Council Charged with the task of selling wartime government programs and war bonds to the American public.

war bonds Issued by the government and purchased by civilians, war bonds functioned as a loan to the government to help finance the war effort.

War Brides Act The 1945 Act that allowed Chinese American veterans to bring brides into the United States.

War Manpower Commission The federal agency charged with balancing the labor needs of agriculture, industry, and the armed forces.

War of 1812 War between the United States and England over trade restrictions, fought between 1812 and 1815.

welfare state Reference to a system of government in which the state assumes primary responsibility for the *welfare* of its *citizens* and accords them services as a matter of entitlement.

Whig Party Political party formed in opposition to the Democrats supporting an active role for the federal government in economic development.

White Rose Home and Industrial Association Formed in 1897 to assist African American women coming to New York in search of work.

white slavery panic A moral panic based on the assumption that thousands of young women were being lured into prostitution and held against their will.

winning plan Formally adopted by the NAWSA in 1916, this strategy introduced targeted key state woman suffrage referenda and simultaneously supported an amendment to the Constitution.

Woman's Central Relief Association Served as the foundation for the United States Sanitary Commission.

Woman's Christian Temperance Union (WCTU) Founded in November 1874 to curtail the use of alcohol and became the largest organization of women in the nineteenth century.

Woman's Convention Organized by women to carry out their social service within the black Baptist Church.

woman's crusade The grassroots component of the temperance campaign that erupted in 1873–1874 that brought thousands of women into activism.

Woman's Peace Party Founded in Chicago in 1915 and chaired by Jane Addams, the WPP formed to protest World War I.

Woman's Work for Woman A phrase representing the agenda of the Woman's Foreign Missionary Society.

women adrift Common reference to women who set up households outside marriage or family.

Women of the Ku Klux Klan (WKKK) the women's auxilary of the racist and nativist Ku Klux Klan

Women Strike for Peace (WSP) A group formed in the 1950s to protest nuclear weapons.

Women's Convention of the Black Baptist Church The locus of the women's movement within the Black Baptist Church.

Women's Division of the Democratic National Committee The group within the National Democratic Party that organized and coordinated women's volunteer efforts for Democratic candidates.

Women's Educational and Industrial Union Founded in 1877 to help women support themselves by offering social services and practical vocational training.

Women's Health Movement (WHM) A movement in the 1970s to bring women greater knowledge of and control over their own health.

women's health protective associations Local groups that sponsored public health initiatives and raised money for building and maintaining hospitals.

Women's International League for Peace and Freedom Formed in 1919, WILPF succeeded the Woman's Peace Party in advocating the end of militarism and world peace.

women's liberation movement The burst of radical feminist groups that formed in the mid- to late 1960s that pioneered an analysis of sexuality and private life.

Women's National Indian Association Founded in 1879 to promote assimilationist policies among Native American women.

Working Women's Protective Union Organized in New York to assist wage-earning women during the Civil War.

Works Progress Administration (WPA) A massive federal relief program launched that created paying jobs for unemployed.

World WCTU Organized in 1891 as a federation of national affiliates of the WCTU to proselytize temperance and woman's rights throughout the world.

World YWCA The U.S. YWCA extended its representation around the world to improve the conditions of women by providing social services and education.

Wounded Knee Massacre The attack by the U.S. 7th Calvary on December 29, 1890 that resulted in the deaths of nearly 190 Indians, the majority of whom were women and children.

yeoman farmer Independent farmer who owns a small plot of land that he works himself.

Young Women's Christian Association Formed in several cities shortly after the Civil War to offer social services to young wage-earning women.

PHOTO AND TEXT CREDITS

Introduction: xxxiv–xxxv: Reprinted with the permission of The Women's College Coalition; xxxiv (bottom); Courtesy of Library of Congress; xxxvi: Corbis/Bettmann; xxxix: New York Times Co./Hulton/Archive; xl: © Bettmann/CORBIS; xlvi: Corbis/SABA Press Photos, Inc.

Chapter 1 *Photos:* 2-3: Service Historique de la Marine, Vincennes, France/The Bridgeman Art Library; 6: The Granger Collection, New York; 9(top): Cahokia Mounds State Historic Site, painting by Michael Hampshire; 9(bottom): Museum HIP; 13: Justin Kerr Associates;17: The Pinpoint Morgan Library/Art Resource, NY; 19: Musée Conde, Chantilly, France, The Bridgeman Art Library; 22: Seattle Art Museum; 27: Courtesy of Library of Congress. *Text:* 16: Richard L. Kagan and Abigail Dyer, eds. and trans. *Inquisitorial Inquiries: Brief Lives of Secret Jews and Other Heretics*, pp. 40–49. Baltimore, Maryland: The Johns Hopkins University Press. Reprinted by permission of The Johns Hopkins University Press.

Chapter 2 *Photos:* 32-33: Breamore House, Hampshire, England; 37: Courtesy of the Library of Congress; 38: "Human Races (Las Castas)," 18th century, oil on canvas, 1.04 x 1.48m. Museo Nacional del Virreinato, Tepotzotlan, Mexico. Schmliwijk/Art Resource, NY; 39: Courtesy of the John Carter Brown Library at Brown University; 42: Thomas Fisher Rare Book Library, University of Toronto; 44: The Public Archives of Canada; 46: © Bettmann/CORBIS; 51: National Potrait Gallery, Smithsonian Instituition, Washington DC/Art Resource, NY; 56: Mrs. Elizabeth Freake and Baby Mary (American), oil on canvas, 1963. 134. Worcester Art Museum, Worcester Massachusetts, Gift of Mr. and Mrs. Albert W. Rice.

Chapter 3 *Photos:* 71: Getty Images Inc.—Hulton Archive Photos; 78: Corbis/Bettmann; 79: Courtesy of the Library of Congress; 82: The Granger Collection, New York; 83: North Wind Picture Archives; 87: Library of Congress; 88: Private Collection/The Bridgeman Art Library. *Text:* 65-66: Quoted in Cynthia Kierner. *Southern Women in Revolution, 1776–1800, Personal and Political Narratives*, pp. 63–64. Columbia: University of South Carolina Press, 1998. Reprinted by permission of University of South Carolina Press; 85: Sharon Harris, ed. Letter of Molly Brandt to Judge Daniel Claus. In *American Women Writers to 1800*, pp. 280–281. New York: Oxford University Press. Reprinted by permission of Oxford University Press, Inc.

Chapter 4 *Photos:* 98-99: Smithsonian Art Museum, Washington, D.C., Art Resource, NY; 101: Courtesy of the Bancroft Library. University of California, Berkeley; 103: Getty Images Inc.—Hulton Archive Photos; 110: Woolaroc Museum; 113: US Mint; 117: Paul and Lulu Hilliard University Art Museum University of Louisiana at Lafayette; 121: Courtesy of the Ohio Historical Society.

Chapter 5 *Photos:* 130-131: Courtesy of the Library of Congress; 133: National Museum of American History Smithsonian; 134: American Textile History Museum, Lowell, Mass.; 141: Dr. Leo Hershkowitz; 143: © American Antiquarian Society; 144: © Courtesy of the Ohio Historical Society; 156: Courtesy of the Library of Congress; 158: © Historical Picture Archive/CORBIS. *Text:* 131-132: Mary H. Blewett. *We Will Rise in Our Might: Working-women's Voices from Nineteenth-Century New England.* Ithaca, NY: Cornell University Press, 1991. Reprinted by permission of Cornell University Press; 147: Lucille Salitan and Eve Lewis Perara, eds. Letter from Elizabeth Chace to Samuel Chace, dated 1854. In *Virtuous Lives: Four Quaker Sisters Remember Family Life, Abolitionism, and Women's Suffrage*. Reprinted by permission of The Continuum International Publishing Group, 1994.

Chapter 6 *Photos:* 164-165: Corbis/Bettmann; 169: From "A House Divided: America in the Age of Lincoln" by Eric Foner, published by Norton and the Chicago Historical Society in 1990. Courtesy of the Library of Congress; 170 (top): © Bettmann/CORBIS All Rights Reserved; 170 (bottom): Courtesy of the Library of Congress; 176: Courtesy of the Library of Congress; 179: Dover Publications, Inc.; 186: Moorland-Spingham Research Center. *Text:* 192: Richard C. Lounsbury, ed. *Louisa S. McCord: Poems, Drama, Biography, Letters*, pp. 293–294. Charlottesville: University of Virginia Press, 1996.

Chapter 7 *Photos:* 196-197: Getty Images Inc.—Hulton Archive Photos; 202: © Southern Baptist Historical Library and Archives; 206: Rosenbach Museum & Library, Philadelphia; 208: The Maryland Historical Society, Baltimore Maryland; 211: From the Collection of the Oneida Community Mansion House, Oneida, NY; 215: Courtesy of the Library of Congress; 217: Courtesy American Antiquarian Society; 219: The University of Massachusetts Lowell, Center for Lowell History; 221: © Punch Limited. *Text:* 212: "E.E. Porter to the New York Female Moral Reform Society Corresponding Secretary, April 21, 1838." *Advocate of Moral Reform.* June 15, 1838. Reprinted in Daniel Wright and Kathryn Kish Sklar. "What Was the Appeal of Moral Reform to Antebellum Northern Women 1835-1841?" Women and Social Movements Website. Alexander Street Press. http://wasm.alexanderstreet.com.

Chapter 8 *Photos:* 228-229: Bibliothèque Nationale, Paris France/The Bridgeman Art Library; 232: © Queen Mary, University of London; 234: Mary Evans/Fawcett Library; 236: Getty Images Inc.—Hulton Archive Photos; 238: Courtesy of the Library of Congress; 241: Brown Brothers; 244 (top): Courtesy of Library of Congress; 244 (bottom): Courtesy of Library of Congress; 246: Courtesy Earl Vandale Collection, CN09569, Center for American History,

University of Texas at Austin; 251: Corbis/Bettmann; 252: © The Harper's Magazine Foundation. All rights reserved; 253: Courtesy of the Library of Congress. *Text:* 240: "Sally Rudd to Caroline Mary Rudd, March 26, 1836." Oberlin College Archives. Reprinted in Carol Lasser and the Students of History 266 at Oberlin College. "How Did Oberlin Women Students Draw on Their College Experience to Participate in Antebellum Social Movements, 1831-1861?" Women and Social Movements Website. Alexander Street Press. http://wasm.alexanderstreet.com.

Chapter 9 *Photos:* 260-261: The Granger Collection, New York; 265: Courtesy of the Library of Congress; 267: Getty Images Inc.—Hulton Archive Photos; 271: Provided courtesy HarpWeek., LLC; 272: Getty Images Inc.—Hulton Archive Photos; 273: Corbis/Bettmann; 276: © Bettmann/CORBIS; 278 (left): © National Portrait Gallery, Smithsonian Institution/Art Resource; 278 (right): Courtesy of the Library of Congress; 281: Courtesy of the Library of Congress; 284: Courtesy of the Library of Congress; 285: Courtesy of the Library of Congress; 287: © Mary Evans Picture Library/Edwin Wallace/The Image Works. *Text:* 275-276: Kate Cumming. A *Journal of Hospital Life in the Confederate Army of Tennessee from the Battle of Shiloh to the End of the War* , 44-45. Louisville, KY: John P. Morton & Co., 1966.

Chapter 10 *Photos:* 294-295: Courtesy of the Library of Congress; 299: Library of Congress; 305: Courtesy of the Library of Congress; 308: Courtesy of the Library of Congress; 311: Courtesy of the Library of Congress; 313: The Brechin Group Inc.; 314: © Betmann/CORBIS All Rights Reserved; 316: Courtesy of the Library of Congress; 317: Picture History; 318: Courtesy of the Library of Congress; 323: Courtesy of the Library of Congress; 324: Courtesy of the Library of Congress.

Chapter 11 *Photos:* 333: Courtesy of the Library of Congress; 337: Photo Researchers Inc.; 340: Used by Permission, Utah State Historical Society, all rights reserved; 343: Courtesy of the Library of Congress; 346: Courtesy of the Library of Congress; 348: Nebraska Historical Society, Solomon T. Butcher Collection; 349: © Betmann/CORBIS All Rights Reserved; 353: Courtesy of the Library of Congress; 356 (left and right): National Anthropological Archives; 357: Courtesy of the Library of Congress.

Chapter 12 *Photos:* 366: Courtesy of the Library of Congress; 369: Courtesy of the Library of Congress; 372: North Baker Research Library/California Historical Society; 373: Courtesy of the Library of Congress; 375: Courtesy of the Library of Congress; 382: Courtesy of the Library of Congress; 383: Schlesinger Library, Radcliffe Institute, Harvard University; 385: © CORBIS/All Rights Reserved; 387: Courtesy of the Library of Congress; 391: Duke University.

Chapter 13 *Photos:* 398-399: Photograph courtesy of the Pocumtuck Valley Memorial Association, Memorial Hall Museum, Deerfield, Massachusetts; 401: © CORBIS/All Rights Reserved; 403: Courtesy of Teachers College, Columbia University; 404: University of Delaware Library, Special Collections Department; 405: Special Collections, Cleveland State University Library; 407: Courtesy of the Library of Congress; 409: Courtesy of the Library of Congress; 412: Schlesinger Library, Radcliffe Institute, Harvard University; 417: © CORBIS/All Rights Reserved; 419: The Granger Collection; 423: Courtesy of the Library of Congress; 427: Courtesy of the Library of Congress.

Chapter 14 *Photos:* 435: Courtesy of the Library of Congress; 438: Courtesy of the Library of Congress; 441: Courtesy of the Library of Congress; 442: Photograph courtesy Newberry Library, Congress; 444: Swathmore College Peace Collection; 446: Courtesy of the Library of Congress; 448: Carlson Library, University of Toledo; 449: Courtesy of the Library of Congress; 452: Courtesy of the Library of Congress; 453: © Bettmann/CORBIS All Rights Reserved; 459: Lebrecht Music & Arts Photo Library. *Text:* 436-437: Sherna Gluck, ed. *From Parlor to Prison: Five American Suffragists Talk about Their Lives*, pp. 98–103. New York: Vintage Books, 1976.

Chapter 15 *Photos:* 464-465: Courtesy of the Library of Congress; 469 (top): © Betmann/CORBIS; 469 (bottom): Courtesy of the Library of Congress; 471: Courtesy of the Library of Congress; 473: Courtesy of the Library of Congress; 475: Courtesy of the Library of Congress; 476: Courtesy of the Library of Congress; 480: Courtesy of the Library of Congress; 483: Courtesy of the Library of Congress; 485: Courtesy of the Library of Congress; 487: Courtesy of the Library of Congress; 490: Courtesy of the Library of Congress; 496: Courtesy of the Library of Congress. *Text:* 478-479: Rosey Safran. "The Washington Place Fire." *The Independent* 70 (April 20, 1911). 840–841.

Chapter 16 *Photos:* 502-503: Courtesy of the Library of Congress; 506: Courtesy of the Library of Congress; 507: Corbis/Bettmann; 510: Courtesy of the Library of Congress; 515: Courtesy of the Library of Congress; 517: Courtesy of the Library of Congress; 520: The Granger Collection; 522: Courtesy of the Visiting Nurse Association of Boston; 526: The Marcus Garvey & UNIA Papers; 527: Corbis/Bettmann; 529: Courtesy W.A. Swift Photograph Collection, Archives and Special Collections, Ball State University; 534: Getty Images Inc.—Hulton Archive Photos. *Text:* 519-520: Dorothy Dunbar Bromley. "Feminist-New Style." *Harper's Magazine* (October 1927).

Chapter 17 *Photos:* 540-541: The Granger Collection, New York; 543:Courtesy of the Library of Congress; 544: National Archives and Records Administration Special Collections & Archives; 553: Special Collections & Archives, Georgia State University Library; 557: © Bettmann/CORBIS All Rights Reserved; 559: Courtesy Virginia S. Bourne, Castine, ME; 561: Corbis/Bettmann;

INDEX

A

Immigrants—*continued*
  Italians, 373–374
  Jazz Age, 508
  Post-Civil War, 370–376
  See also Slavery; *specific countries*
Imperialism, 421–427
Indentured servants, 45, 48
Independence (from Britain), 77–88
Indian Allotment Act, 352
Indian Country, 101–111
Indian removal, 218–220
Indian Removal Act, 111
Indian reservations, 102
Indian schools. *See* Reservation boarding schools
Indian territory, 101–102
Industrial revolution, 132, 133–137, 142–150
Industrial Workers of the World, 476, 477
Infant Care, 389
Infanticide, 19
Inheritance, 17, 56, 69–70, 74, 92, 107–111, 235–236
Inner light, 205
Inquisition, 16
Integration, 624. *See also* Segregation
Intermarriage
  antebellum south, 187
  colonization, 28, 35, 36–37, 38, 41, 42, 44, 50, 51–52
  frontier, 118, 120, 343–345
  law, 50, 117, 449–450
  See also Miscegenation
International Association of Machinists, 583
International Council of Women, 400–401
International Council of Women of the Darker Races of the World, 525–526
International feminism. *See* Global feminism
International Ladies Garment Workers Union, 474–476, 554
International Women's Year, 730
Internet, 755
Internment camps, 577–578, 597–601
Interracial relationships. *See* Intermarriage
Interracial Women's Committee, 528
Iraq, 751
Irish, 152–153
Iroquois, 7
Isabella of Castile, 14, 19
Islam, 23
Issei, 597
Italians, 373–374

J
Jackson, Andrew, 229
Jackson, Helen Hunt, 351
Jackson, Thomas "Stonewall", 278
Jacobs, Harriet, 188, 270, 286
Jacques-Garvey, Amy, 524–526
James I (England), 46
Jamestown (colony), 46
Jane, 759
Jane club, 437
Japanese Americans, 577–578, 597–601, 608–610
Jay, Karla, 695
Jazz Age, 502–505
  manners and morals, 505–513
  modernity, culture of, 530–533
  Rainey, Gertrude "Ma," 534
  woman's movement during, 517–523
  women and work, 513–517
  women's activism during, 524–530

Jefferson, Thomas, 111
Jeffersonian Republicans, 86
Jewish immigrants, 374–376
Jezebel, 175
Jim Crow, 655
  woman movement (1880–1900) and, 401, 405, 410, 415, 419–420
  work segregation, 623, 627
  World War II and, 585, 595
Job discrimination, 580–586, 619–621
Johnson, Andrew, 296
Johnson, Joyce, 617–618, 641
Johnson, Lady Bird, 730
Johnson, Lyndon, 668, 694, 718
Johnson, Virgina, 693
Jones, Hettie, 641
Jong, Erica, 642
Jook joints, 439
Joplin, Janice, 641
Jordan, Ann Haseltine, 202
Jordan, Barbara, 730
Joy of Sex, 694
Judaism, 206–207
Juvenile court system, 481
Juvenile delinquency, 602

K
Kanal Ikal (Mayan princess), 12
Kansas-Nebraska act, 167
Keckley, Elizabeth, 186, 188–189
Kelley, Florence, 491
Kemble, Fanny, 155, 251, 286
Kennedy, John F., 666, 667
Kennedy, Robert, 662
Kenney, Lucy, 245
Kerouac, Jack, 641
Keys, Elizabeth, 50
King, Billie Jean, 681
King, Martin Luther, Jr., 657–658, 662
Kingston, Maxine Hong, 704–705, 757
Kinsey, Alfred, 511, 601, 639, 693
Kitchen Table: Women of Color Press, 702
Kivas, 9
Knights of St. Krispin, 321
Koedt, Anne, 707
Komarovsky, Mirra, 621
Koop, C. Everett, 732
Korean War, 632
Ku Klux Klan, 303, 449, 524, 528–530

L
L-85, 591
Labor protests, 217–218
Labor rights, 318–321, 665–673. *See also* Unions
Labor segmentation, 367
Ladies Industrial Aid Association of Union Hall, 272
Ladies Federal Labor Union, 407
Lady of Cofachiqui, 12
Lady Xoc, 12, 13
La familia, 343
LaHaye, Beverly, 730, 732
Lake, Handsome, 106
Lake, Veronica, 589
La malinche, 37
Lange, Dorothea, 567–568
Lange, Sister Mary Elizabeth, 208
Larson, Nella, 532